BEYOND SECTARIANISM

BEYOND SECTARIANISM

The Realignment of American Orthodox Judaism

ADAM S. FERZIGER

WAYNE STATE UNIVERSITY PRESS
DETROIT

© 2015 by Wayne State University Press, Detroit, Michigan 48201.

All rights reserved.

No part of this book may be reproduced without formal permission.

19 18 17 16 15   5 4 3 2 1

Library of Cataloging Control Number: 2015934523

ISBN 978-0-8143-3953-4 (paperback)
ISBN 978-0-8143-3954-1 (ebook)

Designed and typeset by Adam B. Bohannon
Composed in Adobe Caslon Pro

Gratitude is hereby expressed for permission to republish revised versions or extracts from these essays:

"Beyond Bais Ya'akov: Orthodox Outreach and the Emergence of Haredi Women as Religious Leaders," *Journal of Modern Jewish Studies* 14, no. 1 (2015): 140–59.

"Hungarian Separatist Orthodoxy and the Migration of Its Legacy to America: The Greenwald-Hirschenson Debate." *Jewish Quarterly Review* 105, no. 2 (2015) 250–83.

"From Lubavitch to Lakewood: The 'Chabadization' of American Orthodoxy." *Modern Judaism* 33, no. 2 (2013): 101–24.

"'Outside the Shul': The American Soviet Jewry Movement and the Rise of Solidarity Orthodoxy (1964–1986)." *Religion and American Culture* 22, no. 1 (2012): 83–130.

"Holocaust, *Hurban*, and Haredization: Pilgrimages to Eastern Europe and the Realignment of American Orthodoxy." *Contemporary Jewry* 31, no. 1 (2011): 25–54.

"Feminism and Heresy: The Construction of a Jewish Meta-Narrative." *Journal of the American Academy of Religion* 77, no. 3 (2009): 494–546.

"From Demonic Deviant to Drowning Brother: Reform Judaism in the Eyes of Orthodoxy (1983–2007)." *Jewish Social Studies* 15, no. 3 (2009): 56–88.

"Between Outreach and Inreach: Redrawing the Lines of the American Orthodox Rabbinate." *Modern Judaism* 25, no. 3 (2005): 237–63.

"The Lookstein Legacy: An American Orthodox Rabbinical Dynasty?" *Jewish History* 13, no. 1 (1999): 127–49.

לנעמי, כי אל אשר תלכי אלך
For Naomi, wherever you go I go

CONTENTS

Acknowledgments ix

Introduction: The Church/Sect Divide and American Orthodoxy Reconsidered 1

I. Division

1. Between Hungarian Orthodoxy and American Modern Orthodoxy 19
2. A Modern Orthodox Rabbinical Dynasty 42
3. The Rise and Fall of Solidarity Orthodoxy 58

II. Realignment

4. Pilgrimages to Eastern Europe and Haredization 85
5. Counter-Feminism and Modern Orthodoxy 114
6. Reform in the Eyes of Orthodoxy 130
7. Rabbinical Training and Role Reversal 151
8. The Chabadization of Haredi Orthodoxy 175
9. Women and Haredi Outreach: A Silent Revolution 195

Conclusion: Beyond Outreach: Post-Denominationalism, Open Orthodoxy, and Realignment 211

Notes 225

Bibliography 301

Index 331

ACKNOWLEDGMENTS

Many individuals played roles in the evolution of this book, and I owe each of them a debt of gratitude. They cannot all be listed, but numerous figures deserve special recognition. I apologize in advance if I have inadvertently missed mentioning someone who belongs here.

I had the great privilege of conducting my initial research on Orthodox Judaism under the mentorship of the legendary late Professor Jacob Katz. His model of rigorous engagement with texts, discerning assessment of contextual factors, and introduction of insightful analytical methodologies, which did not prevent him from addressing subjects about which he cared deeply, remains my gold standard. Since I began my doctoral work under his guidance, I have gained a great deal from my relationship with the outstanding historian Professor Gershon Bacon, who is today a close colleague and friend. His vast erudition and appreciation of the subtleties involved in writing about the history of modern and contemporary Jewish religious life continued to be a decisive influence on the preparation of this book.

My intensive scholarly engagement with North American Jewry began in 2001 when I received a wonderful invitation to serve as a fellow at Bar-Ilan University's Rappaport Center for Assimilation Research from its director, Professor Zvi Zohar. The generous research funding enabled me to carry out fieldwork throughout North America and to produce a series of studies that contain some of my initial examinations of American Orthodoxy. It was at this time that I had the honor of developing a close intellectual bond with the late Professor Charles S. Liebman. He was unusually giving with his time, and no less strident in rendering his frank assessments of my work. Soon after, I began to teach on a full-time basis in Bar-Ilan's Graduate Program in Contemporary Jewry. Professor Judy Baumel-Schwartz, the chair of the program, has ever since been a consistently encouraging but honest critic and a genuine friend. My position was facilitated initially through appointment as the Gwendolyn and Joseph Straus Fellow in Jewish Studies. The personal connection that subsequently developed

ACKNOWLEDGMENTS

with Moshael and Zahava Straus, who created this early-career fellowship in memory of his parents, has only grown over the ensuing years. I am honored to count among my closest mentors and exemplars Rabbi Professor Daniel Sperber, the renowned academic Talmudist and religious thinker and Israel Prize laureate.

Bar-Ilan University is my academic home. There I have had the good fortune to meet many individuals who took a deep interest in my work and offered me the encouragement and support that enabled me to move forward. Among the numerous people at Bar-Ilan who deserve thanks, I mention prominently Professor Moshe Kaveh, the former president; former rectors Professors Yoseph Yeshurun and Haim Taitelbaum; Professors Joshua Schwartz, Moisés Orfali, Eliezer Tauber, and Elie Assis—each of whom has served as dean of the Faculty of Jewish Studies during my tenure; and Professor Yaron Harel, the chairman of my current disciplinary framework, the recently integrated Department of Jewish History and Contemporary Jewry. I have learned a great deal from interactions with additional Bar-Ilan colleagues: Benjamin Bar-Tikva, Albert Baumgarten, Kimmy Caplan, Stuart Cohen, Yitzhak Conforti, Noah Efron, Shmuel Feiner, Emanuel Friedheim, Menachem Friedman, Aryeh A. Frimer, Judah Galinsky, Zehavit Gross, Moshe Hellinger, Elliott Horowitz, Meirav Tubul Kahana, Ari Kahn, Michael Kramer, Yitzhak Kraus, James Kugel, Nissim Leon, Lilach Lev-Ari, David Malkiel, Dan Michman, Jonathan Rabinowitz, Moshe Rosman, Ben-Zion Rosenfeld, Avi Sagi, Dov Schwartz, Ephraim Tabory, Joel Walters, Jeffrey Woolf, and Bernard Zisser.

During the winter/spring term of 2013, I served as co-convener of a seminar on Orthodox Judaism and theology at the Oxford Centre for Hebrew and Jewish Studies, an affiliate of University of Oxford. I am grateful to the president of the center, Professor Martin Goodman, to former president Dr. David Ariel, and to my co-convener, Dr. Miri Freud-Kandel, for this gracious invitation, and particularly for enabling me to travel back and forth to Israel during an exceedingly difficult period for me and my family. Especially in light of the considerable personal challenges, the serenity of the Yarnton Manor environment, along with the constant supportive and constructive interfaces with fellow members of the research group, sustained me as I labored toward completion of this manuscript.

My friend and colleague and fellow investigator of American Orthodoxy, Dr. Yoel Finkelman, devoted extensive time to reading and remarking on the entire manuscript. His abundant suggestions added essential elements to the final draft. The following scholars, friends, and relatives have been kind enough to read parts of the text at various stages of preparation and to share their comments with me (of course I bear full responsibility for any inaccuracies): Yaakov Ariel, Elisheva Baumgarten, Shalom Z. Berger, Joshua A. Berman, Alan Brill,

ACKNOWLEDGMENTS

Menachem Butler, Zev Eleff, David H. Ellenson, Cliff M. J. Felig, Ari A. Ferziger, Ben-Zion Ferziger, Jonathan H. Ferziger, Naomi Ferziger, Fred Gottlieb, Sandra Ferziger Gottlieb, Jeffrey S. Gurock, Samuel C. Heilman, Alan Jotkowitz, Lawrence Kaplan, Shnayer Z. Leiman, Naphtali Lowenthal, Michael A. Meyer, David N. Myers, Tamar Ross, Jonathan Sarna, Jacob J. Schacter, Marc Shapiro, Michael K. Silber, Shaul Stampfer, Chaim I. Waxman, Jack Wertheimer, and Ephraim Zuroff. I have drawn considerable knowledge and insight from additional friends, colleagues, and family, including David Berger, Rabbi Jack Bieler, Miriam Bloom, Andreas Braemer, Steven M. Cohen, Arye Edrei, Seth Farber, Reuven Ferziger, Minna Ferziger Felig, Meira Shulman Ferziger, Philip Fishman, Sylvia Barack Fishman, Gershon Greenberg, Irving "Yitz" Greenberg, Micah Halperin, Isaac "Zahi" Hershkowitz, Miriam Hershlag, Jenna Joselit, Michael L. Miller, Yehudah Mirsky, Marc Lee Raphael, Rachelle Rohde, Yoseph Salmon, Burton (Baruch) Weinstein, and Esther Weinstein. Special thanks to Aroma G–Kfar-Sava. The staff of the Judaica Reading Room in the Wurzweiler Library of Bar-Ilan University, led by Menashe Elyashiv, together with Dr. Ronit Shoshani and David Ben-Naim, has always been extremely accommodating and helpful. Most of the ideas developed in the following pages were first presented to my undergraduate and graduate students. Their questions, suggestions, and the extraordinary cerebral catharsis that only face-to-face classroom interaction can produce generated some of the most novel analyses and conceptualizations in this book. I want to thank personally the many individuals who agreed to be interviewed or provided firsthand information. They may not agree with all my analyses, but I hope they will find them valuable and informed.

From the moment of our first correspondence, the entire staff and editorial board of the Wayne State University Press, led by Editor-in-Chief and Associate Director Kathryn Wildfong, have conducted the process of evaluation, publication approval, revision, copyediting, and production with utmost earnestness, sensitivity, and professionalism. The critical observations of the anonymous evaluators vastly improved the final product.

My mother, Sandra Ferziger Gottlieb, and father, of blessed memory, Daniel Ferziger, created a home characterized by unconditional love toward all family members, Jewish commitment, hospitality, intellectual curiosity, and cultural openness. I cannot thank them enough for these precious gifts. An outstanding illustration of the fruits of their efforts is that each one of my four siblings and their spouses have assisted me in my work and been unusually supportive of me, my wife, Naomi, and our children. Dr. Fred Gottlieb, my mother's husband

and himself a published author on twentieth-century German Jewish life, shows sincere interest in my research and is always eager to help me with deciphering German-language materials.

Since we met more than twenty-seven years ago, my father-in-law, David G. Weiss, often discussed Jewish history with me, especially issues pertaining to his native Hungary, the Holocaust, which he unfortunately experienced firsthand, and American Jewish synagogue life. The entire family is still recovering from his recent passing. May my mother-in-law, Bernice Weiss, and all their offspring draw strength from his blessed memory.

When I published my first book in 2005, our children—Ben-Zion, Yoel, Aviad, Dovie, Avital, and Adi—ranged in age from four to fifteen. Only the older boys had any real inkling of what I was doing. Today they are all far more aware of the scholarly endeavor—its benefits, and excitement, as well as its challenges. Their lives have been touched on various levels by both the private and public aspects of the research and university teaching of both of their parents. All considered, Naomi and I have striven to communicate that notwithstanding the efforts that serious academic activity demands, our fundamental priorities are family well-being and living a life of spiritual and ethical meaning.

This book is dedicated to Naomi, the beautiful human being with whom I have been blessed to share life and the only one in the world who fully understands.

לה' הארץ ומלואה
Bar-Ilan University
Ramat-Gan, Israel
Sivan 5775—June 2015

Introduction

The Church/Sect Divide and American Orthodoxy Reconsidered

Until the mid-twentieth century, most researchers of American Jewry relegated the Orthodox segment to no more than a dwindling and insignificant remnant of traditional Eastern European Jewish life. The future of American Judaism was to be identified in the liberal streams that were attracting the majority of those who sought to join a synagogue. As prominent sociologist Marshal Sklare remarked regarding the Orthodox in 1955, "the history of their movement can be written in terms of a case study of institutional decay."[1] The year 1965 marked a turning point. A study was published that not only undermined the prevailing approach but also spawned a new subdiscipline that has since garnered considerable scholarly and popular interest. In a pathbreaking investigation titled "Orthodoxy in American Jewish Life," a young social scientist named Charles S. Liebman declared boldly that "the only remaining vestige of Jewish passion in America resides in the Orthodox community.... [It is] the only group which today contains within it a strength and will to live that may yet nourish all the Jewish world."[2] Liebman, who went on to an award-winning career as one of the keenest interpreters of contemporary Jewry, provided a wellspring of data to support his argument and established definitions and foundational distinctions that set the agenda for the burgeoning investigation of American Orthodoxy over the next four decades.[3]

INTRODUCTION

The turn of the twenty-first century actually demonstrated a resurgence of "Jewish passion" and creativity among liberal denominations and independent groups that Liebman did not foresee. Fresh religious energies sprouted through the increased involvement of women, as well as via nondenominational frameworks including "emergent communities," "Jewish Renewal," and various "New Age" approaches.[4] To be sure, the numbers of unaffiliated and the rates of intermarriage among non-Orthodox Jews also achieved unprecedented proportions.[5] American Orthodoxy, in parallel, continued to grow in geographical, institutional, and political strength, and a generation of outstanding academics has deepened understanding of this stream dramatically. In as far as demographics are concerned, the 2013 Pew Survey of U.S. Jewry, along with two local studies, demonstrate that all denominations declined in comparison to the growth of unaffiliated Jews, but—as opposed to previous studies—the Orthodox unequivocally had the highest retention rate. Moreover, while the Orthodox remained at 10 percent of the overall Jewish population, their median age (40) is considerably younger than that of their liberal counterparts (54–55), and Orthodoxy is the only denomination in which younger members (under 50) have higher rates of retention of their religious identities than the older generation. Thus, unless there is a dramatic reverse in the current trends, it would appear that Orthodoxy's place among the active and strongly connected American Jewish population will only expand in the coming decades.[6]

Despite the proliferation of scholarship, Liebman's once "revolutionary" understanding of American Orthodoxy's character and divisions remains the accepted view of the ongoing trajectory of this Jewish stream. To a degree, this work pursues a similar path by presenting fresh materials that build on and lend support to Liebman's original observations. The crucial contention here, however, is that one of his principal perceptions needs to be reassessed in light of events and new initiatives that have arisen particularly since the 1990s.

Based on the classic dichotomy between "church" and "sect" first articulated by Max Weber and Ernst Troeltsch,[7] Liebman proposed that the "committed Orthodox"—observant rather than nominally affiliated—could be divided into two main streams: "church" or Modern Orthodoxy, and "sectarian" or right-wing Orthodoxy. The churchlike inclusive behavior of the Modern Orthodox was reflected most in their efforts to emphasize what they shared with the non-Orthodox rather than what divided them. The sectarian Orthodox, in opposition, were vigilant in maintaining their distance from the majority of American Jews—their leaders and educational institutions catered nearly exclusively to the needs of their cohesive collective.[8]

INTRODUCTION

Notwithstanding this fundamental division, Liebman noted a steady increase in religious fervor and punctiliousness among some within the more acculturated Modern Orthodox that was bringing them closer to their sectarian counterparts. The "shift to the right" of the Modern Orthodox has indeed received a great deal of attention from prominent researchers in recent decades. This work supports and offers fresh nuances to this appraisal, but it stands out in highlighting the ways that significant elements within what will be referred to throughout as "Haredi Orthodoxy" have simultaneously abandoned certain strict and seemingly uncontested norms.[9] Both sides, then, have contributed toward a narrowing of the former gap between them and in so doing engendered a realignment of American Orthodox Judaism.

Orthodox Judaism: A Modern Mosaic

In the eyes of its strict adherents, Orthodoxy was and remains simply the direct heir to an authentic, historic Judaism that has long been characterized by uniformity in matters of religious behavior and core theological principles. Alternatively, all forms of present-day Orthodoxy are voluntary, "modern" trends that emerged out of choices resulting from the interface of long-held traditions with the changing world of the last three centuries. This in no way contradicts the fact that Orthodoxy stands out in comparison to other contemporary Jewish movements in levels of continuity of deeply entrenched practices and beliefs.[10]

"Allegiance to Jewish law" is certainly a foundational principle of Orthodoxy. Yet Conservative Judaism also historically mandated the observance of the halakhah as proper religious behavior.[11] Therefore, this expansive category cannot necessarily serve as a singular criterion for defining Orthodoxy. The more narrow description, however, of those modern Jews who accept Rabbi Yosef Caro's sixteenth-century *Shulhan Arukh* (along with the glosses of Rabbi Moses Isserles that add the Ashkenazi interpretation and custom) as the main source of legitimate Jewish behavior is an exclusive trait of Orthodox constituencies. In addition, most Orthodox Jews are more literal in their views of the nature of the Torah. They consider the Pentateuch (Five Books of Moses) to be a divine statement rendered to Moses through direct prophecy (*Torah min ha-Shamayim*), and the Oral Law (*Torah she-be'al peh*) as reflected by the Mishnaic and Talmudic Sages to be of divine origin.[12]

The terms "movement" and "denomination" can be applied to Orthodoxy, but they are certainly less precise than in reference to Conservative or Reform Judaisms. While these liberal streams have certainly known heterogeneity in practice and ideological outlooks, in both cases a basic common denominator

3

existed. Once specific national denominational associations that set policies for its memberships were established, almost all Conservative and Reform congregations and their rabbis affiliated with these respective structures. American Orthodoxy too has produced a number of unique organizational and institutional bodies that played key roles in its evolution, and often affiliation with them correlated with specific religious worldviews as well. Nevertheless, even before the mass settlement of Jews in America at the turn of the twentieth century, the European society from which Orthodoxy drew its numbers included Sephardim and Ashkenazim, Hasidim and Mitnagedim (non- or anti-Hasidim), Hungarian antimodernists and German Hirschian synthesists, and an almost limitless number of subgroups within each faction.[13] Before World War II, but particularly after the influx of refugees in the late 1930s and 1940s, this variety also came to characterize American Orthodoxy. Thus, official guideline statements, charters, and platforms tell us about specific parties but are often less instructive in understanding the general phenomenon of American Orthodoxy than is the case regarding other denominations. The presentation here, as such, offers a window into the mosaic of American Orthodoxy.

Historical Background

The first Jews to settle in New Amsterdam in 1654 (renamed New York by the British in 1664) were Spanish and Portuguese refugees descended from conversos or *anusim*—Jews who had been forced to accept Christianity. The collective structure for Jewish life that they established—as well as those founded over the following century along the Atlantic seaboard by the hundreds of fellow Jews who followed them to the New World (Savannah, Charleston, Philadelphia, Newport)—was designed (with some significant distinctions) according to the community model prevalent among their brethren in Amsterdam, London, Hamburg, and other significant concentrations of the "Western Sephardic Diaspora."[14] These "all-encompassing" congregational institutions spoke for the entire Jewish population in a given area and took responsibility for most aspects of internal Jewish life: public prayer, lifecycle events, dietary standards, supervision of religious and ritual facilities (synagogue, mikveh, matzah bakery, and cemetery), education, and charity.

Concerted efforts were made to replicate with as much exactitude as possible the synagogue customs of their European forefathers. Yet considerable numbers of America's early Jewish settlers were less than stringent in regard to such personal observances as dietary laws, Sabbath and festival restrictions, and even intermarriage.[15] Despite this diversity in individual religious conduct, there was no question for the first 170 years of American Jewish life that the entire active local Jewish population maintained membership in a united community that gathered in one synagogue for all public worship. This situation changed in the 1820s when the first Ashkenazi synagogue was established in New York and the original American Reform congregation was formed in Charleston, South Carolina.[16]

From 1830 to 1880 the Jewish population in America expanded from approximately four thousand to close to three hundred thousand.[17] The majority originated in the German-speaking countries of Central Europe, although a considerable number of Eastern European Jews who spoke Yiddish also immigrated during that period. There were even thirty thousand Jews from the Balkans, Turkey, and Greece.[18] Many of these immigrants were poor and uneducated Jews from rural areas. Some of the German speakers, however, had internalized the changing political and social ethos of emancipation in Europe prior to settling in America and had been exposed as well to the nascent Reform movement. Among them were individuals who soon achieved financial success, which facilitated their entrance into mainstream society and brought with it intensive exposure to American democratic ideals. By 1870, 30 of the 152 active synagogues in the United States already had organs. Moreover, in 1869 a conference of Reform-minded rabbis was held in Philadelphia; in 1873 the Union of American Hebrew Congregations (UAHC), which became the umbrella organization for Reform synagogues, was established; in 1875 the Hebrew Union College, which was destined to be the main Reform rabbinical seminary, opened in Cincinnati.[19] As Jonathan Sarna put it, "Reform's passionate embrace of modernity looked like the wave of the future in the 1870s."[20] This period also beheld the arrival of the first ordained Orthodox rabbis on American soil. These figures sought, with limited success, to sustain and even invigorate Orthodox Judaism within the American sphere.

The last decades of the nineteenth century witnessed a vast influx of Jews from Eastern Europe, and by 1900 the American Jewish population reached approximately one million.[21] Some of the fresh arrivals had already adopted the social norms of general society before reaching America. Others were set on detaching themselves from the religious culture and demands of their communities of origin as soon as they reached their new habitat. The largest contingent was not hostile to religion, but nonetheless did not perceive a religiously observant lifestyle as compatible with the economic and social conventions of American society. All the same, there were thousands of immigrants who remained committed to upholding the standards of traditional Jewish law, including an increasing number of European-trained rabbis and scholars.[22]

Initially, the main focus of those who served the Orthodox community was on maintaining basic functions such as kosher dietary supervision and encouraging regular synagogue attendance. New religious and educational frameworks gradually appeared that provided an infrastructure for those who felt obligated by tradition but were not antagonistic toward American social and intellectual culture. During the first decades of the twentieth century, elementary and high schools as well as institutions for higher Torah learning, national synagogue organizations, and rabbinical associations were established in large cities, some of which continue to serve as the core infrastructure for Modern Orthodoxy until today. The Jewish Theological Seminary (JTS), which opened its doors in the late 1880s, was originally conceived as an advanced school for training Americanized, English-speaking rabbis who could relate to immigrants and, especially, their offspring. Over time it developed an identity independent of mainstream Orthodoxy and spawned the Conservative movement.[23] A few yeshivas and secondary schools were also founded that reflected a more rigid religious outlook and a less sympathetic perception of the American environment. Until the mid-twentieth century only a small contingency of American Jews identified ardently with these policies. The mass entry of Eastern European refugees in the period immediately surrounding World War II brought with it a number of prominent rabbinical authorities and Hasidic leaders as well as a high proportion of deeply observant individuals.[24]

This group will be referred to throughout the forthcoming chapters of this book as Haredi Orthodoxy. The term *haredi* is translated from biblical Hebrew as "one who trembles" (see Isaiah 66:2). In explaining its application to the contemporary Orthodox coalition bearing this title, sociologist Samuel Heilman describes this loose collection as "anxiously and fervently religious."[25] Other labels that are utilized for its subgroups include right wing, ultra-Orthodox, *hasidish, yeshivish,* the yeshiva world (*welt* in Yiddish), the Torah world, and the generally pejorative "black hatters." Although there were representations of the current approaches from the late nineteenth century, the growth and influence of American Haredi Orthodoxy is primarily a post–World War II phenomenon.

Despite their own historic conflicts, today both Mitnagedic and Hasidic factions are generally included under the broad rubric of American Haredi Orthodoxy (and in Israel, Western Europe, and parts of Latin America the Eastern–Mizrahi Shas party followers as well). This fusion is reflected geographically in shared neighborhoods, and politically by the fact that they join forces to advocate for common interests, including mass public events organized in partnership by figures from both camps.[26] On an elite educational level as well, increasingly, talented young Hasidic Torah scholars are choosing to study at banner Lithuanian-style yeshivas like Beth Medrash Govoha in Lakewood, New Jersey, and the Yeshiva of South Fallsburg, New York. All the same, other than among Chabad Hasidism, on the whole graduates of Mitnagedic yeshivas and Bais Yaakov women's schools and seminaries are less antagonistic and insular vis-à-vis secular society and culture than are their Hasidic counterparts.[27] As such, in his 2011 study of Orthodox popular literary culture Yoel Finkelman chose to formalize distinctions between American Hasidim and Haredim.[28] Within the context of heterogeneous American Jewish life, however, the term "Haredi"—or as social linguist Sarah Benor recently put it, "the black hat pole"[29]—generally serves to distinguish the many Hasidic and Mitnagedic subtrends from both the Modern Orthodox and non-Orthodox populations. Since this is the main division that will be addressed in this book, the term that will be used is "Haredi Orthodoxy." That said, the majority of the discussions will focus on the non-Hasidic groups.

Committed Orthodoxy: Two Trends

In 1965, Charles Liebman published his pioneering study in which he applied the church/sect typology to the main components of American Orthodoxy. Like the more established and all-encompassing church, the Modern Orthodox adherents were relatively wealthy and acculturated, and they accepted a broad range of interpretations in matters of religious dogma. Their collective roots lay in the efforts of primarily second-generation Orthodox Jews in the initial decades of the twentieth century to create a formula that would enable them to integrate fully into American society without abandoning an observant lifestyle. Accomplishing such a task inevitably involved shedding aspects of the religious segregation and particularism they had inherited from Eastern Europe, and adapting to, in the words of Samuel Heilman, a "contrapuntal" lifestyle of "competing loyalties to potentially rivalrous institutions and cultures."[30] The organizational homes of Modern Orthodoxy were to be found in "Americanized" frameworks such as Yeshiva University (YU), the Young Israel synagogue movement, and the Rabbinical Council of America (RCA), as well as the numerous full-time dual curriculum "day schools" (many of them coeducational) that sprang up from the late 1930s.[31] Support for the State of Israel and adoption of a positive religious outlook in regard to modern Zionism also became trademarks of this Jewish sector.[32]

Among these "accommodating" but steadfast Jews, Liebman uncovered diversity in degrees of religious observance as well as a nonmonolithic approach to a variety of ideological issues.[33] All the same, he distinguished between them and the so-called nonobservant Orthodox—primarily immigrants and some of their offspring—whose "folk" religious orientation impelled them to the Orthodox synagogue but who were really not very different from the core Conservative constituency. Although in the first half of the twentieth century the majority of members of a good number of Modern Orthodox synagogues worked on the Jewish Sabbath, from the 1960s the more meticulous began to dominate in most major urban centers of Orthodox life.[34]

Liebman's sectarian Orthodoxy, in contrast, was nurtured in the yeshivas and Hasidic courts that were transplanted from European to American soil in the mid-twentieth century. Sectarian Orthodoxy's rise was a direct result of the influx of Eastern European refugees that took place due to the Holocaust. Had it not been for Hitler, these Jews would have been perfectly satisfied to remain within the environments in which they were born. Having found themselves in America, they had no desire to integrate. Their aims were to survive and to rebuild the religious way of life that had been destroyed. Any necessary compromise with societal realities was to be minimized, and there was certainly no room for variation and heterogeneity as far as religious fundamentals were concerned.[35]

Above the aforesaid cultural and theological differences, Liebman argued, lay the key factor that distinguished the two groups: their respective attitudes toward interaction with other Jews. The churchlike behavior of the Modern Orthodox was reflected in their efforts to emphasize what they shared with the non-Orthodox rather than what divided them. One way this was expressed was in a willingness to cooperate with non-Orthodox groups regarding issues of mutual concern. This consideration for all Jews, said Liebman, was also articulated by the many Modern Orthodox rabbis who chose to serve primarily nonobservant constituencies, and it found further expression in the then rising number of Modern Orthodox programs aimed at bringing unaffiliated Jews closer to Judaism. The sectarian Orthodox, in opposition, were guided by an isolationist approach that entailed a far more selective attitude regarding who could claim membership in their collectives. As such, their educational institutions and clergy focused their efforts almost exclusively on their own narrow "natural" constituency.[36] Recognition of or cooperation with non-Orthodox public bodies was certainly out of the question.[37]

Despite the sectarians' strong cadre of adherents and ideological consistency, opined Liebman, they would at best survive but would never experience widespread growth. He attributed this, in part, to their lack of the kind of "intellectual-philosophical perspective" that would broaden their appeal. He admitted that the younger members had experienced some level of acculturation, and many of them had certainly grown financially secure. This had not drawn them closer to non-Orthodox Jews. It had, however, enabled them to communicate their more clear-cut religious vision to the products of the less doctrinal Modern Orthodox. The result was a steady shift to the right on the part of the entire committed Orthodox community. Liebman predicted that this rightward turn would continue. Hence, American Orthodoxy was destined to remain vibrant, but in the process it would become more sectarian and cloistered within its own self-enclosed environment.[38] Indeed, today the Haredi sector accounts for nearly two-thirds of those categorized by the 2013 Pew Report as Orthodox.[39]

Continuity and Realignment

American Orthodoxy's shift to the right is by now well documented.[40] It is generally agreed that this process has only intensified over time.[41] Indeed the search for rigorous explanations for this phenomenon has inspired some of the most original and persuasive discussions and analyses of the roots and character of American Orthodoxy. Additional factors not yet present in the mid-1960s, such as the influence on Orthodox life of the many modern day-school graduates who study in the more monolithic environments of post–high school yeshivas in Israel, have recently buttressed this trend.[42]

Modern Orthodoxy's shift to the right is exemplified in a wide variety of areas that move beyond those described by Liebman. Separation of the sexes in formal educational frameworks, previously a characteristic of schools found in sectarian precincts, is increasingly the norm within "banner" Modern Orthodox communities.[43] At the university level, students once considered "natural" candidates for YU are instead attending institutions of higher education that emphasize their minimal liberal arts course requirements.[44] YU's own "yeshivish" ambience is illustrated by the black felt yarmulkes and dark sport jackets that dominate scenes once containing knitted kippahs and jeans. Evening home games of the YU Maccabees basketball team, once a major attraction for the "Americanized" students, cannot compete with voluntary study in the *beis medrash* (study hall)—the "in" place to be until the wee hours of the night.[45] Halakhic observances associated with Liebman's sectarian Orthodox have become the accepted standard within Modern Orthodox circles as well.[46] Liebman himself noted in the 1960s the disappearance of mixed-gender social dancing at Orthodox weddings.[47] Today, however, it is rare—at least within major

Orthodox centers such as the greater New York area, Los Angeles, Chicago, Toronto, and southeastern Florida—to attend an Orthodox wedding in which there is no *mehizah* (physical divider) on the dance floor to prevent both physical and visual contact between the sexes.[48] After marriage it is quite possible that the bride will wear a wig or head covering in public, once again halakhic behavior formerly associated exclusively with sectarian Orthodoxy.[49] Indeed, a vocal and apparently sustainable backlash to the slide to the right has emerged in the last decade. To date, its main institutions such as Yeshivat Chovevei Torah (YCT) rabbinical seminary remain on the periphery for most of those who are within the mainstream Modern Orthodox constituency. That said, its very existence has already played a role in the realignment at the center of this study and will be addressed in detail in chapter 7 and in the conclusion of this work.

The adoption of stringent ritual and social practices by people from within the Modern Orthodox orbit has blurred the lines between the various American Orthodox camps at numerous levels. Liebman predicted this, yet the distinctions that he drew between the modernists and the sectarians were not predicated exclusively on differences in personal religious behavior and educational and cultural orientations. According to Liebman the fundamental line of demarcation was that which emerged most definitively from the church/sect divide. Modern Orthodoxy's churchlike quality was best exemplified through its willingness to work together with non-Orthodox Jews and to address a broad constituency within its own institutions as well. The sectarians closed themselves off and took little interest in those who differed from them.[50] From this perspective, I suggest that the church/sect divide no longer offers accurate insight into the nature of American Orthodoxy.[51]

Since the late 1980s, and with increasing intensity in the last two decades, a realignment has taken place within American Orthodoxy, offering an alternative to the dichotomy that was previously applied. While Modern Orthodoxy has adopted numerous ideological positions and patterns of religious and social behavior formerly particular to the traditionalists, there are strong indications that the latter faction has become less monolithic and adopted manners of conduct and attitudes formerly associated with the Modern Orthodox. The bulk of Haredi Orthodox Jews remain situated in the ever-expanding neighborhoods of Brooklyn, as well as Rockland County, New York, and Passaic and Lakewood, New Jersey.[52] Yet since the 1970s Haredi concentrations have sprouted or expanded dramatically throughout North America: Baltimore, Maryland; Toronto, Ontario, Canada; West Rodgers Park in Chicago, Illinois; West Los Angeles, California; and even Houston and Dallas, Texas. Unlike Liebman's sectarian Orthodox, as well, the majority of contemporary American Haredi Jews were born in the United States. The central area of change that directly challenges the "sectarian" label, however, is the relationship of Haredi Orthodoxy toward non-Orthodox and nonobservant Jews. Offspring of the same Jews who strove to create cloistered communities, where they could focus exclusively on self-survival, are demonstrating an enhanced sense of concern and responsibility for other Jews who stand outside their own natural milieu.

The earliest example of adjustment in the relationship of traditionalists toward other Jews was in the adoption of "kiruv," or outreach to fellow Jews, as a core value. The pioneers in such endeavors were actually the Modern Orthodox and the highly independent-minded Chabad Hasidic movement.[53] By the 1970s the Haredi world had begun to get involved too.[54] Today kiruv is a central goal of this community. Numerous educational institutions, organizations, and publications have been created with the aim of bringing Jews closer to religious observance. The Haredi media also devote considerable space to discussions regarding the inherent value of such efforts and the practical methodologies that can make them most effective.

The key position that outreach now occupies within the formerly "sectarian" Orthodox ethos points to a more basic change that began to emerge within this sector in the late twentieth century. The survivalist approach that had dominated the efforts made by World War II refugees began to give way to a new outlook. The more confident the leaders were that their style of Orthodoxy was not threatened with extinction, the more sensitive they became to sharp increases in assimilation and loss of Jewish identity around them. Indeed, they may have seen outreach as a tool for strengthening their own group through "mass conversion." Yet the shift in priorities certainly implies greater cognizance of the issues confronting the broader Jewish collective than was previously the case.[55]

Introversionists and Reformists

The rise of outreach within Haredi Orthodox circles does not, in and of itself, demand a reassessment of the continued application of the church/sect dichotomy to American Orthodoxy. In his study of Jewish sectarianism in the Second Temple period, Albert I. Baumgarten makes the following comments regarding the general nature of sects: "I therefore define a sect as a voluntary association of protest, which utilizes boundary marking mechanisms—the social means of differentiating between insiders and outsiders—to distinguish between its own members and those otherwise normally regarded as belonging to the same national or religious entity."[56] Thus seen, the sect constantly seeks to distance itself from others and is concerned almost exclusively with its own internal dynamics and ideology. Its contacts with the outside world are often limited to issues crucial to physical survival or to situations that offer the opportunity to deepen the chasm between its own membership and the "evil" or "ignorant" outsiders.

Yet the "ideal" sect does not encompass within it the variety of "sectarian type" groups that exist. Indeed, sociologists have sought to articulate subcategories of sects that take into account the limitations of applying one rubric to a wide range of religious and social frameworks that all seem to share certain common characteristics. Baumgarten himself employs just such a distinction in order to encompass groups as far apart as the Pharisees and the Qumran community within the borders of sectarianism. Adopting the terminology of Bryan Wilson, he suggests that the Pharisees should be characterized as a "reformist sect," while the Dead Sea group approximates more closely to the classical mold of an "introversionist sect": "The former hold hopes of reforming the larger society, and have not given up on it or renounced it totally, still perceiving themselves as members of the whole.... The introversionist sort of sect, by contrast, has so finally rejected the institutions of the society as a whole as to turn in on itself completely, and to rank those outside its bounds as irredeemable."[57]

Applying these subcategories to American Orthodoxy, one may suggest that the elevation of outreach to a pivotal role in Haredi Orthodox society does not undermine its basically sectarian character. After all, the majority of Haredi Orthodox still live in relatively cloistered environments. Nevertheless, their creation of specialized institutions and training of individuals dedicated to strengthening the religious identity of others does signify this sect's movement from an "introversionist" to a "reformist" status.[58] This should by no means be interpreted as a conferment of legitimacy on the non-Orthodox lifestyle or as an expression of willingness to work as partners with non-Orthodoxy on issues of common interest. But it does articulate a change. While still convinced of both its authenticity and unique group identity, Haredi Orthodoxy has become sufficiently connected to the broader collective to encourage others to join its ranks.

The novel initiatives that have arisen since the 1990s and that are addressed in this book indicate that the trends taking place within Haredi Orthodoxy move beyond a reformist stance. Rather than simply aiming to bring new recruits into their own ranks, there is a growing appreciation for positive expressions of Jewish identity on the part of the broader Jewish collective, even if they do not lead to adoption of an Orthodox lifestyle. Moreover, various institutional boundary markers that were considered sacrosanct in previous generations—such as not entering a Reform synagogue even to teach Judaism—have been blurred in the effort to engage other Jews. Like many religious movements, Orthodoxy possesses a strong sense of what is considered to be ideal religious behavior. In the mid-twentieth century, all Haredi Orthodox energies were trained on buttressing the narrow group that conformed to these standards. Today, in contrast, there is greater understanding that those who "fall short" are also deserving of the attention necessary to sustain them, even minimally, within the collective.

If the evolution in Haredi Orthodoxy reflects a distancing from strict sectarianism, the core Modern Orthodox versions exemplify a retreat of this sector into survivalist mode. While the Haredi yeshivas have redirected their students away from their historic introspection and toward promoting unity among Jews of all orientations, graduates of banner Modern Orthodox institutions have been drafted primarily to buttress their own educational and communal institutions. Liebman's "church" Orthodox, who first championed the role of addressing the broader Jewish community, have actually refocused their efforts toward their own core observant constituency.

Many within the Modern Orthodox camp now admit to the lack of well-defined ideological principles and charismatic leadership, which Liebman identified as major sources of Orthodoxy's weakness. Some children of Modern Orthodoxy have responded by moving closer to the more doctrinaire Haredi Orthodox approach,[59] while others have been attracted to alternative social and intellectual frameworks that have led to a weakening in their Jewish commitment.[60] Whichever the case, the common result has been a sense of "crisis" that has been articulated by Modern Orthodoxy's strongest supporters and leading spokesman.[61]

Notwithstanding this dulling in the expansive "church" quality that was once a hallmark of Modern Orthodoxy, it would be wrong to suggest that this branch of American Judaism has simply morphed into a sort of "sect" while sectarian Orthodoxy has become more "church" like. In each camp, numerous characteristics—such as differing attitudes toward American culture, leisure, education, and acceptable intellectual pursuits—remain consistent with Liebman's dichotomy. The 2013 Pew Survey notes, for example, that even as Haredi (Ultra-)Orthodox individuals are increasingly earning university degrees, the percentage of college graduates within this camp is still less than half that of Modern Orthodox adherents.[62] More significantly for the current discussion, while outreach has become part and parcel of the Haredi ethos, the same study also demonstrates that sectarian attitudes are still far more prevalent among its rank and file than among their Modern Orthodox counterparts.[63] This can only partially be accounted for by distinguishing between the Mitnagedic yeshiva world and the more enclavist Hasidim.[64] I offer, then, that changes that have occurred within American Orthodoxy have resulted in a more fluid and less easily categorized religious stream than that which Liebman described in the mid-1960s. Like any religious trend it is variable and continues to adjust in response to evolving internal and external realities. In as far as the relationship of American Orthodoxy's various factions to other Jewish groups is concerned, it would appear that each camp's position is as much a reflection of its own self-confidence and sense of security as it is a product of deeper ideological convictions.

* * *

American Orthodoxy's development is presented in this volume through a series of historical and sociological case studies that focus on seminal aspects of this religious branch primarily in the twentieth century and reaching until the second decade of the twenty-first century. Each chapter can stand alone and offers insight into a special event, individual, institution, or phenomenon. Taken together, they produce a fresh interpretation of the evolution of American Orthodoxy during this period.

The bulk of the book is split into two main sections. The first, titled "Division," concentrates on the period up to the 1980s and illustrates the process by which Orthodoxy in America transformed from an appendage to the preeminent established European communities into an independent entity with its own voice and ultimately to the new "Babylon" in parallel to Israeli Orthodoxy. These discussions highlight distinctions between the Modern Orthodox and sectarian camps. Nonetheless, individuals and trends are also detected that evoke porous borderlines between the sectors that emerged more prominently toward the end of the century. The second section, "Realignment," begins with two chapters that portray striking aspects of the "Haredization" or the "shift to the right" of Modern Orthodoxy that have not drawn the attention of others. The next four chapters concentrate on the Haredi Orthodox world and put forward crucial evidence for the abandonment by key segments within this camp of the predominant sectarianism that had long prevailed. The conclusion raises additional analytical points and considers some of the possible scenarios for the future.

Methodology

In 1991 an entire volume of the academic journal *American Jewish History* was dedicated to reviewing the contributions of Charles Liebman to the study of contemporary Jewish life. After the piercing essays of prominent colleagues,

INTRODUCTION

Liebman penned a response titled "A Perspective on My Studies of American Jews." Beyond engaging the main points of each critique, he introduced some broader methodological remarks regarding his own approach. Somewhat counterintuitively in light of his own training as a social scientist, he asserted the primacy of historical study and familiarity with prior models of Jewish life in modern times for gaining a deep appreciation for the character and unique qualities of American Judaism:

> To understand the present one must compare it with the past and this requires historical knowledge. In addition, I believe that the careful reading of texts, which is part of the historical method, is the best preparation one can have for developing one's "sociological" sensitivity. The American Jewish sociologist needs to develop an ear and an eye to appreciate what one is "really being told" in an interview or what is "really taking place" in a social setting. At the risk of offending many of my good friends and most American Jewish sociologists, I believe that modern European Jewish history and American Jewish history are more important prerequisites for the student of American Jewish sociology than sociology in general and the study of quantitative methods in particular ... it is the discipline of history which, in my opinion, should shape the orientations of the American Jewish sociologist.[65]

I read these sentences just as I began to address twentieth-century American Judaism more rigorously. As my initial academic research focused on the intellectual and social history of nineteenth-century European Judaism—religious denominations in particular—Liebman's words quite naturally resonated to my ears. I was privileged to study both on the master and doctoral levels with outstanding historians, Jacob Katz and Gershon Bacon, both meticulous historical observers who made insightful use of concepts emanating from the social sciences in their analyses of historical episodes and Jewish societies. In point of fact, the central thesis of my doctoral dissertation and my first book was predicated on theories that originated in the works of sociologist Emile Durkheim and social anthropologists Mary Douglas and Louis Dumont. Moreover, throughout this book, indeed beginning with this chapter, I draw from sociological tools both for gathering data—participant observation, personal interviews, and quantitative surveys conducted by others—and for analysis of the information. Nonetheless, like my main mentors—and unlike most scholars of contemporary American Jewish life—my core scientific instruments are, in Liebman's words, "historical knowledge" and "the careful reading of texts, which is part of the historical method."

By no means do I claim that my distinctively historical orientation offers the exclusive vantage point from which to address contemporary Orthodoxy. All the same, the comparative and contextual understandings that illuminate almost every chapter facilitate distinct appreciation for both the continuities and the departures from prior models or norms that characterize contemporary Orthodoxy. Thus, some precedents for late twentieth-century Haredi Orthodoxy are found in the worldview of a Hungarian immigrant rabbi from the 1920s; a Modern Orthodox rabbinical family is compared to Hasidic and Mitnagedic dynasties from the nineteenth century; Haredi opposition to Orthodox Soviet Jewry activism in the 1960s and 1970s is examined in the context of the experiences of Eastern European rabbis under communist rule; seemingly novel expressions of antagonism to Orthodox feminism are addressed through the lens of Ultra-Orthodox demonization of moderates in nineteenth-century Hungary; new Haredi approaches to Reform Jews are evaluated as a component of the ongoing tension over the past two centuries between Orthodox and Reform; cutting-edge rabbinical training programs are assessed as part of the history of the modern rabbinate; and the influence of Chabad houses on the emergence of Mitnagedic community-outreach kollels is analyzed through the prism of Mitnagedic responses to early Hasidism among the students of the Gaon of Vilna.

Undoubtedly, American Orthodox Judaism is in many ways an unprecedented phenomenon. But it is simultaneously an outgrowth and expression of trends and evolutions whose initial formative moments long preceded the current products. By introducing an interdisciplinary orientation that highlights historical context and close reading but is duly cognizant of the prevailing scholarship and utilizes social scientific theories and perspectives when they can shed light, I aim to contribute to a richer and more thorough critical narrative of American Orthodoxy in the twentieth and early twenty-first centuries.

I
DIVISION

I

Between Hungarian Orthodoxy and American Modern Orthodoxy

This chapter offers fresh insight into the division between the sectarian Orthodox and Modern Orthodox streams that was evolving during the early twentieth century. The starting point is an impassioned debate that transpired in the 1920s between two of American Orthodoxy's most prolific authors, Rabbi Hayyim Hirschenson and Rabbi Yekutiel Yehudah "Leopold" Greenwald. The formal topic of their heated interchange was their discordant evaluations of the Hungarian separatist Orthodox ideology that each independently encountered prior to their immigration to America. It becomes clear that their seemingly historical dispute actually reveals alternative visions for American Judaism. Most of the chapter focuses on the heretofore minimally studied Greenwald and the efforts of this scholar-rabbi to differentiate between his brand of Orthodoxy and the upstart "imposters" that he described as "Modern Orthodox." On the one hand, the positions that he articulated laid the groundwork for the Haredi Orthodox worldview that emerged more emphatically after World War II. On the other hand, the tensions between his declared ideology and the actual situation of the community that he served are suggestive of the realities that have led to more recent adjustments in the policies of contemporary American Haredi Orthodoxy—and which will be addressed in part 2 of this book.

Introduction

Amid the myriad Jewish efforts to accommodate modern Europe's novel realities, Hungarian Orthodoxy stood out, according to Jacob Katz, in promoting "enhancement of the tradition ... limitation of contact with the outside world ... [and] exclusion of the recalcitrants."[1] Over the course of the late nineteenth and early twentieth centuries, prominent disciples of this stream spread its influence to other parts of the continent as well as to the "yishuv" in Jerusalem.

Within descriptions of the burgeoning United States Jewish religious life, however, Hungarian religious ideologues played relatively minor roles. To be sure, many Hungarians could be found among the thousands of Central European Jews who reached the shores of North America from the mid-nineteenth century, including influential rabbis.[2] But the rabbinic elite that arose in America alongside the millions of Eastern European Jews who arrived between the 1870s and 1924 was dominated by Polish and Lithuanian Orthodox figures.[3] This dynamic only began to change in wake of World War II, particularly with the establishment of large Hungarian Hasidic courts—most prominently the Satmar dynasty—on American soil.[4]

Nevertheless, there were a few conspicuous early twentieth-century American rabbis whose outlooks and policies were shaped or inspired by their exposures to Hungarian Orthodoxy. This chapter concentrates on one of them, Rabbi Yekutiel Yehudah "Leopold" Greenwald (1889–1955) of Columbus, Ohio, a native Hungarian who was nurtured within its Torah academies. The various ways that his Hungarian background manifested itself within the American Jewish landscape offer novel perspectives on the initial rise of American Modern Orthodoxy and its clash with its European precursors during the early twentieth century. Indeed, this chapter provides evidence of the tensions inherent in seeking to cultivate a core sectarian worldview within the realities of local American communal life before World War II.

Hungarian Orthodoxy

By the mid-nineteenth century, Hungarian Jewry was deeply divided along ideological lines. The Neologue movement that supported cultural integration along with educational reform and moderate ritual adjustments developed into the religious base for liberal-minded Jews. Opposing this group was a vocal and noncompromising Orthodoxy that refused to give any modicum of legitimacy to the outlook or lifestyle of their acculturated counterparts. A less militant Orthodox minority also existed and contested the positions of its zealous counterparts.[5] The split between the Neologue and the Orthodox became official political reality when a government-sponsored "Jewish Congress" in 1868–69 was abandoned by the Orthodox. Ultimately, the Hungarian government recognized two completely separate national Jewish communal bodies, one carrying the flag of the Neologue, the other under Orthodox auspices.[6] Later, a third strand known as the Status Quo also arose. Every individual local community had to decide to which religious organization it would declare allegiance.[7]

The most militant Hungarian traditionalists have become known within scholarship as the Ultra-Orthodox. This group articulated an ideology that was predicated on demonization of all aspects of modernity. Moreover, they listed among the enemies of the Torah not only those who reinterpreted it or abandoned traditional observance, but even figures who identified with accepted Orthodox legal standards and theology but sought to minimize its conflict with outside culture and non-Orthodox Jews.[8]

In the wake of the Congress of 1868–69, Ultra-Orthodox perceptions were integrated more centrally into the normative outlook of the Hungarian Orthodox religious leadership and its communal policies. This is not to say that all of the Ultra-Orthodox positions were adopted—rather, that the core stances of alienation from modern culture and erection of sharp boundaries between loyal Orthodox Jews and all others achieved dominant and almost exclusive status as the accepted Hungarian Orthodox way.[9]

Some of the most ideologically motivated Ultra-Orthodox emigrated from Hungary and established a community of the faithful in Turkish-controlled Jerusalem. This small but fiercely loyal collective and its rabbinical leaders achieved profound influence on the religious atmosphere within non-Zionist "old settlement" circles during the late nineteenth and early twentieth centuries.[10]

The Greenwald-Hirschenson Exchange

In the summer of 1928, an "open letter" by Yekutiel Yehudah Greenwald that was addressed to Rabbi Hayyim Hirschenson (1857–1935) of Hoboken, New Jersey, appeared in the American rabbinical journal *Apiryon*. Greenwald said that he owed his correspondent an explanation. In the fall of the previous year, 1927, an edition of the same publication had been printed that was dedicated to Hirschenson on the occasion of his seventieth birthday. In Hirschenson's printed words of thanks to those involved in this project, he wondered "aloud" how the editor even knew when his birthday was in the first place.[11] Greenwald's subsequent letter offered an answer.

Greenwald let out that he had supplied the date and had actually been the one to suggest that a collection of writings by fellow rabbis and scholars would be a suitable birthday honor for Hirschenson.[12] Yet provision of this information actually put Greenwald in an awkward position. If he—already a copious author in his own right—was the one who had initiated the anthology, why did he refrain from contributing an essay in honor of Hirschenson?

Greenwald did not skirt this issue. On the contrary, he offered an explicit explanation for his actions that included a highly personal accusation against Hirschenson:

> I did not participate in this work, why? . . . In your talmudic novellae . . . you wrote "And terrible trouble was brought by the Hungarian sages upon Israel. . . ."[13] [And] in the fourth volume of your work *Malki ba-Kodesh* . . . you recorded that "Ever since our brothers the sons of Hungary settled in the Land of Israel, infighting and division have grown . . . sectarian dissention and multiplication of irreparable splits has long been the national sickness of the children of Hungary."[14] Forgive me honorable one for your pen has spilled an inadvertent sin. You that labors to find goodness among the lighthearted evildoers who publicly desecrate the Sabbath, while regarding the brilliant rabbis of Israel that saved the country from total destruction, you find no redeeming qualities? . . . From these words I could only conclude that you possess hatred toward our brothers the children of Israel from my birthplace, that stems from ignorance as to the reason for the division and the fissures. When I recognized this I made an about face—for I thought am I not one of them, a person from that same country that brought terrible misery upon Israel?[15]

Greenwald added that on numerous occasions since his arrival in America he had heard such accusations "against Hungarian Jewry" but he was especially surprised to see them written by Hirschenson.

The rest of Greenwald's letter is a five-page exposition on the merits and correctness of the Hungarian Orthodox approach to communal separatism from the days of the Hungarian Jewish Congress of 1868–69 onward. Among others, Greenwald deflected an additional critique of hypocrisy rendered by Hirschenson against the Hungarians for adopting the non-Jewish titles "Orthodox" and "Neologue" as the designations for the opposing groups rather than the Hebrew *"shomrei Torah"*—Torah keepers—and *"mefirei Torah"*—Torah violators.[16] Hirschenson, no stranger to controversy, did not sit idly by. In the following edition of *Apiryon* he published his retort in which he forthrightly rejected Greenwald's defense of Hungarian Orthodoxy and expanded further his original assessment.[17] The fact that the two protagonists could be considered kindred souls with many ostensive similarities indicates the need to delve into the roots of their conflict.

Rabbinical Scholars in a Strange Land

Hirschenson, born in 1857, was thirty-two years older than Greenwald, yet the two shared much in common. In fact, in explaining why he chose to respond to his younger adversary, Hirschenson emphasized that he felt obligated to do so because it was written by "an ideological companion in a number of areas." He also noted that Greenwald had visited him personally at his home in New Jersey.[18]

The two men were members of the Agudath ha-Rabbonim (Union of Orthodox Rabbis of the United States and Canada), an organization that only accepted foreign ordained rabbis into its fraternity and saw its role as defending tradition against the trials of American acculturation.[19] In addition, both were highly qualified scholars of Jewish law and religious life who served as rabbis of Orthodox synagogues in secondary American communities, and whose main pursuits and contributions were through their copious literary outputs. All the same, Greenwald was more proactive in asserting his rabbinic leadership.

The Safed-born Hirschenson spent his early years in Jerusalem before moving briefly to Turkey and then immigrating to the United States in 1904. He authored over thirty books and countless articles, and he made his intellectual mark in particular as a halakhic theorist and religious thinker. His creative approach to fundamentals of Jewish law was inspired by his search over the course of more than thirty years in the American rabbinate for ways to navigate the spread of secularization, critical scientific theory, nationalism and Zionism, American democracy, women's rights, fresh economic circumstances, and technology. Although apparently not overly adept at communicating with his Americanizing congregants, he was very sensitive to their plights and struggles and sought solutions that would enable them to maintain connections to Jewish tradition. His writings are for the most part explorations of the intricacies of Jewish law and thought geared to knowledgeable rabbinic colleagues and beyond the grasp of the vast majority of his synagogue membership.[20] They present a radically tolerant "churchlike" position, even bordering at times on pluralism.

Significant contributions to the study and practice of Jewish law can be found as well among the corpus of forty-five books and more than five hundred articles authored by Greenwald, who was born in Sziget (Maramarossziget; currently Romania). His main areas of concentration, however, were religious histories of Central European Jewry and literary efforts to preserve the legacy of his native Hungarian Jewish life.[21] As rabbi of Columbus's Beth Jacob congregation, he taught weekly classes, preached regularly in Hebrew and Yiddish, and was extremely active in communal welfare projects, yet Greenwald never became a proficient English orator. Like Hirschenson, he seems to have maintained a certain degree of cultural isolation from his surroundings by engrossing himself in his intellectual pursuits.[22]

Of the two, Hirschenson's reputation was decidedly more the maverick. His innovative suggestions for adjusting Jewish law raised the eyebrows of numerous colleagues, as did his often defiant writing style.[23] Indeed, today he has been adopted by liberal factions in Israeli Orthodoxy as an ideological forerunner of sorts. Greenwald, nonetheless, also did not fit easily the stereotype of a Hungarian Orthodox rabbi.[24] His father was a deeply committed religious individual, imbued with Ultra-Orthodox animosity toward outside culture and education. While the son too was dedicated to Torah study and absorbed a great deal of traditional knowledge during his formative years, by his mid-teens he already expressed considerable interest in modern political movements and enlightened Jewish learning.

As a fourteen-year-old, Greenwald participated in the 1903 convention of the religious-Zionist Mizrahi party in Pressburg (Bratislava), and, like Hirschenson, he remained a Zionist activist throughout his career.[25] His position was especially bold in light of the predominant antagonism of Hungarian Orthodoxy to the Zionist movement.[26] He also studied at Pressburg's famed yeshiva. This, despite his father's glaring opposition. The Pressburg yeshiva's long-held reputation as a stronghold of traditionalism was by the early twentieth century compromised by a fair share of "individuals who reeked with the scent of enlightenment."[27] Indeed, still during his teens, Greenwald made his way from Pressburg to the Frankfurt am Main yeshiva of the *gemeindeorthodoxe* (nonseparatist) rabbi Nehemiah Nobel. A fellow Hungarian expatriate, Nobel was a student of the moderate rabbi Esriel Hildesheimer and a major German Zionist leader, as well as an intellectual protégé of the neo-Kantian theorist Hermann Cohen.[28] Alongside his Frankfurt yeshiva studies, Greenwald attended classes in history and philosophy at the local university. By the age of nineteen he had already published a biography of the controversial eighteenth-century rabbi Yonatan Eibeschütz, and until his 1924 migration to America, he served briefly as a rabbi in a Hungarian community, but he also worked as a journalist and as an army radio operator during World War I.[29]

Once in America, Greenwald concentrated his prolific pen on preserving the legacy of Hungarian Jewry. A review of his historical works makes clear that he supported the Orthodox position unequivocally. In fact, the term "apologist" could be applied. Yet he also demonstrated greater tolerance for diversity than the official party line disseminated when he grew up there. Among others, he referred to controversial rabbinical figures as upstanding scholars and prized students of major authorities, and he sought to offer reasonable explanations for the zealous actions of some of Hungarian Orthodoxy's central authorities.[30]

As to his policies and performance as rabbi in Columbus, once again there are two perspectives from which they can be analyzed. He clearly represented strict Orthodoxy within the community. Famously, he condemned kosher butchers from the Beth Jacob pulpit who opened their stores too soon after the Sabbath. In addition, upon finding out that one of the attendees at his Friday night lecture forum had driven to the synagogue he canceled the entire season of presentations. And when Mordecai M. Kaplan's new Reconstructionist Sabbath prayer book was published in 1945, he declared that it should be burned, that its author should be excommunicated, and that any rabbi who defended it should lose the right to use this title.[31]

Notwithstanding, when it came to cultural and intellectual discourse Greenwald displayed a level of openness to diversity that would have found little support within the Hungarian Orthodox milieu in which he was nurtured. His public lectures included titles such as "George Washington and the Jews" and "The History of Medieval Jewish Philosophy," and in 1933 he participated in a debate over whether Shakespeare's play *The Merchant of Venice* was anti-Semitic. His synagogue also held special events in memory of Theodor Herzl and Hayyim Nahman Bialik, the first an assimilated Jew of Hungarian descent and the second a former Lithuanian yeshiva student who had abandoned the observance of his youth. More dramatically, he helped bring secular Zionist leaders to the community for speaking engagements. Not just Golda Meir (then Meyerson) was welcomed, but even Abba Hillel Silver, one of the most prominent Reform rabbis in America and longtime spiritual leader of Cleveland's famed The Temple.[32] The very idea of being involved, even for a common cause, with a renowned Reform figure is a total anathema to the Hungarian separatist Orthodox worldview. In

CHAPTER 1

Hungary, Polish Hasidic figures were even condemned for associating with the anti-Zionist Orthodox Agudath Israel movement because the Neo-Orthodox Germans were part of the coalition.[33] Greenwald also maintained an ongoing correspondence with the well-known Reform rabbi and scholar Solomon Freehof. As an Ohio native and historical researcher, Greenwald sought out the best Judaica library in the region, which meant periodic visits to the Reform Hebrew Union College in Cincinnati.[34]

During the mid-twentieth century, mixed-gender seating in the synagogue became a contentious issue within American Judaism.[35] The pressure to remove the *mehizah* barrier and integrate the male and female sections was especially pervasive in the midwestern states, starting with Ohio.[36] In fact, a traditional synagogue named Agudas Achim existed in Columbus in which mixed seating was eventually instituted in parts of the sanctuary. Greenwald was the fiercest local opponent of this innovation and, following classic Hungarian separatist doctrine, refused to set foot in the Agudas Achim edifice. In 1948, and with his synagogue Beth Jacob in decline, intense negotiations took place with the intention of merging the two "traditionalist" houses of worship. Ultimately, however, the agreement fell through. This was due primarily to the fierce opposition of Greenwald, who garnered a core group of supporters around him and won the day. Nonetheless, when the new Beth Jacob synagogue was being built two years later numerous of Greenwald's own loyal congregants demanded that it too adopt mixed seating. In the end, he agreed that as long as male and female sections remained separate the *mehizah* could be removed—a compromise that was, once again, completely foreign to the Hungarian Orthodox worldview.[37]

The American custom of holding weddings inside sanctuaries raises additional evidence regarding Greenwald's fickle steering between adherence to Hungarian Orthodox norms and adjusting to American realities. He begins an undated responsum published in 1942 by acknowledging that in Hungary, based on an opinion explicated by the authoritative Rabbi Moses Sofer, the Hatam Sofer, there was strong consensus forbidding such rituals in the synagogue. Thus, when Greenwald first arrived he would only perform ceremonies in people's homes or gardens. "However, afterward I was no longer able to stop and fight against the current, . . . and since then I have lowered my head and performed ceremonies in the synagogue, but I warned and requested that the sanctity of the synagogue be preserved, and commanded that the women go to their separate gallery."[38] He then goes on to offer both legal reasoning and historical evidence that explains why the impetus for the Hungarian prohibition does not apply to the American religious culture.

Characterizing Greenwald's relationship to his Hungarian Orthodox separatist heritage, then, is not a simple matter. A closer look at his 1928 letter to Hirschenson offers insight into the seeming internal contradictions between Greenwald's staunch loyalty to Orthodox separatist ideology and his own operative deviations during the course of his American career.

A Condensed and Heroic History of Hungarian Orthodoxy

Greenwald's 1928 letter of protest to Hirschenson that appeared in *Apiryon* was published just four years after his arrival in the United States. In it he adopted a form that he had already begun to develop in Hungary and which he utilized throughout his career. His sympathetic approach to the Hungarian Orthodox separatism was articulated through a neatly packaged story. It begins in the early nineteenth century with the spread of the Haskalah and Reform from Germany to other parts of Europe and describes the manifestations of these trends within mid-nineteenth-century Hungary. It then gives an account of the Congress of 1868–69, the "courageous" behavior of the Orthodox, and the subsequent dramatic encounter of its sages with the Kaiser Franz Josef that led to the decision to free them to create their own national framework. In words meant to chide Hirschenson directly, Greenwald exclaimed, "I am deeply pained to say that a Christian king had a greater understanding of the issue than many Jews and even some rabbis.... He did not perceive the separation as a sickness. On the contrary, it was the most complete and safe remedy."[39]

Greenwald summed up his heroic narrative as follows: "Since then there is peace and serenity in each and every town, there are no grievances and no invectives.... In truth the assimilationists soon recognized the mistake of their approach, and they still seek to reunite, but why would we want such a problem?"[40] Strikingly he does not portray in any detail the ongoing hostility of the Orthodox toward the Neologue in Hungary, and even more so the visceral battles between the Orthodox and the Status Quo that only began after the events described and continued at the time this letter was written in 1928. Outlining the contemporary situation would have been much easier, one would think, since rather than relying on the testimony of others, Greenwald himself could have served as a firsthand witness. Nonetheless, he chose to omit any discussion of more recent events.

As far as Greenwald was concerned, then, a powerful confrontation had transpired during the late 1860s and early 1870s in which the valiant Orthodox had won the day, and since then all was tranquil and quiet. The proof was found in the fact that throughout Hungary numerous communities could still be found that were characterized by fear of God and commitment to Torah study. If not for the separation it was unlikely that this would have come to fruition.

At the end of his letter, Greenwald draws a parallel between the Hungarian Orthodox policies and the secessionist campaign carried out by Rabbi Samson Raphael Hirsch in Frankfurt-am-Main, Germany, that culminated in 1876.[41] Moreover, Greenwald expresses hope that the policy of separation would be applied to America as well. In this context, he reprimands Hirschenson for maintaining friendly relations with the Eastern European scholar Rabbi Hayyim Tchernowitz (Rav Za'ir), who was employed by Rabbi Stephen Wise in his Reform Jewish Institute of Religion. All the same, Greenwald admits that his knowledge of the role of the Hungarian Orthodox in the Land of Israel—the central source for Hirschenson's familiarity with this group—was limited.[42]

Greenwald was so dismayed by the "ignorance" of his colleagues regarding the correctness of the Hungarian Orthodox approach that soon after publishing the letter to Hirschenson in *Apiryon* he set out to author a more detailed volume on the subject. The result was his 1929 work, *Li-Felagot Yisrael be-Hungariyah* (The Divisions of Israel in Hungary), whose subtitle was "On the condition of the Torah in the Land of Hungary, the battles of the God fearers against the Reform, the arguments between the communities and the rabbis . . . and the reason for the division into two parties." There, on the first page of the introduction, he notifies the reader that his interchange with Hirschenson gave the initial impetus for him to compose the new volume.[43] Although this was not Greenwald's first time addressing this topic in a monograph,[44] it was his initial full-length engagement with the issue since he arrived in America. Despite its clear Orthodox slant, this volume—which was dedicated in memory of his father—remains an important repository for scholars seeking information on the Hungarian Jewish schism.[45] Moreover, it was recognized as an authoritative historical account within the Orthodox literary canon. The fact that Rabbi Abraham Frankel, the Budapest-based president of the Orthodox national communal organization, penned a letter of support that appears at the beginning of the text likely contributed to the book's renown within traditionalist circles.[46]

In light of his own early deviations from the intellectual and cultural milieu of Hungarian Ultra-Orthodoxy, as well as aspects of his subsequent American rabbinical career, Greenwald's ongoing dedication to Orthodox separatism is perplexing. How could the same individual who later maintained contacts with secular Zionists and more dramatically Reform figures and institutions so staunchly defend Hungarian Orthodox sectarianism—even to the point of fueling a feud with Hirschenson?

One consideration that must inform any attempt at addressing this conundrum is to reiterate that while Greenwald grew up in a vociferously Ultra-Orthodox environment, he was never a typical Hungarian yeshiva student or rabbi. Indeed, as noted, his interests, activities, and associations from as far back as his early teen years digressed from the conventional path of this camp, and he left home specifically to expand his intellectual horizons. Thus, what might appear to the reader as an inconsistency was actually the idiosyncratic way he conducted himself throughout his life.

It should also be borne in mind that Greenwald's letter to Hirschenson was written early in his American tenure. As time went on the realities of American Jewish life at least partially softened his resolve. Certainly, his acquiescence toward the end of his life to serve in a synagogue with separate seating but no *mehizah* would support this perception. All the same, as late as 1948—just three years before the new synagogue was opened—he published a work that essentially reaffirmed his commitment to the righteousness of the Hungarian separatist approach.[47] There are additional factors, however, that emerge directly from his letter to Hirschenson and offer broader insight into Greenwald's outlook regarding the Hungarian Orthodox approach and its relevance to American life.

Despite the many incidents related to the schism that had transpired between 1871 and 1928, as emphasized above, Greenwald's letter focused nearly exclusively on the initial events. Clearly he was aware of the subsequent infighting and demonization of those Hungarian Jews, even with strong Orthodox pedigree, who questioned the policies of the Orthodox bureau in Budapest. Yet what Greenwald sought to defend, or for that matter construct, was the most poignant legacy of the separation—and not every last detail. It was the heroic version whose initial formulation appeared in the writings of some of the protagonists of the original battles themselves (including Rabbi Moses "Maharam" Schick, about whom Greenwald later penned a biography).[48] No doubt there were some prominent rabbis in Hungary at the time of the Congress, such as Hildesheimer, who had deep reservations regarding the outcome. In subsequent decades, by contrast, the correctness of the original decision of their leadership to abandon the Congress and to embark on a campaign in its aftermath aimed at securing a separate communal framework became almost indisputable for the vast majority of Hungarian Orthodoxy. This was the foundational narrative upon which all Hungarian Orthodox Jews had been nurtured since the 1870s and which few dared to question.[49] The idea put forward by Hirschenson that this fundamental principle of existence—what might even be termed a doctrine or article of faith—was rotten at the core, and for that matter had polluted the rest of the Jewish world through its proliferation, was unfathomable to Greenwald, and had to be refuted unequivocally. If this demanded homing in on the less internally controversial episodes, so be it.

To be sure, Greenwald did not simply pay lip service to the ideology of Orthodox separatism. As already seen, simultaneously with his self-appointed position as the constructor of an official Orthodox version of the Hungarian schism, throughout his career he continued to play the role of guardian of the tradition in the face of the many challenges that it met on American soil. Sometimes he did so in ways that were wholly consistent with the policies of his Hungarian Orthodox brethren. At other times, he charted an alternative practical path. As far as he was concerned, his actions were inspired by the principal sectarian worldview that emerged in Hungary during the 1870s.

Hungarian Separatism Meets American "Modern Orthodoxy"

This idea that the Hungarian Orthodox outlook remained ingrained in Greenwald's worldview even as the specifics of his public actions may have digressed from its norms receives further support from another element that shouts out from the letter to Hirschenson. Greenwald, the same person who did not refrain from certain associations with Reform leaders and institutions, simultaneously called for imposition of Hungarian-style separatism in America.

A close examination of the section in which he makes this proposal is instructive. The example that he offers for justifying an official schism is not of a Reform spokesman who spreads his heterodox ideology, but of rabbis who preach ideas that are contrary to legitimate Orthodox theology in ostensibly Orthodox synagogues. These figures speak critically of the great Sages and exegetes of the past and in the process disseminate heresy from the pulpit. A clear demarcation, therefore, needed to be established in order to neutralize this American phenomenon that he encountered incessantly.[50] Who were these rabbis "who preach heresy," and why did they inspire Greenwald to promote a Hungarian separatist model as the best remedy for the future of American Jewish life?

At first glance, it would be reasonable to surmise that Greenwald was referring to graduates of the Jewish Theological Seminary (JTS) at a period of time, the late 1920s, when distinctions between American Orthodoxy and the nascent Conservative movement were hazy at best. The liminal border was expressed institutionally, for example, through the efforts of backers of the staunchly Orthodox yet Americanized Yeshiva College and JTS to facilitate a merger.[51] This, while Mordecai Kaplan—who had already made his official break from Orthodoxy—was simultaneously cultivating the next generation of seminary graduates through his position as head of its Teacher's Institute and his dynamic lectures in homiletics and midrash.[52] Recall that Greenwald later expressed the desire that Kaplan's prayer book be burned and its editor excommunicated. Greenwald's introduction of the Hungarian separationist approach to the American scene, then, would have been intended to inspire the Orthodox camp to mark clearer boundaries between itself and the rising, and more theologically heterodox, Conservative stream.[53]

A more compelling reading, however, is that the proposal for separation in Greenwald's letter to Hirschenson was directed, not at wholly new denominations, but against figures and bodies that identified unambiguously with the Orthodox rubric—members of the Orthodox Union, for example—and nonetheless behaved in ways that to his mind undermined core traditional values.[54] Indeed, he could have been alluding to Hirschenson himself, who had achieved infamy in some Orthodox circles for his unconventional theories. Closer to home, Greenwald's call for clarifying internal boundaries most likely stemmed from his own struggles with Agudas Achim, the other Orthodox synagogue in Columbus. During the 1920s this congregation was still a long way off from its late 1940s decision to sanction mixed seating, but it was already a larger, more Americanized congregation than Greenwald's Beth Jacob, and many if not the majority of this "churchlike" institution's members could be termed "nonobservant Orthodox." Some of the rabbis that it hired possessed doctoral degrees from European universities, while others were English-speaking graduates of the Rabbi Isaac Elchanan Theological Seminary (RIETS), the rabbinical academy from which Yeshiva College emerged.[55] Struggling, as Greenwald was, to cultivate a more traditionalist-oriented and religiously homogeneous congregation, his arrows were directed at the adversary whose religious outlook still shared the most in common with his. Note that as late as 1948 serious merger negotiations between the two institutions had taken place, only to be undone by Greenwald and his supporters. Of course, in attacking his neighboring Orthodox synagogue, he was also following the example of his Ultra-Orthodox colleagues in Hungary, who had long ceased focusing their diatribes on the Neologue and instead dedicated most of their efforts to defaming the moderate Orthodox and Status Quo.[56]

The introduction to his 1929 work, *Li-Felagot Yisrael be-Hungariyah*, supports and offers more expansive evidence for the conclusion that the American targets for Greenwald's separatist campaign were formally Orthodox figures and institutions. Echoing and expanding on his letter to Hirschenson from one year earlier, he states that "in publishing this volume here, I am responding to the needs of the hour here in America."⁵⁷ Greenwald then goes on to describe the horrific condition that was to be found: "Orthodox, half Orthodox, Reform, and those who pervert the way of the Lord in one congregation ... the members claim that they are Orthodox, yet in their synagogues they adopt customs of the Reform."⁵⁸ Among these "foreign" behaviors he lists: confirmation ceremonies for girls at twelve and boys at thirteen, English singing by young ladies on Friday night in front of the Torah ark followed by the rabbi's lecture on the latest theater production, or, "far worse," a Christmas Eve rabbinic presentation that speaks with great honor about Jesus.

This description, with its derogatory slant, almost certainly alludes to the late Friday evening "Open Forum" instituted by the highly esteemed Dr. Isaac Werne, the Eastern European–ordained rabbi of Agudas Achim who had earned a PhD at the University of Königsberg in Germany before immigrating to the United States.⁵⁹ In his history of Columbus Jewry, Marc Lee Raphael reports that during these gatherings Werne would "familiarize the members and their families with the more modern day questions" and "sometimes ... review popular motion pictures. . . . [O]n other occasions he would deliver lectures about 'Anthropomorphism in the Bible, 'Higher Criticism and the Bible,' or the 'Humanistic Appeal of Judaism.'"⁶⁰ Werne was a staunch and publicly active Zionist, and his forums were, according to Raphael, "the most popular programs of their kind in the Columbus Jewish community during the 1920s. The non-Jewish press regularly discussed the Open Forums and the Orthodox community generously attended them. Although he would speak English with a terrible accent, he drew a thousand people on a Friday night to listen to his lectures."⁶¹

Werne's Friday night initiative was part of a broader national phenomenon. As second-generation American Jews left the menial jobs of their immigrant parents behind and veered toward entrepreneurship, they were less likely to be forced to work on Sabbath day itself. On the other hand, the regular Friday workday, especially in the winter months, extended far beyond the commencement of the Sabbath. Thus, Reform and Conservative synagogues had initiated "Late Friday night services" that enabled the entire family to participate. This compromise with economic realities proved attractive even to many with a more traditional bent. Fearful of losing core members of their constituency, numerous Orthodox congregations followed suit. Others produced a different compromise, maintaining the legally mandated worship times but introducing an additional "Late Friday Night Forum" that consisted of a few prayers that were not part of the regular evening service, along with educational and social elements. As evidenced by Agudas Achim during Werne's stewardship, this creative navigation between normative practice and socioeconomic realities facilitated a robust Sabbath Eve event for his Americanized congregants.⁶²

Without mentioning Agudas Achim or Werne by name, Greenwald asserted that the innovations that he described had no place within the rubric of Orthodoxy. For, as he made clear in his 1929 work, were it not for a few biblical or Talmudic references that none of the attendees understood, it would be hard to identify such sanctuaries as Jewish prayer halls. More dramatically, these rabbis offered interpretations that contradicted those of the Sages, and in the process their ignorant congregants simply drew the conclusion that all was permitted. "Tragically," Greenwald lamented, this all took place in "Orthodox congregations, for I am not even speaking of the Reform or half-Reform."⁶³ Therefore, he concluded, it was incumbent upon the Agudath ha-Rabbonim organization to create a collective framework that would clarify through its membership policies once and for all "which congregations can justly and legally be termed Orthodox congregations."⁶⁴

Indeed, Werne represented a particular thorn for Greenwald. Recall that the Agudath ha-Rabbonim refused to grant membership to American-ordained rabbis. This was essentially a way to prevent JTS graduates from gaining legitimacy. Yet Werne had bona fide Orthodox credentials from Europe and nonetheless had drifted, according to Greenwald, beyond the margins of legitimate Orthodox conduct. Thus, additional standards had to be enforced in order to defend the faithful Orthodox from those who had conceded to the whims of the times.⁶⁵

No doubt interpersonal and professional tensions contributed to Greenwald's highly negative tone. And, in truth, some of the charges leveled against Werne could have been raised by unwavering Hungarian Ultra-Orthodox ideologues in reference to Greenwald's own concessions to American life as well. All the same, his behavior was surely much closer to the traditionalist approach than that of his prominent neighbor. As such, Greenwald's declaration that American Orthodoxy could learn practical lessons from his historical description of the Hungarian Jewish battles of the previous century was not merely an aside. It reflected, rather, his own modeling of the Hungarian precedent within his new milieu. In Hungary, outstanding moderate rabbinic leaders such as Esriel Hildesheimer had been characterized as "the horse and chariot of the evil inclination,"⁶⁶ and strict tests of loyalty had been instituted in order to clarify who was Orthodox and who was not. Thus, despite his own idiosyncratic ways, when confronted with an "ambitious syncretist's" approach to Orthodox synagogue life,⁶⁷ Greenwald advocated the time-tested Hungarian sectarian model that he had internalized in his youth: demonizing the "enemy" from within and then constructing or reinforcing a more clearly defined framework for housing the loyal minority.

To be sure, the parallel identified here between Greenwald's approach to American Jewish religious disharmony and the subject of his historical writing could reflect the stage in his career. The polemic with Hirschenson as well as his work *Li-Felagot Yisrael be-Hungariyah* both appeared within five years of his arrival in America. Like any new immigrant, it would have been natural for Greenwald to still perceive Jewish life through the lens of his Hungarian upbringing. Over time he might have been expected to adjust to the fresh circumstances of his new environment and abandon those characteristics of his formal culture that did not jibe with American realities. Clearly, as described above, Greenwald did modify his rabbinical posture in numerous areas in order to accommodate his more recent surroundings. There is illuminating evidence, nevertheless, that more than a decade after his written clash with Hirschenson, he was still deeply ensconced in the Hungarian style of sectarian discourse. What did change is that a subdenominational category entered Greenwald's nomenclature, enabling him to define his enemy with greater precision.

In 1939 Greenwald published his halakhic compendium on the laws of burial and mourning, *Ah le-Zarah*.[68] This was a pioneering volume that presented practical ritual guidelines based on highly competent adjudicatory experience along with considerable familiarity with the peculiarities of the American scene. The volume (and especially the revised version that appeared in 1947 titled *Kol Bo al Aveilut*) actually gained for Greenwald far greater stature and long-term exposure in American rabbinic circles than any of his historical works.[69] These texts are groundbreaking not only in how they address American religious realities, but also in that they are among the first examples of the genre of practical guidebooks geared toward American circumstances that have proliferated since the 1980s under Artscroll, Feldheim, and other imprints.[70] In his introduction to *Ah le-Zarah*, Greenwald speaks about the manifold challenges that American funereal and burial norms placed before those loyal to Jewish law and custom. In this context, he returns to the internal Orthodox polemic that he had initiated soon after his arrival, lamenting,

> I myself have heard a speaker who is known by the title rabbi that when eulogizing before the deceased spoke of the greatness of the Russian author Tolstoy. Once upon a time the children of Israel knew well that those who act in this way were called free thinkers, or the deviants of

Israel, Reformers, who have no place among the kosher Israelites. Today, however, they speak in the name of Modern Orthodoxy, and the rabbi is Modern Orthodox, which means that he has the right to change, limit, or add as the times demand as long as he is called Orthodox.

In a footnote he goes out of his way to further define this group:

> Modern Orthodoxy, a plague that does not appear in the Bible. . . . They destroy all that is holy to us. On Sabbath [Friday] evening they gather in the synagogue, arriving in automobiles, they park on all of the surrounding streets. The entire congregation sings tunes, women and men together, young ladies and women chant in front of the Holy Ark and the Modern Orthodox rabbi babbles about Spinoza, Schöpenhauer and other such friends. This is their Sabbath evening worship of God and they throw their spears on all who try to speak out against them. . . . They eat their meals anywhere and even in the homes of women who desecrate the Sabbath in public. . . . They also belittle the adultery laws and without proper investigation and testimony they declare a woman to be eligible for marriage.[71]

By this time, 1939, Werne had moved on to Los Angeles, where he served as chief rabbi of the United Orthodox Rabbinate, but Agudas Achim remained a thorn for Greenwald. Werne's successor, Rabbi Mordechai Hirschsprung (1894–1954), was also an accomplished religious thinker and an outstanding orator. A graduate of City College of New York and Yeshiva College, Hirschsprung was active in many communal organizations including serving as president of Columbus Mizrachi (Religious-Zionists).[72] Greenwald, by contrast, was described by one of his contemporaries as "not very effective as a preacher because he spoke a type of Yiddish which most people could not understand . . . and his English was halting at best."[73] Some of Greenwald's Beth Jacob worshipers could not but wonder why their Orthodox synagogue lacked the flexibility and contemporary tone of the larger and more vibrant neighbor and how come their scholarly rabbi refused to yield to the cultural norms of the surroundings. Thus, the publishing of a new book offered an opportunity to clarify, once again, the boundaries between "real" Orthodoxy and the counterfeiters.

Greenwald's introduction of the designation "Modern Orthodox" is particularly noteworthy. The year 1939 was not the first time that this term was employed within American Jewish religious discourse, but in prior examples, it was generally utilized either in reference to the German "Neo-Orthodox" ideology of Rabbi Samson Raphael Hirsch,[74] or to describe a variety of local examples of a balance between innovation and allegiance to Jewish law that differed from Reform.[75] Indeed, many spokesmen of the nascent Conservative movement portrayed aspects of their approach as modern Orthodox.[76] Greenwald, however, raises "Modern Orthodox" as a formal label for a collective framework or substratum of American Judaism. This is most evident in the distinction that he draws between "free thinkers, or the deviants of Israel, Reformers, who have no place among the kosher Israelites," on one hand, and "Modern Orthodox" on the other.[77]

In applying the tag "Modern Orthodox" to his adversaries Greenwald established that they were different from both the Reform and Conservative, but he simultaneously distinguished them from "true" or "authentic" Orthodox Jewry. This served him well, for it provided a clear branding for those who strayed from his traditionalist European-style Orthodoxy. No longer did he need to complain about these figures and congregations usurping the name Orthodox. Rather, by highlighting or for that matter articulating the formal category of "Modern Orthodox," the genuine Orthodox were cleansed of simply being classified in one broad rubric with less committed Jews. No training ground could have nurtured him better for intuiting this boundary definition tool than his own upbringing in the heart of Hungarian Orthodoxy.

Moving forward, the way in which Greenwald made use of the designation "Modern Orthodox" already in 1939 can be seen as a precursor or harbinger to the subsequent—beginning in the 1950s[78]—wider application of the term referring to a specific stream of American Orthodoxy.[79] For a considerable number of late twentieth-century American Jews, this synthetic designation became a mark of pride.[80] Yet following the pattern initiated by Greenwald, the traditionalist Hasidic and yeshiva refugees who arrived en masse after World War II used "Modern Orthodox" pejoratively. It became a synonym for the sector that feigned religious observance but actually followed a watered-down lifestyle and ideology of convenience and compromise to societal norms that came dangerously close to the Conservative posture.[81]

Hirschenson: The Scars of Youth

Greenwald's initial American iteration in 1928 regarding Hungarian Orthodoxy, recall, was instigated by the severe accusations of his elder colleague Rabbi Hayyim Hirschenson in works published in 1923 and 1926. Among others, Hirschenson had written that "sectarian dissention and multiplication of irreparable splits has long been the national sickness of the children of Hungary."[82] To be sure, this lack of appreciation for the Hungarian Orthodox approach to communal strife is not completely surprising. For as already noted, Hirschenson professed a stridently positive perspective regarding many aspects of modern Jewish life and was highly sympathetic toward the religious and economic challenges faced by his fellow immigrants. Nonetheless, the vociferousness of his critique of Hungarian Orthodoxy is indicative of a more deeply rooted hostility. In point of fact, this virulent antagonism can be attributed to Hirschenson's intensive exposure to Hungarian Ultra-Orthodoxy during his youth and young adulthood prior to his arrival in America. This background draws an additional intriguing parallel with Greenwald, whose empathetic posture toward the Hungarian approach also had its origins in his early years. Yet the conclusions drawn by Hirschenson were diametrically opposed to those of his younger associate. Biographers have chronicled Hirschenson's upbringing and initial development, but none has emphasized the profound negative impressions that lingered from his initial exposure to Hungarian Jewry, nor have they noted a relationship between them and his ultimate articulation of a radically tolerant worldview.

Hirschenson's confrontations with representatives of Hungarian Orthodoxy took place in Turkish-controlled Palestine. The son of a rabbi who was open to some educational reform and was an early supporter of productive settlement in the Land of Israel, Hayyim Hirschenson spent much of his childhood and early adulthood in Jerusalem. There, he received rabbinical ordination in his father's yeshiva and later divided his time among a variety of business ventures, educational initiatives, and religious-intellectual pursuits. His progressive approach to education—which included cooperating with Eliezer Ben-Yehudah's efforts to advance the study and development of the Hebrew language—along with his publication of controversial materials in a journal that he edited, drew the enmity of the religiously zealous contingent in Jerusalem. So much so that in 1887 a *herem* (writ of excommunication) was declared against him to much fanfare at the Western Wall. After nine years of fighting to maintain his position and to support his family under these conditions, in 1896 Hirschenson left Turkish Palestine. He first worked as head of a Jewish school in Istanbul, before migrating permanently to America and settling in as rabbi of the Orthodox synagogue in Hoboken, New Jersey.

The main figures that caused Hirschenson hardship in Jerusalem were affiliated with the Hungarian contingent. Their base was the Batei Ungarin quarter in what is now known as the Meah She'arim neighborhood. One of the people who led the attacks on him was Rabbi Yosef Hayyim Sonnenfeld (1848–1932), the former student of the Pressburg yeshiva who arrived in Jerusalem in 1872—not long after the battles surrounding the Hungarian Jewish Congress.[83] During their formative years, Hungarian natives like Sonnenfeld had experienced the intense conflicts between their leaders and those Jews who supported modern intellectual and political culture. As such, upon immigrating to Jerusalem the Hungarians were highly motivated to prevent any "impurities" from undermining Jewish life in the Holy Land. Sonnenfeld was later to become one of the outspoken ideological adversaries of Rabbi Abraham Isaac Kook, the most prolific rabbinic personality to support the Zionist endeavor, and a figure Hirschenson admired greatly.[84]

Not surprisingly, then, Hirschenson's 1928 defense published in *Apiryon* of his prior deprecating statements regarding the Hungarians highlights the zealous activities in Jerusalem as the central proof for the defective character of the entire Hungarian Orthodox approach. These interactions were so visceral that he was convinced that the behavior of the Jerusalemites could not have emerged merely in response to the local debates. In his opinion, what began in the 1860s as an emergency response had transformed into the core identity of Hungarian Orthodox Jews. While it was fair to assume that the original leaders "did not sense how the ongoing habit of tearing apart (the Jewish collective) would influence their followers," it was undeniable that "most of the splits in Jerusalem emanated from (what had become) the Hungarian's natural love of divisiveness."[85]

The contrast with Greenwald is dramatic, for, as emphasized above, Greenwald's "heroic" narrative celebrates the Orthodox response to the Hungarian Congress of 1868–69 and barely gives details regarding the impact of communal separation on Jewish life either within Hungary or beyond in the following decades. As confident as Greenwald was of the redemptive effect of the founding epoch of Hungarian Orthodox separatism, Hirschenson was convinced that these same actions had facilitated the evolution of a core destructive "schismatic nature."[86]

These sharp distinctions between the respective views of Greenwald and Hirschenson regarding Hungarian Orthodoxy, both fostered in their native lands, play out dramatically in their opposite understandings of Jewish life in their common adopted home. Greenwald proposed instituting Hungarian-style communal separation in America. To his mind, this was necessary in order to differentiate the Reform, Conservative, and Modern Orthodox impostors who deviated from the fundamental principles of Judaism, on the one hand, from those truly Orthodox figures and communities who actually represented authentic Judaism, on the other.

To such propositions Hirschenson retorted, "All the impure blemishes that you detect among the Reformers ... may have come because they were rejected with two hands, and the lack of interest in them.... The sign of this can be seen today regarding assimilation which was the greatest blemish among the Reform, and is being cured among many Reform rabbis through Zionism which does not push away the stone after it has fallen."[87] Instead of focusing on differences and establishing strong ideological boundaries, argued Hirschenson, had the Orthodox rabbinic leaders adopted a more inclusive and accepting "churchlike" stance they could have prevented the wholesale abandonment of Jewish identity by so many modern Jews through assimilation—a far more destructive force than Reform. The Zionist movement's focus on national identity had gained a following among some Reform figures. This demonstrated that a more accepting posture was the key to Jewish survival in America.

On one point Hirschenson did agree with Greenwald: he too was displeased by the fact that rabbis who espoused heretical ideas preached regularly in American Orthodox synagogues. Yet he did not support Greenwald's demand for clearer denominational definitions. On the contrary, Hirschenson actually attributed the phenomenon of "renegade preachers" to the emphasis on official labeling that was rooted in the Hungarian perspective. Instead of evaluating a synagogue based on its ritual standards and the religious integrity of its leaders, Hirschenson claimed, God-fearing people had been duped into assuming that as soon as the title "Orthodox"—itself a non-Jewish term—became associated with a synagogue, all that went on there was acceptable: "If we are Hebrews then we fear the Lord in Heaven, but if we change our names, we turn to foreign Gods."[88] As far as Hirschenson was concerned, not only had the Hungarian Orthodox orientation failed to save Jewish collective life, it had undermined the ability of sincere Jews to discern the proper approach, and many had been turned toward alien ways. All this, he emphasized, had its roots in the ideology of divisiveness that emerged from the original Hungarian Jewish schism in the late 1860s.

Conclusion

At the close of their annual convention in 1914, the association of European-born and yeshiva-trained Orthodox rabbis in America, the Agudath ha-Rabbonim, issued a pronouncement: "The rabbis ... could not hold back any longer and prepared for an intense war against all destroyers of Judaism and enemies of the religion from within and without.... [They] declared that its task was to protest against those organizations whose external face is Orthodox but in truth are Reform and set a net to ensnare the legs of the young generation, to draw them in and bring them under their wings."[89] The main target of this denunciation was the burgeoning Conservative movement. During the previous year, 1913, the chancellor of the Jewish Theological Seminary, Rabbi Solomon Schechter, announced the formation of a new congregational association, the United Synagogue of America, and used the term "Orthodox" to describe his worldview. The organizers of the Agudath ha-Rabbonim convention set out to clarify specific collective religious behaviors that set a synagogue or educational institution outside the margin: mixed seating, placing the bimah at the front of the sanctuary (like in a church), and, of course, associating with the United Synagogue—which was considered from a polemical perspective no different than Reform. In fact, for these figures the Conservatives were far more threatening since the seminary claimed allegiance to Jewish law, and its graduates were culturally more in touch with the younger generation than were their Eastern European adversaries. Truth be told, the Agudath ha-Rabbonim were suspicious of all American-born rabbis, but the establishment of a new, avowedly more liberal congregational framework offered an opportunity to clarify the lines of American Orthodoxy. The aim of the Agudath ha-Rabbonim was to bring to a finish the years of haziness in which all those who opposed Reform could somehow be put together in one basket. Patent definitions, declarations of loyalty, and institutional purity were gaining a bold voice within American Orthodox discourse. This formula, they assumed, could still prevent the masses of recent Eastern European immigrants from abandoning their allegiances to a traditionalist orientation.

Although hardly a monolithic religious and intellectual personality, Rabbi Leopold Greenwald demonstrated with his American career that he empathized with the overall approach expressed by the Agudath ha-Rabbonim. Yet in contradistinction to the stated goals of this organization, the middle decades of the twentieth century saw the Conservative movement establish itself as a major force in American Judaism. To be sure, the boundaries between the Orthodox and the Conservatives remained somewhat porous throughout most of his life, but already from the mid-1920s Greenwald fixed his polemical gaze on an even closer target. Drawing on his Hungarian ideological roots and responding to conditions within his own local community, he assailed officially Orthodox figures and institutions that labored to be inclusive and created innovative social and educational instruments in order to attract the rapidly Americanizing immigrants and their second-generation offspring. Following the position of his Hungarian predecessors vis-à-vis their moderate Orthodox colleagues, Greenwald put forward pejorative descriptions to demonstrate that the novelties of these peers would undermine authentic Judaism. Therefore, those who professed these approaches needed to be marginalized. Moreover, Greenwald buttressed his internal Orthodox boundary-maintenance efforts by designating his adversaries as "Modern Orthodox." This term, which until then had been used primarily as a self-description by Conservative thinkers, was now being utilized in a sectarian manner to censure those internal forces in the mid-twentieth century that were watering down true Orthodoxy through their "churchlike" behaviors.

Commenting on the role of the Agudath ha-Rabbonim in the evolution of American Orthodoxy during the twentieth century, historian Jonathan Sarna wrote, "Their exclusive definition of what constituted an Orthodox rabbi, their resistance to Americanization, and their desire to build, metaphorically, a protective wall around the Torah, an enclave where traditional Judaism would be safe from encroachments, however extreme these seemed at the time, laid the foundation on which later rabbis built fervent or Haredi Orthodoxy, the movement's rightmost wing."[90] By introducing his Hungarian legacy to a wide readership and toiling to implement aspects of its outlook within the community he served, Greenwald's base approach may be seen as well as a forerunner of the Haredi Orthodoxy that emerged in the postwar period. Indeed, his early fundamental distinction between Orthodoxy and Modern Orthodoxy stands as a harbinger of the dichotomy that held sway through much of the late twentieth century. That said, his eclectic intellectual oeuvre and his occasional willingness to join together even with Reform and secular Zionists when common cause was found are suggestive of a less doctrinaire position that has emerged in more recent years and which will be addressed in detail in the second part of this book. The next two chapters, however, will consider developments within mid-twentieth-century Modern Orthodoxy prior to the era of realignment.

2

A Modern Orthodox Rabbinical Dynasty

This chapter focuses on one of the pioneering Modern Orthodox synagogues in the United States and the rabbinical family that consistently steered it in this direction throughout the twentieth and early twenty-first centuries. The discussion considers those elements that, despite the evolutions and vicissitudes of American Jewish life, allowed the Margolies-Lookstein family to maintain its leadership of New York's Congregation Kehilath Jeshurun (KJ) for more than one hundred years. While unique in certain ways, KJ nonetheless serves as an archetypical model for the type of inclusive and Americanized Orthodoxy that emerged particularly in the mid-twentieth century. As such, the story of KJ provides a foil against which to analyze the trends toward "Haredization" within contemporary Modern Orthodoxy that will be considered in part 2.

Introduction

Decades before Greenwald's struggles against his "Modern Orthodox" neighbors in Columbus, Ohio, Congregation Kehilath Jeshurun (henceforth KJ) was established on Manhattan's Upper East Side. From the early twentieth century,

KJ gained prominence as a pathbreaking religious institution dedicated to rejuvenating Orthodoxy on American soil when many foresaw its demise. At a time when masses of immigrants and their offspring were becoming alienated from religion altogether, KJ fostered an atmosphere that attracted these proud new Americans—some of whom adhered to Jewish law and others who were less meticulous. It did so by hiring college-educated rabbis who delivered relevant homiletic messages in nonaccented English; by pioneering a day school that drew both observant and nonobservant parents who valued Jewish knowledge but were unwilling to compromise on their children's secular educations; and by nurturing a service that was intended to be (in the words of the driving force in this renaissance, Rabbi Joseph Lookstein, 1902–79) "as dignified as the most Reform and as pious as the worship in a *shteibbel*."[1] In the late 1950s, his son, Rabbi Dr. Haskel Lookstein, joined him. During Haskel Lookstein's stewardship, he expanded the existing institutions and their activities dramatically, and extended the core vision of Orthodoxy deeply engaged with a wide range of Jews and comfortable within its American surroundings by making public activism integral to synagogue life.

Like Greenwald's adversaries in Ohio, then, the rabbinical family that served this congregation throughout the twentieth century introduced numerous innovations aimed at attracting a broad cross-section of American Jews to its services and functions. In contrast to their midwestern counterparts, however, all along the KJ rabbis remained intent on doing so without abandoning Orthodox affiliation and the fundamental commitments to certain religious standards that this demanded. Navigating the tension between allegiance to tradition and embracement of their Americanized constituency required ideological ingenuity and unique leadership skills. This chapter examines the religious worldview that emerged in KJ during the course of the twentieth century, how it evolved from one generation to the next, and the rabbinical model that sustained the ongoing relationship between this particular family and this religious institution. In doing so, it offers a case study for the type of "church oriented" Modern Orthodox rabbinate that Liebman highlighted in his 1965 study. Unlike similar institutions, however, the Looksteins and KJ have succeeded in preserving the core elements of their worldview into the early twenty-first century.

The foundations from which the KJ version of Modern Orthodoxy arose were established during the thirty-one years that Rabbi Moses Zebulun Margolies served the community. Under the guidance of his granddaughter's husband, Joseph Lookstein, a worldview was articulated that is carried on—with some adjustments—by his son, Haskel Lookstein, until today.[2]

CHAPTER 2

Rabbi Moses Zebulun Margolies—the "RaMaZ" (1851–1936)

At first glance, Margolies seemed to fit the stereotype of the typical late nineteenth-century rabbi who emigrated from Eastern Europe.[3] Dressed in a black frock coat with a majestic white beard flowing to his chest, he spoke publicly only in Yiddish. But while many of his Orthodox contemporaries saw their roles as battling against the "Americanization" of Judaism, this was not the case for "RaMaZ" Margolies.[4]

Indeed, Margolies's acceptance of the KJ position after seventeen years as rabbi of an immigrant community in Boston may be a telling indication of his religious convictions. Established in 1872, KJ was located in the Yorkville section of Manhattan.[5] Its founders were Jews of means who had risen from the tenements of the Lower East Side, the natural first stop off the boat from Europe.[6] The name chosen for the synagogue may reflect the German roots of some of its initial membership.[7] By the turn of the twentieth century, however, the majority of KJ's affiliates were well-off businessmen of Eastern European origin and their families. Most spoke fluent English and sought to mix with the surrounding society.[8] Yet they felt more comfortable at KJ than at a nearby Reform institution such as Manhattan's Temple Emanuel or Rodeph Sholom, either out of allegiance to a traditional Jewish lifestyle or due to sentimental and social factors. Already in 1904, KJ exhibited signs of moving from the familiar traditional immigrant model to a more Americanized congregation.

In that year, the congregation's desire to integrate into American life received distinctive expression when Rabbi Mordecai M. Kaplan, a recent graduate of the Jewish Theological Seminary (JTS) and the future founder of the Reconstructionist movement, was hired as minister and educational supervisor.[9] It was within this setting that Margolies entered KJ a year later.[10] Throughout his time at KJ, an English-speaking rabbi served alongside him and delivered the overwhelming majority of the sermons. Before Joseph Lookstein, they were all JTS graduates.[11]

During Ramaz's thirty-one-year duration as rabbi of KJ, his main role was that of the traditional "*rav*." He taught Torah classes, presented *derashot* (rabbinical discourses) in Yiddish a few times per year, extended personal counseling to members of the congregation, and ruled on issues of ritual law. It is difficult to evaluate his expertise in halakhah and Torah scholarship. He did not leave any responsa or halakhic essays. The single testimony that remains on this issue—from the autobiography of Joseph Lookstein—describes Margolies as "an acknowledged authority on Jewish religious law. Rabbis from all over the country would turn to him for opinions and decisions."[12] Lookstein cites as an example

Margolies's landmark decision permitting Jews to ride an elevator operated by a non-Jew on the Sabbath. According to Lookstein, Margolies always gravitated toward the lenient opinion, which only added to the respect he commanded.[13]

In his role in the synagogue Margolies remained for the most part a "rabbi from the old school"—albeit a compassionate one, but in his interaction with the Jewish community at large he displayed a maverick openness. In particular, he was willing to work in partnership with people of different religious orientations. For this, he endured sharp criticism from his colleagues affiliated with the Agudath ha-Rabbonim—the organization he helped create in 1902 that limited association with non-European rabbis, and whose members were for the most part outspokenly opposed to Americanization of Judaism.[14] In addition, during Margolies's term as president of the Rabbi Isaac Elchanan Theological Seminary (RIETS), the school took its first steps from a traditional yeshiva in the Eastern European mode to Yeshiva University (YU), an institution dedicated to the synthesis of advanced Torah study with academic-level secular education. He publicly declared his support for Zionism and even permitted Judah Magnes (chancellor of the newly established Hebrew University) to speak in the main sanctuary of KJ on Kol Nidre (the solemn, opening prayer on the Day of Atonement) night 1927.[15] Before his emigration to Palestine, Magnes had held rabbinical positions at the Reform Temple Emanuel and the Conservative Bnai Jeshurun. Margolies was also a member of several nondenominational Jewish social and educational organizations and worked in conjunction with non-Orthodox rabbis and other nonobservant Jewish communal leaders.[16]

Margolies did not formulate a new rabbinical model for American Orthodoxy. Nor was he a theoretician of Jewish law in the mode of Rabbi Hayyim Hirschenson. He exemplified, rather, a committed Orthodox rabbi who recognized the needs and complexities with which his American congregants struggled. In a more pragmatic fashion than the relatively detached Hirschenson, he also acknowledged the value of maintaining cooperation with the broader Jewish community on issues of common interest. This outlook would form the cornerstone for an ideology and operative agenda to be articulated more clearly by his successors.[17]

Rabbi Joseph H. Lookstein (1902–79)

With Joseph Lookstein one encounters a new style of American Orthodox rabbi.[18] Beyond demonstrating openness toward the spirit of his times, he was among the central architects and driving forces in the development and spread of a fresh concept in American Orthodox synagogue life. Upon consultation with Dr. Bernard Revel, president of Yeshiva College, in 1923 Margolies invited Lookstein to join him at the KJ pulpit. Just twenty-one years of age and without official rabbinical ordination when he took the post of assistant rabbi and English preacher, Lookstein remained with KJ until his death in 1979. Three years after joining him at the pulpit, Lookstein married Margolies's granddaughter, Gertrude Schlang.

This kinship to Margolies certainly enhanced Lookstein's position within the community, and it made him a natural candidate to inherit the KJ pulpit. It seems unlikely that an individual of Lookstein's talent would have remained assistant rabbi for thirteen years if he did not expect that the post would be his. That said, there was no formal mechanism that set forth that a family member would inherit the post. Lookstein's assumption of the position in 1937 was ensured by his extraordinary rhetorical talent and status as a graduate of RIETS rather than the seminary—by then an official Conservative institution.[19] A multitalented rabbi and educator, he was, among other distinctions, founder of the pioneering Orthodox coeducational Ramaz School, the first president of the Rabbinical Council of America (RCA), president of the cross-denominational Synagogue Council of America, the first chancellor of Israel's Bar-Ilan University, and longtime professor of homiletics at YU/RIETS.[20]

A personal memorandum to his heir and assistant rabbi, Haskel Lookstein, dated October 3, 1968, offers insight into the father's perception of KJ's version of Orthodoxy. The letter was written to check the "extremism" he perceived poking its face within KJ.[21] It appears that the elder Lookstein sensed that his son and others on the synagogue staff felt compelled to apologize for some of the practices that had been instituted in order to add to the aesthetic quality of the service.[22] In the religious ambiance of the late 1960s, some within the Modern Orthodox world had begun to look askance at these innovations. Joseph Lookstein saw an urgent need to guide his chosen successor and protect his own legacy. He turned to his son:

> There seems to be a planned and studied campaign to what I would call the "chnokerization"[23] of our congregation. There is a tendency to introduce what to me is the most odious thing, namely religious extremism into our midst. It is done mildly now but it will become intense. Please trust my intuition.
>
> Hack, what we did in 85th street during over forty years of my incumbency, of which you shared ten with me, was to make Conservatism or Reform unnecessary and undesirable to a substantial number of

families in the neighborhood.²⁴ Some of them came to us from Conservative backgrounds and found themselves very much at home. Some of them would have joined Conservative or Reform temples in this area but found their way to us and now would not go elsewhere.

Some of these families not only have orthodox affiliations at this time, but, as you know, have changed their homes to kosher and their entire home to greater Jewishness. Some of these people sent their children to Ramaz and, because of that, these people and their homes will never be the same.

All of this we were able to do because ... our intention was to conduct the kind of public worship that would be as dignified as the most Reform and as pious as the worship in a "shteibbel." I think that we have succeeded. Before you allow yourself to deviate from that, let us talk.

We have never violated, in our public worship policy, the Jewish law. Whatever we did, we can justify on the basis of law and document our actions accordingly. You know that neither you nor I would do anything that would represent a departure from Jewish law.

That being the case, then I feel that you and I ought to do some real talking and some real heart searching.²⁵

Joseph Lookstein considered KJ-style Orthodoxy to be ideal, and not simply a compromise necessitated by the times. He had a strong belief in the aesthetic, which he conceived of as the key to drawing American Jews into the Orthodox synagogue.²⁶ As opposed to Rabbi Samson Raphael Hirsch of Frankfurt am-Main (1808–88), a personality he loved to present as one of his role models and ideological forerunners, Lookstein opened the doors of KJ to all Jews, without regard to their personal practices or beliefs.²⁷ Moreover, even if he spoke proudly of his success in instilling more Jewish content into their homes, he did not run an "outreach" movement dedicated to encouraging his congregants to adopt a fully halakhically observant lifestyle.

His approach was projected through dramatic sermons, with titles like: "Man, the Unknown—The Jew the Unknown" and "A Religious Definition of Beauty."²⁸ Already early in his tenure, Lookstein and his congregation emerged as models imitated by those within the Orthodox world who viewed modern culture and Americanization positively.²⁹ Indeed, one student who left Yeshiva College for JTS during the interwar period explained that despite Bernard Revel's declared goal of creating a distinctly American Orthodox rabbinate, the majority of the rabbinical faculty at Yeshiva College were "out of sync" with

American society. "The only role model they [at Yeshiva] had of a successful American Orthodox rabbi was Joseph Lookstein."[30]

Joseph Lookstein's letter was written to guide his son and heir. He was convinced that his son would successfully inherit his seat only by adopting the ideology and style he had created. The father maintained this stance in the face of zealous tendencies he identified within American Orthodoxy in the late 1960s. As such, he recognized that his successor's struggles would be focused more on navigating KJ's way inside a changing Orthodox world than in trying to position Orthodoxy in competition with the growing Reform and Conservative movements.

Rabbi Haskel Lookstein (b. 1932)

A review of the changes instituted in KJ during Haskel Lookstein's career demonstrates the ways in which that synagogue has been affected by the general religious atmosphere within American Orthodoxy of the late twentieth and early twenty-first centuries. Today, the community comprises upward of a thousand families, a major increase over the number of families even during the heyday of Joseph Lookstein's tenure.[31] A much larger percentage of these families are meticulous regarding Jewish law—some set out on the path under the guidance of the rabbi and his assistants, while many grew up in fully practicing homes. In conformity with these trends, Lookstein speaks from the pulpit on topics related directly to ritual observance. He has also hired a series of assistant rabbis that excel in Talmudic learning and offer greater traditional text study opportunities for the congregants. Moreover, Lookstein invites *roshei yeshiva* (leading Talmud teachers) from Yeshiva University to present lectures within the walls of KJ on topics of contemporary Jewish law. He even referred to one of them, Rabbi Herschel Schachter, as his *posek* (halakhic adjudicator).[32]

From the 1970s Haskel Lookstein also distinguished himself by adopting some of the tactics that arose out of 1960s American political culture. He was a leading advocate in the struggles for the rights of Soviet Jewry. He traveled to the Soviet Union with his wife, Audrey, to meet with dissidents and local Jews four times between 1972 and 1987, and he turned Soviet Jewry activism into a central motif both in KJ and Ramaz. In 1985 he was arrested at one such demonstration by the New York City police.[33] No doubt his late father would not have been comfortable with such public displays of civil disobedience.[34]

Haskel Lookstein's more intensive promotion of fidelity to Jewish law and political involvement represent digressions from the dignified Upper East Side version of Orthodoxy his father pioneered.[35] At the same time, Lookstein has also thrown his support behind efforts to increase female involvement in synagogue leadership and in ritual life through establishment of a woman's prayer group. Recognizing the diverse population of his synagogue, he has encouraged as well new initiatives such as extensive youth programming, beginner's prayer meetings, and "young couples" services. Finally, showing his awareness of the potential for hyperpunctiliousness in matters of religious law to undermine proper human relations, he has long spoken out on the need to place *"menschliness* before Godliness."[36]

Without underestimating Haskel Lookstein's unique stamp, a strong sense of continuity reigns. For one, his accommodations to new trends such as feminism, as well as his ongoing willingness to partner with non-Orthodox groups, reflect KJ's longtime goal of cultivating an Orthodox environment that engages contemporary American culture positively. What is more, the main showcases of the synagogue, the Sabbath and festival prayer services in the main sanctuary, are almost identical to that of his father's era. They are organized and formal. Sabbath prayers include responsive recitations in Hebrew, while High Holiday worship witness readings in English. All major public rituals are completely managed by the rabbi.[37] Indeed, despite certain adjustments initiated by Haskel Lookstein, by the 1980s many Modern Orthodox practitioners outside the community began to see KJ in much the way Greenwald viewed his more liberal neighbors—as a vestige of a "gray" period when Orthodoxy was forced to compromise in order to ensure its survival.

While Haskel Lookstein would rise to defend the authentically Orthodox credentials of his congregation, he would also readily admit that the changes that have been instituted are minor relative to the deep-seated sense of continuity from his father's tenure through his own: "We are a centrist place as we were when he died. We are an open, tolerant place as we were. We are almost as decorous."[38]

To this point, an ideological line has been drawn from Margolies through Joseph and Haskel Lookstein. Yet there is still quite a gap between a sequence of family members and what can be suitably termed a rabbinical dynasty. A dynasty implies that a specific family has established itself as the natural or legitimate leaders of a particular group or organization. A common basic ideology, while generally a precondition for succession in religious leadership, does not necessarily raise the level of identification between the family and the organization to that which can ensure its continued hold on the reins of leadership.

The Rabbi as CEO (Chief Executive Officer)

The Hasidic rebbe and Lithuanian *rosh yeshiva* are the most prominent models available of rabbinical succession in the modern period. It is perplexing that we find such a basic common denominator between the two rival camps in the battle for the hearts of Eastern European Jewry. Yet upon examination one sees that despite sharp differences in ideology, both groups developed almost identical formulae to ensure that leadership ultimately remained in the family. Surely there were objective criteria for who could be placed at the head, such as the ability to deliver a high-level Talmudic discourse or alternatively conducting oneself as a *tzaddik*. But with these prerequisites met, the primary vehicle through which dynastic families retained their hegemony was through administrative and financial control over the group's or organization's institutions. Contemporary research has demonstrated this phenomenon with regard to the Lithuanian yeshiva,[39] a fact documented as well among the Hasidic dynasties.[40] These rabbis were not spiritual leaders alone. They adopted the expanded role of proprietors of the organizations that they founded and led. This fostered absolute identification between the institutions and governing families, akin to the association of a family business with the principals that direct it.

This facet of dynastic leadership allows insight into the phenomenon that has evolved during the Looksteins' incumbency of the KJ pulpit. In America, the role of the rabbi is multiple; he is the primary Jewish educator, halakhic adjudicator, spiritual leader, and, oftentimes, social worker. Yet most rabbis are quite content to leave the "mundane" aspects of running a congregation—finances, fundraising, maintenance, seating for the High Holidays, board meetings, and so forth—to lay control. Moreover, congregational officials often have an interest in separating the rabbi from these functions, particularly issues of finance. This clarifies the rabbi's status as an employee of the congregation and preserves the ability to check his power or terminate his commission, when necessary.

At KJ, by contrast, the Looksteins created a model of rabbinate that incorporates responsibilities of a quasi–chief executive officer, the rabbi as CEO.[41] For the first three decades of his tenure, Joseph Lookstein oversaw all the affairs of KJ together with the president, Max Etra. Etra's resignation in 1969 after twenty-nine years may have expressed the realization that he had been replaced as Joseph Lookstein's main partner by Kehilath Jeshurun's ascending assistant rabbi, Haskel Lookstein.

Haskel Lookstein asserts that there are virtually no politics in KJ. This, he maintains, is no surprise, as the board of trustees meets only twice a year, and even then, as a "House of Lords." The board is expected to give its stamp of approval on that which has already been concluded between the rabbi and the president and his officers.[42] Here the rabbi is more than a full participant. He sets the agenda for the meeting and authors the subsequent summary that is entered into the official synagogue records.⁴³ Public discussion of the rabbi's salary and benefits, an ordeal that emphasizes the rabbi's dependence on the congregation, simply does not exist in KJ. The terms are known only to the president of the congregation. In other words, the rabbi of KJ is not a typical employee.⁴⁴ To be sure, it is not just the Looksteins who benefit from this situation. The entire congregation is saved from the often acrimonious meetings at which the smallest detail of the clergyman's salary package is examined by all in attendance. It is quite remarkable, nonetheless, that a collective characterized by so many highly accomplished professionals and business people would cooperate with this arrangement.

The Looksteins' active participation in administrative matters is not in itself unique. A survey of American rabbis of all denominations in the early 1980s showed that rabbis often functioned as ad hoc executive directors. All the respondents emphasized, however, that they were compelled to do so for lack of funds to hire a full-time administrator. Rather than offering greater leadership opportunities, respondents felt that the added burden only deepened their sense of being beholden to their congregants. A correlation was demonstrated that the wealthier the congregation, the less likely it was that the rabbi would engage in managerial functions, in sharp distinction to the model that evolved at KJ.⁴⁵ For the Rabbis Lookstein, the role of "rabbi as manager" was cultivated according to their own vision, enabling them to establish a unique identity that practically bridged the chasm between employee and proprietor.

The Looksteins have managed the synagogue with a "hands on" style. The rabbi prepares and supervises the annual budget. The rabbi's acute interest in these issues received expression in a strongly worded internal memorandum by Haskel Lookstein on February 29, 1968, to the executive director, bookkeeper, and sexton of the synagogue, with a copy to his father: "In going over the quarterly report of income and expenditures, I noticed a number of things which I think ought to be considered and on which action should be taken."⁴⁶ He goes on to detail that although income on sales of advertisements for the monthly bulletin was coming in according to projections, this was not the case regarding transactions for new memorial plaques in the sanctuary. Production costs for the bulletin were already reaching the amount budgeted for the entire fiscal year, while outlays for maintenance, obituaries, and office supplies were on the verge of exceeding the full sum allotted. "Perhaps," suggested Haskel Lookstein, "some of the expenses can be cut before it is too late."⁴⁷ Within one day, Joseph Lookstein responded with a memo to his son as well as the other addressees. He expressed dismay "that nobody else, thus far, has become alarmed and disturbed by the financial picture."⁴⁸

The degree of partnership between the two is illustrated in these budget memos. Father and son sensed the urgency in these figures—apparently much more so than did the KJ office staff. It is noteworthy that neither rabbi saw fit to send a copy of his letter to the president or treasurer of the synagogue. The fact that the assistant rabbi initiated the examination of the budget demonstrates that his father had made sure he would be properly trained in all the areas of expertise uniquely demanded of the KJ rabbi. Regarding his first years working in partnership with his father, Haskel Lookstein said: "In those days, it was clear to me that my father ran the shul; if I did things with his approval, that was sufficient—I didn't think I had to clear it with the president of the shul."[49]

Scholarly discussions of Joseph Lookstein have identified his outstanding "administrative and managerial skills."[50] Jenna Joselit catalogued his penchant for keeping statistics of Sabbath service attendance and detailed records on all the members, as well as his scrupulous attention to the physical details of the synagogue: "Lookstein personally inspected the building from top to bottom, making sure that the bathrooms were clean, the brass finishings of the sanctuary polished, and its prayer books untattered and regularly dusted."[51] According to Joselit, this expressed Lookstein's desire to dispel the negative image of the Orthodox synagogue as dirty and lacking aesthetic quality.[52] It also reflects, significantly, on his understanding of what it meant to be the rabbi of KJ. A successful manager, he was not content with the knowledge that he had built an effective organization; he felt a need to personally oversee all aspects of the organization's operations.[53]

For a rabbi to become involved in such issues, he had to have a particular view of his role. Joseph Lookstein saw himself as the ultimate servant of the community and as far more than an employee of the synagogue. In contrast with Eastern European models, however, it must be emphasized that the Looksteins are not the owners of, or even shareholders in, KJ. The financial success of the synagogue does not provide them with the opportunity to accumulate considerable personal wealth. Nonetheless, it does cement the identification between "Lookstein's shul"[54] and the rabbi himself. Like in the Volozhin Yeshiva as described by Shaul Stampfer, the fundraising mechanism set up in order to ensure KJ's ability to function fortified this connection.[55]

The Looksteins' fundraising activities are not limited to extolling the merits of charity from the lectern during the Yom Kippur service. They have always been the central figures in a massive campaign to fill the gap between revenue from membership dues and the costs of running KJ's wide range of religious, educational, and social activities. Each year, before the High Holidays, Haskel Lookstein conducts hundreds of personal phone calls with members of the congregation in order to safeguard that their contribution will at least match that of the previous year. As in most institutions, the more a particular individual is credited with producing income, the greater his overall influence on the organization.[56]

Joseph Lookstein developed the model I have termed "the rabbi as CEO." He perceived that as long as the rabbi serviced the spiritual needs of his congregation and made sure that it stood on firm organizational and financial ground, he could attain almost absolute decision-making authority. As his son Haskel put it: "It is a shul where there is a tradition of great respect for the rabbi. Not crazy veneration, but respect for the fact that the rabbi works all the time for the shul, his whole interest is the synagogue and therefore, if he knows what he is doing, let him lead."[57] Over the years, no doubt this dynamic has also produced numerous detractors among the lay leadership and broader membership. All the same, the very ability of the Looksteins to maintain such a posture is evidence of the predominant sense within the community that such an autocratic approach offers far greater benefits than disadvantages.

This intimate relationship between KJ and the Lookstein rabbinate was never more evident than in the aftermath of one of the darkest moments in KJ's recent history. On July 11, 2011, a fire broke out in the synagogue that caused extensive damage to its historic 85th Street edifice. During the subsequent multiyear renovation, weekday and Sabbath prayers were relocated to the Ramaz Middle School building across the street, while High Holiday services were held at the nearby Metropolitan Museum of Art. As soon as he was informed of the fire, Haskel Lookstein was the central figure in every aspect of the congregation's response to this calamity. His first response was a message of hope communicated to his membership that "out of the ashes of destruction will come the seeds of reconstruction."[58] In chief executive fashion, moreover, he immediately began the process of orchestrating the practical steps toward this rebuilding, including finding alternative venues for prayer and school classrooms, employing architects and engineers to restore and renovate the building as well as add two new floors, and raising the "tens of millions of dollars" necessary to accomplish this. At a meeting one year after the fire, during which he and his staff outlined the reconstruction plan, Lookstein went out of his way to emphasize that the sanctuary "will look exactly like the old synagogue looked."[59]

It would appear that Joseph Lookstein was fully cognizant of the potential for shaping this unique synagogue-rabbi dynamic and strove to create it. His success in founding the Ramaz School in 1937, in memory of the recently deceased Moses Zebulun Margolies, bears evidence to such an outlook. Lookstein faced two problems: the congregation opposed lending financial support to the project, and its members were staunchly opposed to sending their own children to an Orthodox Jewish day school; after all, the neighborhood public schools offered an excellent "American" education.[60] The idea simmered for a few years, but the prospect of Haskel entering the first grade provided the final push to establish the school: "My father started the school for me. No question about it. . . . I was the immediate cause of Ramaz, not the fundamental cause. . . . I think he wanted to start a school. He felt that was the way to influence people and shape lives and he wanted to start a school that would work on Park Avenue."[61] During the first three years of the school's existence, the only KJ member to make significant financial contributions to the school was Joseph Lookstein's future strategic partner, Max Etra, and his family.[62] Enduring these early difficulties, however, brought spectacular results.[63] For the first thirty-five years of its existence, the majority of the Ramaz student body did not come from the KJ family. Nevertheless, "Lookstein's school" became a model for Modern Orthodox education throughout the United States.[64] Ultimately, Joseph Lookstein forged a natural relationship between KJ and the school that came to be its official sponsor.[65] The key player, whose leadership was the glue that joined the two institutions together, was, of course, the rabbi.[66]

Through the founding of Ramaz, Joseph Lookstein educated his own son. The process also allowed him to develop a broader financial base and overall autonomy, comparable to Stampfer's description of Reb Hayyim of Volozhin's role as *rosh yeshiva* and local rabbi of the *kehillah* in Volozhin. The yeshiva's primary funding came from outside its locale, and thus Reb Hayyim was far less dependent on the good graces of his Jewish neighbors than other comparable scholars whose livelihood and ability to attract students were in the hands of the communal board.[67]

From the perspective of rabbinical independence, then, a trend can be discerned common to Margolies and to both Looksteins. Each saw KJ as his main focus and base, but also attained positions of leadership in the greater Jewish community.[68] Their esteem within American and world Jewry brought distinction by association to their congregation. Through yet another vehicle, the rabbi's subservience to the community was greatly diminished.

When Joseph Lookstein decided in 1958 that the time had come for his only son to begin the process of succession, he utilized his managerial skills to ensure a smooth transition.[69] Despite the opposition of his main partner, Max Etra—who felt that that the younger Lookstein needed "seasoning" in another congregation before assuming the KJ pulpit—he drafted the forces necessary to carry the vote and convened a meeting of the board of trustees at his home.⁷⁰ The written transcript of the meeting reports that after Joseph Lookstein left the room, Dr. Samuel Belkin, president of Yeshiva University, "praised" Haskel Lookstein, who had just recently received rabbinical ordination from Yeshiva University, "as a young minister of unusual promise" and proposed that "it would be fitting to elect [him] . . . as the assistant rabbi of Kehilath Jeshurun."⁷¹ The proposal was "carried unanimously," and Joseph Lookstein and Mrs. Lookstein were invited in and informed of the decision: "The Rabbi spoke feelingly about the significance of this occasion, and there were tears in the eyes of many as he reminisced about his three decades of association with Kehilath Jeshurun, climaxed now by the election of his son to the post of assistant rabbi."⁷² The summary concluded, "the meeting was one of the most historic ever held, and when it was adjourned the entire company and guests stayed on for the elaborate collation prepared by Rabbi and Mrs. Lookstein."⁷³

The establishment of a rabbinical family is but one of the Looksteins' creations at KJ. They formulated a new prototype for the American Modern Orthodox rabbi, the rabbi as CEO, and in the process succeeded in nurturing a unique bond of identification between institution and rabbi. This bond has been pivotal to the succession process and justifies viewing their rabbinate as bearing a dynastic quality. All the same, there is no KJ bylaw that requires that the rabbi be a member of the Lookstein family.

Conclusion

In a 1982 article on developments in the spiritual leadership of United States Jewry, Charles Liebman offered comments that bring together the two elements that, as put forward here, underscored the history of the KJ rabbinate through much of the twentieth century: "The rabbi is likely to take on other leadership roles in addition to his position as spiritual leader. He can be an administrative or managerial leader, a political leader, fund-raiser, etc. . . . Even so, there is no doubt that these leadership types will be called into question if the rabbi does not possess the halo of spiritual leadership. If the rabbi does not succeed in re-attaining the crown of spiritual leadership, his status will be undermined."⁷⁴ These words can be applied to virtually all rabbinical dynasties, even when succession is a legal right of birth,⁷⁵ but they are a particularly fitting comment on the recipe for success that was followed in the KJ rabbinate. The bond between the synagogue and the Lookstein/Margolies family came into being because of the rabbis' ability to provide for the spiritual and religious needs of their burgeoning Modern Orthodox synagogue. Indeed, KJ's more recent success in maintaining its "church-oriented" version of Modern Orthodoxy within a broader environment of ongoing Haredi Orthodox ascendancy can be attributed to the strong sense of confidence among the congregants in the judgment and commitment of Rabbi Haskel Lookstein. Despite the deep level of attachment between the Looksteins and KJ cemented by the unique rabbinical model they developed, had doubts emerged concerning the family's capacity to sustain a religious and intellectual platform that was geared to their congregants' needs, their "status would have been undermined."[76]

As of the final editing of this book, it would appear that KJ has concluded that they must look beyond the Lookstein family for a successor to Haskel Lookstein. In order to achieve this goal, on December 7, 2014, a position description was posted on the joint RIETS/RCA list of rabbinic job availabilities. Notwithstanding the decision to hire the first non-family member senior rabbi, the document testifies to the congregation's self-understanding as a model Modern Orthodox synagogue, the crucial role the rabbi plays in this perception, and the overall focus on continuity, even as it sets out on a new leadership path:

> Congregation Kehilath Jeshurun ("KJ") is searching for a Modern Orthodox Rabbi who can build upon its strong history and lead our congregation to new heights. The next Rabbi of KJ must possess superior leadership skills, unquestionable knowledge of halacha, the ability to deliver engaging and inspiring sermons and lectures on topics both Jewish and worldly and the determination to be a prominent voice in the modern Orthodox world.
>
> We seek a Rabbi for whom the pastoral role is second nature, a Rabbi able to guide a diverse group of congregants through all variations of life-cycle events. Our Rabbi must be a "people-person," someone who knows the particular way to connect to a particular person, regardless of that's person's age, gender, or religious background. The Rabbi must have a genuine love of all Jews, and show himself willing and able to work in partnership with other Jewish denominations, as well as other important non-Jewish leaders on the American and international stage.
>
> The next Rabbi of KJ must unite these leadership and pastoral skills to make himself a role model to his congregants. He must be a role model in his faith and commitment to the unique modern Orthodoxy that has defined KJ and has distinguished it from other modern Orthodox shuls worldwide. He must be a role model of how to engage,

inspire, and educate Jews of all diverse backgrounds. He must be a role model in his support for the State of Israel, and his allegiance to the United States. He must be a role model in his commitment to chesed and tikkun olam, unafraid to address social-activist causes both within the Orthodox Jewish community and outside it, including issues of women, conversion, and humanitarianism.

But ultimately, KJ is more than just a synagogue. It is an institution with a deeply formed institutional history, an extensive network of community programming, and a day school that is intricately tied to its hashkafa (religious outlook) and mission. Like his predecessors before him, the next Rabbi of our synagogue must recognize the unique partnership of school and shul that has been the hallmark of our Upper East Side community for nearly eight decades. To keep this partnership together, the KJ Rabbi must believe in the value of a Ramaz education, his hashkafa must define the religious tone of the school, and he must play an advisory role in both the administration and admissions process so that the Ramaz School, in both its mission and composition, can continue to enhance and be enhanced by KJ and the KJ community. We would also expect that the Rabbi's appreciation for Ramaz would include sending his own children to the school, so that Ramaz can be a true part of his family, and he a part of the Ramaz family.

Through a Rabbi with these qualities, we look forward to watching our synagogue grow in numbers, programming, classes, services, outreach and mission ... so that KJ can continue to shine in the broader Jewish community as a prominent example of centrist, modern Orthodoxy for many years to come.[77]

3

The Rise and Fall of Solidarity Orthodoxy

This chapter compares the central role during the 1960s and early 1970s of Modern Orthodoxy in Soviet Jewry activism with that of both non-Orthodox groups and the Haredi Orthodox camp. The main argument is that the Soviet Jewry movement introduced a new level of partnership between Modern Orthodoxy and the rest of American Jewry that went beyond the "churchlike" inclusiveness of synagogues like KJ described in chapter 2. This "solidarity" dynamic stands in sharp contrast to more recent trends in Modern Orthodoxy that will be revealed in part 2. At the same time, the forthcoming chapters will demonstrate that contemporary Haredi Orthodoxy has demonstrated greater openness toward cooperation with broader American Jewry than it did during the height of the struggle for Soviet Jewry.

Introduction

Fourteen years after joining his father as spiritual leader at KJ, Haskel Lookstein's rabbinical career was transformed. In 1972 he and his wife, Audrey, made the first of a series of visits to the Soviet Union. During that trip they had their initial encounter with Jewish "refuseniks" who were being persecuted for their efforts to emigrate to Israel.¹ For the next two decades Lookstein dedicated himself to their cause, both as chairman of the Greater New York Conference for Soviet Jewry and by turning public advocacy into a central tenet of the Ramaz School where he served as principal. "It was the turning point in my life," Lookstein recalled. "It gave me something outside the shul [synagogue]."²

Lookstein's experience may have been a personal breakthrough, but it also reflected broader developments within American Orthodox Judaism. Not only for Lookstein but for an entire generation of young Orthodox Jews who came of age in the 1960s and early 1970s, Soviet Jewry activism was a "turning point." Through their involvement in the campaign to liberate their Soviet brethren, a new cadre of young Modern Orthodox leaders declared their independence from both the American Jewish establishment as well as European-born Orthodox authorities.³ By moving their activities "outside the shul," they reinvented American Orthodoxy as a religious movement whose core ideals could resonate not only within its own parochial habitat, but throughout the American public sphere.

Concern for the plight of Soviet Jewry grew steadily from the early 1950s. The rise of this issue to the forefront of American Jewish consciousness, however, was driven by the broader protest movement that emerged in the mid-1960s. Its central goal was to ensure civic and religious rights for Jewish residents of the Soviet Union, with a particular emphasis on the ability to emigrate. The movement's peak impact was in the 1970s. This decade witnessed the proliferation of grassroots organizations throughout the United States, along with the adoption of a more activist orientation by large segments of the American Jewish establishment. The combined force of the popular and official campaigns was felt in mass solidarity marches, as well as in the passage of the Jackson-Vanek amendment that linked U.S.-Soviet trade with human rights and increased emigration. The February 1986 liberation of Anatoly "Natan" Shcharansky—whose incarceration in a Siberian prison had come to symbolize the overall struggle—was arguably the last major milestone in the history of the movement prior to the reversal of Soviet official policy later in the Gorbachev era.⁴

Since the 1970s works have been published that explored the American Soviet Jewry movement from a broad range of perspectives.⁵ To date, however, minimal attention has been paid to the place of the Soviet Jewry movement in the religious history of American Judaism. This chapter partially confronts this lacuna.⁶ I will first explore the connection between Orthodoxy and the Soviet Jewry movement, particularly during the 1960s and early 1970s. Did American Orthodoxy, as a defined Jewish religious collective, play a significant role in the initial development of the movement? Based on my answer in the affirmative, I will suggest that this specific topic is instructive for a broader understanding of mid- to late twentieth-century American Orthodox Judaism. As part of the analysis, the approach of Modern Orthodoxy toward Soviet Jewry activism will be contrasted with that of both non-Orthodox groups and the sectarian or Haredi Orthodox camp.

The central thesis of this chapter is that the Soviet Jewry movement introduced a new dynamic to the relationship of Modern Orthodoxy and the rest of American Jewry, as well as between Orthodoxy and the broader American public sphere. As part of this process, the Soviet Jewry movement manifested the emergence of a novel religious conceptualization of Jewish solidarity within American Orthodoxy.

The Development of the Soviet Jewry Movement and the Orthodox Role

From the early twentieth century, the two American Jewish groups that took an interest on a consistent basis in the welfare of the Jews of the Soviet Union were the American Jewish labor movement and the Lubavitcher Hasidic sect. The labor activists sought to counter the cultural deprivation being experienced by their Soviet Jewish comrades.[7] The Lubavitchers had cultivated an underground network of followers that provided religious services to Russian Jewry since the Bolshevik Revolution, and they continued to support these activities from their new Brooklyn base.[8] After the conclusion of World War II, other forces within American and international Jewry gradually became aware of rising discrimination against Soviet Jews and embarked on efforts to assist them. In 1952 the Israeli government upgraded its involvement through the establishment of its Liason Bureau (*Lishkat ha-Kesher*). This clandestine department operated under the cover of Israeli diplomatic missions throughout the Communist bloc, providing cultural and religious materials, and encouraging emigration. Henceforth Israel would remain a major force—both openly and behind the scenes—in world efforts for Soviet Jewry.[9]

Over the course of the 1950s reports were also published in America that described the declining predicament of Soviet Jewry. As representatives of major American Jewish organizations and sympathetic elected officials became aware of the situation, increased attempts were made to bring the issue to the attention of the political establishment. In the summer of 1956, two rabbinical delegations received permission from the Soviet government to travel throughout the country. The first was affiliated with the Orthodox Rabbinical Council of America

(RCA).[10] The second came under the auspices of the New York Board of Rabbis, and included representatives of all denominations. Upon their return the reports of both groups garnered considerable publicity in the American press. Unquestionably, however, during the 1950s Soviet Jewry was not at the top of the agenda for the American Jewish establishment—including the Orthodox organizations—and most American Jews were completely ignorant of the issue.[11]

During the 1960s, by contrast, the plight of Soviet Jewry emerged as a major theme for Jews across America. From 1963 in particular, public awareness of Soviet persecution of its Jews increased dramatically.[12] A consensus developed within the American establishment that more concerted efforts needed to be made to alleviate this situation. The change was expressed through public conferences that issued resolutions in support of Soviet Jewry and through the sponsorship by a broad coalition of Jewish groups of a relatively modest framework called the American Jewish Conference on Soviet Jewry (AJCSJ).[13] In addition, more delegations were organized for visits to the Soviet Union—including a second RCA group in July 1965 that was led by Rabbi Israel Miller. By that point, Miller had already served for two years as founding chairman of the AJCSJ.[14] Prominent scientists and other well-known Jewish personalities also made efforts to travel to the USSR for academic conferences, or simply to see for themselves what was really happening to Soviet Jewry. One of the scientists was a Stanford bacteriologist and Orthodox Jew, Dr. David W. Weiss. He subsequently became a central West Coast activist. A more famous Jewish personality who made the trip was author and Holocaust survivor Elie Wiesel. The report he compiled upon his return took the form of his sixth book, *The Jews of Silence*, whose 1966 English publication captured the hearts of American Jewry.[15]

Yet many within the American Jewish establishment maintained great ambivalence regarding the public nature of some of the new initiatives. As a result, they continued to emphasize traditional quiet diplomacy.[16] A more radical expression of heightened American Jewish activity was manifested in the rise of popular grassroots organizations that, in the name of Soviet Jewry, adopted the public protest tactics first championed by the American civil rights movement.[17] Within less than a decade, the outspoken public demonstrations that these activist groups had promoted tenaciously in the mid-1960s had been adopted as official policy by much of the American Jewish establishment. Although significant gaps remained, in retrospect it is clear that by the early 1970s public activism had moved from the periphery to the center of efforts by American Jewry for their Soviet counterparts. Certainly, events such as the Six-Day War and the highly publicized 1970–71 Leningrad trials of Soviet Jewish dissidents inspired mainstream American Jewry to move toward the strategy of popular protest as the anchor of its campaign for Soviet Jewry.[18] But it was the pioneering activists of the 1960s who initiated the approach and set an example that thousands across America would eventually follow.

Orthodox representation among the leadership and troops of the protest movement, particularly in the New York area but in other Jewish communities as well, was from the outset disproportionate to its overall numerical strength within the American Jewish collective. As will be demonstrated below, this rise of an activist American Orthodoxy, and the choice of Soviet Jewry as the framework for its expression, tells a great deal about the evolution taking place at the time in this religious stream.

The Student Struggle for Soviet Jewry (SSSJ)

Since 1986 Malcolm Hoenlein has served as the executive vice chairman of the Conference of Presidents of Major Jewish Organizations. An Orthodox Jew whose path to leadership within the American Jewish establishment began through his Soviet Jewry advocacy, he served from 1971 to 1976 as founding executive director of the Greater New York Conference for Soviet Jewry. In that capacity he orchestrated the mass Solidarity Sunday marches that began in the early 1970s. When asked to comment on the beginnings of American Jewish activism for Soviet Jewry, Hoenlein talked about Jacob "Yaakov" Birnbaum (1926–2014), founder of the SSSJ: "Birnbaum was the father of the movement," he said, "the SSSJ laid the foundation."[19] Along the same lines, Richard Maas, the first chairman of the National Conference on Soviet Jewry, said that the SSSJ was "frequently several steps ahead of the other agencies" in advancing the struggle.[20] Similarly, Sir Martin Gilbert, the late Oxford historian who published extensively on Soviet Jewry, wrote: "As a cautious, pedantic historian, I am naturally reluctant to call anyone the 'Father' of anything ... but I have no hesitation whatever in describing Jacob Birnbaum as the Father of the Soviet Jewry movement."[21]

To be sure, the Cleveland Committee on Soviet Anti-Semitism and other grassroots councils certainly played seminal roles—particularly regarding Jewish communities outside the New York area.[22] Fred Lazin emphasizes nonetheless that the SSSJ, which "drew much of its following from the Orthodox community," was more "committed to civil disobedience" than were the local councils.[23] On the other side of the political spectrum, the short burst of anti-Soviet militancy spearheaded by the Orthodox rabbi Meir Kahane and his Jewish Defense League from 1969 to 1971 had a crucial if notorious function in bringing the cause to the attention of the American public.[24] That said, already in 1973 Abraham Bayer asserted in the *American Jewish Yearbook* that the SSSJ was "the mainstay in the eastern United States in sustaining interest in Soviet Jewry."[25]

What was the SSSJ? Why was its founding so crucial to the emergence of the American Soviet Jewry movement? And what was the Orthodox role in this organization?

The most extensive description of Jacob Birnbaum's career and his original vision for American Jewish activism was produced by the writer and former SSSJ member Yossi Klein-Halevi. Raised on British soil and the grandson of the legendary European Jewish leader Nathan Birnbaum—who is credited with coining the term "Zionism"—Jacob arrived in New York in late 1963 intent on advancing Jewish causes.[26] By then he was already well aware of the suffering of Soviet Jews. Through his initial encounters with the minimal efforts of the American establishment organizations to address the predicament of their Soviet brethren he discovered his own calling.[27]

Birnbaum set out to convince American Jewry to dedicate itself to reclaiming "Let My People Go" as their slogan. He rented a room in Manhattan's Washington Heights area and made contact with the leaders of Yavne—the national Orthodox university student organization—asking them to set up a subcommittee on Soviet Jewry. Simultaneously, he began knocking on the doors of the neighboring YU dormitory.[28] His message to these young adults interspersed righteous indignation at American Jewish apathy during the Holocaust with a seemingly "messianic" confidence in the ultimate triumph of a just cause.[29] Such redemptive virtuousness was unfamiliar to American Jews, and had been expressed until then mainly by the southern preachers who anchored the civil rights movement.[30] Seen in the context of the social and cultural upheavals of the mid-1960s, his words resonated deeply for idealistic students who hoped to change the world.

In April 1964, just a few weeks after the founding by the establishment of the AJCSJ, Birnbaum sent out a letter to Jewish college students throughout Greater New York with the following call:

> Just as we, as human beings and as Jews, are conscious of the wrongs suffered by the Negro and we fight for his betterment, so must we come to feel in ourselves the silent, strangulated pain of so many of our Russian brethren.
>
> We who condemn silence and inaction during the Nazi Holocaust, dare we keep silent now?

CHAPTER 3

> The time has come for a mass grass-roots movement—spearheaded by the student youth. A ferment is indeed at work at this time. There is a time to be passive and a time to act. We believe most emphatically that this is not a time for quietism. We believe that a bold, well-planned campaign, to include some very active measures, can create a climate of opinion, a moral power, which will become a force to be reckoned with.[31]

On April 27, 1964, 250 Jewish students joined together at Columbia University for the first official gathering of the SSSJ.[32] Within four days a rally was held at the Soviet Mission in Manhattan and was attended by 1,100 people.[33] Among the troops of early activists, Glenn Richter immediately became a central figure. A Queens College undergraduate and already a veteran of the civil rights movement, his organizational skills and media savvy complemented Birnbaum's strengths. By 1967 he had completed two semesters of the New York University School of Law before dropping out to spend the next twenty-three years as full-time national coordinator of SSSJ.[34]

From its founding in 1964 to its official closing in 1991, the SSSJ advanced the cause of Soviet Jewry through myriad activities, including maintenance of a database about Soviet Jewish life and repression against it; organization of delegations to visit refuseniks, publication of books, pamphlets, and posters; provision of educational and publicity materials to schools, synagogues, camps, youth groups, and other grassroots organizations throughout the United States; letter-writing campaigns to Congress; and periodic placement of ads in major newspapers. Its pathbreaking contribution was its insistence that only through constant public protest, publicity, and promotion of the cause could American Jews offer substantive assistance to their Soviet brethren.[35] Between April 1964 and December 1965 the SSSJ concretized this policy by organizing more than twenty separate public events.[36]

Any symbol of the Soviet Union on American soil was a viable target for a demonstration. The humiliation of the great Soviet empire by a small cadre of dedicated young people, Birnbaum reasoned, would draw massive media attention. Simultaneously, it would exert pressure on both the American Jewish establishment to upgrade the cause of Soviet Jewry and the U.S. government to turn it into an integral feature of its détente negotiations.[37] Already in 1966 some representatives of mainstream organizations began to show openness to Birnbaum's strategy.[38] By the early 1970s, moreover, much of the establishment had adopted public protest as the central expression of its Soviet Jewry campaigns. Solidarity

Sunday marches to the United Nations and massive rallies in Washington had become key facets of Jewish public life. No longer merely the precinct of idealistic students, they showcased national Jewish leaders, elected officials, and recently released dissidents, and drew crowds of more than a hundred thousand. Despite ongoing disputes between the SSSJ and the establishment over the specifics of when and how to act and who should be making these decisions, clearly the overall direction outlined by Birnbaum in 1964 had become the normative approach of American Jewry.[39]

One of the outstanding features of the SSSJ and the activities that it sponsored was the overt use of religious symbolism. A shofar (ram's horn) that called out figuratively to the Jews of both the Soviet Union and the United States was chosen as the emblem of the organization.[40] SSSJ events featured names like the "Passover Geulah [redemption] March," the "Chanukah Menorah March," and the "Jericho Ride" (which began with the blowing of seven shofars and aimed to march seven times around the Soviet mission before heading to Washington). As part of these events, the demonstrators would sing Hebrew words taken from Psalms according to original tunes, some of them prepared especially for them by the emergent Hasidic folk songwriter Rabbi Shlomo Carlebach.[41] This synthesis between religion and social activism offers an additional illustration of the numerous parallels between the SSSJ and the civil rights movement. Amitai Bin-Nun has noted that "the overt religious nature of the movement, far from limiting the movement's clientele, often had a positive impact on the less religious demonstrators."[42] Needless to say, the prominent place of familiar religious themes is reflective of the makeup of both the SSSJ's leadership and its main constituency—young Modern Orthodox Jews from the Greater New York metropolitan area.

Orthodoxy and the SSSJ

Jacob Birnbaum did not like being labeled Orthodox. He preferred identifying himself as a traditional Jew, in the premodern sense of the word.[43] Indeed, he defined the SSSJ from the outset as a nondenominational organization that aimed to unite the entire spectrum of American Jews under the banner of Soviet Jewry. Not only were the up-and-coming young Orthodox Rabbis Aharon Lichtenstein and Norman Lamm among its board members and sponsors in the 1960s, but so were two Conservative and Reform affiliated theologians, Rabbis Abraham Joshua Heschel and Eugene Borowitz.[44] Among the early student activists, Rabbi Arthur Green, at the time a rabbinical student at the Conservative Jewish Theological Seminary and one of the founders of the Havurah movement,[45] stands out as one who both grew up in a non-Orthodox home and ultimately gained prominence as a non-Orthodox religious leader.[46]

While Birnbaum's vision entailed a nondenominational organization and he sought to avoid being labeled, personally he always observed Judaism according to Orthodox standards and attended an Orthodox synagogue on a regular basis.[47] Moreover, both statistical evidence and the comments of those involved during the 1960s and 1970s draw a picture of the SSSJ as an ostensibly nonsectarian framework whose core activists and leadership stemmed predominantly from New York's Modern Orthodox camp.

Regarding the rank and file, Jim Schwartz's 1973 survey of the SSSJ reported that 65 percent of its members considered themselves Orthodox and "intensely Jewish," most had been educated in Jewish day schools, and most continued to pray daily and attend synagogue on a regular basis.[48] In his highly acclaimed history of the Soviet Jewry movement, Gal Beckerman also describes "the young, mostly yarmulke-wearing ranks of Yaakov Birnbaum's growing army," and makes a point of noting that "Yeshiva students were not the only ones at the Student Struggle rallies."[49] Indeed, Klein-Halevi, who was one of SSSJ's main high school–age activists in the late 1960s, attests in parallel that 90 percent of the attendees at rallies were Orthodox.[50] Similarly, the former chairman of SSSJ, Rabbi Avi Weiss, attributed his own initial involvement to the fact that "Yaakov and Glenn did a lot of their recruiting at YU and Stern College, the largest reservoir in New York of college educated Jewish youth—the prime constituency for the cause they were building."[51] In fact, Birnbaum himself made clear that by the 1970s the main supply of participants at SSSJ rallies came not from a coalition of college students, but from Modern Orthodox high schools throughout the Greater New York metropolitan area.[52] Finally, Malcolm Hoenlein and Rabbi Arthur Green both note the high level of Orthodox involvement. Green even suggested that one of the reasons that he and some of his compatriots from the Conservative Jewish Theological Seminary left the organization was due to their sense that they were not part of the core group.[53]

In as far as the leadership of SSSJ was concerned, like Birnbaum, Glenn Richter is a practicing Orthodox Jew. The longtime national director grew up in a home affiliated with Conservative Judaism but moved closer to Orthodoxy in high school through his involvement in Yeshiva University's Torah Leadership Seminars.[54] He had been inspired at Manhattan's Orthodox Lincoln Square Synagogue by Rabbi Steven "Shlomo" Riskin—one of the rabbis who joined the 1965 Selma civil rights march. Riskin subsequently became the first chairman of the SSSJ, and established the precedent of the chairmanship being occupied by an Orthodox rabbi.[55] During the 1960s, Rabbi Irving "Yitz" Greenberg was vice-chairman, followed by Rabbi Charles Sheer.[56] In 1983 Avi Weiss became SSSJ's chairman and its most visible activist.[57] Quite a few of the other central activists, as will be expanded upon below, also stemmed from the Modern Orthodox camp and themselves went on to auspicious rabbinic and public careers. In the words of Glenn Richter, "like civil rights, SSSJ was a rabbi [clergy] led movement."[58]

It is important to reiterate that outside New York, the Orthodox were not as dominant. There were additional frameworks, such as the Northern California Council for Soviet Jewry and the nonviolent Jewish Defense League chapter supported by Rabbi Saul Berman in Boston, in which Orthodox rabbis did play central roles. But in the grassroots groups and college-campus SSSJ chapters that spread across America, the Orthodox were less prominent. That said, almost all of the central leaders, spokespeople, and activists were based in New York, the main decisions emanated from there, and the majority of high-profile demonstrations took place there or in Washington.[59] As Glenn Richter attests, the SSSJ in New York possessed a strong group dynamic and worked as a team. Outside New York, any collective of Jewish students that agreed with the policy of nonviolent protest and would work with all types of Jews to achieve a common cause was welcome. The non–New York SSSJ member groups, then, were not formal chapters as much as loose associations of Jewish students that received encouragement and materials from the New York office.[60]

To this point I have argued that one of the central forces, even possibly the key initial instigator, that drove American Jewry toward a stand of public advocacy regarding Soviet Jewry was led and populated disproportionately by Orthodox Jews, albeit officially having a nonsectarian grassroots framework. As noted above as well, other well-known Orthodox figures also played central roles in the establishment of the Soviet Jewry movement. Moreover, the person whose actions arguably did the most to land Soviet Jewry in the newspaper headlines, if also casting a dark shadow on the righteousness of the cause, was the radical Orthodox Rabbi Meir Kahane. Not surprisingly, a significant portion of the members of his Jewish Defense League were also Orthodox Jews, although a lower percentage than that found among the SSSJ core group. While most activists and establishment leaders were unified in their condemnation of the violence that he promoted, in retrospect they also agree that the publicity gained through the Kahane-inspired violence between 1969 and 1971 turned Soviet Jewry into an American household word.[61]

CHAPTER 3

Orthodoxy, American Judaism, and the Public Sphere

> Emily Litella: What's all this fuss about Soviet Jewelry?
> Jane Curtin: Emily, it's Soviet Jewry!!!
> Emily: Never mind.[62]

By January 24, 1976, Soviet Jewry had literally entered the American household, as illustrated humorously in this skit broadcast nationwide on NBC's popular *Saturday Night Live* comedy show. The rise of this issue to prominence was actually representative of an overall transformation that had taken place in the American Jewish approach to the public domain. American Jewry had begun to unapologetically assert its own particular interests. By taking a lead in the Soviet Jewry movement, then, American Orthodoxy actually served as a significant force in the revolution of American Jewry's relationship to the public sphere.

This central role in dictating greater Jewish public policy illustrates one of the ways in which Soviet Jewry activism manifested American Orthodoxy's move—recalling the words of Rabbi Haskel Lookstein—"outside the shul." That is, from the 1960s through the 1980s the Soviet Jewry movement engendered a new type of Orthodox expression that differed from the activities whose natural habitat was the synagogue or study hall. Such public behavior had previously been defined and led by other Jewish constituencies.

Up to the mid-1960s the thrust of Jewish establishment efforts in the American public sphere was on advancing liberal, universal issues rather than identifiably Jewish ones.[63] The main reason for this approach was the belief that success in these areas would ultimately benefit the primary Jewish goal of the time: social, economic, and cultural equality and integration. As Peter Medding has argued, only around the time of Israel's 1967 Six-Day War did a "new Jewish politics" emerge in which "American Jews'... growing particularistic concerns with Jewish survival tended to divert attention from universal concerns" and "led directly to a group demand for political power as the only way to ensure that survival."[64] The rise of the Soviet Jewry movement during the 1960s, he adds, is—along with advocacy for the State of Israel—a primary example of the transition that was taking place in American Jewry's approach to the American public sphere.[65]

This idea holds special poignancy for the current discussion of American Orthodoxy and the Soviet Jewry movement. The Orthodox, more than any sector among American Jewry, would have been expected to remain embedded in a more passive approach that perceived the advancement of general American liberal themes of equality as "good for the Jews." As Lawrence Grossman has shown, through the mid-twentieth century, for "Mainstream (Modern) Orthodoxy" there was "no expectation of involvement in the public square unless the rights and welfare of Orthodox Jews were directly at stake."[66] Rather, there was a clear Orthodox tendency to defer to the American Jewish establishment.[67] This approach "was rooted in a 'sense of social inferiority and a habituated posture of subordination to the non-Orthodox in collective Jewish external affairs.'"[68]

From this perspective, its disproportionate and pioneering place in Soviet Jewry activism highlights a new dynamic for American Orthodoxy. A role reversal in the position of this religious subgroup—the origins of which may be identified in the coming-of-age of the English-speaking Orthodox rabbinate after World War II—was taking place in the 1960s. Already in 1964, Jacob Birnbaum's SSSJ exemplified a predominantly Orthodox constituency that had internalized the "new Jewish politics" that both celebrated public protest and shifted priorities from universal to more particularistic issues—years before this ethos gained acceptance among mainstream American Jewry. As pointed out above, however, beyond accepting this principle themselves, the SSSJ saw convincing the American Jewish establishment of the correctness of this position to be one of its primary objectives. Thus, Orthodoxy's pioneering position in the Soviet Jewry movement placed it in a completely new role. Instead of continuing the familiar mode of allowing the non-Orthodox establishment to define Judaism's approach to the public arena, the Orthodox became pacesetters who set the agenda that was eventually adopted by the rest of American Jewry.

Such an understanding is supported by Eli Lederhendler's study of mid-twentieth-century New York City Jewry. He argues that with the move of many Jews away from their original neighborhoods during the 1950s and 1960s, certain common social bonds that had united them began to dissipate. These connections were replaced, in turn, by "the emergence of ideologically driven and generationally driven segregated subgroups."[69] The Orthodox represented one of the main examples of such clusters that were discovering a more independent voice. Based on Lederhendler, then, the Orthodox championing of public protest for Soviet Jewry, particularly when seen in the context of the minority upheavals of the 1960s, reflected a rejection of their previous subordination to the American Jewish establishment. In Lederhendler's words, "Orthodox students, like their parents, were largely alienated from the formal and informal structures of New York Jewish secularized ethnic and intellectual leadership." Thus, "a realignment was taking place ... that was bringing to the fore a group of ethnic activists, many of whom were Orthodox, many of whom were relatively young, and few of whom were committed members of the existing ethnocommunal apparatus."[70]

Here I have suggested that in the context of this reconfiguration, the Orthodox role in the Soviet Jewry movement was especially unique. Not only did its young Modern Orthodox leaders demonstrate their independence from the American Jewish establishment, but they pioneered an approach that was ultimately adopted by those who formerly set the tone.[71] On this level I draw a distinction between Soviet Jewry activism and support for the State of Israel, another cause that galvanized Jewish youth at the time. Indeed, Orthodox involvement in Israel advocacy also grew significantly around the 1967 war. In the case of Israel, however, while the Orthodox certainly demonstrated greater public involvement, for the most part they were following a general trend within American Jewry rather than spearheading it.

Since the 1970s, participation of adherents to Modern Orthodoxy as well as representatives of the Haredi Orthodox world in the public sphere has risen dramatically. To offer but one primary example, the Modern Orthodox–affiliated Orthodox Union, the Haredi Agudath Israel of American organization, and the Hasidic Chabad movement all have full-time representatives in Washington. To be sure, they concentrate on matters of interest to their Orthodox constituencies, but they have increasingly taken stands on issues of broader Jewish and societal concern as well. In retrospect, then, the role adopted by the Orthodox through the Soviet Jewry movement can be seen as a crossroads regarding the public sphere not only for Modern Orthodoxy but for all of American Orthodoxy. It set a precedent for types of Orthodox public behavior that has since been expanded upon by the various subgroups within American Orthodoxy. In its time, however, Soviet Jewry activism actually served to sharpen the internal boundaries between Modern Orthodoxy and its sectarian-oriented Haredi Orthodox counterparts.[72]

American Orthodoxy and Soviet Jewry Activism—The Internal Divide

The Lubavitcher Hasidic sect, as pointed out above, had long maintained a network of emissaries within the Soviet Union that sought to preserve some semblance of religious life.[73] In addition, Rabbi Pinchas Teitz (1908–95) of Elizabeth, New Jersey, who was in close contact with both the Haredi rabbinic elite and YU Modern Orthodox circles, had been making efforts since the 1950s to maintain a connection with Soviet Jewry. From 1965 he traveled regularly to the Soviet Union, teaching classes to local Jews and distributing Jewish religious books.

He also cultivated relationships with Russian officials—an issue that was subsequently criticized severely by the activists.[74]

Both the Lubavitcher rebbe—Rabbi Menachem Mendel Schneerson (1902–94)—and Teitz were vehemently opposed to public protest of the plight of Soviet Jewry, which they considered highly counterproductive. They claimed it would very well endanger the physical welfare of more than three million Jews. No doubt they were also convinced that it would compromise their own rapport with the Soviet government and imperil their clandestine efforts at sustaining religious life. Schneerson expressed his sharp opposition to mass protests in a major address from 1971: "May the one who sits upon high protect Russian Jewry from those who cause disruptions in order to supposedly help them, but whose hearts are oblivious to what constitutes real help and what causes the opposite effect.... It is imperative, instead, to advance secret initiatives like those that until now have brought substantive results."[75]

Regarding R. Teitz's ongoing attempts to influence YU figures to oppose public demonstration, Jacob Birnbaum commented that "R. Pinchas Teitz was a thorn in our side for many years."[76] By contrast, despite their tactical differences with Schneerson, in interviews with Soviet Jewry activists they uniformly expressed admiration for his movement's extensive efforts to sustain Judaism in the Soviet Union throughout the twentieth century. In fact, according to Richter the SSSJ worked for years in coordination with Chabad to send religious materials to Jews in the Soviet Union. Malcolm Hoenlein also commented that he had no criticism of Chabad since "they had the most to lose." Moreover, he described having numerous meetings with Schneerson in which "he was laser sharp and never tried to convince me to change my approach." When Riskin was set to travel to the Soviet Union in 1970, Schneerson invited the then chairman of the SSSJ to a private meeting (*yehidus*). There he gave him contact numbers for local Russian Jews and asked that during his visit he try to set up underground yeshivas in four cities.[77] Upon Israel Miller's return from a 1965 trip to the Soviet Union, the Lubavitcher rebbe had also asked to meet him privately at his Brooklyn headquarters. Schneerson was extremely interested in every detail regarding his journey, but he strongly discouraged Miller from any public activity against the Russians and also urged him to grow a beard.[78]

The ardent anti-activist position articulated by Schneerson and Teitz came to characterize the majority of the leaders of the Haredi Orthodox camp in America.[79] There were certainly exceptions to this rule, most notably when Rabbi Moshe Feinstein, the preeminent American religio-legal authority, sent a message of support that was read publicly by his son in-law Rabbi Moses Tendler at a 1968 rally.⁸⁰ There were also some indications of grassroots pressure within the Haredi world to adopt a more activist position and which even produced a modicum of flexibility. During the crisis that ensued in 1970–71 in light of the Leningrad Trials, the leaders of Agudath Israel took pains to publicize an "all-day meeting of the Moetzes Gedolei HaTorah [Council of Torah Sages] where they had reviewed their position and consulted with 'reliable experts.'"⁸¹ Yet their conclusion was that "representations to alleviate the plight of Russian Jewry which are aggressive and provocative can only harm and aggravate the situation. Accordingly, they are not participating in the general demonstrations since they are not able to control the tone or character of these gatherings."⁸² As such they sponsored a prayer "gathering" in the Manhattan Center on January 10, 1971, at which the press reported an attendance of thirteen thousand people (five thousand inside the building and eight thousand on the street), and they encouraged affiliated institutions outside New York to follow suit. Agudath Israel also asked its members to send "appeal telegrams" to the Russian Ambassador in Washington "beseeching the Russian government for passion and clemency for those convicted in the Leningrad trials."⁸³ Yet, intent on making sure that no one should interpret the New York nonrally as a public protest, the official Agudah spokesman announced afterward that "there was no cry of 'Never Again'" and "When someone at one point shouted *Am Yisrael Chai* [the people of Israel live], he was simply ignored and it did not even cause a ripple."⁸⁴

Despite such reservations, these events suggest that at least at one crucial juncture in the history of the American Soviet Jewry movement, Haredi Orthodoxy manifested behavior that bears similarities to the burgeoning activist strategy. Yet unlike non-Orthodox American Jews, who by the mid-1970s were coming out in droves to the large rallies, the ranks of yeshiva students and young Hasidim that were beginning to swell at the time never became a visible presence at public demonstrations for Soviet Jewry. Ultimately, the one aspect of the Soviet Jewry movement that Agudath Israel did unequivocally embrace was sending clandestine delegations to refuseniks in the Soviet Union.⁸⁵

American Haredi Orthodoxy's preference for working behind the scenes and aversion to public demonstrations have been explained as a reflection of this sector's unwillingness to deviate from the *shtadlanus* (intercession) approach that characterized Jewish-gentile political relations throughout the European Diaspora. Jewish communities traditionally appointed diplomats of sorts whose task was to negotiate communal interests with the local powers. Excluded from mainstream political life and fearful that drawing greater attention could only spell trouble, they cultivated personal connections with members of the court. At times, these *shtadlanim* had to agree to heavy additional financial burdens that would be shared by the entire Jewish collective in return for what was only to be a temporary respite from danger. Particularly since the rise of Modern Zionism, the term *shtadlanus* has acquired a pejorative connotation in many circles.[86]

The "*shtadlanus* instinct" offers a partial explanation for the traditionalist Orthodox aversion to public protest. Nevertheless, I would like to raise an additional avenue of thought that takes greater account of the specific historical circumstances of mid-twentieth-century American Jewry. This approach, in turn, will also shed light on the question of why Soviet Jewry activism had particular appeal to a considerable number of young, American Modern Orthodox Jews in the mid-1960s.

There appear to be both geographical and generational factors at work in the debate between public activism and behind-the-scenes diplomacy that simmered within American Orthodoxy. Schneerson and Teitz, as well as almost all of the major Orthodox rabbinical authorities of the 1960s and 1970s, were born in Eastern Europe.[87] The majority had experienced personally the destructive force of totalitarian communism prior to emigration, and many had been refugees who arrived in America concurrent with the spread of Nazi rule in Europe. This background was evidenced both in their continued approach to the Soviet Union and in their relationship to the United States.

Their fear of communism was limitless, and the thought of Jews actually standing up and challenging the Kremlin beyond comprehension. In describing the difficulties he encountered in presenting the merits of the protest movement to Feinstein, Malcolm Hoenlein explained ironically, "One could not convince him that Hitler was worse than Stalin, because he had lived under Stalin."[88] Glenn Richter added similarly, regarding Rabbi Schneerson, "The Rebbe's concerns regarding public protest were based on his personal experiences living under communist rule."[89] Indeed, in criticizing the relatively passive custom adopted by Soviet Jewry activists of leaving a seat open at the Passover Seder to signify a Soviet Jew who was denied emigration, Schneerson commented: "The Sages said 'do not agitate a young (small) gentile' (*Babylonian Talmud, Ketubot* 111a). Seemingly they should have said 'do not agitate a mature (big) gentile?'The message seems to be clear, then, that if you should refrain from agitating a young gentile, certainly do not do so to a mature one. Yet in our days they have chosen to agitate the mature gentile."[90]

These immigrant rabbis had found security and a new beginning on American soil. Despite their fears of the acculturative attraction of American freedom and materialism, they were highly appreciative of what the country had done for them and their followers. For many, the idea of publicly protesting at a time when such behavior was becoming associated with the radical anti–Vietnam War movement was especially problematic.[91]

It is notable in this light that before the Vietnam era one of the most vehement critics of Soviet Jewry demonstrations had actually joined a public protest in America for a different cause. On August 25, 1963, Rabbi Teitz spoke at a civil rights rally that took place at New York's Polo Grounds and encouraged Jews to join in the march on Washington that was scheduled for the following Wednesday.[92] Unlike some of his Haredi Orthodox colleagues, then, apparently Teitz was sufficiently comfortable in America to take a public stand on controversial matters within the public sphere.[93] When it came to his brethren in the Soviet Union, however, the Latvian native and former Lithuanian yeshiva pupil could not imagine Jews acting with such brashness.

The same geographical and generational factors are instructive in addressing the unwillingness of Rabbi Joseph B. Soloveitchik (1903–93)—YU's central authority during the 1960s—to articulate a plainspoken position regarding Soviet Jewry. By then Soloveitchik had already established his reputation as the most prominent Orthodox ideologue in America to digress significantly from the Haredi line in regard to secular learning, the merits of modern culture, and the State of Israel.[94] Had such a statement been forthcoming from him, it would likely have marginalized the influence of Rabbi Teitz upon the YU faculty and student body. Yet when Soloveitchik's rabbinical pupils approached him in the mid-1960s he suggested that they refrain from public demonstrations—although he allowed that they should consult experts on the subject. According to some accounts, in private conversations he later expressed regret for not supporting the protest movement.[95] In addition, as mentioned above, his son in-law and close disciple Aharon Lichtenstein was on the SSSJ board and attended a number of rallies during the mid-1960s. Nonetheless, even in the 1970s and 1980s, when Soviet Jewry activism became widely accepted by mainstream American Jewry, Rabbi Soloveitchik never came out publicly as a supporter of demonstrations.[96] Certainly, the suggestion that his students consult with experts reflects his reticence from invoking the ultra-authoritative approach regarding political matters known as *da'as Torah* prevalent among the traditionalists.[97] Yet it would appear that like his Eastern European–raised Agudath Israel counterparts, he too perceived the evil of Communist Russia in a way that differed from his predominantly American-born students. This would explain Rabbi Soloveitchik's own reluctance to confront the Soviet Union publicly, as well as his desire to consider the opinions of Sovietologists regarding the dangers that activism might engender for the local Jewish community.⁹⁸ It is notable that his brother, Rabbi Ahron Soloveitchik (1917–2001), did take a open stand in favor of public activism in regard to Soviet Jewry, civil rights, and the Vietnam War. While the younger Soloveitchik was also born in Eastern Europe, he arrived in the United States as a teenager with his parents, and he received an American high school, college, and law school education.⁹⁹

Unlike the immigrant yeshiva heads and Hasidic leaders, the students and their fellow Modern Orthodox Soviet Jewry activists had grown up in a completely different environment. Often the children of immigrants, almost all were American born and took their personal liberties for granted. Coming of age in the wake of the Holocaust and the rise of the early civil rights movement and its righteous "dream" of a better world, they too sought to engender a *tikkun olam* (repair the world). This correction would address both the apathy of the previous generation and the contemporary imperative to spread the values of justice and freedom.¹⁰⁰ Yet unlike their fellow non-Orthodox Jewish students, as Lora Rabin Dagi has demonstrated, for the most part the Modern Orthodox students did not translate their sympathy with the civil rights movement into intense involvement.¹⁰¹ As Americanized as they were, they still emerged from Orthodox Jewish homes and schools where they had been brought up to concentrate on the particularistic and religious concerns of their people. They could appreciate and support the African American desire for equality, but their upbringing still made them gravitate more naturally to Jewish issues.¹⁰² As Glenn Richter put it, "For most Jews, and Orthodox ones in particular, active involvement in the civil rights movement was '*pass nicht*' [unthinkable]. In those days, Jews simply didn't do those things, the very act of protest was a big *hiddush* [novelty]."¹⁰³

Rabbi Irving "Yitz" Greenberg, the former vice-chairman of SSSJ and a prominent theologian and Holocaust scholar, refers to the Soviet Jewry movement as "our version of civil rights."¹⁰⁴ It offered these young Modern Orthodox Americans a cause that enabled them to adopt the strategies and ethos of the peaceful civil rights movements, without moving too far beyond their own natural, religious framework. Other than for the JDL fringe, it also had just enough of an antiestablishment ambiance to connect them with the broader cultural currents of the 1960s, without demanding the radicalization that enveloped much of the antiwar movement as well as the more strident black power campaigns of the late 1960s.¹⁰⁵ Yet it was anti-Soviet as well, and therefore no matter how much pressure they put on the U.S. government to include the issue of Soviet Jewry within its diplomatic demands, no one could doubt that the Jews and America were ultimately on the same side.¹⁰⁶

The Soviet Jewry movement, as such, functioned as a bridge that enabled the Modern Orthodox to move relatively smoothly toward a broader, less parochial type of Jewish activity. Viewed from this perspective, it is notable that for the non-Orthodox it seems to have had exactly the opposite effect. That is, the veterans of the civil rights and antiwar movements discovered the Soviet Jewry movement en masse in the early 1970s. For them it was part of the process of introducing greater particularism and ethnic pride into their solid, universal, liberal foundations. While Soviet Jewry activism may have created a space for Orthodoxy "outside the shul," for the non-Orthodox it actually served to bring them back inside.[107]

Solidarity Orthodoxy

Moving Modern Orthodoxy outside the synagogue, as manifested in its role in the Soviet Jewry movement, represented a broadening of the range of behavior that could be termed its core activities. Implicit in this expansion was a fundamental transformation in the nature of Modern Orthodoxy.[108]

Recall that in 1965 Liebman described the Modern Orthodox as a broad "churchlike" framework, due to their willingness to include within their synagogues many Jews not living according to the ideal religious standards of the Halakhah. The Haredi Orthodox, in contrast, promoted a sectarian type of Orthodoxy that concentrated on self-preservation and tended toward exclusion of anyone who deviates from the uniform behavioral and theological standards of the group.

It would appear that the Orthodox debate over public activism from the 1960s through the 1980s can be understood along the lines that Liebman suggested. Namely, the resistance of the sectarians to becoming involved in a broad-based public protest movement was also fueled by their reluctance to participate in a partnership with nonobservant Jewry. Indeed there is an indication of such a sentiment in the December 30, 1970, Agudath Israel communiqué discussed above. Part of the explanation given by the Council of Torah Sages for their unwillingness to sanction participation was that it was "impossible for us to control the character and nature of these gatherings."[109] Modern Orthodox Soviet Jewry activism, in opposition, highlighted its "churchlike" character in that it was predicated on working together with Jews of all persuasions to advance a common cause.

Further consideration of Liebman's analysis suggests that the Orthodox ethos that emerged through the Soviet Jewry movement actually extended beyond the dynamic that he described. Liebman's Modern Orthodox exhibited "churchlike" qualities primarily through the creation of inclusive religious environments like KJ that provided room for Jews who did not completely adhere to the tenets of the community. All the same, the guidelines and even the physical synagogue frameworks were solely predicated on Orthodox standards. The nonobservant were invited to come in with no strings attached, but this was clearly an Orthodox home, so to speak, albeit an open one.

I suggest that, just as it was a "turning point" in Haskel Lookstein's life that gave this young rabbi an outlet for meaningful self-expression "outside the shul," the Soviet Jewry movement engendered a model for the relationship between Orthodox and nonobservant Jews that could never exist within a synagogue framework. Even if the Orthodox were at times dominant and played key leadership roles, they were not the homeowners. An equal partnership was created that depended purely on the ability of each participant to work toward shared values. By protecting adamantly the nondenominational configuration of the SSSJ, for example, while not standing in the way of disproportionate Orthodox representation, Jacob Birnbaum and his cohorts created a unique framework for expressing solidarity with Soviet Jewry. In the process, they also cultivated a level of Orthodox cooperation with other Jews that could never be expressed in an Orthodox synagogue. The paternalistic dynamic inherent to a synagogue environment was replaced with the goal of achieving freedom for Soviet Jewry that was cherished equally by all involved.

This phenomenon can best be termed "Solidarity Orthodoxy." It was rooted in the religiously motivated desire of Orthodox Jews to "struggle" for their Soviet brethren, but it produced a generation of American Jewish leaders whose religious identity was intertwined with their commitment to working in partnership with other Jews. Unlike additional defining qualities associated with American Modern Orthodoxy—the value of secular education and outside culture for example—few efforts have been made to articulate the ideological underpinnings of an American Orthodox stream that placed partnership with fellow Jews for common goals at the foundation of its religious worldview.[110]

The centrality of the solidarity principle for Modern Orthodoxy from the 1960s through the 1980s can be confirmed by taking a brief look at some of the more prominent Orthodox graduates of the Soviet Jewry movement. What all of these figures shared in common were their backgrounds as Orthodox rabbis and professionals who were dedicated campaigners for Soviet Jewry and the fact that Jewish solidarity remained a fundamental theme throughout their careers. As will become clear, however, when it came to manifesting this outlook within their careers, their paths diverged in significant ways.

CHAPTER 3

Rabbis Israel Miller (1919–2002), Herschel Schacter (1918–2013), and Haskel Lookstein can be considered fusion figures who always maintained solid footing within establishment circles but simultaneously worked in coordination with the more confrontational troops. Those who advocated for more aggressive tactics did not necessarily appreciate this dual status. Miller, Schacter, and Lookstein were each reputable rabbis of veteran New York Orthodox synagogues as well as major players in national Jewish politics. Indeed, Miller and Schacter—who by the 1960s had already achieved renown as Orthodox rabbis in positions of leadership within broader American Jewry—may be seen as "forerunners" of Solidarity Orthodoxy.[111] Miller, who as already mentioned led an Orthodox rabbinical delegation to the Soviet Union in 1965, served alongside others as chair of the Conference of Presidents of Major Jewish Organizations, president of the Holocaust Claims Conference, and founding president of the American Zionist Federation. Throughout, he was also one of the leading administrators of YU. Schacter, who as a twenty-six-year-old U.S. Army chaplain participated in the liberation of Buchenwald, went on to lead the Bronx's Mosholu Jewish Center for fifty-five years while also serving in numerous public positions, including chair of both the AJSCJ and the Conference of Presidents.[112] Stemming from the same generation as many of the Haredi figures who opposed the Soviet Jewry movement, it is notable that both Miller and Schacter were American born.

As time went on Lookstein, younger than Miller and Schacter, gradually adopted approaches identified with activist elements. He took Ramaz students to rallies at the Soviet Mission and even chained himself to the wall, which led to his arrest by New York City police. This was certainly to the chagrin of his father, Joseph Lookstein, who, as seen in the previous chapter, was an architect and pioneer of the "churchlike" approach to Orthodox synagogue culture, but was simultaneously a devotee of "old Jewish politics." Joseph Lookstein, it should be emphasized, attained prominence in the interwar period and considered his son's public activism unbecoming for a Jewish leader in America. The involvement of Modern Orthodox leaders like Miller, Schacter, and Haskel Lookstein served to bridge their focuses on cultivating an Orthodox constituency to careers that navigated between "churchlike" synagogue leadership and solidarity-directed public involvement.

Although they were from the outset less establishment-oriented, the same can be said for the SSSJ's Steven "Shlomo" Riskin and Saul Berman, who inherited Riskin's Lincoln Square Synagogue pulpit in Manhattan (after Riskin moved to Israel). Berman previously held Orthodox rabbinical positions in Berkeley and in Boston and was highly active in both Soviet Jewry and civil rights. Later, he spent nearly ten years as head of Edah, whose Modern Orthodox agenda highlighted Jewish unity and extended to collecting funds for 2005 Hurricane Katrina victims in New Orleans and setting a "slave plate" at the Passover Seder as a reminder of the victims of Darfur.[113]

Throughout his career Avi Weiss too has sought to create frameworks that allowed him to balance a tolerant spiritual leadership of a churchlike nature and a partnership with a broader constituency on common goals. That sometimes uneasy equilibrium is reflected in the Orthodox Hebrew Institute of Riverdale, where he was rabbi from 1975 to 2015.[114] Amcha—the Coalition for Jewish Concerns—is the national organization that he founded in 1992 after the closing of SSSJ, and is the formal framework for his myriad solidarity-oriented activities.[115] In fact, Weiss originally asked Glenn Richter to serve as its executive director.[116] It would appear that one of the aims of Yeshivat Chovevei Torah, the liberal Orthodox rabbinical seminary that he founded, is to cultivate Orthodox rabbis who possess a similar commitment to Solidarity Orthodoxy.

As Jewish chaplain at Columbia University from 1969 to 2003, Rabbi Charles Sheer also split his energies between cultivating a rich religious life for the many Orthodox students and galvanizing all of the Jewish student body in solidarity-type efforts. Sheer, who was the founding president of YU's Soviet Jewry club and subsequent vice-chair of SSSJ, was first introduced to Orthodox solidarity activism during his teenage years growing up in the Berkeley synagogue of Saul Berman.[117]

While other former Soviet Jewry activists remained personally committed to Orthodoxy, their internalization of the solidarity ethos eventually steered the direction of their professional lives away from Orthodox settings. Such was the case with Malcolm Hoenlein, as well as Efraim Zuroff, the Nazi hunter, author, and head of the Simon Wiesenthal Center's Jerusalem office.[118] More pronounced are the examples of Irving "Yitz" Greenberg and the Hasidic music pioneer Shlomo Carlebach, both individuals who began their public careers in Orthodox circles. Concurrent with their Soviet Jewry involvement they evolved into charismatic individuals who reached the pinnacles of their renown as symbols of solidarity rather than as Orthodox leaders.[119] Greenberg—the former pulpit rabbi, theologian, founder of Clal: The National Jewish Center for Learning and Leadership, and chairman of the U.S. Holocaust Memorial Council—describes his life during the 1960s as "a spiritual odyssey—moving not toward withdrawal ... but toward greater involvement": "I was orienting myself to a *Klal Yisrael* community of Orthodox-Conservative-Reform. ... In 1970, I made an abortive attempt to create a Center for Jewish Survival. All Jewish groups were needed to accomplish the task, but Riverdale's [Orthodox] lay leaders were hung up on the participation of the non-Orthodox. I concluded that one cannot turn an Orthodox shul into an intellectual/theological think tank open to all groups."[120] For Greenberg, then, his involvement in the Soviet Jewry movement was part of the process that eventually led him to relocate all his public activities "outside the shul." Numerous Orthodox co-activists did not take such a dramatic step. Yet, as seen above, they too reached the conclusion that sustaining the solidarity ethos demanded moving beyond their familiar Orthodox homes to neutral environments where mutual cooperation could be cultivated.

In the meantime, the individual who inspired so many of the central figures in the rise of Solidarity Orthodoxy remained steadfast in working for the cause that he first brought to their attention in the 1960s. On October 6, 2006, a congressional resolution was proposed that, "Whereas Birnbaum continues to assist institutions for the Jewish education of former Soviet Jews as part of his 'Let My People Know' campaign: Now, therefore, be it Resolved, That on the occasion of his eightieth birthday, the House of Representatives honors the life and six decades of public service of Jacob Birnbaum and especially his commitment to freeing Soviet Jews from religious, cultural, and communal extinction."[121]

Conclusion: Social Capital and the Demise of Solidarity Orthodoxy

Public advocacy for Soviet Jews, inspired in part by the civil rights movement, emerged in the 1960s as a major theme in American Jewish life and played a central role during the subsequent two decades. Modern Orthodox Jews were key players in its rise and development. In doing so they experienced a role reversal in which they helped to redefine the nature of the Jewish relationship to the public sphere. Simultaneously, such activism sharpened the internal divide between Modern Orthodoxy and its Haredi counterparts who opposed demonstrations, encouraged quiet diplomacy, and were loath to work in unison with the broader Jewish community. Through their involvement in a core Jewish activity that entailed partnership with non-Orthodox Jews in efforts for their common brethren, a generation of Modern Orthodox leaders arose that made Jewish solidarity a central expression of their Orthodox religious identities.

In summing up his "Orthodoxy in American Jewish Life," Liebman declares: "The only remaining vestige of Jewish passion in America resides in the Orthodox community.... It is significant that the Student Struggle for Soviet Jewry is directed and led primarily by Orthodox youth."[122] The unique "outside the shul" nature of this fervor is articulated succinctly by Rabbi Dr. Eugene Korn, another

Modern Orthodox individual and former Soviet Jewry advocate who eventually focused on an ecumenical agenda through his position as director of Interfaith Affairs at the American Jewish Congress: "Perhaps because of our commitment to Soviet Jewry and our passion for Israel... we understood that our Torah [religious] values had a trajectory that extended beyond the walls of the *beit midrash* [study hall] and Orthodox Jews. Something greater than Orthodoxy was at stake: *Am Yisrael* [the Jewish people] and God's plan for a chosen people within history were at stake."[123]

American Orthodoxy continues to grow and demonstrate its vitality. Yet Modern Orthodoxy's enthusiasm for solidarity identified here has not been sustained. On the contrary, many within this camp have actually become less comfortable with expressing their religious passion through cooperative frameworks that are predicated on nondenominational Jewish solidarity.[124] As will be seen, for the most part the contemporary constituency associated with YU is more insular than that of the previous generation and less willing to collaborate with their Jewish counterparts unless the activities can be defined as opportunities for bringing the nonobservant closer to Orthodoxy.[125] This may be attributed to the drop in political dependence on the non-Orthodox establishment, a sense of insecurity among some Modern Orthodox in regard to their ability to guide their offspring toward an observant lifestyle, and the ascendant numbers of the Haredi sector and the rising influence of its brand of religion on Modern Orthodox educational institutions. These themes will be expanded upon in subsequent chapters.

In accounting for these changes in Modern Orthodoxy, an additional factor that relates to wider American social trends emerges from the "solidarity" thesis put forward here regarding Orthodox efforts for Soviet Jewry. In his studies of the workings of American society during the last decades of the twentieth century, Robert Putnam highlights the overall decline in social capital as reflected in lower numbers of participants in civic organizations. When pressed by critics to be more exacting, he focused on a particular type of human association endeavor that has deteriorated—what he refers to as "bridging" social capital: the consciousness that facilitates joining with people who are not necessarily like you, especially in order to achieve a values-laden shared objective.[126] Unlike their predecessors of the 1960s and 1970s, as a whole the American public is far less inclined to participate in frameworks that do not relate directly to personal gain, especially when they entail close cooperation with individuals with dissimilar backgrounds and lifestyles. This broader cultural understanding offers an insightful backdrop to the decline of Solidarity Orthodoxy that has been recorded here.

CHAPTER 3

Like their non-Jewish and non-Orthodox American counterparts, members of the generation of Modern Orthodox Jews that emerged in the 1960s and 1970s explored and internalized original forms of cultural, ethical, and spiritual expression. These sometimes put them at odds with principles and norms to which their parents and other figures of authority held fast, but it also offered them a unique sense of purpose that moved beyond notions of personal, social, and financial security. Among the motivating factors in Modern Orthodox activism for Soviet Jewry, for example, was the perception that these struggles could somewhat redress the failure of their predecessors to help fellow Jews abroad who were being persecuted in the 1930s and 1940s. As brought to light in this discussion, the Modern Orthodox young adults developed a unique willingness and even desire to work together with other Jews who did not share the same religious commitment or ideology. The more recent degeneration of this solidarity impulse among contemporary Modern Orthodox Jews (in addition to the reasons mentioned above) may then also reflect the overall waning of "bridging" social capital that formerly connected diverse individuals identified among the broader American public.

While Putnam's perspective certainly sheds light on the passing of the solidarity phase in American Jewish Orthodoxy, the case itself simultaneously challenges aspects of his proof data. One of the main examples presented to sustain his thesis is the decrease of membership in established religious institutions. American Orthodoxy has suffered from "leakage," but the 2013 Pew Report data as well as other studies noted in chapter 1 indicate that high rates of both birth and endogamy, along with strong levels of loyalty among its younger constituents, have enabled it to maintain stability if not grow. Yet this numerical strength has not sustained those forces that facilitated the partnering approach that characterized the Soviet Jewry movement. As such, the distancing from the solidarity ethos by contemporary American Orthodoxy demonstrates a case in which a mainstream religious group was able to preserve continuity or even grow, but in parallel forsake salient elements of its social resources.

Depreciation in social capital, Putnam argues—even in the face of other representations of prosperity that cannot be ignored—portends broader societal deterioration. Similarly, ongoing indications of contemporary American Orthodoxy's spiritual and educational vitality must be assessed alongside the abandonment of those "bridging" qualities that inspired the young leaders of the previous generation.

II

REALIGNMENT

4

Pilgrimages to Eastern Europe and Haredization

This chapter describes and analyzes the evolution of educational trips to Poland for post–high school American Orthodox young adults studying in Israel. It contends that beyond exposing the students to aspects of the Holocaust in an unusually visceral and intense manner, these excursions increasingly serve as "pilgrimages of particularistic Orthodox identity." Indeed, while they are aimed at products of Modern Orthodox homes and schools, over time they have adopted some of the religious stances and celebrated Jewish cultural models that were heretofore more consistent with Haredi Orthodox practice and ideals. As such, these voyages offer insight and may even play a role in the process of religious intensification and distancing from the "solidarity" or the prevalent "churchlike" inclusion models that held sway within American Modern Orthodoxy before the 1990s.

Preface

Like the Soviet Jewry movement in the 1960s, the emergence of educational pilgrimages to Eastern Europe in the 1980s reflected heightened consciousness of American Jews regarding the Holocaust and its implications for contemporary

Jewish life. In point of fact, both targeted collegiate and high school–age Jewish youth from a wide range of religious denominations and levels of observance. Notwithstanding these similarities, the Soviet Jewry movement was fundamentally altruisim oriented, while the Holocaust pilgrimages emphasized acquiring knowledge of the Jewish past and strengthening individual Jewish identity and commitment. Moreover, as this chapter will argue, the trajectory of Modern Orthodox involvement in the trips to Eastern Europe was the reverse of Soviet Jewry activism. The 1960s movement, as emphasized above, inspired within its advocates a sense of solidarity with other Jews whose most compelling expression took place "outside the shul." By contrast, the evolution of the Modern Orthodox excursions to Eastern Europe since the late 1980s demonstrates the advancement of parochial and insular orientations that were previously associated with Haredi Orthodoxy.

Introduction

From the initial rise of the Nazis to power in 1933, their campaign of persecution and efforts to eradicate European Jewry and its living culture have affected profoundly the ebb and flow of Jewish life throughout the world. Clearly, the actual murder and displacement of millions of individual Jews and the destruction of their communities constitute the central and most traumatic period. Nonetheless, new and often unexpected repercussions from these events materialize regularly until this day, and the ways that Jews have responded continue to evolve.

In as far as American Jewry is concerned, scholars have argued that starting in the late 1960s the Holocaust actually gained a more central position than had previously been the case in cultivating collective Jewish identity.[1] One bold manifestation of this direction is the subsequent emergence from the late 1980s of educational trips to Poland and Eastern Europe as rites of passage for Jewish youth. During these pilgrimages young people learn intensively about the events surrounding the Holocaust, visit centers of the pre–World War II European Jewish civilization, encounter directly the locations of the Nazi crimes, and consider the meaning of the experience for their lives as Jews.[2]

Within the Modern Orthodox sector of American Jewry, the 1960s also saw the early stirrings of another tendency that has only grown in subsequent years: the adoption by ever wider circles of strict attitudes toward Jewish law, critical views of secular society and learning, and an emphasis on a particularistic Orthodox identity, all of which were previously largely the precinct of the Haredi camp.

As noted in the introductory chapter, scholars have referred to this trend as the "slide to the right" or "Haredization" of American Orthodoxy.

One of the explanations offered for religious intensification among the Modern Orthodox especially in the past three decades is the popularity of dedicating time to study of Torah in Israel before attending college. From the early 1980s devoting a year to "learning" in an Israeli yeshiva or women's seminary—usually immediately after high school graduation—developed into almost standard practice for Modern Orthodox youth. In fact, by the 1990s there were Modern Orthodox high schools in America that reported upward of 90 percent of their graduates spending a gap year in Israel.[3] While no exact figures exist, there are estimated to be two to three thousand such students in Israel on an annual basis.[4]

The first full-length book to address various aspects of this experience was published in 2007. Its title, *Flipping Out? Myth or Fact: The Impact of the "Year in Israel,"* alludes to the broadly held assumption that many of the Modern Orthodox men and women return home having undergone a religious metamorphosis. For a large contingent of American yeshiva and seminary students in Israel, one of the most intense experiences actually takes place outside the country, usually during the Passover break, when hundreds of them join seminars to Poland and other locations within Eastern Europe.

This chapter describes how supplemental Holocaust education programs evolved into central components of the "year in Israel" for many students. Moreover, it explores numerous modifications that have been instituted over time in the constitutions and contents of these seminars, why the changes were made, how students respond to the experience, and the ways in which this reflects broader developments in contemporary Orthodoxy.

The March of the Living

With the decline of communist rule in the mid-1980s, Western tourism and educational visits to Poland became a less daunting ordeal.[5] After forty years of relative detachment from the rest of the Jewish world, that which was the home to Europe's largest pre–World War II Jewish community and the central scene of Nazi extermination efforts became accessible to those Jews who sought out the scenes where their ancestors and loved ones both lived and died.[6] A variety of Jewish organizations and educational institutions from Israel and the Jewish Diaspora soon began to organize trips for Jewish youth to Poland.[7] Such missions would honor the memory of the victims and deepen the appreciation of the younger generation for the horrors that their predecessors had endured just a few decades before. Simultaneously, they would send a defiant message of Jewish survival to the world.

In 1988 the first "March of the Living" was organized as a cooperative effort between Israeli agencies and Jewish organizations abroad. By 1990 it had established itself as a biannual event attended by more than three thousand high school– and college-age Jewish students. The itineraries of the groups included visits to locations of ghettoes, mass graves, concentration camps, and death camps, as well as major centers of prewar Jewish life. The event was scheduled for the week immediately after Passover. Its high point was the "March" that took place on Yom ha-Shoah, Holocaust Commemoration Day. The entire delegation followed a two-mile path that traversed the Polish town of Oswiecim (Auschwitz in German). They began under the infamous *"Arbeit Macht Frei"* (work makes you free) sign in the Auschwitz I concentration camp, crossed a bridge from which they could view the disproportionately large number of train tracks that converged at the local station, and concluded with a collective ceremony beside the remnants of the crematoria in the massive Auschwitz-Birkenau extermination complex.[8]

By 2004 the now annual event (since 1995) gathered six to seven thousand marchers to Auschwitz.[9] In the meantime, numerous other frameworks had been developed for visiting Poland, including high school trips sponsored by Israel's Ministry of Education and Diaspora Jewish day schools and synagogues, Poland options attached to many summer tours to Israel as well as to Birthright voyages, and even special delegations of Israeli soldiers in active duty. In 2007 the number of Israeli high schoolers alone who visited Poland reached twenty-seven thousand, and by 2009 more than four hundred thousand Israeli pupils had made the trip.[10]

From the outset, the organizers of these excursions made clear that their central goal was to strengthen the Jewish identity of the participants. Among the key lessons that they sought to impart was the importance of Jewish solidarity for Jewish survival. This point was highlighted by the fact that members of the delegations often stemmed from a broad spectrum of Jewish movements. The groups from the United States, for example, could include Reform, Conservative, Reconstructionist, Zionist, and Modern Orthodox youth who marched together with secular and Religious-Zionist Israelis.[11] As one preparation manual for the March of the Living put it, the trip's aims included "teaching *K'lal Yisrael* (the unity of the Jewish people), *Ahavat Yisrael* (the love of one Jew for another), *Tikkun Olam* (making the world a better place for humankind) and *Kol Yisrael Areivim Zeh Bazeh* (every Jew is responsible for every other Jew)."[12]

Since the mid-1990s, scholars have analyzed the Poland trips from a variety of perspectives. Regarding American youth, the data suggest that the goals of strengthening Jewish and Zionist identity are to a great degree achieved.[13] Indeed, this appears to be the consensus among many who formulate Jewish public policy throughout the world. As a former Israeli Minister of Education, Zevulun Orlev, exclaimed during a 2008 Knesset educational committee debate on increasing subsidies for Poland trips, "Research has shown that what establishes the identity of students and connects them to Judaism and Israel is first, Shoah [Holocaust]."[14]

Orthodox Contingents

Among the thousands of Jewish youth who attended the 1990 March of the Living was a small delegation of about forty American college-age female students who had grown up in Modern Orthodox homes and communal environments and had been studying during that year in Israel-based religious seminaries. They were accompanied as well by teachers from their educational institutions. While they were organized as their own bus groups, these Orthodox youth followed itineraries identical to those of the rest of the predominantly non-Orthodox coeducational factions that dominated the delegation. They stayed in the same hotels, joined the others for public lectures and ceremonies, ate the same kosher food that had been shipped specially from Israel, and sat together with them at weekday and Sabbath meals.[15]

By 1991 the Israeli heads of the March of the Living organization began to appreciate the great potential for gaining new participants that existed among the increasing numbers of post–high school Modern Orthodox American male and female students in Israel. Michael Berl, a veteran American Orthodox educator and Jewish camp director who had recently made his home in Jerusalem, was hired to facilitate this constituency. His job entailed, among other duties, recruiting the "yeshiva/seminary" contingent as well as the American college students spending their year abroad at the Hebrew University in Jerusalem, hiring their historical guides and advisors, developing their itineraries, and coordinating the logistics with the main March of the Living office.[16]

During the following two years, the yeshiva/seminary and university groups traveled to Poland under the auspices of the March. The male yeshiva students and female seminarians, many of whom knew one another socially from school and summer camp, functioned as a single subdelegation. While most of the Israeli yeshivas and seminaries requested that their students—who had spent the entire academic year in single-sex educational environments—travel on all-male or all-female buses, the entourage included coed buses as well. Certainly, when the Orthodox participants departed from the buses for the solemn visits to historical and Holocaust-related sites, minimal attention was paid to segregation of the sexes. The young men and women also stayed in the same hotels (on separate floors), shared reactions and feelings in late-night discussion groups, walked together, prayed in the same synagogues (with a partition according to Orthodox practice), ate all their major meals as one contingent, and sang and danced in the same room (separate circles) during festive Sabbath banquets. Such coed programming in informal educational settings was familiar to most of those participants who had grown up in American Modern Orthodox homes and communal environments.

Despite the fact that the Passover break had officially ended and their Israeli institutions had resumed classes, the trips took place after the holiday. This allowed for the yeshiva and seminary students to participate in the March of the Living collective events together with the broad spectrum of Jewish youth who had traveled to Poland from around the world. The culmination of this gathering was, of course, the massive contingent of Jewish teenagers that made its way by foot from Auschwitz I to Birkenau. The American Orthodox young men and women were fully involved in the March, as well as the collective rites at the ruins of the crematoria, which included the recital of the kaddish memorial prayer and the singing of "Hatikvah," the Israeli national anthem.

The yeshiva/seminary group also combined with the university gap-year students for numerous smaller-scale educational programs. In order to facilitate maximum communication and camaraderie between the religiously homogeneous Orthodox and the more varied university participants, Michael Berl requested that during Sabbath meals everyone make sure to sit at tables with representatives from each population. According to his personal educational perspective, there was nothing more appropriate and natural than for a gathering of idealistic Jewish young adults from a variety of backgrounds to come together both to confront their common tragedies and to celebrate their shared legacy.[17]

Beyond the moderate approach to mixed-gender activities, then, one of the educational messages that the pioneering delegations of Modern Orthodox gap-year students to Poland were intended to perpetuate was this sector's tradition of cooperation with other Jews on issues of mutual concern. Paralleling the overall shift to the right of American Orthodoxy that intensified in the 1990s, however, very soon the Poland seminars for Modern Orthodox yeshiva and seminary students veered from their original constitutions. Organizational policies were adopted instead that were more consistent with the stringent approaches to the halakhah associated with Haredi Orthodox and Israeli Religious-Zionist institutions. Educational messages were put forward as well that highlighted particular Orthodox identity and survival rather than Jewish peoplehood.

Separate Orthodox Seminars

In 1993, with the backing of the heads of the two women's schools that had formed the largest contingents in previous years,[18] Michael Berl left the March of the Living and established Heritage Seminars as a privately held, independent framework for organizing trips to Eastern Europe. No longer restrained by the March of the Living bureaucracy and scheduling limitations, he was able to hire the staff that he wanted; focus the itinerary, special programs, and educational literature on the specific needs of his narrower constituency; and cater more directly to its material expectations as well. In the words of Dr. David Bernstein, former director of the Midreshet Lindenbaum seminary and currently the central educational consultant for Heritage Seminars, "We didn't fit in to the March of the Living program. The March itself was not a good use of time. It felt like a Soviet Jewry rally, a lot of waiting around. We sensed that we could do it better on our own."[19] Indeed, during that first year, new sites, many of them related to the religious history of Polish Jewry, were added that had not been part of the March of the Living plans. An option to continue on to Prague after the Poland visit was also introduced. Most significantly, the program was held before Passover, during the official vacation of the yeshivas and seminaries.

By eliminating the scheduling conflict with the beginning of the spring session, a major stumbling block to receiving support for the program from the Israeli Torah study institutions was removed. Rather than causing large numbers of pupils to absent themselves from up to ten days of intensive religious text study, Heritage now offered the yeshivas an informal educational experience that would ensure their students spent their time off in an "appropriate" atmosphere. In addition, running the trip during vacation time lessened the sense of being left out for those students who could not afford to attend or chose not to for other reasons.[20] The other upshot of this scheduling change, however—even if not its initial impetus—was that yeshiva/seminary trips were now exclusively Orthodox. In practice, the heterogeneous Jewish environment that had facilitated the former goal of educating toward Jewish solidarity no longer existed. The result was that rather than serving as an "extracurricular" hedge against the naturally cohesive yeshiva and seminary environments, a process was set into motion whereby Heritage would transform it into an extension or reinforcement of these singular frameworks.

Notwithstanding the implicit particularism of the date changes, during Heritage's maiden voyage the moderate approach to separation of the sexes that had been followed under the March of the Living was not altered dramatically. But by the second year this too was no longer the case, and completely separate men's and women's programs were established. Here the interaction between the economics of the burgeoning market for trips to Poland and the ideological leanings of the leaders of the Israeli institutions combined to facilitate a turn to what were once considered stricter Haredi standards.

Despite Berl's 1993 departure, the March of the Living organization had not been ready to give up on the American Orthodox gap-year students. To this end, they retained one of the educators who had previously worked with Berl, Rabbi Michael Yammer of the Sha'alvim yeshiva. From Yammer's Israeli Religious-Zionist perspective, "the 'mixed' issue was a very difficult problem. I felt that if all year long we were saying 'separate' . . . it would go against this message . . . to do otherwise in Poland."[21] He agreed, therefore, to organize an all men's delegation under the auspices of the March of the Living. Like Heritage, this group also traveled to Poland during the pre-Passover holiday. In fact, he succeeded in recruiting participants from Israel-based Haredi yeshivas for Americans who would never have considered going on a program with Heritage's approach to gender separation.[22]

After one cooperative venture, however, Yammer reunited with Berl. The key to the renewal of their partnership was the latter's commitment that henceforth the men's and women's programs would be absolutely separate.[23] In order to ensure that the strictest religious standards were maintained in regard to programming as well as dietary laws and any other halakhic issues that might arise, Yammer was also appointed the official rabbinical authority of Heritage Seminars.

The new arrangement meant finding different hotels for the women's and men's contingents in each city, creating distinct itineraries, and hiring additional educational, security, and technical staff to facilitate the activities as well as the multiple lodging and eating venues. The policy was so tightly enforced that the male and female delegations were forbidden from visiting sites at the same time—even if they each had their own guides who followed alternative routes. This dynamic demanded a great deal of coordination beyond the already complex task of orchestrating such trips for hundreds of students. At times groups from one of the genders arrived at a venue but were required to remain on their buses until the entire delegation of the opposite sex had left the premises. In the journal that he kept as a Heritage Seminar participant in 1998, Avi Billet protested, "Whenever the girls were somewhere, we had to wait for them to leave. Whenever the girls arrived where we already were, we had to rush out. [An educator] was speaking in Plaszow (concentration camp) at the monument as the girls arrived. He was given 30 seconds, and then he was asked to stop. This was disappointing."[24] From 1993, the gender separation policy, along with Yammer's position as rabbinical authority, became regular components of the Heritage trips.

Among the senior staff, not all were pleased with the decision to completely seal off the men's and women's programs from each other. Vicky Berglas, director of Jerusalem's Midreshet Moriah seminary, asserted that in previous years the students had behaved absolutely appropriately when in mixed settings. In addition, she felt then and continues to maintain that the educational value of keeping the groups together—at least for certain events such as emotion-laden memorial ceremonies and public prayer—far outweighs any unlikely possibility of compromise regarding issues of modesty.[25] According to David Bernstein, the adoption by Heritage of Yammer's position was reflective of the overall marginalization of women: "I understand it in the Haredi world, but with kids from these schools and family backgrounds it is artificial."[26]

By transforming Heritage into a separate-gender program, then, Berl adapted his seminars to norms that had once been associated, at least in America, with Haredi Orthodoxy. Yet this did not necessarily reflect a change in his opinion on these issues. Simply put, Yammer had demonstrated that such a policy would enable more American Orthodox students to be drawn to Heritage. Berl had been convinced that in order to attract the newest products of the yeshivas and seminaries for Americans in Israel, his organization had to operate in regard to gender issues according to the increasingly Haredi-like religious standards of these institutions.[27] As Bernstein asserted, "I tried to fight it but it was a losing battle, the yeshivot were not willing to send their students on a coed program. We were looking reality in the face and we had to accept it."[28]

The evolution during the early 1990s of Poland trips for American Orthodox gap-year students, as such, illustrates the introduction of practices previously identified with Haredi Orthodoxy into ostensibly Modern Orthodox frameworks, as well as the decline of Jewish solidarity as a central educational motif. Furthermore, the description of the actual steps that led to the change in policy at Heritage Seminars offers a window into the dynamic by which, under the influence of Israeli Religious-Zionist Orthodoxy's increasingly strict approach to Jewish law, such transitions actually took place.[29]

In point of fact, once Heritage had established the trips to Poland as a regular component of the year in Israel and adopted strict standards of separation of the sexes, the numbers of participants did increase. At its height, the Heritage pre-Passover yeshiva/seminary delegation numbered more than four hundred students and staff. Over time, however, the success of Heritage, its hefty price tag, and the opportunity to develop a more customized itinerary led some yeshivas and seminaries geared toward Modern Orthodox high school graduates to look for other options for organizing their trips.[30] A few American Modern Orthodox high schools began as well to offer the option of an Eastern European seminar to their students and even made such a voyage into a required "senior trip."[31] Within Israel new organizations arose, some sponsored by public agencies.[32] Others were, like Heritage, for-profit outfits.

One of the privately run programs is called Nesivos of the Gedolim (Paths of the Great Rabbis). It aims to attract American students who attend Haredi-oriented Israeli yeshivas and seminaries, but also those from Modern Orthodox backgrounds who have become more religiously punctilious during their year of study in Israel. Heritage remains by far the largest delegation for gap-year students, but in light—among others—of the rise of Haredi-oriented alternatives, maintaining this position has entailed further adjustments that parallel the broader "slide to the right" of American Modern Orthodoxy.

The subsequent discussion of Nesivos is meant to serve as a "foil" against which certain programmatic changes can be measured. Before doing so, a few words regarding scholarly analyses of Poland trips for the broader American and Israel Jewish populations will be instructive.

The Poland Pilgrimage

Despite the apparent success of the Poland youth missions, the manner by which the various organizers construct the itineraries, arrange site visits, coordinate educational staff, conduct ceremonies, create the atmosphere on the buses, and even utilize security measures in order to shape the memories and value systems of the participants has been viewed critically by some. By referring to the trips as "pilgrimages" rather than educational seminars, and describing "rites" that are observed in the course of the visits, scholars seek to emphasize the performance nature of the seminars.[33] They argue that the focus on a narrow antiassimilationist Jewish survival and Zionist identity narrative to the exclusion of other universal themes is ideological and emotional manipulation that ignores the complex moral and educational issues raised by Poland and the Holocaust. This lack of integrity, they claim, raises questions about the entire efficacy of the endeavor. According to anthropologist Jackie Feldman,

> Israeli state sponsored youth voyages to Poland represent a new kind of Jewish pilgrimage, a pilgrimage of identity. Through on-site testimony of Shoah survivors, symbols and ceremonies imported from the State of Israel, and mass presence of proud Israelis at the crematoria, the pilgrimage transforms the landscape of death into the landscape of sacrifice and assigns meaning to the destruction of the Jewish past through the redemptive act of life in the independent State of Israel. The frameworks of civil commemoration and religious pilgrimage combine in order to root the sanctity of the State in the experience of the Shoah.[34]

Feldman continues: "Regarding the American delegations, Jack Kugelmass describes Poland as, a stage upon which American Jewry performs a rite designed to establish contact with a mythical collective past and acts out the drama of its future.... By identifying with the Shoah dead, the participants seek to affirm their own status as 'victims,' as opposed to their present privileged position in American society, in order to better resist assimilation."[35]

Echoing the criticism of Kugelmass, one former participant in a tour for Orthodox students studying in Israel commented, "I don't know how to explain this, but I often felt that ... the program made this very emotional and dramatic experience into a 'production' that was a little too staged at times ... which wasn't really my thing."[36] Feldman also highlights the manner by which the students are isolated from the contemporary surroundings and are given little opportunity to understand the World War II travails of the Poles. The result is that in the absence of any real Nazis, the Polish gentiles take on the role of the most visible evil other.[37]

While not accepting all of the critical conclusions of these scholars, the language of "pilgrimage" is accurate. These are far from mere sightseeing or informational outings. Rather the itineraries of the trips, along with choice of the staff that are meant to guide the students, and the atmosphere that is established during the time abroad, reflect the clear intention of turning the week to ten days in Eastern Europe into a personally transformative experience.[38]

Nesivos: A "Yeshivish" Pilgrimage

In a 2007 study Aryeh Edrei explored why many of the most prominent Haredi rabbinical authorities in Israel and abroad refused to allow special *kinot* (elegies) written about the Holocaust to be included in the Ninth of Av services, let alone to dedicate a special date in the calendar for such mourning. He does not accept the position that the Haredim merely subsumed the Holocaust within ceremonies dedicated to all other historic Jewish tragedies since the destruction of the Second Temple. Notwithstanding their use of the term *hurban* (destruction)—which references the Temple—rather than "Shoah" or "Holocaust," they too have developed unique forms of Holocaust remembrance.[39] But these Haredi efforts, such as naming Israeli yeshivas and neighborhoods after former centers of Orthodox life and learning, and reprinting numerous rabbinic volumes authored by those who perished, are diametrically opposed in form and meaning to the "memorialization" designed by secular Israeli society. Unlike the Zionists whose focus was on the decimation of Diaspora life as a watershed catastrophe that preceded the birth of a new Jewish world in the State of Israel, "The *Haredi* leadership sought to remember the world that was destroyed and to emphasize its vitality.... [T]hey projected the new society that they were building as a continuation of the world that existed before the Holocaust."[40] They aimed, as such, for the Haredi public to identify totally with Eastern European Orthodox life before the war and to see themselves as the keys to its rejuvenation and continuity: "The destruction itself did not occupy an important place in the remembrance, unless it served to enhance the understanding of Jewish values before Holocaust."[41]

Rabbi Yehuda Fried, founder and director of Nesivos, identifies viscerally with this approach to the Holocaust. In fact, he started the program in 1999 after speaking with students and colleagues who had attended the Heritage yeshiva seminar, and learning that the "yeshivish response ... was lacking." In his opinion, it was crucial to communicate the "Torah view of the *hurban*," so that the students know clearly "what to feel standing at Auschwitz."[42]

Consistent with the Haredi position, Nesivos does not publicize itself as a Holocaust study program at all. The main thrust, rather, is on visiting the former centers of Eastern European premodern and Orthodox Jewry and the graves of outstanding religious personalities from the past: "Being a part of the Nesivos experience means that you will ... get a closer look at the dynamic Torah life of pre-war Europe. You will learn more about and gain a deeper appreciation for some of the greatest leaders of the Yeshiva and Chassidic worlds. You will *daven* [pray] at the *kevarim* [graves] of *tzaddikim* [righteous], and see many other memorable sites."[43]

Here there is a divergence between the male and female versions. The "Yeshivah Bochurim" male tour focuses on Lithuania and Belarus, and offers

Poland as an optional extension, while the "Bais Yaakov" female group spends the entire week in Poland. This gender distinction is reflective of a broader educational dichotomy within the non-Hasidic subdivision of the Haredi sector.

Premodern Poland was certainly the venue of many of the Ashkenazi world's most outstanding and influential rabbinic authorities and Torah scholars.[44] In the nineteenth and early twentieth centuries, however, it became identified more closely with the numerous Hasidic courts and their rebbes that dominated the religious landscape.[45] Lithuania/Belarus, by contrast, emerged as the bastion of the intellectually focused Mitnagedim who opposed the emphasis on personal charisma and the specific mystical orientation of the Hasidic movement. Moreover, this area gained great renown for the world-famous yeshivas that were established there during the nineteenth century, many of which continued to thrive through the first decades of the twentieth century. Recall that the American yeshiva world was established by survivors of this subculture.[46] This connection is articulated emphatically within the portrayal of the Nesivos experience:

> Participants will have the opportunity to literally follow in the footsteps of the great Roshei HaYeshivahs [yeshiva heads] and Gedolim of yesteryear, touring the famous pre-war centers of Torah, including Vilna, Kovno, Slobodka, Ponevich, Telz, Kelm, Radin, Volohzin, Baronovich, Mir, and more.... You will be part of a distinct group ... with a direct link to the Pre-war Torah centers who will join together to revisit their roots. You may read about Eastern Europe, you may hear stories about Eastern Europe, but when you walk the cobblestone streets, our historical Heritage becomes alive.... Our senses will be awakened to the world that although physically may be gone, is spiritually still alive and strong.[47]

For the Nesivos men's tour, then, "establish[ing] contact with a mythical collective past" and "act[ing] out the drama of its future," along the lines drawn by Kugelmass,[48] is more tied up with prewar Orthodox Jewish life in Lithuania/Belarus than with Poland. An additional practical reason for focusing on this region, according to Fried, is that these vistas may attract students spending a second year in an Israeli yeshiva who attended the Heritage Seminar to Poland during the previous term.[49]

Many of the women who join the Nesivos tour actually are from staunch Haredi families who stem from the prewar Eastern European yeshiva world, and they will likely marry alumni of its American institutional heirs. In fact, according to Fried, some of the women's seminaries have asked that a Lithuania component be added to their program.⁵⁰ Yet the focus of the female seminars on Poland is nonetheless consistent with the values of their camp. For one, Haredi women's seminaries do not teach Talmud, nor do they look to the yeshiva hall methodology of study as the model for their curriculums. Thus, while some of the students may have family roots in Lithuania and Belarus, the particular type of religious intellectualism associated with this region resonates more naturally within Haredi male culture. In addition, the educational and spiritual forerunner for the female seminaries was Sarah Schenirer (1883–1935), a Polish Galician woman from a Hasidic family. The institution that she founded in Krakow in 1918 was named Bais Yaakov (House of Jacob), and it first established itself throughout Poland as the pioneer of advanced education for Orthodox women.⁵¹ The visit to Schenirer's grave and to the original site of the Bais Yaakov Seminary, then, is for the Nesivos women the parallel of the men's pilgrimage to the cities and towns of Lithuania and Belarus.

Nevertheless, the central theme of Nesivos is shared unequivocally by both its male and female divisions. While groups visit Auschwitz and Madjanek, the preeminent purpose of the trip to Eastern Europe is to intensify the level of identification between Haredi young adults and an idealized prewar Orthodox elite civilization and its leaders. To offer a stark illustration, most groups spend their Sabbath in Poland in one of the large cities observing both the remnants of premodern and/or prewar life and signs of its destruction (Krakow, Warsaw, or Lodz). By contrast, a female Nesivos participant described a pastoral Sabbath of pure reminiscence and identity formation: "We spent it in Hotel Motyl, the place where the *gedolim* went for the summer. We took a beautiful walk, we walked in the same paths the *gedolim* did."⁵²

In his study of Haredim and the Holocaust, Edrei points out that "as in all remembrance, this remembrance also included forgetting, at times consciously and deliberately. The elements of society that did not enter the halls of the *yeshiva* or the courtyards of the *Hasidim* were completely forgotten.... The *Haredi* leaders projected the old world as a perfect world of Torah and *Hassidut*, to the exclusion of other elements that characterized Jewish life immediately before the Holocaust."⁵³ Indeed, from a review of both 2015 Nesivos itineraries, an uninformed individual could easily draw the conclusion that the millions of Jews who populated Eastern Europe up until World War II were almost all religiously observant.⁵⁴ For that matter, they were likely either aspiring Torah scholars or charismatic Hasidic devotees. The complex social and political environment that existed, and which itself is dramatized in the highly accessible works of I. L.

Peretz, Shmuel Ansky, the Singer brothers, or even those of Chaim Grade, are "forgotten" in the Nesivos "pilgrimage of Haredi identity."[55] As to the Holocaust, the central manifestations of the Nazi atrocities are relegated to a peripheral role within the overall perception of Eastern European Jewish history. When they are encountered more directly, the exclusive focus is on "the Torah perspective and response . . . to those experiences."[56]

Since its inception in 1999, Nesivos has not only continued to cater to institutions clearly identified with the Haredi yeshiva world, but has expanded to work with yeshivas and seminaries that formerly sent their students to Heritage. One is the Ohr Yerushalayim yeshiva, located in Beit Meir on the outskirts of Jerusalem. Its clientele comes almost exclusively from the same Modern Orthodox high schools as the other Heritage stalwarts. For many years it sent a large contingent to Heritage. Today it works with Nesivos. In fact, one of its faculty members has served as a primary guide for the tour. On the female side, the highly regarded Michlalah College for Women in Jerusalem also stopped cooperating with Heritage and sends its overseas students on a tour run by a subsidiary of Nesivos known as Legacy Tours.[57] Partially in order to prevent additional seepage, Heritage has also introduced significant changes into its educational offerings that reflect the increased resonance of Haredi Orthodox culture for its seemingly Modern Orthodox clientele.

Evolving Definitions of "Authentic" Jewish Life

Unlike its Haredi counterpart, for Heritage Seminars the destruction and murder of the Holocaust play a far more central role in the program. The itineraries of the various bus groups of men and women demonstrate that for Heritage, learning about the Holocaust is central to its message and purpose. The list of "primary sites" visited by Heritage delegations includes Warsaw, Treblinka, Madjanek, Belzec, Plaszow, and Auschwitz.[58] In fact, throughout its source books and educational materials, a recurring theme appears in respect to so-called non-Holocaust sites as well: "At the core of the Heritage educational approach is the premise that in order to comprehend the depth of the Holocaust tragedy, one must initially study the richly colored panorama of Jewish life in pre-war Eastern Europe. A thorough analysis of the lifestyles, Jewish communities, personalities, leadership, literature and cultural centers is necessary in order to appreciate the extent of the loss that took place as a result of the Holocaust."[59] In direct contradistinction to the Nesivos Haredi approach, then, the study of prewar Jewish life is essentially a prerequisite for the main task of addressing the Holocaust. The question that needs to be explored, however, is what constitutes the "richly colored panorama of Jewish life" that is vital for comprehending "the depth of the Holocaust tragedy."

As a program geared toward Orthodox students it is natural that connecting to Poland's many rabbinic luminaries, religious institutions, and Hasidic landmarks would find a prominent place in its schedule. Nevertheless, based on its Modern Orthodox roots and clientele, one would also expect that the non-Orthodox population and its significant contributions to Jewish cultural and political life would draw considerable attention as well. Such a programmatic approach would be consistent with Liebman's 1965 description of Modern Orthodoxy as a religious trend that emphasized what it shared with the non-Orthodox rather than what divided them, and especially regarding issues of concern to all. Similarly, the Zionist orientation generally identified with Modern Orthodoxy would imply a desire to learn of those "modernizing" forces that began reevaluating the nature of European Diaspora life long before it was tragically dismembered. The Haredim, in opposition, were guided by an isolationist approach that entailed a far more selective attitude regarding who could claim membership in their collectives. As such, their educational institutions and clergy focused their "sectarian" efforts almost exclusively on their own narrow "natural" constituency.[60]

Over the course of the years since the inception of Heritage in the early 1990s, however, it has increasingly distanced itself from those aspects of prewar Poland that point to diversity, while narrowing in on a predominantly elite Orthodox perspective. In doing so, notwithstanding the aforesaid distinctions from Nesivos, Heritage has gravitated closer to the "Pilgrimage of Haredi identity" described above in respect to its counterpart.

In 1996, Heritage produced *In Their Memory: Introductions, Essays, and Texts for the Study of Jewish Life in Eastern Europe and the Holocaust*, a book-length reader and educational guide for students traveling to Poland.[61] "Written, compiled, and edited" by educational consultant Rabbi Micah Halperin, it contains broad-themed essays regarding the meaning of the Holocaust, including two by the noted philosopher Emil Fackenheim.[62] There are also charts with estimates of the number of Jews killed from each European country, various maps, a brief description of the history of Polish Jewry, an introduction to poetry during the Holocaust, and primary readings related to specific sites—including ones authored by Peretz and Ansky ("I Enlightened the Ghetto"). In addition, there are brief biographies of some of the central Jewish personalities with whom the students are to become acquainted and selected passages from their writings. Those highlighted range from renowned late medieval halakhists as well as

Hasidic rebbes to Sara Schenirer and on to Janus Korczak—the famed secular Jewish educator and author who could have saved himself but chose instead to accompany the children of his Warsaw Ghetto orphanage to the gas chambers in Treblinka. Proportionally, of the 172 pages in the book, 108 focus directly on the Holocaust. Regarding the rest that relate to prewar Polish Jewish life, they are divided almost evenly between items dedicated to specifically religious figures and themes, and those that address broader Jewish culture.

By 2002 a new, more succinct reader and guide, titled *In Search of Our Heritage*, was put out in honor of Heritage's tenth anniversary as an independent framework.[63] This compilation lacks the mosaic quality of its predecessor. Articles and background literature relating to the ghettoes and concentration camps remain at the center, but Fackenheim's original and nonconformist theological discussions were removed. Secular life, non-Orthodox Jewish personalities, and broader Jewish culture are also barely mentioned, while a fully dedicated independent section appears that is titled "Galicia, the Gedolim of Europe, the World of Chassidut." From the perspective of these study guides, then, over time the "richly colored panorama of Jewish life in pre-war Eastern Europe" that is promoted as a necessary prerequisite for appreciating the tragedy of the Holocaust has been scaled down to biographies of elite Orthodox Jewish religious leaders and descriptions of their institutions.

Interviews with key Heritage faculty solidify the impression that with some exceptions little effort is currently expended on aspects of Polish Jewish life besides rabbinic culture and Hasidic lore. All the same, the comments of those charged with guiding subgroups of fifty to ninety students also attest to a degree of independence that they are given in designing the itineraries and choosing the messages that they emphasize to their students.

Rabbi Michael Yammer, the official rabbinical authority of Heritage, strongly advocates concentrating almost exclusively on Orthodox religious themes and personalities. Echoing the "pilgrimage" orientation of the seminar, he suggests that "it gives atmosphere to the trip—more spiritual days. It distinguishes the trip experience from normal day to day life. . . . It is a journey toward holiness."[64] As to the influence of such a framework on the long-term values of the participant, in a similar vein to the Nesivos agenda, he wants a student who attends the trip "to come out with the sense that the world of Torah was destroyed and that he is a part of its rebuilding."[65] In as far as teaching non-Orthodox themes, he is not ideologically opposed: "It's just a question of biting off more than the students can chew. I don't want to overburden them."[66]

Yet such a fear of overburdening may lead to a misrepresentation of the realities of prewar Poland. When asked why in her opinion it was important to learn about "gedolim" and Hasidic rebbes from before the Holocaust, one female Heritage participant explained that "it opened up my eyes to a whole world that used to exist that we really don't have anymore [the equivalent communities today of Me'ah She'arim, Bnei Brak, Borough Park, etc. are not the same]. I think that it allowed me to see the expanse of how many Jews there were, how much of a presence they had, the life they lived—I really felt that it helped to connect me to a part of Jewish history."[67] On the one hand, unlike the classical Haredi approach, there is a clear distinction made here between Polish Orthodox life before the war and the new Haredi strongholds that emerged in the second half of the twentieth century. On the other hand, the instinctual response of this student after her trip to Poland was to equate the "Orthodox" world with "how many Jews there were, how much of a presence they had, the life they lived."

Vicky Berglas, the veteran educator and guide and one of driving forces in Heritage's founding, also feels that homing in on religious subjects is a matter of choosing educational priorities. Yet she apparently succeeds in conveying additional messages as well. According to Ester Blaut Kellman, who traveled with Berglas in 2005, the visit to Poland enabled her "to see how Jews of all kinds were branded together as one regardless of belief or how deeply assimilated they may have been. It made me realize that Jews are Jews and should be proud of that, independently of how they express their Judaism."[68] Nevertheless, Berglas explained that certain decisions regarding which subjects would be at the center were as much a response to the demands of the students themselves as they are an effort to cultivate identification with a particular brand of Judaism. Specifically regarding Heritage's increased focus on Hasidism, she asserted: "That is what kids want, they are 'spiritually hungry.' . . . They identify more with Hasidism because it offers an alternative to the materiality of the American Jewish culture that they come from."[69]

Berglas's response to the spiritual locus of the participants also highlights one of the major aspects of Heritage that continues to distinguish it as a Modern Orthodox–style program. Namely, the staff and institutions that are involved constitute a more diverse collection of Orthodox voices than would be tolerated in Haredi circles. This allows the various faculty members to highlight their own educational and ideological proclivities. Thus, unlike many of his colleagues, Dr. David Bernstein devotes a great deal of his efforts to portraying the complexity and variety of prewar Polish Jewry. In contrast to his peers who are concerned that their students' ability to absorb their central religious messages will be impaired, he maintains that it is important to teach about internal debates and discrepancies among Polish Jewry. Among other things, he argues that it helps them learn how to approach contemporary problems in Jewish communal life.[70]

Heritage's divide from Haredi Orthodoxy is also manifest in its unequivocally positive approach to Zionism and the State of Israel. Yet unlike the "pilgrimage of Zionist identity" described by Feldman regarding the Israeli secular high school trips, none of the Heritage educators presented this theme as the dominant motif of the seminar. Here, however, an interesting distinction was evident between the women's and men's programs. According to Berglas, cultivation of an attachment to Israel and a desire to immigrate is a central educational component throughout the year at the women's seminary that she runs. Thus, in Poland "if I don't bring it up—the girls do."[71] Similarly, Yammer noted the greater excitement regarding aliyah (settlement in Israel) among the female students. As to the men, "unless we put it on the table, for many of them the State of Israel is a non-issue."[72] Rabbi Aryeh Hendler, who works with male American contingents but also escorts numerous Israeli religious high school groups of both genders, was even more emphatic: "For Israelis the issue of the State of Israel is the ultimate topic of the trip and I focus on this agenda.... With the Americans, I don't enjoy making them crazy with this issue. The topics of the State of Israel and immigration arise, but in a far more limited fashion."[73]

The more Zionist bent of Heritage's women's delegations to Poland was reflected in comments by student participants as well. According to Ayelet Kahane, who traveled with the Heritage Seminar for women in 2007, after the trip, "it was never clearer that I was supposed to live in Israel; if the history of the Holocaust proved one thing it was that we cannot fail an opportunity to establish, build, and strengthen our very own Jewish state."[74] Riva, who also joined the Heritage 2007 delegation, reflected that "one of the major things that it cemented was the love of Israel that I had been forming all year. The trip drove home all the things that I had come to really recognize on my own throughout the whole year—how important it is to have our land, our own government, and our own army."[75] Rebecca Weinstein, who traveled with Berglas's contingent, described how these emotions arose within her upon visiting the Western Wall immediately after arriving back from Poland: "More than ever in my life I saw the kotel as a gift, it represented the medinah [state] for me, a place where we would not be persecuted for our Jewish identity, but celebrated for it.... [The trip] definitely added to my desire to live in Israel."[76]

The hesitation of some of the Heritage faculty regarding the introduction of overt Zionist messages may reflect a decline in interest on the part of the participants, especially the male ones. It may also be a function of the difficulty in communicating the Religious-Zionist understanding of the Holocaust to the American Modern Orthodox students. Unlike the Haredim or the secular Zionists who focus respectively on either connection and continuity or commemoration and renewal, the Religious-Zionists resonate to aspects of both of these messages. In the words of Edrei, "Religious-Zionist discourse identifies completely with the desire to memorialize the destroyed world and to rehabilitate the Torah world. At the same time, however, it identifies with [secular] Zionism's desire to build a new and different world."[77] This ambivalence is manifest among others in the way that the Religious-Zionists relate to Yom Hashoah (Holocaust Remembrance Day), which was established by the State of Israel.[78]

Such tensions are present within the Modern Orthodox Heritage Seminar as well. One clear example of Zionist identification is the decision of students—although far fewer than among Israeli groups—to drape Israeli flags on their backs, particularly when marching into Auschwitz-Birkenau. A few, however—especially male staff members—choose instead to don their *tallitot* (prayer shawls). If by no means necessarily in contradiction, the contrast in choice of outwardly displayed symbols manifests the tension between proudly showing the ornaments of a wholly new Jewish society as opposed to connecting directly with an age-old world of the past and mourning its victims.

Studying Torah or "Performing" Hasidism

As a Jewish collective that has been nurtured throughout their lives and especially during their year in Israel to appreciate religious culture and knowledge, it is to be expected that American Modern Orthodox yeshiva and seminary students will demonstrate special interest in significant Polish-Jewish Torah institutions and other locations of spiritual renown. Notwithstanding, a brief comparison between visits to two such landmarks is instructive for analyzing the "memorialization" process that they undergo during the Poland pilgrimage.

Standing at the center of a multiple-acre grassy square at the corner of one of Lublin's busiest thoroughfares, Yeshivat Hakhmei Lublin is one of the most impressive Jewish edifices to remain standing from prewar Poland. Built from funds raised throughout the world by its tireless founder, Rabbi Meir Shapira, the six-story, light-beige stone, 18,310-square-meter complex is fronted by an eight-pillar raised entrance and was constructed to hold up to five hundred students. Its original internal plan included a large study hall/synagogue, a library, classrooms, kitchens and dining hall, ritual baths, dormitory rooms, and even a basement laundry facility.[79] Opened in May 1930, it was intended to serve as an elite institution of learning that would nurture the finest young religious minds of Polish Jewry—primarily Hasidic—into leading Torah scholars. Just nine years later, the September 1939 German invasion led to its permanent closure. During the war it was turned into a base for the local Nazi gendarmerie, and for much of the twentieth century it housed a nursing school—which eventually allowed visits by Jewish groups during lecture breaks. In 2003 the property was returned to the hands of the Polish Jewish community.[80]

With such a rich physical and historical legacy, it is not surprising that most Jewish groups visiting Lublin make a point of going to the yeshiva building and learning its background. For Orthodox gap-year students, however, it is often an experience that resonates deeply with their intensified religious inspiration and commitment to traditional learning. Rabbi Shapira was, among others, the leading force in establishing the seven-year *daf yomi* cycle for completing the Talmud that has gained a great deal of popularity recently.[81] In addition to exploring the building and hearing about the institution, American students will often hear a rabbi teach the portion of the Talmud assigned for that day in the main study hall. Ayelet Kahane recalls, "The *shiur* [lecture] that was given there made a huge impression on me.... Listening to such ideas, in a place that once was bursting with words of Torah and now was empty and bare, made me realize the importance that I, myself, act consistently in my *avodat Hashem* [worship of God], continuing the legacy of the Jews who once lived here. Furthermore ... despite the evident destruction of the Yeshivah community that once existed there, we also celebrated the great Torah learning that once took place there."[82] Similarly, for Avi Billet the visit was something of a culmination of his two years of full-time dedication to Talmud study in Israel that were nearing completion. As he wrote in his journal, "I am sitting in the *beit medrash* of Yeshivat Hakhmei Lublin. I have waited for this moment for a long time.... All I can say is I am in seventh heaven.... This is the highlight for me."[83]

Both of these Heritage participants were fully aware that had they lived in Poland during the 1930s they would not have been among the young Hasidic men who studied at Yeshivat Hakhmei Lublin. Nonetheless, that which they did share with those who once occupied this study hall facilitated a natural connection. The commitment to Torah study that had been cultivated in their Israel-based institutions of learning created a common language and gave meaning to the yeshiva visit that would have been (at least partially) lacking had they come to Poland before their gap year. Such a visit certainly reinforces the internalization of religious learning as a central value that had been developed during the year in Israel. All the same, it does not necessarily celebrate

CHAPTER 4

other characteristics of the institution that are more particular to the Haredi milieu.

The religious intensification process associated with the year in Israel would also seem to account for the raucous dancing and singing that takes place when Heritage groups visit the eastern Galician grave of Rabbi Elimelekh of Leżajsk (pronounced "Lizhensk," 1717–86). Yet the behavior that dominates such encounters would appear to be less reflective of a common language already shared by the students with those who frequented this site before the war. Indeed, the rituals that are performed may actually be intended to encourage the students to develop a new sense of identification with Hasidism that previously did not exist.

"Reb Elimelekh," as he is known, was a central figure in the early development of Polish Hasidism and one of the prime articulators of the Hasidic concept of the *zaddik*.[84] His burial place was a major pilgrimage site for the followers of this movement long before World War II—especially on 21 *Adar*, the anniversary of his death.[85] Today the hillside cemetery—including the large *ohel* (mausoleum) that was built around his tomb—has been rehabilitated and a guesthouse that includes ritual baths, a synagogue, a dining hall, a kitchen, and sleeping facilities has been erected (adjacent to the cemetery) to accommodate the regular flow of Hasidic pilgrims.[86]

Although hardly any of the Heritage participants have direct connection to a Hasidic sect, and few of them know who Reb Elimelekh was before arriving in Leżajsk, visits to his grave have become permanent fixtures within the seminar itineraries—no less likely to be canceled than Auschwitz and Majdanek. Unlike Hasidic pilgrimages to the graves of the *zadikim*, however, the majority of the time is not spent in contemplative prayer with the hope that the spirit of the deceased figure will serve as an intermediary in order to gain divine blessings.[87] On the contrary, the main focus for the Heritage delegations is on creating an ecstatic celebration that most "normative" Hasidic groups would usually confine to the rebbe's Sabbath or festival *tisch* (table) or to weddings and other special events.[88] While some students recall the visit as a unique opportunity for relieving the tension that had built up during the encounters with remnants of the Holocaust horrors, others were actually put off. For Avi Billet, the whole experience of "dancing and giving out alcohol" was troubling, as he recorded in his journal, "I don't understand what it means to dance in front of a grave. I do understand what it means to pray at the grave of a *zaddik*, so that their merit should carry the prayers straight to God. But all else is weird ... the dancing around seemed forced and fake to me."[89] Kugelmass notes that "for Hasidim the graves of *tsadikim* are a meeting point of heaven and earth; one can plead there for divine intervention. Such cosmological mediating links are not active in the cultural repertoire of most American Jews."[90] Even for those who viewed the festivities more positively, then, the question arises as to what messages the program intends to communicate by "staging" a seemingly "Hasidic" style ritual in an environment in which even the Hasidim who visit do not generally behave in this manner.[91]

The Heritage faculty member who since 1998 has placed the greatest emphasis on Hasidism is Rabbi Aryeh Hendler, the associate head of the Sha'alvim yeshiva. His own outlook, while more emphatic than many others, lends insight into the purpose of Heritage's Leżajsk pilgrimage. A tall and strongly built man, Hendler dresses in a white shirt and black pants with *tzizit* strings emerging prominently from his belt on each side. He sports a flowing beard, hair cropped very short, and long, Hasidic-style sidelocks. Indeed, he is considered an expert explicator of the mystical concepts that form the basis for Hasidic thought, and he delivers regular lectures on the topic throughout Israel. His relationship with Heritage, as well as the specific teaching approach that he has developed, underscores his role as a prime representative of the shift that took place over time in the entire program.

Until 1998 Hendler had never set foot in Poland. When he did, it was not to learn about the Holocaust, nor for that matter prewar Polish Jewry. Rather, reflecting his longtime fascination with Hasidic religious ideals, he took advantage of an opportunity that was offered him to join a Haredi trip to Poland that was dedicated exclusively to visiting the graves of the well-known rebbes and Talmudists who were buried there. Only on his second visit, this time as an educator for an Israeli religious high school, did he begin to explore the Holocaust history of Poland more extensively. Subsequently, he enrolled in the course offered by the Yad Vashem Holocaust Authority in Jerusalem that serves as the ministry of education's prerequisite for guiding Israeli high school students in Poland. Today he is one of the most sought-after guides to Poland for Religious-Zionist educational institutions and has been there more than sixty times.[92]

Hendler maintains that Hasidism must play a central role within the educational and personal experience of trips for American Orthodox students to Poland. From a psychological perspective, he feels that the Hasidic orientation toward spiritual happiness offers a much-needed counterbalance to the deep-seated grief that is imminent for a Jew while in Poland. This point, as noted above, was not fully appreciated by all participants. Ayal Kellman, who traveled with Heritage in 2004, commented that this aspect of the trip "made for an emotional roller-coaster jumping between the heart-wrenching experiences in the camps and the dancing and happiness at grave-sites."[93]

From an ideological view, moreover, Hendler asserts that travel in Poland offers the vital promise of learning about the early Hasidic masters in their original geographical milieu. Instead of equating Hasidism with the contemporary sects that are today concentrated in a few large Jewish communities around the globe, these journeys facilitate the student's ability to appreciate the authentic spirituality manifested in Hasidic teachings and charismatic personalities. For most American Orthodox students who come to Israel to study, Hendler maintains, "Hasidism is still a 'foreign language.'"[94] Therefore, as a self-proclaimed follower of the pure, unsullied Hasidism, he believes that it is crucial to find a way for American yeshiva and seminary students to internalize these ideals within their Orthodox religious worldview. The result is that no less than visiting the ghettoes and the central locations of the Nazi crimes, Hendler sees Heritage as an opportunity to encounter Hasidism in its most pristine and untainted state.[95]

Such a "pilgrimage of identity" differs in significant ways from that of the Nesivos Haredi program. Nesivos aims to deepen the sense of a direct link between current-day American Orthodox young men and those of the banner institutions of early twentieth-century Lithuanian Mitnagedism. For that matter, Hendler's approach is also predicated on a different point of departure than that which underlies Heritage's visit to Yeshivat Hakhmei Lublin—a house of study that shares a common language with the Israeli yeshivas and seminaries attended by the Americans. Hendler focuses on the mystical Hasidic traditions of Poland rather than on Eastern European Orthodox Talmudic intellectualism. Yet his aim is not to cement a connection between his American students and the highly established prewar local Hasidic order or their contemporary heirs. Quite the contrary, he actually wants his students to rediscover the so-called original Hasidic spirit and detach them from their, often negative, impressions of the Hasidic sects that they currently encounter in Jerusalem, Bnei Brak, or Brooklyn. Indeed, such a "neo-Hasidic" outlook has become increasingly popular within Israel's Religious-Zionist camp, and Hendler is one of its promulgators.[96]

This nuanced approach to teaching Hasidism in Poland is, among others, reflective of the particular ambivalence felt by Religious-Zionists such as Hendler in bringing youth to Poland in order to deepen their spiritual identities. Having been taught that the Diaspora represents the polar opposite of the redemptive spirit that is pervasive in the Land of Israel, they must justify taking kids who have finally become attached to the Holy Land, and exposing them to the scenes of some of the most "profane" and tragic expressions of the exile.[97] His answer is that it is necessary in order to inspire them to identify more intimately with the spiritual Hasidic movement that began there nearly three centuries ago.

Notwithstanding the originality of Hendler's outlook, for the American Modern Orthodox students this type of intensive identification with Hasidism will most likely be subsumed within their broader "shift to the right." Some of the new Hasidic spirit emanating from Israel has gained popularity in North America, but the atmosphere of a burgeoning multifaceted new religious trend is barely evident within American Modern Orthodoxy. Its primary manifestation is the so-called "Carlebach Minyanim" prayer services that introduce the tunes and style of the late rabbi/songwriter.[98] The faster-growing tendency in America, by contrast, is the above-documented gravitation to a Haredi lifestyle by Modern Orthodox offspring looking for a congenial environment for cultivating their newly found holistic religious tendencies. Hendler and others may hope to germinate the vanguard of an American Neo-Hasidism, yet the more likely scenario is that those yeshiva students who have become enthralled with this type of spirituality will be more inclined to the religious ambiance that characterizes American Haredi and Hasidic circles. Leaving distinctions between Polish Hasidism and Lithuanian Mitnagedism aside, currently both represent Orthodox approaches that demand greater strictness in many areas of observance, denigrate advanced secular learning, and for the most part seek to limit interaction with general culture and society as much as possible.[99]

Hendler eventually left Heritage and created his own independent entity for taking American yeshiva students to Poland, but the festive pilgrimage to the grave of Rabbi Elimelekh of Leżajsk remains a crucial moment in the course of the myriad visits to prewar Jewish landmarks that fill the seminar schedule.

Conclusion: A Critical Week

Unlike the majority of Jewish students who travel to Eastern Europe, Heritage and Nesivos participants are not plucked out of their natural high school or secular college academic environments for a brief, albeit intensive outing. Rather, the trip to Poland takes place in the context of a year in which they have detached themselves—almost always for the first time in their lives—from their parents' homes and watchful eyes and become exposed to all-encompassing environments led by charismatic, spiritually oriented individuals. During this period abroad, students are often exposed to teachers and environments that preach a holistic brand of Orthodoxy that questions the ideals of Americanization and acculturation once championed by Modern Orthodoxy.[100] In addition, some Israeli Religious-Zionist yeshivas that support the State of Israel and send their students to serve in its army are nonetheless highly critical of secular culture and its educational premises. Their tendency is often toward strict interpretations in matters of halakhah, except in areas that relate to the Zionist enterprise.[101] There are also many products of Modern Orthodox homes and schools who attend yeshivas in Israel staffed by American immigrants who have adopted a Haredi lifestyle and are eager to thrust their students in this direction as well. Indeed, according to Yoel Finkelman, the male yeshiva educational programs in Israel often perform the "latent function" of furthering "the students' social and ideological identification with Orthodoxy in general and, in many cases, with a 'yeshivish' kind of Orthodoxy in particular."[102] Psychologist Daniel Jacobson adds that the year in Israel takes place precisely during late adolescence when most people are "solidifying an identity independent of their parents."[103] Samuel Heilman states this even more emphatically: "In this betwixt-and-between state of liminality... the yeshiva experience... became a beacon that led them out of the uncertainty of adolescence toward a new identity, new continuities, connections, commitments, and choices."[104]

The immersion that is experienced during the weeklong seminar in Poland does not in and of itself cultivate new identity formation. It is rather an agent, albeit a uniquely potent one, that can complement or concretize processes that have already begun, or even set into motion new ones. As one female student put it, "It was the icing on the cake."[105]

The particular power of this concentrated week in Poland is highlighted by additional observations regarding recent evolutions in the gap-year yeshiva and seminar experience. Heilman and others have noted that since the late 1990s some of the environmental factors that sustained the isolation of students studying in Israel from their previous settings have been eliminated or at least partially neutralized. In the 1980s and early 1990s, for example, students could go for weeks or even months without direct contact with their parents. Today, however, due to the ubiquity of cellular telephones and relatively low international calling charges, as well as Internet access, rarely do they remain out of touch for more than a few hours. In fact many students attest to speaking or chatting with their families and friends on at least a daily basis. As to actually seeing their friends and families face to face, the relative wealth of the Modern Orthodox community, along with the expansion in travel options and decline in prices of transcontinental flights, have also changed the nature of the experience for many students in Israel. A large portion fly to America for the Passover holiday (often after the Poland excursion), and many visit their homes at least once more during the year. Meanwhile, many parents also make at least one trip to Israel during the course of their children's stay.[106]

Under such circumstances, even if a student becomes enthralled with a particular outlook and begins to reconsider aspects of the home and community in which he or she was nurtured, regular contact with parents and friends may neutralize this tendency or at least lend balance to the process. As such, year-long Israel study programs continue to function as liminal environments that facilitate stricter observance of religious law and spur personal spiritual growth, but the pervasive, almost hermetically sealed quality that once held sway no longer prevails.

From this perspective, not only do the Poland pilgrimages preserve the "sterility" that once dominated throughout the year, they actually offer a more rarefied version. The voyage itself, due to the numerous encounters with the locations in which Nazi persecution and systematic murder led to so much Jewish suffering, is wrought with tension and emotional intensity. The students also remain with their groups during the entire trip, be it on the buses and at the sites by day or in the hotels at night. Throughout this period they are under the supervision and charge of knowledgeable, charismatic, and often spiritually driven educators, who perceive the seminar as a unique environment for disseminating religious ideals. Some, as seen above, even refer to it as a "journey toward holiness."[107] As to communicating with their families while in Eastern Europe, wifi and e-mail access is limited, and sometimes the Israeli cell phones or SIM cards that they have rented for the year do not work.[108]

Like Victor Turner's now classic description of the pilgrimage, then, the Poland trips for American Orthodox yeshiva/seminary youth represent a phase in which one is separated in space and time from normal social frameworks and their limitations. Yet rather than isolated events with limited long-term influence, these pilgrimages to Poland—which take place at the end of the winter-spring term, when students are generally at their most enthused and motivated—actually serve to solidify lessons learned throughout the year. As Turner emphasizes, pilgrimages generally intensify day-to-day religious life: "A pilgrim's commitment, in full physicality, to an arduous yet inspiring journey, is, for him, even more impressive, in the symbolic domain, than the visual and auditory symbols which dominate the liturgies and ceremonies of calendrically structured religion."[109] Reva Wachsman's Heritage diary affirms this understanding,

> The trip drove home all the things that I had come to really recognize on my own throughout the whole year.... [W]hen one is learning for the entire year, and then you go to Poland and you see that you are doing exactly what the Nazis tried to destroy—it just gives you a stronger commitment to your Judaism. It made me think that I am lucky enough to be alive and a Jew today—there were so many Jews who were

killed, and I have a responsibility to live for them. All these thoughts, I believe stemmed from the mindset that I was in being that it was my year in Israel.[110]

Even more so for Ayelet Kahane, the seminar in Poland actually inspired levels of religious yearning that went beyond those she had experienced until that point in her seminary studies:

> My Poland trip was a huge part of my overall "year in Israel" experience. Although the trip was right before Pesach (Passover), it gave me tremendous clarity that colored my last quarter of a year spent in Israel, propelling me forward with this urgent sense of responsibility, which I gained in Poland.... For many American high school students the "year in Israel" experience is about solidifying their Jewish identity, making it their own, making it something personal, instead of something that they were merely taught. The Poland trip is an experience that is such a huge part of that process because it puts everything and everyone in context.[111]

This follows the analysis of the late Erik Cohen, who suggested that "travel to sites of religious significance may be part of a larger religious education program.... In this way the pilgrimage is indeed a continuation of the home community, rather than a complete break from it. The intense group experience ... may serve as a catalyst for increased involvement in the home community."[112] In point of fact, according to Michael Berl, numerous students have told him that their decision to spend a second year learning Torah in Israel was largely in response to the deep, cathartic feelings that arose within them during their relatively brief foray into Poland.[113]

Such comments highlight the vital role that the Poland pilgrimage can play in the religious intensification process that often accompanies the Israel gap-year experience for Modern Orthodox youth. For some students, this inspiration may be integrated into a worldview that synthesizes deep commitment to Torah study and Jewish observance and regular engagement with general culture as well as the human diversity that characterizes contemporary Jewish life. Yet the strict separation of the sexes and decline of Jewish solidarity as a core value that have evolved over time, along with the focus on connecting students to an idealized world of prewar Torah luminaries and Hasidic masters, are consistent with another trend: the introduction of behaviors and values once more closely associated with Sectarian Orthodoxy into mainstream Modern Orthodox educational frameworks. To be sure, as noted throughout, other aspects of the Modern Orthodox seminars, such as centering the program on the destructive events of the Holocaust and supporting Zionist perspectives regarding postwar Jewish life, remain firmly planted within the classical Modern Orthodox worldview.

Poland pilgrimages for Modern Orthodox students studying in Israel, then, by no means reflect a complete abandonment of core values and outlooks long associated with this stream. When viewed together with changes taking place among the Haredi Orthodoxy, however, they exemplify the types of experiences that blur the boundaries between the various sectors, and facilitate the realignment of American Orthodoxy.

5

Counter-Feminism and Modern Orthodoxy

The following discussion highlights the efforts of one of the most prominent rabbinical authorities within the Modern Orthodox camp to reject attempts at upgrading the public religious roles available to women. The legal or "halakhic" position that he expounds is not unto itself exceptional. What is sui generis, rather, is his construction for polemical purposes of a "metanarrative of Jewish heresy" in which a historical chain that begins with the Sadducees in ancient times, includes Reform Judaism, and extends to contemporary Orthodox Jewish feminism is linked through the common complaint of rabbinic discrimination against women. The overall stance put forward resembles—but is by no means identical to—that formerly associated with Haredi Orthodoxy. This chapter can be considered a bookend to chapter 9. They each offer novel and distinct perspectives on the roles that feminism and gender egalitarianism—through both their proponents and antagonists—are playing in the realignment of American Orthodox Judaism.

Introduction

In 1980 the late Israeli religious philosopher Yeshayahu Leibowitz declared, "The question of women and Judaism is more crucial than all the political problems of the people and its state. Failure to deal with it seriously threatens the viability of the Judaism of Torah and Mitzvoth [commandments] in the contemporary world."¹ These reflections came in response to the revolutionary changes that had taken place in the role of women within Orthodox Judaism over the previous century, and particularly the increasing tensions engendered by the campaign of Modern Orthodox women for greater religious egalitarianism. The rise and intensification of religious feminism is one of the most significant revolutions to have taken place in Judaism within the modern period and promises to stand at the center of Orthodox discourse and debate both in North America and in Israel for many years to come. Indeed, it may serve as the strongest counterbalance to the "slide to the right" that has occurred in parallel. Alternatively, following the instincts of Leibowitz, the conflicts surrounding the role of women in Orthodox Jewish ritual and leadership may become so severe that they will stimulate a rupture beyond repair. Ultimately this may spawn not just a realignment, but a full-fledged shattering of the contemporary American Orthodox mosaic.²

A considerable amount of scholarly and ideological discussion has been devoted in the last two decades to various aspects of Orthodox feminism.³ The vast majority has concerned the novel approaches and interpretations of those dedicated to expanding the role of women within Orthodox Judaism. This chapter addresses the major stages and initiatives put forward by the advocates of Orthodox feminism since the 1970s. Its main focus, however, is on the emergence and ongoing development of dramatically negative reactions from one of the most influential figures within contemporary American Modern Orthodoxy to these phenomena since the early 1980s.

Through this description and analysis I will demonstrate that the fresh and creative liberal positions being forwarded by Orthodox feminism have provoked inventive religious thinking among those who are responding negatively as well—in a way that resembles the initial Orthodox response to Reform in the early nineteenth century. This comparison offers additional weight to the evaluation that feminism is arguably the most potent agent of change in contemporary Orthodoxy. Moreover, the reaction portrayed here offers a prime example of the complex dynamic of Haredization and navigation of ideological and social identification taking place within contemporary Modern Orthodoxy.

Orthodox Judaism and Feminism

Religious expression among early modern European Orthodox Jewish women was focused primarily on the private sphere, and through study of a very limited collection of Yiddish homiletic texts.[4] Although religious education for Orthodox young women was provided in German-speaking Central Europe from the mid-nineteenth century, for over half a century this remained a relatively exceptional case.[5] Broader revolutionary changes in traditionalist circles can be traced, however, to the immediate aftermath of World War I and the establishment of the Bais Yaakov (House of Jacob) women's school and seminary network in Poland, whose founder, Sarah Schenirer, and initial location in Krakow were already mentioned in chapter 4. With the approbation of highly respected rabbinical authorities, a framework for women's secondary education and teacher training emerged that included intensive study of practical Jewish law and biblical texts.[6] Graduates of these Bais Yaakov institutions served as institutional leaders and as role models for the ideal educated Haredi Orthodox woman throughout the twentieth century,[7] and variations on this educational model remain the main focus for women's public religious activity within the Haredi sector.[8] Nonetheless, due to these changes, contemporary Haredi policymakers have felt compelled to articulate sociological arguments related to preservation of the traditional family as the basis for placing limits on the canon and scale of female Torah study.[9]

By contrast, starting in the mid-1970s, advanced religious education for Modern Orthodox women not only expanded but transformed dramatically.[10] Numerous institutions were established both in the United States and in Israel that refocused female Orthodox study on rabbinic literature. This vast field forms the central repository for Jewish religious law and theology, and had remained almost exclusively within the male domain. Over the following decades a generation of Modern Orthodox women emerged for whom rabbinic texts and their methodologies were no longer foreign. Indeed, a small cadre of Modern Orthodox women slowly began to appear, women who were both deeply committed to religious observance and in possession of expertise in Talmudic study that exceeded the norm, even among Modern Orthodox males from previous generations.[11] By and large, rabbinical authorities associated with the Modern Orthodox community gave their support to this change.[12]

Opinions were much more divided, however, in regard to parallel requests for greater female participation in public ritual and in positions of religious leadership. From the 1980s, efforts to expand women's opportunities within public prayer became one of the most contentious issues for Modern Orthodoxy. Isolated grassroots initiatives that had already begun in the late 1970s gained popularity and were accompanied by original attempts to reconcile this new phenomenon with accepted Orthodox practice and mores.[13]

The 1981 publication of Blu Greenberg's *On Women and Judaism: A View from Tradition* marked a turning point in this process, as it was the first book-length attempt to articulate a forthright Orthodox feminist program.[14] Beyond wrestling with the ideological tensions between Orthodoxy and feminism, Greenberg advocated greater women's involvement in public ritual and discussed her own experiences as an active participant in an Orthodox women's prayer group.[15] Familiar with Orthodox rhetoric, she noted that her suggestions—regardless of their actual halakhic efficacy—would likely be viewed by Orthodox rabbis as following the path of the Reform, Conservative, and Reconstructionist movements, which had already adopted more egalitarian policies.[16] In point of fact, the advent of women's prayer services in particular inspired prominent rabbinical figures within the Modern Orthodox milieu to issue opinions on the halakhic permissibility and advisability of this new feminism-inspired religious behavior. The consensus was clearly against such innovations, with significant adjudicators forbidding the practice altogether.[17] Significantly, during the early 1980s Rabbi Joseph B. Soloveitchik expressed a clearly negative opinion of women's prayer groups.[18] As to the matter of whether he outright prohibited them, there remains a great deal of debate.[19]

Despite considerable rabbinic opposition, since the 1980s the network of women's prayer services has grown, and they can be found in major Orthodox centers throughout North America, as well as in other Anglo countries and in areas with high concentrations of English speakers in Israel.[20] Moreover, Orthodox feminists and their male supporters have in the meantime advanced new models for female involvement in religious activities that were previously exclusively male. These include leading parts of the prayer and chanting the Torah portion in "egalitarian" or partnership Orthodox (with a partition that separates the men and women) services,[21] reciting the *Ketubah* (writ of marriage) under the wedding canopy,[22] being appointed as "halakhic advisors" regarding Jewish family law,[23] serving as "spiritual leaders" in Orthodox synagogues,[24] and serving as legal advocates in Israeli rabbinic courts.[25] Some of these changes have found support among esteemed rabbis and scholars, while others remain on the fringe.[26] Yet for the most influential rabbinical authorities within Modern Orthodoxy, many of these new efforts to alter traditional practice are considered to be absolutely illegitimate and pose great dangers.[27] As such, feminism has become a major challenge to the future unity of Modern Orthodoxy and its factions.[28]

The Evolution of the Schachter Thesis

Rabbi Herschel (Zvi) Schachter (b. 1941) is, in the words of sociologist Samuel Heilman, "a key figure in shaping the future of and orienting the worldview of the religious leadership of Modern Orthodoxy."[29] His formal position is Talmud lecturer and head of the Marcos and Adina Katz Institute for Advanced Research in Rabbinics (kollel) at Modern Orthodoxy's flagship school for rabbinical training, RIETS at YU.[30] In fact, the image of him teaching his students appears on the letterhead of the RIETS official correspondence stationery.[31] Due to his renown as a Talmudic scholar and religious adjudicator, rabbis and synagogue officers from across North America, in addition to heads of national organizations, consult him regularly on myriad issues relating to Jewish legal decision-making and public policy.[32] Among others, the Israeli Chief Rabbinate recognized him and his RIETS colleague Rabbi Mordechai Willing as the only American authorities who could approve the appointment of rabbinical judges for Orthodox conversion courts in the United States. According to Rabbi Basil Herring, the former Executive Vice President of the Rabbinical Council of America (RCA)—the largest association of Orthodox rabbis in North America—"One can say that they are representative of where Modern Orthodoxy is today."[33]

Schachter's authority is fortified through his identification as one of the preeminent students of Soloveitchik (1903–93) and communicators of his ideas.[34] Yet the nuances of Soloveitchik's Orthodox worldview continue to be the subject of intense debate among both his followers and academic scholars. Indeed, critics complain that through his own publications and lectures, Schachter has sought to deemphasize his mentor's numerous variances from the ideological norms of traditionalist Haredi Orthodoxy.[35] Yet Schachter's credentials as a brilliant Talmudist in his own right and as perhaps the deepest reservoir of knowledge about his teacher are uniformly recognized.[36] As such, many Modern Orthodox rabbis who do not necessarily accept his presentation of the Soloveitchik legacy still consider Schachter's legal decisions to be authoritative.[37] Since the 1980s, he has spoken out vociferously against Orthodox feminism and published a series of prohibitive rulings regarding a variety of ritual innovations advanced by this camp.

Schachter's first major statement on Orthodox feminism was published in 1985. The spread of Orthodox women's prayer groups had led Rabbi Louis Bernstein, then president of the RCA, to turn in 1984 to leading YU rabbis in search of a clear-cut ruling on the permissibility of these ritual gatherings.[38] Notably, the official condemnation of such meetings by the Haredi-affiliated Agudath ha-Rabbonim (Union of Orthodox Rabbis) was already publicized in late 1982.[39] On December 13, 1984, a group of five prominent rabbinic scholars from RIETS—including Schachter—presented their own decision forbidding women's prayer services. During the following year Schachter expanded upon this position in a lengthy responsum titled "*Ze'i lakh be-ikvei ha-zon*" ("Follow you [fem. sing.] in the footsteps of the sheep"),⁴⁰ which was first published in the spring 1985 edition of the RIETS scholarly rabbinic journal, *Beit Yitzhak*.⁴¹

In the essay, Schachter advances numerous reasons for prohibiting Orthodox participation in female prayer groups, as well as in women's *hakafot*—dancing while holding the Torah scroll on the Simhat Torah festival—and public women's readings of the Book of Esther on the Purim holiday.⁴² At a number of junctures, however, he moves beyond technical points to meta-legal or policy considerations. In his opinion, the Orthodox women who promoted the prayer groups had internalized dangerous feminist ideals that had emerged within gentile society and had already been championed by the Conservative and Reform movements, the enemies of Orthodoxy.⁴³ This point is expressed in strongest terms toward the end of the ruling:

> The women's liberation movement has already succeeded in influencing some of the idolaters ... and this influence has already been transferred from the idolatrous nations to our brothers-children of Israel the Conservatives,⁴⁴ until they ruled to include women in a prayer quorum, honor them with being called to recite the blessing on the Torah, and to ordain them as rabbis.... And due to our many sins the hand of the Conservatives has become dominant.... [Thus] if Orthodox women shall participate in such quorums [*minyanim*],⁴⁵ it would appear to all as if they partially accept the counterfeit approach of the Conservatives.... For any issue which unto itself may be deemed permissible, but has become a symbol of destruction of the [true] religion ... such an activity is transformed into a forbidden one.⁴⁶

Schachter's was among the most extensive and forceful responses in its time to the advent of Orthodox feminism. He was unequivocal in judging the entire feminist movement, without distinguishing between various trends, in purely negative terms. As foreseen by Blu Greenberg, the main thrust of his 1985 argument—which is predicated on preventing changes that draw similarities to liberal Jewish denominations—focuses on interdenominational rivalries.⁴⁷ Following a polemical tradition that can be traced to the nineteenth-century struggle with the nascent Reform movement, Schachter disqualifies ceremonial innovation even if legal justification can be found, due to its association with non-Orthodox movements.⁴⁸ This fear of encroachment from Reform and

CHAPTER 5

Conservatives was not new to American Orthodoxy either, and it had influenced the decisions of Schachter's mentor, Soloveitchik, as well.[49] Indeed, due to the 1983 decision by Reform to recognize patrilineal descent as the basis for Jewish identity as well as debates in Israel over the recognition of non-Orthodox conversions, 1985 was a period of particularly intensive interdenominational rivalry.[50] Thus, while Schachter's first major response already testifies to his deep antipathy toward feminism and its Orthodox sympathizers, it can be viewed to a great extent as part of the ongoing struggle of the Orthodox minority to protect itself from the influence of the larger and more powerful liberal factions.[51]

By 1997 direct interdenominational hostilities were beginning to decline,[52] while internal Orthodox conflicts over feminism were only intensifying. A book of Schachter's collected legal writings that appeared that year does not contain any new discussion of feminism, but through its publication he indicated that he saw women's issues as the focal battleground for Orthodoxy. Among the forty legal responsa gathered in the volume, the only one relating to feminism is a republished version of his 1985 decision prohibiting women's prayer groups, along with some notable additions.[53] Nevertheless, he chose to name the entire book *Be-Ikvei ha-Zon* (In the Footsteps of the Sheep), the same phrase that adorns the title of the volume's lone entry regarding feminism and Orthodoxy. By doing so, then, he highlighted both the importance of responding to the challenge of Orthodox feminism and the overall centrality of this issue to his entire Orthodox outlook.[54]

During that same year, 1997, Schachter also delivered a public lecture at YU titled "Woman at Prayer." There he referred to women's prayer groups as an "imitation *mitzvah* [commandment]" and maintained that Soloveitchik unequivocally prohibited such gatherings. Schachter admitted that some of the Orthodox women who attend do so out of sincere religious intentions, but since many of the founders had been influenced by the Reform and Conservative movements, any association was disqualified.[55]

It would appear, then, that by 1997 Schachter had begun to direct both oral presentations and even more so printed publications toward advancing the conflict with feminism to the center of his Orthodox discourse.[56] As yet, however, he had not articulated a theory that viewed this debate in terms that went beyond the denominational struggles that had figured so prominently in previous years—and for that matter the two centuries since the advent of Reform Judaism.[57] His most original and dramatic arguments would emerge in his responses to efforts in the early twenty-first century to integrate women into mixed-gender ritual settings and the support that these initiatives received from highly respected figures within the Orthodox world.

In 2003 Schachter published an essay titled "On the Matter of Masorah."[58] The initial theme is the significance of *masorah*—longstanding traditions of handed-down religious behavior—for deciding normative Jewish law, even when the textual sources may allow for alternative rulings.[59] He then applies this principle as the basis for prohibiting public Torah recital by women, an issue that had risen to the forefront of Modern Orthodox debate after a learned essay sanctioning this practice was published by Rabbi Professor Daniel Sperber in the liberal Orthodox-sponsored *Edah Journal*.[60] The topic had actually already drawn a great deal of attention due to an article by Rabbi Mendel Shapiro that appeared two years earlier in the same journal.[61] At that time, however, Schachter had refrained from responding. Shapiro is a RIETS-trained ordained rabbi, but he is also a practicing lawyer who lives in Jerusalem and was relatively unknown prior to publication of his essay. Sperber, by contrast, is the author of numerous works that have gained acclaim within the Orthodox world. He is also a descendant of a prominent rabbinic family, a world-famous professor of Talmud, an Israel Prize winner, and a longtime rabbi of Orthodox synagogues in Jerusalem.[62] Once Sperber gave his approbation to Orthodox women's public Torah recital, therefore, Schachter apparently saw a greater necessity to respond.[63]

Toward the end of his essay, Schachter reinforced his prohibitive ruling by depicting a "historical tradition" relating to women and Judaism:

> The *Tzdukim* [Sadducees] were apparently bothered with the fact that the Torah discriminated against women regarding the laws of *yerusha* [inheritance], and they attempted to "rectify" this "injustice" somewhat. In later years the early Christians adopted several of the positions of the earlier *Tzdukim*.[64] The Talmud ... records that the early Christians divided *yerushos* [inheritances] equally between sons and daughters. Several centuries later, the Reform movement continued with this complaint against the tradition, that the rabbis were discriminating unfairly against women by having them sit separately in the synagogue, etc. This complaint has developed historically to become the symbol of rebellion against our *masorah*. The fact that this symbolizes *harisus hadas* [destruction of the religion], causes it to become a prohibited activity.[65]

In this narrative, which is unparalleled among Orthodox authorities, feminists have not simply followed the path of their Reform and Conservative contemporaries. Rather, through their behavior they had declared themselves direct heirs to the heretical groups who deviated from normative Judaism since ancient times.[66] For beyond any other areas of dispute with the rabbis, according to Schachter, the complaint that linked all these historical heresies was discrimination against women. As such, anyone who raises objections to accepted rabbinic policy on this topic is clearly aligned with the deviant legacy and intent upon destroying the religion.[67]

During the following year, 2004, Schachter published an additional essay titled "Can Women Be Rabbis?" which dealt with another burgeoning internal Orthodox controversy connected to feminism.[68] Specifically, he attacked a new custom in which Modern Orthodox couples invite a learned woman—sometimes the bride's mentor in Torah studies—to recite the text of the *ketubah* (marriage writ) under the wedding canopy.[69] Following the *masorah* thesis, he argued that the fact that there is no law which requires a male reader[70] does not automatically mean that having a female one is consistent with other hallowed values that emerge from the *halakhah*.[71]

Here, once again, Schachter returned to comparing Orthodox feminists with classical heretics and the common goal of destroying rabbinic Judaism:

> Clearly the motivation to have a woman read the *kesuba* is to make the following statement: the rabbis, or better yet—the G-d of the Jews, has been discriminating against women all these millennia, and has cheated them of their equal rights, and it's high time that this injustice be straightened out.... The Talmud records that during the period of the Second Temple the *Tzdukim* [Sadducees] had many disputes with the *chachamim* [Sages].... One of their big issues was this issue of discrimination against women.... Years later, after the destruction of the Second Temple, the early Christians picked up some of the "shtik" [chicanery] of the *Tzdukim*.... History repeats itself. In recent years, the Reform and the Conservative movements have expressed this same complaint against the rabbis, or better put—against the G-d of the Jews: discrimination against women! Look what has become of the *Tzdukim*, the early Christians, the Reform, and the Conservatives.[72]

Unlike both 1985, when interdenominational tensions were particularly acute, and 1997, when a decline was only beginning to be recognized, scholars have confirmed that by the first years of the twenty-first century American Jewish denominational relations had entered a period of nonconfrontationalism.[73] Not only was there less direct animus, but (as will be discussed in chapter 6) this period saw pioneering Orthodox efforts to interface with broader American Jewry that entailed even greater direct contact with non-Orthodox institutions and leaders. Thus, Schachter's references in 2003 and 2004 to the Reform and Conservative movements should not be understood, primarily, as part of a polemical assault against these groups. Rather, their role is more symbolic: together with the Sadducees and Christians, they constitute factions that found their roots in Jewish tradition, but whose theologies and religious behaviors had placed them irrevocably—in Schachter's opinion—beyond the framework of normative Judaism. By associating the claims of the Orthodox feminists with them, he was declaring that they too were destined for a similar fate.

Indeed, in contrast to the references to the Reform and Conservatives that are ubiquitous within twentieth-century Orthodox polemics, it is the repetitive interjection of the ancient prototypes of Jewish heresy that stands out in Schachter's twenty-first-century critique of Orthodox feminism. As a world-renowned Talmud scholar, he had no trouble identifying sources connecting arguments over the legal status or role of women with all the aforementioned "heretical" groups. Yet he was equally aware that it was only with the emergence of the American Reform and Conservative movements that the status and role of women became a central area of dispute and vehicle for boundary maintenance.[74] The Talmud, for example, certainly records the Sadducee critique regarding distribution of inheritance, but this was by no means among the most prominent of the Sadducee grievances that play out in rabbinic literature.[75]

By expanding the debate over the role of women in Judaism beyond twentieth-century denominational battles, Schachter sought to clarify that feminism had become the main dividing line and the central challenge for the soul of American Judaism. Veritably, his position resembles those spoken in the name of American Haredi Orthodoxy. Rabbi Nisson Wolpin, for example, was the longtime editor of the *Jewish Observer*, the official English-language publication of Agudath Israel.[76] In February 1997 he wrote: "For some proponents of a classical Modern Orthodoxy, who seem to automatically reject any association with rightwingness, the only enticing frontiers seem to be those that border with Conservatism. This includes questioning the rabbinical authority of leading poskim [adjudicators], sponsoring women's prayer groups and Krias HaTorah [Torah reading] gatherings, as well as other gestures of surrender to feminist demands, in total departure from established practice."[77] Similarities notwithstanding, by introducing the analogy between Orthodox feminism and the ancient sectarians,

Schachter's narrative actually bespeaks a more militant tone than that generally associated with American Haredi discourse. In fact, a closer historical precedent for this rhetorical strategy can actually be found among the radical polemical tactics that were championed by zealous Hungarian Ultra-Orthodox Jews during the mid-nineteenth century.

The Ultra-Orthodox Tradition and Counter-Feminism

As well as serving as the birthplace for liberal Jewish religious denominations, nineteenth-century Central Europe also witnessed the rise of Orthodox streams that labored to develop responses to modernity that were consistent with accepted Jewish law and customs. In Germany, Rabbi Samson Raphael Hirsch (1808–88) was the primary architect of a "Neo-Orthodoxy" that synthesized Jewish tradition with European culture.[78] While similar Orthodox models could be found in Hungary as well, as discussed in chapter 1, the prevailing Hungarian approach in the second half of the nineteenth century was that associated with the legacy of Hatam Sofer (Rabbi Moses Sofer, 1762–1839), whose antimodernism was epitomized in the motto "all that is new is biblically forbidden."[79] Not surprisingly, American Modern Orthodoxy has looked to Hirsch as one of the forerunners for its outlook, while American Haredi Orthodoxy has demonstrated greater affinity to Sofer's worldview.[80]

Despite their differences regarding broader modern culture, the Sofer and Hirsch schools in Central Europe shared an absolute antipathy to all forms of Reform or liberal Judaism. In fact, both the late nineteenth-century Hungarians whom scholars refer to as the "Ultra-Orthodox" and Hirsch himself rendered canonical status to a statement by Sofer that is quite reminiscent of those cited above in the name of Schachter.[81] In one of his 1819 correspondences denouncing the advent of the Reform Temple in Hamburg, Sofer declared: "If we had the power over them, my opinion would be to separate them from us [our borders], we should not give our daughters to their sons, and their sons should not be accepted for our daughters so as not to be drawn after them. Their sect should be considered like those of Zadok and Boethus, Anan, and Saul, they among themselves and we among ourselves."[82] From Sofer's perspective, Reform was the archenemy of "authentic Judaism." It was a direct threat to the majority of Jews in his day who were still allegiant to halakhic observance and traditional customs. Therefore, like Schachter's critique of the Orthodox feminists, Sofer delegitimized his contemporary foes by equating them with well-known historical examples of heretical groups, such as the Second Temple–era Sadducees (Zadok), Boethusians, and early Christians (Saul), as well as the medieval

Karaites (Anan), who had all eventually become detached from normative Jewish life. This, in turn, he hoped, would dissuade the majority of Jews from associating with the Reformers and adopting their ideology and religious behavior.

Notwithstanding the fact that both Sofer's Ultra-Orthodox followers as well as Samson Raphael Hirsch identified with this statement,[83] Schachter's construction of a similar narrative in regard to Orthodox feminism is more reminiscent of the Hungarian polemical tradition. Hirsch's late nineteenth-century battles were dedicated primarily to his denominational war against Reform and his efforts to completely separate between them and all Jews who continued to observe the halakhah. By contrast, the main target of Hungarian Ultra-Orthodoxy's campaigns was not the liberal Neologue movement, but rather the observant Jews who aimed to create an Orthodoxy that integrated elements of modern culture into their *Weltanschauung*. While the Hungarian Orthodox continued to delegitimize their liberal foes, by the mid-1870s the denominational boundaries of Hungarian Jewry were fairly concretized. What remained fluid, however, were the varieties of approaches among the Orthodox themselves.[84]

The case of Rabbi Esriel Hildesheimer (noted in chapter 1) offers a fine illustration of this phenomenon. This German-born Orthodox rabbinical figure served from 1851 through 1869 as the rabbi of the Hungarian Jewish community of Eisenstadt (Burgenland region). During this period he founded and orchestrated the first yeshiva in Hungary that included a full program in secular studies. In addition, he advocated for the creation of an Orthodox rabbinical seminary that would include academic and vocational training as part of its educational requirements. Needless to say, these innovations were heavily criticized by his Ultra-Orthodox adversaries. Hildesheimer eventually returned to Germany, where the modern rabbinical seminary that he founded gained him great fame as a champion of Orthodoxy.[85] Yet his Hungarian Ultra-Orthodox opponents feared that even after his departure followers of his approach would remain active. Therefore they made conscious efforts to demonize him and label him as the archenemy of Judaism. In 1872, for example, one of the leading Ultra-Orthodox authorities, Rabbi Hayyim Sofer, declared: "The wicked Hildesheimer is the horse and chariot of the evil inclination, his bravery and success are supernatural, no other than Esau's minister rides with him. All the religious criminals who have arisen over hundreds of years did not labor towards the destruction of religion and faith as he did."[86] Following the model of his mentor Hatam Sofer, he vilified Hildesheimer by comparing him to the historical enemies of Judaism, in this case actually claiming that this latest foe was even worse than his evil predecessors. Yet, as pointed out above, Hildesheimer was a highly competent religious authority who went on to achieve great renown as an architect and defender of Orthodoxy in his native Germany.

It comes as no surprise, then, that the Ultra-Orthodox summoned the association with ancient sectarians—invoked originally by Hatam Sofer regarding the Reform—in reference to their modernist Orthodox adversaries. Historian Michael Silber emphasizes this point in his description of the attacks of Ultra-Orthodox ideologue Rabbi Akiva Yosef Schlesinger on the moderates: "These hypocritical, 'righteous' rabbis, smug in their conviction that cultural synthesis was not only traditionally sanctioned, but also the only proper course to save Orthodoxy, were dubbed by Schlesinger Sadducees. This was a felicitous choice, pregnant with both the implication that the Neo-Orthodox were on the surface 'similar to the Pharisees,' but actually a sect apart."[87]

This Central European scenario lends insight into Schachter's early twenty-first-century American rulings. His interjection of Orthodox feminism into the historical chain of Jewish heresy was not intended primarily to disparage liberal Jewish streams. Recall that such interdenominational tensions had not disappeared, but they were low on the Orthodox agenda. Meanwhile, the internal Orthodox battles over feminism were still heating up. Thus, his comparisons of feminist advocates with ancient sectarians—like those applied by the Ultra-Orthodox to Hildesheimer and his followers—were intended to highlight the destructive quality of this approach for the future viability of Orthodoxy.

Between Right and Left

Having set in bold the parallels between his religious rhetoric and that of nineteenth-century Ultra-Orthodox strategies, I note that from other perspectives, precedent for Schachter's campaign against Orthodox feminism can also be located within Hirsch's German Neo-Orthodox paradigm. Bear in mind the contrast between Hirsch's antagonistic policies toward Reform and his overall embrace of modern culture. Similarly, there is much that distinguishes Schachter's vehement opposition to Orthodox feminism from his attitudes toward other efforts to adjust Orthodoxy to contemporary realities. While Schachter certainly advocates a far more temperate approach to modernity than other disciples of Soloveitchik do, he continues to support positions that would find no adherents within traditionalist Haredi Orthodox circles.[88]

In the introduction to his book *Be-Ikvei ha-Zon*, he writes: "Situations are always changing, history constantly moves forward. Our world is different than that in which our rabbis and parents' parents lived, and if we consistently try to imitate exactly the ways of our fathers, sometimes it will turn out that we have deviated from the tradition. For our rabbis themselves would not have acted that way if they faced today's reality."[89] Schachter's perception of the need to adjust to new historical realities is reflected, on one hand, in his forceful responses to Orthodox feminism, which are far more unequivocal than those of his mentor.[90] On the other hand, however, he also expresses his appreciation for the necessity of at times "deviating from tradition" in his support of positions taken by Soloveitchik that diverged dramatically from those of traditionalist Haredi Orthodoxy. Like his teacher, who set the standard for American Modern Orthodoxy, Schachter identifies forthrightly with Religious-Zionism.[91] He also stands behind his rabbi's support of Yeshiva University, an institution where higher Talmudic learning according to the Lithuanian tradition is integrated with a full-fledged academic program.[92] Most significantly for the current discussion, despite his clear opposition to many aspects of Orthodox feminism, regarding some manifestations of increased religious roles for women he has demonstrated greater tolerance. He defends his teacher for sanctioning Talmudic studies for women,[93] and he also rules—again in the name of his teacher—that women could serve as Orthodox synagogue officers (but not as president).[94] Thus, from the point of view of institutional affiliation, the constituency that looks to him as a religious authority, for significant ideological stands, and even for the education that he has provided for some his own children, Schachter is a leader within Modern Orthodoxy and not the Haredi camp.[95]

Schachter's accommodations to Modern Orthodox norms can be partially attributed to his deep respect for Soloveitchik. While he certainly has made efforts to describe his teacher as less maverick than others do, Schachter nonetheless remains loyal in areas in which Soloveitchik's departure from the Orthodox norms of his Eastern European roots is unequivocal. Yet Schachter has also demonstrated his independence from his mentor, and it would be presumptuous to assume that his public positions on major issues of religious controversy are singularly the result of the esteem with which he holds Soloveitchik.

How then to view the relationship between Schachter's position as a religious leader for Modern Orthodoxy and his adoption of radical rejectionist strategies previously associated with the most zealous Ultra-Orthodox factions? One possible explanation is to understand Schachter as a prime practitioner of the "Haredization" of American Modern Orthodoxy or the "sliding to the right" already encountered in this book. That is, particularly since the 1970s, a significant sector within American Modern Orthodoxy has gravitated toward the sectarian worldview and traditionalist practices previously associated with Haredi Orthodoxy. Some manifestations of this move, as noted, include increased punctiliousness in observance of the halakhah, greater dedication to religious studies combined with deemphasis of secular education, more rigid segregation of sexes, and focus on particularistic Orthodox values to the exclusion of both universal ones and those seemingly shared among Jews of all stripes.

Within YU, Schachter is one of the central exponents of this direction. Many of his students, who themselves were nurtured in Modern Orthodox communities and day schools, have adopted the dress style associated with non-Hasidic traditionalist circles. In addition, like those within the Haredi camp who choose to attain post–high school degrees, they deemphasize the educational value of university studies and perceive college purely as a necessity for earning a living.[96] Schachter himself has consistently highlighted Jewish particularism and has expressed deep appreciation for the religious worldview associated with Haredi Orthodoxy.[97] His repudiation of Orthodox feminism can be viewed, then, as an essential component in his efforts to neutralize more liberal trends within Modern Orthodoxy, thus expediting a realignment of American Orthodoxy that does away with the distinctions between the "right wing" of Modern Orthodoxy and the Haredi sector.

Notwithstanding the possibility that it is a push toward the Haredi worldview that underlies Schachter's antagonism to Orthodox feminism, it is important to distinguish between religious leanings and full identification. Inasmuch as Schachter increasingly puts forward Haredi-like views, he remains, as emphasized above, affiliated with Yeshiva University and has not abandoned key elements in his religious ideology that are squarely associated with Modern Orthodoxy and are disparaged by the traditionalists. Consequently, I suggest a more nuanced account of Schachter that stops short of viewing his rejection of Orthodox feminism as one more indication that he is moving Modern Orthodoxy head first toward the Haredi religious camp.[98]

A return to the model of Orthodoxy articulated by Samson Raphael Hirsch lends insight into that of Schachter as well. Historian Jacob Katz addresses the apparent contradiction between Hirsch's exceedingly positive attitude toward modern culture and his absolute renunciation of those Jewish communities whose exposure to contemporary ideals led them to affiliate with the Reform movement. Katz sees this seeming paradox as reflecting Hirsch's alienation from both the left and the right.[99] Unhappy with the antagonism of the traditionalist rabbis to modern culture, but even more vehemently opposed to the polar approach put forward by the Reform, he advanced a third alternative that was in direct conflict with both extremes. To his mind, this was the only true path for Orthodoxy.

Like Hirsch's approach to those fellow modernists whom he believed to have crossed the boundary beyond authentic Judaism, once Schachter reached the conclusion that feminism was outside the border, he drafted the most lethal rhetorical weapons available within the Orthodox arsenal for attacking its latest archenemy. By listing Orthodox feminists among the historic enemies of normative rabbinic Judaism, he made clear that to his mind there was absolutely no place for them within contemporary Orthodoxy in any of its manifestations.

Schachter is less of a utopian idealist than Hirsch was and is far more sympathetic to the Haredi Orthodox outlook than to the positive approach to non-Jewish culture associated with Modern Orthodoxy. Nevertheless, he is dedicated to advancing a hybrid Orthodoxy that is heavily influenced by Haredi ideals but remains situated within a Modern Orthodox milieu that accepts core positions staked out by his teacher, Soloveitchik. On a personal level as well, Schachter continues to see his mandate as serving a predominantly non-Haredi constituency. Within this role, Schachter's strategy is to bolster a conservative line without necessarily erasing the boundaries that continue to distinguish his camp from its Haredi co-religionists.[100]

6

Reform in the Eyes of Orthodoxy

To this point, the realignment of American Orthodox Judaism has been examined primarily through changes in Modern Orthodoxy that have distanced it from its formerly "churchlike" quality and moved it closer to an insular posture. The next four chapters, in the main, highlight transformations in the Haredi camp that challenge the accuracy of its sectarian characterization.

Over the past two centuries, Orthodox Judaism's attitude toward the Reform movement has been dominated by animosity and polemical efforts at delegitimization and demonization. This chapter demonstrates that, in the past two decades, hostilities have diminished and a new style of Orthodox interaction with Reform has begun to emerge. This dynamic, though by no means leading to harmony between the religious streams, is far removed from prior predictions of "separation-cum-divorce" of these two movements. Conspicuously, the most dramatic changes in approaches to Reform can be identified among prominent representatives and organizations affiliated with Haredi Orthodoxy.

Introduction

In 1984, Orthodox rabbi Reuven Bulka published a book on Orthodox-Reform relations titled *The Coming Cataclysm*.[1] It came out within a year of the landmark decision by the American Reform movement to recognize patrilineal descent as a basis for Jewish identity.[2] Bulka warned that due to "re-entrenchment of the respective positions of the Orthodox and Reform camps, not to mention the movement to the right of Orthodoxy ... a cataclysmic split within the North American Jewish community ... may result in the total renunciation of a significant number within the Jewish community by another group, and the separation-cum-divorce of these two movements into a mainstream Judaism and a new religion."[3]

Subsequent highly publicized pronouncements by various parties within the Orthodox world only buttressed the impression that the Orthodox were on the verge of completely cutting themselves off from Reform as well as other liberal denominations. In May 1988 the RCA—which comprises mainly YU graduates who serve in Modern Orthodox congregations[4]—and the Haredi Orthodox Agudath Israel of America jointly sponsored a full-page advertisement in the *New York Times*. It accused the Reform and Conservative movements of breaking with the definition of Jewish identity that had been accepted throughout history.[5] In the same year, Dr. Yaakov Elman of YU wrote in *Jewish Action*, the official magazine of the consensus-oriented Orthodox Union, "Reform Judaism has been shown to be the sham we have always insisted it is, it is not a 'holding action' stemming assimilation for some Jews. It is a transmission belt for assimilation."[6] In April 1997 the Agudath ha-Rabbonim, the small but albeit well-established national Haredi Orthodox rabbinical organization, declared publicly that "the Reform and Conservative movements are 'not Judaism.'"[7]

By the fall of 1998, however, Rabbi Aharon Lichtenstein offered the more optimistic appraisal that "reciprocal denigration has peaked and the sense of a chasm between mainstream elements in respective factions is receding.... While we may see greater disaffection and splintering at the fringes, the overall climate will be less militant and more congenial."[8] Indeed, in a 2005 study, historian Jack Wertheimer produced data from the late 1990s and the early twenty-first century that supported a similar conclusion and set aside his previous evaluation, published in 1993, that had focused on rising divisiveness.[9] According to his analysis, American Judaism had entered a postdenominational era in which "Jewish denominations [have] shifted from a public posture of confrontation to one of conciliation."[10]

In the following discussion I will draw the contours of a new style of Orthodox interaction with Reform that has begun to emerge, which, while by no means leading to harmony between the religious streams, is also far removed from the prediction cited above of "separation-cum-divorce of these two movements." Before presenting my core data and analysis, I will briefly locate the contemporary discussion within the broader context of the nearly two-hundred-year history of Orthodox-Reform relations.

Orthodoxy and Reform: Two Centuries of Conflict

Rabbi Moses Sofer (1762–1839), the Hatam Sofer, as noted in chapters 1 and 5, was one of the most vociferous opponents of Reform Judaism during its initial rise in early nineteenth-century Central Europe.[11] From Sofer's perspective, Reform was the archenemy of "authentic Judaism." It was a direct threat to the majority of Jews in his day who were still allegiant to observance of the halakhah and traditional customs. Therefore, he sought to delegitimize his contemporary foes by equating them with well-known historical examples of heretical groups who had all eventually become detached from normative Jewish life. This, in turn, he hoped, would dissuade the majority of Jews from associating with the Reformers and adopting their ideology and religious behavior.

Sofer's efforts had a minimal effect on the long-term spread of the Reform movement, yet he was quite successful in drawing a clear boundary between the new enemy and those who professed allegiance to Orthodoxy.[12] Although an all-out ban on marriage to children from Reform homes was never uniformly accepted,[13] there was agreement among all the various Orthodox factions that the Reform religious approach was absolutely invalid. Any official association with its proponents was looked at skeptically, if not completely discouraged—as it might be conceived as expressing a modicum of legitimacy regarding the theological credentials of Reform. Indeed, much of the internal Orthodox debates regarding relationship to Reform over the last two centuries have centered on whether the strict boundaries that divided the two groups could be traversed for the sake of critical issues of common interest such as maintenance of viable shared communal institutions, defense against anti-Semitism, care for Jews in need, and support of Zionism and the State of Israel.[14]

American Orthodoxy's emergence as an independent denomination was also to a great extent a product of efforts by traditionalists to set boundaries between themselves and the nascent Reform. As Jonathan Sarna has pointed out, the term "Orthodoxy" only came into common usage in America after the struggle that took place in 1840 over the introduction of an organ into the synagogue in Charleston, South Carolina.[15] Two decades later, the first ordained Orthodox rabbi with a PhD to reach American shores, Rabbi Bernard Illowy (1814–71), was invited to participate in a conference together with the Reform leadership. His militant refusal echoed the sentiments of his teacher Hatam Sofer: "Chastise those people in public.... Let them change their ways and say 'We have sinned.'"[16]

By the turn of the twentieth century Reform Judaism had succeeded in establishing itself as the religion of America's Jewish elite, most of them of Central European origin. While some cooperation existed between the Reform and the predominantly Eastern European Orthodox leaders regarding social welfare and personal-freedom issues, in as far as religious affairs and theology were concerned, the gulf between the streams had only widened.[17] Toward midcentury, however, much of American Orthodoxy's debating efforts were refocused on differentiating itself and its predominantly immigrant constituency from the nascent Conservative movement—whose leadership actually stemmed from the liberal elements within the traditionalist camp and unlike the Reform had not renounced the binding nature of Jewish law.[18] Yet as the years passed the lines dividing the Orthodox and Conservative movements became more clear-cut. Orthodox polemicists, and to a great degree even more moderate spokesmen such as Joseph Lookstein, tended to deemphasize distinctions between the Conservative and Reform, thus seeking to equate the two in the eyes of their target audience.[19]

This sense of the Orthodox on one side and all other denominations on the other has, on the one hand, been buttressed since the 1980s by Conservative decisions to train women rabbis and team with Reform to promote non-Orthodox conversion in Israel, as well as the most recent move to accept homosexual and lesbian rabbinical candidates.[20] On the other hand, the willingness of Reform rabbis to officiate at mixed marriages, endorse same-sex unions, and particularly the landmark decision to sanction patrilineal descent as a basis for defining Jewishness have highlighted the far more radical departure of Reform from traditional Jewish norms.[21] Such Reform policies brought even liberal-thinking Orthodox leaders such as Lord Jonathan Sacks, the former British United Synagogue Chief Rabbi, to remark in 1993 that "they increase the likelihood that at some time Orthodoxy will see Reform as it saw Christianity: as a separate religion."[22]

While the idea of an official split has found some outspoken Orthodox proponents, predictions that such a policy would become the majority opinion within Orthodoxy have not come to fruition in the second decade of the twenty-first century. To a certain degree, the relative ease with which radical departures from tradition such as patrilineal descent have become normative within the Reform movement may have—somewhat counter-intuitively—actually neutralized the need for the Orthodox to vigilantly attack it. That is, the differences between the two denominations have become so clear that the Orthodox have been relieved of the need to aggressively assert such distinctions.[23] As the late Jacob J. Petuchowski, one of the leading figures in the American Reform rabbinate and a well-regarded scholar, commented in 1986, "There was a time, indeed, when Reform Judaism represented a serious threat to Orthodoxy. But that time is gone."[24] In parallel, internal developments within Reform that will be detailed below, combined with Orthodoxy's increased self-assurance, have actually engendered less confrontational environments for certain types of Orthodox-Reform interactions.

From Confrontation to Kiruv: Confrontation

Rabbi Aharon Kotler (1892–1962) was the founding head of the Beth Medrash Govoha yeshiva in Lakewood, New Jersey—today the largest institution of higher Torah learning in North America.[25] He is considered the main ideologue and architect of the renaissance of Lithuanian Haredi Orthodoxy in North America after the destruction of its Eastern European origins. Upon reaching the United States in 1941, he was appalled to find Orthodox rabbis who sat together with Reform and Conservative colleagues in organizations such as the Synagogue Council of America and the New York Board of Rabbis. In 1956 he took action, leading a move by the Moetzes Gedolei ha-Torah, Agudath Israel's governing Council of Torah Sages, to ban Orthodox participation in such interdenominational frameworks. Although this position was not supported by some prominent figures within the Modern Orthodox camp, eventually the vast majority of Orthodox rabbis adopted Kotler's policy in practice.[26] By 1994 the New York Board of Rabbis officially folded.[27]

Kotler's directives were complemented by legal decisions of other formidable Eastern European–born Orthodox authorities. Rabbi Moses Feinstein (1895–1986), the leading halakhic decisor (*posek*) in America in the mid- to late twentieth century, ruled in the 1950s that it was forbidden for an Orthodox Jew to serve as principal in a non-Orthodox Hebrew School if classes were held in the same building that houses the prayer sanctuary. This, despite Feinstein's stated awareness of the potential benefits for the students from exposure to such a qualified educator.[28] Notably, notwithstanding his clear disagreement with both groups, Feinstein distinguished between the Reform and Conservatives. While to his mind both were dedicated to destroying traditional Jewish life and values, at times he found reason to rule more leniently regarding the Conservative movement.[29] Even Rabbi Joseph B. Soloveitchik—the preeminent rabbinical authority and Talmudic scholar at YU who took a far more positive approach to other aspects of American life than did Kotler—stated during the same decade that it was preferable to pray at home on the High Holidays than to set foot in a non-Orthodox synagogue that did not separate between male and female prayer galleries. In his letter to the RCA on the subject, he admonished that "No pretext, excuse, *ad hoc* formula, missionary complex, or unfounded fear of losing our foothold within the Jewish community, can justify the acceptance of the Christianized synagogue as a bona fide Jewish religious institution."[30]

Such strictures and statements set the standards for Orthodox policy regarding interaction with non-Orthodox public bodies throughout most of the twentieth century.[31] Clearly they expressed the fear of encroachment from the directions of the Reform and Conservative branches that was felt during the 1950s by these captains of American Orthodoxy.[32] The level of insecurity was so great that even opportunities for influencing non-Orthodox Jews were to be abandoned, lest the exposure lead the Orthodox to become attracted to the religious views of their adversaries. To be sure, there were always voices of dissent within Modern Orthodoxy that took a less militant stand on cooperation with Reform and Conservative.[33] Yet from the 1960s the Modern Orthodox increasingly toed the Haredi line in as far as interdenominational issues were concerned.

The late 1990s and early twenty-first century, as will be expanded upon in chapter 7, actually witnessed the resurgence of a more assertive liberal wing within Modern Orthodoxy. One aspect of this countermovement was the promotion of a far less combative stance toward the non-Orthodox. Rabbi Saul Berman's now-defunct Edah organization encouraged interdenominational communication, and Rabbi Avi Weiss's Yeshivat Chovevei Torah (YCT) rabbinical seminary went as far as to hire Conservative- and Reform-affiliated faculty to teach in its pastoral program.[34] By 2003 even YU had invited Rabbi David Ellenson, the newly appointed president of the Reform Hebrew Union College, to offer a presentation to its advanced rabbinical candidates.[35] Indeed, Rabbi Dr. Norman Lamm, then YU president and Rosh Yeshiva (yeshiva head) of YU's Rabbi Isaac Elchanan Theological Seminary, initiated the invitation and attended the session. In a 2007 interview Lamm bemoaned the confrontational approach toward the non-Orthodox that he had adopted during his previous career as a congregational rabbi:

People don't understand that if I treat a person with respect, it doesn't necessarily mean I approve of what he or she is saying. When I was in the rabbinate, when I was much younger, I used to pound the pulpit and storm against Conservative and Reform and secular ideas and practices. In retrospect I think it may have been the wrong approach. Was I really convincing anybody? I don't think so.... The only thing that happened as a result of all these anti-Conservative/Reform/secular groups is that we have less people davening [praying].... I like the idea of having Conservative day schools and Reform day schools. People are afraid these things will attract the Orthodox.[36]

As pointed out above, isolated voices had been heard within American Modern Orthodoxy in the previous decades as well that decried the confrontational stance.[37] This was not the case among the American Haredi Orthodox. A more radical and significant about-face can be discerned, therefore, through a consideration of fresh approaches toward Reform expressed by those who identified more closely with the legacy of Rabbi Aharon Kotler and his mid-twentieth-century Haredi contemporaries.

Reevaluating the Haredi Approach: Rabbi Yaakov Perlow

Rabbi Yaakov Perlow's personal and educational background combines elements of the two forces that dominate Haredi Orthodoxy. An heir to the Novominsker Hasidic dynasty, he received his advanced Talmudic training from one of the leading bastions of Mitnagedic Lithuanian Orthodoxy, the Chaim Berlin yeshiva in Brooklyn.[38] This dual pedigree serves him well in his current position as head of Agudath Israel of America and chair of its Council of Torah Sages, the same position that was held for many years by Kotler.[39] In June 1999, less than a year after his appointment as Rosh Agudath Israel, Perlow published a letter in its official magazine, the *Jewish Observer*, whose heading begins with these words, "*The following thoughts have been percolating in my mind the past few weeks. To some they may seem novel; to some, even questionable. But to me they reflect an unquestionable reality.*"[40] Perlow then offered his response to a series of decisions that had recently been publicized by the two major Reform governing groups, the Union of American Hebrew Congregations (UAHC) and the Central Conference of American Rabbis (CCAR).

The Reform had thrown their support behind efforts "to engage in a dialogue with the sources of our tradition," hoping to create "lives infused with *kedushah*, holiness."[41] Furthermore, in the CCAR *Statement of Principles for Reform Judaism* ratified in Pittsburgh on May 26, 1999, they asserted the centrality of *mitzvot* (ritual commandments) and moved away from universalism toward a "Jewish identity... uncompromisingly rooted in God and Torah."[42] This was a major departure from the religious approach known as American Classical Reform that was advanced at the 1885 Pittsburgh Platform, which focused on Reform's ethical and universal vision and omitted ritual religious acts from its central tenets.[43] The new decisions of the official organs did not require Reform Jews to perform any specific rituals, and total personal autonomy was still advocated. Yet these directives symbolized the rise to dominance of a trend toward greater traditional behavior within Reform Judaism whose earliest expressions can be traced to the late 1930s, but which evolved in particular since the 1970s and has intensified since the 1990s.[44]

For Perlow, the Reform declarations represented a sufficient recant from the movement's long-held positions that they could not be dismissed merely as empty rhetoric. Rather,

> We are witness to a new stirring in the hearts of Jews that deserves our attention and reflection. The fact that this expression, this cry, has the official imprint of the Reform movement is all the more astonishing, given its ideological denial of Revelation and the sanctity of the *mesora* [passed down tradition].... Is this the voice of the citadel of *kefira* [heresy]? No, it is the voice of Jews lost in the wilderness.... We *ma'aminim* [believers] would be totally remiss in our understanding of *Hashgacha* [Divine providence] were we to treat the publication of this manifesto with cynicism.... The call to *mitzvos* should inherently lead to the callers and followers, if they are serious seekers, to real *teshuva*, return. The manifesto is therefore only a beginning, albeit a historic one.[45]

Perlow's central message was that the time had come for the Orthodox to reevaluate aspects of its relationship to Reform. Namely, the nearly exclusive focus on the iniquities of Reform and the danger that it posed, which dominated American Orthodox discourse throughout the twentieth century, was no longer necessarily the proper approach. Despite being fully aware of Reform's continued support for patrilineal descent and for conversions that he would never recognize, for example, he still felt that there were sufficient indications that this epitome of evil was turning a new leaf. As he put it, "The fact that this expression, this cry, has the official imprint of the Reform movement is all the more astonishing.... Is this the voice of the citadel of *kefira* [heresy]?"[46]

Perlow lauded the recent Reform statements as signs of a grassroots revolt from within Reform against its classical alienation from traditional acts and rituals. Moreover, he hoped that this was "only a beginning" and that an increasingly empowered and self-confident Orthodoxy would capitalize on this new situation and tap into the popular thirst for "authentic" religion that had been expressed. This willingness to acknowledge positive elements within Reform and to encourage closer ties with its affiliates was a revolutionary reassessment of the Orthodox-Reform dynamic. Well aware of this, Perlow, already in his opening lines, alluded to the criticism that his innovative spirit was bound to encounter from within his own camp: "To some they may seem novel; to some, even questionable."[47]

In point of fact, Perlow had already spoken similar sentiments soon after his rise to the head of Agudath Israel. In reaction, the Haredi Orthodox–oriented *Jewish Press* had immediately demanded that Agudath Israel "respond forcefully to reports in the Anglo-Jewish media that it is poised to make a rapprochement with the non-Orthodox."[48] As such, the *Jewish Observer* letter may be seen in part as the clarification that the *Jewish Press* had requested. Instead of denying the charges, however, Perlow stated his position in a way that left no doubt as to his commitment to articulating a new orientation for interdenominational relations. Quite paradoxically, in light of the fact that Perlow has subsequently veered Agudath Israel toward a more rejectionist position regarding many areas of non-Jewish culture and modern science, the secular-sponsored *Jewish Daily Forward* volunteered to serve as the rabbi's advocate when it published its own editorial felicitously titled "Perlow's Progress."[49]

The Internal Haredi Debate

The choice of Perlow to lead Agudath Israel can, in fact, be viewed as the affirmation of a position that emerged as a subject of heated debate on the pages of Agudath Israel's *Jewish Observer* during the mid-1990s. Quite in contrast to calls for outreach to the Reform, and consistent with the prior American Haredi Orthodox standard, Rabbi Levi Reisman augured in a 1996 article titled "We Are No Longer One" that due to the Reform's heretical theology and policies, "there might be a time in the not-so-distant future when *kiruv* [outreach] work will be fraught with so many halachic problems arising from questionable Jewish identity that it will simply cease."[50] Rabbi Avi Shafran, Agudath Israel's director of public affairs and one of its chief spokesmen, exhorted his fellow Orthodox to remain militant in delegitimizing the other denominations, "Even we Orthodox can become desensitized . . . and subtly slide into the trap of regarding non-halachic movements as, for some Jews, better than nothing."[51]

During the same period, however, others began to promote the type of approach later lent approbation by Perlow. Rabbi Nisson Wolpin, the editor-in-chief of the *Jewish Observer*, reported positively, if ambivalently, on the UAHC biennial convention that took place in Atlanta in December 1995: "As for the spirituality that informed the UAHC in Atlanta, one should not suspect that the Reform movement traded in Cincinnati for Sinai. Yet one would do well to accept the pronouncements ... as evidence of deep, if undeveloped stirrings amongst these Jews.... We must take these signals seriously."[52] Without condoning Reform theology and public policy, during the following year Rabbi Leonard Oppenheimer (then) of Portland, Oregon, also responded sympathetically within the pages of the *Jewish Observer* to Reform efforts to enhance Jewish identity and knowledge. In direct contradistinction to Shafran, he chided his fellow committed Orthodox:

> Can we not see that virtually all of these are in fact sincere, albeit mistaken, attempts to strengthen Judaism? That virtually all of the young students at the Reform Kollel and the non-Orthodox seminaries have chosen this path because they passionately want to strengthen Judaism, as much as we feel that their career is headed for terrible tragedy. Is it not possible that for them, a trip to Israel for intermarried couples is an attempt to offer some taste of authentic Judaism to the many who are going to consider themselves Jewish, whether we deplore it or not?[53]

These voices at the edge of the millennium encouraged a reconsideration of the long-held Orthodox worldview vis-à-vis Reform canonized in the writings of the Hatam Sofer as well as Samson Raphael Hirsch,[54] and refitted for America by Aharon Kotler.

Another *Jewish Observer* contributor sought to translate these ideas into new pragmatic guidelines that veered away from the halakhic norms established by Moses Feinstein and Joseph B. Soloveitchik. After suggesting that "perhaps, in 1996, we should try to find every possible way to reach Jews before they are even further away from any vestige of Jewish tradition," Rabbi Elchonon Oberstein of Baltimore hypothesized: "Can an Orthodox outreach group go into a non-Orthodox synagogue (not during services and not in the sanctuary) to teach Hebrew, and to explain *mitzvos*? Is there any variation depending on who asks the question and which city we are asking about? How broad is the '*issur*' [prohibition]?"⁵⁵ Without relating explicitly to these very practical questions, Perlow's 1999 pronouncement gave a clear indication that existing precedents ought to be reevaluated.

Kiruv and the Blurring of Boundaries

Indeed, simultaneous with increasingly sympathetic rhetoric regarding Reform, some of the more innovative figures in the burgeoning field of Orthodox outreach to broader American Jewry actually began to traverse boundaries that had previously been sealed. Already in his 1990 work, *Jewish Outreach: Halakhic Perspectives*, Rabbi Moshe Weinberger devoted a subsection to "Cooperation with Non-Orthodox Institutions." He conceded that "one of the most sensitive issues confronting the outreach professional is the question of whether to allow local non-Orthodox institutions to participate in *kiruv* programs. . . . The dilemma is a harrowing one. How can someone in *kiruv* be effective in making Orthodoxy an attractive alternative to Conservative and Reform Judaism if he publicly spurns all non-Orthodox attempts to join forces with him for the purposes of Jewish 'awareness and unity'?"⁵⁶ Despite his apparent desire to reconsider previous standards, at this stage Weinberger was unwilling to go beyond articulating the religious conundrum to formally advance a new approach. Rather, he deferred to the "outspoken . . . disapproval of any such activities" codified by Rabbi Feinstein nearly forty years prior.⁵⁷

By the late 1990s, however, other outreach specialists had moved beyond sympathetic words to behavior that blurs Orthodox denominational boundary markers that had long been clearly demarcated. A major illustration can be found in the activities of a relatively fresh institution within Jewish religious life, the community kiruv kollel. Kollels are generally defined as Orthodox frameworks in which veteran yeshiva students, usually married ones, receive a living stipend in order to study Talmud and Jewish law on a full-time basis. In the new formulation, a group of as many as ten yeshiva students and their families are sent to establish a study hall in a city or neighborhood that lacks intensive Torah-study environments, and for that matter may not have a significant Orthodox population altogether. The fellows continue to devote themselves to daily personal intellectual development, but in contrast to the classical kollels, much of their schedules are dedicated to offering Jewish study opportunities to the broader local Jewish population both within the walls of their *beit midrash* (study hall) and by holding sessions throughout the surrounding area. To date, more than twenty such community-outreach kollels have been established throughout the United States.⁵⁸ In a number of studies I have described these organizations in detail and considered them within the context of both internal Jewish developments and broader themes of American religion.⁵⁹ Here I will present a few examples that testify to their denominational barrier-breaking quality. Chapter 8 will deal more extensively with the evolution of the community kollel and the ways it parallels and distinguishes itself from Lubavitch Hasidic movement's Chabad house.

The Atlanta Scholars Kollel (ASK) is considered the pioneering community kiruv kollel. Founded and led by graduates of Baltimore's Ner Israel yeshiva, its glossy pamphlets and cutting-edge website contain the following invitation: "Whether you're Reform, Conservative, Orthodox, unaffiliated or somewhere in between, the Atlanta Scholars Kollel (ASK) is your most vibrant source for Jewish learning in Atlanta.... By uniting fellow Jews through shared joy in religious education and Judaic tradition, and by extending a friendly, upbeat, nonjudgmental invitation to all Jews, ASK is building bridges in our community."⁶⁰ Such postdenominational language may be seen as pure public relations aimed at lowering the defenses, so to speak, of non-Orthodox Jews. ASK, however, has demonstrated its willingness to meet its constituency on its own terms by actually running a biweekly introductory prayer service in one of Atlanta's largest Reform houses of worship, Temple Sinai of Sandy Springs. To be sure, the meetings take place in a social hall rather than in the synagogue sanctuary.⁶¹ Nevertheless, this is a clear departure from the guidelines set down by Rabbi Feinstein. Similarly, members of the Phoenix Community Kollel have taught classes at the community-sponsored Hebrew High that is housed at the Reform Temple Chai.⁶² Also digressing from Orthodox standards, the head of Pittsburgh's Kollel Jewish Learning Center from 1998 to 2014, Rabbi Aaron Kagan, met on a regular basis with his local rabbinic colleagues from Reform and Conservative synagogues to study Torah together.⁶³ While this may appear less dramatic, it is quite significant in light of the 1956 Kotler ban on interdenominational organizational cooperation among rabbis. Such is the case especially since Kagan is an alumnus of the Lakewood yeshiva. In fact, his father studied with its founder, Rabbi Aharon Kotler, and was originally sent by his son, Rabbi Shneur Kotler, to Pittsburgh in 1978.⁶⁴

Based in Palo Alto, California, the Jewish Study Network (JSN)—one of the most dynamic and rapidly expanding of these kiruv kollels—does not limit its interdenominational contacts to private study. Rather, its fellows work together with Conservative and Reform representatives to create new Jewish learning initiatives throughout the San Francisco Bay area and offer their own programming in non-Orthodox synagogues as well. Rabbi Joey Felsen, the head of JSN and a veteran of five years of full-time Torah study at Jerusalem's venerable Mir yeshiva, made clear that he was not opposed to presenting Torah lectures in a non-Orthodox synagogue sanctuary, although he preferred to teach in the social hall.[65] Indeed, according to Rabbi Yerachmiel Fried, leader of Dallas's highly successful DATA (Dallas Area Torah Association) Kollel and a well-respected halakhist, as far as Jewish religious institutions were concerned, the only boundary that remained hermetically sealed was his unwillingness to teach in a gay synagogue.[66]

Are these merely isolated cases that do not reflect the overall attitude of the Haredi Orthodox camp? Unquestionably, there still exists a great deal of animosity toward the Reform and Conservative movements within all branches of Orthodoxy. But taken together with the comments of Perlow and others, meaningful shifts have occurred. Significantly, from an Orthodox perspective the community kollels have not taken action without backing from Orthodox halakhic authorities. The ASK Kollel in Atlanta was founded under the guidance of Rabbi Yaakov Weinberg (1924–99), the late head of the Ner Israel yeshiva, and the decision to operate within Reform institutions was done with his full consent and following the guidelines that he set down.[67] In addition, Ner LeElef, a Haredi-oriented organization that trains Orthodox outreach workers and provides them with professional guidance and programming materials, has indicated in its literature that there is room for flexibility on such issues.[68] In a discussion of places in which to hold classes, Ner LeElef lists the nondenominational Melton Centers for adult education that have spread throughout the United States. It warns, however, that "the Melton mini-School curriculum is a pluralistic one where the opinions of Reform and Conservative 'scholars' are included." It concludes, therefore, that "it can and has been done, but it is not Glatt [the highest religious dietary standard for meat products]."[69] Building on this metaphor, one can debate whether each of the various new Haredi initiatives contravenes directly the rulings of the authorities of the previous generation. But for a collective that characteristically advances a stricter standard of legal interpretation, the novel approach is far from being "glatt kosher."[70]

Even more significant is the position articulated by Rabbi Shmuel Kamenetsky of the Philadelphia yeshiva—a Lakewood affiliate. He studied with Aharon Kotler and is a prominent member of the Perlow-led Council of Torah Sages. Well aware of Kotler's outlook, he nevertheless permitted—within certain guidelines—a major Haredi-oriented community kollel to run programs in Conservative and Reform institutions. His response to a query from the organization was written on his personal stationery on January 7, 2002, and reads as follows:

> In my opinion it is permitted to give classes in non-Orthodox synagogues of different denominations provided that one gives these classes in a private classroom rather than the sanctuary and one does not share the platform with rabbis of non-Orthodox denominations who are making presentations at the same time ... (a *she'elah* [query] should be asked in every situation since the particulars vary from case to case). It goes without saying that one may not participate in non-Orthodox non-mehizah services in these synagogues. I understand that you and your organization have been highly successful in your first year of operation with large numbers of people being influenced. May you continue your sacred work to be *me-karev aheinu benei Yisrael* [bring closer our brothers the children of Israel] and may everyone work in unison and shalom to achieve this goal.[71]

Despite the limitations that he placed, the letter was considered so radical and unprecedented by some parties that they worked to convince Israeli Haredi authorities to express their opposition. Due to the controversy that ensued, the document was never printed or distributed. All the same, it is known throughout the "outreach community" and serves as a legal precedent for many similar initiatives.

Kamenetsky's overall approach was echoed in a 2012 essay published by his son, Rabbi Sholom Kamenetsky, himself a leading figure in the Philadelphia yeshiva and a highly sought-after guide for Haredi outreach activists. Speaking of the many halakhic challenges that arise in the course of engaging nonobservant Jews on a regular basis, he remarked: "No one should go into kiruv imagining that he will always be able to preserve 'West Point standards' in the field. We are not talking about doing anything in contravention of the *Shulchan Aruch*, just the fact that any kiruv professional in the field will find himself engaged in many types of activities that he never imagined himself doing in yeshiva or [regular] kollel."[72]

To some degree the very design of the community kollel as a vehicle for outreach is indicative of the postdenominational tendencies that have emerged within American Orthodoxy. By creating an institution that focuses on study rather than ritual, the Orthodox have been able to sidestep some of the more directly confrontational aspects of denominational relations as well as specific halakhic issues that are unavoidable in a synagogue framework. One major subject of controversy is intermarriage. The number of Reform Jews who are married to non-Jews but remain active in Jewish life has risen dramatically since the

1970s.[73] Today, most Reform congregations have introduced policies that allow for involvement—with certain limitations—of non-Jewish spouses and children in synagogue services.[74] Orthodox legal authorities, by contrast, not only prohibit non-Jewish participation in public rituals, they also specify sanctions forbidding their Jewish spouses as well from receiving certain religious honors.[75] Thus, those involved in Orthodox outreach struggle to find ways to service intermarried families without trampling on broadly accepted principles of halakhah. Here, the study-centered beit midrash provides a framework that is geared toward engendering increased Jewish involvement, but that is devoid of the normative minefields that occupy the synagogue sanctum.[76] In contrasting the denominational synagogue with the community-outreach kollel, Barton "Bob" Schechter, a lifetime Conservative Jew and veteran Jewish communal executive who is active in the Pittsburgh Kollel Jewish Learning Center, pointed out that synagogues invariably expect their rabbis to focus on developing denominational identification. As such, they "can't do what a kollel can do. They have to cultivate allegiance to the congregation."[77]

Accounting for the Shift: Triumphalism and Beyond

The new willingness of Haredi Orthodoxy to interact directly with Reform Jews and other non-Orthodox Jews, their institutions, and their leaders, is one of the manifestations of what has become known as Orthodox triumphalism. As noted at the outset of this work, until the mid-1960s the consensus among both scholars and lay leaders of American Jewry was that American Orthodoxy was merely a surviving vestige of European traditional Jewry and that its demise on American soil was imminent. This began to change with the appearance of Liebman's 1965 study that emphasized Orthodox vibrancy. Subsequent decades have witnessed ongoing intensive growth in Orthodox-sponsored institutions, political power, and collective wealth.[78] Defying Liebman's analysis, however, the Reform movement has also demonstrated renewed dynamism and expanded significantly since the 1980s. Yet in the eyes of many, and for the Orthodox in particular, these changes have been overshadowed by the steep rise in rates of intermarriage and nonaffiliation among the majority of American Jews, including those who identify as Reform.[79] The results of the 2013 Pew study only strengthened the impression that the non-Orthodox denominations are in steep decline and no longer pose direct danger to the vitality of the Orthodox factions. Under these circumstances, Orthodox leaders have increasingly shed the insecurity that underscored their post–World War II policies. In its place there have arisen a victor's identity and a sense of collective self-confidence. This new stance, in turn, allows for and encourages positive interactions with other Jews and their institutions—sometimes even when it entails entering the ideological adversary's territory—without the vigilance and defensiveness that previously characterized interdenominational encounters.[80]

Consistent with Orthodoxy's triumphalist mood, the perception that by reintroducing traditional outlooks and behaviors "Reform is publicly admitting its failures" could not but have been gratifying for leading Orthodox spiritual and political leaders like Rabbi Yaakov Perlow. Note, however, that unlike many examples from this genre that target Reform weaknesses purely in order to celebrate Orthodoxy's robust condition,[81] Perlow's letter highlights what he considered to be positive developments within Reform.

To this point I have sought to demonstrate that this tone was not merely rhetorical, but reflected a fundamental reevaluation of the nature of Orthodoxy's approach to Reform that manifested itself in policies and activities in which Orthodoxy crossed formerly strict boundaries. Nevertheless, the majority of the examples stem from the field of Orthodox Jewish outreach to the nonobservant. From this perspective, the changes in tone and even behavior may be seen as purely tactical or cosmetic in nature. The kiruv activists reached the conclusion that the largest critical mass of Jews with potential to grow closer to Orthodoxy were those who were already Jewishly involved and affiliated with synagogues of other denominations. By demonstrating understanding and appreciation for their predicament and addressing their desire for increased personal meaning, then, the Orthodox stood a far better chance of winning new members to their ranks.[82]

Financial Imperatives

Within the context of facilitating the expansion of Haredi triumphalist outreach activities, there are also growing economic incentives for the Orthodox to adopt a less combative approach to interdenominational relations. As the Haredi yeshivas produce larger pools of graduates, the pressure to generate employment opportunities for individuals who possess rich stores of religious knowledge but minimal secular education has increased dramatically. Today, for example, there are over 6,500 full-time students in Lakewood's Beth Medrash Govoha.[83] With an average stay in the institution of six to seven years, more than 500 alumni enter the workforce each year.[84] The Orthodox outreach "industry" has opened new vistas for Haredi employment. By lowering the interdenominational tensions, then, more opportunities to market their outreach products are made available to the kiruv workers.[85]

Another financial motivation for the Orthodox to adjust their approach to the non-Orthodox is the need to secure funding for specific programming. As Haredi institutions have expanded, they have increasingly looked to earn capital grants awarded for specific projects by nonsectarian frameworks such as local federations and the Avi Chai Foundation.[86] As one of the conditions for their support, these organizations often demand that those being funded refrain from polemics and demonstrate their commitment to Jewish unity.

To be sure, these fiscal realities certainly played a central role in the reorientation of Orthodox attitudes toward the Reform movement since the 1990s. Nonetheless, there are additional related phenomena that merit consideration in order to appreciate more fully the transformation that has taken place.

The Chabad Factor

Chapter 8 addresses the many parallels between the Lithuanian Orthodox sponsored community kiruv kollel and the Lubavitch movement's Chabad house—the Hasidic outreach center model that made its first appearance in 1969, and continues to multiply throughout the world until today.[87] There I suggest that the rise of the community kiruv kollel illustrates a "chabadization" so to speak of American Orthodoxy. That is, those Haredi Jews who once championed an enclavist/survivalist approach that sought to limit interactions with the majority of American Jewry have more recently adopted much of the outreach orientation that has long stood at the center of the American Chabad movement.

As part of its forerunner role, Chabad also serves as a precursor to the recent willingness within American non-Hasidic Orthodox circles to interact with the Reform movement and its institutions. Like the non-Hasidic Haredim, Lubavitchers do not recognize the Reform movement as a theologically legitimate expression of Judaism. Nevertheless, in the interest of exposing as many individuals as possible to Jewish knowledge and spirit, Chabad representatives have demonstrated flexibility—ignoring denominational boundaries, and thus blazing the trail for their Orthodox counterparts.[88]

Self-Interest or Sustaining Jewish Survival

Following the Chabad example, the increased emphasis within Haredi Orthodoxy on outreach has engendered its willingness to move beyond its natural constituency and focus on groups that were previously seen purely as threats to its survival. Of course, Haredi Orthodoxy's perceptions of the non-Orthodox remain rooted in approaches to Jewish identity whose foundations, as I have shown elsewhere, can be identified in nineteenth-century Europe.[89] Thus, the barrier breaking described here is far from egalitarian or pluralistic in nature. Rather it is more akin to that of a person who chooses to jump into a stormy sea in order to save an estranged brother who is drowning.

Once they have succeeded in attracting non-Orthodox Jews to their programs, Haredi outreach specialists admit openly that they would ideally like to convince their new constituents to embrace full halakhic observance. At the same time they maintain that in light of what they see as alarming rates of intermarriage—like Chabad—they have gained greater appreciation for all forms of Jewish engagement that offer an alternative to complete assimilation. Numerous interviews that I have conducted with non-Orthodox constituents who participate in Haredi community kollel learning programs, for example, indicate that this is their impression of the nature of outreach efforts as well. Nonetheless, one can counter that even when the potential for transforming individuals into Orthodox Jews is minimal, the possibilities for garnering financial support from them remain. Thus, in the long term it may once again be internal interests that drive Haredi willingness to move away from interdenominational confrontation.

Indeed, it is difficult to produce irrefutable evidence for the noncosmetic nature of the changes described here. That said, the about-face that has transpired particularly since the mid-1990s is also noteworthy in that it has manifested itself in ways that appear to be counter to other central Haredi interests. By nevertheless making conscious efforts to minimize tensions, then, Haredi leaders have demonstrated that their commitment to adjusting the dynamics of interdenominational relations is not predicated solely on advancing their own group's internal goals.

To start, it bears repeating that the compromise of significant and long-held Orthodox taboos—most prominently by the heirs to those who established the prior standards—has generated a good deal of internal criticism. After decades of indoctrination regarding the imminent dangers entailed in traversing interdenominational boundaries, the idea of exposing the Haredi world's soldiers to the environments of former archenemies remains controversial.[90] Recall Perlow's introduction in which he admitted that his remarks may seem "*to some . . . novel; to some, even questionable.*"[91] In response to such critiques, part of the intensive training in outreach programming that is now offered within various Haredi yeshivas is focused on how to become involved with the greater American Jewish community without being influenced by it. Consistent with the fear of outreach compromising other hallowed values, in one yeshiva there are actually special sessions offered that map out "how we are different from Chabad."[92]

This last point alludes, among others, to one of the characteristic Haredi attacks on Chabad. Namely, that the intensive exposure of its members to

American culture, along with the high rate of newly religious Jews among its ranks, has introduced influences and behaviors that were formerly considered foreign to Haredi Orthodox society.[93] Consistent with this attitude, one central source of fear among those who question the wisdom of the move toward proactive involvement with non-Orthodox Jews is the recognition that non-Hasidic Haredi society itself is far from immune to contemporary social problems. There are significant numbers of yeshiva dropouts and substance abusers, or what are referred to as "at-risk youth" within the Haredi community, for example, and numerous institutions have been established to address their specific issues. These phenomena, which may have existed in similar proportions in the past but were not spoken of as candidly, are attributed to increased exposure to the outside world.[94] All the same, in the face of such new realities Haredi leaders continue to sanction denominational boundary crossing, at least within the context of outreach.

Finally, concurrent with the decline in interdenominational tension, internal conflicts within Orthodoxy have by no means subsided in the past two decades. One of the central battlegrounds, as discussed in chapter 5, has been over the role of women in Orthodox educational and ritual life. Those representing an assertively Modern Orthodox outlook have sought ways to increase women's involvement in religious leadership and in public ritual. In opposition, the Haredim and those sympathetic to Haredi postures have joined together to portray these efforts as heretical and destructive. Reverting to Orthodox polemical tactics originating in the early nineteenth century, representatives of this camp have declared those who promote Orthodox feminism as aligning with the "Reform" or "Conservative." This point will be expanded upon in chapter 9 and in the concluding chapter of this book.

In such an adversarial atmosphere, in which fellow Orthodox rabbis are vilified for possessing "Reform"-like attitudes, the importance of Haredi authorities supporting increased interaction with Reform Jews cannot be underestimated. On the one hand, it testifies to the major shift that has taken place. Simultaneously, the continued use of non-Orthodox identification within internal Orthodox polemics confirms that such a truce or even tactical partnership—at least from the Orthodox perspective—does not constitute the basis for more fundamental denominational conciliation. Inasmuch as there may be increasing Orthodox appreciation for the need to interact positively with Reform institutions and their constituencies, the fear that such activities will be interpreted as a form of legitimization of the Reform Judaism itself always lurks in the background.

Conclusion: Between Interaction and Legitimization

This point was illustrated clearly in 2002, during a controversy that arose regarding a book whose very existence, paradoxically, exemplified the new Orthodox willingness to look beyond traditional denominational boundaries.

Rabbi Yosef Reinman is an alumnus of the Lakewood yeshiva and a respected Haredi Orthodox educator. Rabbi Ammiel Hirsch is currently rabbi of the Reform Stephen Wise Free Synagogue and former executive director of ARZA, the Reform movement's Zionist Organization. In January 2000, at the behest of a literary agent, they began an e-mail dialogue that lasted the better part of two years. The result was *One People, Two Worlds: A Reform Rabbi and an Orthodox Rabbi Explore the Issues That Divide Them*. Even a cursory reading of the work makes clear that the authors' respective religious worldviews are sharply at odds. Nevertheless, the very act of a Haredi Orthodox rabbi engaging with a Reform representative in theological dialogue that generally avoids nonsubstantive recrimination is testimony to the change of spirit that had evolved since the 1990s. As Reinman writes in his afterword regarding Hirsch, "It was moving to discover a powerful Jewish heartbeat despite the widely reported apathy. It gave me a feeling of hope."[95] In fact, Reinman made sure to clarify to his readers that, while his positions should not be considered the "official views of the Orthodox rabbinate," he wanted "to thank Rabbi Sholom Kamenetsky, who read all the postings and showed many of them to his father, Shmuel Kamenetsky."[96] Recall that the latter is the revered head of the Lakewood-affiliated Philadelphia yeshiva, a central figure in Agudath Israel's Council of Torah Sages, and the person who authored a letter that permits Orthodox outreach work in Reform premises.

This postconfrontational mood made way for traditional boundary placement, however, after the publisher announced in June 2002 that the two authors would embark together on a seventeen-city promotional tour. Days before they were to set out, the same Council of Torah Sages issued the following statement:

> A distressing development has occurred in our community—the publication of a book that presents a debate between, on the one hand, a faithful Jew and *talmid chochom* [Torah scholar] and, on the other, a Reform leader whose premises reflect his denial of the very bases of our faith. The entire gestalt of the book and its promotion, including the strong public emphasis on the warm personal interaction between the two authors and joint promotional appearances before large audiences, represents a blurring of boundaries between darkness and light, and an

undermining of the Jewish religious tradition. That tradition, handed down to us from Sinai, is distorted in the pages of the book through the word of one who falsifies Torah. What is more, the general impression left by the book promotes the unacceptable notion that there is some parity between two legitimate approaches to Judaism, as if to say: "Here, dear reader, are two ways of seeing the world. Feel free to choose as you wish." Such is a debasement of the essence of the Jewish faith.[97]

The council, of course, included Shmuel Kamenetsky, who had himself read "many" of Reinman's postings before they were published.[98] Moreover, the council was led by Yaakov Perlow, the same figure who, in the face of attacks from within his own camp, encouraged Orthodoxy to respond to the 1999 CCAR "call to mitzvos," by reevaluating its own approach to dealing with Reform.[99] Reinman yielded to the edict and withdrew from the book tour.[100]

No doubt, the "coming cataclysm" conjured in response to the denominational struggles of the 1980s did not come to fruition in the following decades.[101] Rather a new age of nonconfrontationalism emerged. Nevertheless, at the inkling that its gestures are granting a modicum of religious legitimacy to Reform, to date the time-honored precedent for Orthodoxy remains to reassert historical denominational boundaries. All the same, as will be demonstrated in the conclusion, the willingness of the Haredi Orthodox to cooperate with the non-Orthodox in areas that do not demand theological legitimization has only grown in subsequent years.

7

Rabbinical Training and Role Reversal

This chapter describes striking changes that have taken place since the late 1980s in the way American Orthodox rabbis are trained. One of the more publicized ones considered here is the establishment of Yeshivat Chovevei Torah as a liberal or "Open Orthodox" alternative to the increasingly inward focus of Modern Orthodoxy's preeminent institution, Yeshiva University. More dramatically, Haredi Orthodoxy has generated a range of frameworks that are dedicated to producing rabbis with skills that are especially geared toward engaging and providing religious services for non-Orthodox and nonobservant Jews. These programs, which receive the imprimatur of some of the most respected and authoritative figures in the Haredi orbit, further challenge the prevailing sectarian label and engender a more nuanced characterization of this stream.

Constituency Definition

Whom do I lead? Whom do I represent? Constituency definition has been a central issue for Orthodox rabbis since the emergence of modern, heterogeneous Jewish life in Europe. If the premodern community rabbi was automatically the religio-legal authority and spiritual leader of all local Jews, the same could not be said for rabbis of subsequent generations. In a society in which religious observance could no longer be legally enforced, only those who volunteered to accept the rabbi's command were necessarily under his jurisdiction. Different approaches developed within the Orthodox rabbinate regarding which Jewish populations should be targeted. While some limited their efforts to cultivating a "community of the faithful" that was committed to preserving traditional values, others felt the imperative to move beyond this "natural constituency." They looked for ways, rather, to continue to function as religious leaders for all Jews.[1]

The following discussion focuses on constituency definition within the contemporary American Orthodox rabbinate. It describes significant changes that have taken place regarding this issue since the 1980s. These, in turn, illuminate the overall transition that has taken place in American Orthodoxy.

Among the generation of American Orthodox rabbis that emerged in the early to mid-twentieth century, following the model of Joseph Lookstein and not that of Leopold Greenwald, there was a strong feeling that Orthodoxy had to try to appeal to as many Jews as possible. At a time when few congregations existed that could boast of a critical mass of fully observant individuals, it was obvious that Orthodoxy would become obsolete if it catered only to the pious. The "broad constituency" approach evolved into part of the ethos of American Modern Orthodoxy's flagship rabbinical training ground, RIETS of YU. Its Americanized, college-educated graduates were dispatched to communities throughout the country with the goal of creating Orthodox congregations that would offer religious services to the entire Jewish population. With this attitude in mind, some even walked a denominational tightrope by accepting pulpits in synagogues with mixed seating.[2]

Alternatively, the survivors and remnants of the leadership of the Lithuanian yeshivas and Hasidic dynasties who arrived around World War II directed their efforts toward re-creating the institutions and lifestyles that had been destroyed. Fearful of the seductive power of the *treife medina* (unkosher state)—which to their minds had tainted the established Modern Orthodox—they set up enclaves in which they could regain their former strength and vitality. As such, their yeshivas and kollels concentrated on producing Torah scholars rather than multitalented pulpit rabbis. If some of their graduates later served in more heterogeneous Orthodox congregations, this was certainly not the primary goal of their mother institutions.[3] The main objective, rather, was to create a cadre of rabbis and teachers who could service the needs of this recently imperiled community of the faithful.

Through its focus on the rabbinate, this chapter offers further evidence for one of the main contentions of this book: that along with Orthodoxy's growth and empowerment, the last decades have witnessed a redrawing of the lines that divide the American Modern Orthodox and Haredi Orthodoxy. To an increasing extent, it is the graduates of what Liebman defined as the sectarian *yeshivish* institutions who are being trained to strengthen the Jewish identity of the broader Jewish community. "Churchlike" Modern Orthodoxy, in contrast, has not completely relinquished this role, but has focused its energies on producing rabbis who can inspire its committed congregants.

This understanding will be illustrated by examining rabbinical training institutions affiliated with each camp. While the particulars of a rabbi's activities are a function of the needs of the specific community that he serves and his personal talents, it is within the various rabbinical seminaries, yeshivas, and training programs that his outlook and skills are initially molded. As such, an examination of what is being taught to the current crop of aspiring Orthodox rabbis is telling regarding the mother institutions and the priorities they assign to various rabbinical pursuits. The chapter describes programs that exemplify the current pattern. In order to appreciate the innovative nature of some of the more recent initiatives, it is necessary to first highlight prior stages in the history of modern rabbinical training.

Rabbinical Training: A Historical Perspective

The loss of judicial authority, asserts Ismar Schorsch, engendered the transformation of the nineteenth-century Central European rabbi from primarily "an expositor of Jewish civil and religious law" to a "teacher/preacher."[4] The transition in the nature of the profession required the rabbi to gain greater familiarity with non-Jewish languages, knowledge, and culture. This was imperative, both to enable him to communicate with his acculturated community members, as well as in order to acquire the minimum prestige necessary to gain their respect.

While the premodern rabbinate gained its judicial know-how by intensive study of the Talmud and codes in a traditional yeshiva, the new skills required by the modern rabbi demanded a fresh educational format. Thus, the mid-nineteenth century saw the rise of a novel framework for advanced Jewish education: the rabbinical seminary. Such institutions adopted a critical, scientific approach to the study of traditional Jewish knowledge and texts. In addition to, or instead of, Talmudic and halakhic studies, rabbinical candidates were required to learn such subjects as biblical exegesis, Hebrew and Aramaic philology, Jewish history, folklore, and literature. This stemmed, among other reasons, from a belief that a rabbi equipped with such knowledge and perspective would be more capable of gaining the respect of his modern congregants. The seminaries also demanded that their students receive a degree from a secular university.[5]

The yeshiva never disappeared from nineteenth-century Europe, and it even rose to great heights in Lithuanian, Polish, and Hungarian milieus.[6] The seminary, however, became the standard institution for rabbinical training in Germany, as well as in Italy, France, and Holland, and it even set down deep roots in Hungary.[7] Indeed, the rise of American Jewry to a position of relative independence within the world community in the late nineteenth and early twentieth centuries paralleled the establishment of rabbinical seminaries among the three major denominations (Reform, Orthodox, and Conservative). Their common mandates were to train homegrown rabbis. The Rabbi Isaac Elchanan Theological Seminary of Yeshiva University (RIETS), the leading American Orthodox rabbinical training institution, evolved a unique approach. This seminary, which began as a Lithuanian-style yeshiva, cultivated a synthetic model in which traditional Talmudic studies during the morning and early afternoon hours in a distinct religious study hall (beit midrash) were combined with secular academics and supplementary professional rabbinical training in the afternoons.[8]

The members of mid-twentieth-century American synagogues, as discussed in chapters 2 and 3, were not of one ilk. Even Orthodox congregations were characterized by a wide variety of lifestyles and religious commitments.[9] Thus, the ideal product of RIETS was a congregational rabbi who could relate simultaneously to a number of different constituencies by offering them a diverse set of religious services.

In general, one of the hallmarks of American rabbinical training has been the introduction of more systematic approaches to acquiring pastoral and professional skills. This resulted from the recognition by figures like Joseph Lookstein, particularly from the mid-twentieth century, that the role of the American rabbi had expanded beyond that of "teacher/preacher." Additional functions, such as social worker, grievance counselor, Hebrew school principal, and even synagogue CEO, had turned the congregational rabbi into a multifaceted religious leader and functionary.[10] The American rabbi had to be equipped with a broad range of proficiencies that would enable him to fulfill this wide variety of responsibilities.[11]

In 1969 Charles Liebman published a study of rabbinical training in America that highlighted the dissonance between what rabbinical students were being taught and what they were being expected to do once they were ordained. He argued that almost no efforts were made to connect textual learning with the more practical elements being taught to the trainees.[12] Recent decades have witnessed a more methodical effort to train rabbis who are equipped for the professional challenges that lie ahead. This can be seen in particular in the innovative rabbinical-training programs that have emerged within American Haredi Jewry. To a limited degree, a similar phenomenon can be identified among Modern Orthodox institutions. All the same, each camp has sought to nurture different skills. The divergence in the educational concentrations of each group's institutions is reflective of their general directions and concerns. Haredi programs have emerged that are entirely dedicated to educating rabbis who can service the needs of Jews with limited religious backgrounds and who are likely candidates for assimilation. The curriculum and structure of RIETS as well have been adjusted to meet some of the challenges facing American Judaism as a whole. In contrast to the Haredi initiatives, however, the RIETS curriculum remains primarily aimed at nurturing budding scholars who can inspire its highly educated and religiously knowledgeable core constituency. Meanwhile, Yeshivat Chovevei Torah (YCT), a new liberal-oriented Modern Orthodox seminary, was established in 1999 and has begun to confront the virtual hegemony of YU/RIETS. Paradoxically, as will be discussed toward the end of this chapter, the approach to constituency definition emerging from YCT actually shares key elements with the novel Haredi training frameworks.

Haredi Orthodoxy and the Training of an "Outreach Rabbinate"

Most of the Haredi yeshivas in the United States are modeled after the Lithuanian centers of learning that flourished from the nineteenth century until the Holocaust. While many practicing rabbis spend their formative years in these institutions of higher learning, like the Lithuanian predecessor institutions, the focus of most American yeshivas is not on training professional rabbis. They follow, rather, the ideal of *Torah li-Shmah* (Torah study for its own sake) articulated by the creator of the prototype Lithuanian yeshiva, Rabbi Hayyim of Volozhin.[13] The main goal is to educate young Jewish men toward the highest level of Talmudic erudition and religious piety. As such, rather than being considered to have achieved a particularly impressive measure of Talmudic mastery, the veteran student who began to study the legal codes that he must know in order to receive rabbinic ordination and become a "licensed" rabbi was often looked down upon. This course of study signals imminent departure from the holy sanctum of the yeshiva, and his efforts were seen as aimed at attaining a formal "professional" degree that will enable him to earn a living in the outside world.

Consistent with this negative perception of those who abandon the way of *Torah li-Shmah*, up until the last two decades of the twentieth century, products of the Haredi yeshivas made up a small minority among the American Orthodox pulpit rabbinate. Serving the needs of the greater American Jewish community meant being willing to compromise on one's own religious values. As Rabbi Emanuel Feldman, a graduate of the Ner Israel Yeshiva and longtime pulpit rabbi in Atlanta, Georgia, explained sympathetically in 1968: "The unfortunate tendency among some of the students must be understood for what it is: an extension of their total commitment to *shlemut* (perfection) and study and service of God which views apparent professionalism and careerism with a jaundiced eye.... As he grows and matures he will come to the understanding that the so-called career rabbi is no less concerned with God and Torah than he."[14]

As mentioned above, there are additional factors that led to the limited numbers of Haredi yeshiva graduates who entered the pulpit rabbinate. First, for most of the twentieth century, American Haredi Orthodoxy dedicated itself toward survival. The generation of Orthodox Jews that arrived in America immediately before, during, and after World War Two still viewed their new home as a place that endangered the continued existence of "Torah Jewry." Therefore, the actions of these Orthodox refugees were inward, seeking preservation rather than expansion. Even after it was clear that these efforts had met with success, the insularity that was engendered remained deeply ingrained in the social ethos of Haredi Orthodoxy. While for some this was purely a practical result of historical circumstances, for others, it was also an ideological statement. Thus, some Haredi ideologues continue to promote the notion that since only "Torah true" Orthodox Jews can be counted upon not to assimilate, all resources should be focused purely on strengthening this group.[15]

By the last two decades of the twentieth century, as highlighted in chapter 6, forces within the American *yeshivish* world that expressed different sentiments began to emerge. Haredi Orthodoxy achieved a level of self-confidence that engendered a rising sense that it was strong enough to extend help to those American Jews who had become alienated from their roots. The late Rabbi Moshe Sherer, the longtime president of Agudath Israel of America, already advanced this point in a 1978 appeal to yeshiva students to become practicing rabbis: "Many [yeshiva students] don't want to go into public Jewish life because they want to spend more time studying Torah. But if we are really engaged in a struggle to survive, something has to give. The alternative is that millions of *neshamos* [souls] that heard the *Aseres ha-Dibros* [Ten Commandments] on *Har Sinai* [Mount Sinai] will enter churches. People have to go into the rabbinate to save them."[16]

By the turn of the twenty-first century, many within the American Haredi world had answered this appeal. Some yeshivas actually began to cultivate an educational posture aimed at producing rabbis who can focus on bringing Judaism to weakly identified individuals. Other yeshiva heads have generally stood firm in their demand that "Torah for Torah's sake" remain the guiding principle within the walls of the yeshiva. Yet, more recently, they have shown greater openness to new supplementary initiatives aimed expressly at training rabbis who can help strengthen Jewish identity among the loosely affiliated. Indeed, according to Jack Wertheimer, in 2013 there were at least two thousand non-Chabad men and women working in Orthodox Jewish outreach throughout North America.[17] Where did this massive workforce learn their trade?

The following pages describe five Haredi frameworks for rabbinical training that were established particularly to address nonobservant and nonaffiliated American Jews.

Maor, Silver Spring, Maryland

In 1999 a graduate of the Ner Israel yeshiva by the name of Rabbi Shaya Milikowsky founded a rabbinical training program for students of Haredi yeshivas called Maor.[18] Unlike classical seminaries, Maor did not offer a full-time rabbinical studies curriculum. Rather, students participated in intensive three-week sessions that met over the course of two successive summers. The reason for this concentrated study schedule was that Maor sought to train rabbis whose formal studies and ultimate ordination took place in one of the traditional Haredi yeshivas, such as Ner Israel, Beth Medrash Govoha in Lakewood, or its subsidiary in Philadelphia. The heads of these institutions, in fact, gave their blessings to this initiative, but only if it did not interfere with the main goal of *Torah li-Shmah*. This was accomplished by running the study sessions during the traditional yeshiva three-week summer break that extends from the ninth of the Hebrew month of *Av* until the first day of *Elul* (and generally falls in July–August).

The skills cultivated by the program reflected an acknowledgment that an effective American rabbi must be equipped with more than a sharp Talmudic mind and a willingness to leave the warm confines of the yeshiva. During the three-week summer sessions, the twenty enrollees met for eight hours per day, five days per week. Their curriculum included the following subjects: public speaking, history, psychology, sociology, American popular culture, pedagogy, public relations, advertising, and fundraising.

In order to fully comprehend the role that the study of these subjects played in shaping the future career of the rabbi, it is necessary to gain an appreciation for the approach to the communal rabbinate that stood at the foundation of Maor. Maor's central aim was to nurture rabbis who could address a broad constituency. Their main skills were ones that could be used to counter assimilation by making Judaism meaningful for all Jews. For some of these constituents, this could ultimately lead to full observance, but Maor emphasized that any movement toward greater involvement and commitment was a success. As such, its graduates were not directed to filling available rabbinical posts in established Orthodox synagogues. The Maor position was that a rabbi who is hired by an existing Orthodox community could rarely be successful at attracting large numbers of unaffiliated Jews toward greater Jewish involvement. The reason was that the main task of such a figure was to serve the needs of the veteran observant congregants who hired him and who expected to gain from his teaching and guidance. Even if such a rabbi were totally committed to boosting the Jewish identity of his unaffiliated neighbors, his hands would be tied. He could never be what Maor sought to create—an "outreach rabbi." At best he could be described as a dilettante, who on occasion steps beyond his natural constituency.[19]

Maor trained its graduates to establish new synagogues in areas with large Jewish populations and in which no Orthodox community existed. In order to create such an institution, pedagogical, homiletic, and intellectual abilities were insufficient. An enterprise of this nature had to be led by an individual who had a keen awareness of what would appeal to highly acculturated American Jews. He needed to know how to use the tools of modern mass media to communicate his message. He had to have the ability, as well, to find the resources to fund such an endeavor.[20]

Milikowsky himself is a veteran outreach worker who was previously the director of AJOP—the Association for Jewish Outreach Professionals. Concurrent with running Maor, he set out to establish his own "outreach rabbinate" twenty miles from Washington, D.C., in Olney, Maryland. The Ohev Shalom Talmud Torah Congregation (OSTT), which describes itself as "a diverse growing synagogue with Orthodox services," has developed considerably and indeed attracted numerous families from non-Orthodox backgrounds.[21] In addition to prayer services it provides a wide range of classes to the broader Jewish community through its affiliated community kollel.[22] In 2011, due to the expansion of the OSTT and the heavy burden of fundraising, Milikowsky closed the Maor program. At the same time, others advanced their own frameworks for training the new style of American Haredi rabbi. Interestingly, much of this activity is concentrated in Jerusalem.

Rabbinical Ordination Leadership Program, Aish Hatorah, Jerusalem

Based in the Jewish Quarter of the Old City of Jerusalem, Aish Hatorah is one of the leading institutions in the world for bringing alienated Jews closer to religious observance (kiruv).[23] It is best known for its representatives who approach students and travelers who have come to the Wailing Wall and invite them to visit the adjacent yeshiva, as well as for its intensive "Discovery" seminars aimed at proving God's existence and the divine authorship of the Torah. Aish Hatorah, however, does not limit its activities to those who visit Israel. In fact, communities have been established throughout the English-speaking world where the methods and beliefs studied at the mother institution are being utilized in order to attract as many Jews as possible to traditional religious observance.[24]

The yeshiva was established in 1975 after its founder, Rabbi Noah Weinberg, broke away from the Ohr Somayach yeshiva.[25] According to his followers, the split came about due to differences regarding the goals of the yeshiva. Ohr Somayach felt that success was determined by whether a newly observant student dedicated himself to a life of learning. Rabbi Weinberg, in contrast, hoped that once a student had adjusted to religious life, he would either become a kiruv worker or join the secular workforce. Through his interaction with other Jews, he would have the ability to help the weakly affiliated become observant.[26]

Aish Hatorah has developed an entire ideology and system of outreach. In order to make sure that its approach is properly implemented, its leaders foster an "Aish culture" among their students, who are viewed as the future of the institution. It is, indeed, this "Aish culture" that is the most distinctive characteristic of Aish Hatorah's Rabbinical Ordination Leadership Program (ROLP). Even the more traditional classes on such subjects as Talmud and Jewish legal codes focus on what one needs to know in order to become an effective outreach rabbi.

It takes a student one and a half to two years to complete ROLP. Graduation is contingent upon passing a halakhah examination administered by two rabbis appointed by Aish Hatorah, as well as receiving a positive evaluation of the accomplishments of the student by the yeshiva administration. The curriculum is divided into three parts: traditional rabbinic learning, practical rabbinics, and vocational training. The traditional learning portion is dedicated to sharpening the students' study skills and increasing their halakhic knowledge. In addition, a major focus is placed on the study of the Bible. This emphasis is based on the premise that the ability to prepare a Bible class that highlights the Torah's relevance to modern life is crucial for recruiting Jews to the Aish world as well as for cultivating financial supporters. The practical rabbinics portion consists of students leading various programs offered by Aish Hatorah in Israel. This is, essentially, the same kind of work that they will be doing in America.

The training section is the most extensive part of the program and amounts to 40 percent of the curriculum. There are classes dedicated to the daily responsibilities of being a rabbi. Courses are also offered in pedagogy, public speaking, counseling, writing, and dealing with contemporary issues. In addition, students participate in workshops that teach them how to establish Aish Hatorah communities of their own in America. Subjects such as demographics are taught in order to enable graduates to best determine what their target audience is for a city where a new Aish community is under way. The rabbis-in-training also learn fundraising skills. In the context of the development of the proper tools for leading a viable and successful "Aish" community, students are required to take classes in computers and business management. Finally, each newly ordained rabbi is given an "Aish bag," which consists of numerous lectures on the weekly Torah portions, ideas for activities, literature on an array of topics, and many other Aish-approved supplies to help him in the field. Once they go into the field, the rabbis will have the support of Aish.com, which, together with Chabad.org, offers the most sophisticated Jewish outreach materials on the web.

A particularly unique aspect of the Aish ordination program is the significant amount of time spent training the students to deal with questions that they will be asked when they are out in the field. The students play simulation games in which they debate their position against rabbis who assume the roles of non-affiliated Jews, Reform rabbis, potential donors, and so forth.

Although most of the students are Aish Hatorah products, individuals from some of the traditional Haredi yeshivas have been accepted as well. The program's goal is not to create rabbis who will go on to have congregational pulpits; Aish Hatorah, rather, views its ordination program as the most effective way to supply manpower for its centers in the Diaspora. Therefore, its graduates will either join one of the preexisting Aish centers or travel to other cities to launch new programs.[27] There are currently two hundred students in the Aish Hatorah yeshiva, of which twenty are in the ordination program. Over the last decade, more than 160 rabbinic graduates have been placed primarily in one of the twenty Aish Hatorah centers throughout North America.[28]

This description of ROLP certainly strengthens the impression that this is not a classic rabbinical seminary or yeshiva. Focus on "recruitment," on the "Aish approach" and the "Aish system," and in particular on the development of debating and rhetorical skills is unique. In addition, even a cursory examination of the curriculum makes clear that "Aish" rabbis are unlikely to stand out as Torah scholars. In this way, they differ dramatically from the Maor graduates, who only attended the program after a considerable number of years engrossed in a yeshiva environment.

Ner LeElef World Center for Jewish Leadership Training and Outreach, and The Jerusalem Kollel

Ner LeElef (literally, "a candle to a thousand," henceforth NLE) was established in Jerusalem in 1998 by Rabbi Avraham Edelstein. Today it claims to be "the single largest source of Jewish leadership training in the world, thereby providing critical manpower and resources worldwide to the Rabbinate, Jewish Educational Institutions at all age levels, and outreach to the growing numbers of Jews who have no affiliation with any Jewish institution."[29] The organization, which receives considerable financial backing from the Wolfson family of New York and Elie Horn of Sao Paulo, has succeeded both by developing its own training program and by partnering with others.

Within its Jerusalem base, NLE has exploited a burgeoning human resource: young married English speakers studying in Jerusalem's Haredi yeshivas and kollels. Modern Orthodox high school graduates, as discussed in chapter 4, come to Israeli yeshivas and seminaries during their gap year prior to entering secular college. While numerous Haredi students do the same, a common practice within this sector is to first spend time in an American post–high school yeshiva environment, and then come to Israel for a few years after getting married. Subsequently, many will go on for further study in American yeshivas and kollels. Others return to North America with minimal secular education but a strong desire to set out on a career in the rabbinate and education. NLE recognized this phenomenon and designed a weekly training course that would both not interfere with regular Talmudic study and offer a supplement to the minimal stipend tendered by the core institutions. A parallel women's program is available for wives. In addition to its English department, NLE prepares emissaries for Spanish-, Portuguese-, French-, and Russian-speaking locales.[30]

The NLE English program is a two-year track that meets on one evening and on Friday mornings—so as not to interfere with full-time Talmud study—for a total of six and a half weekly hours. The curriculum combines text-based study of Jewish thought, ethics, Bible, and law with practical courses in public speaking, programming and management, computers and technology, communication, and counseling. The aim is to provide a rigorous curriculum that prepares students for "all areas of Jewish outreach work, including working within existing outreach organizations, interfacing with communities, and creating and developing new programs and opportunities."³¹ According to NLE, there are currently twelve hundred couples working in Jewish religious leadership who underwent its training. During the years 2006–8, NLE also organized a comparable program in Lakewood, New Jersey.³²

Alongside its supplementary initiative, in 2002 NLE teamed up with Rabbi Yitzchak Berkowitz, the former *menahel ruhani* (spiritual director) and one of the heads of the ordination program at Aish Hatorah, to create The Jerusalem Kollel (TJK). Unlike NLE's structure of biweekly meetings, TJK is a full-time Torah learning institution for married Haredi men that aims to "train some of the finest products of the yeshiva system to stand at the forefront of the battle against assimilation."³³ The curriculum combines traditional study of Talmud and halakhah with professional rabbinical and outreach education. A parallel women's program focuses on education, mentoring, and counseling. There are currently seventy full-time students in TJK and more than one hundred TJK graduates are already working in North America and Europe, almost all of them in outreach-related positions.³⁴

Maor, ROLP, NLE, and TJK all demonstrate the considerable efforts being made by the Haredi community to nurture a rabbinate that can connect with the nonobservant population and provide attractive Jewish content. From a pedagogic perspective as well, these models actually respond to the critique advanced by Charles Liebman already in 1969 in his study of American rabbinical seminaries. That is, as opposed to a disconnect between theory and practical rabbinics that he highlighted, these initiatives seek to integrate practical rabbinics with study of traditional rabbinical texts. These innovations are fueled by the keenness of significant elements within American Haredi Orthodoxy to abandon their formerly arch-sectarian worldview and address the needs of the nonobservant and weakly affiliated Jewish population

Rabbinical Seminary of America, Yeshivas Chofetz Chaim, Kew Gardens Hills, New York

Unlike the majority of American-based Haredi institutions, Chofetz Chaim yeshiva has long placed emphasis on nurturing religious leaders who could serve a broad spectrum of American Jews. All the same, since the late 1990s these efforts have been upgraded and the yeshiva has expanded significantly.

Rabbinical Seminary of America, or Chofetz Chaim (CC), was established in 1933 by Rabbi Dovid Leibowitz, a student of the famed Knesset Yisrael yeshiva located in the town of Slobodka outside Kaunas, Lithuania, and of Rabbi Meir Kagan's (the Chofetz Chaim) yeshiva in Radin.³⁵ From the founder's death in 1941 until 2008 CC was led by his son, Rabbi Henoch Leibowitz. Later Henoch Leibowitz was joined by Rabbi David Harris, who continues to head the institution with Rabbi Akiva Grunblatt.[36] Initially the yeshiva was located in Williamsburg, Brooklyn. In 1955 it relocated to Forest Hills, Queens, and more recently to its Kew Gardens Hills campus.

CC is ostensibly a traditional yeshiva in that the educational focus is on *Torah li-Shmah*. Following the Slobodka model of a *mussar* (ethics) yeshiva, a great deal of emphasis is also placed on formal activities aimed to build proper religious and moral character,[37] with the students dedicating time each day to the study of ethical literature. Beyond its dedication to *mussar* study, CC's unique place among Haredi yeshivas is reflected in its greater openness to modern society and culture. The yeshiva runs cooperative master's degree programs in education and administration with secular universities.[38] Its students also stand out in comparison to other yeshivas through their more modern attire. The most significant way through which CC has distinguished itself, however, is in the area of public service. Students are encouraged to take time out during the week from their Torah studies, for example, in order to run Jewish culture hours in New York-area public schools, as well as to volunteer in the Queens HATZOLAH emergency ambulance corps and the Queens Hevrah Kadisha (Jewish burial society).[39] No doubt, students from other Haredi institutions also participate in these types of programs; in the case of CC, the students are expected by the leaders of the yeshiva to participate.

CC's unique place within the American yeshiva world is not merely a reflection of its willingness to allow its students greater interaction with outside society. Its emphasis on formal character development is part of a process by which CC sets out to nurture rabbis who embody the main goal of the yeshiva: dedication to the religious and educational leadership of their fellow Jews. In order to receive rabbinical ordination one must complete a long and rigorous course of study that usually lasts for twelve to fifteen years. The lengthiness of the program is partly due to the slow, plodding method of Talmudic study that CC promulgates. Moreover, the extended period of residence within the confines of the yeshiva is aimed at cultivating a CC rabbinical emissary, that is, a person willing to occupy the type of rabbinical positions that the yeshiva deems most important for the perpetuation of American Jewish life.

Since the late 1970s, CC has invested considerable effort in founding schools and synagogues in locales where there is no Orthodox community or where the community has become severely weakened. Starting with the CC center established in 1978 in Rochester, New York, successive models have been created in

Milwaukee; Cherry Hill, New Jersey; Los Angeles; San Diego; Buffalo Grove, Illinois (outside Chicago); and Las Vegas. The educational and religious institutions that have been built cater to both observant and less affiliated Jewish youth and adults. The rabbis and staffs are CC graduates who have been sent to these communities. By going as a group, as opposed to an individual rabbi establishing a synagogue, they ensure the existence of an infrastructure that will give the young rabbinical families a social and religious environment that is sustainable over a long period of time. In addition, they bring together a core of highly motivated rabbis who, due to their long and intensive years of common training, share a basic ideological and religious mind-set.

The CC rabbi is not sent to an outlying community as part of a career track that will eventually bring him back to an established East Coast Orthodox congregation. Rather, he hopes to create a permanent base for himself, and together with a group of other like-minded CC alumni to raise the level of religious consciousness of a locale whose Jewish population is highly prone to assimilation.

Despite its heavy demands, rabbinical training at CC has become increasingly popular. Until recently, anywhere between two and twelve new rabbis were ordained in a given year. In the last few years, however, the total yeshiva population has grown to nearly five hundred full-time students.[40]

Chabad-Lubavitch

Reference has already been made in chapter 6 to the profound and continually expanding role that Chabad-Lubavitch Hasidism has had in American Jewish life. This theme will be explored further in the next chapter. Here, I will describe the unique approach of Chabad to rabbinic training.[41]

A candidate for Chabad ordination has to complete three years of full-time post–high school Torah study in a Chabad yeshiva. Assuming that he has demonstrated the proper intellectual and religious qualities, at the age of twenty or twenty-one he is permitted to study the Jewish legal codes that he will be tested on in order to receive ordination. In addition to the sections on the dietary laws, the four tests that he must pass include the laws of Sabbath and prayer.

Officially, there are no other "supplementary" courses of study in the Chabad rabbinical training program. How then do Chabad rabbis often display such a unique talent for communicating with nonobservant Jews and for bringing their message to a wide public? The answer, according to R. Eli Hecht, a veteran Chabad rabbi in Southern California, is that the training of a Chabad rabbi/emissary begins years before he actually studies the material required for ordination. From the age of fourteen, male Chabad high school students throughout the world are given what is known as a "route." Every Friday they finish school early, but instead of going home or relaxing, they are assigned to a local area—a few streets, a town square, a group of stores, a meeting place of Jews—where they are expected to help nonobservant Jews perform *mitzvos* (commandments). Generally, this means distributing Sabbath candlesticks to women, enabling men to don tefillin (ritual phylacteries), or offering the opportunity to Jews to perform the blessing on the four species on Sukkot. Over long periods of time they return every week and develop relationships with the local Jewish population. Moreover, they learn to rid themselves of adolescent shyness and to cultivate communication skills and to become more comfortable with the colloquial language of the public. By the time they receive ordination, they will have been working as "junior" *sheluhim* (emissaries) for as long as eight years. They are then not only intellectually and religiously equipped, but they have also devoted far more time—albeit with little accompanying theoretics—to learning how to approach a Jewish public that is prone to assimilation than does the average graduate of any other rabbinical program. Indeed, they also share experiences with their friends and their teachers and receive advice as to how to deal with the various situations that they encounter. Clearly, when they become emissaries they will move to new locales and face fresh challenges, but they will bring with them a wealth of hands-on experience.

Chabad training cannot be duplicated within other sectors of the American Orthodox population. It is predicated on the cultivation of certain personality traits and skills from an age at which few young men have thought seriously about going into the rabbinate, let alone championing the cause of outreach.

Modern Orthodoxy and the Inreach Rabbi

While American Haredi Orthodoxy and its Jerusalem expatriates are increasingly training rabbis who are capable of reaching out far beyond its boundaries, the leading institution of Modern Orthodoxy focuses most of it energies on inreach—servicing the highly specific intellectual and ideological needs of its natural constituents, observant Jews. The continued expansion of the Jewish day school and high school movement, and particularly the large number of graduates who dedicate at least one year to intensive post–high school Torah study,[42] have produced an unprecedented generation of knowledgeable Modern Orthodox Jews. For such individuals, a college diploma is a given, and a high percentage have professional and other advanced degrees. In order to cater to this burgeoning population, efforts have been directed toward producing scholar-rabbis who can challenge the minds of their congregants no less than spiritually inspire them and comfort them in times of sorrow.

In the following section, two Modern Orthodox rabbinical seminaries are presented. The first, RIETS, is the largest institution for the training of Orthodox rabbis in America. The second, Yeshivat Chovevei Torah (YCT), was founded in 1999 by a prominent RIETS alumnus who felt that it no longer espoused a coherent Modern Orthodox philosophy. A comparison of the two institutions highlights the ideological conflicts that have emerged within Modern Orthodoxy.

Rabbi Isaac Elchanan Theological Seminary (RIETS), Yeshiva University, New York

Over the past century nearly three thousand rabbis have received RIETS ordination.[43] Today, there are more than 1,000 students in the YU advanced Talmud tracks and 195 enrolled in the RIETS ordination program, although some will only complete one or two years before going to professional schools or joining the workforce.[44] On average, forty to fifty new rabbis are ordained each year, of which approximately ten enter the pulpit rabbinate.[45] RIETS enrollment has benefited greatly from the trend of Modern Orthodox high school graduates studying at Israeli yeshivot for one or two years before entering college. Many of the students return with intense devotion to Torah study and join the professional rabbinate. That said, in order to attract candidates who are less interested in the secular and professional co-requisites that RIETS historically demanded, alternative study tracks that focus almost entirely on traditional text study have been added or expanded. Moreover, contemporary Modern Orthodox Jews present unique challenges to their rabbis. As a group they are culturally urbane and highly educated in both religious and secular disciplines. In addition, the Modern Orthodox sector is increasingly concerned that its offspring will not be able to maintain the synthetic balancing act that their parents championed.[46] RIETS graduates must be equipped to address the complex intellectual and spiritual needs of their sophisticated congregational families. Such multiple demands have led this institution, which once was the vanguard of outreach toward the broader American Jewish collective, to focus its efforts toward cultivating rabbinic skills that will facilitate "inreach" within their own natural constituency.[47]

RIETS accepts students who possess a bachelor's degree or are in their last year of college courses and have simultaneously already learned the Talmud on a post–high school level for at least four years. The main disciplines of study are Talmud, Jewish legal codes, and practice (minimally thirty-three hours per week). In order to produce well-rounded rabbis, students are required to attend classes in a wide variety of areas relevant to rabbinic functions and leadership. These include pastoral psychology, survey of professional rabbinics, survey of the American Jewish community, public speaking, and Jewish communal leadership.[48]

RIETS also has a series of academic co-requisites. Students must spend their afternoon hours in one of three study environments. They may return to the study hall for an additional four hours per day of Talmudic learning; they may work toward a master's degree in Judaic studies, education, or social work; or they may attend classes in traditional Jewish thought.[49]

A notable reflection of the flexibility of the RIETS program is the option offered to a student to fulfill the bare minimum of supplementary rabbinic requirements and spend most of his time focused purely on studying Talmud and codes. The very fact that this option has been offered for more than a decade expresses the changes in the directions of Modern Orthodoxy over the last twenty years. For one, this acquiescence to a "Torah only" approach seems to have come in response to the general "slide to the right" of American Modern Orthodoxy. A result is that students who were once natural candidates for RIETS ordination are now more likely to consider studying at Haredi yeshivas like Ner Israel.[50] Fearful of challenges to its predominant role in training Orthodox rabbis, RIETS has sought to accommodate those who might otherwise look elsewhere.

Another implication of the "Torah only" option is that the leaders of RIETS feel the need to produce a stronger and larger cadre of Talmud scholars. This effort is directed at catering to the needs of the growing number of communities whose core populations are capable and desirous of hearing high-level Talmud and Halakhah lectures from their rabbi on a regular basis. Once again, it should be noted that as more products of Haredi yeshivas enter the Orthodox pulpit rabbinate, the opportunity for a community to find a rabbi who qualifies as a Torah scholar increases. As such, in order to remain the primary source for Modern Orthodox pulpit rabbis, RIETS focuses greater efforts on training "scholar-rabbis." This intensive effort on the part of RIETS to nurture Talmud scholars who can service the highly educated Orthodox public is illustrated through the evolution of its Kollel Elyon (advanced Torah-study institute). From its founding in 1982, a select group of newly ordained RIETS graduates was offered the equivalent of a generous postdoctoral fellowship in order to continue to dedicate themselves fully to high-level Talmud study. This institute was meant to serve as the breeding ground for the next generation of *roshei yeshiva* (professors of Talmud) who would take up positions within RIETS. Indeed, the current RIETS faculty has a number of Kollel Elyon alumni among its staff. Additionally, it would appear that its purpose was, from the outset, to ensure that the credentials of RIETS as an institution geared to churning out highly qualified rabbinical graduates would compare favorably with its Haredi counterparts. As Rabbi Aharon Kahn, the former head of the program, declared, "The *Kollel Elyon* is the crown jewel of the institution. It gave the Yeshiva [RIETS] the opportunity to train *talmidei chachamim* (Talmud scholars) that can hold their own in comparison to the superior element in any yeshiva."[51]

In 1998 the study program and the goals of the Kollel Elyon were revamped. A change in benefactors who endowed the institute brought along with it the appointment of two new *roshei kollel* (institute heads), as well as new qualifications for awarding fellowships. The reconstituted Kollel Elyon was now divided into two. A small group continued to focus almost exclusively on advanced Talmudic scholarship, while the majority entered a program that "combines intensive Torah learning for future rabbinic leaders with courses in skills such as counseling, advanced public speaking and writing, business ethics and conflict resolution."[52] In other words, while continuing to nurture advanced Torah scholars, the new Kollel Elyon participants are no longer being trained primarily to serve as *roshei yeshiva*. Instead, they are an elite group of talented men who are being directed toward careers as "scholar-rabbis."

Alongside the core Talmud and law study, as well as the academic co-requisites, during their second year of enrollment RIETS students are required to choose from five specializations: education, pulpit rabbinate, organizational leadership, chaplaincy, and community outreach and campus leadership. Each demands participation in additional weekly courses or workshops.[53] The "community outreach and campus leadership" option stands out in particular. It reflects the fact that since 2005 RIETS has become more conscious of the lack of concentration on addressing additional Jewish constituencies within its training program.[54] Nonetheless, the group is limited to twelve students per year. More notably, rather than using its own human and financial resources, RIETS actually contracted with Ner LeElef to run the outreach courses. Indeed, the YU official website emphasizes that "the program, which is supported by and operates under the guidelines of Ner LeElef, is geared toward professionalizing the students practice, exposing them to major personalities in the field, and helping them develop skills and strategies to utilize in a successful outreach career."[55] The description there of the curriculum—including parallel sessions for wives—is almost identical to that implemented at the Ner LeElef center in Jerusalem and in the Jerusalem Kollel. No doubt, the joint venture stemmed in part from the willingness of Ner LeElef and its high-powered and motivated donors to offer financial coverage. The fact remains that Modern Orthodoxy's flagship institution, which had once pioneered outreach, felt the need to turn to a Haredi Orthodox framework that had only been established in 1999 to teach outreach to its RIETS rabbinical candidates.

YU's historically groundbreaking role in Jewish outreach was orchestrated during the mid- to late twentieth century through its Max Stern Division of Communal Services (MSDCS). The main figures who ran its events were RIETS students. In 2003 Richard Joel was named the fourth president of YU. His prior post was president and international director of Hillel, the foundation for Jewish campus life. One of Joel's goals was to reassert YU's role within the broader Jewish community. To this end, he founded the Center for the Jewish Future (CJF) as a successor to the MSDCS and hired Rabbi Kenneth Brander, a well-regarded rabbi of a diverse Orthodox congregation in Boca Raton, Florida, to lead it. During close to a decade of existence, the CJF has infused the YU campuses with a spirit of social and religious activity that was lacking in previous decades and has inaugurated or revamped a host of programs, a few of which have outreach components. A review of its array of offerings, however, makes clear that the main thrust is inreach—strengthening the Modern Orthodox orientation of its student body and servicing the Modern Orthodox communities throughout the United States that remain YU's primary sources of undergraduates and funders.[56]

The emphasis by YU/RIETS on its Orthodox constituency does not mean that it is opposed to addressing the needs of other sectors. Yet by comparing its program to the recent innovations within the Haredi sector it has become clear that engaging a diverse range of American Jews remains a nominal goal among YU's list of priorities.[57]

Assuming that Modern Orthodoxy continues to, on the one hand, produce large numbers of individuals who are highly conversant in Talmudic learning and, on the other hand, feel insecure about its ability to maintain the loyalties of its youth, it is likely that the "scholar-rabbi" who can dazzle the minds of the educated Orthodox will continue to be cultivated for years to come. This is not, however, the only model that is being put forward in Modern Orthodoxy. A relatively new and more liberal-oriented Orthodox rabbinical seminary is gradually making inroads. While also responding to trends in Orthodoxy, the model rabbi that it seeks to develop is not necessarily an outstanding Talmudist, but rather an individual whose skills are intended to address multiple American Jewish constituencies, and particularly those who are not part of mainstream Modern Orthodoxy.

Yeshivat Chovevei Torah, New York

New York–based Yeshivat Chovevei Torah (YCT) was founded in 1999 by the prominent synagogue rabbi and activist Avi Weiss.[58] In 2013 he was succeeded by Rabbi Asher Lopatin, a former Rhodes scholar who previously led an Orthodox synagogue with a diverse constituency in Chicago.[59] Both of them, as well as the rosh yeshiva and dean Rabbi Dov Linzer and much of the faculty, were trained in RIETS.[60]

YCT arose as a liberal Orthodox response to the cultural insularity and the move to the right that its leaders believe has characterized American Modern Orthodoxy in recent decades. Specifically, the sense among Weiss and likeminded Orthodox Jews is that RIETS has succumbed to these forces and no longer represents a forthright philosophy of Modern Orthodoxy.[61] YCT's outlook is expressed in its official mission statement that includes, among other points,

> Encouraging intellectual openness, questioning, and critical thinking as essential components of one's full service to God.... Affirming the shared covenantal bond between all Jews. Promoting love of all Jews (ahavat Yisrael) and actively pursuing the positive and respectful interaction of all Jewish movements.... Recognizing the need to enhance and expand the role of women in talmud Torah, the halakhic process, religious life and communal leadership within the bounds of Halakha.... Affirming the shared divine image (tzelem Elokim) of all people, our responsibility to improve the world and our capacity to be enriched by it.[62]

Like RIETS, intensive study of Talmud and Halakhah are the predominant activities at YCT. Similarly, significant time is set aside to pursue a graduate academic degree. Study of the Bible and Jewish thought—including classes on the history of Jewish denominations and "the Challenges of Modern Orthodoxy," as well as "professional" courses in homiletics, pedagogy, and orchestrating Jewish lifecycle events—are also integral parts of the YCT study program.[63] While it is hard to consider these curricular additions revolutionary, they imply an effort to broaden the scope of the rabbi's expertise. The highlighting of "historical and source-critical methodologies" suggests that there is greater willingness to integrate academic approaches to the study of Jewish texts than is acceptable within the confines of the RIETS division of YU.[64]

YCT's goal of creating a well-rounded Modern Orthodox rabbi is not limited to the intellectual sphere. A great deal of emphasis is placed on pastoral counseling through a program designed and coordinated by a psychiatrist who specializes in Jewish communal life.[65] This curriculum highlights topics that have come to the fore of public awareness in the past decade: "Students explore the impact of having a disabled child, the spiritual life of young children, adolescence, dating, courtship and the creation of mature intimate relationships. Issues of infertility, adoption, infidelity, and domestic violence are also examined."[66] In addition to attending classes, students are required to do fieldwork in health facilities and to participate in counseling workshops.

Beyond ideological declarations and some innovative course requirements, is the rabbinical product that YCT nurtures dramatically different from that of RIETS? More specifically, in the context of the current discussion, does the education that YCT provides offer an Orthodox rabbinical model that is particularly geared toward addressing a broader constituency of American Jews?

Unquestionably, studying and having contact with Weiss, as well as Lopatin, offer special opportunities for those looking to develop an appreciation and love for all Jews.[67] Weiss's outspoken and consistent commitment over five decades to serving the entire Jewish people is unique within the Orthodox landscape. The general emphasis on the role that an "open Orthodox" rabbi can play within the entire Jewish collective orients students toward such a direction.[68]

A review of the placements of the more than eighty rabbis to receive YCT ordination since its inception demonstrates a preponderance of graduates working within broad constituency nonsynagogue frameworks such as campus Hillel houses, nonsectarian community day schools, and chaplaincies, as well as both Orthodox- and Conservative-affiliated educational and academic institutions. Sixteen are serving as pulpit rabbis, primarily in officially Orthodox synagogues that are oriented toward a broad spectrum of Jews and are located outside densely populated Orthodox neighborhoods. Of the four in New York, two work for Weiss's Hebrew Institute of Riverdale.[69] In addition, some YCT rabbis are affiliated with synagogues that do not officially define themselves as Orthodox, such as the Northbrook Community Synagogue outside Chicago, which—like numerous Midwest houses of prayer—uses an Orthodox prayer book but permits mixed seating.[70]

A list of recent alumni placements distributed by the RIETS placement department in August 2013 tells quite a different story.[71] Of the more than seventy

CHAPTER 7

rabbis listed, only seven entered posts outside large Orthodox strongholds. The rest stayed in the Greater New York area, with a few venturing to other major Orthodox concentrations in Chicago, Los Angeles, Atlanta, and southern Florida. Furthermore, at most five positions could be defined as primarily outreach rabbinates. Indeed, among the current RIETS ordination student body of 195, only 8 have expressed a clear desire to pursue a career in Jewish outreach.[72] Even among the four graduates who went to work on university campuses, they did so as the official "Orthodox" rabbi within the Hillel center or as representatives of the Orthodox Jewish Learning Initiative on Campus (JLIC). In either case, their primary function is inreach toward the Orthodox student constituency, as the JLIC official website explains: "JLIC places Orthodox Rabbinic couples to serve as Torah educators within the Hillels on local college campuses ... the JLIC educators strive to enhance the learning opportunities available to students, and also to bolster an infrastructure for Orthodox life to flourish.... While the primary impetus of JLIC has been to serve the Orthodox, rather than Kiruv in a classic sense, we have found that the educators have had a substantive and positive impact on a broader population as well."[73]

Juxtaposed with the RIETS list, the array and character of YCT's placements demonstrate that, notwithstanding the more dominant rightward trend within Modern Orthodoxy, considerable opportunities remain for liberal-oriented Modern Orthodox figures to serve as rabbis. All the same, the fact that so many YCT alumni are working in nonaffiliated institutions or congregations without a strong observant presence is not due purely to their professional or ideological preferences. Rather, it reflects the struggle by "mainstream" Modern Orthodoxy against this liberal rabbinical school. The most concrete example is the refusal to date of both the RCA to accept YCT graduates as members, and the National Council of Young Israel to permit its synagogue branches to hire YCT rabbis.[74] After considerable efforts to gain acceptance for its students into the RCA, YCT withdrew its application and banded together with likeminded figures to establish an alternative organization: the International Rabbinical Fellowship (IRF).[75]

Along with complaints regarding YCT's commitment to aspects of Orthodox theology and its willingness to hire non-Orthodox instructors for its pastoral training program,[76] one of the main bones of contention has been Weiss's efforts to ordain women as Orthodox clergy.[77] In 2010 he conferred the title of "Rabba" on Sara Hurwitz, who had completed the same course of study as YCT students. Today she uses this title in her position as one of Weiss's rabbinical associates at the Hebrew Institute of Riverdale. Subsequently, he changed the title for women clergy and established Yeshivat Maharat ("*Manhigah Hilkhatit Rukhanit Toranit*, a teacher/leader in Jewish law and spirituality"), whose self-described aim is "to ordain Orthodox women as spiritual leaders and halakhic authorities" and thus change "the communal landscape by actualizing the potential of Orthodox women as rabbinic leaders."[78] Hurwitz is dean and Rabbi Jeffrey Fox, the first rabbi ordained by YCT, is yeshiva head. Both YCT and Yeshivat Maharat are presently housed on the campus of the Hebrew Institute of Riverdale, and its students and graduates intern or have gained employment in synagogues led by YCT graduates. In light of the discussion in chapter 5 regarding the vociferous response of leading RIETS figures to Orthodox feminism, it is clear that the deep connections between YCT and Yeshivat Maharat buttress those within Modern Orthodoxy who oppose accreditation.[79] The decision to make a leadership transition at YCT from Weiss to Lopatin, then, may in part reflect a desire to neutralize such claims and shore up the institution's position within mainstream Modern Orthodoxy.[80]

Conclusion: Between YCT and the Haredi Outreach Rabbi

Placing the discussion within overall trends, the ongoing development of YCT demonstrates that—despite the limited focus of RIETS on outreach—Modern Orthodox rabbis still have a role to play in servicing the broader Jewish community. Ironically, from a professional perspective the liberal YCT rabbi actually has more in common with Haredi outreach-oriented figures than the inreach-focused RIETS graduates. YCT rabbis are to a great extent, like their Haredi outreach counterparts (along with Chabad), specialists who gravitate to peripheral Jewish communities that lack a strong Orthodox infrastructure.[81] Neither of these cutting-edge rabbinical products would reject more "mainstream" congregants, but the skill sets and outlooks that they internalize through their rabbinical training tailor them to attract and address the concerns of the wider Jewish community. To be sure, the YCT and Haredi worldviews diverge dramatically on multiple issues. Yet both frameworks demonstrate that in order for Orthodoxy to deliver a relevant message to the majority of American Jews it must cultivate environments and train leaders who are in touch with the needs of this body.

Notwithstanding the common denominators, it is important to reiterate the distinctive backdrops that led to the emergence of the new Haredi and YCT rabbinates. The Haredi "outreach specialist" training programs emerged as manifestations of strength. The vastly improved self-image of a triumphant Haredi Orthodoxy has engendered the creation of a new type of rabbi. One who feels that he can afford to concentrate on dealing with problems that stand outside the immediate concerns of his natural constituency. YCT, in contrast, came about because prominent Modern Orthodox leaders sensed a weakening in the ideological and spiritual fiber of their core constituency. Its main justification for existence is to serve as a corrective to what is seen as a Modern Orthodoxy gone astray. In this context, part of the attempt to reformulate its priorities is the need for greater involvement with the weakly affiliated Jewish population. But unlike the Haredi model, this is not necessarily an expression of vitality. It stems from a conviction, rather, that without this element American Modern Orthodoxy is lacking a crucial ideological mandate that was for many years at the root of its own self-identity.

All the same, the idea that this common "outreach" ideal could forge a bond between the ideologically polar but similarly innovative elements within American Orthodoxy based on a shared broad constituency discourse is tantalizing. That said, the next chapter, which analyzes parallels between Chabad and Haredi outreach activists, suggests that on a practical level such commonalities more often than not sharpen competition rather than afford a sense of shared mission.

8

The Chabadization of Haredi Orthodoxy

Long before the rise of the outreach rabbinate, at a time when most of the Haredi world was still deeply entrenched within a sectarian outlook and lifestyle, one major exception existed: the Chabad movement of Lubavitch Hasidism. This chapter details the sharp ideological divide that distinguished Chabad from the predominant post–World War II American Haredi outlook. It then demonstrates how the evolution from the late 1980s of the Haredi worldview from defensive sectarianism to increasing involvement with broader Jewish life manifests adoption of perceptions and educational models initially championed by Chabad. All the same, the significant distinctions that still exist between the ways they design their outreach models can be attributed to the ongoing influence of each group's historical roots and core ideologies.

The year 1941 witnessed the arrival in America of two Eastern European refugee rabbinical figures destined to reshape the landscape of American Judaism: Rabbi Menachem Mendel Schneerson and Rabbi Aharon Kotler.[1] Within a decade both stood at the helms of their respective constituencies. Schneerson was formally chosen as the rebbe (central spiritual figure and political leader) of the

Brooklyn-based Lubavitcher Hasidic sect, while Kotler led the Beth Medrash Govoha yeshiva in Lakewood, New Jersey, and was head of the Council of Torah Sages (*Moetzes Gedolei ha-Torah*) of Agudath Israel of America. In these capacities, he was widely acknowledged as the driving force in the renaissance of Lithuanian Haredi Orthodoxy on American soil. Despite their common commitments to Orthodox interpretation of Jewish law, as outstanding representatives of Hasidic and Mitnagedic (non or anti-Hasidic) traditions, there were certainly significant differences in their personal religious orientations. Indeed, one of the sharpest divides was expressed in their polar visions of how to mold the future of American Judaism.[2]

Kotler, as described in chapter 6, positioned himself in direct opposition to all American Jewish religious movements—including Modern Orthodoxy—that had emerged in the early twentieth century. In his estimation, they all accommodated to local cultural and intellectual norms as a price for social acceptance. Authentic Judaism would develop in America, he argued, only if a core population separated itself physically from society and its members concentrated on enriching their own Jewish knowledge and commitment. In light of the destruction of European Jewry and its Torah centers, the key to achieving this goal was to establish yeshivas and, even more so, kollels—institutions where married men receive a regular stipend in return for dedicating themselves exclusively to Talmud study.[3] He claimed that the young scholar who secluded himself in the pursuit of Torah knowledge was not only growing intellectually and spiritually, but this very feat was making a critical contribution to the welfare of the Jewish people. As such, any activities that distracted him from this pursuit were to be discouraged.[4] In 1961, a year before his passing, he reiterated this vision:

> For our generation, the generation of the destruction [hurban] that lost the majority of its finest and most outstanding sons during the years of rage ... the importance of sustaining the study hall is multiplied. This was the idea behind the establishment of the Beth Medrash Govoha in Lakewood; that it should serve as a site for growing in understanding of the Torah through in-depth analysis as we were instructed by our mentors. In order for this [to be achieved] it was necessary to prepare the location and surrounding environment such that it would match the spiritual aspirations of the learners ... the more those absorbed in Torah proliferate—who fling the indulgences of this world from their backs, and they have no involvements in this world other than Torah,

since they have savored the taste of Torah and it is appealing to them—others will follow in their paths and Torah learning will spread.[5]

Schneerson was no less disturbed than Kotler by the integration of Jews into American society and their widespread abandonment of traditional Jewish practice. His solution, however, was expressive of a completely different educational and ideational orientation. He proclaimed the main goal of his generation to be the spread (*"u-faratzta"*) of the wellsprings (*"ma'ayanot"*) of the Torah to every Jew regardless of his or her personal level of observance, and he categorically rejected the enclavist position put forward by Kotler.[6] A 1957 sermon demonstrates explicit antagonism toward Kotler's Lakewood outlook:

> Even regarding a single Jew, we cannot give in. If there exists a single Jew who does not act in the ways of the Torah, then this touches on the entire collective since all Israelites are responsible one for another.... If they (the Children of Israel at Sinai), had been even one less than 600,000, be it who it be, even the lowest of the low, the Torah would not have been given heaven forbid even to the greatest of great ones, like Moses our teacher. Therefore, we cannot be satisfied with limiting the Torah within the four cubits of Torah observant Jews, rather it is incumbent upon us to go outside and do all within our powers, and even beyond, until we work among all the Jews.[7]

Paradoxically, Schneerson considered materialistic America to be the ideal framework for fulfilling this challenge. Starting in 1951, he systematically transformed Lubavitch Hasidism from an insular sect to the multifaceted Chabad religious movement.[8] The vanguard were his *shluchim* and *shluchos* (personal emissaries), who were commanded to leave the warm confines of the rebbe's Crown Heights neighborhood and settle in areas that were often devoid of any Orthodox infrastructure.[9] There they were to dedicate themselves to touching the souls of the local Jews, while remaining absolutely committed to the strict religious regimens of their Hasidic order. Needless to say, Kotler was reported to be highly critical of Lubavitch activism.[10]

In his 1965 analysis of American Orthodoxy, Charles Liebman highlighted Chabad's focus on addressing the "potentially devout" as a unique phenomenon within the Haredi world. In contrast, Kotler's isolationism was the accepted Haredi view. All the same, Liebman predicted that along with the accelerated growth of the Torah world, the enclavist outlook would continue to dominate the future.[11] The last five decades have witnessed significant growth and expansion in American Haredi Orthodoxy. In the course of this enlargement, as emphasized in this book, many of the heirs to Kotler's legacy have become less insular and adopted significant aspects of the outreach ideal first championed on American soil by Schneerson. This transformation, which is not without its critics within the yeshiva world, has entailed the assimilation and adaptation by America's Mitnagedic elite of institutions and methodologies that parallel those conceived within the Lubavitch Hasidic milieu. It is particularly noteworthy since it has taken place simultaneously with the sharp attacks of Kotler's camp on Chabad and the ongoing messianic tension surrounding its late leader.[12] Put more succinctly, alongside what Chaim Waxman has called a "Haredization" process,[13] there has also been a *Chabadization* of American Haredi Orthodoxy. This is not a matter of adopting ritual or theological behaviors that were once considered inappropriate or even problematic, but of a worldview reorientation from a formerly sectarian direction toward a more inclusive, outreach posture.

The Chabadization of American Orthodoxy is illustrated most clearly through an analysis of and comparison between banner institutions of each party, the Chabad house and the community-outreach kollel. I begin with a brief description of the development and main characteristics of the Chabad house in its position as an extension of Schneerson's educational ideology. This is followed by a similar discussion of the community-outreach kollel, which focuses on its departure from the approach articulated by Kotler. Here I will highlight the main areas in which the yeshiva world institution shares common traits with the Lubavitcher one. I will argue that the community-outreach kollel can actually be seen as an attempt at creating a Mitnagedic style alternative that is nourished by the Chabad house model, but does so without reneging on a distinctly non-Hasidic character. The next section will draw parallels with prior interactions between Hasidism and Mitnagedism, and analyze how initial distinctions continue to play out in the alternative outreach frameworks of each of these Haredi groups. The final discussion will address a Modern Orthodox version of the community kollel and how its orientation once again highlights the inreach direction that has come to dominate American Modern Orthodoxy.

The Chabad House

Menachem Mendel Schneerson's Shluchim have been settling in Jewish communities throughout America since the 1950s. Even before then, there were figures who traveled widely, making contact with a broad spectrum of Jewish populations. Notable among the pioneers were Rabbi Shlomo Carlebach,

Rabbi Zalman Schachter Shalomi, and Rabbi Shmuel David Raichik.[14] All three actually began their careers in the 1940s under the leadership of the previous Lubavitcher rebbe, Rabbi Joseph Isaac Schneerson, and continued in the 1950s under his son-in-law and successor.[15] The Chabad emissaries established schools, camps, and other educational programs. They worked on campuses and in synagogues, spearheaded "mitzvah" campaigns that concentrated on the spread of a specific traditional practice (such as Sabbath lamps or phylacteries),[16] and opened up their homes.

The term "Chabad house" was first coined by the West Coast *shliach* (emissary), Rabbi Shlomo Cunin, in reference to the center that he set up on the UCLA campus in 1969.[17] Yet it would appear that Menachem Mendel Schneerson had already been dedicating considerable thought toward finding a creative way to address Jewish students on campus since the early 1960s. Notably in regard to the trends highlighted in this book, in June 1960 the Lubavitcher leader actually invited Joel Levine and Rivka (Teitz) Blau to a private meeting in order to learn more about how to attract nonobservant students to Jewish activities. At the time Levine was the president and Blau was the vice president of the Yavneh Modern Orthodox college campus organization.[18] According to Chabad lore, when Cunin presented a symbolic key to the UCLA Chabad house to Schneerson, the latter professed that such frameworks would spread like a supermarket chain.[19]

Today there are over three thousand Chabad houses throughout the world, with new ones being established on a monthly basis.[20] In the interim, however, the main venue for Chabad centers has changed. More than one hundred campus houses exist, but the majority of Chabad houses are located in areas where Jewish families live or in major travel destinations.[21] To a certain degree this adjustment is a response to the transition of the baby boomers of the 1960s and early 1970s from campus rebels to adult "seekers."[22] Simultaneously, the economics of supporting a Chabad house certainly encourage servicing a larger and more financially secure constituency.[23]

Although each Chabad chapter has its own unique character and focus, and there are numerous variations, there is a relatively standard mode of operation that characterizes the majority. A shliach couple arrives and rents or purchases a large space in an area where Jews live or frequently pass through. It is sometimes in the vicinity of an established denominational synagogue, but physical and operational independence is almost always maintained. A limited area of the house is dedicated to private living quarters for the shliach family, while most of the structure functions dually as residence and public outreach center. Often the main room serves as a prayer hall, classroom, and kindergarten, as well as the only place large enough to seat the family and the many guests who arrive for Sabbath and holiday meals, or just drop in.[24]

This fusion of familial warmth with religious and educational activity—centered on the enthusiastic shliach couple and their children—is one of the keys to the success of the Chabad house. This framework is informal, inviting, and for many inspiring. It offers spiritual and intellectual stimulation in a relaxed, social environment. The individual who enters is given the opportunity to interact with a knowledgeable Jew on a level that is rare in a large, established congregation.[25] Questioning is encouraged, and the tenor of the discussions, sometimes peppered with raucous Hasidic melodies and alcoholic refreshments, is intended to be motivating but nonjudgmental. Of great significance as well, there are no obligatory membership fees or demands regarding observance, and attendance is not limited to official business hours.[26] In all these ways, the Chabad house fills a void that is felt by many who are left in the cold by the typical synagogue experience.[27]

The friendliness and independence of the Chabad house also set the tone for many of the additional activities that are promoted. It gives parents the confidence to send their children to Chabad preschools, camps, after-school programs, or even just to a Sunday morning matzah-baking workshop. It enables those generally apprehensive about Jewish singles mixers to attend a class or function geared to this population. The warmth and energy of the Chabad couple may also lead some to turn to them at times of personal crisis or tragedy. The focus on positive reinforcement and the Chabad house's lack of official association with any major denomination are also part of the reason why some Reform and Conservative rabbis and congregations are comfortable allowing Chabad representatives to run programs in their synagogues.[28] Moreover, those Jews who find their experiences at the Chabad house to be particularly fulfilling are most likely to want to duplicate this warmth and spirituality in their own homes. On all these levels, the unique physical and organizational framework of the Chabad house, and the human environment orchestrated by the resident shliach and shlucha (female emissary)—independent of Chabad's deeper theological underpinnings—facilitate touching the souls of other Jews.[29]

Like the original eighteenth-century Hasidic courts and their *zaddikim*, the character of a given Chabad house is to a great extent a function of the personalities and proclivities of the shliach couple. Yet unlike the earlier models, it is much more than common ideological roots or even a shared reverence for a charismatic figure that defines the individual chapters as being part of one movement. Each emissary couple is responsible for the financial viability of their local frameworks. Over the years, however, Chabad has created an overarching structure that trains shluchim and strategically places them; helps in acquiring seed money and major donations; provides an enormous amount of programming, educational materials, and religious objects; advertises nationally; operates a sophisticated website with links to every Chabad house and representative;[30] and sponsors yearly conferences for both shluchim and shluchos, who are flown in to Brooklyn for a "a weekend of study, networking, and morale-boosting."[31] The openness and familial warmth of the Chabad house, then, is backed up by a sophisticated federation that fuels the existing centers while constantly setting the groundwork for expansion.

The emergence of the Chabad house testifies to the success of Schneerson in communicating his outreach message to his followers and creating an organizational infrastructure that can sustain it. The evolution of this institution also epitomizes the ability of Chabad to pay attention to changing trends within American Jewry. In light of these innovative qualities, it is striking that this framework also echoes Hasidism's initial development through establishment of "courts" that facilitated the spread of the founder's ideals.[32]

Outreach specialists and communal leaders from the yeshiva world admire Chabad for its advanced promotional abilities, and for its centralized and highly effective organizational backbone. Some are even willing to recognize Chabad's influence on their own camp. As Rabbi Avi Shafran, spokesman of Agudath Israel, remarked in 2008: "I think there's a lot to learn from Chabad.... [T]he idea of active outreach that Chabad pioneered has, over recent decades, become very much part of the stance of mainstream Orthodox American Judaism."[33] The criticisms by the Mitnagedic sector, however, are far from limited to the theological realm. They feel, among other things, that beyond the rare individuals who themselves become "chabadnikim" (full-fledged followers), Chabad houses are not conducive to engendering ongoing involvement and greater personal commitment among the majority of Jews who enter their realms. These centers, rather, offer a pleasant but rather fleeting and tangential experience. Yet the Lithuanian-style scholar-activists who emerged from the late twentieth century on are less comfortable acknowledging the degree to which the novel model they promote is in many ways a Mitnagedic alternative that draws upon many of the same educational and organizational principles as the Chabad house.[34]

The Community-Outreach Kollel

Like the development of the Chabad house among the Lubavitchers, the community-outreach kollel is the culmination of a process that began within Haredi

Orthodoxy after World War II. Unlike its Hasidic parallel, along with important manifestations of continuity, it has departed in significant ways from the educational concept put forward by its yeshiva-world forerunners. Indeed, as will be shown, this new institution shares much in common with the Chabad house model that was already flourishing before it.

Rabbi Aharon Kotler's vision, recall, was to build up Torah learning centers in which young scholars, particularly married ones, receive funding that would enable them to remain devoted exclusively to personal intellectual and religious growth. In his lifetime most of these kollels were connected to large yeshivas, and located in neighborhoods with high concentrations of Orthodox Jews, or within reasonable distance by car (Lakewood, New Jersey, for example). By the early 1970s the heirs to Kotler's legacy believed that his mission had succeeded. An American yeshiva world espousing a sectarian Orthodoxy that rejected popular culture was a reality. No longer preoccupied with mere survival, they were ready to move toward expansion.[35]

Independent bodies known as community kollels were established in locales with Orthodox congregations where Torah study had until then been the precinct of a small minority. Sometimes they were preceded by short-term study seminars, such as the Torah Umesorah–sponsored SEED program, in which yeshiva students would spend a few weeks during the summer studying in a community.[36] After fundraising efforts had created a viable financial base, groups of five to ten veteran fellows and *rashei kollel* (kollel leaders or instructors), and their families, were recruited from existing institutions. They were then transplanted as a collective to highly populated Jewish communities outside the New York area, such as Toronto (1970), Los Angeles (1975), Pittsburgh (1978), and Chicago (1981).[37] There, they set up a beit midrash.

Undoubtedly the growth of these new institutions represented an increased effort on the part of the yeshiva world to directly influence American Jewish life. In fact, partly due to this new strategy, Los Angeles, Toronto, and Chicago are today major destinations for Haredi Orthodox Jews who want to leave the New York hub.[38] From the perspective of educational ideology, however, the early community kollel model should be seen as a reasonable extension of the approach promulgated by Kotler, not a major digression. The predominant activity and daily schedule of the young scholars remained the same. The kollel fellows were expected to occupy the study hall as full-time Talmud students. Organized interaction with the lay community was generally limited to select evenings when the local Orthodox were invited to the beit midrash to join the fellows in learning partnerships or to hear lectures. Moreover, by making its way into broader Jewish society via a critical mass of kollel families, the enclave concept was not completely abandoned. Rather mini-Haredi enclaves were created within Modern Orthodox communities. Certainly in comparison to the Chabad houses that were spreading their rebbe's outreach message to the broadest spectrum of Jews in locations that had no Orthodox infrastructure, the early community kollels remained highly segregationist. Whatever popular education they carried out was inreach, aimed at a slightly less homogeneous Orthodox constituency than was previously the case. Rabbi Shneur Kotler, the son and heir to the Lakewood founder, is reported to have declared that the goal was "to transform the committed Jews into Torah Jews."[39]

As noted in chapter 6, a revolution in the community kollel concept began in 1987 with the opening of ASK—the Atlanta Scholars Kollel—as a community kiruv kollel. It is here that the resemblance to the Chabad house becomes more pronounced. With the encouragement of his mentors and the backing of a prominent Atlanta Orthodox rabbi, twenty-eight-year-old Ner Israel yeshiva graduate Rabbi Menachem Deutsch set out to create a kollel that would be more proactive than its predecessors and involve its fellows intensively in outreach, as well as inreach.[40]

The first concrete indication of a change in emphasis in Atlanta was the decision to require the fellows to devote only three to four hours of their day to personal Talmud study. During the rest of the time, they were expected to be involved in a broad range of formal and informal educational activities. Over time, a multifaceted outreach program was developed that included a daily open *beit medrash* where Jews possessing all levels of knowledge were invited to join in private study partnerships; Hebrew crash reading courses; adult beginners services, including one in a Reform Temple; singles events; lunch and learn classes in corporations, hospitals, and schools; women's study groups; Torah for Teens; home study meetings; young couples events; and campus activities in four different universities. The current male ASK staff consists of sixteen full-time kollel members, each responsible for a different aspect of the program. In 2003 the kollel's annual budget reached $850,000. Its officially stated goal is "to heighten Jewish identity through hands-on educational experiences that respect all Jews."[41]

Today there are more than twenty outreach kollels throughout North America.[42] Some of them are modeled directly after ASK, while others—such as JSN and DATA[43]—have developed alternative styles and study schedules. Yet in addition to their basic outreach premise, they all share common traits that sharpen the comparison to the Chabad house.

Like the Chabad house, the new community kollel emphasizes inclusiveness. The staff clearly possesses an Orthodox orientation, but all Jews are invited to participate with no ideological strings attached. In direct contrast to the establishment synagogue, the kollel celebrates this nondenominational quality. Once again like the Chabad house, and in contradistinction to the established synagogue, there are no regular membership dues and no events in which all must participate.

Moving further in emphasizing the similarities to the Chabad house, most community kollels do not function out of a local Orthodox synagogue. They make a point instead to set up in homes within neighborhoods with a high percentage of Jews. This is done in order to create a neutral environment that is devoid of the stigma that the marginally affiliated often possess in regard to formal synagogue life. Furthermore, by setting up as an independent entity, it is hoped that the community kollel can dissociate itself from the denominational or congregational fractures that plague so many Jewish communities. Finally, the kollel building is meant to serve as a warm and inviting open house to which Jews can drop in when they desire. The residential quality of many of the kollel's physical facilities highlights its role as a friendly neighbor within the community.

The parallels between the community-outreach kollel and the Chabad house move beyond outreach orientations, common constituencies, physical settings, and similarities in programming of the individual chapters. A broader national community kollel infrastructure has begun to emerge as well. Institutions such as Kotler's own Lakewood yeshiva have created frameworks that are responsible for selecting the future kollel members, offering them advanced training, and hunting out new venues. In addition, they help raise the local funds to support these endeavors and troubleshoot for the first few years. Torah Umesorah, the Haredi Orthodox national educational organization, also established a multimillion-dollar seed-money fund.[44]

Particularly since 2004, initiatives have been taken to coordinate campaigns in different kollels, thus sharing educational and promotional resources. A most effective example was the hiring of a marketing and public relations specialist. Individual kollels are offered guidance regarding preparing flyers and advertising, as well as in designing the community kollel's website. This consultant received accolades for spearheading a highly successful campaign adopted by at least seven kollels that transformed the March 2005 completion of the seven-year *daf yomi* Talmud study cycle into a "celebration of Jewish unity." At the event sponsored by the Phoenix kollel, "Unity Awards" were given by the kollel to the leaders of local nondenominational institutions including the Federation of Jewish Philanthropies, Jewish Community Center, United Jewish Committee, and Jewish National Fund. The regional director of the Anti-Defamation League chaired the evening, which was "designed to bring Jews of all backgrounds together in celebration of that which truly unites us—our Torah."[45] While Aharon Kotler would have agreed with this last statement, it is highly questionable whether he would have approved of the direct association with non-Orthodox entities.

Even Chabad's yearly shluchim conference has a yeshiva-world parallel. AJOP, the Association of Jewish Outreach Professionals, meets each winter in a convention center. Like at the Chabad conventions, numerous individuals involved in various frameworks for Jewish Outreach join together for their own "weekend of study, networking, and morale-boosting."[46] In recent years a special section has been dedicated to the community kollels, with sessions being held for community kollel fellows, as well as coordination meetings among their leaders.[47]

A Mitnagedic Alternative

Identification of similarities or even imitation does not necessarily imply duplication. Along with the many parallels between the Chabad house model and the community kiruv kollel concept, there are also significant differences. These distinctions reflect the diverse lifestyles and religious behaviors of the Mitnagedic *jungerleit* (fellows) as opposed to the Hasidic shluchim. They can also be viewed as addressing some of the lacunae identified by the yeshiva world in the Chabad house framework.

The most basic issue that divides the two institutions is the central focus of activity. While the community-outreach kollels have expanded to include a wide variety of informal programming, much of it pioneered by the Chabad house, they are at the core learning communities. First, the kollel fellows themselves are required to devote a block of a few hours of their daily schedules to advancing their personal Talmudic acumen. Moreover, the main pursuit of the community kollel remains promoting study of Jewish texts and ideas.[48] The goal is to enable Jews to learn about Judaism in an active way. Thus it is the creation of a study hall that is inviting and stimulating to a broad cross-section of Jews, or by taking the beit midrash to the people through programs like weekly "lunch and learns"—in which kollel members conduct a lunchtime study session in a local office—that the community kollel seeks to inspire other Jews.

This emphasis on study explains why the community kollel—in an alternative but complementary way to Chabad house warmth—may hold particular attraction to the postmodern, seeking individual. Jews of every persuasion and level of commitment or affiliation are encouraged to join with a kollel member in a one-to-one textual study session or *hevrutah*. Certainly, the kollel member will share his understanding of the material, but as opposed to frontal lectures, such text learning is oriented to give and take.[49] Implicit within this dynamic is the recognition that the opinion of both individuals is valuable and worthy of expression. Even in larger settings such as the "lunch and learns," the classes are generally geared toward discussions that enable the participants to express themselves regarding the topic at hand. This orientation toward study contrasts starkly with the classical synagogue environment, where the central activity is public prayer. A visit to the most inviting synagogue of any denomination can leave a Jew who is unaffiliated and uneducated in Jewish ritual with a feeling of inadequacy or illegitimacy. The community kollel, in contrast, offers contemporary Jews an environment that can facilitate their personal religious quest.[50]

Beyond satisfying the intellectually and spiritually curious, argue the Mitnagedic community kollel outreach specialists, the emphasis on study directly enhances overall Jewish commitment in a more substantive manner than the Chabad approach. By framing their outreach around open-ended Torah learning, the community kollels have neutralized fears of religious coercion while encouraging consistency and increasing commitment to religious activity. Some participants may see their Torah sessions as isolated weekly events, but others will find themselves segueing smoothly from study to intensified religious practice. Such a transition, it is claimed, is far less likely to take place even among Chabad house regulars. For one, Chabad's emphasis on group activity does not orient itself toward greater active personal commitment. In addition, since much of the direct study that takes place in Chabad houses emphasizes Lubavitcher Hasidic ideals, only those enthralled with this lifestyle and worldview will be moved toward more concrete commitment.[51]

Human resources are also a factor to consider in comparing the community kiruv kollel to the Chabad house. The entire Chabad house enterprise generally revolves around the shliach couple. Only after achieving financial viability and developing demand for manpower-oriented activities (such as schools) will the shliach consider adding additional staff. Alternatively, a young Chabad yeshiva graduate may be hired to produce income for the Chabad house, for example, through kosher supervision of local stores and factories. The Chabad rabbi leads all the prayers, and together with his wife instructs the attendants in Jewish ritual and belief, teaches all the classes, orchestrates the meals, and is the chief conversationalist. In most cases it is primarily a one-couple show that welcomes all comers but does not engender a sense of partnership. In all likelihood, the personalities of the shliach couple will appeal to some people more than others. Those with whom they do not click, then, will be less likely to want to become more involved.

By sending out delegations of five to ten couples, the community kollel neutralizes some of the potential pitfalls of the sole-practitioner Chabad house approach. Different kollel members may appeal to varying constituencies. Some may be more charismatic, others more cerebral. Some may be more philosophically oriented, while others possess musical and theatrical talents. In addition, the kollel automatically provides a critical mass of fellows and families to occupy the study hall and attend events. This emphasizes the collective nature of the body. As such, the community-outreach kollel is populated by a diverse range of fellows, who are meant to complement each other's talents and can attract people with different intellectual and human proclivities. Once the person enters this realm, he or she is presented with an instant community that offers friendship and a sense of common purpose.[52]

This point was illustrated to me in a conversation with an individual who became observant through Chabad but now is an active member of an establishment Modern Orthodox congregation. When I asked why he no longer attends Sabbath services in the Chabad house, he remarked that the latter was a wonderful environment for initial exposure to many positive elements of religious life. Nonetheless, in order to adopt an observant lifestyle he needed community. The Chabad house, with its collection of minimally committed Jews orchestrated by a charismatic Hasidic rabbi, did not offer the stability and camaraderie that he sought. Central figures within the community kollel movement have commented as well that many people who began in Chabad moved to them out of a desire for more substance and a greater sense of connection to a cohesive group.

The collective nature of the community kollel also has advantages in recruiting fellows to serve as outreach workers. For most kollel couples, the very act of leaving the warm enclave of the establishment kollel is daunting. By sending groups together, the intensity of the new encounter with greater society is lessened. The kollel framework offers safeguards and checks that are meant to counterbalance any negative influence of society on the fellows and their families. Chabad enthusiasts would counter that their successes are direct results of the willingness of the shluchim to leave familiar environments in order to touch Jewish souls in every corner of the earth. At the same time, the financial model of the community-outreach kollel severely limits its potential to spread as a popular movement. Sending a young shliach couple to a given locale and demanding that they find funding for their endeavors is much more feasible than relocating and attaining communal support for five to ten young families.

In relation to broader environmental issues, the development of both the Chabad house and the community-outreach kollel can be viewed in the context of central motifs within contemporary American religion and culture. To the "generation of seekers" who came of age in the 1980s and 1990s, the Chabad house and the community kollel had a unique attraction. Robert Wuthnow has described contemporary America's communal orientation as one of "loose connections."[53] Growing numbers of people throughout the country are uncomfortable with the level of commitment that membership in more traditional social and religious organizations generally entails. Nonetheless, many are not satisfied with the extreme individualism that Putnam described as "bowling alone" and still desire to create associations based on common values.[54] One response, claims Wuthnow, is the rise of "porous institutions" that enable those involved to move in and out more smoothly.[55] It would appear that both the Chabad house and the community kollel—neither of which requires formal membership or exclusive allegiance—can be viewed as "porous institutions" that speak to American Jews who are satisfied with "loose connections." Wuthnow also suggests that there is a growing tendency within the religious and cultural spheres of this generation of "loose connections" to move away from huge mega-churches and toward "small groups" that often meet in private homes or store fronts. These collectives offer a sense of caring and community but make minimal demands in return. Here too, both the Chabad house and the community kollel appear to meet the criteria that Wuthnow set out for these associations.[56]

Positive Anti-Hasidism

Once Haredi Orthodoxy began to try to expand its own influence on American Jewry, it had no choice but to pay attention to the success of the Chabad house. Chabad had "put outreach on the map,"[57] and no Orthodox group that planned to become a force in this field could do so without being aware of Chabad's achievements. Notwithstanding this, the yeshiva world was also keenly critical of both theological and practical aspects of the Chabad approach. The result was an effort to create an alternative framework that expressed simultaneously both emulation and sharp criticism. The community-outreach kollel, as such, is to a certain degree a Mitnagedic response to a Hasidic institution that it could not ignore. In order to develop this idea more clearly it is instructive to first look at an earlier stage in the conflict between Hasidism and Mitnagedism.

Rabbi Elijah, the Gaon of Vilna (1720–97), was the most authoritative Lithuanian rabbinical figure of his time and is the person most closely associated with the emergence of Mitnagedism as a unique worldview.⁵⁸ During the course of his career he expressed total opposition to the burgeoning Hasidic movement, and even supported excommunication of those who associated with it.⁵⁹ Rabbi Hayyim of Volozhin (1749–1821) was considered by many to be the main heir to the Gaon. The yeshiva that he founded in Volozhin (Belarus) became the model for future Lithuanian institutions of higher Torah study. Like the Gaon, he too was opposed to the Hasidic religious approach. Unlike his mentor, however, he recognized that Hasidism had tapped into a spiritual vacuum among Eastern European Jewry. As Immanuel Etkes has argued, Hayyim of Volozhin's literary and educational efforts should be viewed as direct responses to the rise of Hasidism. Through the ideology articulated in his *Nefesh ha-Hayyim*, and the yeshiva that he founded in Volozhin, he promoted a "positive anti-Hasidim." That is, even as he expressed an anti-Hasidic theology and created an alternative framework for disseminating Judaism, he was actually building on the social and spiritual insight of those he opposed.⁶⁰

One of the most striking aspects of this understanding of Hayyim of Volozhin's enterprise is the suggestion that in many ways the yeshiva that he founded paralleled the Hasidic courts whose popularity he hoped to stymie. Unlike Torah study institutions of the past, and like the Hasidic court, the yeshiva was an independent body that was often funded by sources beyond the local Jewish community. Moreover, the yeshiva was intended not only to spur growth in Torah knowledge, but also to serve as a formative spiritual environment where students would develop in their personal piety. This was achieved through the emphasis placed on both devotion to Torah study and to *yira*, fear of God. Regarding the latter in particular, Rabbi Hayyim was responding to the Hasidic critique of the dry, intellectual tenor of the traditional study halls of previous centuries. At the center of this framework was the *rosh yeshiva*, who—similar to the Hasidic rebbe—drew his authority and financial sustenance from his own institution and not from the community. While the rosh yeshiva's leadership was dependent on exceptional mastery of Talmudic texts, like his Hasidic counterpart, he was also the chief spiritual guide and controlled organizational aspects of his independent learning community.⁶¹

The rise of the nineteenth-century Lithuanian yeshiva as a reaction to Hasidism, I suggest then, is highly instructive in evaluating the influence of the late-twentieth-century Chabad house on the development of the community kiruv kollel. Clearly, historical contexts and the specifics of the institutional parallels differ, but following the earlier example, the recent Mitnagedic innovation draws heavily on the spiritual and social insight of its Hasidic predecessor. The many educational and organizational similarities between the Chabad house and the emergent community kiruv kollel have been spelled out in detail above. An additional analogy that should be highlighted here is that, as in the case of Lithuanian Mitnagedism's founder, the Gaon of Vilna, the original framer of American Mitnagedism, Aharon Kotler, also promoted a worldview that was completely antithetical to the Chabad Hasidic outreach approach. Like the students of the Gaon, moreover, the actions of some of the heirs to Kotler's legacy have demonstrated that they too saw that those who differed from their mentor actually possessed a deep appreciation for the needs of the Jewish society around them. Moving one step further, Hayyim of Volozhin did not become a Hasid, but rather tried to create a model that drew from the Hasidic framework without duplicating it. So too, as shown above, the community kiruv kollel is a Mitnagedic alternative that builds on the Chabad house but departs from it in ways that highlight both the intellectual orientation of its architects and their criticisms of their Hasidic precursor.

Indeed, discussions with individuals connected with the community kollel movement support this understanding of their relationship to their Hasidic predecessors and current competitors. As pointed out above, they do not credit Chabad as an inspiration for their own institutions, but they cannot ignore at least some aspects of the parallels between them. At the most basic level, the nonobservant Jews that they encounter are often unable to distinguish between the kollel *jungerleit* and the Chabad shluchim. Surely these people are not conversant in the theological rifts or even the nuances in attire that divide the two. What they see are energetic, friendly, Orthodox-looking young men who offer them opportunities to experience and learn about Judaism. Alternatively, they perceive these religious activists as extremists intent on recruiting them and their children. In either case, most American Jews would not be able to tell the difference between the two types of outreach specialists. In her bachelor's thesis on campus outreach at Emory University in Atlanta, Dara Gever described the reaction of her parents after hearing about her experience on a Haredi-sponsored seminar in Israel in which she participated: "When I returned from my Israel trip and told my parents about my classes, they were taken aback; they consulted with resources from our Jewish community, and concluded that this trip was a function of the Lubavitch Jews."[62]

The community kollel leaders recognize the futility and counterproductiveness of trying to dwell in public upon where the two groups diverge. Yet among themselves, they admit to engaging in intensive discussions about what distinguishes them from Chabad.[63] This behavior, it would appear, is an isolated acting out of the "positive anti-Hasidism" that is at the core of their community kiruv kollel enterprise. Implicit in the emphasis on distinctions is recognition of the strong degree of commonality that exists. Similarly, awareness of the ostensive comparisons to Chabad has reached beyond local chapters to those who train fellows in the more traditional yeshivas in advance of outreach assignments. Among the topics that are covered in an ongoing series of *schmoozim* (educational, homiletical addresses) given at one prominent yeshiva is "how we are different from Chabad." Conversely, in its websites and official publications, Chabad has made a point of celebrating the fact that the Lithuanian yeshiva world both in the United States and Israel eventually adopted outreach activities originally pioneered by Chabad.[64]

The Chabadization of American Haredi Orthodoxy should not be viewed as a full acceptance by the latter of the theology or religious ideology of the followers of Schneerson. It is, rather, a novel illustration of the "positive anti-Hasidism" first pioneered by one of the founders of Lithuanian Orthodoxy.

The Modern Orthodox Community-Inreach Kollel

Alongside Haredi Orthodoxy's development of "Chabad-like" community outreach kollels that attenuate its sectarian ways, Modern Orthodoxy began to sponsor community kollels in North America. However, like the emphasis of YU/RIETS rabbinical training, so too the American Modern Orthodox–sponsored community kollels focus almost exclusively on inreach to synagogues and schools populated by observant constituencies.[65]

In 1994 the Cleveland Torat Tzion Kollel (Torah of Zion, henceforth CTTK) was opened through a collaborative effort between a local philanthropist and Orthodox activist, and the leaders of Yeshivat Har Etzion, one of the oldest and best-known Israeli *hesder* yeshivas.[66] Har Etzion committed to sending senior rabbis to Cleveland for two-year stints, along with a group of post-army students.[67] There they established a study hall in a local day school that served as a base both for advancing their own Talmudic erudition and for educational activities with the student body. In addition, they created an open beit midrash to offer Torah learning opportunities in the evenings and on weekends for the surrounding Orthodox community.[68] Shortly after, the Torah MiTzion organization (henceforth TMZ) was inaugurated in Jerusalem. Under the guidance of founding executive director Ze'ev Schwartz, also a former Har Etzion student, it became a worldwide movement that today encompasses seventeen such Religious-Zionist kollels. They range now from Moscow to Montevideo and from Melbourne to Memphis, with seven of them located in North America.[69]

CHAPTER 8

From early on, YU/RIETS partnered with TMZ and since 2008 it has become the main sponsor of some of the Modern Orthodox kollel branches with the cooperation of TMZ. The Chicago YU TMZ Kollel offers a good example of the evolution of such kollels and their roles in American Modern Orthodoxy.

Rabbi Dr. Leonard A. Matanky is the dean of Chicago's Ida Crown Jewish Academy and rabbi of the Orthodox Congregation KINS of West Rogers Park. He has served as the driving force in creating and sustaining the Chicago TMZ kollel since its inception in 1997. In August 2006 Matanky and Rabbi Yehuda Sussman, a former rosh kollel who currently heads a yeshiva for Americans in Jerusalem, produced an informative retrospective on their experience with TMZ in Chicago. They affirmed that the founding of the kollel was in response to Haredi initiatives such as the highly successful Chicago Community Kollel,[70] one of the original community kollels that has been targeting the Modern Orthodox community since its inception in the 1970s:

> Major communities have witnessed the emergence of community kollelim. Whether staffed by alumni of Ner Yisrael, Beth Medrash Govoha of Lakewood, Chafetz Chaim or other charedi yeshivot, these kollelim have made tremendous in-roads, not only among like-minded lay leaders, but also among those who in the past, had identified with Modern Orthodoxy/Religious-Zionism. In essence, for many, these community kollelim and the ideals that they represented became the prime source of an authentic Jewish voice, but one that was often at odds with modernity, and the hashkafa (worldview) of Tzionut Datit (Religious-Zionism). In response to this, a group of lay leaders and rabbis in our community sought to establish a community kollel that would not only be a serious voice of Torah, but also reflect the values of Tziyonut and Modern Orthodoxy.[71]

The authors list the many benefits that Chicago's Modern Orthodox community has gained from the TMZ's existence, including "strengthening both the Torah atmosphere and Religious-Zionist identity of the high school." Despite these achievements there had also been problems in maintaining an Israeli-based kollel, including the cultural differences between Israelis and Americans and the lack of permanent local staff.

With these issues in mind, in 2008 Matanky worked with YU to reconstitute the kollel such that it would be led by an American YU/RIETS-trained rabbinic scholar and would draw primarily from RIETS graduates to serve as kollel members. Under the guidance of Matanky and the new rosh kollel, Rabbi Reuven Brand, there was a resurgence of activity and highly positive communal responses to the renewed framework. That said, like its predecessor, the vast majority of its resources and programming were directed toward sustaining the existing Modern Orthodox communities in the Chicago environs and inspiring pupils at Modern Orthodox schools to remain loyal to this path. As the kollel's official mission statement announces: "The mission of the Yeshiva University Torah Mitzion Kollel of Chicago is to enrich and engage the greater Chicago Jewish community with inspired Torah living and learning. The Kollel is an open community of learning that celebrates three core values: the primacy of Torah, the importance of positive interaction with general society and culture and the religious significance of the State of Israel."[72] In July 2013 Matanky was elected president of the RCA. In an interview immediately after being chosen, he vowed to strengthen the Orthodox alternative to the Haredi approach and "stand up for the values we have in the Orthodox world."[73]

Matanky's statement echoes the overall tenor of many within the Modern Orthodox camp since the late 1980s who lamented the lack of well-defined ideological principles and charismatic leadership. In Chicago, Toronto, Montreal, Memphis, and other venues where Modern Orthodoxy thrived in the past, the community kollel—with its "battle-hardened" Sabra Torah students or YU "Torah u-Madda" (Torah and science) patriots—has been advanced as one possible cure to the ideological malaise and lack of inspiring Modern Orthodox role models that the community sorely feels.

If the emergence of the new Haredi kollels reflects a move away from sectarianism, the Modern Orthodox versions exemplify a retreat of this sector into survivalist mode. While Lakewood and Ner Israel have redirected their students beyond their historic introspection and toward promoting unity among Jews of all orientations—adopting and adjusting in the process strategies and tools initiated by Chabad—YU and Israeli yeshiva graduates have been drafted primarily to buttress Modern Orthodox educational and religious institutions. Liebman's "church" Orthodox, who first championed the role of addressing the broader Jewish collective, have refocused their efforts inward toward their own core observant constituency.

Finally, it is notable that one of the boldest challenges to the 2013 Pew study emanated from a prominent Chabad spokesman and activist, Rabbi David Eliezrie of Orange County, California. He argues, among other things, that the report does not take sufficient account of the growing number of self-identifying Reform and Conservative Jews who attend services or participate regularly in activities sponsored by Chabad houses. The upshot is that unlike the liberal denominations that for the most part address only those who formally affiliate with them, Chabad's role extends to many American Jews who would never consider themselves Hasidic or "Chabadnikim." Thus, measuring Orthodoxy's role in American Jewish life primarily based on the self-definition of those who were surveyed—especially without asking a separate question regarding additional Chabad connections—does not offer a sufficiently accurate and insightful accounting.[74] Here I would add that rather than limiting such a question to Chabad, the data and analysis in this chapter suggest that it should include both Chabad and the many community kollels and other Haredi outreach enterprises that work consistently with the broader local Jewish populations but do not necessarily cause most of them to adopt Orthodox lifestyles or identities.

9

Women and Haredi Outreach

A Silent Revolution

Feminism and gender egalitarianism have figured centrally in Modern Orthodox discourse and communal life since the early 1980s. For the most part, it has been assumed that Haredi Orthodoxy was relatively immune to these trends. Only in recent years has greater attention been drawn to the emergence of new types of Haredi female figures. Chabad women emissaries constituted one of the first groups to draw notice in this transformation. This chapter is the first account of a "silent" revolution taking place among non-Hasidic Haredi women who increasingly are taking on more prominent religious leadership roles. One of the main frameworks for these transformations is the field of outreach to the broader American Jewish population. The rise of the female outreach activist is an additional manifestation of the ways that Haredi Orthodoxy's abandonment of sectarian approaches to nonobservant Jews has led to less rigid religious and social norms on the part of members of its core constituency. The new roles taken on by female outreach activists raise conflicts and engender complex hybrid identities that digress in notable ways from accepted notions within this sector.

Introduction

The twentieth century witnessed fresh models of Jewish women's educational and religious leadership. Quite understandably, the majority of the scholarly focus has been on burgeoning egalitarian trends featured in the new roles for women within liberal Jewish denominations and among the Modern Orthodox. Most prominently, women rabbis, but also cantors, heads of yeshivot or midrashot, halakhic advisors, congregational interns, Israeli rabbinic advocates, and women's lay leaders in liberal synagogues, have all drawn considerable attention.[1] As elucidated in chapter 5, efforts by Orthodox feminists to expand female ritual functions and formal leadership have met with fierce criticism by some of Orthodoxy's most prominent rabbinical figures.

Increased appreciation for gendered perspectives within Jewish studies has also led to recognition that seemingly traditional female roles—once viewed as purely supportive in nature—have evolved into platforms for voicing uniquely feminine styles of Jewish authority. Pioneering studies of the Bais Yaakov educational network and its graduates,[2] as well as discussions of the American rebbetzin,[3] the Chabad shluchah (female emissary),[4] female Haredi authors of self-help books and quasi-secular novels,[5] and both Israeli and American Haredi female preachers who address exclusively women's audiences, have all highlighted the positions of such individuals as both religious activists and agents of change.[6] This chapter builds on and adds to these prior examples.

A "silent" revolution is taking place in which Haredi women are taking on more central religious roles. One of the main frameworks for these transformations is the field of Haredi Orthodox outreach to the broader American Jewish population.

More than a Rebbetzin: The Female Kollel Activist

As a rule, membership in an outreach kollel demands a greater level of involvement from the female spouse than the wife of a fellow in a traditional kollel setting. Minimally, the decision to move from a center of Orthodox life to a less established community entails the willingness to forego closeness to family and familiar comforts, as well as access to the widest variety of religious services, kosher products, and educational options for children. In return one enters a heterogeneous Jewish collective that often lacks the basic infrastructure deemed necessary for a Haredi Orthodox Jewish family. In addition, beyond the daily kollel study routine, much of community kollel outreach work centers on the homes and Sabbath tables of the fellows and their families. Kollel spouses are expected to prepare meals for company on a weekly basis, and they and their children must be willing to model the warm religious family atmosphere that will inspire unaffiliated or non-Orthodox Jews to upgrade their Jewish involvements. Another role often taken on by kollel spouses is administrative work in the kollel office. This brings them closer to the center of activity, but it remains essentially a supportive position.

To a great degree, this description of the outreach kollel spouse is reminiscent of the helpful rabbinical wife portrayed and analyzed by Shuli Rubin Schwartz in her work on the *rebbetzin*.[7] One can even point to a distinct benefit possessed by the kollel wife over a woman married to a congregational rabbi. Namely, unlike the latter, the kollel spouse is not alone. She is part of a group of young families who can offer one another an automatic social network and mutual assistance. For many female kollel spouses, however, their involvements extend far beyond their homes and other forms of buttressing their husbands' endeavors. Rather they serve as full-fledged outreach professionals alongside their husbands.

Most outreach kollels sponsor women's divisions that offer an extensive array of classes and study opportunities. Some are geared to local Orthodox women, but much of the efforts are directed toward the broader Jewish female population. Generally speaking, these departments are run by the wives of kollel heads and fellows who also serve as the main instructors. At the website of the TORCH Kollel in Houston, for example, the individual pictures and bios of the kollel's female activists, most of them wives of fellows, appear on the same page as those of the male faculty. Both divisions are included under the title "our team."[8] In appealing to Greater Houston Jewry, the "ASCENT Institute," as the women's division is called, beckons: "If you'd like to learn and reclaim your heritage with other like minded women, or to set up a class or learning group with your own friends, please contact us. We'd love to help!"[9] ASCENT's programming parallels and augments that of its male counterpart, including weekly classes, group study sessions, and "lunch and learns," as well as special inspirational public lectures by dynamic female Haredi "stars" flown in for the occasion and the annual "Houston Conference for Jewish Women." The latter is cosponsored by the nondenominational Houston Federation and Jewish Family Services.[10]

The activities of female kollel spouses are not necessarily limited to single-gender environments. Kollel female activists orchestrate and take part in collective Torah study, often in mixed-gender settings, by serving as study partners to women in the groups (*hevrutot*). While most formal lectures presented by women are to female groups, exceptions are made to this rule as well. Kollel female activists also play central roles in the planning and direction of the myriad events and activities that fall under the rubric of kollel education in the various branches. These include campus outreach with university students, singles get-togethers and weekend seminars, young professionals meetings, family getaways, and special holiday events.

At JSN, the Jewish Study Network in Palo Alto, 80 percent of the classes and activities are mixed gender. Kollel female activists not only cook for and cater events, they are often the people who organize, orchestrate, and make the key decisions on most aspects of the educational and social programs that will be presented. According to Rabbi Joey Felsen, the head of the kollel, while there is no prohibition on women teaching mixed-gender audiences of any age, most of the female activists do not do so.[11]

Female Training and Guide Books

Two typologies of women's leadership have already been mentioned that are relevant to an analysis of the Haredi female outreach activists, the rebbetzin and the Chabad shluchah. Among the numerous distinctions between the two is the fact that the wives of congregational rabbis rarely, at least until recently, had any formal preparation for their roles. By contrast, the shluchos receive extensive training in advance of setting out to run a Chabad house with their husbands. From this perspective as well, the Haredi female outreach activist model is closer to that of Chabad.

As discussed in chapter 7, two of the main programs for training Haredi outreach specialists, and for that matter female activists, are based in Jerusalem. Many young American Haredi couples choose to live and study in Jerusalem for the first few years of their married lives. The men attend traditional kollels, while the women often attain American university professional degrees through local Israeli extensions. This population is considered particularly suited for careers in Jewish outreach. The frameworks that have been established to train them for their future vocation are under the auspices of Ner LeElef and its affiliated Jerusalem Kollel. Both institutions offer separate male and female courses. In exchange for participation in a two-year part-time program, the young marrieds receive a generous stipend.[12]

Like the men, the women learn how to address the manifold types of Jews that they will encounter within the complex mosaic of American Jewry. Particular emphasis is placed on controversial questions that will arise in the course of their work with the nonobservant, and how to present Orthodox practice and theology in response in such a way that it will appeal to contemporary American sensitivities.

The literature produced by Ner LeElef for use by its students and graduates reveals original booklets numbering hundreds of pages, including extensive footnotes and sources, on topics such as American society, science and Judaism, evolution, suffering, the Holocaust, and the Chosen People.[13] Two book-length pamphlets are titled "Women's Issues" and address topics such as male-female relationships, women's Torah study, women's liberation, and the Orthodox feminist movement.[14] The halakhic positions posited open up room for leniencies that go far beyond normative Haredi standards. Regarding women wearing pants in public, for example, one Ner LeElef book offers the following approach: "Although [Torah *banot* (girls)] universally do not wear women's slacks, some say that there may be a Halachic source to tell someone that it is O.K. as an intermediate step."[15] These publications, as such, offer an additional window into how the focus on outreach has forced the Haredi world to navigate and sometimes adjust its boundaries in meaningful ways—including those relating to the very delicate issues of gender and female modesty.[16]

Women's Outreach Organizations and Conferences

Chapter 8 highlighted parallels between the Chabad house and its emissaries and the community-outreach kollel and its activists. Like Chabad, efforts have been made to go beyond individual institutions and local bodies in order to create networks that organize and support those in the field. Just as Chabad has created frameworks—including an annual conference—for supporting its shluchos, Haredi outreach has also crafted associations and events intended to cultivate and sustain its female religious emissaries.[17]

WIK—"women in kiruv"—exemplifies such an initiative. Its mission is "to encourage and support women engaged in Torah education by offering them connections, information, and inspiration that nurture the Torah teacher and support her growth both personally and as a guide for others."[18] Notwithstanding its Haredi orientation, and in keeping with the "silent" feminist "revolution" identified in this chapter, WIK declares unabashedly that it "affirms the significance of the contribution of women to the education, ingathering and guidance of Jews as they take their place in the framework of a Torah life."[19] In other words, women are genuine leadership figures in the outreach industry and need to be emboldened.

The now annual WIK conference took place for first time in 2010 and was organized in conjunction with AJOP, the Association of Jewish Outreach Professionals. The 2012 event was held in Baltimore, Maryland, and attended by a hundred women from nineteen states as well as Canada and Israel. Topics covered included "How does one stay inspired while inspiring others?" "Technology and outreach," and "How to fight burnout while being far from family and friends." Like any conference, in addition to content meetings, there were social and recreational activities. According to an official WIK report: "A special moment of the conference came on Sunday night, when Stacey Spigelman of LA Style Hair Salon arrived to take 46 of the women's sheitels [wigs] to wash and blow dry before their departure on Tuesday morning."[20] No doubt, this testifies to the strict levels of observance of the participants. Yet it also reflects the fact that most of these women have left the enclaves of Brooklyn, Lakewood, Monsey, and Baltimore. As the report noted, "the women come from communities where there are no sheitel machers, coming to Baltimore was an opportunity for them to pamper their often neglected, and often worn, headwear."[21]

Conflicts

Along with their novel roles, fresh conflicts have also arisen for Haredi women as a result of their involvement in outreach. Some outreach kollel wives are unhappy with the new expectation that they must become full-fledged partners in their husband's career. According to Elky Langer, wife of one of the heads of Pittsburgh's Kollel Jewish Learning Center and herself a regular speaker at Kollel events, "This is an area of some tension. Some are more involved, some hardly do anything.... There is a definite interest in making it clear to new kollel wives that they are expected to actively participate.... Of course the Rosh Kollel would be delighted ... sort of like getting two for one! Sounds ideal, but in fact not every Kollel wife is cut out for a community-expanded role."[22] The female outreach activist represents a new type of feminine "voice" within Haredi Jewry. The rejection of this role by some spouses suggests, among other things, that this redefinition sufficiently challenges normative Haredi notions to cause discomfort for some who were nurtured within its corridors.[23]

While some kollel wives have not adjusted to the new expectations thrust upon them, the very success of others has caused them to reflect on its broader social and religious implications. A case in point is the JSN in Palo Alto. As noted above, JSN's female faculty is intensely involved in many aspects of the kollel, including teaching, as well as planning and implementation of informal programming. Such endeavors demand intensive and ongoing cooperation between members of the male and female kollel staffs, and not necessarily those who are married to each other. While such working relationships may be the norm in general society and even among Modern Orthodox educators, they deviate from the strict separation of the sexes and general approach to modesty that is idealized in the contemporary Haredi world. For Rabbi Joey Felsen, the JSN head, this posed a problem. From the perspective of developing successful outreach to weakly affiliated Jews, as well as from an organizational standpoint, it is crucial that the women activists play central roles. Yet crossing this boundary, from his view, might endanger the spiritual makeup of the members of the kollel staff itself. His compromise was to establish a rule whereby kollel families are forbidden to socialize with each other unless a third party from their outreach constituency is also present. Similarly, the JSN policy is for the men to address the wives of other kollel members as "Mrs."[24]

Partially in light of these types of conflicts, even after the families move on to kollels or other outreach centers throughout North America, both the Jerusalem Kollel and Ner LeElef continue to supervise and offer professional support to their graduates. In fact, Ner LeElef maintains a full-time female staff member who travels throughout North America to meet and support the female alumni activists in their endeavors.

Returning to the 2012 Women in Kiruv conference, two additional topics addressed at length were balancing work and home life and dealing with domestic conflicts that can arise when women take on public roles.[25] These issues, once again, highlight the complexities that have arisen alongside the emergence of the new female Haredi outreach leadership.[26] By choosing to confront them head-on, the organizers made clear that despite the difficulties, they did not consider the possibility that Haredi women ought to choose between increased female activism and family stability. On the contrary, since neither of these valuable aspects of life should be abandoned, it was necessary to help those in the field develop skills for addressing these challenges.

The Female Future of Haredi Outreach

One reflection of the growing importance of female activists to Haredi outreach is the decision made by Rabbi Avraham Edelstein, the head of Ner LeElef, to fly from Israel to Baltimore to speak at the 2012 WIK conference. Another featured lecturer was Lori Palatnik, who is considered to be a "superstar" of women's outreach. The former radio and television copywriter has spent more than a decade traveling the world to speak to Jewish audiences at various outreach centers, synagogues, and college campuses about their Jewish heritage. Simultaneously, she and her husband founded outreach communities in Denver, Colorado, and Washington, D.C., that were affiliated with Aish Hatorah. In 2008 she and seven friends—some observant some not—founded the Jewish Women's Renaissance Project (JWRP), which is modeled after the Taglit-Birthright program and offers subsidized trips to Israel for married women from primarily non-Orthodox backgrounds. More than three thousand Jewish women have participated in JWRP Israel trips that include considerable programming to "promote Jewish continuity." The 2013 trips were oversubscribed. The goal of the organization is that by 2020 ten thousand Jewish women will go annually on these "trips of female Jewish empowerment." In addition to her involvement in JWRP and her myriad speaking engagements, Palatnik has also created a video blog, *Lori Almost Live,* which is featured on Aish Hatorah's Aish.com site and combines parenting and family advice with Jewish inspiration. It receives an average of fifty thousand monthly hits.[27]

When the editors of *Klal Perspectives,* the Haredi journal founded in 2011 to address pressing contemporary issues facing Orthodoxy, decided to dedicate the fall 2012 issue to an assessment of the state of Jewish outreach, they turned to Lori Palatnik to author one of the articles. In her essay, she posits that in order to reach a wider audience of American Jews and make a longer-lasting impact, Jewish outreach should place less emphasis on college campuses and refocus its efforts on targeting Jewish mothers:

> If you connect a 20-year-old young man to his Judaism, and he becomes a committed Jew, you have now impacted a 20-year-old. But what about his 17-year-old sister, his 15-year-old brother and his mother and father? ... Throughout our kiruv careers it became crystal clear that the key to impacting a family is through the Jewish woman; the wife, the mother. The woman of the home, in general, is the one who is the main decider of some of the most important choices a family will make: where to live, what schools children will attend, who they will socialize with, and the list goes on and on. The impact of these choices is literally the difference between one lifestyle and another.... During the trips, we strongly emphasize that the women must take this inspiration home and assume spiritual responsibility for their families, communities and even for the Jewish people.[28]

To prove her thesis, Palatnik described the follow-up process from JWRP and produced numbers to support its success: "We track the women closely after the trip, offering support and follow-up through our many partner organizations throughout the country. These local partners, such as Aish branches, community kollels, shuls and kiruv organizations, are an essential part of our vision.... City leaders from among our partners participate in monthly conference calls to share best practices and explore each other's challenges.... Each organization submits quarterly reports on the events they have with their women, attendance, and other important information regarding the women's progress in their post-trip learning and growth."[29] Statistically, the data from the JWRP 2011 annual report sustain the claim that one year after going on the trip, 86 percent of the women say being Jewish is more important to them, 42 percent have placed their kids into Jewish youth groups, 23 percent of those with school-aged children switched them from a public or non-Jewish private school to a Jewish day school, 75 percent increased their observance of Shabbat, 90 percent expanded their Jewish study, and 68 percent of their husbands became more Jewishly involved. JWRP has succeeded in gaining the support of many local Jewish federations. In this light, the report noted that 39.2 percent of the women raised their financial support for their local federation after their trips, and 37.3 percent participated in more federation events.[30]

Palatnik's success has not gone unnoticed by the broader Jewish community. The fall 2013 edition of *Jewish Woman* magazine—a publication of the nondenominationally affiliated Jewish Women International—named Lori Palatnik along with nine others as their annual "Women to Watch."[31] More spectacularly, in tribute to Women's History Month 2014, Hadassah Women inscribed a few new personalities in its official honor roll of "Most Outstanding Jewish American Women of Our Time." Palatnik was among them, and is portrayed on the Hadassah website as "an activist for Jewish women's rights and the founder of 'Birthright for Women.'" Her name is now listed prominently together with leading feminists of the twentieth century, including Gloria Steinhem, Betty Friedan, and Ruth Bader Ginsburg.[32]

Feminism, Counter-Feminism, and Outreach

Lori Palatnik presents compelling evidence for the effective fusion of women's empowerment within Orthodox outreach. At the same time, American Haredi leaders have been categorically critical of religious feminism and women's leadership initiatives emanating from Modern Orthodoxy. The following accusatory statement appears, for example, at the end of a discussion of Orthodox feminism in a sourcebook on Jewish women published by Ner LeElef: "It is quite amazing that while some women will devote enormous time and resources to working out how a woman can get to read the Megillah, 100 million females are dying [in developing countries due to poor medical attention] and not a word is being said by these same 'women's liberators'. Given these facts, the smell of egocentricity reaches a veritable stench."[33] How do the same forces that sanction the printing of such bellicose expressions come to terms with Palatnik's brand of

Haredi female activism? No doubt the fact that the Haredi female figures do not assert themselves within male-dominated ritual roles distinguishes them from their Modern Orthodox counterparts—although as seen above, outreach has been used as a justification for religious leniencies. Nonetheless, one of the major debates within Modern Orthodoxy is regarding efforts to cultivate female spiritual guides who play almost identical roles to rabbis. The Haredi world would appear eager to establish especially vigilant boundaries against similar incursions of contemporary norms by cracking down on the emergence of religious leadership figures such as Palatnik. The few academic studies that have been published on other Jewish female outreach figures and how they navigate their relationship to their religious milieus offer valuable points for comparison.[34]

Historian Shuli Rubin Schwartz has analyzed the career of Rebbetzin Esther Jungreis (b. 1936), arguably the forerunner of contemporary non-Hasidic Orthodox women's outreach.[35] Along with working with her husband to establish an Orthodox congregation in North Woodmere, New York, Jungreis developed a career as an inspirational speaker and highly popular writer and columnist. In 1973, decades before outreach became a mainstay within American Haredi culture, this Hungarian-born Holocaust survivor and Bais Yaakov graduate founded an independent organization called Hineni (I am here). Through this framework she disseminates her teachings that emphasize the importance of remembering the Holocaust, the joy of Torah, traditional Jewish family life, and Sabbath observance, and are directed to observant and nonobservant Jews alike. Based in Manhattan's Upper West Side, Hineni sponsors a wide range of popular religious programming that regularly attracts hundreds of participants, especially single Jewish professionals.

According to Rubin Schwartz, if in practice Jungreis herself has long digressed from traditional Orthodox female roles, she hedges this "deviance" by focusing her messages on seemingly "authentic" Orthodox values. In this vein, Jungreis has always been careful to present herself as an extension of her husband's rabbinical work rather than an independent leader. "These attitudes," according to Rubin Schwartz, "enable Jungreis to remain safely ensconced within the traditional world while continuing to subvert its notions of the appropriate women's role."[36]

Jungreis's rhetorical model of balancing between public female religious persona and firm allegiance to core traditional postures has been adopted by the fresh troops of female leaders that have arisen within American Haredi Orthodoxy since the 1990s. In doing so, they neutralize apprehensions that they, like their Modern Orthodox counterparts, are crossing dangerous lines or undermining fundamental Orthodox ideals. That said, unlike the community kollel wives and Ner LeElef graduates of the twenty-first century, Jungreis has long been a hybrid figure who does not sit squarely in the Haredi world. Inasmuch as she and her late husband both emerged from the same traditionalist Hungarian Orthodox rabbinical family, the synagogue they established is Modern Orthodox and today is served by a graduate of Yeshiva University. Indeed, Rabbi Jungreis himself received his doctoral degree from that banner institution of Modern Orthodoxy. While Jungreis is often invited to speak at various Haredi-sponsored outreach events, her primary venues are Modern Orthodox or nonsectarian forums. In fact, long before Haredi outreach figures contemplated engaging non-Orthodox denominations directly, she appeared at official Reform and Conservative public events. As such, Jungreis's "balancing act" certainly provides insight into the new female Haredi outreach activists, but her specific example does not necessarily explain the apparent acceptance by the Haredi world of this "revolutionary" female archetype.

An additional avenue for consideration is the way Chabad shluchos, who work in partnership with their emissary husbands at drawing Jews closer to observance, address the feminism implicit in their roles. Some studies of Chabad women reach comparable conclusions to those of Rubin Schwartz regarding Jungreis. These investigations note, however, that unlike Jungreis, the Chabad figures seek to demonstrate that their posture is not necessarily contrary to all versions of feminism. In her 1998 portrayal of the central themes in the writings and actions of Chabad female representatives, women's studies scholar Bonnie Morris explains that especially through the many formerly nonobservant women (repentant Jews) who have joined them, Chabad women have absorbed the values of "greater female autonomy and self-determination" that are at the foundation of American "second wave" feminism. Yet the "Lubavitchers" refute the notion that these principles demand taking on the same roles as males. On the contrary, this would mean imposing what they consider to be "Christian" perceptions of feminism and equality on them. By maintaining traditional matrilineal forms, the Lubavitcher women argue, they are not abandoning self-determination. Rather, they are asserting the differences between themselves and the non-Jewish majority and through this fighting the battle against assimilation.[37]

This resourceful "feminist anti-feminism," as described by sociologist Debra Kaufman,[38] has enabled Chabad to articulate a message that is highly attractive to many contemporary women: far from arcane or primitive, Judaism actually preceded more recent trends in celebrating the uniquely feminine voices of Jewish women. It is ingenious as well in its fusion of female distinctiveness with

CHAPTER 9

Chabad's primary goal of attracting alienated Jews toward increasing religious activity.

Various articulations of this "separate but equal" dynamic fill the pages of Haredi publications dedicated to promoting Orthodoxy to contemporary women as well.[39] But like the Chabad literature described by Morris, the main targets of these communications are those who have been brought up on secular egalitarian values and must now be convinced that traditional Judaism does not discriminate against women. Certainly women who have been nurtured in Chabad or Haredi environments are not immune to contemporary social mores and also may seek to understand why their groups do not affirm the prevalent contemporary ethos regarding women. Regardless, the "separate but equal" explanation does not sufficiently account for the egalitarian dynamic that is reflected in the roles of the Chabad shluchos and female Haredi outreach activists, both of whom display behaviors more closely identified with the "male" sphere of religious leadership. The challenge to accepted norms is inherent in these figures—especially when their Modern Orthodox foils are simultaneously pushing the envelope so openly.

Here the scholarship of Hasidism expert Naftali Loewenthal provides valuable comparative tools for assessing the non-Hasidic Haredi phenomenon. In a series of articles, Loewenthal asserts that over the course of the twentieth century a fresh understanding of women as religious personalities developed within Lubavitch-Chabad. Instead of being seen purely as the "wife and daughter of a Hasid (adherent to a grand rabbi and member of his sect)," there emerged "the woman or girl who considers herself to be a hasidic follower or activist in her own right."[40] This process began in the early part of the century through alliances of learned Chabad women in Poland, Latvia, and the United States who engaged in the study of Hasidic mystical texts, and were encouraged and given guidance in this endeavor by the sixth Lubavitcher rebbe, Rabbi Joseph Isaac Schneerson (1880–1950).[41] Loewenthal asserts that these Chabad women went a crucial step beyond the revolutionary Bais Yaakov movement that emerged at the same time. Not only did the Lubavitch women study the Bible and other basic canonical books, they also immersed themselves in mystical Hasidic texts. According to Loewenthal, this initial intellectual facilitation for women to encounter the spiritual depths of the Hasidic worldview eventually served as a "portal of entry" for Chabad women into spheres of leadership that had previously been almost exclusively male.[42]

The full transformation in Chabad's perception of women took place, however, under the inventive leadership of the seventh rebbe, Rabbi Menachem Mendel Schneerson (1902–94), who articulated original theological conceptualizations that empowered his female followers to serve as religious activists.

The main goal of his generation, as highlighted in the previous chapter, was the spread ("*u-faratzta*") of the wellsprings ("*ma'ayanot*") of the Torah to every Jew regardless of his or her personal level of observance. Starting in 1951, he systematically transformed Lubavitch Hasidism from an insular sect to the multifaceted Chabad religious movement. The vanguard were his shluchim—emissaries who were commanded to leave the warm confines of their Crown Heights, Brooklyn, neighborhood and settle in areas that were often devoid of any Orthodox infrastructure. There they were to dedicate themselves to touching the souls of the local Jews, while remaining absolutely committed to the strict religious regimens of their Hasidic order.[43]

Early on, Schneerson acknowledged that women had a role to play in this movement, but especially from the 1980s he cultivated the idea that Chabad shluchos were no less agents of this calling than their emissary husbands. In fact, he asserted that women possess characteristics that make them potentially more effective outreach agents. Loewenthal maintains that Schneerson strived to advance his original perception without undermining more traditional female functions. To this end, he articulated a unique dual ideal for Chabad women: at once the traditional Jewish mother, homemaker, and hostess, while simultaneously an activist deeply involved in a wide gamut of pursuits—including those once exclusively in the male domain—aimed at engaging weakly affiliated Jews.[44]

The Chabad shluchos have evolved into an empowered female vanguard that defies long-held Haredi notions of gendered division of labor. That said, it is crucial to emphasize that Schneerson's iteration of the ideal Jewish woman, novel that it is and notwithstanding the theological explanations that he offered, emanates from his core agenda: enabling as many Jews as possible to fulfill as many religious commandments as possible. Just as he recognized in the late 1960s that college campuses were fertile environments for attracting religiously alienated Jews toward stronger commitment, so too did he understand in the 1980s—notably around the same time that the Conservative movement voted to ordain female rabbis and Modern Orthodox women began to campaign for greater religious involvement—that attracting contemporary Jews to religion demanded fostering female religious leadership.

This analysis of Lubavitch Hasidism's approach to its female emissaries lends considerable insight into the more recent non-Hasidic Haredi phenomenon of women's outreach activists. The key to analyzing the relatively seamless emergence of these female leaders within American Haredi culture is that it is less reflective of a change in Haredi attitudes toward women's roles than of the overall embrace of outreach as a central communal value. Just as the Lubavitcher rebbe realized that the success of his major endeavor was dependent on expanding the profile and mission of his female followers, similarly the emergence of female Haredi outreach professionals reflects the acknowledgment of their communal leaders that extensive women's involvement is crucial to achieving their goals. Once this recognition took place the path was paved for the appearance of Lori Palatnik and others like her.

As such, the rise of female Haredi outreach activists is certainly indicative of a transformation in Haredi thinking. But unlike the prior and parallel changes in the non-Orthodox and Modern Orthodox streams, it is only indirectly a result of the broader reorientation toward gender equality that began in the twentieth century. Societal realities dictated that in order to bring women (and their families) closer to Judaism, Haredi women needed to play pivotal roles in the process. But this was a functional change. The more fundamental transformation in Haredi Orthodoxy was the move from a strictly enclavist worldview toward greater engagement with the broader Jewish population.

From a historical perspective, the turn-of-the-twenty-first-century "silent revolution" implicit in the development of Haredi women's outreach leaders shares common characteristics with the previous revolution in Haredi women's religious involvement, which took place through the establishment of the Bais Yaakov schools and teacher's seminaries during the interwar period. There too, the initial impetus of its founder, Sarah Schenirer, was not a positive desire to raise the religious stature of Jewish women. Rather, her acute awareness of the alienation from religion characteristic of many daughters of Polish Hasidic families led her to initiate a framework that would invigorate their spiritual and Jewish intellectual lives. Indeed, this was the reason that some of the most prominent rabbinical authorities of the time gave their imprimatur to this groundbreaking effort. That said, the net result was an essential revision in the professional and religious norms of Haredi Orthodox women. This, in turn, blazed the trail for more radical enterprises that arose during the second half of the twentieth century.[45]

Conclusion: The Challenge of Female Leadership

Will figures such as Lori Palatnik serve as agents of change for more profound adjustments in the Haredi approach to female religious leadership? While an unequivocal answer is impossible at this point, some insight may be provided by Haredi responses to ostensibly internal Modern Orthodox debates regarding women. One example is the vociferous rejoinder of Agudath Israel of America to the 2010 decision of Rabbi Avi Weiss to confer the title "Rabba" upon his student Sara Hurwitz after her completion of the study requirements for Orthodox ordination. At first glance, this would appear to have been a purely in-house Modern Orthodox issue. Some Modern Orthodox Jews have long advocated for female religious leadership within the synagogue, but this has never been the case regarding Agudath Israel-affiliated individuals or institutions. Nonetheless, Agudath Israel issued three separate statements condemning Weiss's actions.[46]

One explanation for Agudath Israel's outspokenness is that despite criticisms of the Modern Orthodox, it recognizes the basic legitimacy of most Modern Orthodox rabbis and acknowledges that the two sectors—Haredi and Modern—together make up the broader rubric of American Orthodoxy. Thus, it was necessary to clarify that appointment of female rabbis was a boundary marker that would distinguish between any type of Orthodoxy and the alternatives. As the original statement declares unequivocally, "Any congregation with a woman in a rabbinical position of any sort cannot be considered Orthodox."[47] For the same reason, Agudath Israel did not relent until the president of the RCA clarified that it was absolutely "unacceptable for an Orthodox synagogue to have a woman on its rabbinic staff."[48]

A parallel but not mutually exclusive understanding of the militant Agudath Israel response relates more directly to the new phenomenon of female Haredi outreach activists highlighted in this chapter. Agudath Israel's statement was intended as much for internal Haredi consumption as to make sure that Modern Orthodoxy continued to toe the line. While no Haredim have broached the idea of women rabbis, in practice, dynamic figures like Lori Palatnik and other female outreach activists have emerged as charismatic religious leaders whose activities contest Haredi norms. They inspire and serve as religious authorities for hundreds and sometimes thousands of Jews—and not exclusively women—and are increasingly the key figures in creating outreach networks. Sometimes they even articulate their agenda in the context of the feminist revolution. The description of the (Palatnik-led) JWRP's foundational concept that appears on its official website, for example, posits a direct continuum from late twentieth-century feminism to early twenty-first-century female outreach: "Just as Jewish women were the leadership of the feminist movement in the 1970s that created real social change, so too Jewish women must be the leaders in a new social movement based on values."[49] With such rhetoric being espoused by vibrant female figures within Haredi Orthodoxy itself, the leaders of Agudath Israel may have felt an especially strong imperative to clarify the distinctions between women rabbis and other types of female leaders.

Chapter 5 portrayed the fierce struggle of a central Modern Orthodox rabbinical authority against Orthodox feminism. Here I have suggested that the emergence of the female outreach activist is an additional manifestation of the ways that American Haredi Orthodoxy's abandonment of sectarian approaches to nonobservant Jews has led to less-rigid religious and social norms on the part of members of its core constituency. The new roles taken on by female outreach activists raise conflicts and engender complex hybrid identities that digress in notable ways from accepted notions within this community. Notwithstanding the numerous distinctions between the training and activities of women rabbis and outreach activists, both are challenging long-held standards of their particular sectors. Moreover, they are both implicitly, and sometimes explicitly, drawing on the feminist movement as inspiration for their own initiatives. The force of Haredi criticism of Modern Orthodox feminism may partially reflect its concerns over the progressively more liminal character of its own camp regarding the role of women in religious life. Thus, not only is the rise of new types of female religious leadership a phenomenon that is shared by contemporary Modern Orthodoxy and Haredi Orthodoxy, so too are the visceral alarms sounded by their respective rabbinic elites.

Conclusion

Beyond Outreach

Postdenominationalism, Open Orthodoxy, and Realignment

In the summer of 2013 a prominent Orthodox synagogue rabbi in Baltimore, who is a disciple of the Ner Israel yeshiva and well respected in local Haredi circles, put forward a fresh vision for peaceful coexistence within American Jewish communal life. Writing in *Klal Perspectives,* Rabbi Moshe Hauer declared: "It is well established that principle limits Orthodox participation with other streams in religious matters, including joint membership on communal Boards of Rabbis.... It nevertheless remains possible and appropriate for leaders and members of these various streams to build and maintain friendships and working relationships that build understanding, retain a sense of community between Jews of all streams and facilitate working together on issues of common concern."[1]

Hauer both reinforces one of the central themes in this book and goes beyond it. On one level, his statement exemplifies the transformation that has taken place within American Haredi Orthodoxy regarding the terms of its engagement with the broader non-Orthodox community. Notwithstanding formal restrictions regarding membership in cross-denominational organizations that essentially pay lip service to policies of old, a respected rabbi in Baltimore's Haredi circles forthrightly endorsed the need for both Orthodox rabbis and laypeople to connect with all Jews—regardless of their degrees of observance or denominational affiliations.

On a second level, however, Hauer's essay moves further than the majority of examples identified in previous chapters in a highly significant way. For his discussion does not focus at all on outreach efforts aimed ultimately at drawing Jews closer to full observance and Orthodox identification. On the contrary, his main thrust is that in order to avoid tension and rivalries and sustain a peaceful internal Jewish atmosphere, "organizations and the community should adopt a posture that ranges from working together cooperatively to 'live-and-let-live.'"[2] In fact, not only does he advocate tolerance of other groups that digress from Orthodox ideals, he acknowledges their constructive elements: "When we reject others entirely without regard for their positive contributions, it confuses our constituents greatly."[3] Referring back to the introductory chapter of this book, even the "reformist" sectarian label no longer encompasses the degree of tolerance articulated in Hauer's Haredi Orthodoxy.

Hauer's novel outlook may be attributed in part to factors that have been cited in the course of this volume, in the introduction and especially in chapter 6. The first is the Haredi "triumphalism" that has arisen in light of the sharp contrast between the decline of liberal denominations and rising intermarriage, on the one hand, and the ongoing demographic and geographic expansion of Haredi Orthodoxy, growth of its institutions, and much higher retention rates, on the other. As Hauer noted, "This posture requires a sense of confidence and security, to the point that one is not fearful that any assistance to, or recognition of, the other would confuse or dilute one's own message."[4] The second consideration is economic. Haredi Orthodoxy recognizes that as its population and institutions grow, its financial burdens rise as well. In such a scenario, drawing on the infrastructure of the broader Jewish community becomes attractive if not imperative but also requires a taming of formerly bellicose rhetoric. Here too, Hauer's composition relates to this angle: "An Orthodox community preoccupied with building institutions of religious life and education such as schools and shuls may welcome the commitment of a local Federation to build agencies to provide much-needed social services."[5] The third issue is the overall atmosphere of postdenominationalism within American Jewish life. Fewer American Jews define their identity through a specific denomination, and among those who do, the distinctions between Orthodox synagogue life and that of other streams are clearer than ever. At the same time, there is growing recognition that many active Jews see no contradiction between maintaining membership in a non-Orthodox congregation while attending activities sponsored by Chabad or Haredi outreach

CONCLUSION

initiatives, for example. Indeed, there is a willingness of non-Orthodox frameworks to cooperate with these Orthodox bodies in order to provide positive portals of entry for as many Jews as possible. This decline in competition has lessened the need for the Orthodox to accentuate differences in ideology and practice.⁶

From the perspective of postdenominationalism, the fact that Hauer's comments were not made specifically in relation to outreach is of considerable consequence. For it buttresses the sense that the changes described in this book are not fleeting or peripheral, but are integrating into the normative social structure of Haredi life. The abandonment of the sectarian outlook that once characterized Haredi Orthodoxy may have been inspired by the outreach impulse, which still facilitates the most radical departures from prior stances. Yet Hauer's proposals offer that the new position is becoming sufficiently rooted—at least in some Haredi sectors—that it is no longer predicated purely on instrumental motivations.

This last point has considerable pragmatic implications. If the exclusive foundation for the revision in the Haredi stance is outreach, then were forces within Haredi Orthodoxy that support such activities to decline, this might cause a retreat from these changes. Indeed, the dominant role played by a few wealthy Orthodox benefactors in supporting the outreach movement illustrates the financial Achilles' heel of this enterprise. Were these individuals or families to lose interest or confidence in the value of outreach, it is uncertain whether much of its activity would be sustainable. Parallel with the massive expansion of Haredi outreach and internalization of its ethos, there have arisen multiple voices within this sector that question the high place it now occupies within the spectrum of Haredi priorities. When kollels, yeshivas, and day schools need to meet expanding enrollments, including so-called off the *derekh* kids, and multiple other social welfare and cultural challenges confront this community, some wonder why so much time, energy, and resources are invested in the weakly connected Jewish population.⁷ In fact, the precarious long-term stability of Orthodox outreach was also demonstrated by the alarmed reaction of prominent Haredi kiruv specialists to the results of the 2013 Pew Study of American Jewry. Rather than focusing triumphantly on the distinctions between the Orthodox position of strength and the testimony to non-Orthodox—especially Conservative—decline, outreach activists expressed exasperation at their own inability to curtail in significant ways the ongoing assimilatory trends among American Jews.⁸ Thus, Hauer's call for a core communal approach that sits somewhere between "working

CONCLUSION

together cooperatively" and "live-and-let-live" implies an alternative condition to an ongoing correlation between the decline in sectarianism and Haredi Orthodox focus on outreach to the non-Orthodox.

No doubt numerous caveats can be introduced to my analysis of Hauer's essay. For one, within the Haredi world, the Ner Israel yeshiva and the community that grew around it in Baltimore is perceived as more moderate than Haredi strongholds in New York, Lakewood, Cleveland, Chicago, Toronto, and Los Angeles. Furthermore, even if he is a well-respected figure in the Haredi community, Hauer is rabbi of a synagogue that is predominantly Haredi but includes Modern Orthodox congregants as well, and therefore he may refrain from putting forward the most rigorous Haredi positions.[9] That said, Ner Israel is still very much seen as part of the Haredi world and generally joins forces with the other yeshivas on core issues.[10] Indeed, as evidenced in this book, while Ner Israel may have been at the vanguard of new initiatives such as the community-outreach kollel, these activist models were soon adopted by Lakewood and other yeshivas and have established themselves within the consensus of the American Haredi outlook. Moreover, Rabbi Hauer's somewhat liminal position as a Haredi-oriented communal rabbi of a mixed constituency Orthodox synagogue actually strengthens the broader understanding of overall trends in American Orthodoxy put forward in this work. Namely, that the realignment of American Orthodoxy has entailed a "move to the right" of considerable elements with Modern Orthodoxy coupled with a decline in strict sectarianism within Haredi Orthodoxy. The result has been a blurring of the ideological, behavioral, cultural, and social boundaries that separated the two and the emergence of a more fluid Orthodox core, albeit with critical masses of outspoken ideological groups still occupying the margins on each side. Hauer's location at the convergence of the Haredi and Modern Orthodox lay populations suggests that his vision very much exemplifies the emerging realignment as well as its limitations.

This depiction of the Haredi and Modern Orthodox mainstreams coalescing around a broad-based consensus is supported by another aspect of Hauer's essay not addressed until this point. Along with his call for greater interaction with non-Orthodox Jewish individuals and groups, he also identifies certain factions with whom the Orthodox should forbid any interface:

> There may be situations where a movement is actually beyond the pale (Jews for J, for example), and should not be included in the community at all. In this regard an important distinction is to be made ... between developing and established movements. One may wish to oppose and

stand firm against the development of a movement that is diverting people away from the path of Torah, while being more helpful to an existing constituency that is already established on a different path. For example, including the founders of a new "partnership minyan" is not in the same category as working with the leadership of an existing, non-Orthodox community school.[11]

To be sure, no Orthodox factions—nor for that matter almost all Jewish groups of any orientation—would condone communal relationships with Jews for Jesus, but this is absolutely not the case regarding a "partnership minyan" (literally quorum but colloquially service). In a partnership minyan a partition separates the male and female participants, but both genders participate in leading the prayers and Torah recital. However, women only do so for those sections in which the halakhah does not specifically require a quorum of men or that a man performs the ceremonial act. This novel setting is a prime example of the efforts of Orthodox feminists to navigate between increasing female participation in public ritual and adherence to religious legal requirements. While the majority of Orthodox rabbis oppose such frameworks, they have received the imprimatur of well-regarded individual Orthodox rabbis and scholars.[12] The demonization of such initiatives through a loose parallel drawn with Jews for Jesus exemplifies what sociologists refer to as the functional model of deviance definition.[13] By asserting that both Jews for Jesus and partnership minyanim are "beyond the pale," Hauer sought to unite all those who oppose liberal Orthodox innovations as sharing in an authentic Orthodox identity.

The distinction that Hauer elucidates between relationships with "developing" versus "established" movements offers considerable insight regarding the current realignment of Orthodoxy and the ongoing role of denominational categories even in an increasingly postdenominational environment. For Hauer, at least, the battle against the Reform and Conservative movements is a thing of the past. While on a technical level their rabbis and institutions may espouse heretical ideas and promote non-halakhic approaches to Jewish practice, no one would mistake these ideas for Orthodox theology or normative Jewish law. The boundaries are clear, and therefore there is no need to harp on previous policies that were intended to clarify the differences between the movements. As such, the Orthodox could even reconceive non-Orthodox movements as neutral "infants taken captive" who were not to be held accountable for their transgressions—much the same as nineteenth-century rabbis redefined nonobservant individuals who lacked traditional education and whose deviations were not ideologically motivated.[14] The Haredi

Orthodox could go as far as engage the nonobservant within their non-Orthodox environments for the sake of strengthening Jewish identity.

Yet along with the end of competition with the Reform and Conservative movements and the strengthening of Haredi Orthodoxy, a new entity emerged from within Modern Orthodoxy that increasingly describes itself as "Open Orthodoxy."[15] Many of its leaders were educated in YU but are now officially connected to YCT or at least support the same types of innovations, such as female clergy and partnership minyanim. This American faction is also nourished by the numerous liberal institutions and thinkers that have sprouted within Israeli Religious-Zionism.[16] For the Haredi Orthodox, the "development" of the Open Orthodox stream must be dealt with completely differently than "established" denominations. Indeed, their reactions recall the diatribes of Rabbi Leopold (Yekutiel Yehudah) Greenwald aimed at his upstart "Modern Orthodox" neighbors and described in chapter 1. To a certain degree, Hauer's directives recall as well the attitudes of Greenwald's Hungarian predecessors toward the early Reform and Neologue movements.

The October 2013 installation event in honor of Rabbi Asher Lopatin's ascendancy to the presidency of YCT (at which representatives from the liberal denominations were invited to speak) coincided with a public call on his part for an inclusive approach within Orthodoxy, and inspired just such polemical expressions. Lopatin bemoaned the tendency toward "dividing up and tossing others outside of the tent" and appealed for the broad spectrum of American Orthodoxy to unite around common goals.[17] In response, Avi Shafran, the spokesman of Agudath Israel of America, published an article in the *Jewish Daily Forward* titled "'Open Orthodoxy' Is Not Really Orthodox at All." There, he specified the criteria for a Jewish religious group to be identified as "Orthodox" and why YCT does not meet them. In fact, he made clear that from his perspective YCT belongs elsewhere: "There already exists an 'open' movement that seeks to 'conserve' what it likes of the mesorah but to respect the Zeitgeist and embrace different approaches and practices from those of the Jewish past."[18] Following the outlook put forward in Hauer's blueprint for communal harmony, theoretically once YCT and the Open Orthodox would abandon claims of an "Orthodox" identity and join the Conservative movement, the Haredi Orthodox would no longer feel a necessity to assail them. Notwithstanding, Safran's comments illustrate that even if key Haredi Orthodox figures have a postdenominational approach to relations with the Conservatives and Reform themselves, these denominations still maintain their status as symbols of deviation from tradition that can be drawn upon for polemical ammunition during internal Orthodox controversies.

CONCLUSION

The Haredi campaign against liberal elements within American Orthodoxy communicated through Shafran's column received far greater publicity in May 2014, at the annual Agudath Israel of America dinner. During his address, Rabbi Yaakov Perlow, the president of the Council of Torah Sages and the same figure who in 1999 expressed appreciation for renewed Reform interest in traditional ritual and a desire to engage its constituencies (see chapter 6), rendered a blistering attack on "Open Orthodoxy." He proclaimed that its leaders and institutions were "steeped in *apikorsus* [heresy]" and that "There's a grave danger out there ... outside New York City, that positions of leadership amongst Orthodox Jews are being taken over by people who have completely deviated from [the preservation of holiness]." Perlow called upon the Modern Orthodox to "stand up and reject these new deviationists, cloaking themselves in the mantle of Orthodoxy."[19] From the perspective of YCT and its sympathizers, nothing could attest more clearly than the alarm sounded by Perlow to its own incremental inroads into mainstream Orthodox communal life—especially in communities beyond the greater metropolitan New York area that have been targeted by Haredi community kollels and Chabad houses, and where YU has had trouble finding willing candidates. Within the context of the thesis put forward in this book, moreover, Perlow's call on the Modern Orthodox to "stand and reject these deviationists" exemplifies a further intensification of the realignment and forging of a broad-based nucleus that includes mainstream representations of both what Liebman once referred to as "churchlike" Modern Orthodoxy and sectarian Orthodoxy.[20]

Similarly, as part of the process of outcasting the Open Orthodox, Agudath Israel spokesman Shafran offered a relatively broad list of who does fit into the Orthodox rubric that exemplifies the postsectarian realignment examined in this study: "An adherent of the late Lubavitcher Rebbe, a Satmar chassid, a 'Litvish' yeshiva graduate and a student of Yeshiva University's Rabbi Isaac Elchonon Theological Seminary are all unified by the essence of what the world has called Orthodoxy for generations. But 'Open Orthodoxy,' despite its name, has adulterated that essence, and sought to change both Jewish belief and Jewish praxis."[21] Taken in light of past Haredi attacks on both Chabad messianism and Yeshiva University, this is quite a historic document.

No less significant than Shafran's October 2013 publication is the fact that a day after his Haredi Orthodox invective against YCT appeared, a petition was publicized attacking YCT and those who identify with "Open Orthodoxy" that was signed by more than forty members of the RCA, most of them YU/RIETS graduates. The main point of the declaration is that rather than decrying those "Ultra-Orthodox" who are set on excluding them from Orthodoxy, Lopatin and his cohorts should recognize that they are to blame for adopting positions that "distance" themselves from "mainstream Orthodoxy." Although the letter leaves more room for Open Orthodoxy to mend its ways than both the Shafran document and the Perlow oral address, the bottom line of the RCA petition utilizes similar outcasting rhetoric to reach essentially the same conclusion: the Open Orthodox have "plunged ahead, again and again, across the border that divides Orthodoxy from neo-Conservatism."[22]

The "Modern Orthodox" identity of the RCA member petition is supported by the fact that it lists well-regarded YU/RIETS graduates who serve in banner institutions, including individuals with doctoral degrees in Jewish studies from distinguished Ivy League universities. Thus, it would be inaccurate to claim that it represents a "Haredi" fringe of YU. Although some of the signers, such as Rabbi Ilan Feldman of Atlanta and Rabbi Yitzchok Adlerstein of Los Angeles, are graduates of Haredi yeshivas like Ner Yisrael and Chofetz Chaim, quite a few fit into the "mainstream" Modern Orthodox category.

Early 2014 witnessed two additional controversies that illustrated the intensification of the internal Modern Orthodox divide and the narrowing of the gap between its more conservative elements and Haredi Orthodoxy. A dispute erupted in February 2014 in response to a letter penned by Rabbi Tully Harcsztark, the principal of the esteemed Modern Orthodox SAR High School in Riverdale, New York, to the institution's parent body regarding women wearing tefillin. He explained that, although school policy followed the Orthodox practice that only males don tefillin during morning prayer, two female students who had been putting on tefillin privately on a daily basis since their bat-mitzvahs had now requested to do so in school. He then listed the authorities upon which he based his positive response, and clarified that his permissive decision was for the specific students, and not a general recommendation. Shortly after, the Ramaz School issued its support for this position. Harcsztark is a highly respected YU/RIETS graduate and studied there with Rabbi Herschel Schachter, who has become the leading voice of the camp within YU that seeks to stymie the liberalizing elements (see chapter 5). Ramaz (as told in chapter 2), is the well-known Manhattan school sponsored by the Lookstein-led Kehilath Jeshurun, a congregation that has in the past turned to Schachter for halakhic guidance.[23]

Not coincidentally, Schachter subsequently came out with a strongly worded judgment that forbids women from wearing tefillin. Along with highlighting the literary sources for his opinion, his five-page discussion focuses on two points. First, that it should be clear to all that the approach to Jewish law reflected in such policies matched that adopted by the Conservative movement years before.

CONCLUSION

Second, apparently directing himself to Harcsztark and other YU/RIETS graduates who sympathize with the latter's approach, he declared that "even if his intentions are good, not every person with rabbinical ordination or a rabbi of a local synagogue should offer his [halakhic] opinion on such questions, and certainly he shouldn't publicise his private view in the press or on the Internet."[24]

Almost at the same time, on January 13, 2014, Rabbi Menachem Penner, the acting dean of RIETS, sent a disciplinary letter to a student named Shalom (no last name appears on the letter itself) who was to be awarded his rabbinical ordination less than two months later. From the content of the communication (and confirmed by later discussions of the episode), it transpires that the addressee had attended a "partnership minyan" at a private home at which women had been called to bless the Torah. Penner explained the seriousness of this act of deviance for someone who wanted the "stamp of approval" of YU/RIETS to rule on religious-legal matters according to accepted norms. He demanded that Shalom send a signed letter "affirming or denying your ability to agree to these principles."[25] When the exchange reached the Internet and the Jewish press, there were outcries on both sides. Some said that this demand of a "loyalty oath" was draconian, and was evidence of YU's "Haredization," while others—including Haredi spokesmen—applauded YU for drawing a clear line.[26] In response YU issued a statement that the main issue was not the one-time attendance at the partnership minyan but concern that the student had not internalized the fundamental approach of YU/RIETS to adjudication and authority. That said, the official announcement proceeded: "We are pleased to share that an agreement has been reached with the student reflective of his commitment to the principles of our institution stated above. The student will, with over 225 others, receive his ordination as part of a record class of graduates at our quadrennial Chag Hasemikhah celebration next month."[27]

Concurrent with Penner's letter, Schachter authored a nine-page Hebrew responsum that declared "partnership minyanim" to be unequivocally forbidden. The essay is predicated almost completely on the same arguments that he put forward in his rulings from 1983 and 1997 regarding women's prayer groups, and especially the English discussions of Orthodox feminism published in 2003 and 2004—and analyzed in detail in chapter 5—including his focus on comparisons to heretical groups of the past. Schachter states that not all Torah scholars have the authority to render decisions on sensitive areas of halakhah. He compares the process by which the "partnership minyanim" have received halakhic imprimatur to the permissive decisions regarding the initial changes to the synagogue service enacted by the Reform movement in early nineteenth-century Germany. Once again, he states that the motivation behind much of the contemporary initiatives is the sense that the rabbis have historically discriminated against women. Such claims, he warns, can be traced to the Sadducees who disputed the Sages' understanding of the Torah during the Second Temple period, and subsequently to the early Christians. In the last three pages he raises a number of specific legal reservations based on standards of female modesty and established ritual custom. Seemingly recognizing that in the end the main issue of dispute is not a specific technical issue but one of overall outlook, he concludes by citing his fundamental approach to women's prayer groups composed nearly forty years earlier: "Even if a specific act can in truth be permitted halakhically, once it becomes the symbol of breaking barriers and destruction of the religion, this embodiment [of deviance] itself makes it forbidden."[28]

Schachter's ruling was met with a flurry of responses, including a point-by-point rejoinder by Rabbi Ysoscher Katz, the head of the Talmud department at YCT.[29] One of the most detailed discussions was published by Yitzchok Adlerstein. In many ways, this essay may be considered a formal call for unification between the conservative segments of Modern Orthodoxy and Haredi Orthodoxy. His words, therefore, deserve to be cited directly:

> Rabbi Schachter's piece is a wonderful contribution. There are tens of thousands of Orthodox Jews in the Modern Orthodox world (and certainly in the Haredi world) who view the tearing down of all barriers by YCT and Open Orthodoxy with horror. However, they regard a simple recitation of *chadash assur min ha-Torah* (that which is new is biblically forbidden) as an insufficient answer, but they are open to listening to a presentation of where guidelines need to be drawn, and by whom. Rabbi Schachter's presentation ought to be a wonderful beginning. This will be more important in the long run than the existence or disappearance of partnership minyanim. It will not be enough to take Rabbi Schachter's formulation and use it to rally the troops. The challenge will be to take it and build upon it, at least to those who do not reject the idea of contemporary rabbinic authority. Before this essay, making the case for limitation was an issue of each Rabbi for himself. Rabbi Schachter's contribution could allow for a common platform upon which others can build and explain, if enough people react favorably and embrace it. It creates a simple (but not simplistic) image that can be shared by the entire community, excepting the outliers.[30]

CONCLUSION

What stands out is Adlerstein's description of a constituency that includes both Modern and Haredi Orthodox, and his emphasis on the "common platform ... shared by the entire community" who "do not reject the idea of rabbinic authority." To be sure, the call to the Modern Orthodox a few months later by the Agudah president Perlow to stand up against the changes of Open Orthodoxy reflects significant official Haredi acknowledgment of the religious integrity of YU figures. Nonetheless, Alderstein's campaign to create a common bloc comprising the conservative ranks of Modern Orthodoxy and Haredi Orthodoxy is farther reaching. It encourages a burgeoning partnership relationship that is the next step in the process observed and analyzed in this book.

The controversies surrounding YCT, Open Orthodoxy, and Orthodox feminism are expanding and accelerating the realignment of American Orthodoxy. If throughout most of this volume the move to the right of Modern Orthodoxy and the decline of Haredi sectarianism have been presented primarily as parallel but not interdependent phenomena that have reached a certain degree of confluence, the shared challenge of "Open Orthodoxy" has facilitated a more synchronized coordination. As Emile Durkheim explained in 1892, "the deviant act then, creates a sense of mutuality among the people of a community by supplying a focus for group feeling. Like a war, a flood, or some other emergency, deviance makes people more alert to the interests they share in common and draws attention to those values which constitute the 'collective conscience' of the community."[31]

Based on the strident positions shared by Agudath Israel and the RCA petitioners, it is not difficult to envision a day coming soon when YCT and its supporters will find themselves completely alienated from all of the other components of the Orthodox world including the majority of those who align themselves with YU. Such a scenario would conceivably push the "Open" contingent to form a new coalition with the growing trend toward nondenominationally affiliated synagogue communities that aim to be both fully egalitarian and halakhic.[32] The intellectual base for this burgeoning coalition is found in the egalitarian yeshiva Mechon Hadar, which is located in New York and is led by a group of learned products of the Conservative movement, one of whom has Orthodox rabbinical ordination from the Israeli chief rabbinate.[33] An indication of such a scenario is the joint lecture series titled "Why Learn Talmud?" that was held from late October through early November 2014. It was cosponsored by YCT, Yeshivat Maharat, Mechon Hadar, and the Drisha Institute for advanced Torah study for women.[34]

CONCLUSION

Alternatively, the future of Open Orthodoxy and for that matter a less Haredi-sympathetic Modern Orthodoxy altogether may be determined just as much by geographic and economic considerations than by clarifying theological beliefs and synagogue standards. Even if Haredi Orthodoxy has expanded its reach and language of discourse, it still remains concentrated geographically around a few locations in Brooklyn and Rockland County in New York, and Lakewood and Passaic in New Jersey, as well as smaller but considerable representations in Baltimore, Cleveland, Chicago, Toronto, and Los Angeles.[35] At the same time, an active and significant group of Orthodox Jews still exists that—regardless of whether they resonate with the ideals of Open Orthodoxy—sees cross-cultural interaction and secular education as part of an ideal.[36] Some of them live in neighborhoods with sizable Haredi populations and institutions. Others, however, can be found in Upper Manhattan, Riverdale, and Westchester, New York; Teaneck and Englewood, New Jersey; and Skokie, Illinois, and Silver Spring, Maryland. These communities continue to expand and offer vibrant and diverse opportunities for intellectual and spiritual enhancement. The families may likely send their children to study in a post–high school yeshiva in Israel. They will invest equal energy into gaining acceptance for their children into Columbia University, New York University, or the University of Pennsylvania, for example. At Penn they will be exposed to a rigorous academic education and attend any of the numerous Orthodox *minyanim* hosted by the OCP (Orthodox Community at Penn).[37] In addition, not only Haredi Orthodox communities and educational institutions are expanding. In New York, the forthrightly Modern Orthodox KJ community of Manhattan featured in chapter 2 continues to grow, and its coeducational Ramaz School is still oversubscribed.[38] So too is its more recent rival for the cream of the crop of Modern Orthodox youth, SAR in Riverdale. There, a postcollegiate beit midrash/kollel exists in which men and women are given generous stipends to study Talmud and Halakhah side by side five days per week.[39] For many of these Orthodox Jews, YU is their standard for a Modern Orthodox institution. Even if they do not necessarily approve of all the innovations associated with YCT and Open Orthodoxy, they may sympathize with some of its core ideals—especially those related to gender—and appreciate its place within the broad spectrum of American Orthodoxy.

Notwithstanding the realignment highlighted in this volume, then, at this juncture it is premature to declare that Modern Orthodoxy will disappear as a distinctive educational ideal and lifestyle. Indeed in the end Modern Orthodoxy's future may be primarily a function of its financial feasibility far more than its capacity to inspire ideological allegiance. According to the 2013 Pew Report, the Modern Orthodox have the highest per-capita income of all American Jewish sectors (37 percent earn over $150,000), have the largest percentage of college graduates (65 percent), and are the most attached to Israel (79 percent). Living within the Modern Orthodox community—joining its synagogues, educating children, sending them to camp, visiting Israel, and covering their college and graduate school tuitions—is an especially heavy economic burden. Were there to be a major financial upheaval, Modern Orthodox families and institutions would be particularly vulnerable to these changes.[40]

Returning to Charles Liebman's monumental 1965 study with which I began, not only was Liebman correct in his appraisal of rising Orthodox religious passion. He also envisaged that the Orthodox would increasingly seek to "nourish all the Jewish world."[41] What he could not foresee was that the crucial figures in the development of Orthodox outreach would be his "sectarian" Orthodox, and that in the process of engaging the broader American Jewish community, they themselves would undergo changes that would make their sectarian label obsolete.

Notes

Introduction

1. Marshal Sklare, *Conservative Judaism* (Glencoe, Ill.: Free Press, 1955), 43. Similarly, see Nathan Glazer, *American Judaism* (Chicago: University of Chicago Press, 1957), 142.
2. Charles S. Liebman, "Orthodoxy in American Jewish Life," *American Jewish Year Book* 66 (1965): 92.
3. On Liebman's rise to prominence, see, for example, Lawrence Grossman, "Charles S. Liebman, the Scholar and the Man," *American Jewish History* 80, no. 4 (1991): 465; Chaim I. Waxman, "An Ambivalent American Jewish Sociologist: The Perspectives of Charles S. Liebman," *American Jewish History* 80, no. 4 (1991): 494–95.
4. On emergent communitees, see Steven M. Cohen, J. Shawn Landres, Elie Kaunfer, and Michelle Shain, *Emergent Jewish Communities and Their Participants* (Van Nuys, Calif.: Synagogue 3000 and Mechon Hadar, 2007), www.synagogue3000.org/files/NatSpirComStudyReport_S3K_Hadar.pdf. On New Age approaches, see, for example, Jeffrey K. Salkin, "New Age Judaism," in *The Blackwell Companion to Judaism*, ed. Jacob Neusner and Alan J. Avery-Peck, 354–70 (Oxford: Blackwell, 2004).
5. Jonathan D. Sarna, *American Judaism: A History* (New Haven: Yale University Press, 2004), 272–355. See the provocative study of Barry A. Kosmin and Ariela Keysar, "American Jewish Secularism: Jewish Life beyond the Synagogue," *American Jewish Year Book 2012* (2013): 3–54.
6. *A Portrait of Jewish Americans: Findings from a Pew Research Center Survey of U.S. Jews* (Washington, D.C.: Pew Research Center, 2013), 51 (henceforth Pew 2013). The Pew study also details that more than 85 percent of American Jews are U.S. born. While the Orthodox numbers are not specified and may be lower, they are certainly much higher than among those studied by Liebman. See also the data on Orthodox growth in Jacob B. Ukeles, Ron Miller, and Pearl Beck, *Young Jewish Adults in the United States Today: Harbingers of the American Jewish Community of Tomorrow?* (New York: AJC, 2013); Ira M. Sheskin and Arnold Dashefsky, "Jewish Population in the United States, 2013," in *American Jewish Year Book* 113 (2013): 201–77. The latter highlights a 2012 study of Greater Metro West, New Jersey, that points to a measurable increase in Orthodox synagogue membership and a concurrent decrease among both Conservative and Reform institutions. The New York study demonstrates that since 2002 the Orthodox have remained 20 percent of the total population; this stands in sharp contrast to the major decreases among the other denominations that have lost considerable

numbers—especially among those under forty—to the "just Jewish" category. More dramatically, the number of Orthodox Jews has increased over a decade by 30 percent, from 378,000 to 493,000, a statistic that clearly points to further population expansion in the future. These studies can be accessed at www.jewishdatabank.org. For a provocative challenge to the Pew Study that highlights, among others, the lack of attention paid to Orthodox frameworks like Chabad that service nonobservant Jews, see Dovid Eliezrie, "Pew Asked the Wrong Questions," *Times of Israel*, October 17, 2013, http://blogs.timesofisrael.com/rescind-the-pew-r/.

7. For a general appreciation of the development of this theory, see William H. Swatos Jr., "Weber and Troeltsch? Methodology, Syndrome, and the Development of Church-Sect Theory," *Journal for the Scientific Study of Religion* 15, no. 2 (1976): 129–44.

8. Liebman, "Orthodoxy in American Jewish Life," 42–47.

9. The use of the term "Haredi Orthodoxy" is explained below.

10. On traditional, premodern Judaism and Orthodoxy, see, for example, Adam S. Ferziger, *Exclusion and Hierarchy: Orthodoxy, Nonobservance, and the Emergence of Modern Jewish Identity* (Philadelphia: University of Pennsylvania Press, 2005), 1–2; Jacob Katz, "Orthodoxy in Historical Perspective," in *Studies in Contemporary Jewry*, ed. Peter Medding, 2:3–17 (Bloomington: Indiana University Press, 1986); Charles S. Liebman, "Religion and the Chaos of Modernity," in *Take Judaism for Example*, ed. Jacob Neusner (Chicago: Chico, 1983), 148; Yosef Salmon, "Jacob Katz's Approach to Orthodoxy: The Eastern European Case," *Modern Judaism* 32, no. 2 (2012): 129–54; Moshe Samet, "The Beginnings of Orthodoxy," *Modern Judaism* 8 (1988): 249–69. For a critique of this methodological paradigm, see Avi Sagi, "Ha-Orthodoksiyah ke-ba'ayah," in *Ha-Orthodoksiyah ha-Yehudit: Hebetim Hadashim*, ed. Yoseph Salmon, Avi Ravitzky, and Adam S. Ferziger, 21–53 (Jerusalem: Magnes Press, 2006).

11. See the "Preamble to the Constitution of the United Synagogue (1913)," in *Tradition and Change: The Rise of the Conservative Movement*, ed. Mordecai Waxman (New York: Burning Bush Press, 1958), 173.

12. Charles S. Liebman, "Orthodox Judaism," in *The Encyclopedia of Religion*, ed. Mircea Eliade, 11:114–15 (New York: Macmillan, 1987). I am aware that individual Orthodox figures in both Israel and North America have recently expressed greater latitude regarding the parameters of these dogmas and the relative legitimacy of aspects of higher biblical criticism. These remain, nonetheless, minority opinions on the periphery of Orthodox consensus. See, for example: http://thetorah.com; http://kavvanah.wordpress.com/2013/08/19/interview-with-prof-jacob-wright-of-emory-university.

13. See Jeffrey S. Gurock, "Resisters and Accommodators: Varieties of Orthodox Rabbis in America, 1886–1983," *American Jewish Archives* 35, no. 2 (1983): 100–187 (reprinted in Jacob Rader Marcus and Abraham Peck, eds., *The American Rabbinate: A Century of Continuity and Change: 1883–1983*, 10–97 [Hoboken, N.J.: Ktav, 1985]); Samuel C. Heilman, "The Many Faces of Orthodoxy: Part 1," *Modern Judaism* 2, no. 1 (1982): 23–51; and Samuel C. Heilman, "The Many Faces of Orthodoxy: Part 2," *Modern Judaism* 2, no. 2 (1982): 171–98.

14. On these communities, see Yosef Kaplan, *An Alternative Path to Modernity: The Sephardi Diaspora in Western Europe* (Leiden: Brill, 2000).

15. David H. Ellenson, "A Jewish Legal Decision by Rabbi Bernard Illowy of New Orleans and Its Discussion in Nineteenth-Century Europe," *American Jewish History* 69, no. 2 (1979): 174–95; Jeffrey S. Gurock, *Orthodox Jews in America* (Bloomington: Indiana University Press, 2009), 21–47.
16. Sarna, *American Judaism*, 52–61.
17. Ibid., 375.
18. Hasia R. Diner, *The Jews of the United States, 1654–2000* (Berkeley: University of California Press, 2004), 82–88.
19. Michael A. Meyer, *Response to Modernity* (New York: Oxford University Press, 1988), 235–63.
20. Sarna, *American Judaism*, 128.
21. Ibid., 375.
22. Jeffrey S. Gurock, "Twentieth-Century American Orthodoxy's Era of Non-Observance (1900–1960)," *Torah U-Madda Journal* 9 (2000): 87–107.
23. Sarna, *American Judaism*, 184–93.
24. Gurock, *Orthodox Jews in America*, 109–99.
25. Samuel C. Heilman, *Sliding to the Right: The Contest for the Future of American Orthodoxy* (Berkeley: University of California Press, 2006), 4, 314n.9.
26. See, for example, Jonathan Nathan-Kazis, "Ultra-Orthodox Host Mega-Rally in U.S. for a More Kosher Internet," *Haaretz*, May 21, 2012, www.haaretz.com/jewish-world/jewish-world-news/ultra-orthodox-host-mega-rally-in-u-s-for-a-more-kosher-internet-1.431644.
27.. For a self-description that more accurately portrays the Mitnagedic sector, see Avi Shafran, "Statement from Agudath Israel of America," July 4, 2013, www.cross-currents.com/archives/2013/07/04/statement-from-agudath-israel-of-america/.
28. Yoel Finkelman, *Strictly Kosher Reading: Popular Literature and the Condition of Contemporary Orthodoxy* (Boston: Academic Studies Press, 2011), 23–25, divides American Orthodoxy into three camps: Hasidic, Haredi, and Modern Orthodox, with the former being the most sectarian in their worldview and social behavior.
29. Sarah Bunim Benor, *Becoming Frum: How Newcomers Learn the Language and Culture of Orthodox Judaism* (New Brunswick: Rutgers University Press, 2012), introduction.
30. S. Heilman, *Sliding to the Right*, 3 (see also 40–47).
31. Liebman, "Orthodoxy in American Jewish Life," 42–67. On the history of the Orthodox "day school movement," see Doniel Z. Kramer, *The Day Schools and Torah Umesorah: The Seeding of Traditional Judaism in America* (New York: Yeshiva University Press, 1984); Alvin I. Schiff, *The Jewish Day School in America* (New York: Jewish Education Committee Press, 1966).
32. Lawrence Grossman, "Decline and Fall: Thoughts on Religious-Zionism in America," in *Religious-Zionism Post-Disengagement: Future Directions*, ed. Chaim I. Waxman, 34–38 (New York: Yeshiva University Press, 2008).
33. Steven M. Cohen and Samuel C. Heilman, *Cosmopolitans and Parochials: Modern Orthodox Jews in America* (Chicago: University of Chicago Press, 1989).
34. Gurock, "Twentieth-Century American Orthodoxy's Era of Non-Observance."
35. Liebman, "Orthodoxy in American Jewish Life," 67–89.

NOTES TO INTRODUCTION

36. For a discussion of "constituency definition" as a central theme in the emergence of the Orthodox rabbinate in the nineteenth century, see Adam S. Ferziger, "Constituency Definition: The Orthodox Dilemma," in *Jewish Religious Leadership: Image and Reality*, ed. Jack Wertheimer, 2:535–67 (New York: JTS, 2005).
37. Liebman, "Orthodoxy in American Jewish Life," 42–89; see also Charles S. Liebman, "Left and Right in American Orthodoxy," *Judaism* 15, no. 1 (1966): 106–7.
38. Liebman, "Orthodoxy in American Jewish Life," 91; see also Charles S. Liebman, "Orthodox Judaism Today," *Midstream*, August/September, 1979, 19–26.
39. Pew 2013, 48.
40. Liebman himself returned to this theme in his *Deceptive Images: Toward a Redefinition of American Judaism* (New Brunswick, N.J.: Transaction Books, 1988), 25–42.
41. See Chaim I. Waxman, "From Institutional Decay to Primary Day: American Orthodox Jewry since World War II," *American Jewish History* 91 (2003): 415–18.
42. See, for example, S. Heilman, *Sliding to the Right*; Charles Selengut, "By Torah Alone: Yeshiva Fundamentalism in Jewish Life," in *Accounting for Fundamentalisms*, ed. Martin E. Marty and R. Scott Appleby, 236–63 (Chicago: University of Chicago Press, 1994); Haym Soloveitchik, "Rupture and Reconstruction: The Transformation of Contemporary Orthodoxy," *Tradition* 28, no. 4 (1994): 64–130 (reprinted in Roberta Rosenberg and Chaim I. Waxman, eds., *Jews in America: A Contemporary Reader*, 320–76 [Hanover, N.H.: University Press of New England, 1999]); Chaim I. Waxman, "The Haredization of American Orthodox Jewry," *Jerusalem Letter/Viewpoints*, Jerusalem Center for Public Affairs, February 15, 1998, www.bjpa.org/Publications/details.cfm?PublicationID=2373. Chaim I. Waxman and Joshua Turetsky subsequently raised questions regarding the characterization of this process as "Haredization." They suggest that while greater stringency is evident in some communities, the more significant development is a liberal countermovement that has recently arisen within Modern Orthodoxy. See Turetsky and Waxman, "Sliding to the Left? Contemporary American Modern Orthodoxy," *Modern Judaism* 31 (May 2011): 119–41. This rise of a new, self-consciously liberal group, which sometimes refers to itself as "Open Orthodoxy," will be discussed in chapter 7 and in the conclusion.
43. Samuel I. Freedman, *Jew vs. Jew: The Struggle for the Soul of American Jewry* (New York: Simon and Schuster, 2000), 224.
44. The Lander College for Men in Queens, New York, is a Touro College affiliate that promotes its ability to offer advanced Talmudical studies in a less heterogeneous environment than Yeshiva University. See http://lcm.touro.edu.
45. See Jeffrey S. Gurock, *Judaism's Encounter with American Sports* (Bloomington: Indiana University Press, 2005), 129.
46. Freedman, *Jew vs. Jew*, 224–25.
47. Liebman, "Orthodoxy in American Jewish Life," 59.
48. For a halakhic discussion that challenges this norm, see Leebie Mallin, "Separation Anxiety: Mechitzot at Weddings," *JOFA Journal* 4, no. 2 (2003), www.jofa.org/pdf/JofaSummer2003.pdf.
49. Even the wives of Modern Orthodox rabbis of the previous generation were not expected to cover their hair on a regular basis. See the collection of essays in Lynne

Schreiber, ed., *Hide and Seek: Jewish Women and Hair Covering* (Jerusalem: Urim Publications, 2003).
50. Liebman, "Orthodoxy in American Jewish Life," 42–89.
51. In 1974 "Orthodoxy in American Jewish Life" was reprinted with two other Liebman studies as a book under the title *Aspects of the Religious Behavior of American Jews* (New York: Ktav, 1974). In his introduction (xi) Liebman wrote that after reviewing the Orthodoxy article he did not feel any need to change his basic description. He did acknowledge (xii) that since moving to Israel he realized that the "sectarian Orthodox" had also gone through a process of Americanization, though in a subtler way. A broader critique of Liebman's use of sociological categories to support his understanding of American Orthodoxy appears in Norman B. Mirsky, "Categories and Ceremonies: The Rules of the Liebman Method," *American Jewish History* 80, no. 4 (1991): 479–90.
52. See *The Jewish Community Study of New York 2011: Geographic Profile* (New York: UJA/Federation, 2012), www.ujafedny.org/geographic-profile-report/.
53. Liebman noted, in "Orthodoxy in American Jewish Life," 79–82, that the Chabad Hasidic movement did not easily fit into either camp. On Chabad, see chapter 8.
54. On the growth of the Orthodox outreach movement, see M. Herbert Danzger, *Returning to Tradition: The Contemporary Revival of Orthodox Judaism* (New Haven: Yale University Press, 1989). Zev Eleff's history of the National Council for Synagogue Youth (NCSY), sponsored by the Orthodox Union (OU), offers a fine illustration of the transition in outreach. While most of the NCSY participants were from nonobservant homes, through the 1970s the core of the NCSY college-age advisors were observant Modern Orthodox students from Yeshiva University and other secular colleges. Although some of the Haredi yeshiva heads supported involvement, there was also much ambivalence regarding the organization's coeducational activities. Eventually, however, a strong contingent—and even the majority in some regions—stemmed from Haredi institutions. See Zev Eleff, *Living from Convention to Convention: A History of the NCSY, 1954–1980* (Jersey City, N.J.: Ktav, 2009), 44–45, 49–53, 73.
55. Two esteemed colleagues with whom I have been privileged to share in ongoing conversation for the past decade regarding these issues, Chaim I. Waxman and Jack Wertheimer, have published important studies that support my interpretation of the changes in Haredi Orthodoxy described in this work. See, for example, Chaim I. Waxman, "From Institutional Decay to Primary Day," 416–17; Chaim I. Waxman, "American Modern Orthodoxy: Confronting Cultural Challenges," *Edah Journal* 4, no. 1 (2004), www.bjpa.org/Publications/details.cfm?PublicationID=2024; Jack Wertheimer, "The Outreach Revolution," *Commentary*, April 2013, 20–26, www.commentarymagazine.com/article/the-outreach-revolution/.
56. Albert I. Baumgarten, *The Flourishing of Jewish Sects in the Maccabean Era: An Interpretation* (Leiden: Brill, 1997), 7.
57. Ibid., 13; Bryan Wilson, *Magic and the Millennium* (London: Heinemann, 1973), 18–26.
58. Of course there remain significant minorities that are dedicated to a thoroughly introversionist model. See, for example, David Myers, "Commanded War: Three Chapters

in the 'Military' History of Satmar Hasidism," *Journal of the American Academy of Religion* 81, no. 2 (2013): 311–56.

59. Beryl Wein highlighted this point in his "Ultra-Orthodoxy Isn't a Problem," *Jerusalem Post*, May 26, 2004, 1.

60. See a pamphlet regarding the ill effects of college campus life on Orthodox students that was circulated by two Orthodox graduate students from Harvard and MIT: Gil Perl and Yaakov Weinstein, *A Parent's Guide to Orthodox Assimilation on University Campuses*. A subsequent version published by Yaakov Weinstein appears on the Beyond Teshuva: Jewish Spiritual Growth website as "Orthodox Assimilation on Campus Part 1," February 22, 2007, www.beyondbt.com/2007/02/22/orthodox-assimilation-on-campus-part-1/ and "Orthodox Assimilation on Campus Part 2," March 15, 2007, www.beyondbt.com/2007/03/15/orthodox-assimilation-on-campus-part-2/. For some of the many reactions to the pamphlet, see, for example, Harvey Blitz, "Answering Orthodox Assimilation on Campus," *Jewish Action*, Summer 2003, www.ou.org/publications/ja/5763/5763summer; Shalom Berger (moderator), "Orthodox Assimilation on University Campuses," *Lookjed Archive*, May–July 2003, http://lookstein.org/lookjed/read.php?1,3011,3072; Alan Mittleman, "Fretful Orthodoxy," *First Things* 136 (October 2003): 23–26, www.firstthings.com/article/2007/01/fretful-orthodoxy-30; Julie Wiener, "Debauchery U.," *Jewish Week*, June 20, 2003, www.beliefnet.com/Faiths/Judaism/2003/06/Debauchery-U.aspx#.

61. See, for example, William B. Helmreich and Reuel Shinnar, "Modern Orthodoxy in America: Possibilities for a Movement under Siege," *Jerusalem Letter/Viewpoints*, June 1, 1998, http://jcpa.org/article/modern-orthodoxy-in-america-possibilities-for-a-movement-under-siege/; Jonathan Sacks, "Modern Orthodoxy in Crisis," *Le'eyla* 2, no. 17 (1984): 20–25; Edward S. Shapiro, "Modern Orthodoxy in Crisis: A Test Case," *Judaism* 51, no. 3 (2002): 347–61.

62. Pew 2013, 46, records that 65 percent of the Modern Orthodox reported being college graduates, as opposed to 25 percent of Haredi Orthodoxy. This statistic itself tells only part of the story, since many Haredi students gain their degrees through university online correspondence programs. This allows them to gain a fully recognized degree with minimal exposure to outside society and culture. See, for example, the popular program in communicative disorders at Utah State University, http://comd.usu.edu/htm/distance-education/online-bach/onlinebach-overview. See as well the comparisons between Haredi and Modern Orthodoxy presented in the chart titled "Essentials of Jewish Identity" found in Pew 2013, 57.

63. Pew 2013, 59, states: "96 percent of Modern Orthodox say a person can be Jewish and work on the Sabbath, far fewer Ultra-Orthodox Jews share this view (64 percent)." Although the National Jewish Population Studies (1960, 1970–71) of the past did not relate to such a question, nor for that matter did they differentiate between the two Orthodox sectors, it is reasonable to surmise that 64 percent is a rise from past Haredi attitudes. Nonetheless, it is still notably below the figure among the Modern Orthodox.

64. According to Pew 2013, 178, 60 percent of the Haredi (Ultra-Orthodox) collective is Hasidic. *The Jewish Community Study of New York 2011* puts the figure at 70 percent Hasidic.

65. Charles Liebman, "A Perspective on My Studies of American Jews," *American Jewish History* 80, no. 4 (1991): 530.

Chapter 1

1. Jacob Katz, "Religion as a Uniting and Dividing Force in Jewish History," *Jewish Emancipation and Self-Emancipation* (Philadelphia: Jewish Publication Society, 1986), 29.
2. See, for example, Ellenson, "A Jewish Legal Decision by Rabbi Bernard Illowy," 174–95; Gurock, *Orthodox Jews in America*, 54–55, 82–83; Moshe D. Sherman, "Bernard Illowy and Nineteenth-Century American Orthodoxy," PhD diss., Yeshiva University, 1991.
3. Rabbi Phillip Klein (1844–1907), who immigrated to the United States in 1890, is an exception, although he identified with the more moderate wing of Hungarian Orthodoxy. See Gurock, *Orthodox Jews in America*, 133–35; Kimmy Caplan, *Orthodoksiyah be-Olam Hadash* (Jerusalem: Merkaz Shazar, 2002). The Moravian-born Rabbi Leo Jung (1892–1987) studied in Hungarian yeshivas, but his upbringing was closer in outlook to the Neo-Orthodoxy promulgated by Rabbi Samson Raphael Hirsch. See Leo Jung, *The Path of a Pioneer: The Autobiography of Leo Jung* (London: Soncino Press, 1980), 1–37. Another Hungarian native, Rabbi Moses Weinberger (1854–1940), arrived in America in 1880 and had a tumultuous rabbinic career before turning to the matzah baking business. His literary descriptions of Jewish immigrant society have become a valuable primary source for this period. See Moses Weinberger, *People Walk on Their Heads: Moses Weinberger's Jews and Judaism in New York*, trans. and ed. Jonathan D. Sarna (New York: Holmes Meir Publishers, 1982). Rabbi Alexander Kohut was probably the most prominent Hungarian rabbi to immigrate to the United States in the late nineteenth century (he arrived in 1883). His scholarly renown and rabbinical stature enabled him to play a crucial role in the founding of the Jewish Theological Seminary of America (JTS) in 1886 as an alternative to the Reform-sponsored Hebrew Union College. Indeed, his premature death in 1893 likely exacerbated the fledgling institution's struggles during that period as well. In Hungary, however, Kohut was clearly identified with the Neolog movement, although in the United States he was most comfortable with moderate Orthodox figures such as his cofounder of JTS, Rabbi Sabato Morais. See, most recently, Howard Lupovitch, "Navigating Rough Waters: Alexander Kohut and the Hungarian Roots of Conservative Judaism," *AJS Review* 32, no. 1 (2008): 49–78.
4. Sarna, *American Judaism*, 296–98. On Satmar, see Norman Lamm, "The Ideology of the Neturei Karta: According to the Satmarer Version," *Tradition* 13 (1971): 38–53; Allan Nadler, "Piety and Politics: The Case of the Satmar Rebbe," *Judaism* 31, no. 2 (1982): 135–52; Allan Nadler, "The Riddle of Satmar," *Jewish Ideas Daily*, February 17, 2011, www.jewishideasdaily.com/content/module/2011/2/17/main-feature/1/the-riddle-of-the-satmar; Zvi Jonathan Kaplan, "Rabbi Joel Teitelbaum, Zionism, and Hungarian Ultra-Orthodoxy," *Modern Judaism* 24, no. 2 (2004): 165–78; Jerome R. Mintz, *Hasidic People: A Place in the New World* (Cambridge, Mass.: Harvard University Press, 1992); Myers, "Commanded War."
5. The process that led to the divide has been described with great erudition in Michael K. Silber, "Shorshei ha-Pilug be-Yahadut Hungariyah," PhD diss., Hebrew University

of Jerusalem, 1985. Also see Michael K. Silber, "The Historical Experience of German Jewry and Its Impact on Haskalah and Reforms in Hungary," in *Toward Modernity*, ed. Jacob Katz, 107–57 (New Brunswick, N.J.: Transaction Press, 1987).

6. On the Hungarian Jewish Congress and its repercussions, see Adam S. Ferziger, "The Hungarian Jewish Congress," in *YIVO Encyclopedia of the Jews in Eastern Europe*, ed. Gershon Hundert, 826–28 (New Haven: Yale University Press, 2008); Jacob Katz, *A House Divided: Orthodoxy and Schism in Nineteenth-Century Central Europe* (Hanover, N.H.: Brandeis University Press/University Press of New England, 1998), 89–215; Nathaniel Katzburg, "The Hungarian Jewish Congress of 1868–1869," in *Hungarian Jewish Studies*, ed. Randolph Braham, 2:1–34 (New York: World Federation of Hungarian Jews, 1969).

7. Some of the larger cities maintained Orthodox, Neolog, and Status Quo synagogues. On the Status Quo, see Y. Yosef Cohen, *Hakhmei Transylvaniyah* (Jerusalem: Machon Yerashalayim, 1989), 210–19; Y. Yosef Cohen, *Hakhmei Hungariyah* (Jerusalem: Machon Yerushalayim, 1997), 146–58; Yekutiel Yehudah Greenwald, *Le-Toldot ha-Reformazion be-Germanyah u-ve-Hungariyah* (Columbus, Ohio: L. Greenwald, 1948), 87–112; J. Katz, *A House Divided*, 204–14; Howard Lupovitch, "Between Orthodox and Judaism and Neology: The Origins of the Status Quo Movement," *Jewish Social Studies* 9, no. 2 (2003): 123–53.

8. On Hungarian Ultra-Orthodoxy, see Michael K. Silber, "The Emergence of Ultra-Orthodoxy: The Invention of a Tradition," in *The Uses of Tradition*, ed. Jack Wertheimer, 23–84 (New York: Jewish Theological Seminary of America, 1992). Also see Adam S. Ferziger, "Religious Zealotry and Religious Law: Reexamining Conflict and Coexistence," *Journal of Religion* (January 2004), 48–77; J. Katz, *A House Divided*, 56–85; Allan Nadler, "The War on Modernity of R. Hayyim Elazar Schapira of Munkacz," *Modern Judaism* 14, no. 3 (1994): 233–64.

9. See Adam S. Ferziger, "The Road Not Taken: Rabbi Salamon Zvi Schück and the Legacy of Hungarian Orthodoxy," *Hebrew Union College Annual* 79 (2011): 107–40.

10. See Mordechai Eliav, *Erez Yisrael ve-Yishuvah ba-Meah ha-19* (Jerusalem: Keter, 1978), 132–33, 161–66; Menachem Friedman, *Hevrah va-Dat* (Jerusalem: Yad Yitzhak Ben-Zvi, 1978), 1–32.

11. Hayyim Hirschenson, "Todah le-Mekhabdani," *Apiryon* 5 (Fall 1927): 87.

12. Yekutiel Yehudah Greenwald, "Mikhtav Galui," *Apiryon* 5 (1927/28): 282.

13. See Hayyim Hirschenson, *Hiddushei RaHa"H* 3 [halifat mikhtavim] (Jerusalem: Ha-Ivri, 1926), 23.

14. See Hayyim Hirschenson, *Malki ba-Kodesh* 4 (St. Louis: Moinester Printing, 1923), 56–57. The comments appear at the end of an extensive interchange with Rabbi Zvi Pessah Frank, the chief rabbi of Jerusalem, regarding the status of public Sabbath desecrators in contemporary times.

15. Greenwald, "Mikhtav Galui," 282–83.

16. Ibid., 283–84.

17. Hayyim Hirschenson, "Teshuvah giluyah le-mikhtav galuy," *Apiryon* 5 (1927/28): 309–15.

18. Ibid., 309–10.

NOTES TO CHAPTER 1

19. On the Agudath ha-Rabbanim, see Gurock, *Orthodox Jews in America*, 118–19, 135.
20. The most comprehensive account of Hirschenson and his worldview is David Zohar, *Mehuyavut Yehudit be-Olam Moderni: Ha-Rav Hirschenson ve-Yahaso el ha-Modernah* (Jerusalem: Shalom Hartman Institute and the Faculty of Law at Bar-Ilan University, 2003). See review essays: Adam S. Ferziger, "Ha-Zionut ha-Datit bat zemanenu ve-ha-heepuss ahar 'avar shimushi': Heker Ha-Rav Hayyim Hirschenson Ke-Mikre Mivhan," in *Yosef Da'at: Mekhkarim be-Historiyah Yehudit Modernit Mukdashim le-Professor Yoseph Salmon le-Hag Yovelo*, ed. Yoseph Goldstein, 261–75 (Be'er Sheva: Ben-Gurion University, 2011); Meir Roth, "Ha-Ish she-heekdeem et tekufato," *De'ot* 17 (2003): 31–34, 37; Marc Shapiro, "'Jewish Commitment in a Modern World: Rabbi Hayyim Hirschenson and His Attitude to Modernity' by David Zohar (Jer. 2003)," *Edah Journal* 5, no. 1 (2005), www.edah.org/coldfusion/backend/journalArticle/5_1_shapiro.pdf. Also see Ari Ackerman, "'Judging the Sinner Favorably': R. Hayyim Hirschensohn on the Need for Leniency in Halakhic Decision Making," *Modern Judaism* 22, no. 3 (2002): 261–80; Avi Sagi and Zvi Zohar, *Ma'agalei Zehut Yehudit ba-Sifrut ha-Hilkhatit* (Tel Aviv: Hakibbutz Hameuchad, 2000), 177–85; Eliezer Schweid, *Democratiyah ve-Halakhah: Pirkei Iyun be-Mishnato shel ha-Rav Hayyim Hirschenson* (Jerusalem: Magnes, 1978); Yossi Turner, "Samkhut ve-otonomiyah be-tefisato ha-hilkhatit shel ha-Rav Hayyim Hirschenson," in *Bein Samhut le-Otonomiyah be-Masoret Yisrael*, ed. Avi Sagi and Ze'ev Safrai, 181–95 (Tel Aviv: Ha-Kibbutz ha-Meuhad/Ne'emanei Torah va-Avodah, 1997); Yossi Turner, "Ma'amad mekorot Torat ha-hinukh ha-Yisraeli shel ha-Rav Hayyim Hirschenson," *Hagut be-Hinukh Yehudi* 2 (2000): 201–23; Yossi Turner, "'Koakh ha-zibbur' be-mishnato ha-datit Ziyonit shel ha-Rav Hayyim Hirschenson," in *Yahadut Pnim u-Huz—Dialogue bein Olamot*, ed. Avi Sagi, Dudi Schwarz, and Yedidia Stern, 31–57 (Jerusalem: Magnes, 2000); Yossi Turner, "Samkhut ha-am ve-samkhut ha-Torah be-tefisat ha-Medinah shel ha-Rav Hayyim Hirschenson," in *Dat u-Medinah ba-Hagut ha-Yehudit ba-Me'ah ha-Esrim*, ed. Avi Ravitzky, 193–219 (Jerusalem: Israel Democratic Institute, 2005).
21. The most detailed biographical essay on Greenwald, with an emphasis on his early years is Akiva Ben-Ezra, "Yekutiel Yehudah Greenwald," addendum to Yekutiel Yehudah Greenwald, *Ha-Shohet ve-ha-Shehitah ba-Sifrut ha-Rabbanut*, 185–92 (New York: Feldheim, 1955). For a list of Greenwald's main publications as well as biographical data, see Moshe D. Sherman, *Orthodox Judaism in America: A Biographical Dictionary and Sourcebook* (Westport, Conn.: Greenwood Press, 1996), 83–84, and the sources cited there. In addition, see Shmuel Miller, "Ha-Rav Yekutiel Yehudah Greenwald: ahad ha-olim," *Apiryon* 1 (Fall 1924): 312; Sid Z. Leiman, "Rabbi Leopold Greenwald: Tish'ah be-Av at the University of Leipzig," *Tradition* 25, no. 4 (1991): 103–6. On the unfortunate disposal of Greenwald's personal papers by his family after his passing, see the letter written by Marvin Fox in 1955 and reproduced by Marc Shapiro, "Some Assorted Comments and a Selection from My Memoir, Part 2," *The Seforim Blog*, November 1, 2009, http://seforim.blogspot.com/2009/11/some-assorted-comments-and-selection.html.
22. Marc Lee Raphael, *Jews and Judaism in a Midwestern Community: Columbus, Ohio, 1840–1975* (Columbus: Ohio Historical Society, 1979), 262–65.

23. See the ambivalent comments of Hirschenson's friend, the scholar and communal leader Judah David Eisenstein, in his biographical introduction to the volume dedicated to Hirschenson upon his seventieth birthday, *Apiryon* 5 (1927): 4–13 (reprinted in Judah David Eisenstein, *Ozar Zikhronotai* [New York: J. D. Eisenstein, 1930], 29–34).
24. His outward appearance conformed more to Westernized rabbinic norms than to the Hungarian traditionalist style. He wore a contemporary tie and jacket and sported a goatee rather than a full beard. See the photograph in the *Ohio Jewish Chronicle*, May 28, 1948, 4, www.ohiomemory.org/cdm/compoundobject/collection/ojc/id/12247/rec/4.
25. Raphael, *Jews and Judaism in a Midwestern Community*, 264, 313.
26. See, for example, Livia Bitton Jackson, "Zionism in Hungary: The First Twenty-Five Years," *Herzl Yearbook* 7 (1971): 285–320.
27. Ben-Ezra, "Yekutiel Yehudah Greenwald," 187; Leiman, "Rabbi Leopold Greenwald," 104. See Jacob Katz's detailed personal description of student life at the Pressburg yeshiva during the 1920s in his autobiography, *With My Own Eyes: The Autobiography of an Historian* (Hanover, N.H.: Brandeis University Press/University Press of New England, 1995), 49–61.
28. On Nobel, see Rachel Heuberger, "Orthodoxy and Reform: The Case of Rabbi Nehemiah Anton Nobel of Frankfurt a. Main," *Leo Baeck Institute Year Book* 37 (1992): 45–58.
29. Ben-Ezra, "Yekutiel Yehudah Greenwald"; Raphael, *Jews and Judaism in a Midwestern Community*, 262–63.
30. Greenwald, *Le-Toldot ha-Reformazion*, 16 n.36.
31. Raphael, *Jews and Judaism in a Midwestern Community*, 262–63.
32. Ibid., 263–64.
33. Nadler, "The War on Modernity of R. Hayyim Elazar Shapira," 239–42.
34. See Marvin Fox's letter in Shapiro, "Some Assorted Comments."
35. See Jonathan Sarna, "The Debate over Mixed Seating in the American Synagogue," in *The American Synagogue: A Sanctuary Transformed*, ed. Jack Wertheimer, 363–94 (Cambridge: Cambridge University Press, 1987).
36. It is noteworthy that while the *mehizah* undoubtedly attained the status of a central boundary maintenance symbol that distinguished between American Orthodox and Conservative synagogues, within the Midwest the hybrid "traditional synagogue"—which is led by an Orthodox rabbi and follows Orthodox ritual guidelines but allows mixed seating—has maintained a presence. See the discussion in Marc B. Shapiro, *Saul Lieberman and the Orthodox*, 14–15n.51 (Scranton: University of Scranton Press, 2006).
37. Raphael, *Jews and Judaism in a Midwestern Community*, 347–48. In 1969, under the leadership of Rabbi David Stavsky, Beth Jacob built a new synagogue building whose sanctuary once again was divided by a *mehizah*. See Kerry Olitzky, *The American Synagogue: A Historical Dictionary and Sourcebook* (Westport, Conn.: Greenwood, 1996), 289; David Stavsky, "A Mechitza for Columbus," *Jewish Life* 41, no. 1 (1974): 22–27.
38. Yekutiel Yehudah Greenwald, *Ozar Nehmad* (Columbus, n.p., 1942), 52.
39. Greenwald, "Mikhtav Galui," 286.

40. Ibid., 287.
41. See Robert Liberles, *Religious Conflict in a Social Context: The Resurgence of Orthodox Judaism in Frankfurt am Main, 1838–1877* (Westport, Conn.: Greenwood Press, 1985).
42. Greenwald, "Mikhtav Galui," 288.
43. Yekutiel Yehudah Greenwald, *Li-Felagot Yisrael be-Hungariyah* (Deva: Markovits and Friedmann, 1929), vii n.1.
44. See Yekutiel Yehudah Greenwald, *Korot ha-Torah ve-ha-Emunah be-Hungariyah* (Budapest: Katzburg, 1921).
45. Greenwald noted that he gleaned much of his initial perspective regarding the Congress of 1868–69 from his father, who was at the time of the event a student of one of the leading Orthodox figures, the Ketav Sofer (Rabbi Abraham Shmuel Binyamin Sofer) of Pressburg.
46. Greenwald, *Korot ha-Torah ve-ha-Emunah be-Hungariyah*, vi.
47. Greenwald, *Le-Toldot ha-Reformazion*.
48. Greenwald's *Le-Toldot ha-Reformazion* is subtitled *Ha-Maharam Shick u-venei Doro*—Maharam Schick and His Generation. For Schick's heroic "Purim" version of the events, see Moses Schick, *She'elot u-Teshuvot Maharam Schick: Orah Hayyim* (Munkacs: Bleier, 1880), 103a–103b [entry #309] (henceforth, Maharam Schick, OH). On this responsum, see Louis Jacobs, *Theology in the Responsa* (London: Routledge, 1975), 232–34; Jacob Katz, "Sources of Orthodox Trends," in his *The Role of Religion in Modern Jewish History* (Boston: Association of Jewish Studies, 1975), 33.
49. For an example of a figure who initially supported the Orthodox policies during and after the Congress but evolved into a vocal internal critic, see Ferziger, "The Road Not Taken."
50. Greenwald, "Mikhtav galui," 287.
51. See Jeffrey S. Gurock, "An Orthodox Conspiracy Theory: The Travis Family, Bernard Revel, and the Jewish Theological Seminary," *Modern Judaism* 19, no. 3 (1999): 241–53.
52. See Jeffrey S. Gurock and Jacob J. Schacter, *A Modern Heretic and a Traditional Community: Mordecai M. Kaplan, Orthodoxy and American Judaism* (New York: Columbia University Press, 1997).
53. By 1929 the JTS-affiliated United Synagogue organization had 229 member congregations. See Gurock, *Orthodox Jews in America*, 158.
54. The Orthodox Union (OU) was founded in the late nineteenth century and was led initially by figures affiliated with JTS. By the second decade of the twentieth century, and especially after the establishment of the United Synagogue in 1913, the JTS contingency declined, and graduates of more squarely Orthodox institutions asserted their leadership, though as late as the 1940s, JTS graduates could still be found serving in OU-affiliated synagogues. On the liminal boundaries between the Orthodox and Conservative streams during the first half of the twentieth century, see the materials gathered in Jeffrey S. Gurock, "From Fluidity to Rigidity: The Religious Worlds of Conservative and Orthodox Jews in Twentieth-Century America," David W. Belin Lecture in American Jewish Affairs, University of Michigan (2000) (reprinted in *American Jewish Identity Politics*, ed. Deborah Dash Moore, 159–206 [Ann Arbor: University of Michigan Press, 2008]).
55. Raphael, *Jews and Judaism in a Midwestern Community*, 174–76.

56. See, for example, Silber, "The Emergence of Ultra-Orthodoxy," 67; Ferziger, "The Road Not Taken," 129–30.
57. Greenwald, *Li-Felagot Yisrael be-Hungariyah*, vii–viii.
58. Ibid., viii.
59. For details on Werne's education and scholarly and public endeavors, see Julius Schwartz and Solomon Kaye, eds., "Isaac Werne," *Who's Who in American Jewry 1926* (New York: Jewish Biographical Bureau, 1927), 644.
60. Raphael, *Jews and Judaism in a Midwestern Community*, 176.
61. Ibid.
62. See the extensive discussion in Gurock, *Orthodox Jews in America*, 157–62.
63. Greenwald, *Li-Felagot Yisrael be-Hungariyah*, viii. The term "half-Reform" may refer to Conservative.
64. Ibid.
65. See Schwartz and Kaye, "Isaac Werne," 644. Werne studied in the yeshivas in Slonim, Vilna, and Warsaw, and was ordained by Rabbi Shmuel Zangwill Klapfish, the head of Warsaw's rabbinical court.
66. Comment of Rabbi Hayyim Sofer that appears in a letter of Rabbi Hillel Lichtenstein, *Responsa Beit Hillel* (Satu-Mare: Z. Schwartz Publishers, 1908), entry 13.
67. See Samuel C. Heilman's typological study, "The Many Faces of Orthodoxy, Part 1," 30: "Others [syncretists] sought to create a new form of Judaism—something that brought together the various worlds, values and practices they considered valuable. These latter represented the most ambitious among the modern Orthodox."
68. Yekutiel Yehudah Greenwald, *Ah le-Zarah* (St. Louis: Quality Printing, 1939).
69. Yekutiel Yehudah Greenwald, *Kol Bo al Aveilut* (New York: Moria Printing, 1947).
70. See Jeremy Stolow, *Orthodox by Design: Judaism, Print Politics, and the Art Scroll Revolution* (Berkeley: University of California Press, 2010). Similar volumes that were produced previously by immigrant rabbis generally focused on recording the accepted customs in Europe. On such works, see Yosef Goldman, *Hebrew Printing in America, 1735–1926* (New York: YG Books, 2006).
71. Greenwald, *Ah le-Zarah*, 6–7. The mention of leniencies regarding Jewish marital law likely refers to debates raging at the time over the initiative of Rabbi Louis Epstein, a JTS alumnus and halakhic scholar, to promote a new solution to the problem of the *agunah* (anchored wife) who is prevented from remarrying because her husband refuses to issue a divorce writ, or due to incertitude regarding whether her husband is alive. See Sarna, *American Judaism*, 240; Shapiro, *Saul Lieberman and the Orthodox*, 11–13.
72. Raphael, *Jews and Judaism in a Midwestern Community*, 260–62.
73. Marc Lee Raphael, "Interview with Rabbi Samuel Rubinstein," *Columbus Jewish History Society—Oral History Project*, May 10, 1974, http://columbusjewishhistory.org/?post_type=oral_histories&p=416.
74. See "Rabbi Solomon Breuer, Leader of German Orthodoxy, Dies," *JTA*, July 21, 1926, http://archive.jta.org/article/1926/07/21/2762611/rabbi-solomon-breuer-leader-of-german-orthodoxy-dies. For a discussion as late as 1960, see Simon Noveck, "Editor's Introduction: Emergence of Modern Orthodoxy," in his *Great Jewish Personalities in Modern Times* (Clinton, Mass.: Bnai Brith, 1960), 61–68. In the biographical article on Hirsch in

Noveck's volume, Edward W. Jelenko, "Samson Raphael Hirsch," 94, the author merely notes the extension of the Hirschian approach among his German descendants who settled in New York City's Washington Heights. See also Zev Eleff, "American Orthodoxy's Lukewarm Embrace of the Hirschian Legacy," *Tradition* 45, no. 3 (2012): 35–53.

75. I have not examined every example of the use of the term "Modern Orthodox" in the early twentieth century but through searches on the JTA website (www.jta.org/search), NYTimes.com, and Google books (books.google.com), I have compiled a good deal of material. I thank my colleagues Jonathan Sarna and Alan Brill for suggesting these digital avenues for addressing this subject. In a chapter titled "Modern Orthodoxy," for the book he is preparing on the varieties of Jewish Orthodoxies over the past two centuries, Alan Brill explores in detail the various uses of the designation "modern Orthodox." In addition to its application to German neo-Orthodoxy and the early American Conservative movement, he notes its introduction in the 1892 description by British Reform spokesman Claude Montefiore of those affiliated with London's Jews College. Brill shares my appraisal that the the association of "Modern Orthodox" (often with a capitalized M) with a unique American religious substream is for the most part—Greenwald being a notable exception—a post–World War II phenomenon. I thank Professor Brill for sharing his work with me before its publication.

76. See, for example, Joseph Silverman, "Up-to-Date Judaism: The Religion of the Reformed Jews," *New York Times*, May 15, 1910. See also the description of the famed union organizer and Jewish institutional leader Joseph Barondess, "Achievements and Failings of Borough Park Jews," *Jewish Forum* 7, no. 4 (April 1924): 243–44, who writes of "the half-Reform," the so-called Modern Orthodox. In the following paragraph, by contrast, he describes the "Ultra-Orthodox" and notes that the most progressive synagogue within this category is the "Congregation Young Israel."

77. Of course, Greenwald always remained vehemently opposed to Reform Judaism and at times attacked it head-on. His main focus, however, was not on undermining Reform—which he appraised as already too strong and organized to be undone—but on clarifying Orthodoxy loyalty. See, for example, the introduction to his work *Ozar Nehmad*, 7–13, in which he details his concern regarding the many successes of the Reform as well as the Conservatives. Nonetheless, he is most frustrated with those who claim to be Orthodox but are willing to cooperate with non-Orthodox colleagues and even enter their sanctuaries. In this case he does not use the term "Modern Orthodox," but the description is consistent with his prior admonitions and his Hungarian emphasis on the "holiness" of the name Orthodox: "Whoever believes in Orthodoxy is forbidden to tolerate crossing boundaries or allowing them to disintegrate.... [W]eren't we warned by the lights of the Diaspora over one hundred years ago about the strict rules preventing contact between us and them?" (10).

78. See, for example, Robert Gordis, *Conservative Judaism: A Modern Approach to Jewish Tradition* (New York: National Academy for Adult Jewish Studies, 1956), 10: "Conservatism exerts a potent influence upon the other wings of Jewish religious thought, as recent trends within modern Orthodoxy and contemporary Reform abundantly demonstrate"; Marshall Sklare, *The Jews: Social Patterns of an American Group*, 388–92 (Glencoe, Ill.: Free Press, 1958).

79. See Charles S. Liebman, "A Sociological Analysis of Contemporary Orthodoxy," *Judaism* 13, no. 3 (1964): 300–303; Liebman, "Orthodoxy in American Jewish Life"; Sklare, *The Jews*, 388–92.
80. See the discussion of the conflicts within the Modern Orthodox camp from the 1990s regarding the degree of compromise to American realities and how this is reflected in the term "Modern Orthodox" in S. Heilman, *Sliding to the Right*, 96–101. The now defunct Edah organization (www.edah.org) coined the slogan, "The courage to be modern and Orthodox." See also Marc Angel, "Are We 'Modern' or 'Centrist' or 'Open'... Who Are We?" website of the Institute for Jewish Ideals and Ideas, March 2009, www.jewishideas.org/blog/are-we-modern-or-centrist-or-open-orwho-are-we.
81. See, for example, Nisson Wolpin, "Orthodoxy's Move to the Right: Grappling with the Helmreich Principle," *Jewish Observer* 30, no. 1 (1997): 19–24. Indeed, during the 1980s some within the Modern Orthodox camp were so taken aback by the negative religious connotations that had become associated with the appellation of their group that they suggested renaming their movement "Centrist Orthodoxy." See Norman Lamm, "Centrist Orthodoxy: Judaism and Moderationism, Definitions and Desideratum," in *Orthodoxy Confronts Modernity*, ed. Jonathan Sacks, 48–61 (Hoboken, N.J.: Ktav, 1991); Walter S. Wurtzburger, "Centrist Orthodoxy: Ideology or Atmosphere?" in *Covenantal Imperatives: Essays by Walter S. Wurzburger on Jewish Law, Thought and Community*, ed. Eliezer L. Jacobs and Shalom Carmy, 212–19 (Jerusalem: Urim, 2008).
82. Hirschenson, *Malki ba-Kodesh* 4, 56–57.
83. On Sonnenfeld, see Hillel Danziger, *Guardian of Jerusalem: The Life and Times of Yosef Chaim Sonnenfeld* (New York: Mesorah Publications, 1983). The former is a condensed English version of Shlomoh Zalman Sonnenfeld, *Ha-Ish al-ha-Homah*, 3 vols. (Jerusalem: n.p., 1971). Also see Menahem Mendel Gorlitz, *Mara de-Ara de-Yisrael* (Jerusalem: Y. M. Sofer, 2003).
84. Sonnenfeld is one of the central protagonists in Menachem Friedman's now classic analysis of pre-State non-Zionist Jewry in the Land of Israel, *Hevrah ve-Dat: Ha-Orthodoksiyah ha-lo Zionit be-Erez Yisrael* (Jerusalem: Yad Yitzhak Ben-Zvi, 1978).
85. Hirschenson, "Teshuvah Geluyah le-Mikhtav Galuy," 311.
86. Ibid., 310.
87. Ibid., 312.
88. Ibid., 313. The reference is to the well-known rabbinic homily in Vayikra Rabba 32:5 that asserts that the Children of Israel were worthy of redemption because throughout their Egyptian exile they did not change, among other things, their names.
89. *Sefer ha-Yovel shel Agudath ha-Rabbanim ha-Orthodoksim de-Arzot ha-Berith: Le-Mele'at Esrim ve-Hamesh Shanim le-Hivasdah [5662–5687]* (New York: Ariam Press, 1927/28), 51–52.
90. Sarna, *American Judaism*, 193.

Chapter 2

1. Joseph Lookstein, "Memorandum to Haskel Lookstein," October 3, 1968, KJ Archive.
2. Jeffrey Gurock and Jenna Joselit have both published important historical studies with particular focus on KJ. See Jeffrey S. Gurock, "The Ramaz Version of American

Orthodoxy," in *Ramaz: School, Community, Scholarship and Orthodoxy*, ed. Jeffrey S. Gurock, 40–82 (Hoboken, N.J.: Ktav, 1989); Jeffrey S. Gurock, "The Orthodox Synagogue," in *The American Synagogue: A Sanctuary Transformed*, ed. Jack Wertheimer, 37–84 (Cambridge: Cambridge University Press, 1987); Jenna Weissman Joselit, *New York's Jewish Jews: The Orthodox Community in the Interwar Years* (Bloomington: Indiana University Press, 1990); Jenna Weissman Joselit, "Of Manners, Morals, and Orthodox Judaism: Decorum within the Orthodox Synagogue," in Gurock, *Ramaz: School, Community, Scholarship and Orthodoxy*, 20–39; Jenna Weissman Joselit, "The Special Sphere of the Middle-Class American Jewish Woman: The Synagogue Sisterhood, 1890–1940," in *The American Synagogue: A Sanctuary Transformed*, ed. Jack Wertheimer, 219–21 (Cambridge: Cambridge University Press, 1987).

3. For biographical information on Margolies, see *Kehilath Jeshurun Bulletin: Special Memorial Issue for the Fiftieth Yahrzeit of Rabbi Moses Zevulun Margolies* (Summer 1986); Joseph H. Lookstein, "Rabbi Moses Zebulun Margolies: High Priest of Kehilath Jeshurun," in *Congregation Kehilath Jeshurun, Diamond Jubilee Yearbook*, 1946, 48–51; Gurock, "Resisters and Accommodators"; Gurock and Schacter, *A Modern Heretic and a Traditional Community*, 49–51; Joselit, *New York's Jewish Jews*, 64–66; *Encyclopaedia Judaica* (Jerusalem: Keter, 1971–72), 959; "Biographical Sketches of Rabbis and Cantors Officiating in the United States," *American Jewish Yearbook* 5 (1903–4): 77–78, 79; Sherman, *Orthodox Judaism in America*, 143–44. Ramaz's Boston years are described in relative detail in Samuel Nathaniel Behrman, *The Worcester Account* (New York: Chandler House Press, 1954), 14–16, 71, 104–5, 136–39. Among the notable points is the fact that Margolies arrived in the United States in 1886, but after a short period he returned to Eastern Europe. Only in 1889, after feeling the wrath of his Eastern European colleagues for leaving the first time, did he permanently emigrate.

4. Kimmy Caplan, "Ha-Rav Yitzhak Margaliyot: Mi-Mizrah Eiropah le-Amerika," *Zion* 58, no. 2 (1993): 215–40, argues that anyone who left Eastern Europe despite the warnings of many leading rabbinical figures against emigration to the *treife medina* (United States, the "un-kosher state") had to have been inspired by positive reasons. Those who saw America in wholly negative terms would generally stay put in Eastern Europe, even with the financial hardships and physical dangers. That said, once they landed at the New York harbor, they generally adopted the position of defenders of the faith against the influences of American society. Gurock, "Resisters and Accomodators," 30, describes Margolies, along with two other immigrant rabbis, Philip Hillel Klein and Bernard Levinthal, as "highly influential pre–World War I Orthodox leaders who simply did not fit the mold of the transplanted Eastern European rabbi."

5. The original name of the synagogue was Anshe Jeshurun. See "Milestones in the History of Kehilath Jeshurun," in *Congregation Kehilath Jeschurun Diamond Jubilee Yearbook*, 1946, 58; Joselit, *New York's Jewish Jews*, 29.

6. See Jeffrey Gurock's discussion of the membership of KJ at the turn of the century in "The Emergence of the American Synagogue," in *The American Jewish Experience*, ed. Jonathan D. Sarna, 219–34 (New York: Holmes and Meier, 1997); Gurock and Schacter, *A Modern Heretic and a Traditional Community*, 38–42.

7. The dominant ethnic group in Yorkville consisted of people of German origin; see Joselit, *New York's Jewish Jews*, 12; Stanley Nadel, *Little Germany: Ethnicity, Religion, and Class in New York City, 1845–1880* (Urbana: University of Illinois Press, 1990), 161–62. For a description within contemporary fiction of the German atmosphere of Yorkville, see Michael Chabon, *The Amazing Adventures of Kavalier and Clay* (London: Harper-Collins/Fourth Estate, 2000), 197–205.
8. Joselit, *New York's Jewish Jews*, 9.
9. On Kaplan's career at KJ, see Gurock and Schacter, *A Modern Heretic and a Traditional Community*, 31–54. On page 50, the working relationship between Ramaz and Kaplan is described: "Indeed, Ramaz was more sympathetic than some of Kehilath Jeshurun's lay leaders toward the modifications in procedure and ritual that Kaplan defended as permissible within Orthodox teaching. In fact, the minister and the rabbi worked well together as public advocates of American Orthodoxy and humanitarian causes in general, even as Kaplan was privately drifting further and further away from his faith in the tradition that spawned them both." Jacob J. Schacter, "Mordecai M. Kaplan's Orthodox Ordination," *American Jewish Archives* 46, no. 2 (1994): 1–11; Mel Scult, "Controversial Beginnings: Kaplan's First Congregation," *The Reconstructionist*, July–August 1985, 21–26.
10. It is possible that Margolies was hired by KJ due to pressure exerted on the more traditional members of the congregation by the "Ridbaz," Jacob David Willowski, a prominent Eastern European rabbi who spoke out vehemently against the institution of English-language sermons in Orthodox synagogues. Willowski even succeeded in procuring an invitation to deliver the sermons instead of Kaplan at the KJ Rosh Hashanah (Jewish New Year) services in 1904. This was seen as an affront to Kaplan and the many congregants who wanted English-language sermons and caused a minor controversy within New York Jewish circles during the fall of that year. On Willowski, see Aaron Rothkoff, "The American Sojourns of Ridbaz: Religious Problems within the Immigrant Community," *Proceedings of the American Jewish Historical Society* 57, no. 4 (1968): 557–72; Abraham J. Karp, "The Ridwas: Rabbi Jacob David Wilowsky, 1845–1913," in *Perspectives on Jews and Judaism: Essays in Honor of Wolfe Kelman*, ed. Arthur A. Chiel, 215–39 (New York: Rabbinical Assembly, 1978); *Encyclopaedia Judaica* (Jerusalem: Keter, 1972), 16:518–19; Bezalel Landau, "Ridbaz," in *Shu"t ha-Ridbaz*, Ridbaz, 5–34 (Jerusalem: Mossad ha-Rav Kook, 1995); Sherman, *Orthodox Judaism in America*, 217–19; Caplan, "Ha-Rav Yitzhak Margaliyot," 71–72. For discussions of Willowski's involvement with KJ, see Joselit, *New York's Jewish Jews*, 29–31; Gurock and Schacter, *A Modern Heretic and a Traditional Community*, 47–50.
11. Joselit, "Of Manners, Morals, and Orthodox Judaism"; Joselit, *New York's Jewish Jews*, 25–53; Gurock, "Resisters and Accomodators," 89 n.98.
12. Joseph H. Lookstein, "A Rabbi of the Old School," *Kehilath Jeshurun Bulletin: Special Memorial Edition in Memory of Rabbi Moses Zevulun Margolies upon His Fiftieth Yahrzeit*, Summer 1986, 10.
13. Ibid. See also Rafael Medoff, *Rav Chesed: The Life and Times of Rabbi Haskel Lookstein*, ed. Rafael Medoff (Jersey City, N.J.: Ktav, 2008), 390–91.

14. See Joshua Hoffman, "The Changing Attitude of Rabbi Gavriel Zev Margolis toward RIETS," *The Commentator*, December 22, 2004, http://admin2.collegepublisher.com/preview/mobile/2.2469/2.2843/1.299300; Jonathan Krasner, "The Rise and Fall of the Progressive Talmud Torah: The Central Jewish Institute and Interwar American Jewish Identity," in *Rav Chesed: Essays in Honor of Rabbi Dr. Haskel Lookstein*, ed. Rafael Medoff, 411–68 (Jersey City, N.J.: Ktav, 2009).
15. *Congregation Kehilath Jeschurun Diamond Jubilee Yearbook*, 1946, 59. On Magnes, see Norman Bentwich, *For Zion's Sake: A Biography of Judah L. Magnes, First Chancellor and First President of the Hebrew University of Jerusalem* (Philadelphia: Jewish Publication Society, 1954); William M. Brinner and Moses Rischin, *Like All the Nations? The Life and Legacy of Judah L. Magnes* (Albany: State University of New York Press, 1987). On Margolies's connection to Zionism as well as that of other members of the Agudath ha-Rabbanim, see the extensive note in Gurock, "Resisters and Accomodators," 76n21; Jeffrey S. Gurock, "Ha-Irgunim ha-Orthodoksim be-Amerika ve-temikhatam ba-Zionut, 1880–1930," in *Zionut ve-Dat*, ed. Shmuel Almong, Judah Reinharz and Anita Shapira, 263–85 (Jerusalem: Merkaz Shazar, 1994). According to Haskel Lookstein, Interview with Rabbi Haskel Lookstein on July 19, 1995 (henceforth Interview HL), until meeting Margolies, Joseph Lookstein was an Agudist (member of Agudath Israel).
16. Gurock, "Resisters and Accomodators," 30–34.
17. Gurock, *Orthodox Jews in America*, 135.
18. See S. Heilman, "The Many Faces of Orthodoxy: Part 1," 23–31. According to Heilman's typology, Margolies would be characterized as a "tolerator" or "transitional-tolerator," while Joseph Lookstein would be considered a highly active "syncretist."
19. See Joselit, *New York's Jewish Jews*, 13–14, where she suggests that Joseph Lookstein was hired because by the 1920s synagogue attendance was dwindling as the population of KJ was aging, and they hoped that "his personality would serve to draw a more youthful element." Joselit points out that this tactic was successful. Whereas in 1921 barely 200 people attended the Sabbath morning service in a sanctuary built to hold 1,000, by 1946 there were more than 650 regular seat holders. Joseph Lookstein, who supervised every detail of KJ (see later discussion), was particularly captivated by the issue of synagogue attendance. In fact, Haskel Lookstein pointed out that throughout his youth he was the official counter (Interview HL). This entailed tallying the total number of Sabbath morning attendees, as well as how many of each gender. At the conclusion of the Sabbath, he would fill out an index card with these statistics as well as the weather or any other factor that might have influenced the figures. Joseph Lookstein's penchant for details is described in Joselit, *New York's Jewish Jews*, 65.
20. Full disclosure: this author is a graduate of the Ramaz Upper School. For biographical information on Joseph Lookstein, see Bernard Schientag, "Rabbi Joseph H. Lookstein: A Character Study by a Congregant," in *Congregation Kehilath Jeschurun Diamond Jubilee Yearbook*, 53–57 (1946); *Kehilath Jeshurun Bulletin: Special Memorial Issue for Rabbi Joseph H. Lookstein*, Fall 1979, www.ckj.org/docs/Rabbi%20Joseph%20Lookstein%20Memorial.pdf; Gurock, "Resisters and Accomodators," 46–49; Joselit, *New York's Jewish Jews*, 64–72; *Encyclopaedia Judaica*, 487–88; Joseph H. Lookstein,

"God Owes Me Nothing," typescript, New York; Sherman, *Orthodox Judaism in America*, 139–41.
21. J. Lookstein, "Memorandum to Haskel Lookstein."
22. The particular issue that gave impetus to this memo was Haskel Lookstein's "apologetic" remarks regarding KJ's deemphasis of the *avodah* (sacrificial service of the High Priest) in its Yom Kippur service. Joseph Lookstein was piqued by the fact that "you [Haskel Lookstein] made some veiled reference to the 'spirit of the times' and, therefore, you suggested that a compromise be made."
23. A variation on the Yiddish slang "khinyuk," a pejorative reference to someone who is unnecessarily strict in his or her observance.
24. For Joseph Lookstein's view of Conservative Judaism, see "A Critique and a Plea," *Judaism* 26, no. 3 (1977): 390–95.
25. J. Lookstein, "Memorandum to Haskel Lookstein."
26. See Joselit, "Of Manners, Morals, and Orthodox Judaism," 20–39; Joselit, *New York's Jewish Jews*, 25–53.
27. This was not necessarily the case throughout the history of the American Orthodox synagogue. See Gurock, "The Orthodox Synagogue," 37–39. Indeed, the 1903 bylaws of KJ itself state that only a Jew "who properly observes the Jewish Sabbath and is not married contrary to the Jewish law shall be eligible for membership in this congregation," "Article Two: Membership," By-Laws of the Congregation Kehilath Jeshurun, 1903, 3–4 (cited in Joselit, *New York's Jewish Jews*, 28). The ineligibility of intermarried Jews for KJ membership was maintained in practice during Joseph Lookstein's career (Interview HL). On Joseph Lookstein's dependence on the ideas or at least slogans of Hirsch, see Joselit, *New York's Jewish Jews*, 22–23. The most glaring example is his adoption of the declaration in *Mishnah* Tractate *Avot* 2:2: "yafeh Talmud Torah im derekh erez"—which was interpreted as "it is good to integrate Torah study with the ways [culture] of the land"—as the motto of the Ramaz School. Joselit claims that there was little originality in the thinking of Lookstein and some of his "pathbreaking" interwar peers. While Lookstein certainly could look to Hirsch for his synthetic conception of the ideal Orthodox Jew, Lookstein's "Americanization" of Orthodox Judaism went beyond Hirsch's example. Hirsch's articulation was limited to "high German culture." Lookstein, on the other hand, encouraged a broader involvement in American life. An outstanding example is his initiation of a Thanksgiving Service in 1939, in which special prayers for Thanksgiving were inculcated into the regular Thursday prayer service. Lookstein sought to show that for a Jew, being a good American meant being a good Jew and vice versa, in the same way as an American Christian made the connection between his country and his religion. In so doing he expressed a particular formulation of an American Jewish civil religion. On Hirsch's ideal Jew, see Noah H. Rosenbloom, *Tradition in an Age of Reform* (Philadelphia: Jewish Publication Society, 1976), 351–52; Mordechai Breuer, *Modernity within Tradition* (New York: Columbia University Press, 1992), 27; Isidor Grunfeld, *Horeb* (London: Soncino Press, 1962), 271–72. On the KJ Thanksgiving service, see "Milestones in the History of Kehilath Jeshurun," 60; https://kavvanah.files.wordpress.com/2014/11/thanksgiving-service-at-kj-1940-edited.pdf. See

Gurock's discussion of Joseph Lookstein's synthesis of Orthodoxy and American culture regarding the KJ-sponsored Ramaz School in Gurock, "The Ramaz Version of American Orthodoxy," 47–48. On Judaism and civil religion in the United States, see Jonathan S. Woocher, *Civil Judaism in the United States* (Jerusalem: Center for Jewish Communal Studies, 1978); Jonathan S. Woocher, *Sacred Survival* (Bloomington: Indiana University Press, 1986); S. Daniel Breslauer, *Judaism and Civil Religion* (Atlanta: Rowman and Littlefield, 1993).

28. *Kehilath Jeshurun Bulletin, Rosh Hashona*, 1936/5697, cover page; Joseph H. Lookstein, "A Religious Definition of Beauty," transcript of radio broadcast, *United Jewish Layman's Committee: Message of Israel*, American Broadcasting Company, December 18, 1949, 1.
29. Lawrence Grossman, "American Orthodoxy in the 1950s: The Lean Years," *Rav Chesed*, 259–60.
30. Cited in Gurock, *Orthodox Jews in America*, 165.
31. Interview HL; Steve Lipman, "Kehilath Jeshurun's Old Look, New Materials," *Jewish Week*, July 17, 2012, www.thejewishweek.com/news/new-york-news/kehillat-jeshuruns-old-look-new-materials.
32. For a detailed biography of Haskel Lookstein, see Medoff, *Rav Chesed*, 367–523. On Schachter, see chapter 5.
33. Ibid.; Gurock, "The Ramaz Version of American Orthodoxy," 45–46, 76.
34. On Lookstein's activism for Soviet Jewry, see Medoff, *Rav Chesed*, 423–70.
35. It should be noted that the Orthodox presence in the Upper East Side became significantly more visible in the 1990s. Within a three-block radius of KJ there are now a few kosher restaurants and a Jewish bookstore with the full range of classical Jewish texts in stock. Moreover, a large number of young families who in the past would have migrated to the suburbs have chosen to establish their permanent homes in KJ territory. This phenomenon is, no doubt, partially a function of economic capability. Yet central to it has also been Lookstein's recognition of the needs of this highly educated and generally more observant young Orthodox population.
36. Medoff, *Rav Chesed*, 417.
37. See the website titled "How to Daven as A Ba'al Tefillah," http://ramaz.org/nusach/, which contains Haskel Lookstein's recordings of KJ's traditional liturgical tunes as taught to him by the cantors of the synagogue as well as his father.
38. Interview HL. See also Medoff, *Rav Chesed*, 414.
39. Shaul Stampfer, *Lithuanian Yeshivas of the Nineteenth Century: Creating a Tradition of Learning* (London: Littman Library, 2012), describes how the battle over which of Reb Hayyim Volozhin's offspring would succeed as the head of the yeshiva in 1853 really came down to a decision as to who would control the finances of the yeshiva. In addition, according to Stampfer, Rabbi Hayyim Soloveitchik of Brisk was not chosen as the heir in Volozhin to his grandfather-in-law, the *Neziv*, Rabbi Naftali Zvi Yehudah Berlin, because he lacked skills and experience in financial management.
40. See David Assaf, *The Regal Way: The Life and Times of Rabbi Israel of Ruzhin* (Stanford: Stanford University Press, 2002), chap. 2; Mendel Piekarz, *Hasidut Polin* (Jerusalem: Mossad Bialik, 1990), 190–95.

41. Joseph Lookstein's rabbinate combined two aspects that Stavridis considered necessary for the ideal leader: "charisma" and "administrative" ability. See James G. Stavridis, "Closing the Gaps in Naval Leadership," *Proceedings of the U.S. Naval Institute*, July 1982, 76–78. For a similar dichotomy between what he termed "leadership" and "management," see Carl E. Welte, "Management and Leadership: Concepts with an Important Difference," *Personnel Journal* 11 (1990): 57.
42. Interview HL: "There is no such thing in our synagogue as someone coming into office whom my father would not have approved of or whom I am not happy to have.... It's not that I pick every trustee or officer but it's just understood. Nobody picks them without considering my opinion."
43. Ibid.: "I don't remember fights in our shul. My father ran the shul.... There's a certain tradition in the congregation now that my father I think started that has tremendous reverence for the rabbi.... He attended every single board meeting, he ran the board meeting. The President ran the board meeting but my father prepared the whole agenda—he set up everything and everything was prepared in advance. The board meetings in the congregation are basically extremely boring." See, by contrast, the description of the usual dynamic between the rabbi and the lay leadership in Menachem Friedman, "The Changing Role of the Community Rabbinate," *Jerusalem Quarterly* 25 (Fall 1982): 90: "The almost total dependence of the rabbi on the president of the synagogue and the members of the board . . . may be a source of great frustration."
44. Interview HL.
45. See Daniel Elazar and Rena Geffen Monson, "The Evolving Roles of American Congregational Rabbis," *Modern Judaism* 2, no. 1 (1982): 73–89.
46. Haskel Lookstein, "Memorandum to Mr. Joseph Glatt, Mr. Israel D. Rosenberg and Mrs. Lillian Finkelberg," February 29, 1968, KJ Archives.
47. Ibid.
48. Joseph H. Lookstein, "Memorandum to Rabbi Haskel Lookstein, Mr. Joseph Glatt, Mr. Israel D. Rosenberg and Mrs. Lillian Finkelberg," March 1, 1968, KJ Archives.
49. Interview HL.
50. Joselit, *New York's Jewish Jews*, 65.
51. Ibid.
52. Ibid.
53. Micha Popper, *Al Menahalim ke-Manhigim* (Tel Aviv: Ramot, 1994), 12, describes how the previously held notion known as the "normative" theory of leadership has been dispelled. This approach presented the manager as a conductor of an orchestra whose ultimate goal was to enable his musicians to play without him. Since the 1970s it has been commonly acknowledged that successful management in reality entails a much higher degree of personal involvement on a regular basis than that recommended by the "normative" school. On the "normative" approach and its weaknesses, see Henry Mintzberg, *The Nature of Managerial Work* (New York: HarperCollins, 1973); Henry Mintzberg, "The Manager's Job: Folklore and Facts," *Harvard Business Review*, July–August 1975, 53.
54. This term has long been in use by both members and outsiders as interchangeable with the name KJ.

55. Stampfer, *Lithuanian Yeshivas of the Nineteenth Century*, 40–42, describes the revolutionary approach of Reb Hayyim Volozhin to fundraising, in which he sat at the head of a pyramid of professional fundraisers who represented him in various regions of Europe. When it came to wealthy individuals, it was generally Reb Hayyim who personally asked for their support.
56. Haskel Lookstein pointed out to me that the shul went through some financially difficult times during the Depression and subsequent years. In fact, there was a period of three years when Joseph Lookstein's assistant rabbi salary was not paid. According to the younger Lookstein, "I think the shul got on a sound financial basis through my father's fundraising ability" (Interview HL).
57. Interview HL.
58. Joseph Berger, "Blaze Shatters a Heart of New York Jewish Life," *New York Times*, July 12, 2011, www.nytimes.com/2011/07/13/nyregion/blaze-shatters-a-heart-of-new-york-jewish-life.html.
59. Lipman, "Kehilath Jeshurun's Old Look, New Materials."
60. Gurock, "The Ramaz Version of American Orthodoxy," 41–42.
61. Interview HL; J. Lookstein, "God Owes Me Nothing," 68; Joselit, *New York's Jewish Jews*, 133.
62. Medoff, *Rav Chesed*, 371.
63. In his autobiography, Joseph Lookstein described his commitment to found Ramaz despite the community's objections ("God Owes Me Nothing," 51): he told the KJ board, "If you will not help me to start the school I will have to go elsewhere where I can get help." On the same page he described Max Etra's early support. See also Haskel Lookstein, "To Kehilath Jeshurun with Love," *Ramaz School: Forty-Eighth Annual Dinner Dance Sponsored by the Parents Council, January 13, 1985* (1985): 3, as quoted in Gurock, "The Ramaz Version of American Orthodoxy," 41.
64. Gurock, "The Ramaz Version of American Orthodoxy," 54; Joselit, *New York's Jewish Jews*, 141.
65. Gurock, *Orthodox Jews in America*, 200.
66. Another Orthodox rabbinical family in the United States that has handed over succession to the third or fourth generation is the Teitzes of Elizabeth, New Jersey. Here as well, the rabbinate entails leadership of both a synagogue and a community-sponsored day school. While this rabbinical family deserves further exploration, it would appear that the Teitz rabbinate initially was much closer to the European communal model, in which there is one chief rabbi who is expected to supervise all aspects of religious life for the community. On the Teitz rabbinate in Elizabeth, New Jersey, see Rivka Teitz Blau, *Learn Torah, Love Torah, Live Torah: Harav Mordechai Pinchas Teitz* (Hoboken, N.J.: Ktav, 2001); Rabbi Yaakov M. Dombroff, "An Appreciation of Rabbi Mordechai Pinchas Teitz zz"l," *Jewish Observer* 29 (Tammuz 5756/June 1996): 18–26.
67. Stampfer, *Lithuanian Yeshivas of the Nineteenth Century*, 41; Friedman, "The Changing Role of the Community Rabbinate," 85: "The great yeshiva of the Volozhin type was different. It was not a community yeshiva, but was established on the initiative of the head of the yeshiva and supported by people from near and far. The monies were received directly by the head of the yeshiva, in his name.... Thus the head had almost

total and exclusive authority in the yeshiva, not only in academic matters but in questions of finances, staff and the like."
68. See Haskel Lookstein, "Words of Eulogy," *Kehilath Jeshurun Bulletin: Special Memorial Issue in Memory of Rabbi Joseph Lookstein*, Fall 1979, 6: "No matter how far my father traveled or how high he went in the Jewish community, Kehilath Jeshurun was his home base." One focus of outside involvement shared by Margolies and both Looksteins is YU. While Margolies and the elder Lookstein were directly involved in the running of the institution, Haskel Lookstein has focused almost exclusively on training young rabbis in his position as holder of the Joseph H. Lookstein Chair in Homiletics. Regarding this position he commented, in Interview HL: "It's one of the things in which I feel that I carry on his tradition."
69. While Haskel Lookstein is adamant that his father did not speak to him about inheriting the position until he was far along in his rabbinical studies, he did mention an anecdote that indicates that his father always harbored the hope that he would join him. In the main sanctuary of KJ there are two seats for the rabbis, one on each side of the ark. When Margolies was alive, he and Joseph Lookstein occupied these chairs. After Margolies died, his seat remained empty. None of the assistant rabbis or rabbinical assistants who served under Joseph Lookstein was permitted to sit in Margolies's place—until Joseph's son Haskel was appointed assistant rabbi in 1958. When queried by congregants, Joseph Lookstein would quote the words of the blessing recited upon completion of the reading of the portion from the Prophets (*haftarah*) which refers to the Davidic dynasty, "*al kiso lo yeshev zar*" (on his seat, a stranger—i.e., not of the davidic line—shall not sit). According to Joseph Lookstein, "God Owes Me Nothing," 42, even Margolies, who died when Haskel was three years old, had hoped that the child would someday become a rabbi. Margolies affectionately referred to baby Haskel (who was named after Hatzkel Lifshitz, the rabbi of Kalish, Poland, who officiated with Margolies at Joseph Lookstein's wedding and died the week of Haskel's birth) as "Reb Hatzkel." According to Joseph Lookstein, "a name to my grandfather was no mere label. It was a holy symbol, a tribute to someone past, *a hope and an augury for a bearer's future*" (my emphasis). One senses from his autobiography that Joseph Lookstein gave much thought to the issue of succession and inheritance; the work contains broad discussions of the transition from Margolies to himself and then from himself to his son (91–95, 119–26). Moreover, he relates that his master's thesis in sociology, written for Columbia University, was on the subject of "primogeniture in Jewish law and society" (19).
70. The relative ease with which he succeeded in achieving this goal demonstrates the degree to which he had established his authority in the community. See Saemy Jaephet, "The Secession from the Frankfort Community under Samson Raphael Hirsch," *Historia Judaica* 10 (1948): 123–34, where he asserts that Samson Raphael Hirsch's loss of popularity in the IRG community in Frankfurt a. m. despite having built the community over the course of more than twenty-five years was partially due to the fact that he tried to make sure that his son-in-law would inherit his position.
71. "Regular Meeting, Board of Trustees," May 19, 1958, KJ Archives.
72. Ibid.

73. Ibid.; Medoff, *Rav Chesed*, 383–84.
74. Charles S. Liebman, "Temurot be-manhigut ruhanit shel Yehudei Arzot ha-Berit," in *Manhigut Ruhanit be-Yisrael*, ed. Ella Belfer, 171 (Ramat-Gan: Bar-Ilan, 1982).
75. Stampfer, *Lithuanian Yeshivas of the Nineteenth Century*, 61, tells of a son of Reb Yitzhak of Volozhin, the son and successor of Reb Hayyim, who did not receive a position in the yeshiva for lack of objective qualifications; similarly, see Assaf's discussion of the Rizhin Hasidic dynasty, *The Regal Way*, 113.
76. Liebman, "Temurot."
77. www.jcareersrabbinics.org/job-category/pulpit/.

Chapter 3

1. "Refusenik" is the popular term that was used to describe Soviet citizens, particularly Jews, who were denied the right to emigrate. See Louis Rapoport, "The Refuseniks," in *Encyclopaedia Judaica Year Book, 1988/89* (Jerusalem: Keter, 1990), 76–83.
2. Interview HL. On this trip in detail, see Medoff, *Rav Chesed*, 428–35.
3. The term "American Jewish establishment" is itself open to interpretation. Generally this refers to the major organizations and their leaders who served as the quasi-official representatives of American Jewry in public life throughout much of the twentieth century. Until the 1970s they rarely had an Orthodox figure at their helms. Most of these bodies are members of the Conference of Presidents of Major American Jewish Organizations that was set up as an umbrella group in 1953. See J. J. Goldberg, *Jewish Power: Inside the American Jewish Establishment* (Reading, Mass.: Addison-Wesley, 1996); Arthur Goren, *The Politics and Public Culture of American Jews* (Bloomington: Indiana University Press, 1999), 110–31; Alan Mittleman, Jonathan D. Sarna, and Robert Licht, eds., *Jewish Polity and American Civil Society* (Lanham, Md.: Rowman and Littlefield, 2002).
4. In his unpublished memoir, Rabbi Avi Weiss, the activist and former chairman of the Student Struggle for Soviet Jewry, describes the decision in the late 1970s to reinvigorate the American campaign for Soviet Jewry by focusing on the Shcharansky case. See Avraham Weiss, "Avi," chap. 7: "With Avital and Anatoly," unpublished memoir, 1–4.
5. Some may point to the December 1987 Washington rally attended by more than 250,000 people as an alternative event for marking the conclusion of the movement. For the most comprehensive work to date on the efforts to revive Soviet Jewry and facilitate emigration, see Gal Beckerman, *When They Come for Us, We'll Be Gone: The Epic Struggle to Save Soviet Jewry* (New York: Houghton, Mifflin, and Harcourt, 2010). Other principal critical studies and collections on the American Soviet Jewry movement include Stuart Altshuler, *From Exodus to Freedom: The History of the Soviet Jewry Movement* (Lanham, Md.: Rowman and Littlefield, 2005); Marc E. Frey, "Challenging the World's Conscience: The Soviet Jewry Movement, American Political Culture, and U.S. Foreign Policy, 1952–1967," PhD diss., Temple University, 2002; Murray Friedman and Albert D. Chernin, eds., *A Second Exodus: The American Movement to Free Soviet Jews* (Hanover, N.H.: Brandeis University Press, 1999); Andrew Harrison, *Passover Revisited: Philadelphia's Efforts to Aid Soviet Jews, 1963–1998* (Cranbury, N.J.: Associated University Presses, 2001); Fred Lazin, *The Struggle for Soviet Jewry in American Politics:*

Israel versus the American Establishment (Lanham, Md.: Lexington Books, 2005); William W. Orbach, *The American Movement to Aid Soviet Jews* (Amherst: University of Massachusetts Press, 1979); Yaakov Ro'i, *The Struggle for Soviet Jewish Emigration (1948–1967)* (Cambridge: Cambridge University Press, 1991).

6. A recent exception is the fine study by Shaul Kelner, "Ritualized Protest and Redemptive Politics: Cultural Consequences of the American Mobilization to Free Soviet Jewry," *Jewish Social Studies* 14, no. 3 (2008): 1–37. In Sarna's brief treatment of the topic, *American Judaism*, 317–18, he directs attention to the role of Soviet Jewry in "religious action programming" of the 1970s and 1980s. Eli Lederhendler and Charles Liebman also highlight the significance of the central role played by the Orthodox in the Soviet Jewry movement. See Eli Lederhendler, *New York Jews and the Decline of Urban Ethnicity, 1950–1970* (Syracuse: Syracuse University Press, 2001), 188; Liebman, "Orthodoxy in American Jewish Life," 92.

7. Orbach, *The American Movement to Aid Soviet Jews*, 19; Ro'i, *The Struggle for Soviet Jewish Emigration*, 91, 97.

8. See Sue Fishkoff, *The Rebbe's Army: Inside the World of Chabad Lubavitch* (New York: Schocken, 2003), 68, 143; Zusha Wolf, ed., *Diedushka: Ha-Rebbe mi-Lubavitch ve-Yahadut Russiyah* (Kfar Chabad: Yad ha-Hamishah, 2006), 36–112.

9. Lazin, *The Struggle for Soviet Jewry in American Politics*, 23–28; Ro'i, *The Struggle for Soviet Jewish Emigration*, 101–5, 115–16.

10. For detailed descriptions of the trip, see Louis Bernstein, *Challenge and Mission: The Emergence of the English Speaking Orthodox Rabbinate* (New York: Shengold Publishers, 1982), 167–78.

11. Unlike most scholars, Frey ("Challenging the World's Conscience," x, 28) dates the beginnings of the Soviet Jewry movement to various responses of American Jewry to the plight of Soviet Jewry beginning in 1952.

12. See Moshe Decter, "The Status of Jews in the Soviet Union," *Foreign Affairs* 41, no. 2 (1963): 3–13. There was actually one public rally for Soviet Jewry held on April 12, 1962, to protest the denial of matzah distribution before Passover—both locally baked and shipped from abroad—by the Soviet authorities. The demonstration took place at the Soviet Mission in Manhattan and was organized and led by Orthodox students of the Yeshiva University High School (MTA). See Orbach, *The American Movement to Aid Soviet Jews*, 18.

13. On the AJCSJ, see Frey, "Challenging the World's Conscience," 77–80; Lazin, *The Struggle for Soviet Jewry in American Politics*, 28–30; Orbach, *The American Movement to Aid Soviet Jews*, 24–27; Ro'i, *The Struggle for Soviet Jewish Emigration*, 193–202.

14. Ro'i, *The Struggle for Soviet Jewish Emigration*, 240–41. On Miller as chairman of the AJCSJ and later chairman of the Conference of Presidents of Major Jewish Organizations, see Frey, "Challenging the World's Conscience," 94–94, 117, 121; Orbach, *The American Movement to Aid Soviet Jews*, 30, 33, 72; Ro'i, *The Struggle for Soviet Jewish Emigration*, 201, 211, 219, 400 n.292.

15. Elie Wiesel, *The Jews of Silence* (New York: Holt, Rinehart and Winston, 1966). It appeared originally in Hebrew as a series of articles in the Israeli daily *Yediot Aharonot*.

16. Orbach, *The American Movement to Aid Soviet Jews*, 27. In 1966 Rabbi Dr. Irving "Yitz" Greenberg, then full-time rabbi at the Orthodox Riverdale Jewish Center, professor of history at Yeshiva University, and vice chairman of the Student Struggle for Soviet Jewry (SSSJ), decided to take a partial sabbatical from his rabbinical duties in order to raise funds for the Soviet Jewry movement. He and Mel Stein created the Center for Soviet Jewry and set out to convince the Jewish establishment of the need to lend significant financial support to this endeavor. The response to their appeals was very weak. Greenberg, who later championed the role of an Orthodox rabbi with great standing among broader American Jewry, recalls commenting at the time, "Now I know why the Shoah happened, due to the apathy of the American establishment." Interview with Rabbi Dr. Irving "Yitz" Greenberg, Jerusalem, June 10, 2006.
17. On the rise of grassroots organizations, see Altshuler, *From Exodus to Freedom*; Harrison, *Passover Revisited*; Douglas Kahn, "Advocacy on a Communal Level," in *A Second Exodus: The American Movement to Free Soviet Jews*, ed. Murray Friedman and Albert D. Chernin, 181–99 (Hanover, N.H.: Brandeis University Press, 1999); Micah Naftalin, "The Activist Movement," in *A Second Exodus: The American Movement to Free Soviet Jews*, ed. Murray Friedman and Albert D. Chernin, 224–42 (Hanover, N.H.: Brandeis University Press, 1999); Ro'i, *The Struggle for Soviet Jewish Emigration*, 206–12; Walter Ruby, "The Role of Nonestablishment Groups," in Friedman and Chernin, *A Second Exodus*, 200–223.
18. On the Leningrad trials and their influence on the movement, see Friedman and Chernin, *A Second Exodus*, 116, 173, 233; Orbach, *The American Movement to Aid Soviet Jews*, 52–58.
19. Telephone interview with Malcolm Hoenlein, May 26, 2006. See also "Selections from 120 letters received for the commemoration of Jacob Birnbaum's 40 years of service to the Jewish people," typescript.
20. "Selections from 120 letters." See also Freedman, *Jew vs. Jew*, 280.
21. "Selections from 120 letters." See Ro'i, *The Struggle for Soviet Jewish Emigration*, 203, 212.
22. See Beckerman, *When They Come for Us*, 42–49, 55–60, 68–72, 135–40; Albert D. Chernin, "Making Soviet Jewry an Issue: A History," in *A Second Exodus: The American Movement to Free Soviet Jews*, ed. Murray Friedman and Albert D. Chernin, 32 (Hanover, N.H.: Brandeis University Press, 1999); Frey, "Challenging the World's Conscience," 79, 86–87; Freedman, *Jew vs. Jew*, 4; Naftalin, "The Activist Movement," 229; Orbach, *The American Movement to Aid Soviet Jews*, 20–21, 25, 30–33, 41–42; Ro'i, *The Struggle for Soviet Jewish Emigration*, 208–9.
23. Lazin, *The Struggle for Soviet Jewry in American Politics*, 41.
24. On Kahane, Soviet Jewry, and the reaction of American Jewry, see Beckerman, *When They Come for Us*, 155–64, 167–71, 228–36; Janet Dolgin, *Jewish Identity and the JDL* (Princeton: Princeton University Press, 1977), 32–40; Shlomo M. Russ, "The 'Zionist Hooligans': The Jewish Defense League," PhD diss., City University of New York, 1981, 149–92, 306–526; Yossi Klein Halevi, *Memoirs of a Jewish Extremist* (Boston: Little, Brown and Company, 1995), 77–79, 83–89, 114–20, 155–62; Orbach, *The American Movement to Aid Soviet Jews*, 55–58; Ruby, "The Role of Nonestablishment Groups,"

207–8. See the ambivalent comments of Lazin, *The Struggle for Soviet Jewry in American Politics*, 41.
25. Abraham Bayer, "American Response to Soviet Anti-Jewish Policies," *American Jewish Yearbook 1973* (Philadelphia: American Jewish Committee, 1973), 211; cited in Lazin, *The Struggle for Soviet Jewry in American Politics*, 41.
26. On Nathan Birnbaum, the early Zionist and Yiddishist leader who subsequently became an Orthodox activist, see Joshua A. Fishman, *Ideology, Society and Language: The Odyssey of Nathan Birnbaum* (Ann Arbor, Mich.: Karoma, 1987).
27. Yossi Klein Halevi, "Jacob Birnbaum and the Struggle for Soviet Jewry," *Azure* 17 (Spring 5764/2004): 27–57. See also Klein Halevi, *Memoirs of a Jewish Extremist*, 52–54; Beckerman, *When They Come for Us*, 72–85; Jonathan Mark, "Yakov Birnbaum's Freedom Ride," *Jewish Week*, April 30, 2004, 1, 16–17. See the 2012 tribute including historic footage and interviews, "Dr. Jacob Birnbaum—RAJE 2012 Dinner video," www.youtube.com/watch?v=K8F8mrA96FA. Birnbaum's passing on April 9, 2014—nearly fifty years to the date after the first student rally he organized in New York—inspired a number of former Soviet Jewry activists to reflect personally on his unique contributions and the minimal credit extended to him. See, for example, Jonathan Mark, "Yaakov Birnbaum: 'A Hero of Biblical Proportions,'" *Jewish Week*, April 17, 2014, www.thejewishweek.com/news/international/yaakov-birnbaum-hero-biblical-proportions.
28. On early Soviet Jewry activism at YU, see Lora Rabin Dagi, "'Justice, Justice You Will Pursue?' Orthodox Jewry and the Civil Rights Movement, 1954–1970," BA thesis, Harvard University, 2006, 70–74; N. Lightman, "A Call to End the Apathy towards Our Brethren," *Hamevasser* 3, no. 2 (1965): 5; H. L. Michaelson, "Plight of Soviet Jewry Arouses Concern, Confusion," *Hamevasser* 2, no. 5 (1964): 3; Stanley Raskas, "From Out of Town," in *My Yeshiva College: 75 Years of Memories*, ed. Menachem Butler and Zev Nagel, 250 (New York: Yashar Books, 2006).
29. On American Jewish responses during the Holocaust, see Seymour M. Finger, ed., *American Jewry during the Holocaust* (New York: Holmes and Meier, 1984); Haskell Lookstein, *Were We Our Brother's Keepers? The Public Response of American Jews to the Holocaust* (New York: Hartmore, 1986); Rafael Medoff, *The Deafening Silence: American Jewish Leaders and the Holocaust* (New York: Shapolsky, 1987).
30. See, for example, David J. Garrow, *Bearing the Cross: Martin Luther King Jr. and the Southern Christian Leadership Conference* (New York: Vintage Books, 1988). The outspoken Rabbi Abraham Joshua Heschel was a notable exception to the generally apathetic mode of most American Jewish leaders in the early 1960s. See Beckerman, *When They Come for Us*, 64–68; Sarna, *American Judaism*, 310–11, 317.
31. The transcript of the original letter was provided by Jacob Birnbaum.
32. See the file "SSSJ Founding Meeting—4/27/64," SSSJ Archive, Gottesman Library, Yeshiva University, box 1, file 1.
33. A video recording in DVD format of the May 1, 1964, rally can be found in the SSSJ Archive, box 7.
34. Beckerman, *When They Come for Us*, 79–80; Klein Halevi, "Jacob Birnbaum and the Struggle for Soviet Jewry," 35, 36, 41.

35. Copies of most of the printed materials are preserved in the SSSJ Archive at Yeshiva University.
36. Ro'i, *The Struggle for Soviet Jewish Emigration*, 211–12. See SSSJ Archive, box 1, files 1–14, box 197, files 1 and 2.
37. Ronald I. Rubin, "Student Struggle for Soviet Jewry," *Hadassah Magazine* 48, no. 4 (1966): 7, 34–35.
38. Jacob Birnbaum, "Jewish Redemption Ritual in Jacob Birnbaum's Struggle for Soviet Jewry in the 1960s: The Role of His Family Heritage," typescript, May 22, 2006, 3.
39. See, for example, Richard Bernstein, "Thousands in March on 5th Ave. Support Jews in Soviet Union," *New York Times*, March 23, 1983, 1.
40. Birnbaum, "Jewish Redemption Ritual," 3, refers to the first two years of the SSSJ as "the Shofar Period."
41. See Sherwood Goffin, "Songs of Hope for Soviet Jews," recorded July 30, 1970, SSSJ Archive, Reel to Reel Case, side 2. On Carlebach, see Yaakov Ariel, "Hasidism in the Age of Aquarius: The House of Love and Prayer in San Francisco, 1967–1977," *Religion and American Culture* 13, no. 2 (2003): 139–65; Beckerman, *When They Come for Us*, 125–28; Danzger, *Returning to Tradition*, 50.
42. Amitai Bin-Nun, "Motivations and Symbols of the Early Student Struggle for Soviet Jewry (SSSJ), 1964–1970," BA paper, Yeshiva College, January 11, 2004, 19; Beckerman, *When They Come for Us*, 129–30. See the extensive discussion of the role of religious symbolism and "ritualization" in Kelner, "Ritualized Protest and Redemptive Politics," 8–23.
43. Yaakov Birnbaum, e-mail correspondence (June 6, 2006).
44. Lichtenstein (1933–2015) was a leading figure and thinker in contemporary Orthodoxy and Religious-Zionism, and was the son-in-law of the preeminent theologian of American Modern Orthodoxy, the late Rabbi Dr. Joseph B. Soloveitchik. During the 1960s he was the head of the kollel (advanced Talmudic fellows program) at YU/RIETS and an instructor in English Literature at Stern College for Women. See Alan Brill, "An Ideal Rosh Yeshiva: *By His Light: Character and Values in the Service of God* and *Leaves of Faith* by Rav Aharon Lichtenstein (KTAV)," *Edah Journal* 5, no. 1 (2005), www.edah.org/backend/JournalArticle/5_1_Brill.pdf; *Tradition* 47, no. 4 (2015). Lamm, a leading ideologue of American Orthodoxy, is the former chancellor and president of YU (1976–2003). See Norman Lamm, "There Is Only One Yeshiva College: A Memoir," in *My Yeshiva College: 75 Years of Memories*, ed. Menachem Butler and Zev Nagel, 219–25 (New York: Yashar Books, 2006). On Heschel, see most recently Shai Held, *Abraham Joshua Heschel: The Call of Transcendence* (Bloomington: Indiana University Press, 2013). On Borowitz, see, for example, David H. Ellenson, "Eugene B. Borowitz: A Tribute," *Jewish Book Annual* 51 (1993–94): 125–36.
45. Riv-Ellen Prell, *Prayer and Community: The Havurah in American Judaism* (Detroit: Wayne State University Press, 1989), 92–93; telephone interview with Rabbi Professor Arthur Green (May 25, 2006).
46. See "Information Sheets 1965–1972," in SSSJ Printed Materials Collections, SSSJ Archive, box 2; Birnbaum, "Jewish Redemption Ritual"; Klein Halevi, "Jacob Birnbaum and the Struggle for Soviet Jewry," 37; Phil Spiegal, "Mobilizing a Critical Mass

in New York: The Seminal Activity of the Student Struggle for Soviet Jewry (SSSJ), 1964–1966," typescript, September 18, 2005, 3, 4, 10, 11.
47. Birnbaum, e-mail.
48. Orbach, *The American Movement to Aid Soviet Jews*, 28.
49. Beckerman, *When They Come for Us*, 128, 131.
50. Telephone interview with Yossi Klein Halevi (May 21, 2006).
51. Weiss, "Avi," chap. 4, p. 16; Kelner, "Ritualized Protest and Redemptive Politics," 13.
52. Birnbaum, "Jewish Redemption Ritual," 2. See also Frey, "Challenging the World's Conscience," 79–80, who describes the SSSJ as "drawing its members largely from New York's Orthodox community."
53. Green interview.
54. Telephone interview with Glenn Richter (May 5, 2006); Glenn Richter, transcript of responses to Lora Rabin Dagi (July 26, 2005).
55. In our interview, Richter referred to Riskin as the "chief inspirer," due to his role as a central speaker at many of the rallies. Similarly, Birnbaum, in e-mail correspondence, highlighted Riskin's "thunderous speech making at events." Birnbaum met Riskin originally in Israel in 1960 when they lived in the same building. On Riskin, see Edward Abramson, *Circle in a Square* (Jerusalem: Urim, 2008).
56. On Greenberg, see, for example, Steven T. Katz, "Irving (Yitzchak) Greenberg," in *Interpreters of Judaism in the Twentieth Century*, ed. Steven T. Katz, 59–90 (Washington, D.C.: Bnai Brith Books, 1993); Steven T. Katz and Steven Bayme, eds., *Continuity and Change: A Festschrift in Honor of Irving (Yitz) Greenberg's 75th Birthday* (Lanham, Md.: University Press of America, 2011). On Sheer, the longtime chaplain of Columbia University, see www.rabbis.org/news/article.cfm?id=100797.
57. On Weiss, see Beckerman, *When They Come for Us*, 460–63, 475–76; Ruby, "The Role of Nonestablishment Groups," 215–18.
58. Richter interview; Birnbaum, e-mail; Birnbaum, "Jewish Redemption Ritual"; interview with Rabbi Shlomo Riskin, Jerusalem (May 29, 2006); Greenberg interview; telephone interview with Rabbi Avi Weiss (May 9, 2006); Weiss, "Avi," chap. 5, p. 5.
59. Regarding New York as the center of the Soviet Jewry movement, see Rafael Medoff, *Jewish Americans and Political Participation* (Santa Barbara, Calif.: ABC-CLIO, 2002), 163.
60. Richter interview.
61. See Judith Tydor Baumel, "Kahane in America: An Exercise in Right-Wing Urban Terror," *Studies in Conflict and Terrorism* 22 (1999): 317–19, 323.
62. See *Saturday Night Live* Transcripts, season 1, episode 11, January 24, 1976, http://snltranscripts.jt.org/75/75k.phtml.
63. See Marc Dollinger, *Quest for Inclusion: Jews and Liberalism in Modern America* (Princeton: Princeton University Press, 2000); Stuart Svonkin, *Jews against Prejudice: American Jews and the Fight for Civil Liberties* (New York: Columbia University Press, 1997).
64. Peter Medding, "The New Jewish Politics in America," in *Terms of Survival: The Jewish World since 1945*, ed. Robert S. Wistrich, 92–93 (London: Routledge, 1995). See also Ezra Mendelsohn, *On Modern Jewish Politics* (New York: Oxford University Press, 1993), 95–103; J. Goldberg, *Jewish Power*, 133–62; Joshua Michael Zeitz, "'If I am not

for myself...': The American Jewish Establishment in the Aftermath of the Six-Day War," *American Jewish History* 88, no. 2 (2000): 253–86. Zeitz offers a slight adjustment to Medding's position by arguing that the emphasis on broad liberal considerations within the Jewish approach to the public domain did not dissipate even after the introduction of greater particularism.

65. Medding, "The New Jewish Politics in America," 94–95.
66. Lawrence Grossman, "Mainstream Orthodoxy and the American Public Square," in *Jewish Polity and American Civil Society*, ed. Alan Mittleman, Jonathan D. Sarna, and Robert Licht, 284 (Lanham, Md.: Rowman and Littlefield, 2002).
67. See Goren, *The Politics and Public Culture of American Jews*, 191–92. A significant exception to the Orthodox tendency to follow the lead of the American Jewish establishment was the advocacy led by traditionalist Orthodox figures for government rescue efforts and changes in immigration policies during World War II. Although the main vehicle used by the Orthodox was *shtadlanus*, quiet diplomacy, they were also responsible for the 1943 "Rabbi's March on Washington." This was the only major public demonstration by American Jews against government policy that took place during the entire war period. As noted in the notes to chapter 1, Rabbi Yekutiel Yehudah (Leopold) of Columbus, Ohio, attended this march. On the Washington March, see David Kranzler, *Thy Brother's Keeper: The Orthodox Jewish Response during the Holocaust* (New York: Mesorah, 1987), 99–102. Efraim Zuroff argues, however, that most of the Orthodox rescue activities were focused on saving the remnants of the yeshivas and Hasidic courts. Thus they follow the pattern of cases in which Grossman ("Mainstream Orthodoxy and the American Public Square," 284) would suggest, "the rights and welfare of Orthodox Jews were directly at stake." See Efraim Zuroff, *The Response of Orthodox Jewry in the United States to the Holocaust: The Activities of the Vaad ha-Hatzala Rescue Committee, 1939–1945* (New York: Yeshiva University Press, 2000). For alternatives to Zuroff's view, see David Kranzler, "Orthodoxy's Finest Hour," *Jewish Action* 63, no. 1 (2002), www.ou.org/publications/ja/5763/5763fall/ORTHODOX.pdf.
68. Saul Bernstein, *Renaissance of the Torah Jew* (Hoboken, N.J.: Ktav, 1985), 194–95 (cited in Grossman, "Mainstream Orthodoxy and the American Public Square," 191).
69. Lederhendler, *New York Jews and the Decline of Urban Ethnicity*, 191–92.
70. Ibid., 188, 191.
71. See, for example, Deborah E. Lipstadt, "From Noblesse Oblige to Personal Redemption: The Changing Profile and Agenda of American Jewish Leaders," *Modern Judaism* 4, no. 3 (1984): 295–309.
72. See James D. Besser, "With God on Their Side: Is the Growing Orthodox Influence in D.C. Good for All of the Jewish Community?" *Jewish Week*, October 17, 2003, www.thejewishweek.com/news/newscontent.php3?artid=8563; Fishkoff, *The Rebbe's Army*, 184–200; Samuel C. Heilman, "Haredim and the Public Square," in *Jewish Polity and American Civil Society*, ed. Alan Mittleman, Jonathan D. Sarna, and Robert Licht, 328–33 (Lanham, Md.: Rowman and Littlefield, 2002); "Symposium: Orthodoxy and the Public Square," *Tradition* 38, no. 1 (2004): 6–52.
73. See Orbach, *The American Movement to Aid Soviet Jews*, 24; Ro'i, *The Struggle for Soviet Jewish Emigration*, 197. For an extensive discussion, albeit from a Lubavitch

perspective, of all aspects of this Hasidic movement's activities in regard to Russian-speaking Jewry, see Wolf, *Diedushka*.

74. Another Orthodox figure who gained notoriety for his willingness to engage the Soviet apparatus was Rabbi Arthur Shneier of Manhattan's Park East Synagogue. On Schneier's activities, see Lazin, *The Struggle for Soviet Jewry in American Politics*, 223, 238 n.57. Regarding his involvement with Russian-speaking Jewry, see Blau, *Learn Torah*, 243–300. See also Orbach, *The American Movement to Aid Soviet Jews*, 76; Leon Shapiro, "Soviet Jewry since the Death of Stalin: A Twenty-Five Year Perspective," *American Jewish Yearbook 1979* (New York: American Jewish Committee and Jewish Publication Society, 1979), 83, 86, www.policyarchive.org/handle/10207/bitstreams/17740.pdf. Blau (295) suggests that by the late 1970s her father, Rabbi Mordechai Pinchas Teitz, recognized the need for both quiet diplomacy and public protest. Rabbi Dr. Shalom Berger told me that Rabbi Teitz sent items with him when he traveled to the Soviet Union for Passover in 1983. He also offered advice regarding which sacred books to bring for the local Jews and how to make sure they were not confiscated by the border authorities.

75. Menachem Mendel Schneerson, *Sihos Kodesh 5731* (1971), www.hebrewbooks.org/4603, 1:473–74. See the Hebrew translation of the original Yiddish, with slight variations from my English translation, in Wolf, *Diedushka*, 143. On Schneerson's position, see Wolf, *Diedushka*, 124–71, 395–97; Fishkoff, *The Rebbe's Army*, 190.

76. Birnbaum, "Jewish Redemption Ritual."

77. Richter interview; Hoenlein interview; Riskin interview.

78. Telephone interview with Rabbi Dovid Miller (May 17, 2006). According to an alternative version of this meeting that appears in Wolf, *Diedushka*, 461 (based on an interview with Rabbi Israel Miller in the *Kfar Chabad* publication), Schneerson said that if you are going to go public at least make sure that it gets to the front page of the *New York Times*.

79. For contemporary records of early Haredi Orthodox opposition to public protest for Soviet Jewry, see Ben Meir, "The Conference on Jews in the Soviet Union," *Jewish Observer* 1, no. 7 (1964): 23–24; Morris N. Kertzer, "Religion," *American Jewish Year Book* 65 (1964): 77; Simcha A. Neuschloss, "Soviet Jewry and Jewish Responsibility: The Historical and Torah Dimensions of the Problem," *Jewish Observer* 11, no. 9 (1965): 3–5.

80. Birnbaum, "Jewish Redemption Ritual," 6; Hoenlein interview; Avraham Weiss, "Public Protest and Soviet Jewry," *Midstream* 33 (February 1987): 26–27. On Feinstein, see, for example, David H. Ellenson, "Two Responsa of Rabbi Moshe Feinstein," *American Jewish Archives* 52, nos. 1 and 2 (2000–2001): 112–28; Norma Baumel Joseph, "Jewish Education for Women: Rabbi Moshe Feinstein's Map of America," *American Jewish History* 83, no. 2 (1995): 205–22; Jacob Chinitz, "Reb Moshe and the Conservatives," *Conservative Judaism* 41, no. 3 (1989): 5–26; Wolfe Kelman, "Moshe Feinstein and Postwar American Orthodoxy," *Survey of Jewish Affairs 1987* (1988): 173–87; Ira Robinson, "Because of Our Many Sins: The Contemporary Jewish World as Reflected in the Responsa of Moses Feinstein," *Judaism* 35, no. 1 (1987): 364–73.

81. Rabbi Moshe Sherer, "Emergency Memorandum to Branch Presidents and Zeirei Agudath Israel [Re: Russian Situation]," December 30, 1970, Agudath Israel archive.
82. "A Call from the Moetzes Gedolei HaTorah (Council of Torah Authorities)," *Day-Jewish Journal*, December 31, 1970.
83. Sherer, "Emergency Memorandum."
84. "Orthodox Youth Group Says Russian Jewry Harmed by Provocative, Arrogant Actions," *JTA Daily News Bulletin*, January 12, 1971.
85. Rabbi Avi Shafran, Director of Public Affairs, Agudath Israel of America, e-mail correspondence (May 11, 2006); Richter interview.
86. See Gideon Shimoni, *The Zionist Ideology* (Hanover, N.H.: University Press of New England, 1995), 98. Regarding *shtadlanus* and American Orthodox involvement with Soviet Jewry, see Irving Greenberg, "Yeshiva in the 60s," in *My Yeshiva College: 75 Years of Memories*, ed. Menachem Butler and Zev Nagel, 180 (New York: Yashar Books, 2006); Orbach, *The American Movement to Aid Soviet Jews*, 34, 76; Avi Weiss, *Principles of Spiritual Activism* (Hoboken, N.J.: Ktav, 2002), 9. Neuschloss, "Soviet Jewry and Jewish Responsibility," offers an explication of the Aguda position that centers on defense of the traditional value and effectiveness of *shtadlanus*. On the practice of *shtadlanus* in Jewish history, see David Biale, *Power and Powerlessness in Jewish History* (New York: Schocken, 1986), 71–72. On the development of traditionalist Orthodox *shtadlanus* in early modern and modern Europe, see David Assaf and Israel Bartal, "Shtadlanut ve-Ortodoksiyah: Zadikei Polin be-Mifgash im ha-Zemanim ha-Hadashim," in *Zadikim ve-Anshei Ma'aseh*, ed. Rachel Elior, Israel Bartal, and Chone Shmeruk, 69–90 (Jerusalem: Mossad Bialik, 1994); Gershon C. Bacon, *The Politics of Tradition: Agudat Yisrael in Poland, 1916–1939* (Jerusalem: Magnes Press, 1996), 228–30, 235–37; Alan L. Mittleman, *The Politics of Torah: The Jewish Political Tradition and the Founding of Agudat Israel* (Albany: State University of New York Press, 1996), 79; Marcin Wodzinski, "Hasidism, Shtadlanut, and Jewish Politics in Nineteenth-Century Poland: The Case of Isaac of Warka," *Jewish Quarterly Review* 95, no. 2 (2005): 290–320.
87. All five of those who signed on "A Call From The Moetzes Gedolei," cited above (in order of signatures), were born and raised in Eastern Europe: Rabbis Yaakov Kamenetsky of Yeshiva Torah Voda'ath, Yaakov Yitzchok Halevi Ruderman of Ner Israel Rabbinical College (Baltimore), Yitzchok Hutner of Yeshiva Chaim Berlin, Yisroel Shapira (the Bloshaver Rebbe), Moshe Feinstein, and Nochum Mordechai Perlow (the Novominsker Rebbe).
88. Hoenlein interview.
89. Richter interview.
90. M. Schneerson, *Sihos Kodesh 5730*, part 2, 107. See the translation in Wolf, *Diedushka*, 154. See also *Diedushka*, 479–83.
91. S. Heilman, "Haredim and the Public Square," 321. Schneerson, in particular, developed a theology that emphasized the divine inspiration that stood at the foundation of American democracy. See Wolf, *Diedushka*, 173; Fishkoff, *The Rebbe's Army*, 192–93. Clearly the Eastern European–born but German-educated and JTS-affiliated

Abraham Joshua Heschel digressed from this characterization regarding both Soviet Jewry and Vietnam. See Sarna, *American Judaism*, 310–17. On Orthodox patriotism and reluctance to become involved in antiwar demonstrations, see I. Greenberg, "Yeshiva in the 60s," 181. On internal Jewish conflicts regarding Vietnam protests, see Michael Staub, introduction to *The Jewish 1960s: An American Sourcebook*, ed. Michael Staub, 137–64 (Waltham, Mass.: Brandeis University Press, 2004); Michael Staub, *Torn at the Roots: The Crisis of Jewish Liberalism in Postwar America* (New York: Columbia University Press, 2002), 14.

92. See Blau, *Learn Torah*, 302; Rabin Dagi, "'Justice, Justice You Will Pursue?'" 23, 79; Richter interview.

93. For an analysis of Orthodox ambivalence regarding the civil rights movement in the early 1960s, see Marvin Schick, "The Orthodox Jew and the Negro Revolution: A Hard Look at Religious Jewry's Attitudes," *Jewish Observer* 11, no. 9 (1964): 15–17.

94. On the role of Rabbi Soloveitchik as the central ideologue and authority figure for 1960s American Modern Orthodoxy, see Liebman, "Orthodoxy in American Jewish Life," 50–51, 53, 87–89.

95. Telephone interview with Rabbi Saul Berman, May 15, 2006; Richter telephone interview; Malka Zeiger, "The Student Struggle for Soviet Jewry: The Grassroots Movement to Aid Soviet Jews, 1963–1968," BA paper, Stern College, 2004, 4 n.3. According to Riskin, Soloveitchik considered the question a "political issue" rather than one demanding a "religious directive" and suggested that they consult with Professor Erich Goldhagen of Columbia University.

96. In other public issues of contention within Orthodoxy, however, he was far more forthright. See his major statement in support of Zionism and the State of Israel: Joseph B. Soloveitchik, *Kol Dodi Dofek: Listen My Beloved Knocks*, ed. Jeffrey Woolf, trans. David Gordon (Hoboken, N.J.: Ktav, 2006), delivered originally on Israel Independence Day in 1956. See Joseph B. Soloveitchik, "Confrontation," *Tradition* 6, no. 2 (1964): 5–29, penned in the wake of the Second Vatican Council, in which he expressed his unequivocally negative appraisal of interreligious dialogue.

97. On *da'as Torah* in America, see S. Heilman, *Sliding to the Right*, 103–4, 109, 137. On the development of the concept in general, see Bacon, *The Politics of Tradition*, 43–69; Binyamin Brown, "Doktrinat da'at Torah: sheloshah shelabim," *Mekhkarei Yerushalayim be-Makhshavet Yisrael* 19, no. 2 (2005): 537–600; Lawrence Kaplan, "*Daas Torah*: A Modern Conception of Rabbinic Authority," in *Rabbinic Authority and Personal Autonomy*, ed. Moshe Sokol, 1–60 (Northvale, N.J.: Jason Aronson, 1992); Jacob Katz, "*Da'at Torah*: The Unqualified Authority Claimed for Halachists," The Gruss Lectures: Jewish Law and Modernity, October 26–November 30, 1994, www.law.harvard. edu/programs/Gruss/katz.html.

98. For Soloveitchik's views of the evil of Communist Russia, see, for example, Joseph B. Soloveitchik, *Festival of Freedom: Essays on Pesah and the Haggadah* (Jersey City, N.J.: Toras Horav Foundation, 2006), 10, 49; Abraham R. Besdin, *Reflections of the Rav* (Jerusalem: World Zionist Organization, 1979), 180–81; Aaron Rakeffet-Rothkoff, *The Rav: The World of Rabbi Joseph B. Soloveitchik* (Jersey City, N.J.: Ktav, 1999), 2:24–26, 107–9.

99. Grossman, "Mainstream Orthodoxy and the American Public Square," 293, 307–8 n.25; Berman interview; Rabin Dagi, "'Justice, Justice You Will Pursue?'" 26–27, 47; Liebman, "Orthodoxy in American Jewish Life," 44.
100. Frey, "Challenging the World's Conscience," 110; I. Greenberg, "Yeshiva in the 60s," 180–81; Klein Halevi, "Jacob Birnbaum and the Struggle for Soviet Jewry," 33; Klein Halevi, *Memoirs of a Jewish Extremist*, 11; Weiss, "Avi," chap. 3, pp. 14–16. The foreign-born Jacob Birnbaum, of course, was a notable exception.
101. Rabin Dagi, "'Justice, Justice You Will Pursue?'" 49–72. On Jewish involvement in the civil rights movement, see Mark K. Bauman and Berkely Kalin, eds., *The Quiet Voices: Southern Rabbis and Black Civil Rights, 1880s to 1990s* (Tuscaloosa: University of Alabama Press, 1997); Seth Forman, *Blacks in the Jewish Mind: A Crisis of Liberalism* (New York: New York University Press, 1998); Meyer, *Response to Modernity*, 364–69; Debra L. Schultz, *Going South: Jewish Women in the Civil Rights Movement* (New York: New York University Press, 2001); Clive Webb, *Fight against Fear: Southern Jews and Black Civil Rights* (Athens: University of Georgia Press, 2001).
102. According to Rabbi Charles Sheer, the former president of YU's SSSJ chapter, the primary concern of Orthodox Jewry in the 1960s was survival. Soviet Jewry was defined as part of this struggle, while civil rights fit less easily into this mind-set. See Charles Sheer, e-mail correspondence with Laura Rabin Dagi (August 21, 2005).
103. Richter interview. Of course there were also many college-educated Orthodox students who supported the approach of the Agudath Israel authorities. See, for example, David Luchins, "The Urge to Protest," *HaMevaser* 9 (February 1967) (cited in Rabin Dagi, "'Justice, Justice You Will Pursue?'" 69).
104. Greenberg interview.
105. In his interview, Greenberg said that some of the members of the Riverdale Jewish Center were vehemently opposed to his efforts as rabbi during the late 1960s to invite black rights activists to speak in the synagogue. These members had fled other sections of the Bronx and moved to Riverdale due to the violence that they had experienced on the part of their African American neighbors.
106. See Frey, "Challenging the World's Conscience," 51–57. Frey also points out that already during the 1950s the American Jewish establishment organizations saw protest over Soviet anti-Semitism as a way to dispel the image of the American Jew as a communist sympathizer (7–10). This was consistent with their cooperation with Senator Joseph McCarthy's House Un-American Activities Committee, and their endorsement of the death penalty for Ethel and Julius Rosenberg. See Naomi W. Cohen, *Not Free to Desist: The American Jewish Committee, 1906–1966* (Philadelphia: Jewish Publication Society, 1972), 499; Dollinger, *Quest for Inclusion*, 133–37; Deborah Dash Moore, "Reconsidering the Rosenbergs: Symbol and Substance in Second-Generation American Jewish Consciousness," *Journal of American Ethnic History* 8 (Fall 1988): 21–22.
107. Jack Wertheimer, *A People Divided: Judaism in Contemporary America* (New York: Basic Books, 1993), 29. Sarna, *American Judaism*, 318–23, introduces his description of the rise of the Havurah communal movement immediately after Soviet Jewry. The Havurah, he suggests (318), exemplifies the move of American Jewry, in the words

of Wertheimer (29), "from universalistic concerns to a preoccupation with Jewish particularism."
108. Kelner, "Ritualized Protest and Redemptive Politics," 22, remarks that "Ritualization constructed the act of protesting as a sacred obligation and resituated the protestors from actors in the domain of secular politics to an assemblage of the faithful responding to a command they were duty bound to answer."
109. Sherer, "Emergency Memorandum."
110. Joseph B. Soloveitchik addresses this issue through his dichotomy between communities of "fate" and "destiny," although his main context is not American Jewry but the Holocaust and its implications for a religious understanding of the State of Israel. See Joseph B. Soloveitchik, *Fate and Destiny: From the Holocaust to the State of Israel*, trans. Lawrence Kaplan (Hoboken, N.J.: Ktav, 2000); J. Soloveitchik, *Kol Dodi Dofek*. A number of the articles written by Rabbi Avi Weiss over the years could be considered an effort in this direction. See Weiss, *Principles of Spiritual Activism*, 19–21, 31–35, 68–71, 72–75, 99–101.
111. Amy Sara Clark, "Rabbi Israel Miller, Advocate for Restitution, Dies at 83," *Jewish News Weekly of California*, May 29, 2002, www.jewishsf.com/content/2-0-/module/displaystory/story_id/17971/edition_id/358/format/html/displaystory.html.
112. Chernin, "Making Soviet Jewry an Issue," 45, 51, 57, 59, 63; Orbach, *The American Movement to Aid Soviet Jews*, 105. On Schacter, see L. Bernstein, *Challenge and Mission*, 19, 69, 113, 163, 168–79, 216, 222, 244, 246, 253, 262; Margalit Fox, "Rabbi Herschel Schacter Is Dead at 95; Cried to the Jews of Buchenwald: 'You Are Free,'" *New York Times*, March 26, 2013, www.nytimes.com/2013/03/27/nyregion/rabbi-herschel-schacter-who-carried-word-of-freedom-to-buchenwald-dies-at-95.html?pagewanted=all&_r=0.
113. See Edah's website at www.edah.org; Adam Dicter, "Modern Orthodox Think Tank to Fold," *Jewish Week*, June 30, 2006, www.thejewishweek.com/news/newscontent.php3?artid=12665.
114. See his October 2014 announcement that he would leave his position in June 2015: http://failedmessiah.typepad.com/failed_messiahcom/2014/10/full-text-of-rabbi-avi-weiss-speech-announcing-his-retirement-123.html.
115. For the Hebrew Institute of Riverdale, see www.hir.org/aboutus.html. For Amcha, see www.amchacjc.org.
116. Richter interview; Weiss interview; Weiss, "Avi," chap. 3, p. 19.
117. Rabbi Charles Sheer, telephone interview (May 5, 2006); Sheer, e-mail correspondence.
118. See Efraim Zuroff, *Occupation: Nazi-Hunter: The Continuing Search for the Perpetrators of the Holocaust* (Jersey City, N.J.: Ktav, 1994); Klein Halevi interview; Efraim Zuroff, telephone interview (May 25, 2006).
119. Regarding Carlebach, since his passing in 1994 his legacy as a contemporary Hasidic master has for the most part been cultivated by the Orthodox.
120. I. Greenberg, "Yeshiva in the 60s," 181, 184, 186. For more information on Clal, see www.clal.org/.
121. "Rep. Nadler Introduces Resolution Honoring Founder of Student Struggle for Soviet Jewry," *U.S. Fed News Service*, October 2, 2006, www.highbeam.com/doc/1P3-1138672641.html.

122. Liebman, "Orthodoxy in American Jewish Life," 92.
123. Korn, "God, Torah, and Yeshiva in the Sixties," *My Yeshiva College*, 213. For an analysis of YU student activism in the 1960s regarding Vietnam in particular, see Jeffrey S. Gurock, *The Men and Woman of Yeshiva* (New York: Columbia University Press, 1988), 213–45.
124. Addressing developments in Conservative and Reform Judaism in particular, Neil Gillman suggests that the "peoplehood agenda" that dominated mid-twentieth-century American Judaism is dead and has been replaced by a "God-centered" one that is focused on "Jewish religion." If Orthodoxy has indeed moved away from the solidarity ethos, this would parallel the phenomenon described by Gillman. See Gillman's comments in Elliott Abrams and David G. Dalin, eds., *Secularism, Spirituality, and the Future of American Jewry* (Washington, D.C.: Ethics and Public Policy Center, 1999), 43–46.
125. Weiss's Yeshivat Chovevei Torah seminary, as noted, is attempting to fortify the solidarity approach. In this regard, see Amy Eilberg, "*Spiritual Activism: A Jewish Guide to Leadership and Repairing the World* (Review)," *Conservative Judaism* 63, no. 4 (2012): 108–10. Since 2005 Yeshiva University, under the leadership of President Richard Joel and Rabbi Kenneth Brander, Vice President and Dean of the Center for the Jewish Future, has in turn also sponsored initiatives aimed at encouraging its students to become involved in humanitarian action beyond their parochial interests. For the most part, these programs do not, however, entail cooperation with non-Orthodox entities.
126. Robert D. Putnam, *Bowling Alone: The Collapse and Revival of American Community* (New York: Touchstone, 2001), 22–24. For a summary of some of the main lines of critique, see Margot Talbot, "Who Wants to Be a Legionnaire," *New York Times Book Review*, June 25, 2000, www.nytimes.com/books/00/06/25/reviews/000625.25talbott.html. See also David A. Schultz, Manfred Steger, and Scott L. Maclean, *Social Capital: Critical Perspectives on Community and "Bowling Alone"* (New York: New York University Press, 2002).

Chapter 4

1. Michael R. Marrus, *The Holocaust in History* (Hanover, N.H.: University Press of New England, 1987), 4–6; Peter Novick, *The Holocaust in American Life* (Boston: Houghton Mifflin, 1999), 127–45; Jeffrey Shandler, *While America Watches: Televising the Holocaust* (New York: Oxford University Press, 1999), 81–132, 155–78.
2. See Rona Sheramy, "From Auschwitz to Jerusalem: Re-enacting Jewish History on the March of the Living," in *Polin*, vol. 19: *Polish-Jewish Relations in North America*, ed. Mieczslaw B. Biskupski and Antony Polonsky, 307–26 (Oxford: Littman Library for Jewish Civilization, 2007); Rona Sheramy, "The March of the Living: Where Is It Now?," *Jewish Educational Leadership* 8, no. 1 (2009), www.lookstein.org/online_journal_toc.php?id=16.
3. On the origins and historical development of the year in Israel programs, see Chaim Waxman, "Year in Israel and the Orthodox Community," in Shalom Z. Berger, Daniel

Jacobson, and Chaim I. Waxman, *Flipping Out? Myth or Fact: The Impact of the "Year in Israel,"* 160–63 (New York: Yashar Books, 2007).

4. See Michelle Chabin, "Fast Times at Gap Year High," *Jewish Week*, January 12, 2010, www.jewishindependent.ca/archives/Jan10/archives10Jan29-03.html.

5. The discussion draws upon personal interviews and written communications with participants and staff who had gone on the trips subsequent to their return, as well as a broad review of printed educational literature and websites dedicated to Poland seminars, the growing secondary literature on the topic, and ethnographic observations carried out during the eleven trips that I made to Poland between 1991 and 2004. In the majority of cases, I served as one of the historical guides for the delegation. I participated in the entire gamut of activities and kept records and wrote notes that related to choices of itinerary, nature of visits and ceremonies, and reactions of participants. I also recorded my impressions after returning home in notes and personal correspondences.

6. There were a few Israeli youth trips to Poland in the 1960s, but these efforts ended completely in wake of the Six-Day War of 1967, when Poland cut off diplomatic relations with Israel. See Tovah Zur, "Ha-Masa le-Polin ke-si'o shel tahalikh hinukhi," *Be-Shevilei ha-Zikkaron* 7 (October 1995): 5. On the varieties of Jewish "tourism" to Poland, see Jack Kugelmass, "The Rites of the Tribe: The Meaning of Poland for American Tourists," *Yivo Annual* 21 (1993): 395–443 (reprinted in Christine M. Kreamer and Steven D. Lavine, eds., *Museums and Communities: The Politics of Public Culture*, 382–427 [Washington, D.C.: Smithsonian Institution Press, 1992]).

7. The first groups were sponsored in 1983 by the Israeli Kibbutz ha-Artzi movement. See Avraham Azilei, "Masa le-hidud arakhim ziyoni'im, yehudi'im, tenuati'im," *Be-Shevilei ha-Zikkaron* 7 (1995): 7–8.

8. On the history of the March of the Living, see Sheramy, "From Auschwitz to Jerusalem," 307–26. On the Israeli groups, see Zur, "Ha-Masa le-Polin ke-si'o shel tahalikh hinukhi," 5–7.

9. Sheramy, "From Auschwitz to Jerusalem," 310, 313.

10. Yehonatan Wender, "Ashirim ve-dati'im yozim yoter le-'masaot le-Polin," *Makor Rishon*, January 31, 2008, 24.

11. Regarding the original educational goals, see Sheramy, "The March of the Living," 309–10; Jackie Feldman, "Shoah, Security, Victory: A Critique of Israeli Youth Voyages to Poland," *Jewish Educational Leadership* 8, no. 1 (2009), www.lookstein.org/online_journal/index.php?id=293.

12. Central Agency for Jewish Education, Miami, Florida, *March of the Living Adult Manual* (Miami, 1995), 1 (cited in Sheramy, "From Auschwitz to Jerusalem," 320).

13. See, for example, William B. Helmreich, "Visits to Europe, Zionist Education, and Jewish Identity: The Case of the March of the Living," *Journal of Jewish Education* 61, no. 3 (1995): 16–20; Sheramy, "From Auschwitz to Jerusalem," 323.

14. Cited in Wender, "Ashirim ve-dati'im." Regarding Israeli youth, however, some studies suggest that the influence of the trips on the knowledge of the students as well as their attitudes toward Jewish and national identity is short lived. That said, researchers acknowledge that independent of such trips, Israeli youth possess relatively strong feelings and familiarity with the Holocaust and a deep commitment toward Israeli

national identity. See Shlomo Romi and Tamar Lev, "Experiential Learning of History through Youth Journeys to Poland: Israeli Jewish Youth and the Holocaust," *Research in Education* 78 (2007): 88–102; Alon Lazar, Julia Chaitin, Tamar Gross, and Dan Bar-On, "Jewish Israeli Teenagers, National Identity, and the Lessons of the Holocaust," *Holocaust and Genocide Studies* 18, no. 2 (2004): 188–204.

15. Telephone interview with Michael Berl, Director, Heritage Seminars, January 30, 2008. Transcripts of all interviews are stored at the Bruce and Ruth Rappaport Faculty for Jewish Studies, Bar-Ilan University, Ramat-Gan, Israel, room 37.
16. Ibid.
17. Ibid.
18. Telephone interview with Vicky Berglas, Director, Midreshet Moriah (June 19, 2008); interview with Dr. David Bernstein, Dean, Pardes Institute (former Director, Midreshet Lindenbaum), Jerusalem (June 26, 2008).
19. Bernstein interview. Dr. Bernstein is presently the dean of the Pardes Institute, a non-affiliated yeshiva in Jerusalem that attracts post–college age male and female students from a variety of religious backgrounds. Like Bernstein, the majority of the leaders and staff are Orthodox Jews. See the institute's website at www.pardes.org.il/.
20. Berglas interview.
21. Telephone interview with Rabbi Michael Yammer, Yeshivat Sha'alvim (June 19, 2008).
22. Ibid.
23. Ibid.
24. Entry from Avi Billet, personal journal of 1998 Heritage Seminar to Poland and Lithuania (April 3, 1998), sent in e-mail correspondence on April 26, 2009.
25. Berglas interview.
26. Bernstein interview.
27. Berl interview.
28. Ibid.
29. On distinctions between American Modern Orthodoxy and Israeli Religious-Zionism, see Eliezer Don-Yehiya, "Orthodox Jewry in Israel and in North America," *Israel Studies* 10, no. 1 (2005): 157–87. On the rise of the so-called *hardal* (*Haredi-leumi*) camp within Israeli Religious-Zionism, see Adam S. Ferziger, "The Role of Reform in Israeli Orthodoxy," in *Between Jewish Tradition and Modernity: Essays in Honor of David H. Ellenson*, ed. Michael A. Meyer and David Myers, 51-66 (Detroit: Wayne State University Press, 2014); Yoel Finkelman, "On the Irrelevance of Religious-Zionism," *Tradition* 39, no. 1 (2005): 21–44.
30. Rabbi Dr. Shalom Berger, e-mail correspondence, June 26, 2008.
31. Heritage actually organizes some of these tours. While there is some customization involved, the basic itinerary is the same as that prepared for the students spending a year in Israel. That said, according to Michael Berl the age and context of the high school students have a profound influence on the nature of their experiences. For one, unlike those who go during their year in Israel, rarely does a high school student arrive in Poland after experiencing a prior intensive religious awakening. This does not mean that the pilgrimage will not be meaningful, but it contrasts sharply with the unique transformative quality of the trip for those

who have already been studying in an Israeli religious environment throughout the academic year.

32. One example is the "Israel Experience," a subsidiary of the Jewish Agency. See www.israelexperience.org.il//pages/aboutus.asp.
33. See, for example, Oren Baruch Stier, "Lunch at Majdanek: The March of the Living as a Contemporary Pilgrimage of Memory," *Jewish Folklore and Ethnology Review* 17, nos. 1–2 (1995): 57–66.
34. Jackie Feldman, "'It Is My Brothers Whom I Am Seeking': Israeli Youths' Pilgrimages to Poland and the Shoah," *Jewish Folklore and Ethnology Review* 17, nos. 1–2 (1995): 33. Similarly, see Sheramy, "From Auschwitz to Jerusalem," 314–16. Feldman is the most prolific observer of Israeli youth trips to Poland. His full-length monograph on the subject appeared as Jackie Feldman, *Above the Death Pits, Beneath the Flag: Youth Voyages to Poland and the Performance of Israeli National Identity* (Oxford: Berghahn Books, 2008).
35. The quote is from J. Feldman, "'It Is My Brothers Whom I Am Seeking,'" 33, where he summarizes a central thesis that appears in Kugelmass's "The Rites of the Tribe," 432–33. See, however, Jack Kugelmass, "Bloody Memories: Encountering the Past in Contemporary Poland," *Cultural Anthropology* 10, no. 3 (1995): 281, where he questions some of the premises of his previous article.
36. Shoshana Balk, e-mail correspondence, April 2, 2009.
37. J. Feldman, "'It Is My Brothers Whom I Am Seeking,'" 34. See also Amiram Barkat, "Youth Trips to Poland; Under Polish Pressure, Government Considering Changes to Camp Visits," *Ha'aretz*, May 5, 2005, www.haaretz.com/print-edition/news/youth-trips-to-poland-under-polish-pressure-government-considering-changes-to-camp-visits-1.157670; Sheramy, "From Auschwitz to Jerusalem," 324–25. For an attempt to construct an alternative type of Jewish visit to Poland, see Erica Lehrer and Hannah Smotrich, "Jewish? Heritage? in Poland? A Brief Manifesto and an Ethnographic Design Intervention into Jewish Tourism to Poland," *Bridges* 12, no. 1 (2007): 36–41.
38. For analyses of the broader theme of "religious tourism" and education that includes discussion of Jewish trips to Eastern Europe, see Erik H. Cohen, "Religious Tourism as an Educational Experience," in *Tourism, Religion, and Spiritual Journeys*, ed. Daniel H. Olsen and Dallen J. Timothy, 78–93 (London: Routledge, 2006); Mara W. Cohen Ioannides and Dmitri Ioannides, "Global Jewish Tourism: Pilgrimages and Remembrance," in *Tourism, Religion, and Spiritual Journeys*, ed. Daniel H. Olsen and Dallen J. Timothy, 156–71 (London: Routledge, 2006).
39. See, for example, the title of a Hebrew Haredi textbook that is unique in the degree to which it details the destructive aspects of the Holocaust: R. Lichtenstein, *Edut: Hurban Yahadut Eiropah* (New York: Mossad Ha-RI"M Levine, 2000); Nehemia Polen, "Theological Responses to the Hurban from within the Hurban," in *Jewish Perspectives on the Experience of Suffering*, ed. Robert Hirt and Shalom Carmy, 277–95 (Northvale, N.J.: Jason Aronson, 1999).
40. Arye Edrei, "Holocaust Memorial: A Paradigm of Competing Memories in the Religious and Secular Societies in Israel," in *On Memory: An Interdisciplinary Approach*, ed. Doron Mendels (Oxford: Peter Lang, 2007), 88. For additional discussions of

the Haredi approach to the Holocaust, see, for example, Menachem Friedman, "The Haredim and the Holocaust," *Jerusalem Quarterly* 53 (Winter 1990): 86–114; Kimmy Caplan, "Have 'Many Lies Accumulated in History Books'? The Holocaust in Ashkenazi *Haredi* Historical Consciousness in Israel," *Yad Vashem Studies* 29 (2001): 321–75; Kimmy Caplan, "The Holocaust in Contemporary Israeli Haredi Popular Religion," *Modern Judaism* 22, no. 2 (2002): 142–68.

41. Arye Edrei, "Keizad zokhrim? Zikhron ha-Shoah ba-hevrah ha-datit u-vahevrah ha-hilonit," *Tarbut Democratit* 11 (2007): 15, notes that Rabbi Joseph B. Soloveitchik, the most influential rabbinical figure in Yeshiva University, similarly expressed opposition to special Holocaust prayers. For an expanded discussion of this position and a contrast to that of other prominent Religious-Zionist and Modern Orthodox rabbinical personalities, see Jacob J. Schacter, "Holocaust Commemoration and *Tish'a be-Av*: The Debate over *Yom ha-Sho'a*," *Tradition* 41, no. 2 (2008): 174–79.

42. Telephone interview with Rabbi Yehuda Fried, Director, Nesivos of the Gedolim (June 19, 2008).

43. Nesivos Tours: Jewish Legacy Tours, "Beis Yaakov Tours," www.nesivos.com/beis-yaakov-tours-2/.

44. See Ya'akov Elboim, *Petihut ve-Histagrut: Ha-Yezirah ha-Ruhanit-ha-Sifrutit be-Polin u-ve-Arzot Ashkenzaz be-Shilhei ha-Meah ha-Shesh Esreh* (Jerusalem: Magnes Press, 1990).

45. On Polish Hasidism, see, for example, Glenn Dynner, *Men of Silk: The Hasidic Conquest of Polish Jewish Society* (Oxford: Oxford University Press, 2006).

46. On the transformation of this ideology in America, see Yoel Finkelman, "An Ideology for American Yeshiva Students: The Sermons of R. Aharon Kotler," *Journal of Jewish Studies* 58, no. 2 (2007): 314–32; Finkelman, *Strictly Kosher Reading*, 99–122.

47. Nesivos Tours: Jewish Legacy Tours, "Yeshiva Tours," www.nesivos.com/yeshiva-tours/.

48. Kugelmass, "The Rites of the Tribe," 432–33.

49. Yehuda Fried interview.

50. Ibid.

51. On Sarah Schenirer and the Bais Yaakov educational movement, see Pearl Benisch, *Carry Me in Your Heart: The Life and Legacy of Sarah Schenirer, Founder and Visionary of the Bais Yaakov Movement* (New York: Feldheim Publishers, 2003); Deborah R. Weissman, "Bais Ya'akov as an Innovation in Jewish Women's Education," *Studies in Jewish Education* 7 (1995): 278–99; Shoshana Pantel Zolty, *"And All Your Children Shall Be Learned": Women and the Study of Torah in Jewish Law and History* (Northvale, N.J.: Jason Aronson, 1997), 55–95.

52. E-mail correspondence, April 8, 2009. The transcript is filed with the other communications and interview materials, but the correspondent asked specifically not to be identified by name.

53. Edrei, "Holocaust Memorial," 89.

54. For the itineraries, see www.nesivos.com/Yeshivaeritage.asp#itinerary; www.nesivos.com/BeisYaakov.asp#Tour%20Itinerary.

55. J. Feldman, "It Is My Brothers Whom I Am Seeking," 33–37.
56. Nesivos Tours: Jewish Legacy Tours, "Beis Yaakov Tours," www.nesivos.com/beis-yaakov-tours-2/.
57. See Nesivos Tours: Jewish Legacy Tours, "Legacy Seminary Tours," www.nesivos.com/legacy-seminary-tours/.
58. Heritage Seminars: Educational Seminars in Eastern Europe, "Heritage Highlights," http://heritageseminars.org/heritage-highlights/.
59. Heritage Seminars: Educational Seminars in Eastern Europe, http://heritageseminars.org.
60. Liebman, "Orthodoxy in American Jewish Life," 67–89; S. Heilman, *Sliding to the Right*, 4–5, 47–62; Finkelman, "An Ideology for American Yeshiva Students," 314–32.
61. Micah D. Halperin, *In Their Memory: Introductions, Essays, and Texts for the Study of Jewish Life in Eastern Europe and the Holocaust* (Jerusalem: Heritage Seminars, 1996).
62. For his original approach, see, for example, Emil Fackenheim, *To Mend the World: Foundations of Post-Holocaust Thought* (Bloomington: Indiana University Press, 1994).
63. *In Search of Our Heritage* (Jerusalem: Heritage Seminars, 2002).
64. Yammer interview. See Justine Digance, "Religious and Secular Pilgrimage: Journeys Redolent with Meaning," in *Tourism, Religion, and Spiritual Journeys*, ed. Daniel H. Olsen and Dallen J. Timothy, 38 (London: Routledge, 2006): "All pilgrims share the common trait in that they are searching for . . . a moment when they experience something out of the ordinary that marks a transition from the mundane secular humdrum world of our everyday existence to a special and sacred state."
65. Yammer interview.
66. Ibid.
67. Riva Wachsman, e-mail correspondence, April 2, 2009.
68. Ester Blaut Kellman, e-mail correspondence, January 10, 2010.
69. Berglas interview.
70. Bernstein interview. See his nuanced discussion in David I. Bernstein, "Teaching the Role of the Poles in the Shoah," *Jewish Educational Leadership* 8, no. 1 (2009), www.lookstein.org/online_journal.php?id=285.
71. Berglas interview.
72. Yammer interview.
73. Hendler interview. Regarding attitudes of American year in Israel students toward Israel, see Shalom Z. Berger, "Engaging the Ultimate: The Impact of Post–High School Study in Israel," in Berger, Jacobson, and Waxman, *Flipping Out?*, 57. On page 54, he addresses gender distinctions in respect to this issue.
74. Ayelet Kahane, e-mail correspondence, March 15 and April 2, 2009.
75. Wachsman e-mail.
76. Rebecca Weinstein, e-mail correspondence, January 10, 2010.
77. The section on Religious-Zionism only appears in the Hebrew version of his essay, Edrei, "Keizad zokhrim?," 45.
78. See the discussion in Schacter, "Holocaust Commemoration and *Tish'a be-Av*."

79. See the photograph from 2009 on Leszek Kozlowski's Flickr stream, www.flickr.com/photos/bilk/3421059959/.
80. See Andrzej Trzciński, *Yeshivat Chachmei Lublin* (Warsaw: Adrem Books/Warsaw Jewish Community, 2007).
81. On the massive increase in study of the *daf yomi* among American Orthodox Jews during the late twentieth century as a manifestation of "religious resurgence," see H. Soloveitchik, "Rupture and Reconstruction."
82. Kahane e-mail, March 15, 2009.
83. Billet, Personal journal.
84. See Norman Lamm, *The Religious Thought of the Hasidim* (New York: Yeshiva University Press, 1999), 254–70.
85. See Slawomir Kapralski, "Battlefields of Memory: Landscape and Identity in Polish-Jewish Relations," *History and Memory* 13, no. 2 (2001): 50–51.
86. See Hachnassas Orchim Lizensk, http://sites.torahindex.com/lizensk/en/about_en.html.
87. Lamm, *The Religious Thought of Hasidism*, 261–64; Yoram Shemer, "Notes on Filming a Hasidic Pilgrimage to Poland," *Jewish Folklore and Ethnology Review* 17 (1995): 53–56.
88. Lamm, *The Religious Thought of Hasidism*, 323–36.
89. Billet, Personal journal.
90. Kugelmass, "The Rites of the Tribe," 437.
91. For an interesting juxtaposition, see the discussion of Polish gentile visits and myths regarding the grave of Reb Elimelekh of Leżajsk in Aline Cala, "The Cult of Tzaddikim among Non-Jews in Poland," *Jewish Folklore and Ethnology Review* 17 (1995): 16–19.
92. Hendler interview.
93. Ayal Kellman, e-mail correspondence, January 18, 2010.
94. Ibid.
95. Ibid. Another senior Heritage guide who highlights Hasidic life is Rabbi Avraham Krieger. Yet unlike Hendler, Krieger does so by using his own parents' background as members of the Gerrer Hasidic community in prewar Lodz, and their experiences before, during, and after the Holocaust as the backdrop to the historical narrative that he puts forward. See Yammer interview.
96. On "neo-Hasidic" directions within contemporary Israeli Religious-Zionist circles, see Finkelman, "On the Irrelevance of Religious Zionism"; Yehonatan Garb, "Tehiyatah ha-movnet shel ha-mistikah be-yameinu," in *Tarbut Yehudit be-Ein ha-Se'arah: Sefer ha-Yovel le-Yoseph Ahituv*, ed. Avi Sagi and Nahem Ilan, 172–99 (Tel Aviv: Ha-Kibbutz ha-Me'uhad, 2002); Moshe Hellinger, "Individualism, datiyut, ruhaniyut, be-idan post-moderni," *Akdamot* 14 (December 2004): 9–14; Yair Sheleg, "Aliyatah shel Hasidut Ginzburg" (September 9, 1989), 12; Yair Sheleg, "Mered kadosh be-Kefar Etzion," *Nekudah*, July 1998, 12–13.
97. See Jackie Feldman, "Marking the Boundaries of the Enclave: Defining the Israeli Collective through the Poland Experience," *Israel Studies* 7, no. 2 (2002): 102. On the ideology of "negation of the exile" in Religious-Zionist thought, see Eliezer

Don-Yehiya, "The Negation of the *Galut* in Religious Zionism," *Modern Judaism* 12 (1992): 129–55.

98. See Natan Ofir (Offenbacher), *Rabbi Shlomo Carlebach: Life, Mission, Legacy* (Jerusalem: Urim Publications, 2014); Avraham Arieh Trugman, "Probing the Carlebach Phenomenon,'" *Jewish Action* 63 (Winter 2002): 9–12.

99. Congregation Aish Kodesh in Woodmere, New York, is a fascinating example of an initiative aimed at integrating Hasidic/Haredi ideals into a bastion of Modern Orthodoxy. Its charismatic leader, Rabbi Moshe Weinberger, is a YU graduate who subsequently studied in Hasidic institutions and adopted this approach. Indeed, the synagogue edifice is modeled after a Polish Hasidic house of prayer and study. See www.aishkodesh.org/about.html. In 2013 Weinberger was appointed to the position of mashpia (literally influencer, but essentially spiritual coach) for the RIETS division of Yeshiva University.

100. S. Heilman, *Sliding to the Right*, 112–23; C. Waxman, "Year in Israel and the Orthodox Community," 169–70. S. Berger, "Engaging the Ultimate," 73–77, takes issue with Heilman's thesis. One Israeli yeshiva with a large American contingent that has not adopted this approach is Yeshivat Har Etzion, known popularly as Gush. Notably, a few years ago they opted to organize their own Poland trip guided by an alumnus who shares the institution's worldview. See Adam S. Ferziger, "Religious Zionism, *Galut*, and Global Jewry: Exploring 'Gush' Exceptionalism," in *How I Love Your Torah: Essays in Honor of Yeshivat Har Etzion on the Forty-fifth Anniversary of Its Founding*, ed. Yitzhak Recanati, Shaul Barth, and Reuven Ziegler, 111–41 (Alon Shevut: Yeshivat Har Etzion, 2014).

101. Even in this area, there is less willingness—particularly since the 2004 disengagement from Gaza—to follow the lenient rulings once championed in order to allow for maximum partnership with Israeli society and the state's agencies. See Finkelman, "On the Irrelevance of Religious-Zionism"; Aviad Hacohen, "'Religious Zionist Halakhah': Is It a Reality or Was It a Dream," in *Religious Zionism Post-Disengagement: Future Directions*, ed. Chaim I. Waxman, 342–45 (New York: Yeshiva University Press, 2008).

102. Yoel Finkelman, "Virtual Volozhin: Socialization versus Learning in Israel Yeshiva Programs," in *Wisdom from All My Teachers: Challenges and Initiatives in Contemporary Torah Education*, ed. Jeffrey Saks and Susan Handelman, 362 (Jerusalem: ATID and Urim, 2003).

103. Daniel Jacobson, "In Search of Self: Psychological Perspectives on Change," in Berger, Jacobson, and Waxman, *Flipping Out?*, 138.

104. S. Heilman, *Sliding to the Right*, 116. On the liminal quality of pilgrimages, see Victor Turner, "The Center Out There: Pilgrim's Goal," *History of Religions* 12, no. 3 (1973): 204–14.

105. E-mail correspondence, July 7, 2009. The correspondent asked that her name be withheld.

106. Dodi Tobin, "The Impact of One-Year Israel Study on American Day School Graduates," PhD diss., Fairleigh Dickinson University, 1997.

107. Yammer interview.
108. See J. Feldman, "Shoah, Security, Victory," for a description of the isolation of the students during the Poland pilgrimages. Occasionally parents accompany their children on the trips, but this is a tiny minority.
109. V. Turner, "The Center Out There," 221.
110. Wachsman communication.
111. Kahane e-mail, March 15, 2009.
112. E. Cohen, "Religious Tourism as an Educational Experience," 87.
113. Berl interview.

Chapter 5

1. Yeshayahu Leibowitz, "The Status of Women in Halakhah and Meta-Halakhah," in *Judaism, Human Values, and the Jewish State*, ed. Eliezer Goldman, 128 (Cambridge, Mass.: Harvard University Press, 1982).
2. The same may be true in Israel as well, although this topic is beyond the scope of the current study.
3. Two major works in English to appear in the last decade, both produced by Orthodox academics who are also widely respected as religious thinkers and practitioners, are Tamar Ross, *Expanding the Palace of the Torah: Orthodoxy and Feminism* (Waltham, Mass.: Brandeis University Press/University Press of New England, 2004) and Chaim Trachtman, ed., *Women and Men in Communal Prayer: Halakhic Perspectives* (Jersey City, N.J.: JOFA/Ktav, 2010), which features articles by Daniel Sperber, Mendel Schapiro, Eliav Schochetman, and Shlomo Riskin. See the fine summary discussion of Orthodoxy and feminism up to 2009 in Gurock, *Orthodox Jews in America*, 273–311.
4. See Tova Cohen, "Iris Parush's *Reading* Women," *Journal of Israeli History* 21, nos. 1–2 (2002): 175–79; Natalie Davis, *Women at the Margins* (Cambridge, Mass.: Harvard University Press, 1995), 5–62; Paula Hyman, *Gender and Assimilation in Modern Jewish History* (Seattle: University of Washington Press, 1995), 56–57; Marion Kaplan, *The Making of the Jewish Middle Class: Women, Family, and Identity in Imperial Germany* (New York: Oxford University Press, 1991), 233. On Jewish women in early modern Poland, see Moshe Rosman, "Poland: Early Modern, 1500–1795," in *Jewish Women: A Comprehensive Historical Encyclopedia* [online version] (Jerusalem: Shalvi Publishers, 2006), http://jwa.org/encyclopedia/article/poland-early-modern-1500-1795.
5. See Breuer, *Modernity within Traditon*, 120–25.
6. See Weissman, "Bais Ya'akov as an Innovation in Jewish Women's Education," 278–99; Pantel Zolty, *"And All Your Children Shall Be Learned,"* 55–95.
7. See Judy Baumel-Schwartz, *Double Jeopardy: Gender and the Holocaust* (London: Valentine Mitchell, 1998), 242–43; Benisch, *Carry Me in Your Heart*.
8. As in many areas, the Chabad Lubavitch Hasidic sect is a noteworthy exception. See the discussion in chapter 9.
9. Iris Brown (Hoisman), "Bein 'teva ha-ishah' le 'marut ha-ba'al': ha-ideologiyah ha-hinukhit ha-Haredit ve-gevulot ha-haskalah ha-Toranit le-banot," *Zehuyot* 3 (2013): 97–124.

10. For distinctions between Haredi Orthodox and Modern Orthodox perceptions of women's religious roles, see Lynn Davidman, *Tradition in a Rootless World: Women Turn to Orthodox Judaism* (Berkeley: University of California Press, 1991), 26–48.
11. On developments in higher religious learning among Modern Orthodox and Israeli Religious-Zionist women, see, for example, Tamar El-Or, *Next Year I Will Know More: Literacy and Identity among Young Orthodox Women in Israel* (Detroit: Wayne State University Press, 2002); Rochelle Furstenberg, "The Flourishing of Higher Jewish Learning for Women," *Jerusalem Letter* 429 (May 2000): 1–11; Joel Wolowelsky, *Women, Jewish Law and Modernity: New Opportunities in a Post-Feminist Age* (Jersey City, N.J.: Ktav, 2003), 111–22.
12. See, for example, Baumel Joseph, "Jewish Education for Women," 205–22; Moshe Meiselman, *Jewish Women in Jewish Law* (New York: Ktav/Yeshiva University Press, 1978), 34–42. For a brief history of Orthodox feminism, see Ross, *Expanding the Palace of the Torah*, 25–31.
13. The first concerted effort by a Modern Orthodox rabbinical figure and scholar to come to terms with feminism was Saul Berman, "The Status of Women in Halakhic Judaism," *Tradition* 14, no. 2 (1973): 5–28. This article inspired a vociferous response by Rabbi Moshe Meiselman, who like Rabbi Berman was a student of Rabbi Joseph B. Soloveitchik. Meiselman's initial argument can be found in Moshe Meiselman, "Women and Judaism: A Rejoinder," *Tradition* 15, no. 3 (1975): 52–68. The first responsum of Rabbi Moshe Feinstein, the preeminent American Orthodox halakhic authority of the mid-twentieth century, is from 1976; see Moshe Feinstein, "Be-Inyan ha-tenuah ha-hadashah shel nashim ha-sha'ananot ve-ha-hashuvot," in *Igerot Moshe*, vol. 4: *Orah Hayyim* (Bnei Brak: Yeshivat Ohel Yosef, 1981), #49. See the discussion in Ilan Fuchs, *Jewish Women's Torah Study: Orthodox Religious Education and Modernity* (Oxford: Routledge, 2014), 110–29. Yet the proliferation of publications on the subject can be dated to the 1980s and has only increased by leaps and bounds since then. For a rich bibliography on Orthodoxy and feminism through 2006, see the Hebrew version of Tamar Ross's study on Orthodoxy and feminism, *Armon ha-Torah mi-Ma'al Lah: Al Orthodoksiyah ve-Feminism* (Tel Aviv: Alma College and Am Oved, 2007), 420–57.
14. Blu Greenberg, *On Women and Judaism: A View from Tradition* (Philadelphia: Jewish Publication Society, 1981). An earlier, less strident statement by Greenberg can be found in her "Jewish Women: Coming of Age," *Tradition* 16, no. 4 (1977): 79–94.
15. B. Greenberg, *On Women and Judaism*, 95–97.
16. Ibid., 93.
17. The main opinions published up to 1998 have been summarized and analyzed by Aryeh A. Frimer and Dov I. Frimer, "Women's Prayer Services: Theory and Practice," *Tradition* 32, no. 2 (1998): 5–118.
18. See Eli Turkel, "Partial Bibliography of Works by and about Rabbi Joseph B. Soloveitchik Zt"l," last updated October 22, 2013, www.math.tau.ac.il/~turkel/engsol.html.
19. For an analysis of this issue, see Frimer and Frimer, "Women's Prayer Services," 40–45. For subsequent discussions, see Moshe Meiselman, "The Rav, Feminism, and Public Policy: An Insider's View," *Tradition* 33, no. 1 (1998): 5–30; Ross, *Expanding the*

Palace of Torah, 73–78; Zvi (Herschel) Schachter, *Mi-Peninei ha-Rav* (Jerusalem: Beit Midrash de-Flatbush, 2001), 67–68, 142; Mayer Twersky, "Halakhic Values and Halakhic Decisions: Rav Soloveitchik's Pesak Regarding Women's Prayer Groups," *Tradition* 32, no. 3 (1998): 5–18.

20. See Aileen Cohen Nusbacher, "Efforts at Change in a Traditional Denomination: The Case of Orthodox Women's Prayer Groups," *Nashim*, Spring, 5759/1999, 95–113. For a list of Orthodox women's prayer groups up to 2006, see Edah, "Women's Tefilla Groups," www.edah.org/tefilla.cfm.

21. See the directory of partnership minyanim at JOFA, "Partnership Minyanim," www.jofa.org/Resources/Partnership_Minyanim.

22. Irit Koren, "The Bride's Voice: Religious Women Challenge the Wedding Ritual," *Nashim* 10 (2005): 29–52. For a discussion of various suggestions to introduce a more egalitarian character to the Orthodox wedding ceremony without contravening religious law, see Dov Linzer, "*Ani li'Dodi vi'Dodi Li:* Towards a More Balanced Wedding Ceremony," *JOFA Journal* 4, no. 2 (2003): 4–7.

23. See, for example, Nishmat: Women's Health and Halacha, "About Us," www.yoatzot.org/about.php. For a broad discussion of women's leadership in Israeli Orthodoxy, see Tova Cohen, "And All the Women Followed Her," in *Jewish Religious Leadership: Image and Reality*, ed. Jack Wertheimer, 2:715–56 (New York: JTS, 2004).

24. See, for example, The Hebrew Institute of Riverdale, "Who Is the Madricha Ruchanit?" www.hir.org/madricha_ruchanit.html. See the discussions in Shmuel Rosner, "Mazav ha-Judaism: Mah bein rav le-ven morah ruhanit," *Ha'aretz*, February 2, 2008, http://cafe.themarker.com/view.php?t=332968; Joel Wolowelsky, "Rabbis, Rebbetzins and Halakhic Advisors," *Tradition* 36, no. 4 (2002): 54–63.

25. See, for example, the Kibbutz movement site, www.kibbutz.org.il/itonut/2007/haver/070125_m_falk.htm.

26. See Rabbinical Council of America, "RCA Statement Regarding Recent Developments at Yeshivat Maharat," May 7, 2013, www.rabbis.org/news/article.cfm?id=105753.

27. Another controversial issue that has received more support from some conservative authorities is recitation of the mourner's prayer (kaddish) by women in mainstream Orthodox public prayer services. See the discussion and sources in Rahel Berkovits, *A Daughter's Recitation of Mourner's Kaddish* (New York: JOFA, 2011).

28. For an exploration of the ways in which Orthodox feminism is redefining Orthodox concepts of boundaries and authority, see Yehudah Mirsky, "Modernizing Orthodoxies: The Case of Feminism," in *To Be a Jewish Woman*, ed. Tova Cohen, Kolech Proceedings 4, 37–51 (Jerusalem: Kolech, 2007). See also Gurock, *Orthodox Jews in America*, 273–311.

29. S. Heilman, *Sliding to the Right*, 58.

30. In March 2014 it was announced that Lord Rabbi Jonathan Sacks, the former chief rabbi of the Britain's United Synagogue, and Schachter would receive the Katz Foundation Award for their "contributions to the practical analysis and application of halakha [Jewish law] in modern life." See *YU News*, March 11, 2014, http://blogs.yu.edu/news/2014/03/11/yu-torah-scholars-to-receive-katz-prize/.

31. See Letter of Rabbi Menachem Penner (Acting Dean of RIETS) to RIETS Alumni, September 3, 2013, http://yu.convio.net/site/MessageViewer?em_id=42361.0&dlv_id=52601.
32. See his official biography at www.yutorah.org/bio.cfm/80153/Rabbi_Hershel_Schachter.
33. Debra Nussbaum Cohen, "RCA Seen as Caving In," *Jewish Week*, February 27, 2008, www.thejewishweek.com/features/rca_seen_caving_conversions.
34. Gurock, *Orthodox Jews in America*, 270. See Zvi (Herschel) Schachter, *Nefesh ha-Rav* (Jerusalem: Hoza'at Reshit Yerushalayim, 1994), and Schachter, *Mi-Peninei ha-Rav*, where he describes the religious customs and outlook of his mentor that he witnessed during his many years as a devoted student and follower. See also Schachter's published notes of Soloveitchik's Talmud lectures available through the Torahweb foundation, www.torahweb.org/ravSet.html.
35. See Lawrence Kaplan, "The Multi-Faceted Legacy of the Rav: A Critical Analysis of Hershel Schachter's Nefesh ha-Rav," *BDD (Bekhol Derakhekha Daehu: Journal of Torah and Scholarship)* 7 (Summer 1998): 51–85; Lawrence Kaplan, "Revisionism and the Rav: The Struggle for the Soul of Modern Orthodoxy," *Judaism* 48, no. 3 (1999): 294–95.
36. See David Landes, "Traditional Struggles: Studying, Defining and Performing the Law at the Rabbi Isaac Elchanan Theological Seminary," PhD diss., Princeton University, 2010, 73.
37. See, for example, "Women Elected Officers for First Time at KJ," *Kehilath Jeshurun Bulletin* 68, no. 6 (1999), www.ckj.org/docs/June%2018,%201999&20(kjo699).pdf. Rabbi Haskel Lookstein explains in the article that the synagogue's decision was made after consultation with Schachter, who said that a woman can serve as an officer, but not as president of the synagogue. Schachter maintained that this was the position of Soloveitchik. Paradoxically, the same synagogue bulletin lists the schedule for the synagogue's longstanding women's prayer service.
38. On the background to the RCA decision to clarify this issue, see. Frimer and Frimer, "Women's Prayer Services," 15; Avraham Weiss, *Women at Prayer: A Halakhic Analysis of Women's Prayer Groups* (Hoboken, N.J.: Ktav, 1990), xv.
39. See the pronouncement in *The Jewish Press*, December 10, 1982, 3, cited by Jeffrey S. Gurock, "The Orthodox Synagogue," in *The American Synagogue*, 84 n.108.
40. *Song of Songs* 1:8.
41. Zvi (Hershel) Schachter, "Ze'i lakh be-ikvei ha-zon," *Beit Yitzchak* 17 (5745–1985): 118–34. The original prohibition is dated 19 Kislev, 5745 (December 13, 1984). The five RIETS authorities who signed it were Rabbis Zalman Alpert, Abba Bronspigel, Mordechai Willig, Yehuda Parnes, and Zvi (Herschel) Schachter. It was first published in *Ha-Darom* (Sivan/June 5785/1985): 49. See also, in brief, Zvi (Herschel) Schachter, "Be-Inyanei Beit ha-Knesset u-Kedushato," *Or Hamizrach* 34, nos. 1–2 (Tishrei 5746/September 1985): 66–68. The halakhic approach of these sources has been addressed in detail in the following works: Frimer and Frimer, "Women's Prayer Services," 15–32; Weiss, *Women at Prayer*, xvi, 55–56 n.45, 99–122. For an extensive discussion and critique of Schachter's responsum that introduces feminist theory of law, see Rachel Adler, "Innovation and Authority: A Feminist Reading of the 'Women's Minyan'

Responsum," in *Re-Examining Progressive Halakhah*, ed. Walter Jacob and Moshe Zemer, 3–32 (New York: Berghahm Books, 2001).
42. Similarly, see Schachter, *Nefesh ha-Rav*, 145; Schachter, *Mi-Peninei ha-Rav*, 67–68, 142.
43. Schachter, "Ze'i lakh be-ikvei ha-zon," 126.
44. On Schachter's approach to distinctions betweens Jews and gentiles, see S. Heilman, *Sliding to the Right*, 58–60.
45. As others have pointed out, the use of the term *minyan* (quorum) suggests that the women's prayer groups are seen by their participants as equal in the eyes of Jewish law to a service predicated on a quorum of men. In fact, this is not the case and this issue remains a major boundary between all Orthodox groups that seek to be more inclusive of women and normative non-Orthodox practice. The Orthodox partnership minyanim as well, as opposed to fully egalitarian services, only count males for the quorum.
46. Schachter, "Ze'i lakh be-ikvei ha-zon," 132–33.
47. On the slippery slope argument in connection to Orthodox feminism, see the comments of Neriah Gutel, "Kaddish yetomah (teguvah)," *Tzohar* 8 (Fall 2001): 25–26.
48. See, for example, David H. Ellenson, "A Disputed Precedent: The Prague Organ in Nineteenth-Century Central European Legal Literature and Polemics," *Leo Baeck Institute Year Book* 40 (1995): 252–64; Alexander Guttman, *The Struggle over Reform in Rabbinic Literature* (Jerusalem: World Union for Progressive Judaism, 1977); Moshe Samet, "Ha-Shinuyim be-sidrei beit ha-knesset: emdat ha-rabbanim ke-neged 'ha-Mehadshim' ha-Reformim," *Assufot* 5 (1991): 253–96.
49. For a nuanced appraisal of the motivations and particular nature of Soloveitchik's antagonism toward the non-Orthodox movements, see Farber, "Reproach, Recognition and Respect," 193–214.
50. See, for example, Freedman, *Jew vs. Jew*, 105–6; Wertheimer, *A People Divided*, 108–9, 176–78.
51. The fear of legitimizing non-Orthodox streams was emphasized in 1989 by Schachter's YU colleague and Orthodox legal authority J. David Bleich, *Contemporary Halakhic Problems* (New York: Ktav, 1989), 3:90: "The issue in the United States is not that of possible negative influence but of legitimization." An exception to Schachter's strident prohibitive tone can be found in a brief comment regarding women's prayer services that appears in Zvi (Herschel) Schachter, *Erez ha-Zvi* (New York: Yeshiva University, 1992), 99. There he clearly rejects the practice but demonstrates understanding for the sincere intentions of some of the Orthodox women who choose to participate.
52. In 1998, one of the more influential thinkers within Modern Orthodoxy commented: "Reciprocal denigration has peaked and the sense of a chasm between mainstream elements in respective factions is receding ... while we may see greater disaffection and splintering at the fringes, the overall climate will be less militant and more congenial." See Aharon Lichtenstein, "Symposium: Our Next 100 Years—The Future of American Orthodoxy," *Jewish Action* 59, no. 1 (1998): 52. See the discussion in chapter 6.

53. Zvi (Herschel) Schachter, *Be-Ikvei ha-Zon* (Jerusalem: Hoza'at Beit Midrash D'Flatbush, 1997), 21–36.
54. This is also suggested by his decision to reprint the original 1984 ruling of the five RIETS yeshiva heads at the conclusion of his own essay.
55. The audio tape is available at YUTorah Online, www.yutorah.org/showShiur.cfm/703731/Rabbi_Hershel_Schachter/Women_at_Prayer.
56. Similarly, see Mayer Schiller, "Symposium: Our Next 100 Years—The Future of American Orthodoxy," *Jewish Action* 59, no. 1 (1998): 58: "Feminism represents a central Rubicon for Orthodoxy.... I deeply fear that the unwillingness of many Modern Orthodox leaders to courageously reject the zeitgeist's dogmas in this area will lead to a fundamental break between them and the rest of *Klal Yisrael* [the Israelite collective]."
57. On the early struggle between Orthodoxy and Reform, see, for example, Jacob Katz, "The Controversy over the Temple in Hamburg and the Rabbinical Assembly in Braunschweig: Milestones in the Development of Orthodoxy," in his *Divine Law in Human Hands* (Jerusalem: Magnes, 1998), 216–30; Samet, "The Beginnings of Orthodoxy," 249–69. On the relationship between American Orthodoxy and other denominations through the mid-twentieth century, see, for example, Liebman, "Orthodoxy in American Jewish Life," 38–68.
58. Herschel Schachter, "On the Matter of Masorah," Torahweb.org, 2003, www.torahweb.org/torah/special/2003/rsch_masorah.html. See the "The Torah Web Foundation" page of Torahweb.org, www.torahweb.org/about.html, where Schachter is listed as one of the board members of this site, which was founded in 1999, and whose contributors are primarily senior Talmudic lecturers (roshei yeshiva) at RIETS. The site's goal is "to disseminate *divrei Torah* [words of Torah] and *hashkafa* [religious outlook] with special attention to contemporary religious and social issues." Furthermore, it is stated explicitly that "the *divrei Torah* on this site were written by the respective rabbis themselves."
59. This understanding of *masorah*, which he attributes to his mentor Soloveitchik, is a dominant theme in much of Schachter's writings. See, for example, Schachter, *Nefesh ha-Rav*, 19–58 (note that already on page 23, Schachter acknowledges and seeks to explain the fact that on numerous issues Soloveitchik had indeed deviated from the Lithuanian tradition upon which he had been nurtured); Schachter, *Mi-Peninei ha-Rav*, 142; Schachter, *Be-Ikvei ha-Zon*, 1–2. See the extensive discussion in Landes, "Traditional Struggles," 98–126.
60. Daniel Sperber, "Congregational Dignity and Human Dignity: Women's Public Torah Reading," *Edah Journal* 3, no. 2 (2003), www.edah.org/backend/JournalArticle/3_2.pdf. Sperber expanded upon his argument in his 2007 monograph, *Darkah shel Halakhah* (Tel Aviv: Reuven Mass, 2007). An English translation of a good part of this book appeared in Daniel Sperber, "Congregational Dignity and Human Dignity: Women and Public Torah Reading," in *Women and Men in Communal Prayer: Halakhic Perspectives*, 27–206.
61. Mendel Shapiro, "Qeri'at Torah by Women: A Halakhic Analysis," *Edah Journal* 1, no. 2 (2001), www.edah.org/backend/JournalArticle/1_2_shapiro.pdf. The essay was reprinted in *Women and Men in Communal Prayer: Halakhic Perspectives*, 207–90.

62. Sperber's rabbinic credentials were deemed sufficiently reliable for his audio lectures to be among the offerings of the RIETS official website for Torah study, see www.yutorah.org/searchResults.cfm?types=ALL&teacher=80189&dates=ALL&submitType=advanced. His biography appears as well at www.yutorah.org/bio.cfm/80189/Professor_Daniel_Sperber.
63. Schachter alludes to this in a comment in which he denigrates scholars who take on the role of halakhic adjudicators. See Schachter, "On the Matter of *Masorah*," where he relates the words of Moshe Feinstein from a 1973 decision, "the fact that some 'scholar,' not particularly known for his strength in *psak* [adjudication], published a paper in which he was prepared to permit a centuries-honored prohibition universally accepted by *Klal Yisroel*, would itself seem to indicate that the author of the paper probably belonged to that group of individuals who are *gaas libam b'hora'ah* [arrogantly enjoy deciding questions of Jewish law]." See Moshe Feinstein, *Igerot Moshe*, vol. 3: *Yoreh Deah* (Bnei Brak: Yeshivat Ohel Yosef, 1981), #155.
64. Jewish historian Susannah Heschel actually lends support to Schachter's interpretation; see Susannah Heschel, "The Impact of Feminist Theory on Jewish Studies," in *Modern Judaism in Historical Consciousness*, ed. Andreas Gotzmann and Christian Wiese, 528–48 (Leiden: Brill, 2007): "Attention to the position of women within Judaism seems to have originated as part of Christian traditions of anti-Judaism. One of the earliest statements appears in the *Juden Büchlein* of Victor von Karben (1519), in which he mocks the refusal of Jews to include women in the prayer quorum.... The inferior status of women within Judaism was discussed not only to denigrate Judaism, but also to elevate Christianity with the claim that Jesus' positive treatment of women stood in stark contrast to the Jewish men of his day."
65. Schachter, "On the Matter of *Masorah*."
66. Note, however, that John B. Henderson, *The Construction of Orthodoxy and Heresy* (Albany: State University of New York Press, 1998), 157–60, describes such an association of the new target with an "already defeated heresy" as a common heresiological strategy found in numerous religions.
67. See Landes, "Traditional Struggles," 107, where he transcribes a section of an oral presentation by Schachter to his students on April 13, 2003, in which Schachter connects between the broader theme of heresy during the Second Temple period and contemporary heresy: "After the Anshe Ke'nesses ha-Gedolah [men of the Great Assembly] succeeded in being *me'vatel* the *yetzer hara* for *avodah zarah* [canceling the evil inclination based on idolatry], so there was *mi-shekil'kalu ha-minim* [the spoiling by the heretics], then there was a period that we are still in, a period of *kefirah* [heretical denial], or *apikursus* [heretical skepticism], of *mi'nus* [heretical sectarians], *mi-shekil'kalu ha-minim*, and the antidote to this *yetzer hara* is the *Torah she-Be'al Peh* [Oral Law]."
68. Herschel Schachter, "Can Women Be Rabbis?" Torahweb.org, 2004, www.torahweb.org/torah/2004/parsha/rsch_dvorim2.html.
69. See Koren, "The Bride's Voice."
70. Schachter, "Can Women Be Rabbis?," illustrates the absence of a codified prohibition against women reading the marriage writ by alluding to a rabbinic statement (see

Mishnah *Yadayim* 1:5) regarding the lack of status requirements for certain religious tasks: "Yes, even if a parrot or a monkey would read the *kesuba*, the marriage would be one hundred percent valid.... [T]here's absolutely no mention whatsoever that anything is wrong with a woman reading the *kesuba*. Yes, a monkey could also read the *kesuba*." This analogy was deemed highly offensive and evoked sharp criticism even from some who actually sympathized and supported Schachter and the underlying religious principles that he put forward. Subsequently, the editor of Torahweb.com where the essay was published introduced the following note before the text: "The statement about monkeys or parrots reading the *kesuba* was clearly intended to dramatize the *halachic* [legal] insignificance of the reading of the *kesuba* from the standpoint of the *siddur kiddushin* (legal marriage orchestration). It was not intended to imply or insinuate anything else. And his analogy applies equally for men or women reading the *kesuba*."

71. Regarding Schachter's assertion that halakhic propriety entails avoiding behavior that does not have direct precedent in previous generations, see the discussion and extensive notes in Sperber, *Darkah shel Halakhah*, 102–5. See also the insightful typology of halakhic approaches to change articulated by Michael Avraham, "Ha-im yesh avodah zarah ne-urah? Al ha-yahas le-goyim ve-al shinuyim ba-halakhah," *Akdamot* 19 (Sivan 5767/June 2007): 66–69, www.bmj.org. il/files/1331292103800.pdf.

72. Schachter, "Can Women Be Rabbis?"

73. See Jack Wertheimer, *All Quiet on the Religious Front: Jewish Unity, Denominationalism, and Postdenominationalism in the United States* (New York: American Jewish Committee, 2005), 3. See also Sarna, *American Judaism*, 372.

74. See, for example, Sarna, "The Debate over Mixed Seating," 363–94; Wertheimer, *A People Divided*, 12–13.

75. On legal issues that divided the Sadducees and Pharisees, see Eyal Regev, *Ha-Z'dukim ve-Hilkhatam* (Jerusalem: Yad Yitzhak Ben-Zvi, 2005), 59–202. The discussion of women's inheritance is treated comprehensively in four pages, 109–13. Note that the tannaitic *Tosefta* (*Yadayim* 1, 20) attributes this opinion to the Boethusians. The amoraic literature is divided, with the Babylonian Talmud (*Bava Batra* 115b) listing this as a complaint of the Sadducees, while the Jerusalem Talmud (*Bava Batra* 8, 1) sees this opinion as characteristic of "gentile wisdom." Notably, the introduction of the Sadducees as a usable prototype for mistaken Jewish approaches to modernity is not an exclusively Orthodox practice. Prominent nineteenth-century German Reform theologian Abraham Geiger argued that the Pharisees were religious reformers, while the Sadducees were conservatives unwilling to adapt to changing circumstances. See Abraham Geiger, *Sadducaer und Pharisaer* (Breslau: Schletter'sche Buchhandlung, 1863).

76. The *Jewish Observer* was published from 1963 to 2009. See "Jewish Observer, in 'Transitional Phase,' to Be Honored for Distinguished Service to Torah," *Yeshiva World News*, May 14, 2009, www.theyeshivaworld.com/article.php?p=34261.

77. Nisson Wolpin, "Orthodoxy's Move to the Right: Grappling with the Helmreich Principle," *Jewish Observer* 30, no. 1 (1997): 24. Similarly, see Nisson Wolpin and Levi Reisman, "Feminism and Orthodoxy: How Promising a Shidduch," *Jewish Observer*

30, no. 3 (1997): 8–15, "Behind the question of Orthodox feminism, there is the much larger issue, of whether or not 'Orthodox Judaism' stands for the uncontested authority of the *halacha* as we understand it."

78. For an extensive list of secondary literature written about Hirsch up to 2004, see Carsten Wilke, *Die Rabbiner der Emanzipationszeit in den deutschen, böhmischen und grofspolnischen Ländern, 1781–1871* (Munich: K. G. Saur, 2004), 1:442–45. Subsequently, see Ferziger, *Exclusion and Hierarchy*, 117–32.

79. On Sofer, see, for example, Jacob Katz, "Towards a Biography of the Hatam Sofer," in *Divine Law in Human Hands*, 403–42, and the sources listed on 404–5; Moshe Samet, "Kavim nosafim le-biographiah shel ha-Hatam Sofer," in *Torah Im Derekh Eretz*, ed. Mordechai Breuer, 65–74 (Ramat Gan: Bar-Ilan University, 1987).

80. Examples that reflect Hirsch's influence include Gurock, "The Ramaz Version of American Orthodoxy," 40–82; and S. Heilman, *Sliding to the Right*, 18–19. For those who follow Sofer, see, for example, Gurock, "Resisters and Accommodaters"; S. Heilman, "The Many Faces of Orthodoxy: Part 2," 171–98; S. Heilman, *Sliding to the Right*, 19–20; Liebman, "Orthodoxy in American Jewish Life," 45–46, 67–85; Nadler, "Piety and Politics," 135–52.

81. Silber, "The Emergence of Ultra-Orthodoxy," 30 n.11. Silber's article is the most comprehensive discussion of Hungarian Ultra-Orthodoxy.

82. Moses Sofer, *Shu"t Hatam Sofer* [Likutim] (Jerusalem: Hod, 1972), 6: #89.

83. Rabbi Jacob Ettlinger, who was one of Hirsch's mentors, also referred to Reform and nonobservant Jews as Sadducees. Regarding the latter, at least, I believe that there were different motivations that led him to draft this term. See Ferziger, *Exclusion and Hierarchy*, 101–2.

84. See J. Katz, *A House Divided*; Silber, "The Emergence of Ultra-Orthodoxy," 33–37, 79–82.

85. The most comprehensive biography of Hildesheimer is David H. Ellenson, *Rabbi Esriel Hildesheimer and the Creation of a Modern Jewish Orthodoxy* (Tuscaloosa: University of Alabama Press, 1990).

86. Published in a letter of Rabbi Hillel Lichtenstein, *Responsa Beit Hillel*, #13. See also Silber, "The Emergence of Ultra-Orthodoxy," 68 n.94. On Hayyim Sofer, see Adam S. Ferziger, "Religious Zealotry and Religious Law: Reexamining Conflict and Coexistence," *Journal of Religion*, January 2004, 48–77.

87. Silber, "The Emergence of Ultra-Orthodoxy," 67.

88. For examples of his ridicule of other more liberal students of Soloveitchik, see Schachter, *Erez ha-Zvi*, 2; Schachter, *Mi-Peninei ha-Rav*, 68.

89. Schachter, *Be-Ikvei ha-Zon*, 1. Listen as well to his audio lecture titled "Modern Orthodoxy," available at Torahweb.org, September 14, 2003, www.torahweb.org/audio/rsch_091403.html, where he addresses this theme.

90. See Frimer and Frimer, "Women's Prayer Services," 42–47. See the discussion of Schachter's approach to rabbinical authority to adjust laws for their generation in Landes, "Traditional Struggles," 114–16.

91. Unlike his mentor, however, his position is more closely aligned with the nationalist "redemptive" school of Religious-Zionist thought. See, for example, Schachter,

"Be-Gidrei ha-Medinah u-milhamotehah," in *Be-Ikvei ha-Zon*, 205–20; Schachter, *Nefesh ha-Rav*, 62n.4; Schachter, "The Significance of the State of Israel: Celebrating Yom Ha'atzmaut," audio lecture available at Torahweb.org, April 17, 2002, www.torahweb.org/audio/rsch_041402.html (Yom Ha'atzmaut is Israel Independence Day). On the distinction between Soloveitchik's brand of Religious-Zionism and the redemptive school identified with Rabbi Abraham Isaac Kook, see Lawrence Kaplan, "Rabbi Abraham Isaac Kook, Rabbi Joseph B. Soloveitchik and Dr. Isaac Breuer on Jewish Identity and the National Jewish Revival," in *Jewish Identity in the Postmodern Age*, ed. Charles Selengut, 47–66 (New York: Paragon, 1999).

92. See Schachter, *Erez ha-Zvi*, 3–4; Schachter, *Nefesh ha-Rav*, 23.
93. Schachter, *Mi-Peninei ha-Rav*, 167–68.
94. "Women Elected Officers for First Time at KJ." See also his discussion of whether women are required to recite the "*kiddush le-vanah*" sanctification of the new moon prayer in Schachter, *Mi-Peninei ha-Rav*, 81–82.
95. Schachter has sent a number of his children to YU and its affiliated schools, and he proudly acknowledges the fact that some of them married YU graduates as well. See Schachter, *Erez ha-Zvi*, 2–3; Schachter, *Nefesh ha-Rav*, 19. He also has sons who attend the Haredi-oriented Ner Israel yeshiva in Baltimore. A comparison of the introductions to his four monographs suggests that over time he has made increasing efforts to emphasize the commonalities between his teacher's worldview and that of the American non-Hasidic Haredi world. This point comes across most clearly in his introduction to *Mi-Peninei ha-Rav*, published in 2001.
96. See William Helmreich, *The World of the Yeshiva* (New York: Free Press, 1982); Landes, "Traditional Struggles," 82–84.
97. See S. Heilman, *Sliding to the Right*, 58–60; L. Kaplan, "The Multi-Faceted Legacy of the Rav." See Pini Dunner and David N. Myers, "A Haredi Attack on Rabbi Joseph Ber Soloveitchik, *Jewish Quarterly Review* 105, no. 1 (2015): 131–38.
98. For an example of the complex relationship of Schachter to YU, which demonstrates his deep institutional allegiance on one hand, and his efforts to minimize areas of study that he considers to be contrary to Orthodoxy on the other, see Zev Eleff and Eitan Kastner, "Reconciling Institutional Divides: Rosh Kollel and YC Dean Begin Dialogue," *The Commentator*, September 11, 2006.
99. Jacob Katz, "Ha-Rav Shimshon Raphael Hirsch: Ha-mi-yamin u-mi-sema'iel," in *Torah im Derekh Eretz*, ed. Mordechai Breuer, 13–32 (Ramat Gan: Bar-Ilan University Press, 1987) (republished in *Ha-Halakhah be-Meizar: Mikhsholim al Derekh ha-Orthodoksiyah be-Hithavutah*, ed. Mordechai Breuer, 228–46 [Jerusalem: Magnes Press, 1992]).
100. The last ten minutes of Schachter's audio lecture "Modern Orthodoxy" buttress this.

Chapter 6

1. Reuven P. Bulka, *The Coming Cataclysm: The Orthodox-Reform Rift and the Future of the Jewish People* (Oakville, Ont.: Mosaic Press, 1984).
2. Sarna, *American Judaism*, 438.

3. Bulka, *The Coming Cataclysm*, 13. While omitting any judgment as to what traditions qualified as "mainstream Judaism," historian Jack Wertheimer leaned toward a similar conclusion nearly ten years later in his *A People Divided*, 176–79, as did journalist Samuel I. Freedman in *Jew vs. Jew*, 354. More recently, see Dana Evan Kaplan, "Trends in American Judaism from 1945 to the Present," in *The Cambridge Companion to American Judaism*, ed. Dana Evan Kaplan, 71–74 (New York: Cambridge University Press, 2005). See also Irving Greenberg, "Will There Be One Jewish People in the Year 2000?" *Perspectives*, CLAL, June 1985, 1–8, http://rabbiirvinggreenberg.com/wp-content/uploads/2013/02/Will-There-Be-One_red.pdf.
4. On the history of the RCA, see L. Bernstein, *Challenge and Mission*.
5. Cited in Freedman, *Jew vs. Jew*, 77.
6. Yaakov Elman, "Reform Judaism's Cheshire Grin," *Jewish Action* (September 1988): 27–28.
7. Debra Nussbaum Cohen, "How a Small Orthodox Group Wrote a National Story," *Jewish Telegraphic Agency*, April 4, 1997, www.jewishsf.com/content/2-0-/module/displaystory/story_id/5883/edition_id/109/format/html/displaystory.html. See Sarna, *American Judaism*, 191–93, where he argues that despite relegation to a minor role since the mid-twentieth century, it was the constant pressure of the Agudath ha-Rabbonim faction that eventually led to the complete detachment of Orthodoxy from Conservative Judaism after World War II. See also Liebman, "Orthodoxy in American Jewish Life," 32–34; Gurock, "Resisters and Accommodators," 114–22.
8. Lichtenstein, "Symposium: Our Next 100 Years," 52.
9. The earlier work is Wertheimer, *A People Divided*.
10. Wertheimer, *All Quiet on the Religious Front*, 3. See also Sarna, *American Judaism*, 372.
11. On Sofer's approach to Reform, see, for example, David Ellenson, "Traditional Reactions to Modern Jewish Reform: The Paradigm of German Orthodoxy," in *History of Jewish Philosophy*, ed. Daniel Frank and Oliver Leaman, 651–74 (London: Routledge, 1997); David Ellenson, "The Orthodox Rabbinate and Apostasy in Nineteenth-Century Germany and Hungary," in his *Tradition in Transition* (Lanham, Md.: University Press of America, 1989), 165–66; Ferziger, *Exclusion and Hierarchy*, 63–64, 67–69, 71–75; Jacob Katz, "Towards a Biography of the Hatam Sofer," in his *Divine Law in Human Hands*, 403–5; Moshe Samet, "Ha-Shinuyim be-Sidrei beit ha-knesset," 273–96; Silber, "Shorshei ha-Pilug be-Yahadut Hungariyah," 17–48.
12. See J. Katz, "Orthodoxy in Historical Perspective," 2:3–17; Liebman, "Religion and the Chaos of Modernity," 148; Liebman, "Orthodox Judaism," 11:123; Samet, "The Beginnings of Orthodoxy," 249–69.
13. See Ferziger, *Exclusion and Hierarchy*, 94–95.
14. On communal institutions, see, for example, ibid., 117–19, and the sources listed on 241–42 n.9; J. Katz, *A House Divided*. On support for Zionism, see Ellenson, *Rabbi Esriel Hildesheimer and the Creation of a Modern Jewish Orthodoxy*, 94–95, 99–100, 109–12.
15. Sarna, *American Judaism*, 86–87.
16. Ibid., 110. On Illowy, see Ellenson, "A Jewish Legal Decision by Rabbi Bernard Illowy," 174–95; Sherman, *Orthodox Judaism in America*, 101–3.

17. Sarna, *American Judaism*, 193–201.
18. See, for example, Jeffrey Gurock, "The Winnowing of American Orthodoxy," in his *American Jewish Orthodoxy in Historical Perspective*, 299–316 (Hoboken, N.J.: Ktav, 1996); Sarna, *American Judaism*, 237–42.
19. See, for example, Moses Feinstein, *Igerot Moshe*, vol. 2: *Yoreh Deah* (New York: n.p., 1959), #4; Liebman, "Orthodoxy in American Jewish Life," 53–54, 89; Sarna, "The Debate over Mixed Seating," 363–94; Wertheimer, *A People Divided*, 12–13, 27–29.
20. On women rabbis, see, for example, Simon Greenberg, *The Ordination of Woman Rabbis* (New York: Jewish Theological Seminary, 1988); Wenger, "The Politics of Women's Ordination: Jewish Law, Institutional Power, and the Debate over Women in the Rabbinate"; Wertheimer, *A People Divided*, 145–50, 158. On non-Orthodox conversion in Israel, see Ephraim Tabory, "The Legitimacy of Reform Judaism: The Impact of Israel on the United States," in *Contemporary Debates in American Reform Judaism: Conflicting Visions*, ed. Dana Evan Kaplan, 228 (New York: Routledge, 2001). On homosexual and lesbian rabbinical candidates, see Rebecca Spence, "Conservative Panel Votes to Permit Gay Rabbis," *Jewish Daily Forward*, December 6, 2006, http://forward.com/articles/9576/conservative-panel-votes-to-permit-gay-rabbis/.
21. On officiating at mixed marriages, see, for example, Hillel Cohn, "Why I Officiate at Mixed Marriage Ceremonies," in *Contemporary Debates in American Reform Judaism: Conflicting Visions*, ed. Dana Evan Kaplan, 161 (New York: Routledge, 2001), where he notes that of the one hundred marriages he conducted in 1996, sixty-four were between a Jew and a non-Jew; Wertheimer, *A People Divided*, 100–102, 107–9. On endorsing same-sex unions, see Wertheimer, *All Quiet on the Religious Front*, 22–23. On patrilineal descent, see Wertheimer, *A People Divided*, 158, 171. On Reform's departure from norms, see also Sarna, *American Judaism*, 372. In December 2014, a prominent Conservative rabbi created an uproar when he raised the possibility of performing mixed marriages. Due to pressure from some of his congregants, he later backed down. See Uriel Heilman, "Causing Stir, Prominent Conservative Rabbi Considers Breaking Intermarriage Ban," *JTA* (Dec. 14, 2014), www.jta.org/2014/12/18/news-opinion/united-states/causing-stir-prominent-conservative-rabbi-considers-breaking-intermarriage-ban.
22. Jonathan Sacks, *One People? Tradition, Modernity and Jewish Unity* (London: Littman Library, 1993), 224.
23. Wertheimer, *All Quiet on the Religious Front*, 17.
24. Jacob J. Petuchowski, "Reform Judaism's Diminishing Boundaries: The Grin That Remained," *Journal of Reform Judaism* (Fall 1986): 15.
25. On Kotler and the founding and early history of his yeshiva, see, for example, Herbert Bomzer, *The Kolel in America* (New York: Shengold Publishers, 1985), 26–35; Yoel Finkelman, "Haredi Isolation in Changing Environments: A Case Study in Yeshivah Immigration," *Modern Judaism* 22, no. 1 (2002): 61–82; Yoel Finkelman, "Religion and Public Life in 20th-Century American Jewish Thought," PhD diss., Hebrew University in Jerusalem, 2002, 101–15 (especially the many additional biographical sources cited in n.2); Finkelman, "An Ideology for American Yeshiva Students," 314–32; Helmreich, *The World of the Yeshivah*, 40–45; Liebman, "Orthodoxy in American Jewish Life," 67–69; Sarna, *American Judaism*, 302–4.

26. See Liebman, "Orthodoxy in American Jewish Life," 52.
27. See L. Bernstein, *Challenge and Mission*, 141–56; Sarna, *American Judaism*, 303.
28. Moses Feinstein, *Igerot Moshe*, vol. 1: *Yoreh De'ah* (New York: Balshon, 1960), #139 (nd).
29. See Ilan Fuchs, "'Bein ish le-isha ha-kol le-fi ha-ma'ase she-hu oseh kakh ruah ha-kodesh shurah alav': Yahasam shel sheloshah posekim Amerika'im Orthodoksim le-sugiyat talmud Torah le-nashim be-mahazit ha-me'ah ha-sheniyah shel ha-me'ah ha-Esrim," MA thesis, Bar-Ilan University, 2003, 55–57; Fuchs, *Jewish Women's Torah Study*, 120–29; Yael Levine, "Ha-Tenuah ha-Conservativit ke-fi she-mishtakefet be-teshuvotav shel ha-Rav Moshe Feinstein," in *Sefer Aviad*, ed. Yitzhak Raphael, 281–93 (Jerusalem: Mossad ha-Rav Kook, 1986); I. Robinson, "Because of Our Many Sins," 40–41, and the responsa of Feinstein cited in Robinson's nn. 27–35.
30. See Joseph B. Soloveitchik, "Message to a Rabbinic Convention," in *The Sanctity of the Synagogue*, ed. Baruch Litvin, 110–11 (New York: Spero Foundation, 1959). For a nuanced appraisal of the motivations and particular nature of Soloveitchik's antagonism toward the non-Orthodox, see Farber, "Reproach, Recognition and Respect." For a rigorous analysis of the controversy over mixed seating, see Sarna, "The Debate over Mixed Seating."
31. Regarding specific members of non-Orthodox congregations, already in the nineteenth century, efforts had been made to distinguish between individuals and institutions. See Ferziger, *Exclusion and Hierarchy*, 90–133.
32. Joselit, *New York's Jewish Jews*, 81–82.
33. See Liebman, "Orthodoxy in American Jewish Life," 49; David Singer, "Debating Modern Orthodoxy at Yeshiva College: The Greenberg-Lichtenstein Exchange," *Modern Judaism* 26, no. 2 (2006): 117.
34. For Edah, see the vision statement available at "Our Vision Statement," Edah, www.edah.org/vision.cfm, which speaks of trying to "reach out to and interact with Jews of all movements." For YCT, see Yeshivat Chovevei Torah, www.yctorah.org/content.
35. The meeting took place on November 13, 2003. The information was confirmed by Rabbi Robert S. Hirt, former vice president of Yeshiva University on November 13, 2007, in an e-mail communication to Nicole Vandestienne, Office of the President, Hebrew Union College. The latter forwarded me Hirt's text.
36. Yoni Lipshitz, "Recollections and Reconsiderations: Revisiting the Path of Rabbi Norman Lamm," *The Commentator*, December 12, 2007, 7–8.
37. See David Singer, "Emanuel Rackman: Gadfly of Modern Orthodoxy," *Modern Judaism* 28, no. 2 (2008): 134–48. Aharon Lichtenstein, the son-in-law of Joseph B. Soloveitchik, who moved to Israel in 1971, also expressed less combative attitudes toward the non-Orthodox when this was not a popular Orthodox position. See Adam S. Ferziger, "On Fragmentary Judaism: The Jewish 'Other' in the Worldview of Rabbi Dr. Aharon Lichtenstein," *Tradition* 47, no. 4 (2015): 34–68.
38. On Mitnagedism as a unique Orthodox ideology, see Immanuel Etkes, *The Gaon of Vilna* (Berkeley: University of California Press, 2002); Norman Lamm, *Torah Lishma: Torah for Torah's Sake* (New York: Yeshiva University Press/Ktav, 1989); Nadler, *The Faith of the Mithnagedim*. On Ner Israel, see Helmreich, *The World of the Yeshiva*, 32–36; Eliyahu Stern, *The Genius: Elijah of Vilna and the Making of Modern Judaism* (New Haven: Yale University Press), 2013.

39. On Perlow, see, for example, Staff, "Forward 50," *Jewish Daily Forward*, November 11, 2005, www.forward.com/articles/the-forward-50/.
40. Yaakov Perlow, "The following thoughts . . ." *Jewish Observer* 32, no. 6 (1999): 40 (italics in original).
41. Peter Haas, "Reform Judaism and Halacha: A Rapprochement," in *Platforms and Prayer Books*, ed. Dana Evan Kaplan, 243 (Lanham, Md.: Rowman and Littlefield, 2002).
42. Herbert Bronstein, "Platforms and Prayerbooks: From Exclusivity to Inclusivity in Reform Judaism," in *Platforms and Prayer Books*, ed. Dana Evan Kaplan, 37–38 (Lanham, Md.: Rowman and Littlefield, 2002).
43. See Meyer, *Response to Modernity*, 265–70, 388–89.
44. For efforts in the 1970s, see Wertheimer, *A People Divided*, 102–4. For the 1990s, see Dana E. Kaplan, "The Reform Theological Enterprise at Work: Debating Theory and Practice in the American Market Place," in *Platforms and Prayer Books*, ed. Dana Evan Kaplan, 6–7 (Lanham, Md.: Rowman and Littlefield, 2002); Dana E. Kaplan, *American Reform Judaism: An Introduction* (New Brunswick: Rutgers University Press, 2003), 64–112; Sarna, *American Judaism*, 324–25; Jack Wertheimer, "What Does Reform Judaism Stand For?" *Commentary*, June 2008, www.commentarymagazine.com/article/what-does-reform-judaism-stand-for/.
45. Perlow, "The following thoughts . . ."
46. Ibid.
47. Ibid.
48. "Novominsker Rebbe Emerges as New Sage of Aguda: Perlow Assumes Mantle of Sherer as Movement Seeks to Improve Relations with Secular Jewry," *Jewish Daily Forward*, December 4, 1998, www.highbeam.com/doc/1P1-22213037.html.
49. "Perlow's Progress," *Jewish Daily Forward*, January 8, 1998, 6. On Perlow's rejectionist position, see, for example, Joseph Berger, "Rabbis Who Were Sages Not Saints," *New York Times*, April 26, 2003, http://query.nytimes.com/gst/fullpage.html?res=9504E4D C143DF935A15757C0 A9659C8B63&sec=&spon=&pagewanted=print.
50. Levi Reisman, "We Are No Longer One," *Jewish Observer* 29, no. 4 (1996): 29–30.
51. Avi Shafran, "Why 'Jewish Religious Pluralism' Must Matter to Us," *Jewish Observer* 29, no. 9 (1996): 6. Since Perlow's appointment, however, Shafran has deferred to the latter's judgment; see Avi Shafran, "Burning Issues: The Revised Version," *Cross-Currents*, February 5, 2007, www.cross-currents/archives/2007/02/05.
52. Nisson Wolpin, "Surprising Settings, Yearning Souls: A Search for the Spiritual at Federation's General Assembly, in Pursuit of Torah within the Ranks of Reform," *Jewish Observer* 28, no. 10 (1996): 9–10. Wolpin could not resist pointing out that (10), "according to the Jewish Telegraphic Agency story, Shabbat dinners were offered to delegates, but many well-heeled couples from the biennial were seen making reservations for dinner that night at local non-kosher restaurants."
53. Leonard Oppenheimer, "Do We Really Have all the Answers," *Jewish Observer* 29, no. 6 (1996): 28. Similarly, see Eric Simon, "Of Coats and Fires: An Erstwhile Reform Jew's Challenge," *Jewish Observer* 33, no. 2 (2000): 31–34.
54. On Hirsch's approach to Reform, see, for example, Judith Bleich, "The Frankfurt Secession Controversy," *Jewish Action*, Winter, 1991–92, 22–27, 52; Ferziger, *Exclusion*

and Hierarchy, 113–32; Jaephet, "The Secession from the Frankfort Jewish Community," 99–122; J. Katz, *A House Divided*; Leo Levi, "The Relationship of the Orthodox to Heterodox Organizations: From A Halakhic Analysis by Rabbi S. R. Hirsch," *Tradition* 9, no. 3 (1967): 95–102; Liberles, *Religious Conflict in Social Context*, 219–25.

55. Elchonon Oberstein, "Defining the Agenda with Reform: Beyond the Battlefield," *Jewish Observer* 29, no. 8 (1996): 40.

56. Moshe Weinberger, *Jewish Outreach: Halakhic Perspectives* (Hoboken, N.J.: Ktav, 1990), 64.

57. Ibid.

58. For a list of Haredi kollels, see www.kerenyehoshuavyisroel.com/ajop/KollelDoc.cfm.

59. See Adam S. Ferziger, *The Emergence of the Community Kollel: A New Model for Addressing Assimilation*, Position Paper 13 (Ramat-Gan: Rappaport Center for Assimilation Research—Bar-Ilan University, 2006); Adam S. Ferziger, *Centered on Study: Typologies of the American Community Kollel*, Position Paper 18 (Ramat-Gan: Rappaport Center for Assimilation Research—Bar-Ilan University, 2009); Adam S. Ferziger, "Holy Land in Exile: The Torah MiTzion Movement: Toward a New Paradigm for Religious Zionism," in *Religious Zionism Post Disengagement: Future Directions*, ed. Chaim I. Waxman, 373–414 (New York: Yeshiva University Press, 2008).

60. See *Come Learn with Us* brochure, Atlanta Scholars Kollel, n.d., www.atlantakollel.org/about.htm. For a relatively balanced journalistic view of ASK's activities, see Melanie A. Lasoff, "Men in Black: How the Atlanta Scholars Kollel Turns People on to Our 3,000-Year-Old Tradition," *Atlanta Jewish Times*, April 13, 2001. Eleff, *Living from Convention to Convention*, 52, notes regarding Rabbi Yaakov Weinberg, the head of the Ner Israel yeshiva, "More than others, Weinberg and his rabbinical school kept close associations with NCSY."

61. Interview with Rabbi Menachem Deutsch, Founder and Rosh Kollel of ASK, Atlanta, September 18, 2003.

62. Leisah Mann, "Oasis in the Desert," *Jewish News of Greater Phoenix*, December 15, 2000.

63. Adam Reinherz, "Longtime Leader Leaving Pittsburgh Kollel," *Jewish Chronicle*, May 2014, http://thejewishchronicle.net/view/full_story/24975563/article-Longtime-Leader-Leaving-Pittsburgh-Kollel.

64. Interview with Rabbi Aaron Kagan, Rosh Kollel, Kollel Jewish Learning Center—Kollel Beis Yitzchak, Pittsburgh, September 9, 2003.

65. Interview with Rabbi Joey Felsen, Rosh Kollel/Executive Director, Jewish Study Network, Jerusalem, February 2, 2008.

66. Interview with Rabbi Yerachmiel Fried, Rosh Kollel, DATA Kollel, Dallas, Texas, February 10, 2008. Fried, however, would not present in a Reform sanctuary. Fried has authored numerous books on contemporary Jewish law, and serves as head of the religious court in Dallas that is authorized by both the RCA and the Israeli Chief Rabbinate to sanction local conversions.

67. Deutsch interview.

68. See the discussion of Ner LeElef in chapter 7.

69. "Alternative Locations for Holding Shiurim," *Ner LeElef Monthly Newsletter*, May–June 2002, www.nerleelef.com/Nitzotzot/alternative.doc.
70. On the promotion of strict halakhic interpretation as a characteristic of American Haredi Orthodoxy and the historical background to this phenomenon, see H. Soloveitchik, "Rupture and Reconstruction," 64–130. A parallel version with less extensive footnotes appeared as Haym Soloveitchik, "Migration, Acculturation, and the New Role of Texts," in *Accounting for Fundamentalisms: The Dynamic Character of Movements*, ed. Martin E. Marty and R. Scott Appleby, 197–235 (Chicago: University of Chicago Press, 1994).
71. The letter was shared with me by the addressee and its content is published here for the first time. Due to the sensitivity of the matter he did not permit me to photocopy it but allowed me to read it aloud and record it word for word on a digitial device. A further condition was that I leave out any identifying information regarding the addressee and his organization.
72. "A Rosh Yeshiva's View: An Interview with Rabbi Sholom Kamenetsky," *Klal Perspectives* (December 2012), http://klalperspectives.org/harav-sholom-kamenetsky-shlita/. Part of this citation appears in the title of an article that offers an initial glimpse into the halakhic issues arising from Orthodox outreach. See Jack Wertheimer, "Between 'West Point Standards' and Life in the Trenches: The Halakhic Dilemmas of Orthodox Outreach Workers," in *Between Jewish Tradition and Modernity: Essays in Honor of David H. Ellenson*, ed. Michael A. Meyer and David Myers, 67-79 (Detroit: Wayne State University Press, 2014). The author cites a wide range of additional questions that appear in two volumes dedicated to this new subtopic within contemporary Jewish law.
73. Wertheimer, "What Does Reform Judaism Stand For?"
74. See Michael A. Meyer, "Mekomo ve-zehuto shel ha-lo-Yehudi be-veit ha-kenesset ha-Reformi," *Gesher* 146 (Winter 2003): 66–74; Shmuel Rosner, "U.S. Jewish Movement Embraces Mixed Marriages, Reaches Out to Kids," *Ha'aretz*, March 24, 2008, www.haaretz.com/hasen/spages/967339.html.
75. See Ferziger, *Exclusion and Hierarchy*, 199–200; Ariel Picard, *Ha-Pesikah ha-Hilkhatit bat Zemanenu ve-Hitmodedutah im Ba'ayat ha-Hitbolelut*, Position Paper 3 (Ramat-Gan: Rappaport Center for Assimilation Research, 2003), 22–29.
76. Interview with David Luderman, Participant—DATA Kollel, Dallas, Texas, February 10, 2008.
77. Interview with Barton "Bob" Schechter, Pittsburgh, September 9, 2003. In October 2014 a new project was brought to the United States by Rabbi Warren Goldstein, the chief rabbi of South Africa, after its successful inauguration the prior year in his home country. Known as the Shabbos Project, the idea was to encourage as many Jews as possible to observe "just" one full Sabbath according to traditional law. No doubt there was hope that some would be inspired to continue this behavior in the future. But the central message was that "keeping it together" was an act of Jewish unity. The main local organizers of the Shabbes Project in Atlanta, Dallas, Houston, Seattle, Scottsdale (Arizona), and numerous other venues were the community kollels. See www.theshabbosproject.org/.

78. See, for example, Wertheimer, *A People Divided*, 118–23.
79. Sarna, *American Judaism*, 324–25, 363; Wertheimer, "What Does Reform Judaism Stand For?"
80. On Orthodox triumphalism, see, for example, Freedman, *Jew vs. Jew*, 338–43; Jonathan Sarna, "The Future of American Orthodoxy," *Shma.Com*, February 2001, http://shma.com/2001/02/the-future-of-american-orthodoxy/; Wertheimer, *A People Divided*, 118–23.
81. For a stark example of this type of Orthodox triumphalism, see Rabbi Berel Wein's comments in "The Sea Change in American Orthodox Judaism: A Symposium," *Tradition* 32, no. 4 (1998): 122–25.
82. See Steven M. Cohen and Arnold Eisen, *The Jew Within* (Bloomington: Indiana University Press, 2000), 183–85.
83. National Center for Education Statistics, School Search, Beth Midrash Govoha, http://nces.ed.gov/globallocator/col_info_popup.asp?ID=183804.
84. On the Lakewood yeshiva today, see David Landes, "How Lakewood, N.J., Is Redefining What It Means to Be Orthodox in America," *Tablet*, June 5, 2013, www.tabletmag.com/jewish-life-and-religion/133643/lakewood-redefining-orthodoxy?all=1.
85. On employment issues within American Haredi Orthodoxy, see Amiram Gonen, "From Yeshiva to Work: The American Experience and Lessons for Israel," *Floersheimer Institute Policy Studies* nos. 4/5 (2000), www.fips.org.il/Site/p_publications/item_en.asp?doc=&iss=&iid=569.
86. For Haredi-directed programs funded by the Avi Chai Foundation, see http://avichai.org/aboutus/activities/.
87. Chabad appears according to the spelling used by the organization in its official publications.
88. See, for example, Fishkoff, *The Rebbe's Army*, 38; Alison Klayman, "United, Chabad, Reform Promote Beijing Jewish Life," *Jerusalem Post*, April 2, 2008, www.jpost.com/Jewish-World/Jewish-Features/United-Chabad-Reform-promote-Beijing-Jewish-life; Jack Wertheimer, "Why the Lubavitch Movement Thrives in the Absence of a Living Rebbe," *Jewish Action*, June 16, 2014, www.ou.org/jewish_action/06/2014/lubavitch-movement-thrives-absence-living-rebbe/. For a critique of Chabad for "increasingly ... operat[ing] in a framework of postdenominational Judaism," see Marvin Schick, "Where Is Habad Heading," *Jerusalem Post*, January 9, 2008, http://mschick.blogspot.co.il/2006/01/where-is-chabad-heading.html.
89. See Ferziger, *Exclusion and Hierarchy*, 186–92.
90. See, for example, Marvin Schick, "An Essay on Contemporary Jewish Life," *Tradition* 35, no. 2 (2001): 14–35.
91. Perlow, "The following thoughts..."
92. In preparing this chapter, I conducted interviews with numerous individuals affiliated with specific community kollels and with the community kollel movement. However, a number of them asked that they remain anonymous out of a desire not to be associated with hostility or ill feelings toward other Jews. All the sources are recorded and preserved.
93. See, for example, Robert Eisenberg, *Boychiks in the Hood: Travels in the Hasidic Underground* (San Francisco: Harper, 1997), 14–15.

94. See, for example, Joshua Fogel, "Illegal Drug Use in Orthodox Jewish Adolescents," *Journal of Ethnicity in Substance Abuse* 3, no. 3 (2004): 17–31; Gerald Cromer, "Secularism Is the Root of All Evil: The Haredi Response to Crime and Delinquency," in *Language and Communication in Israel*, ed. Hana Herzog and Eliezer Ben-Raphael, 259–72 (Piscataway, N.J.: Transaction Publishers, 2001); Benzion Twerski, "Orthodox Youth and Drug Abuse: Shattering the Myths," *Jewish Action*, Spring 1998, www.jacsweb.org/article-8.html.
95. Ammiel Hirsch and Yaakov Yosef Reinman, *One People, Two Worlds: A Reform Rabbi and an Orthodox Rabbi Explore the Issues That Divide Them* (New York: Schocken Books, 2002), 308.
96. Ibid, x.
97. Quoted in Benzion N. Chinn, "Towards One People in One World," *The Commentator*, December 31, 2002, http://commie.droryikra.com/v67i7/culture/book.html.
98. Ibid.
99. Perlow, "The following thoughts . . ."
100. See, for example, Dan Pine, "Reform-Haredi Collaboration Ends in Bitter Brouhaha," *JWeekly.com*, February 21, 2003, www.jweekly.com/article/full/19371/reform-Haredi-collaboration-ends-in-bitter-brouhaha/.
101. Bulka, *The Coming Cataclysm*.

Chapter 7

1. Ferziger, "Constituency Definition," 535–67.
2. See, for example, Gurock, *Orthodox Jews in America*, 124, 16–163.
3. One clear exception, as noted in chapter 6 and expanded upon in chapter 8, is Chabad Hasidism.
4. Ismar Schorsch, "Emancipation and the Crisis of Religious Authority," in *Revolution and Evolution: 1848 in German-Jewish History*, ed. W. E. Mosse, 207–14 (Tübingen: Mohr Siebeck, 1981).
5. For a general discussion of the emergence of the seminaries, see Simon Schwartzfuchs, *A Concise History of the Rabbinate* (Oxford: Blackwell, 1993), 86–122. For specific studies, see Guy Miron, ed., *Mi-Breslau le-Yerushalayim: Batei Midrash le-Rabbanim, Pirkei Mehkar ve-Hagut* (Jerusalem: Machon Schechter and Leo Baeck Institute, 2009). For memoirs, see Asaf Yedidya, ed., *Batei Midrash Nusah Ashkenaz* (Jerusalem: Ha-Karmel, Machon Schechter, and Leo Baeck Institute, 2010).
6. For a vast collection of essays on the yeshiva in modern Europe, as well as Orthodox rabbinical seminaries, see Samuel K. Mirsky, ed., *Mosdot Torah be-Eiropah be-Vinyanam u-ve-Hurbanam* (New York: Egen, 1956).
7. See, for example, Moshe Carmilly Weinberger, ed., *The Rabbinical Seminary of Budapest* (New York: Sepher-Hermon Press, 1986).
8. On the history of Yeshiva University and its RIETS affiliate, see Jeffrey S. Gurock, *The Men and Women of Yeshiva* (New York: Columbia University Press, 1988); Gilbert Klapperman, *The Story of Yeshiva University* (New York: Macmillan, 1969); Aaron Rakeffet-Rothkoff, *Bernard Revel: Builder of American Orthodoxy* (Philadelphia: Jewish Publication Society, 1972).

9. Gurock, "The Winnowing of American Orthodoxy."
10. See chapter 2.
11. Elazar and Monson, "The Evolving Roles of American Congregational Rabbis," 73–89; Friedman, "The Changing Role of the Community Rabbinate," 90–94.
12. Charles S. Liebman, "The Training of American Rabbis," *American Jewish Year Book* 70 (1969): 3–112.
13. On this approach, see Immanuel Etkes, "The Relationship between Talmudic Scholarship and the Institution of the Rabbinate in Nineteenth-Century Lithuanian Jewry," in *Scholars and Scholarship: The Interaction between Judaism and Other Cultures*, ed. Leo Landman, 107–32 (New York: Yeshiva University Press, 1990); Lamm, *Torah Lishmah*.
14. Emanuel Feldman, "Trends in the American Yeshivot," *Tradition*, Spring 1968, 59 (quoted in Helmreich, *The World of the Yeshiva*, 244).
15. This tension can be illustrated through the "Symposium on the Priorities for the Years Ahead" published in the *Jewish Observer* (Tammuz-Av 5757/Summer 1997). While twelve of the seventeen participants raised outreach as a major priority, others encouraged strengthening and serving the core constituency. As Marc Shapiro has demonstrated, probably the most zealous figure in America until his passing in 2012 was the Hungarian-born Rabbi Menashe Klein, author of the eighteen-volume *Shu"t Mishne Halakhos*. Among others, Klein opposed outreach to the nonobservant due to halakhic problems regarding marriage to those whose parents did not observe ritual purity laws. Marc Shapiro, "Hungarian Ultra-Orthodoxy and Its Post–World War II Halakhic Legacy: The Case of Rabbi Menashe Klein," lecture at the Sixteenth World Congress for Jewish Studies, Jerusalem, August 1, 2013.
16. Interview of Sherer by William Helmreich, December 14, 1978, in *The World of the Yeshiva*, 243. Eleff, *Living from Convention to Convention*, 50–52, notes that during the 1960s and 1970s some Haredi yeshiva heads did encourage their students to become involved in outreach through NCSY. At the same time, the leaders expressed considerable ambivalence regarding the perceived compromised religious standards of this organization.
17. Jack Wertheimer, "The Outreach Revolution," *Commentary*, April 2013, 20–26, www.commentarymagazine.com/article/the-outreach-revolution/.
18. The information gathered here is based on personal communications with people connected with the Maor program, as well as with a student at the Ner Israel Rabbinical College in Baltimore.
19. Numerous discussions with pulpit rabbis of Modern Orthodox synagogues who would like to forge stronger connections with the broader community have confirmed their frustration at this predicament.
20. In an interview held with Rabbi Yaakov Shulman of the Beth Medrash Gadol in Lakewood, September 11, 2003, he described a similar program that was instituted by staff of the Lakewood yeshiva itself.
21. See the OSTT website at www.osttolney.org/.
22. See Community Resources, The Friedman Kollel of Metropolitan Washington, OSTT website, www.osttolney.org/community/kollel/.
23. On Aish Hatorah and the approach of its founder, Rabbi Noah Weinberg, see Janet Aviad, *Return to Judaism* (Chicago: University of Chicago Press, 1983), 28–29, 38–41;

Aaron Joshua Tapper, "The 'Cult' of Aish Hatorah: *Ba'alei Teshuva* and the Newly Religious Movement Phenomenon," *Jewish Journal of Sociology* 44, nos. 1–2 (2002): 5–29.

24. The initial information regarding the ROLP program was gathered during an interview conducted with Rabbi Yaakov Blackman, former director of ROLP, that took place in Jerusalem in the early afternoon (Israel time) of September 11, 2001. An updated account was provided through e-mail correspondence with Rabbi Eric Coopersmith, Director of ROLP (July 15, 2013).

25. On Ohr Somayach, see Aviad, *Return to Judaism*, 23–28. For an "in-house" description of its history and activities, see *The Ohr Somayach Story* (Jerusalem: Joseph and Faye Tannenbaum College of Jewish Studies, 1982).

26. Ohr Somayach runs its own outreach rabbi training institute, Ohr Lagolah. See "They Laughed When They Heard I Wanted to Be a Rebbe, but When I Started to Teach . . . ," Ohr Somayach, Ohr Lagolah: Hertz Institute for International Training, http://ohr.edu/study_in_israel/advanced/ohr_lagolah/4311.

27. Tapper, "The 'Cult' of Aish Hatorah," 10–11, notes this distinctive aspect of the Aish Hatorah ordination program.

28. Coopersmith e-mail.

29. "Welcome to Ner LeElef," Ner LeElef website, www.nerleelef.com/index.htm.

30. Ibid.

31. Ibid.

32. "Ner Le'Elef Programs," Ner LeElef website, www.nerleelef.com/programs/Dn.html.

33. The Jerusalem Kollel website, http://thejerusalemkollel.com.

34. See the list at "Jerusalem Kollel Alumni Serving Am Yisrael," The Jerusalem Kollel website, www.thejerusalemkollel.com/placements.php.

35. On the yeshiva in Slobodka, see Stampfer, *Lithuanian Yeshivas in the Nineteenth Century*. On the Chofetz Chaim and his yeshiva in Radin, see, for example, Lester Eckman, *Revered by All* (New York: Shengold, 1974).

36. On the history of the Chofetz Chaim yeshiva in America, see Helmreich, *The World of the Yeshiva*, 28–29.

37. On the *mussar* movement, see, for example, Immanuel Etkes, *Rabbi Israel Salanter and the Mussar Movement* (Philadelphia: Jewish Publication Society, 1993). On the *mussar* yeshivas, see Stampfer, *Lithuanian Yeshivas in the Nineteenth Century*.

38. Ner Israel also runs cooperative academic programs and allows its students to attain degrees at neighboring universities.

39. Queens Hatzolah Ambulance Service website, www.queenshatzolah.org/about.php.

40. National Center for Education Statistics, School Search, Rabbinical Seminary of America, http://nces.ed.gov/globallocator/col_info_popup.asp?ID=194763.

41. The main source for this description of the Chabad approach to rabbinical training is an extensive telephone interview held in September 2001 with R. Eli Hecht. In 1973 R. Hecht established a community in Lomita, California, to date still the only Orthodox synagogue in the area. In addition to holding weekly synagogue services with an attendance of more than 150 nonobservant Jews, R. Hecht has built a Jewish day school and a mikveh. He is also a prolific author and publicist whose articles appear

regularly in the nationally syndicated secular press. Finally, his two grown sons have themselves recently completed the Chabad rabbinical training program. See www.chabadsb.org/templates/articlecco_cdo/aid/61321/jewish/About-Rabbi-Hecht.htm.

42. See Shalom Z. Berger, "The Impact of One-Year Israel Study on American Day School Graduates," *Ten Da'at* 12 (1999): 3–14.
43. The information gathered is based on official RIETS publications, details provided by the rabbinical placement office, and this writer's personal experience and familiarity with the institution. Also see Avi Robinson, "Students Choose between RIETS and Chovevei Torah," *The Commentator* 67, no. 7 (2002), www.yctorah.org/component/option,com_docman/task,doc_view/gid,97/.
44. See Letter of Rabbi Menachem Penner (Acting Dean of RIETS) to RIETS Alumni, September 3, 2013, http://yu.convio.net/site/MessageViewer?em_id=42361.0&dlv_id=52601.
45. These figures appear in a chart sent to me on October 24, 2013, by Rabbi Ari Weitz, Assistant to the Dean, RIETS.
46. See Perl and Weinstein, *A Parent's Guide to Orthodox Assimilation on University Campuses*; "Orthodox Assimilation on Campus Part 1," and "Orthodox Assimilation on Campus Part 2."
47. Danzger, *Returning to Tradition*, 33–50.
48. "Rabbi Isaac Elchanan Theological Seminary: Semikhah Requirements," www.yu.edu/uploadedfiles/semikhah_requirements_final.pdf.
49. Ibid.
50. See Zev Eleff, "Ten Sha'alvim Alumni Depart Yeshiva after a Year for Less Academic Alternatives," *The Commentator*, February 12, 2007, http://admin2.collegepublisher.com/preview/mobile/2.2469/2.2828/1.298324. A greater challenge came from the decision earlier in the decade of two prominent *roshei yeshiva* at RIETS, Rabbi Yehuda Parnes and Rabbi Abba Bronspigel, to leave the institution after more than thirty years of association and help found Lander College for Men in Queens, New York. This Touro College affiliate promotes its ability to offer advanced Talmudic studies in a less heterogeneous environment than Yeshiva University. See www.touro.edu/landercollege.
51. Noah Streit, "Kollel Elyon Disbanded," *The Commentator* 62, no. 10 (2001), http://commie.droryikra.com/archives/v62iA/news/kollelelyon.html.
52. Yeshiva University, Kollellim, Bella and Harry Wexner Kollel Elyon and Semikhah Honors Program, www.yu.edu/riets/kollellim/wexner/.
53. "Rabbi Isaac Elchanan Theological Seminary."
54. Full disclosure: during that period I presented my initial research findings to a number of YU forums that addressed this issue, and I held individual and group consultations with relevant staff members.
55. Yeshiva University, Graduate Programming, Ner Le'Elef, http://yu.edu/cjf/graduate/ner_eleff/.
56. See Yeshiva University, Center for the Jewish Future, http://yu.edu/cjf/.
57. For additional comparisons, see the discussion in chapter 8 of the community kollels.

58. See the biographical interview of Weiss: Gary Rosenblatt, "Between a Rav and a Hard Place," *Jewish Week*, June 26, 2009, www.thejewishweek.com/editorial_opinion/gary_rosenblatt/between_rav_and_hard_place. See also Gurock, *Orthodox Jews in America*, 290–93.
59. Uriel Heilman, "Can Asher Lopatin Secure Yeshivat Chovevei Torah's Place in the Orthodox World?" *JTA*, September 7, 2013, www.jta.org/2012/09/07/life-religion/can-asher-lopatin-secure-yeshivat-chovevei-torahs-place-in-the-orthodox-world#ixzz2brbpDv7d.
60. The information gathered is based on official publications of Yeshivat Chovevei Torah, journalistic reports, and personal communications with leading teachers in the institution.
61. Weiss himself served for many years as a lecturer in Jewish Studies at Yeshiva University's Stern College for Women.
62. "Mission and Values," Yeshivat Chovevei Torah website, www.yctorah.org/content/view/1/49/.
63. "Curriculum Overview," Yeshivat Chovevei Torah website, www.yctorah.org/content/view/640/47/.
64. Ibid.
65. Yeshivat Chovevei Torah website, www.yctorah.org/content/view/39/47/.
66. "Curriculum Overview," Yeshivat Chovevei Torah.
67. For a sense of Lopatin's synthesis of intellectual nimbleness with social sensity, see Asher Lopatin, "How Orthodoxy and Orthodox Synagogues Can Meet the Needs of the Odyssey Generation," in *The Next Generation of Modern Orthodoxy*, ed. Shmuel Hain (New York: Yeshiva University/Ktav, 2012), www.yutorah.org/lectures/lecture.cfm/777847/Rabbi_Asher_Lopatin/How_Orthodoxy_and_Orthodox_Synagogues_Can_Meet_the_Needs_of_the_Odyssey_Generation#.
68. Dov Linzer and Avraham Weiss, "Creating an Open Orthodox Rabbinate," *Shma.Com*, January 1, 2003, http://shma.com/2003/01/creating-an-open-orthodox-rabbinate/.
69. "Alumni Placement as of August 2013," Yeshivat Chovevei Torah website, www.yctorah.org/images/yct%20placement%20sheet.pdf; "Our Alumni," Yeshivat Chovevei Torah website, www.yctorah.org/content/view/44/49/.
70. See the Northbrook Community Synagogue's website at http://northbrookcommunitysynagogue.com/; "The Guide to Jewish Living in Chicago: Traditional Congregations/Synagogues," JUF.org, www.juf.org/guide/category.aspx?id=16098. There is a separate seating service as well.
71. "Mazel Tov to Our Rabbis!" Yeshiva University website, http://yu.convio.net/site/MessageViewer?em_id=41481.0&dlv_id=51441.
72. Weitz communication (see n. 45, above).
73. "JLIC Overview," Heshie and Harriet Seif Jewish Learning Initiative on Campus, http://jliconline.org/jlic-overview/.
74. Uriel Heilman, "Is Yeshivat Chovevei Torah Kosher Enough?" *JTA*, September 7, 2012, www.jta.org/2012/09/07/news-opinion/the-telegraph/is-yeshivat-chovevei-torah-kosher-enough.

75. "A Few Words from IRF Leadership," International Rabbinic Fellowship, www.internationalrabbinicfellowship.org/.
76. In 2014, Rabbi Dov Lerea was appointed dean and "mashgiach ruchani" (spiritual supervisor) at YCT. Lerea, who was the longtime head of Jewish studies at the nondenominational Heschel School in New York, received his first rabbinical ordination from JTS and a second ordination from RIETS. He is currently a doctoral candidate at JTS. See www.jtsa.edu/The_Davidson_School/Rabbi_Dov_Lerea.xml?ss=print.
77. From late October to mid-November 2014, a public lecture series titled "Why Learn Talmud?" was held at the Drisha Institute for women's Torah study in Manhattan. The program was jointly sponsored and staffed by YCT, Yeshivat Maharat, Drisha, and the non-Orthodox Mechon Hadar. The lecturers included faculty members from both HUC and JTS. See http://drisha.org/whylearntalmud.php.
78. "About Yeshivat Maharat," Yeshivat Maharat website, http://yeshivatmaharat.org/.
79. See Weiss's response to attacks that appeared after Yeshivat Maharat's first ordination ceremony: Avraham Weiss, "Mesorah and Making Room: A Journey to Women's Spiritual Leadership," *Times of Israel*, June 17, 2013, http://blogs.timesofisrael.com/mesorah-and-making-room-a-journey-to-womens-spiritual-leadership/. Note that the RCA statement (as well as Weiss's initial discussion) focuses on the concept of *mesorah* (handed-down tradition). Recall that one of Rabbi Herschel Schachter's forceful and original attacks on the concept of women rabbis was titled "On the Matter of *Masorah*."
80. U. Heilman, "Can Asher Lopatin Secure?" For an interesting effort to analyze Weiss and his institutions within the context of the history of American Jewish denominational splits, see Zev Eleff, "The Maharat Moment," *Torah Musings*, September 9, 2013, www.torahmusings.com/2013/09/the-maharat-moment-3/. Eleff's article responds, in part, to accusations that Weiss's institutions are "Neo-Conservative" leveled in Moshe Averick, "American Jewry at the Crossroads: Isaac Mayer Wise, Solomon Schechter, and now . . . Avi Weiss and Sara Hurwitz," *The Algemeiner*, July 18, 2013, www.algemeiner.com/2013/07/18/american-jewry-at-the-crossroads-isaac-mayer-wise-solomon-schechter-and-now-avi-weiss-and-sara-hurwitz/.
81. See Gurock, *Orthodox Jews in America*, 318–21.

Chapter 8

1. Authorized Chabad accounts of Rabbi Schneerson's life are vague regarding many basic facts prior to his being chosen to lead the movement. It is difficult as well to gather substantial autobiographical information from Rabbi Schneerson's voluminous writings. For a rigorous attempt to decipher his biography, see Samuel C. Heilman and Menachem Friedman, *The Rebbe: The Life and Afterlife of Menachem Mendel Schneerson* (Princeton: Princeton University Press, 2010). Also see Shaul Shimon Deutsch, *Larger than Life: The Life and Times of the Lubavitcher Rebbe Rabbi Menachem Mendel Schneerson*, 2 vols. (New York: Chasidic Historical Productions, 1995–97); Avrum M. Ehrlich, *The Messiah of Brooklyn* (Jersey City, N.J.: Ktav, 2004); Fishkoff, *The Rebbe's Army*; Elliot R. Wolfson, *Open Secret: Postmessianic Messianism and the Mystical Revision of Menahem Mendel Schneerson* (New York: Columbia University Press, 2012).

2. The introduction to the biography and collection of the writings of Rabbi Nissan Waxman (1904–82), *Shevilei Nissan* (Jerusalem: Mossad Ha-Rav Kook), 7–9, relates an interesting confluence. This Lithuanian-born figure, who was ordained in 1926 by the RIETS, actually played a role in the establishment of both the Lubavitch Hasidic dynasty and the Lakewood yeshiva in America. Rabbi Joseph Isaac Schneerson, the sixth Lubavitcher Rebbe, escaped from Warsaw to New York in March 1940. He spent his first Passover holiday in Lakewood, New Jersey, and was hosted by Waxman, then the local rabbi. Subsequently, Waxman helped Schneerson arrange visas to America for his daughter Chaya Mushke and son-in-law, Menachem Mendel Schneerson. During his young adult years, Waxman had spent considerable time in Slutzk, where Kotler taught in the yeshiva of his father-in-law, Rabbi Isser Zalman Meltzer. After Kotler's arrival in the United States he met Waxman periodically. Waxman soon began a successful campaign to convince Kotler to establish a new yeshiva in Lakewood. I thank Chaim Waxman, the noted sociologist of American Jewry and editor of the new volume about his father, for sharing this information with me. See also Helmreich, *The World of the Yeshiva*, 359n.54; "The History of Chof Ches Sivan," in a pamphlet titled *Living with the Rebbe*, 7, www.crownheights.info/media/2/20100610-Leben%20%20 28%20Sivan.pdf.

3. Yaakov Yosef Reinman, "Remembering Reb Shneur Kotler," in *The Torah Profile*, ed. Nisson Wolpin (Brooklyn: Mesorah, 1988), 236. On the history of the kollel, see Bomzer, *The Kolel in America*; Mordechai Breuer, *Ohalei Torah: Ha-Yeshiva, Tavnitah ve-Toldotehah* (Jerusalem: Merkaz Shazar, 2004), 28, 149; Stampfer, *Lithuanian Yeshivas of the Nineteenth Century*.

4. Finkelman, "Religion and Public Life," 118–20, 142–47; Helmreich, *The World of the Yeshiva*, 43–44, 284.

5. Aharon Kotler, *Mishnat Rabbi Aharon*, vol. 4: *Ma'amarim ve-Sihot Mussar* (Lakewood, N.J.: Makhon Mishnat Rabbi Aharon, 2005), 192–94.

6. Jonathan Sacks, "The Man Who Turned Judaism Outwards," *Wellsprings* 41 (Summer 1994): 7–8.

7. Menachem Mendel Schneerson, *Likutei Sihos* 10 (Brooklyn: Kehot Press, 1993), 254–56 (quoted in Yitzhak Kraus, Ha-Shevi'i, 61–65 [Tel Aviv: Yediot Aharonot, 2008]).

8. Kraus, *Ha-Shevi'i*, 34–92. Kraus points out that unlike his son-in-law, the previous Lubavitcher Rebbe had initially directed his followers' educational efforts primarily to *anshei shelomeinu* (roughly "those within the fold"). Indeed, Rabbi Joseph Isaac Schneerson stated that he delayed moving to the United States due to his reluctance to associate with heterogeneous American Jewry. Once he arrived on American soil in 1940, however, he began the process of refocusing Lubavitch Hasidism on outreach toward all Jews. In fact, he even suggested that eventually other groups would follow suit. See Joseph Isaac Schneerson, *Sefer ha-Sihot Kayitz ha-Ta"sh[1940]* (Brooklyn: Ma'arekhet Ozar ha-Hasidim, 1956), 88–89.

9. Kraus, *Ha-Shevi'i*, 92–131; Fishkoff, *The Rebbe's Army*, 27–32, 111–17.

10. Regarding Rabbi Kotler's opinion of Chabad, I found agreement between two sources that are at sharp odds regarding their overall evaluation of the movement; see David Berger, *The Rebbe, the Messiah, and the Scandal of Orthodox Indifference* (London:

Littman Library, 2001), 7; Chaim Dalfin, *Attack on Lubavitch: A Response* (Brooklyn: Jewish Enrichment Press, 2002), 71–72.
11. Liebman, "Orthodoxy in American Jewish Life," 79–82, 89–92.
12. See D. Berger, *The Rebbe, the Messiah, and the Scandal*, 7. See the penetrating and nuanced analysis of Schneerson's messianism in Wolfson, *Open Secret*. Deutsch, *Larger than Life*, 117–23, argues that former allies such as Rabbi Isaac Hutner of the Chaim Berlin Yeshiva and Rabbi Joseph B. Soloveitchik of Yeshiva University distanced themselves from Rabbi Schneerson already at the outset of his tenure due to their discomfort with his messianic ideology. Chaim Rapoport, *The Messiah Problem: Berger, the Angel, and the Scandal of Reckless Indiscrimination* (Ilford: self-published, 2002), reproduces a tremendous amount of material regarding the late twentieth-century controversy.
13. C. Waxman, "The Haredization of American Orthodox Jewry."
14. Prior to becoming a Lubavitcher Hasid, Carlebach had studied with Kotler. See Danzger, *Returning to Tradition*, 50. Carlebach left the Chabad movement in the 1960s and gained wide popularity as a Hebrew songwriter and performer. Simultaneously, he created his own brand of New Age Hasidism that appealed primarily to young unaffiliated Jews. See Ariel, "Hasidism in the Age of Aquarius," 139–65. Like his compatriot Carlebach, Schachter Shalomi also eventually moved away from mainstream Chabad—and for that matter Orthodoxy—and emerged as one of the main figures in the American Jewish New Age movement. See Micha Odenheimer, "Wise Guy, Wise Man," *Haaretz*, October 10, 2005, www.haaretz.com/news/wise-guy-wise-man-1.171162.
15. Danzger, *Returning to Tradition*, 2, 58–62; Eisenberg, *Boychiks in the Hood*, 183–85; Fishkoff, *The Rebbe's Army*, 94, 112.
16. On the development of the *mivtzoim* (mitzvah campaigns), see Fishkoff, *The Rebbe's Army*, 46–58; Kraus, *Ha-Shevi'i*, 132–77.
17. Fishkoff, *The Rebbe's Army*, 94.
18. Telephone interview with Mrs. Rivka (Teitz) Blau, May 7, 2006. On Yavne, see Benny Kraut, *The Greening of American Orthodox Judaism: Yavneh in the Nineteen Sixties* (Cincinnati: Hebrew Union College Press, 2011).
19. Dalfin, *Attack on Lubavitch*, 83.
20. Ibid. View the full list through the search function of the official Chabad website: www.chabad.org.
21. Fishkoff, *The Rebbe's Army*, 96–97.
22. See Cohen and Eisen, *The Jew Within*, 130–34; Diner, *Jews of the United States*, 315–16; Roof, *A Generation of Seekers*, 241–62; Chaim I. Waxman, *Jewish Baby Boomers: A Communal Perspective* (Albany: State University of New York Press, 2001).
23. On Chabad fundraising, see Fishkoff, *The Rebbe's Army*, 160–83.
24. Ibid., 88–93, 108–10.
25. Critics of Chabad claim that many of the shluchim are not sufficiently learned in Jewish law. All the same, their knowledge is certainly far richer than that of the average American Jew.
26. Funds are certainly solicited, but services are not conditional on individuals giving donations.

27. This analysis is based on numerous visits to Chabad houses throughout the world and is buttressed by evidence offered in Fishkoff's work.
28. Fishkoff, *The Rebbe's Army*, 38.
29. On the role of women emissaries in Chabad, see chapter 9.
30. See www.chabad.org.
31. Fishkoff, *The Rebbe's Army*, 9. For the conference, see *Kinus.com*, www.kinus.com/templates/kinus/default.htm.
32. On the role of "decentralization" in the spread of early Hasidism, see, for example, Shmuel Ettinger, "The Hasidic Movement: Reality and Ideals," *Journal of World History* 11, nos. 1–2 (1968): 226–43 (reprinted in *Essential Papers on Hasidism*, ed. Gershon David Hundert, 238–42 [New York: New York University Press, 1991]); Ada Rapoport-Albert, "Hasidism after 1772, Structural Continuity and Change," in *Hasidism Reappraised*, ed. Ada Rapoport-Albert, 76–140 (London: Littman Library of Jewish Civilization, 1996).
33. Cited in Uriel Heilman, "Chabad Outreach Admired by Other Orthodox, Reform," *The Jewish Review*, May 12, 2008, www.jewishreview.org/node/7880.
34. In preparation for this chapter, I conducted interviews with numerous individuals affiliated with specific community kollels and with the community kollel movement. A number of them asked that they remain anonymous out of a desire not to be associated with hostility or ill feelings toward other Jews. All the sources are preserved with me.
35. For a more detailed discussion of the stages in the development of the American kollel, see Ferziger, *The Emergence of the Community Kollel*, 15–55.
36. Bomzer, *The Kolel in America*, 33–34; Wolpin, "The Community Kolel," 20.
37. For Toronto, see "Kollelim," *Nitzotzot Min HaNer* 16 (January–March 2004): 3, which reports that the Toronto Community Kollel was founded in 1972. The first community kollel was actually begun in Johannesburg, South Africa, by alumni of the Gateshead Yeshiva in England. On this institution, see Moishe Sternbuch, "The Kollel Phenomenon and Its Significance," in *Halachic Discourses on Masechte Beitzo*, 5–16 (Bnei Brak: Kollel Yad Shaul, 1982). For Los Angeles, see an expansive description of this kollel in Bomzer, *The Kolel in America*, 112–15.
38. Regarding Toronto, see Etan Diamond, *And I Will Dwell in Their Midst: Orthodox Jews in Suburbia* (Chapel Hill: University of North Carolina Press, 2000), 48–54.
39. Interview with Rabbi Shaya Milikowsky, Jerusalem, August 2, 2003.
40. Deutsch interview.
41. Ibid. See the ASK website, www.atlantakollel.org, for a mission statement and a detailed description of its activities.
42. "Kollelim," *Nitzotzot Min HaNer*, 5. See a list that includes both traditional community and outreach kollelim at www.kerenyehoshuavyisroel.com/ajop/KollelDoc.cfm.
43. See JSN, www.jsn.info/; DATA, http://datanet.org.
44. Interview with Rabbi Nate Segal of Torah Umesorah, Staten Island, New York, September 14, 2003.
45. Leisah Mann, "Jewish Unity 2005 Makes World Debut," *Jewish News of Greater Phoenix*, February 18, 2005.

46. Fishkoff, *The Rebbe's Army*, 9.
47. See information on the upcoming AJOP convention at www.ajopconvention.com.
48. In his last full-length monograph, Charles Liebman (together with Bernard Susser) identified Orthodoxy's emphasis on learning as one of the keys to its survival, as well as one of the values that non-Orthodox Jews should emulate in order to stem assimilation. See Bernard Susser and Charles S. Liebman, *Choosing Survival: Strategies for a Jewish Future* (New York: Oxford University Press, 1999), 133–44, 146–49.
49. Danzger, *Returning to Tradition*, 279, describes the *hevrutah* approach to study as follows: "It does not simply bind one person to the other, although it does that too. It binds one directly to the learning experience. You have not just passively absorbed; you have created, you have understood a view, argued for it, transmitted it, defended it. It is now you as much as anything else."
50. On the role of individual quest in contemporary American Jewish life, see, for example, Cohen and Eisen, *The Jew Within*; Diner, *Jews of the United States*, 356–58; Sarna, *American Judaism*, 348–52; Steven Sharot, "Assimilating, Coalescing and Spiritual-Seeking: Recent Trends among American Jews," *Studies in Contemporary Jewry* 18 (2002): 240–46.
51. The difference between the teaching approaches of the Chabad house and the community kollel may be connected to their divergent outlooks on the nature of Torah study in general. Hasidism's focus on teaching their philosophy reflects its emphasis on the Torah as a tradition handed down directly from their Rebbe. The willingness of the Mitnagedim to open up the text to analysis, on the other hand, is consistent with the value placed in their circles on innovation (*hiddush*).
52. See Danzger, *Returning to Tradition*, 42, "Becoming Orthodox means not only learning and accepting beliefs and practices. It also means becoming part of a community of people who support each other's common customs, beliefs, values, and life-style."
53. Robert Wuthnow, *Loose Connections: Joining Together in America's Fragmented Communities* (Cambridge, Mass.: Harvard University Press, 1998), esp. 9–57.
54. Putnam, *Bowling Alone*.
55. Wuthnow, *Loose Connections*, 58–82.
56. Robert Wuthnow, ed., *"I Come Away Stronger": How Small Groups Are Shaping American Religion* (Grand Rapids, Mich.: Wm. B. Eerdmans Publishing, 1994); Robert Wuthnow, *Sharing the Journey: Support Groups and America's New Quest for Community* (New York: Free Press, 1994).
57. Telephone interview with Rabbi Aaron Kagan, Rosh Kollel, Kollel Jewish Learning Center, Pittsburgh, Pennsylvania, September 10, 2005.
58. For a recent rigorous academic biography that offers a fresh view of this figure, see Stern, *The Genius*.
59. On the Gaon's opposition to Hasidism, see, for example, Immanuel Etkes, "The Vilna Gaon and the Beginning of the Struggle against Hasidism," in his *The Gaon of Vilna*, 73–95.
60. Etkes, "Rabbi Hayyim of Volozhin's Response to Hasidism," in *The Gaon of Vilna*, 151–208. See also Breuer, *Ohalei ha-Torah*, 46–49; Friedman, "The Changing Role of the

NOTES TO CHAPTER 8

Community Rabbinate," 10. Other scholars are less inclined to view anti-Hasidism as a central motivating factor. See, for example, Lamm, *Torah Lishma*, 9–28.

61. Etkes, "Rabbi Hayyim," in *The Gaon of Vilna*, 205–8.
62. Dara Gever, "Contemporary Campus Kiruv at Emory: Departing from 'Outreach' and 'Returning' to Judaism," BA thesis, Emory University, 2013. I thank Professor Michael Berger for calling my attention to this source—which is based on excellent fieldwork and contains important data—and to Dara Gever for sending it to me.
63. Telephone interview with Rabbi Menachem Deutsch, Rosh Kollel, ASK Kollel, Atlanta, Georgia, September 15, 2005.
64. See, for example, Shturem, http://shturem.net/index.php?section=news&id=65257.
65. This is not necessarily the case regarding the TMZ kollels in Australia, Europe, and South America.
66. See interview with Robert L. Stark, Beachwood, Ohio, September 6, 2003; Dianne Chabbot, "Kollel with a Modern Twist," *Jewish Action* (Winter 2002), http://ou.org.s3.amazonaws.com/publications/ja/5763/5763winter/ITTAKESA.pdf. On Yeshivat Har Etzion, see David Morrison, *The Gush: Center of Modern Religious Zionism* (Jerusalem: Gefen, 2003).
67. See "Site Visit by David Roth and Ze'ev Schwartz to Cleveland, November 2001," TMZ Cleveland File, TMZ Jerusalem Office, 54 King George St., Jerusalem 91710, entrance floor; interview with Rabbi Binyamin Blau, former Rosh Kollel (Kollel Head) and Principal of Fuchs-Mizrachi High School, Cleveland Heights, Ohio, September 8, 2003.
68. B. Blau interview; interview with Vicky Epstein Frolich, Kollel Administrator, Cleveland Heights, Ohio, September 8, 2003.
69. On the Memphis shlichim, see Torah MiTzion, Communities: Memphis, Tennessee, https://torahmitzion.org/communities/memphis-tennessee-2-2/. For background on TMZ, see "About Torah MiTzion," Torah MiTzion, http://torahmitzion.org/about.
70. See Chicago Community Kollel, www.cckollel.org/contactus.shtml. In February 2011 I visited Chicago, and observed the Chicago Community Kollel and conducted interviews with its leaders, Rabbi Moshe Francis, Rabbi Dovid Zucker, some of the fellows, and lay community members who study in its programs.
71. Leonard A. Matanky and Yehuda Sussman, "Creative Solutions to Educational Challenges: The Torah MiTzion *Kollel*s II," *Lookjed Forum*, August 28, 2006, http://listserv.biu.ac.il/cgi-bin/wa?A3=ind0608&L=LOOKJED&E=8bit&P=12870 2&B=—&T=TEXT%2FPLAIN;%20charset=ISO-8859-8&header=1.
72. Yeshiva University Torah Mitzion Kollel of Chicago, "Our Mission," http://chicagotorah.org/about/. During my February 2011 visit to Chicago, I observed the YU/TMZ Kollel and conducted interviews with Rabbi Matanky, Rabbi Brand, some of the fellows, and lay Modern Orthodox community members.
73. Josh Nathan Kazis, "Leonard Matanky, Chicago Rabbi, Named to Head RCA," *Jewish Daily Forward*, July 9, 2013, http://forward.com/articles/180146/leonard-matanky-chicago-rabbi-named-to-head-rca/#ixzz2cdyeLY65.

74. David Eliezrie, "Pew Asked the Wrong Questions," *Times of Israel*, October 17, 2013, http://blogs.timesofisrael.com/rescind-the-pew-r/. See the rebuttal by the lead authors of the Pew Report, Alan Cooperman and Greg Smith, "Pew Research Center: Our Research Is Sound," *Times of Israel*, October 18, 2013, http://blogs.timesofisrael.com/pew-research-center-our-research-is-sound/.

Chapter 9

1. Sylvia Barack Fishman with Daniel Parmer, *Matrilineal Ascent/Patrilineal Descent: The Growing Gender Imbalance in American Jewish Life* (Waltham, Mass.: Cohen Center for Modern Jewish Studies, 2008). For a bibliography of both primary and secondary sources in English that have been published on women and Judaism up until 2008, see Phyllis Holman Weisbard, "Annotated Bibliography and Guide to Archival Resources on the History of Jewish Women in America," March 1, 2009, http://jwa.org/encyclopedia/article/annotated-bibliography-and-guide-to-archival-resources-on-history-of-jewish-wom.
2. See chapter 5.
3. Shuli Rubin Schwartz, *The Rabbi's Wife: The Rebbetzin in American Jewish Life* (New York: New York University Press, 2006).
4. Fishkoff, *The Rebbe's Army*, 148–60; Naftali Loewenthal, "Women and the Dialectic of Spirituality in Hasidism," in *Within Hasidic Circles, Studies in Hasidism in Memory of Mordecai Wilensky*, ed. Immanuel Etkes, David Assaf, Israel Bartal, and Elhanan Reiner, 7–65 (Jerusalem: Machon Bialik, 1999); Naftali Loewenthal, "Hasidic Woman," *Journal of World Union of Jewish Studies* 40 (2000): 21–28; Bonnie Morris, *Lubavitcher Women in America: Identity and Activism in the Postwar Era* (Albany: State University of New York Press, 1999).
5. Finkelman, *Strictly Kosher Reading*, 68–69, 90–91.
6. Kimmy Caplan, "The Internal Popular Discourse of Israeli Haredi Women," *Archives de sciences sociales des religions* 123 (July–September 2003): 77–101, http://assr.revues.org/1069.
7. Rubin Schwartz, *The Rabbi's Wife*, 51–87.
8. "Our Team," TORCH: Connecting Jews and Judaism, www.torchweb.org/team2.php.
9. "ASCENT: The Women of TORCH," TORCH: Connecting Jews and Judaism, www.torchweb.org/ascent.php.
10. "Celebration of Judaism Unites Houston Women," *Jewish Herald-Voice* (January 3, 2008), http://jhvonline.com/celebration-of-judaism-unites-houston-women-p3812.htm.
11. Felsen interview; interview with Sarah Apt, Palo Alto, Calif. (February 11, 2011); fieldwork observation, Palo Alto, Calif. (February 2011).
12. "Ner Le'Elef Programs: English Speaking Programs," Ner LeElef website, www.nerleelef.com/programs/english.html; "Women's Program," The Jerusalem Kollel, www.thejerusalemkollel.com/womens_program.php.
13. See "Ner LeElef Booklets," Ner LeElef website, www.nerleelef.com/booklets.htm.
14. *Women's Issues—Book One: The Female and Her Characteristics* (Jerusalem: Ner Leelef, 2007), www.nerleelef.com/books/Women%20Book%20One.pdf; *Women's Issues—Book Two: Women in Mitzvos* (Jerusalem: Ner Leelef, 2007), www.nerleelef.com/books/Women%20Book%20One.pdf.

15. *Women's Issues—Book One*, 167.
16. See Wertheimer, "Between 'West Point Standards' and Life in the Trenches."
17. See, for example, photo gallery from the International Conference of Shluchos 2012, Chabad Lubavitch of Greater Boynton Beach, www.chabadboynton.com/templates/photogallery_cdo/aid/1789097/jewish/International-Conference-of-Shluchos-2012.htm#!6274841.
18. "About WIK," WomenInKiruv.org, www.womeninkiruv.org/about/.
19. Ibid.
20. "Women in Kiruv Conference," Matzav.com, November 15, 2012, http://matzav.com/women-in-kiruv-conference.
21. Ibid.
22. Interview with Elky Langer, Pittsburgh (September 9, 2003).
23. Apt interview.
24. Felsen interview; Apt interview.
25. "Women in Kiruv Conference."
26. These conflicts regarding female religious figures are, of course, connected to the broader issue of the Haredi family and expanding employment opportunities for women. See Caplan, "The Internal Popular Discourse of Haredi Women," 88–94; S. Heilman, *Sliding to the Right*, 173–79.
27. *Lori Almost Live*, www.aish.com/sp/lal/.
28. Lori Palatnik, "Kiruv: If We Do Not Change, We Will Lose," *Klal Perspectives*, Fall 2012, http://klalperspectives.org/lori-palatnik/.
29. Ibid.
30. Jewish Women's Renaissance Project, Annual Report, 2011, available at ISSUU.com, http://issuu.com/juliefarkasgraphicdesign/docs/jwrp_annual_nofinancials2.
31. Editors, "Ten Women to Watch in 5774," *Jewish Woman Magazine*, Fall 2013, http://jwi.org/page.aspx?pid=1889#sthash.s6YeMxkN.nB56xAwb.dpbs.
32. "March Is Women's History Month," Hadassah.org, March 2014, www.hadassah.org/site/c.keJNIWOvElH/b.6606301/k.4698/March_Is_Womens_History_Month.htm. For an Israeli female figure whose activities and style raise parallels to Lori Palatnik, see the discussion of Rabbanit Yemima Mizrachi in Nissim Leon and Aliza Lavie, "*Hizuk*—The Gender Track: Religious Invigoration and Women Motivators in Israel," *Contemporary Jewry* 33, no. 3 (2013): 201–2.
33. *Women's Issues—Book Two*, 165.
34. Leon and Lavie, "*Hizuk*—The Gender Track," 209–13, ask similar questions regarding the response among Israeli male Haredi figures to the Israeli female activists whom they describe. The authors suggest that opinions are divided, with some figures fully supportive and others highly critical. Furthermore, they raise the question of whether these female religious personalities actually challenge the strictly male-dominated hierarchy of Israeli Haredi society, but they do not reach a conclusive answer. There is definitely room for a comparative study of these parallel Israeli and American phenomena.
35. Rubin Schwartz, *The Rabbi's Wife*, 200–208; Shuli Rubin Schwartz, "Ambassadors without Portfolio? The Religious Leadership of Rebbetzins in Late-Twentieth-Century

American Jewish Life," in *Women and American Judaism: Historical Perspectives*, ed. Pamela Suzanne Nadell and Jonathan D. Sarna, 235–67 (Hanover, N.H.: Brandeis University Press/University Press of New England, 2001).
36. Rubin Schwartz, "Ambassadors without Portfolio," 252.
37. Morris, *Lubavitcher Women in America*, 100–122.
38. Debra R. Kaufman, "Engendering Orthodoxy: Newly Orthodox Women and Hasidism," in *New World Hasidism: Ethnographic Studies of Hasidic Jews in America*, ed. Janet S. Belcove-Shalin, 135–60 (Albany: State University of New York Press, 1995).
39. See, for example, Ner LeElef's *Women's Issues—Book Two*, 8–19.
40. Naftali Loewenthal, "'Daughter/Wife of Hasid' or 'Hasidic Woman'?" *Jewish Studies* 40 (2000): 28. See also Loewenthal, "Women and the Dialectic of Spirituality in Hasidism," 7–65; Loewenthal, "From 'Ladies' Auxiliary' to 'Shluhot' Network: Women's Activism in Twentieth-Century Habad," in *A Touch of Grace: Studies in Ashkenazi Culture, Women's History, and the Languages of the Jews Presented to Chava Turniansky*, 69–93 (Jerusalem: Zalman Shazar Center for Jewish History; Hebrew University, Center for Research on Polish Jewry, 2013).
41. See the discussion of new approaches to women among the fifth and sixth Lubavitcher rebbes in Ada Rapoport-Albert, "On Women in Hasidism, S. A. Horodecky, and the Maid of Ludmir Tradition," in *Jewish History: Essays in Honour of Chimen Abramsky*, ed. Ada Rapoport-Albert and Steven J. Zipperstein, 495–525 (London: Peter Halban, 1988).
42. Loewenthal, "From 'Ladies' Auxiliary' to 'Shluhot' Network," 74–79.
43. For extensive discussions of Chabad outreach, see Fishkoff, *The Rebbe's Army*; Heilman and Friedman, *The Rebbe*, 1–28; Kraus, *Ha-Shevi'i*.
44. Loewenthal, "From 'Ladies' Auxiliary' to 'Shluhot' Network," 80–93.
45. Fuchs, *Jewish Women's Torah Study*, 31–62.
46. "Recent Statements by Agudath Israel and the Rabbinical Council of America Regarding Women Rabbis," *Hakirah* 11 (Spring 2011), www.hakirah.org/vol%2011%20rca%20agudah.pdf.
47. Ibid.
48. Ibid.
49. "About the JWRP," JWRP: Jewish Women's Renaissance Project, www.jwrp.org/about-us.

Conclusion

1. Moshe Hauer, "Idealistic Realism in Communal Leadership," *Klal Perspectives* 2, no. 2 (2013): 37.
2. Ibid., 38.
3. Ibid.
4. Ibid.
5. Ibid.
6. Wertheimer, *All Quiet on the Religious Front*. One of the new terms that has been adopted to self-describe the obsolescence of classical labels is "Reconformadox." See, for example, http://jfsa.org/community/community-directory/beth-shalom-temple-center-of-green-valley.

7. The skeptical stance toward kiruv has been articulated consistently by well-known Haredi educator and social commentator Marvin Schick. See, for example, Marvin Schick, "An Essay on Contemporary American Jewish Life" (August 1, 2001); "Rethinking Outreach" (October 16, 2003); "Is Outreach Out of Our Reach (June 6, 2005); "RJJ Newsletter—January 2010" (January 1, 2010). All are available at http://mschick.blogspot.co.il. Probably the most zealous figure in America until his passing in 2012 was the Hungarian-born Rabbi Menashe Klein (1924–2011), author of the eighteen-volume *Shu"t Mishne Halakhot* (Brooklyn: Makhon Mishne Halakhot Gedolot, 1998–2004). Among others, Klein opposed outreach to the nonobservant due to halakhic problems regarding marriage to those whose parents did not observe ritual purity laws; see Marc Shapiro, "Hungarian Ultra-Orthodoxy and its Post–World War II Halakhic Legacy."
8. On October 15, 2013, a veteran activist and musician affiliated with Aish Hatorah named Tzvi Gluckin responded to the Pew report on the Torah kiruv network for outreach workers. Reacting to the sharp rise in intermarriage and decline in synagogue affiliation documented in the report, he commented that "we are not reaching the masses. And if we miss the masses we are not really doing much of anything.... Most Jews will live their entire lives and die and never know what they had and threw away. And it is our fault." www.denverjewish.com/mailman/listinfo/torahkiruv.
9. See the website of Bnai Jacob Shaarei Zion, www.bjsz.org/.
10. See, for example, the insider report on the September 2013 rally against Israeli government cuts of financial support of yeshiva students: "PHOTOS: Over 7000 Gather in Lakewood at Historic Rally on Behalf of Yidden in Eretz Yisroel," *Lakewood Scoop*, September 3, 2013, www.thelakewoodscoop.com/news/2013/09/photos-over-7000-gather-in-lakewood-at-historic-rally-on-behalf-of-yidden-in-eretz-yisroel.html.
11. Hauer, "Idealistic Realism in Communal Leadership," 38.
12. See, for example, Sperber et al, *Women and Men in Communal Prayer*.
13. See, for example, David Downes and Paul Rock, *Understanding Deviance* (Oxford: Oxford University Press, 1982); Emile Durkheim, *The Division of Labor in Society*, trans. George Simpson (Glencoe, Ill.: Free Press, 1960), 70–110; Kai T. Erikson, *Wayward Puritans: A Study in the Sociology of Deviance*, rev. ed. (Boston: Allyn and Bacon, 2004).
14. See Ferziger, *Exclusion and Hierarchy*.
15. See Linzer and Weiss, "Creating an Open Orthodox Rabbinate." As noted throughout this book, more moderate voices have always existed within Modern Orthodoxy and at times—such as regarding Soviet Jewry—even set its agenda. Nonetheless the current initiatives come in the wake of the more pronounced trend toward a more Haredi-sympathetic position that emerged since the 1980s. Moreover, until the advent of YCT, the various forces all found an institutional home in YU.
16. See Adam S. Ferziger, "The Role of Reform in Israeli Orthodoxy," in *Between Jewish Tradition and Modernity: Essays in Honor of David H. Ellenson*, ed. Michael A. Meyer and David Myers, 51–66 (Detroit: Wayne State University Press, 2014); Yitzhak Geiger,

"Ha-Zionut ha-Datit ha-Hadashah," *Akdamot* 11 (2002): 51–77; Maayana Miskin, "Study: Religious-Zionist World Is Changing," *Arutz Sheva*, May 20, 2011, www.israelnationalnews.com/News/News.aspx/144354#.UnDBe3Ayooc; Yair Sheleg, *Ha-Dati'im ha-Hadashim* (Jerusalem: Keter, 2000).

17. Asher Lopatin, "Orthodox and Here to Stay," *Haaretz*, October 23, 2013, www.haaretz.com/opinion/.premium-1.553902.
18. Avi Shafran, "'Open Orthodoxy' Is Not Really Orthodox at All," *Jewish Daily Forward*, October 28, 2013, http://forward.com/articles/186369/open-orthodoxy-is-not-really-orthodox-at-all/.
19. Josh Nathan-Kazis, "Orthodox Rabbi Stuns Agudath Gala with 'Heresy' Attack on Open Orthodoxy," *Jewish Daily Forward*, May 28, 2014, http://forward.com/articles/199010/orthodox-rabbi-stuns-agudath-gala-with-heresy-atta/. Perlow also noted the dire condition of the non-Orthodox movements, but unlike that reported in some media outlets, this was by no means the main thrust of his diatribe. This point was emphasized in a follow-up statement by Agudath Israel responding to widespread criticism of Perlow's speech; see statement of Agudath Israel of America, "Rabbi Perlow's Remarks at Agudath Israel Dinner: Ensuring the Jewish Future," May 30, 2014, http://myemail.constantcontact.com/Rabbi-Perlow-s-Remarks-at-Agudath-Israel-Dinner—Ensuring-the-Jewish-Future.html?soid=1116045723924&aid=jdWY_uO7KKE.
20. In February 2014, AJOP sponsored a conference for synagogue rabbis involved in kiruv, which was held in Scottsdale, Arizona. An entire session was dedicated to "Dealing with the Challenges of Open Orthodoxy." See http://ajoprabbis.weebly.com/.
21. Shafran, "'Open Orthodoxy' Is Not Really Orthodox at All."
22. Gidon Rothstein, "Violating Orthodox Law and Custom, Dividing Our Community," *Haaretz*, October 29, 2013, www.haaretz.com/opinion/.premium-1.555014.
23. The resources for this cited paragraph are available at "Crowd-Sourced Bibliography on Tefilin, Partnership Minyanim, and the Future of Orthodoxy," Morethodoxy: Exploring the Breadth, Depth and Passion of Orthodox Judaism, February 28, 2014, http://morethodoxy.org/2014/02/28/crowd-sourced-bibliography-on-tefilin-partnership-minyanim-and-the-future-of-orthodoxy/.
24. Zvi "Herschel" Schachter, "Rabbi Hershel Schachter on Women Wearing Tefillin," *Yutopia*, February 8, 2014, www.joshyuter.com/2014/02/08/judaism/rabbi-hershel-schachter-women-wearing-tefillin/.
25. Menachem Penner, "Letter from Rabbi Menachem Penner to Shalom," January 14, 2014. A scanned copy of the signed letter was sent to me by e-mail.
26. See, for example, Gary Rosenblatt, "'Your Semicha or Your Wife': YU Withholding Ordination from Rabbinic Student Who Participated in 'Partnership Minyan,'" *Jewish Week*, February 26, 2014, www.thejewishweek.com/news/new-york/your-semicha-or-your-wife; Avi Shafran, "Partnership Minyan Is an Innovation Too Far," *Haaretz*, February 19, 2014, www.haaretz.com/opinion/.premium-1.575144.
27. "Statement from YU and RIETS," February 27, 2014, http://blogs.yu.edu/news/2014/02/27/statement-from-yu-and-riets/.
28. Zvi "Herschel" Schachter, "Al da'at ha-minyanim ha-meshutafim," January 2014, www.rcarabbis.org/pdf/Rabbi_Schachter_new_letter.pdf.

29. The responses have been collected at "Crowd-Sourced Bibliography on Tefilin, Partnership Minyanim, and the Future of Orthodoxy."
30. Yitzchok Adlerstein, "Rav Schachter's Bright-Line Rule on Halachic Innovation," *Cross-Currents*, February 10, 2014, www.cross-currents.com/archives/2014/02/10/rav-schachters-bright-line-rule-on-halachic-innovation/#ixzz2t1tNBpPo.
31. Durkheim, *The Division of Labor in Society*, 92.
32. Elie Kaunfer, *Empowered Judaism: What Independent Minyanim Can Teach Us about Building Vibrant Jewish Communities* (Woodstock, Vt.: Jewish Lights, 2010).
33. "About Us," Mechon Hadar, www.mechonhadar.org/about-us1.
34. "Why Learn Talmud" Announcement, http://drisha.org/whylearntalmud.php.
35. See Diamond, *And I Will Dwell in Their Midst*.
36. One inside observer, whose 2014 essay received a great deal of publicity, suggests that entrenched ideological and theological positions of any sort are really anathema to many self-proclaimed Modern Orthodox Jews. The issues that drive them are simply how to sustain a lifestyle that combines full involvement with American culture and society with maintenance of the same set of social frameworks, human values, and basic ritual tradition restrictions that are identified with their religious stream. See Jay P. Lefkowitz, "The Rise of Social Orthodoxy: A Personal Account," *Commentary*, January 1, 2014, www.commentarymagazine.com/article/the-rise-of-social-orthodoxy-a-personal-account/. Interestingly, such a description is in certain ways reminiscent of the portrayals of the residual folk constituency within American Orthodoxy in Liebman's classic 1965 article. See also the discussion of folk versus elite religion among American Jews in Charles S. Liebman, "Reconstructionism in American Jewish Life," *American Jewish Year Book 1969* (1970): 90–97, www.bjpa.org/Publications/downloadFile.cfm?FileID=1906. See also David Sable, "Why We Need Reform to Redefine Orthodoxy," *Jewish Week*, February 11, 2015, www.thejewishweek.com/editorial-opinion/opinion/why-we-need-redefine-orthodoxy.
37. See the OCP's website at http://pennocp.org/.
38. There are presently more than nine hundred family members in KJ and more than eleven hundred full-time students in Ramaz; see Congregation Kehilath Jeshurun, "Mission Statement," www.ckj.org/KJ_Mission_Statement.php.
39. Interview with Rabbi Naftali Hartcztak, Principal of the SAR Academy High School, September 17, 2003.
40. Pew 2013, 43, 57; see the thoughtful essay of Elli Fischer, "Modern Orthodoxy Has Its Costs—Not Just Financial," *Jewish Week*, February 17, 2015, www.thejewishweek.com/editorial-opinion/opinion/modern-orthodoxy-has-its-costs-not-just-financial.
41. Liebman, "Orthodoxy in American Jewish Life," 92.

Bibliography

Primary Materials

Archival Resources (specific locations of materials are listed in the notes)
Agudath Israel of America Archives, New York
ajcarchives.org
archive.jta.org
bjpa.org
hebrewbooks.org
Kehilath Jeshurun (KJ) Archive, New York
Lookjed Archive
ohiomemory.org/cdm/compoundobject/collection/ojc/id/12247/rec/4
snltranscripts.jt.org
SSSJ Archive, Gottesman Library, Yeshiva University
The Seforim Blog
Torah Mi-Tzion Archive, Jerusalem

Interviews and Direct Communications (if no location cited then via Skype or telephone)
Apt, Sarah (Palo Alto, Calif., February 11, 2011)
Balk, Shoshana (e-mail correspondence, April 2, 2009)
Berger, Shalom (e-mail correspondence, June 26, 2008)
Berglas, Vicky (June 19, 2008)
Berl, Michael (January 30, 2008)
Berman, Saul (May 15, 2006)
Bernstein, David (Jerusalem, June 26, 2008)
Billet, Avi (e-mail correspondence, April 26, 2009)
Birnbaum, Yaakov (e-mail correspondence, June 6, 2006)
Blackman, Yaakov (Jerusalem, September 11, 2001)
Blau, Binyamin (Cleveland Heights, Ohio, September 8, 2003)
Blau, Rivka (Teitz) (May 7, 2006)
Coopersmith, Eric (e-mail correspondence, July 15, 2013)
Deutsch, Menachem (Atlanta, September 18, 2003)
———. (September 15, 2005)
Felsen, Joey (Jerusalem, February 2, 2008)
Fried, Yehuda (June 19, 2008)

Fried, Yerachmiel (Dallas, February 10, 2008)
Frolich, Vicky Epstein (Cleveland Heights, Ohio, September 8, 2003)
Green, Arthur (May 25, 2006)
Greenberg, Irving "Yitz" (Jerusalem, June 10, 2006)
Hartcztak, Naftali (Riverdale, N.Y., September 17, 2003)
Hendler, Aryeh (June 22, 2008)
Hoenlein, Malcolm (May 26, 2006)
Kagan, Aaron (Pittsburgh, September 9, 2003)
———. (September 10, 2005)
Kahane, Ayelet (e-mail correspondence, March 15 and April 2, 2009)
Kellman, Ayal (e-mail correspondence, January 18, 2010)
Kellman, Ester Blaut (e-mail correspondence, January 10, 2010)
Klein Halevi, Yossi (May 21, 2006)
Langer, Elky (Pittsburgh, September 9, 2003)
Lookstein, Haskel (Jerusalem, July 19, 1995)
Luderman, David (Dallas, February 10, 2008)
Milikowsky, Shaya (Jerusalem, August 2, 2003)
Miller, Dovid (May 17, 2006)
Richter, Glenn (transcript of responses to Lora Rabin Dagi, July 26, 2005)
Richter, Glenn (May 5, 2006)
Riskin, Shlomo (Jerusalem, May 29, 2006)
Schechter, Barton (Pittsburgh, September 9, 2003)
Segal, Nate (Staten Island, New York, September 14, 2003)
Shafran, Avi (e-mail correspondence, May 11, 2006)
Sheer, Charles (May 5, 2006)
——— (e-mail correspondence with Laura Rabin Dagi, August 21, 2005)
Stark, Robert L. (Beachwood, Ohio, September 6, 2003)
Wachsman, Riva (e-mail correspondence, April 2, 2009)
Weinstein, Rebecca (e-mail correspondence, January 10, 2010)
Weiss, Avi (May 9, 2006)
Yammer, Michael (June 19, 2008)
Zuroff, Efraim (May 25, 2006)

Printed and Online Periodicals and Journals, News Sites, and Blogs (specific references are listed in the notes)
Apiryon (1924–28)
beyondbt.com
blogs.timesofisrael.com
commentarymagazine.com
Conversations
cross-currents.com
fednews.com
forward.com
haaretz.com
Hadarom (1957–94)
hakirah.org
hirhurim.blogspot.com
Jewish Morning Journal (1901–71)

Jewishideas.org
jewishindependent.ca
jewishjournal.com
jewishpress.com
jewishsf.com
jhvonline.com
jpost.com
jta.org
jwi.org
kavvanah.wordpress.com
Kehilath Jeshurun Bulletin
klalperspectives.org
kolhamevaser.com
lookstein.org/lookjed
morethodoxy.org
mosaicmagazine.com
mschick.blogspot.co.il
nytimes.com
ohiojewishchronicle.com
ou.org/jewish_action
Perspectives, CLAL (June 1985)
Rabbiirvinggreenberg.com
text.rcarabbis.org/
seforim.blogspot.com
shma.com
tabletmag.com
The Jewish Observer (1963–2010), www.shemayisrael.com/jewishobserver/archives.htm
thejewishweek.com
theyeshivaworld.com
torahmusings.com
traditiononline.org
facebook.com/Algemeiner
ynet.co.il
yucommentator.org

Memoirs and Autobiographies
Barondess, Joseph. "Achievements and Failings of Borough Park Jews." *Jewish Forum* 7, no. 4 (1924): 242–44.
Billet, Avi. Personal Journal of 1998 Heritage Seminar to Poland and Lithuania. April 3, 1998.
Birnbaum, Jacob. "Jewish Redemption Ritual in Jacob Birnbaum's Struggle for Soviet Jewry in the 1960s: The Role of His Family Heritage." Typescript. May 22, 2006.
Butler, Menachem, and Zev Nagel, eds. *My Yeshiva College: 75 Years of Memories*. New York: Yashar, 2006.
Greenberg, Irving. "Yeshiva in the 60s." In *My Yeshiva College: 75 Years of Memories*, ed. Menachem Butler and Zev Nagel, 179–87. New York: Yashar Books, 2006.
Jung, Leo. *The Path of a Pioneer: The Autobiography of Leo Jung*. London: Soncino Press, 1980.
Kehilath Jeshurun Bulletin: Special Memorial Issue for the Fiftieth Yahrzeit of Rabbi Moses Zevulun Margolies. Summer 1986.

Kehilath Jeshurun Bulletin: Special Memorial Issue in Memory of Rabbi Joseph Lookstein. Fall 1979. www.ckj.org/docs/Rabbi%20Joseph%20Lookstein%20Memorial.pdf.
Klein Halevi, Yossi. *Memoirs of a Jewish Extremist.* Boston: Little, Brown and Company, 1995.
Korn, Eugene. "God, Torah, and Yeshiva in the Sixties." In *My Yeshiva College: 75 Years of Memories,* ed. Menachem Butler and Zev Nagel, 211–14. New York: Yashar Books, 2006.
Lamm, Norman. "There Is Only One Yeshiva College: A Memoir." In *My Yeshiva College: 75 Years of Memories,* ed. Menachem Butler and Zev Nagel, 219–25. New York: Yashar Books, 2006.
Lipshitz, Yoni. "Recollections and Reconsiderations: Revisiting the Path of Rabbi Norman Lamm." *The Commentator,* December 12, 2007, 7–8.
Lookstein, Haskel. "Words of Eulogy." *Kehilath Jeshurun Bulletin: Special Memorial Issue in Memory of Rabbi Joseph Lookstein,* Fall 1979, 6–8.
Lookstein, Joseph. "God Owes Me Nothing." Typescript. New York, n.d.
———. "Rabbi Moses Zebulun Margolies: High Priest of Kehilath Jeshurun." In *Congregation Kehilath Jeshurun, Diamond Jubilee Yearbook,* 1946, 48–51.
———. "A Rabbi of the Old School." *Kehilath Jeshurun Bulletin: Special Memorial Edition in Memory of Rabbi Moses Zevulun Margolies upon His Fiftieth Yahrzeit,* Summer 1986, 10.
Raskas, Stanley. "From Out of Town." In *My Yeshiva College: 75 Years of Memories,* ed. Menachem Butler and Zev Nagel, 248–52. New York: Yashar Books, 2006.
Schientag, Bernard. "Rabbi Joseph H. Lookstein: A Character Study by a Congregant." In *Congregation Kehilath Jeschurun, Diamond Jubilee Yearbook,* 1946, 53–57.
"Selections from 120 Letters Received for the Commemoration of Jacob Birnbaum's 40 Years of Service to the Jewish People." Typescript, 2004.
Stavsky, David. "A Mechitza for Columbus." *Jewish Life* 41, no. 1 (Winter 1974): 22–27.
Weinberger, Moses. *People Walk on Their Heads: Moses Weinberger's Jews and Judaism in New York.* Trans. and ed. Jonathan D. Sarna. New York: Holmes Meir Publishers, 1982.
Weiss, Avraham. "Avi." Unpublished memoir. N.d.

Surveys, Demographic Reports, and Data Banks (all available at Berman Data Bank, www.jewishdatabank.org/)

The Jewish Community Study of New York 2011: Geographic Profile. New York: UJA/Federation, 2012. www.ujafedny.org/geographic-profile-report/.
National Jewish Population Survey (NJPS). 1971, 1989–90, 2000–2001.
A Portrait of Jewish Americans: Findings from a Pew Research Center Survey of U.S. Jews. Washington, D.C.: Pew Research Center, 2013.
Sheskin, Ira M., and Arnold Dashefsky. "Jewish Population in the United States, 2013." *American Jewish Year Book* 113 (2013): 201–77.
Ukeles, Jack B., R. Miller, and P. Beck. *Young Jewish Adults in the United States Today: Harbingers of the American Jewish Community of Tomorrow?* New York: AJC, 2013.

Records and Source Collections

By-Laws of the Congregation Kehilath Jeshurun. 1903.
Congregation Kehilath Jeschurun, Diamond Jubilee Yearbook. 1946.
Halperin, Micah D. *In Their Memory: Introductions, Essays, and Texts for the Study of Jewish Life in Eastern Europe and the Holocaust.* Jerusalem: Heritage Seminars, 1996.
In Search of Our Heritage. Jerusalem: Heritage Seminars, 2002.
"Milestones in the History of Kehilath Jeshurun." In *Congregation Kehilath Jeschurun, Diamond Jubilee Yearbook.* 1946.

BIBLIOGRAPHY

Websites of Organizations and Institutions
Aish.com
aishkodesh.org
ajc.org
ajop.ccsend.com
ajopconvention.com
atlantakollel.org
avichai.org
bjsz.org
ccarnet.org
cckollel.org
chabad.org.
chabadboynton.com
chicagotorah.org
ckj.org
comd.usu.edu/htm/distance-education/online-bach/onlinebach-overview
crownheights.info
datanet.org.
edah.org
heritageseminars.org
huc.edu
internationalrabbinicfellowship.org
israelexperience.org.il
jewishideas.org
jliconline.org
jofa.org
jsn.info
jtsa.edu
juf.org
jwrp.org
kibbutz.org.il
kinus.com
lcm.touro.edu
lubavitch.com
mechonhadar.org
nces.ed.gov
nerleelef.com
nesivos.com.
northbrookcommunitysynagogue.com
ohr.edu
osttolney.org
pennocp.org
queenshatzolah.org
rabbis.org
ramaz.org
shturem.net
sites.torahindex.com/lizensk/en/
thejerusalemkollel.com

thelakewoodscoop.com
theshabbosproject.org
thetorah.com
torahmitzion.org
torchweb.org
touro.edu/landercollege
ujafedny.org
womeninkiruv.org
yctorah.org
yeshivatmaharat.org
yoatzot.org
yu.edu
yutorah.org

Rabbinical Literature and Ideological Writings
Angel, M. "Are We 'Modern' or 'Centrist' or 'Open'... Who Are We?" Institute for Jewish Ideals and Ideas, March 2009, www.jewishideas.org/blog/are-we-modern-or-centrist-or-open-orwho-are-we.
Berkovits, Rahel. *A Daughter's Recitation of Mourner's Kaddish*. New York: JOFA, 2011.
Besdin, Abraham R. *Reflections of the Rav*. Jerusalem: World Zionist Organization, 1979.
Dalfin, Chaim. *Attack on Lubavitch: A Response*. Brooklyn: Jewish Enrichment Press, 2002.
Feinstein, Moshe. *Igerot Moshe*. Vol. 1: *Yoreh De'ah*. New York: Balshon, 1960.
———. *Igerot Moshe*. Vol. 2: *Yoreh Deah*. New York: n.p., 1959.
———. *Igerot Moshe*. Vol. 3: *Yoreh Deah*. Bnei Brak: Yeshivat Ohel Yosef, 1981.
———. *Igerot Moshe*. Vol. 4: *Orah Hayyim*. Bnei Brak: Yeshivat Ohel Yosef, 1981.
Greenberg, Blu. "Jewish Women: Coming of Age." *Tradition* 16, no. 4 (1977): 79–94.
Greenberg, Irving. "Will There Be One Jewish People in the Year 2000?" *Perspectives, CLAL*, June 1985, 1–8, http://rabbiirvinggreenberg.com/wp-content/uploads/2013/02/Will-There-Be-One_red.pdf.
Greenwald, Yekutiel Yehudah (Leopold). *Ah le-Zarah*. St. Louis: Quality Printing, 1939.
———. *Kol Bo al Aveilut*. New York: Moria Printing, 1947.
———. *Korot ha-Torah ve-ha-Emunah be-Hungariyah*. Budapest: Katzburg, 1921.
———. *Le-Toldot ha-Reformazion be-Germanyah u-ve-Hungariyah*. Columbus, Ohio: L. Grenwald, 1948.
———. *Li-Felagot Yisrael be-Hungariyah*. Deva: Markovits and Friedmann, 1929.
———. "Mikhtav galui." *Apiryon* 5 (1927/28): 282–88.
———. *Ozar Nehmad*. Columbus, Ohio: n.p., 1942.
Grunfeld, Isidor. *Horeb*. London: Soncino Press, 1962.
Gutel, Neriah. "Kaddish yetomah (teguvah)." *Tzohar* 8 (Fall 2001): 25–26.
Hauer, Moshe. "Idealistic Realism in Communal Leadership." *Klal Perspectives* 2, no. 2 (2013): http://klalperspectives.org/rabbi-moshe-hauer-4/.
Hirsch, Ammiel, and Yaakov Yosef Reinman. *One People, Two Worlds: A Reform Rabbi and an Orthodox Rabbi Explore the Issues That Divide Them*. New York: Schocken Books, 2002.
Hirschenson, Hayyim. *Hiddushei RaHa"H* 3 [halifat mikhtavim]. Jerusalem: Ha-Ivri, 1926.
———. *Malki ba-Kodesh* 4. St. Louis: Moinester Printing Co., 1923.
———. "Teshuvah geluyah le-mikhtav galuy." *Apiryon* 5 (1927/28): 309–15.
———. "Todah le-mekhabdani." *Apiryon* 5 (Fall 1927): 87–91.
Kotler, Aharon. *Mishnat Rabbi Aharon*. Vol. 4: *Ma'amarim ve-Sihot Mussar*. Lakewood, N.J.:

Makhon Mishnat Rabbi Aharon, 2005.
Lamm, Norman. "Centrist Orthodoxy: Judaism and Moderationism, Definitions and Desideratum." In *Orthodoxy Confronts Modernity*, ed. Jonathan Sacks, 48–61. Hoboken, N.J.: Ktav, 1991.
Lichtenstein, Hillel. *Responsa Beit Hillel*. Satu-Mare: Z. Schwartz Publishers, 1908.
Linzer, Dov, and Avraham Weiss. "Creating an Open Orthodox Rabbinate." *Shma.Com*, January 1, 2003, http://shma.com/2003/01/creating-an-open-orthodox-rabbinate/.
Litvin, Baruch, ed. *The Sanctity of the Synagogue*. New York: Spero Foundation, 1959.
Lookstein, Haskel. "To Kehilath Jeshurun with Love." *Ramaz School: Forty-Eighth Annual Dinner Dance Sponsored by the Parents Council, January 13, 1985* (1985): 3.
Lookstein, Joseph. "A Critique and a Plea." *Judaism* 26, no. 3 (1977): 390–95.
———. "A Religious Definition of Beauty." Transcript of radio broadcast, *United Jewish Layman's Committee: Message of Israel*. American Broadcasting Company. December 18, 1949, 1.
Lopatin, Asher. "How Orthodoxy and Orthodox Synagogues Can Meet the Needs of the Odyssey Generation." In *The Next Generation of Modern Orthodoxy*, ed. Shmuel Hain. New York: Yeshiva University/Ktav, 2012. www.yutorah.org/lectures/lecture.cfm/777847/Rabbi_Asher_Lopatin/How_Orthodoxy_and_Orthodox_Synagogues_Can_Meet_the_Needs_of_the_Odyssey_Generation#.
Meiselman, Moshe. *Jewish Women in Jewish Law*. New York: Ktav/Yeshiva University Press, 1978.
Mishnah Avot.
The Ohr Somayach Story. Jerusalem: Ohr Somayach, 1982.
Perl, Gil, and Yaakov Weinstein. *A Parent's Guide to Orthodox Assimilation on University Campuses*. N.p.: n.p., 2003.
Rakeffet-Rothkoff, Aaron. *The Rav: The World of Rabbi Joseph B. Soloveitchik*, vol. 2. Jersey City, N.J.: Ktav, 1999.
Rapoport, Chaim. *The Messiah Problem: Berger, the Angel, and the Scandal of Reckless Indiscrimination*. Ilford: self-published, 2002.
Reisman, Levi. "We Are No Longer One." *Jewish Observer* 29, no. 4 (1996): 29–30.
Schachter, Herschel (Zvi). "Al da'at ha-minyanim ha-meshutafim." January 2014. www.rcarabbis.org/pdf/Rabbi_Schachter_new_letter.pdf.
———. *Be-Ikvei ha-Zon*. Jerusalem: Hoza'at Beit Midrash D'Flatbush, 1997.
———. "Be-Inyanei beit ha-knesset u-kedushato." *Or Hamizrach* 34, nos. 1–2 (1985): 66–68.
———. "Can Women Be Rabbis?" Torahweb.org. 2004. www.torahweb.org/torah/2004/parsha/rsch_devorim2.html.
———. *Erez ha-Zvi*. New York: Yeshiva University, 1992.
———. *Mi-Peninei ha-Rav*. Jerusalem: Beit Midrash de-Flatbush, 2001.
———. *Nefesh ha-Rav*. Jerusalem: Hoza'at Reshit Yerushalayim, 1994.
———. "On the Matter of Masorah." Torahweb.org. 2003. www.torahweb.org/torah/special/2003/rsch_masorah.html.
———. "The Significance of the State of Israel: Celebrating Yom Ha'atzmaut." Audio lecture available at Torahweb.org. April 17, 2002. www.torahweb.org/audio/rsch_041402.html.
———. "Ze'i lakh be-ikvei ha-zon." *Beit Yitzchak* 17 (1985): 118–34.
Schick, Moses. *She'elot u-Teshuvot Maharam Schick: Orah Hayyim*. Munkacs: Bleier, 1880.
Schneerson, Joseph Isaac. *Sefer ha-Sihot Kayitz ha-SH"T [1940]*. Brooklyn: Ma'arekhet Ozar ha-Hasidim, 1956.
Schneerson, Menachem Mendel. *Likutei Sihos*. 39 vols. Brooklyn: Kehot Press, 2014.
———. *Sihos Kodesh*. Brooklyn, N.Y.: Kehot Press, 1951–92.

Sefer ha-Yovel shel Agudath ha-Rabbanim ha-Orthodoksim de-Arzot ha-Berith: Le-Mele'at Esrim ve-Hamesh Shanim le-Hivasdah [5662–5687]. New York: Ariam Press, 1927/28.

Shafran, Avi. "Why 'Jewish Religious Pluralism' Must Matter to Us." *Jewish Observer* 29, no. 9 (1996): 6–7.

Shapiro, Mendel. "Qeri'at Torah by Women: A Halakhic Analysis." *Edah Journal* 1, no. 2 (2001), www.edah.org/backend/JournalArticle/1_2_shapiro.pdf.

Sofer, Moses. *Shu"t Hatam Sofer*. Jerusalem: Hod, 1972.

Soloveitchik, Joseph B. "Confrontation." *Tradition* 6, no. 2 (1964): 5–29.

———. *Fate and Destiny: From the Holocaust to the State of Israel*. Trans. Lawrence Kaplan. Hoboken, N.J.: Ktav, 2000.

———. *Festival of Freedom: Essays on Pesah and the Haggadah*. Jersey City, N.J.: Toras Horav Foundation, 2006.

———. *Kol Dodi Dofek: Listen My Beloved Knocks*. Ed. Jeffrey Woolf. Trans. David Gordon. Hoboken, N.J.: Ktav, 2006.

———. "Message to a Rabbinic Convention." In *The Sanctity of the Synagogue*, ed. Baruch Litvin, 11–12. New York: Spero Foundation, 1959.

Sperber, Daniel. "Congregational Dignity and Human Dignity: Women's Public Torah Reading." *Edah Journal* 3, no. 2 (2003), www.edah.org/backend/JournalArticle/3_2.pdf.

———. *Darkah shel Halakhah*. Tel Aviv: Reuven Mass, 2007.

Sternbuch, Moishe. "The Kollel Phenomenon and Its Significance." In *Halachic Discourses on Masechte Beitzo*, 5–16. Bnei Brak: Kollel Yad Shaul, 1982.

Tosefta—Yadayim.

Trachtman, Chaim, ed. *Women and Men in Communal Prayer: Halakhic Perspectives*. Jersey City, N.J.: JOFA/Ktav, 2010.

Turkel, Eli. "Partial Bibliography of Works by and about Rabbi Joseph B. Soloveitchik Zt"l." Last updated June 25, 2013. www.math.tau.ac.il/~turkel/engsol.html.

Vayikra Rabba.

Waxman, Nissan. *Shevilei Nissan*. Jerusalem: Mossad Ha-Rav Kook, 2013.

Weinberger, Moshe. *Jewish Outreach: Halakhic Perspectives*. Hoboken, N.J.: Ktav, 1990.

Weinstein Yaakov. "Orthodox Assimilation on Campus, Part 1." February 22, 2007. www.beyondbt.com/2007/02/22/orthodox-assimilation-on-campus-part-1/

———. "Orthodox Assimilation on Campus, Part 2." March 15, 2007. www.beyondbt.com/2007/03/15/orthodox-assimilation-on-campus-part-2/.

Weiss, Avraham. *Principles of Spiritual Activism*. Hoboken, N.J.: Ktav, 2002.

———. "Public Protest and Soviet Jewry." *Midstream* 33 (February 1987): 26–27.

———. *Women at Prayer: A Halakhic Analysis of Women's Prayer Groups*. Hoboken, N.J.: Ktav, 1990.

Wolpin, Nisson. "The Community Kolel: Reaching out with Torah." *Jewish Observer* 14, no. 3 (1979): 20–26.

———. "Orthodoxy's Move to the Right: Grappling with the Helmreich Principle." *Jewish Observer* 30, no. 1 (1997): 19–24.

———. "Surprising Settings, Yearning Souls: A Search for the Spiritual at Federation's General Assembly, in Pursuit of Torah within the Ranks of Reform." *Jewish Observer* 28, no. 10 (1996): 9–10.

Women's Issues—Book One: The Female and Her Characteristics. Jerusalem: Ner LeElef, 2007. www.nerleelef.com/books/Women%20Book%20One.pdf.

Women's Issues—Book Two: Women in Mitzvos. Jerusalem: Ner LeElef, 2007. www.nerleelef.com/books/Women%20Book%20One.pdf.

BIBLIOGRAPHY

Secondary Literature

Books, Dissertations, and Theses

Abrams Elliot, and David G. Dalin, eds. *Secularism, Spirituality, and the Future of American Jewry.* Washington, D.C.: Ethics and Public Policy Center, 1999.

Abramson, Edward. *Circle in a Square.* Jerusalem: Urim, 2008.

Altshuler, Stuart. *From Exodus to Freedom: The History of the Soviet Jewry Movement.* Lanham, Md.: Rowman and Littlefield, 2005.

Antler, Joyce. *The Journey Home: Jewish Women and the American Century.* New York: Free Press, 1997.

Assaf, David. *The Regal Way: The Life and Times of Rabbi Israel of Ruzhin.* Stanford: Stanford University Press, 2002.

Aviad, Janet. *Return to Judaism.* Chicago: University of Chicago Press, 1983.

Bacon, Gershon C. *The Politics of Tradition: Agudat Yisrael in Poland, 1916–1939.* Jerusalem: Magnes Press, 1996.

Barack Fishman, Sylvia. *Changing Minds: A Study of the Impact of Feminism on American Orthodox Jewish Communities.* New York: American Jewish Committee, 2000.

Barack Fishman, Sylvia, with Daniel Parmer. *Matrilineal Ascent/Patrilineal Descent: The Growing Gender Imbalance in American Jewish Life.* Waltham, Mass.: Cohen Center for Modern Jewish Studies, 2008.

Bauman, Mark K., and Kalin Berkely, eds. *The Quiet Voices: Southern Rabbis and Black Civil Rights, 1880s to 1990s.* Tuscaloosa: University of Alabama Press, 1997.

Baumel-Schwartz, Judith. *Double Jeopardy: Gender and the Holocaust.* London: Valentine Mitchell, 1998.

Baumgarten, Albert B. *The Flourishing of Jewish Sects in the Maccabean Era: An Interpretation.* Leiden: Brill, 1997.

Beckerman, Gal. *When They Come for Us, We'll Be Gone: The Epic Struggle to Save Soviet Jewry.* New York: Houghton, Mifflin, and Harcourt, 2010.

Behrman, Samuel Nathaniel. *The Worcester Account.* New York: Chandler House Press, 1954.

Benisch, Pearl. *Carry Me in Your Heart: The Life and Legacy of Sarah Schenirer, Founder and Visionary of the Bais Yaakov Movement.* New York: Feldheim Publishers, 2003.

Benor, Sarah Bunim. *Becoming Frum: How Newcomers Learn the Language and Culture of Orthodox Judaism.* New Brunswick: Rutgers University Press, 2012.

Bentwich, Norman. *For Zion's Sake: A Biography of Judah L. Magnes, First Chancellor and First President of the Hebrew University of Jerusalem.* Philadelphia: Jewish Publication Society, 1954.

Berger, Shalom Z., Dan Jacobson, and Chaim I. Waxman. *Flipping Out? Myth or Fact: The Impact of the "Year in Israel."* New York: Yashar Books, 2007.

Berger, Shalom Z. "Engaging the Ultimate: The Impact of Post–High School Study in Israel." In Shalom Z. Berger, Daniel Jacobson, and Chaim I. Waxman, *Flipping Out? Myth or Fact: The Impact of the "Year in Israel,"* 5–78. New York: Yashar Books, 2007.

Bernstein, Louis. *Challenge and Mission: The Emergence of the English Speaking Orthodox Rabbinate.* New York: Shengold Publishers, 1982.

Bernstein, Saul. *Renaissance of the Torah Jew.* Hoboken, N.J.: Ktav, 1985.

Biale, David. *Power and Powerlessness in Jewish History.* New York: Random House, 1986.

Blau, Rivkah Teitz. *Learn Torah, Love Torah, Live Torah: Harav Mordechai Pinchas Teitz.* Hoboken, N.J.: Ktav, 2001.

Bleich, J. David. *Contemporary Halakhic Problems.* Vol. 3. New York: Ktav, 1989.

BIBLIOGRAPHY

Bomzer, Herbert. *The Kolel in America*. New York: Shengold Publishers, 1985.
Breslauer, S. Daniel. *Judaism and Civil Religion*. Atlanta: Rowman and Littlefield, 1993.
Breuer, Mordechai. *Modernity within Tradition*. New York: Columbia University Press, 1992.
———. *Ohalei Torah: Ha-Yeshiva, Tavnitah ve-Toldotehah*. Jerusalem: Merkaz Shazar, 2004.
Brinner, William M., and Moses Rischin. *Like All the Nations? The Life and Legacy of Judah L. Magnes*. Albany: State University of New York Press, 1987.
Bulka, Reuven P. *The Coming Cataclysm: The Orthodox-Reform Rift and the Future of the Jewish People*. Oakville, Ont.: Mosaic Press, 1984.
Caplan, Kimmy. *Orthodoksiyah be-Olam Hadash*. Jerusalem: Merkaz Shazar, 2002.
Chabon, Michael. *The Amazing Adventures of Kavalier and Clay*. London: HarperCollins/Fourth Estate, 2000.
Cohen, Naomi W. *Not Free to Desist: The American Jewish Committee, 1906–1966*. Philadelphia: Jewish Publication Society, 1972.
Cohen, Steven M., and Arnold Eisen. *The Jew Within*. Bloomington: Indiana University Press, 2000.
Cohen, Steven M., and Samuel C. Heilman. *Cosmopolitans and Parochials: Modern Orthodox Jews in America*. Chicago: University of Chicago Press, 1989.
Cohen, Steven M., J. Shwan Landres, Elie Kaunfer, and Michelle Shain. *Emergent Jewish Communities and Their Participants*. Van Nuys, Calif.: Synagogue 3000 and Mechon Hadar, 2007. www.synagogue3000.org/files/NatSpirComStudyReport_S3K_Hadar.pdf.
Cohen, Y. Yosef. *Hakhmei Hungariyah*. Jerusalem: Machon Yerushalayim, 1997.
———. *Hakhmei Transylvaniyah*. Jerusalem: Machon Yerashalayim, 1989.
Danzger, M. Herbert. *Returning to Tradition: The Contemporary Revival of Orthodox Judaism*. New Haven: Yale University Press, 1989.
Danziger, Hillel. *Guardian of Jerusalem: The Life and Times of Yosef Chaim Sonnenfeld*. New York: Mesorah Publications, 1983.
Davidman, Lynn. *Tradition in a Rootless World: Women Turn to Orthodox Judaism*. Berkeley: University of California Press, 1991.
Davis, Natalie. *Women at the Margins*. Cambridge, Mass.: Harvard University Press, 1995.
Deutsch, Shimon S. *Larger than Life: The Life and Times of the Lubavitcher Rebbe Rabbi Menachem Mendel Schneerson*. 2 vols. New York: Chasidic Historical Productions, 1995–97.
Diamond, Etan. *And I Will Dwell in Their Midst: Orthodox Jews in Suburbia*. Chapel Hill: University of North Carolina Press, 2000.
Diner, Hasia R. *The Jews of the United States, 1654–2000*. Berkeley: University of California Press, 2004.
Dolgin, Janet. *Jewish Identity and the JDL*. Princeton: Princeton University Press, 1977.
Dollinger, Marc. *Quest for Inclusion: Jews and Liberalism in Modern America*. Princeton: Princeton University Press, 2000.
Downes, David, and Paul Rock. *Understanding Deviance*. Oxford: Oxford University Press, 1982.
Durkheim, Emile. *The Division of Labor in Society*. Trans. George Simpson. Glencoe, Ill.: Free Press, 1960.
Dynner, Glenn. *Men of Silk: The Hasidic Conquest of Polish Jewish Society*. Oxford: Oxford University Press, 2006.
Eckman, Lester. *Revered by All*. New York: Shengold, 1974.
Ehrlich, Avrum M. *The Messiah of Brooklyn*. Jersey City, N.J.: Ktav, 2004.
Eisenberg, Robert. *Boychiks in the Hood: Travels in the Hasidic Underground*. San Francisco: Harper, 1997.

BIBLIOGRAPHY

Elboim, Yaakov. *Petihut ve-Histagrut: Ha-Yezirah ha-Ruhanit-ha-Sifrutit be-Polin u-ve-Arzot Ashkenzaz be-Shilhei ha-Meah ha-Shesh Esreh.* Jerusalem: Magnes Press, 1990.

Eleff, Zev. *Living from Convention to Convention: A History of the NCSY, 1954–1980.* Jersey City, N.J.: Ktav, 2009.

Eliav, Mordechai. *Erez Yisrael ve-Yishuvah ba-Meah ha-19.* Jerusalem: Keter, 1978.

Ellenson, David H. *After Emancipation: Jewish Religious Responses to Modernity.* Cincinnati: HUCA Press, 2004.

———. *Rabbi Esriel Hildesheimer and the Creation of a Modern Jewish Orthodoxy.* Tuscaloosa: University of Alabama Press, 1990.

———. *Tradition in Transition.* Lanham, Md.: University Press of America, 1989.

El-Or, Tamar. *Next Year I Will Know More: Literacy and Identity among Young Orthodox Women in Israel.* Detroit: Wayne State University Press, 2002.

Encyclopaedia Judaica. Jerusalem: Keter, 1971–72.

Encyclopaedia Judaica. 2nd ed. Jerusalem: Keter/Gale, 2006.

Erikson, Kai T. *Wayward Puritans: A Study in the Sociology of Deviance.* Rev. ed. Boston: Allyn and Bacon, 2004.

Etkes, Immanuel. *The Gaon of Vilna.* Berkeley: University of California Press, 2002.

———. *Rabbi Israel Salanter and the Mussar Movement.* Philadelphia: Jewish Publication Society, 1993.

Fackenheim, Emil. *To Mend the World: Foundations of Post-Holocaust Thought.* Bloomington: Indiana University Press, 1994.

Feldman, Jackie. *Above the Death Pits, Beneath the Flag: Youth Voyages to Poland and the Performance of Israeli National Identity.* Oxford: Berghahn Books, 2008.

Ferziger, Adam S. *Exclusion and Hierarchy: Orthodoxy, Nonobservance, and the Emergence of Modern Jewish Identity.* Philadelphia: University of Pennsylvania Press, 2005.

Finger, Seymour M., ed. *American Jewry during the Holocaust.* New York: Holmes and Meier, 1984.

Finkelman, Yoel. "Religion and Public Life in 20th-Century American Jewish Thought." PhD diss., Hebrew University in Jerusalem, 2002.

———. *Strictly Kosher Reading: Popular Literature and the Condition of Contemporary Orthodoxy.* Boston: Academic Studies Press, 2011.

Fishkoff, Sue. *The Rebbe's Army: Inside the World of Chabad Lubavitch.* New York: Schocken, 2003.

Fishman, Joshua A. *Ideology, Society and Language: The Odyssey of Nathan Birnbaum.* Ann Arbor, Mich.: Karoma, 1987.

Forman, Seth. *Blacks in the Jewish Mind: A Crisis of Liberalism.* New York: New York University Press, 1998.

Freedman, Samuel I. *Jew vs. Jew: The Struggle for the Soul of American Jewry.* New York: Simon and Schuster, 2000.

Frey, Marc E. "Challenging the World's Conscience: The Soviet Jewry Movement, American Political Culture, and U.S. Foreign Policy, 1952–1967." PhD diss., Temple University, 2002.

Friedman, Menachem. *Hevrah va-Dat: Ha-Orthodoksiyah ha-lo Zionit be-Erez Yisrael.* Jerusalem: Yad Yitzhak Ben-Zvi, 1978.

Friedman, Murray, and Albert D. Chernin, eds. *A Second Exodus: The American Movement to Free Soviet Jews.* Hanover, N.H.: Brandeis University Press, 1999.

Fuchs, Ilan. "'Bein ish le-isha ha-kol le-fi ha-ma'ase she-hu oseh kakh ruah ha-kodesh shurah alav': Yahasam shel sheloshah posekim Amerika'im Orthodoksim le-sugiyat talmud Torah le-nashim be-mahazit ha-ma'ah ha-sheniyah shel ha-me'ah ha-Esrim." MA thesis, Bar-

Ilan University, 2003.

———. *Jewish Women's Torah Study: Orthodox Religious Education and Modernity.* Oxford: Routledge, 2014.

Garrow, David J. *Bearing the Cross: Martin Luther King Jr. and the Southern Christian Leadership Conference.* New York: Vintage Books, 1988.

Gever, Dara. "Contemporary Campus Kiruv at Emory: Departing from 'Outreach' and 'Returning' to Judaism." BA thesis, Emory University, 2013.

Glazer, Nathan. *American Judaism.* Chicago: University of Chicago Press, 1957.

Goldberg, J. J. *Jewish Power: Inside the American Jewish Establishment.* Reading, Mass.: Addison-Wesley, 1996.

Goldman, Yosef. *Hebrew Printing in America, 1735–1926.* New York: YG Books, 2006.

Gordis, Robert. *Conservative Judaism: A Modern Approach to Jewish Tradition.* New York: National Academy for Adult Jewish Studies, 1956.

Goren, Arthur. *The Politics and Public Culture of American Jews.* Bloomington: Indiana University Press, 1999.

Gorlitz, Menachem Mendel. *Mara de-Ara de-Yisrael.* Jerusalem: Y. M. Sofer, 2003.

Greenberg, Blu. *On Women and Judaism: A View from Tradition.* Philadelphia: Jewish Publication Society, 1981.

Greenberg, Simon. *The Ordination of Woman Rabbis.* New York: Jewish Theological Seminary, 1988.

Gurock, Jeffrey S. *American Jewish Orthodoxy in Historical Perspective*, 299-316. Hoboken, N.J.: Ktav, 1996.

———. *Judaism's Encounter with American Sports.* Bloomington: Indiana University Press, 2005.

———. *The Men and Women of Yeshiva.* New York: Columbia University Press, 1988.

———. *Orthodox Jews in America.* Bloomington: Indiana University Press, 2009.

Gurock Jeffrey S., and Jacob J. Schacter. *A Modern Heretic and a Traditional Community: Mordecai M. Kaplan, Orthodoxy, and American Judaism.* New York: Columbia University Press, 1997.

Guttman, Alexander. *The Struggle over Reform in Rabbinic Literature.* Jerusalem: World Union for Progressive Judaism, 1977.

Harrison, Andrew. *Passover Revisited: Philadelphia's Efforts to Aid Soviet Jews, 1963–1998.* Cranbury, N.J.: Associated University Presses, 2001.

Heilman, Samuel C. *Sliding to the Right: The Contest for the Future of American Orthodoxy.* Berkeley: University of California Press, 2006.

Heilman, Samuel C., and Menachem Friedman. *The Rebbe: The Life and Afterlife of Menachem Mendel Schneerson.* Princeton: Princeton University Press, 2010.

Held, Shai. *Abraham Joshua Heschel: The Call of Transcendence.* Bloomington: Indiana University Press, 2013.

Helmreich, William. *The World of the Yeshiva.* New York: Free Press, 1982.

Henderson, John B. *The Construction of Orthodoxy and Heresy.* Albany: State University of New York Press, 1998.

Hyman, Paula. *Gender and Assimilation in Modern Jewish History.* Seattle: University of Washington Press, 1995.

Jacobs, Louis. *Theology in the Responsa.* London: Routledge, 1975.

Joselit, Jenna W. *New York's Jewish Jews: The Orthodox Community in the Interwar Years.* Bloomington: Indiana University Press, 1990.

Kaplan, Dana Evan. *American Reform Judaism: An Introduction.* New Brunswick: Rutgers University Press, 2003.

———, ed. *The Cambridge Companion to American Judaism*. New York: Cambridge University Press, 2005.

———. *The New Reform Judaism: Challenges and Reflections*. Lincoln: University of Nebraska Press, 2014.

———, ed. *Platforms and Prayerbooks: Theological and Liturgical Perspectives on Reform Judaism*. New York: Rowman and Littlefield, 2002.

Kaplan, Marion. *The Making of the Jewish Middle Class: Women, Family, and Identity in Imperial Germany*. New York: Oxford University Press, 1991.

Kaplan, Yosef. *An Alternative Path to Modernity: The Sephardi Diaspora in Western Europe*. Leiden: Brill, 2000.

Katz, Jacob. *Divine Law in Human Hands*. Jerusalem: Magnes, 1998.

———. *A House Divided: Orthodoxy and Schism in Nineteenth-Century Central Europe*. Hanover, N.H.: Brandeis University Press/University Press of New England, 1998.

———. *The Role of Religion in Modern Jewish History*. Boston: Association of Jewish Studies, 1975.

———. *With My Own Eyes: The Autobiography of an Historian*. Hanover, N.H.: Brandeis University Press/University Press of New England, 1995.

Katz, Steven T., and Steven Bayme, eds. *Continuity and Change: A Festschrift in Honor of Irving (Yitz) Greenberg's 75th Birthday*. Lanham, Md.: University Press of America, 2011.

Kaunfer, Elie. *Empowered Judaism: What Independent Minyanim Can Teach Us about Building Vibrant Jewish Communities*. Woodstock, Vt.: Jewish Lights, 2010.

Klapperman, Gilbert. *The Story of Yeshiva University*. New York: Macmillan, 1969.

Kramer, Doniel Z. *The Day Schools and Torah Umesorah: The Seeding of Traditional Judaism in America*. New York: Yeshiva University Press, 1984.

Kranzler, David. *Thy Brother's Keeper: The Orthodox Jewish Response during the Holocaust*. New York: Mesorah, 1987.

Kraus, Yitzhak. *Ha-Shevi'i: Meshihiyut be-Dor ha-Shevi'i shel Habad*. Tel Aviv: Yediot Aharonot, 2007.

Kraut, Benny. *The Greening of American Orthodox Judaism: Yavneh in the Nineteen Sixties*. Cincinnati: Hebrew Union College Press, 2011.

Lamm, Norman. *The Religious Thought of the Hasidim*. New York: Yeshiva University Press, 1999.

———. *Torah Lishma: Torah for Torah's Sake*. New York: Yeshiva University Press/Ktav, 1989.

Landes, David. "Traditional Struggles: Studying, Defining and Performing the Law at the Rabbi Isaac Elchanan Theological Seminary." PhD diss., Princeton University, 2010.

Lazin, Fred. *The Struggle for Soviet Jewry in American Politics: Israel versus the American Establishment*. Lanham, Md.: Lexington Books, 2005.

Lederhendler, Eli. *New York Jews and the Decline of Urban Ethnicity, 1950–1970*. Syracuse: Syracuse University Press, 2001.

Leibowitz, Yeshayahu. *Judaism, Human Values, and the Jewish State*. Ed. Eliezer Goldman. Cambridge, Mass.: Harvard University Press, 1982.

Liberles, Robert. *Religious Conflict in a Social Context: The Resurgence of Orthodox Judaism in Frankfurt am Main, 1838–1877*. Westport, Conn.: Greenwood Press, 1985.

Lichtenstein, Ruth. *Edut: Hurban Yahadut Eiropah*. New York: Mossad Ha-RI"M Levine, 2000.

Liebman, Charles S. *Aspects of the Religious Behavior of American Jews*. New York: Ktav, 1974.

———. *Deceptive Images: Toward a Redefinition of American Judaism*. New Brunswick, N.J.: Transaction Books, 1988.

Lookstein, Haskel. *Were We Our Brother's Keepers? The Public Response of American Jews to the Holocaust*. New York: Hartmore, 1986.

Marrus, Michael R. *The Holocaust in History*. Hanover, N.H.: University Press of New England, 1987.
Medoff, Rafael. *The Deafening Silence: American Jewish Leaders and the Holocaust*. New York: Shapolsky, 1987.
———. *Jewish Americans and Political Participation*. Santa Barbara, Calif.: ABC-CLIO, 2002.
———. *Rav Chesed: The Life and Times of Rabbi Haskel Lookstein*. Jersey City, N.J.: Ktav, 2008.
———, ed. *Rav Chesed: Essays in Honor of Rabbi Dr. Haskel Lookstein*. Jersey City, N.J.: Ktav, 2009.
Mendelsohn, Ezra. *On Modern Jewish Politics*. New York: Oxford University Press, 1993.
Meyer, Michael A. *Response to Modernity: A History of the Reform Movement*. New York: Oxford University Press, 1988.
Mintz, Jerome R. *Hasidic People: A Place in the New World*. Cambridge, Mass.: Harvard University Press, 1992.
Mintzberg, Henry. *The Nature of Managerial Work*. New York: HarperCollins, 1973.
Miron, Guy ed. *Mi-Breslau le-Yerushalayim: Batei Midrash le-Rabbanim, Pirkei Mehkar ve-Hagut*. Jerusalem: Machon Schechter and Leo Baeck Institute, 2009.
Mirsky Samuel K. ed. *Mosdot Torah be-Eiropah be-Vinyanam u-ve-Hurbanam*. New York: Egen, 1956.
Mittleman, Alan. *The Politics of Torah: The Jewish Political Tradition and the Founding of Agudat Israel*. Albany: State University of New York Press, 1996.
Mittleman, Alan, Jonathan D. Sarna, and Robert Licht, eds. *Jewish Polity and American Civil Society*. Lanham, Md.: Rowman and Littlefield, 2002.
Morris, Bonnie. *Lubavitcher Women in America: Identity and Activism in the Postwar Era*. Albany: State University of New York Press, 1999.
Morrison, David. *The Gush: Center of Modern Religious Zionism*. Jerusalem: Gefen, 2003.
Nadel, Stanley. *Little Germany: Ethnicity, Religion, and Class in New York City, 1845–1880*. Urbana: University of Illinois Press, 1990.
Novick, Peter. *The Holocaust in American Life*. Boston: Houghton Mifflin, 1999.
Ofir (Offenbacher), Natan. *Rabbi Shlomo Carlebach: Life, Mission, Legacy*. Jerusalem: Urim Publications, 2014.
Noveck, Simon, ed. *Great Jewish Personalities in Modern Times*. Clinton, Mass.: Bnai Brith, 1960.
Olitzky, Kerry. *The American Synagogue: A Historical Dictionary and Sourcebook*. Westport, Conn.: Greenwood, 1996.
Orbach, William W. *The American Movement to Aid Soviet Jews*. Amherst: University of Massachusetts Press, 1979.
Pantel Zolty, Shoshana. *"And All Your Children Shall Be Learned": Women and the Study of Torah in Jewish Law and History*. Northvale, N.J.: Jason Aronson, 1997.
Piekarz, Mendel. *Hasidut Polin*. Jerusalem: Mossad Bialik, 1990.
Popper, Micha. *Al Menahalim ke-Manhigim*. Tel Aviv: Ramot, 1994.
Prell, Riv-Ellen. *Prayer and Community: The Havurah in American Judaism*. Detroit: Wayne State University Press, 1989.
Putnam, Robert D. *Bowling Alone: The Collapse and Revival of American Community*. New York: Touchstone, 2001.
Rabin Dagi, Laura. "'Justice, Justice You Will Pursue?' Orthodox Jewry and the Civil Rights Movement, 1954–1970." BA thesis, Harvard University, 2006.
Rakeffet-Rothkoff, Aaron. *Bernard Revel: Builder of American Orthodoxy*. Philadelphia: Jewish

Publication Society, 1972.
Raphael, Marc Lee. *Jews and Judaism in a Midwestern Community: Columbus, Ohio, 1840–1975*. Columbus: Ohio Historical Society, 1979.
Regev, Eyal. *Ha-Z'dukim ve-hilkhatam*. Jerusalem: Yad Yitzhak Ben-Zvi, 2005.
Ro'i, Yaakov. *The Struggle for Soviet Jewish Emigration (1948–1967)*. Cambridge: Cambridge University Press, 1991.
Roof, Wade Clark. *A Generation of Seekers*. San Francisco: Harper, 1993.
Rosenbloom, Noah H. *Tradition in an Age of Reform*. Philadelphia: Jewish Publication Society, 1976.
Ross, Tamar. *Armon ha-Torah mi-Ma'al Lah: Al Orthodoksiyah ve-Feminism*. Tel Aviv: Alma College and Am Oved, 2007.
———. *Expanding the Palace of the Torah: Orthodoxy and Feminism*. Waltham, Mass.: Brandeis University Press/University Press of New England, 2004.
Rubin Schwartz, Shuli. *The Rabbi's Wife: The Rebbetzin in American Jewish Life*. New York: New York University Press, 2006.
Russ, Shlomo M. "The 'Zionist Hooligans': The Jewish Defense League." PhD diss., City University of New York, 1981.
Sacks, Jonathan. *One People? Tradition, Modernity and Jewish Unity*. London: Littman Library, 1993.
Sagi Avi, and Zvi Zohar. *Ma'agalei Zehut Yehudit ba-Sifrut ha-Hilkhatit*. Tel Aviv: Hakibbutz Hameuchad, 2000.
Salmon, Yoseph, Aviezer Ravitzky, and Adam S. Ferziger, eds. *Ha-Orthodoksiyah ha-Yehudit: Hebetim Hadashim*. Jerusalem: Magnes Press, 2006.
Sarna, Jonathan D. *American Judaism: A History*. New Haven: Yale University Press, 2004.
Schiff, Alvin I. *The Jewish Day School in America*. New York: Jewish Education Committee Press, 1966.
Schreiber, Lynn, ed., *Hide and Seek: Jewish Women and Hair Covering*. Jerusalem: Urim Publications, 2003.
Schultz, David A., Manfred Steger, and Scott L. Maclean. *Social Capital: Critical Perspectives on Community and "Bowling Alone."* New York: New York University Press, 2002.
Schultz, Debra L. *Going South: Jewish Women in the Civil Rights Movement*. New York: New York University Press, 2001.
Schwartzfuchs, Simon. *A Concise History of the Rabbinate*. Oxford: Blackwell, 1993.
Schweid, E. *Democratiyah ve-Halakhah: Pirkei Iyun be-Mishnato shel ha-Rav Hayyim Hirschenson*. Jerusalem: Magnes, 1978.
Shandler, Jeffrey. *While America Watches: Televising the Holocaust*. New York: Oxford University Press, 1999.
Shapiro, Marc B. *Saul Lieberman and the Orthodox*. Scranton: University of Scranton Press, 2006.
Sheleg, Yair. *Ha-Dati'im ha-Hadashim*. Jerusalem: Keter, 2000.
Sherman, Moshe D. "Bernard Illowy and Nineteenth-Century American Orthodoxy." PhD diss., Yeshiva University, 1991.
———. *Orthodox Judaism in America: A Biographical Dictionary and Sourcebook*. Westport, Conn.: Greenwood Press, 1996.
Shimoni, Gideon. *The Zionist Ideology*. Hanover, N.H.: University Press of New England, 1995.
Silber, Michael K. "Shorshei ha-Pilug be-Yahadut Hungariyah." PhD diss., Hebrew University of Jerusalem, 1985.

BIBLIOGRAPHY

Sklare, Marshall. *Conservative Judaism*. Glencoe, Ill.: Free Press, 1955.

———. *The Jews: Social Patterns of an American Group*. Glencoe, Ill.: Free Press, 1958.

Sonnenfeld, Shlomo Zalman. *Ha-Ish al-ha-Homah*. 3 vols. Jerusalem: n.p., 1971.

Stampfer, Shaul. *Lithuanian Yeshivas of the Nineteenth Century: Creating a Tradition of Learning*. London: Littman Library, 2012.

Staub, Michael, ed. *The Jewish 1960s: An American Sourcebook*. Waltham, Mass.: Brandeis University Press, 2004.

———. *Torn at the Roots: The Crisis of Jewish Liberalism in Postwar America*. New York: Columbia University Press, 2002.

Stern, Eliyahu. *The Genius: Elijah of Vilna and the Making of Modern Judaism*. New Haven: Yale University Press, 2013.

Stolow, Jeremy. *Orthodox by Design: Judaism, Print Politics, and the Art Scroll Revolution*. Berkeley: University of California Press, 2010.

Susser, Bernard, and Charles S. Liebman. *Choosing Survival: Strategies for a Jewish Future*. New York: Oxford University Press, 1999.

Svonkin, Stuart. *Jews against Prejudice: American Jews and the Fight for Civil Liberties*. New York: Columbia University Press, 1997.

Tobin, Dodi. "The Impact of One-Year Israel Study on American Day School Graduates." PhD diss., Fairleigh Dickinson University, 1997.

Trzciński, Andrzej. *Yeshivat Chachmei Lublin*. Warsaw: Adrem Books/Warsaw Jewish Community, 2007.

Waxman, Chaim I. *Jewish Baby Boomers: A Communal Perspective*. Albany: State University of New York Press, 2001.

Waxman, Mordechai, ed. *Tradition and Change: The Rise of the Conservative Movement*. New York: Burning Bush Press, 1958.

Webb, Clive. *Fight against Fear: Southern Jews and Black Civil Rights*. Athens: University of Georgia Press, 2001.

Weinberger, Moshe Carmilly, ed. *The Rabbinical Seminary of Budapest*. New York: Sepher-Hermon Press, 1986.

Wertheimer, Jack. *All Quiet on the Religious Front: Jewish Unity, Denominationalism, and Postdenominationalism in the United States*. New York: American Jewish Committee, 2005.

———. *A People Divided: Judaism in Contemporary America*. New York: Basic Books, 1993.

Wiesel, Elie. *The Jews of Silence*. New York: Holt, Rinehart and Winston, 1966.

Wilke, Carsten. *Die Rabbiner der Emanzipationszeit in den deutschen, böhmischen und grofspolnischen Ländern, 1781–1871*. Vol. 1. Munich: K. G. Saur, 2004.

Wilson, Bryan. *Magic and the Millennium*. London, Heinemann: 1973.

Wolf, Zusha, ed. *Diedushka: Ha-Rebbe mi-Lubavitch ve-Yahadut Russiyah*. Kfar Chabad: Yad ha-Hamishah, 2006.

Wolfson, Elliot R. *Open Secret: Postmessianic Messianism and the Mystical Revision of Menahem Mendel Schneerson*. New York: Columbia University Press, 2012.

Wolowelsky, Joel. *Women, Jewish Law and Modernity: New Opportunities in a Post-Feminist Age*. Jersey City, N.J.: Ktav, 2003.

Woocher, Jonathan S. *Civil Judaism in the United States*. Jerusalem: Center for Jewish Communal Studies, 1978.

———. *Sacred Survival*. Bloomington: Indiana University Press, 1986.

Wuthnow, Robert, ed. *"I Come Away Stronger": How Small Groups Are Shaping American Religion*. Grand Rapids, Mich.: Wm. B. Eerdmans Publishing, 1994.

———. *Loose Connections: Joining Together in America's Fragmented Communities*. Cambridge,

Mass.: Harvard University Press, 1998.

———. *Sharing the Journey: Support Groups and America's New Quest for Community*. New York: Free Press, 1994.

Yedidya, Asaf, ed. *Batei Midrash Nusah Ashkenaz*. Jerusalem: Ha-Karmel, Machon Schechter, and Leo Baeck Institute, 2010.

Zohar, David. *Mehuyavut Yehudit be-Olam Moderni: Ha-Rav Hirschenson ve-Yahaso el ha-Modernah*. Jerusalem: Shalom Hartman Institute and the Faculty of Law at Bar-Ilan University, 2003.

Zuroff, Efraim. *Occupation: Nazi-Hunter: The Continuing Search for the Perpetrators of the Holocaust*. Jersey City, N.J.: Ktav, 1994.

———. *The Response of Orthodox Jewry in the United States to the Holocaust: The Activities of the Vaad ha-Hatzala Rescue Committee, 1939–1945*. New York: Yeshiva University Press, 2000.

Articles and Chapters

Ackerman, Ari. "'Judging the Sinner Favorably': R. Hayyim Hirschensohn on the Need for Leniency in Halakhic Decision Making." *Modern Judaism* 22, no. 3 (2002): 261–80.

Adler, Rachel. "Innovation and Authority: A Feminist Reading of the 'Women's Minyan' Responsum." In *Re-Examining Progressive Halakhah*, ed. Walter Jacob and Moshe Zemer, 3–32. New York: Berghahn Books, 2001.

Ariel, Yaakov. "Hasidism in the Age of Aquarius: The House of Love and Prayer in San Francisco, 1967–1977." *Religion and American Culture* 13, no. 2 (2003): 139–65.

Assaf, David, and Israel Bartal. "Shtadlanut ve-Orthodoksiyah: Zadikei Polin be-mifgash im ha-zemanim ha-hadashim." In *Zadikim ve-Anshei Ma'aseh*, ed. Rachel Elior, Israel Bartal, and Chone Shmeruk, 69–90. Jerusalem: Mossad Bialik, 1994.

Avraham, Michael. "Ha-im yesh avodah zarah ne-urah? Al ha-yahas le-goyim ve-al shinuyim ba-halakhah." *Akdamot* 19 (Sivan 5767/June 2007), www.bmj.org.il/files/1331292103800.pdf.

Azilei, Avraham. "Masa le-hidud arakhim ziyoni'im, yehudi'im, tenuati'im." *Be-Shevilei ha-Zikkaron* 7 (1995): 7–8.

Baumel Joseph, Norma. "Jewish Education for Women: Rabbi Moshe Feinstein's Map of America." *American Jewish History* 83, no. 2 (1995): 205–22.

Bayer, Abraham. "American Response to Soviet Anti-Jewish Policies." In *American Jewish Yearbook 1973*, 210–25. Philadelphia: American Jewish Committee, 1973.

Ben-Ezra, Akiva. "Yekutiel Yehudah Greenwald." Addendum to Yekutiel Yehudah Greenwald, *Ha-Shohet ve-ha-Shehitah ba-Sifrut ha-Rabbanut*, 185–92. New York: Feldheim, 1955.

Berger, Shalom Z. "The Impact of One-Year Israel Study on American Day School Graduates." *Ten Da'at* 12 (1999): 3–14.

Berman, Saul. "The Status of Women in Halakhic Judaism." *Tradition* 14, no. 2 (1973): 5–28.

Bernstein, David I. "Teaching the Role of the Poles in the Shoah." *Jewish Educational Leadership* 8, no. 1 (2009), www.lookstein.org/online_journal.php?id=285.

Bin-Nun, Amitai. "Motivations and Symbols of the Early Student Struggle for Soviet Jewry (SSSJ), 1964–1970." BA Paper, Yeshiva College, 2004.

"Biographical Sketches of Rabbis and Cantors Officiating in the United States." *American Jewish Yearbook* 5 (1903–4): 40–105.

Bleich, Judith. "The Frankfurt Secession Controversy." *Jewish Action*, Winter 1991–92, 22–27, 52.

Brill, Alan. "An Ideal Rosh Yeshiva: *By His Light: Character and Values in the Service of God* and *Leaves of Faith* by Rav Aharon Lichtenstein (KTAV)." *Edah Journal* 5, no. 1 (2005), www.edah.org/backend/JournalArticle/5_1_Brill.pdf.

———. "Modern Orthodoxy." Unpublished book chapter. 2014.
Bronstein, Herbert. "Platforms and Prayerbooks: From Exclusivity to Inclusivity in Reform Judaism." In *Platforms and Prayer Books*, ed. Dana Evan Kaplan, 25–40. Lanham, Md.: Rowman and Littlefield, 2002.
Brown, Binyamin. "Doktrinat da'at Torah: sheloshah shelabim." *Mekhkarei Yerushalayim be-Makhshevet Yisrael* 19, no. 2 (2005): 537–600.
Brown (Hoisman), Iris. "Bein 'teva ha-ishah' le 'marut ha-ba'al': Ha-ideologiyah ha-hinukhit ha-Haredit ve-gevulot ha-haskalah ha-Toranit le-banot." *Zehuyot* 3 (2013): 97–124.
Cala, Alina. "The Cult of Tzaddikim among Non-Jews in Poland." *Jewish Folklore and Ethnology Review* 17 (1995): 16–19.
Caplan, Kimmy. "Ha-Rav Yitzhak Margaliyot: Mi-Mizrah Eiropah le-Amerika." *Zion* 58, no. 2 (1993): 215–40.
———. "Have 'many lies accumulated in history books'? The Holocaust in Ashkenazi 'Haredi' Historical Consciousness in Israel." *Yad Vashem Studies* 29 (2001): 321–75.
———. "The Holocaust in Contemporary Israeli Haredi Popular Religion." *Modern Judaism* 22, no. 2 (2002): 142–68.
———. "The Internal Popular Discourse of Israeli Haredi Women." *Archives de sciences sociales des religions* 123 (July–September 2003): 77–101, http://assr.revues.org/1069.
Chernin, Albert D. "Making Soviet Jewry an Issue: A History." In *A Second Exodus: The American Movement to Free Soviet Jews*, ed. Murray Friedman and Albert D. Chernin, 15–69. Hanover, N.H.: Brandeis University Press, 1999.
Chinitz, Jacob. "Reb Moshe and the Conservatives." *Conservative Judaism* 41, no. 3 (1989): 5–26.
Chinn, Benzion N. "Towards One People in One World." *The Commentator*, December 31, 2002, http://commie.droryikra.com/v67i7/culture/book.html.
Cohen, Erik H. "Religious Tourism as an Educational Experience." In *Tourism, Religion, and Spiritual Journeys*, ed. Daniel H. Olsen and Dallen J. Timothy, 78–93. London: Routledge, 2006.
Cohen, Tova. "'And All the Women Followed Her . . .': On Women's Religious Leadership in Israeli Modern Orthodoxy." In *Jewish Religious Leadership: Image and Reality*, ed. Jack Wertheimer, 2:715–56. New York: JTS, 2004.
———. "Iris Parush's *Reading Women*." *Journal of Israeli History* 21, nos. 1–2 (2002): 169–91.
Cohen Ioannides, Mara W., and Dmitri Ioannides. "Global Jewish Tourism: Pilgrimages and Remembrance." In *Tourism, Religion, and Spiritual Journeys*, ed. Daniel H. Olsen and Dallen J. Timothy, 156–71. London: Routledge, 2006.
Cohen Nusbacher, Aileen. "Efforts at Change in a Traditional Denomination: The Case of Orthodox Women's Prayer Groups." *Nashim*, Spring 5759/1999, 95–113.
Cohn, Hillel. "Why I Officiate at Mixed Marriage Ceremonies." In *Contemporary Debates in American Reform Judaism: Conflicting Visions*, ed. Dana Evan Kaplan, 160–70. New York: Routledge, 2001.
Cromer, Gerald. "'Secularism Is the Root of All Evil': The Haredi Response to Crime and Delinquency." In *Language and Communication in Israel*, ed. Hana Herzog and Eliezer Ben-Raphael, 259–72. Piscataway, N.J.: Transaction Publishers, 2001.
Dash Moore, Debra. "Reconsidering the Rosenbergs: Symbol and Substance in Second-Generation American Jewish Consciousness." *Journal of American Ethnic History* 8 (Fall 1988): 21–37.
Decter, Moshe. "The Status of Jews in the Soviet Union." *Foreign Affairs* 41, no. 2 (1963): 3–13.
Digance, Justine. "Religious and Secular Pilgrimage: Journeys Redolent with Meaning." In

Tourism, Religion, and Spiritual Journeys, ed. Daniel H. Olsen and Dallen J. Timothy, 36–48. London: Routledge, 2006.

Dombroff, Yaakov M. "An Appreciation of Rabbi Mordechai Pinchas Teitz zz"l." *Jewish Observer* 29 (Tammuz 5756/June 1996): 18–26.

Don-Yehiya, Eliezer. "The Negation of the *Galut* in Religious Zionism." *Modern Judaism* 12 (1992): 129–55.

———. "Orthodox Jewry in Israel and in North America." *Israel Studies* 10, no. 1 (2005): 157–87.

Edrei, Arye. "Holocaust Memorial: A Paradigm of Competing Memories in the Religious and Secular Societies in Israel." In *On Memory: An Interdisciplinary Approach*, ed. Doron Mendels, 37–100. Oxford: Peter Lang, 2007.

———. "Keizad zokhrim? Zikhron ha-Shoah ba-hevrah ha-datit u-va-hevrah ha-hilonit." *Tarbut Democratit* 11 (2007): 7–50.

Eilberg, Amy. "*Spiritual Activism: A Jewish Guide to Leadership and Repairing the World* (Review)." *Conservative Judaism* 63, no. 4 (2012): 108–10.

Eisenstein, Judah David. "Rabbi Hayyim Hirschenson." *Apiryon* 5 (1927): 4–13. Reprinted in Judah David Eisenstein, *Ozar Zikhronotai*, 29–34. New York: J. D. Eisenstein, 1930.

Elazar, Dan, and Rena Geffen Monson. "The Evolving Roles of American Congregational Rabbis." *Modern Judaism* 2, no. 1 (1982): 73–89.

Eleff, Zev. "American Orthodoxy's Lukewarm Embrace of the Hirschain Legacy." *Tradition* 45, no. 3 (Fall 2012), 35-33.

———. "The Maharat Moment." *Torah Musings*, September 9, 2013, http://mosaicmagazine.com/picks/2013/09/a-maharat-moment/?utm_source=Mosaic+Daily+Email&utm_campaign=2e3e8bd7a8-Mosaic_2013_9_11&utm_medium=email&utm_term=0_0b0517b2ab-2e3e8bd7a8-41174565.

———. "Ten Sha'alvim Alumni Depart Yeshiva after a Year for Less Academic Alternatives." *The Commentator*, February 12, 2007.

Eleff, Zev, and Eitan Kastner. "Reconciling Institutional Divides: Rosh Kollel and YC Dean Begin Dialogue." *The Commentator*, September 11, 2006.

Ellenson, David H. "A Disputed Precedent: The Prague Organ in Nineteenth-Century Central European Legal Literature and Polemics." *Leo Baeck Institute Year Book* 40 (1995): 252–64.

———. "Eugene B. Borowitz: A Tribute." *Jewish Book Annual* 51 (1993–94): 125–36.

———. "A Jewish Legal Decision by Rabbi Bernard Illowy of New Orleans and Its Discussion in Nineteenth-Century Europe." *American Jewish History* 69, no. 2 (1979): 174–95.

———. "Traditional Reactions to Modern Jewish Reform: The Paradigm of German Orthodoxy." In *History of Jewish Philosophy*, ed. Daniel Frank and Oliver Leaman, 651–74. London: Routledge, 1997.

———. "Two Responsa of Rabbi Moshe Feinstein." *American Jewish Archives* 52, nos. 1 and 2 (2000–2001): 112–28.

Etkes, Immanuel. "The Relationship between Talmudic Scholarship and the Institution of the Rabbinate in Nineteenth-Century Lithuanian Jewry." In *Scholars and Scholarship: The Interaction between Judaism and Other Cultures*, ed. Leo Landman, 107–32. New York: Yeshiva University Press, 1990.

Ettinger, Shmuel. "The Hasidic Movement: Reality and Ideals." *Journal of World History* 11, nos. 1–2 (1968): 226–43. Reprinted in *Essential Papers on Hasidism*, ed. Gershon David Hundert, 238–42. New York: New York University Press, 1991.

Farber, Seth. "Reproach, Recognition and Respect: Rabbi Joseph B. Soloveitchik's Mid-Century Attitude toward Non-Orthodox Denominations." *American Jewish History* 89, no. 2 (2001): 193–214.

Feldman, Emanuel. "Trends in the American Yeshivot." *Tradition*, Spring 1968, http://traditionarchive.org/news/article.cfm?id=105182.
Feldman, Jackie. "'It Is My Brothers Whom I Am Seeking': Israeli Youths' Pilgrimages to Poland and the Shoah." *Jewish Folklore and Ethnology Review* 17, nos. 1–2 (1995): 33–36.
———. "Marking the Boundaries of the Enclave: Defining the Israeli Collective through the Poland Experience." *Israel Studies* 7, no. 2 (2002): 84–114.
———. "Shoah, Security, Victory: A Critique of Israeli Youth Voyages to Poland." *Jewish Educational Leadership* 8, no. 1 (2009), www.lookstein.org/online_journal/index.php?id=293.
Ferziger, Adam S. *Centered on Study: Typologies of the American Community Kollel*, Position Paper 18. Ramat-Gan: Rappaport Center for Assimilation Research—Bar-Ilan University, 2009.
———. "Constituency Definition: The Orthodox Dilemma." In *Jewish Religious Leadership: Image and Reality*, ed. Jack Wertheimer, 2:535–67. New York: JTS, 2005.
———. *The Emergence of the Community Kollel: A New Model for Addressing Assimilation*, Position Paper 13. Ramat-Gan: Rappaport Center for Assimilation Research—Bar-Ilan University, 2006.
———. "Ha-Zionut ha-Datit bat zemanenu ve-ha-heepuss ahar 'avar shimushi': heker Ha-Rav Hayyim Hirschenson ke-mikre mivhan." In *Yosef Da'at: Mekhkarim be-Historiyah Yehudit Modernit Mukdashim le-Professor Yoseph Salmon le-Hag Yovelo*, ed. Yoseph Goldstein, 261–75. Be'er Sheva: Ben-Gurion University, 2011.
———. "Holy Land in Exile: The Torah MiTzion Movement: Toward a New Paradigm for Religious Zionism." In *Religious Zionism Post-Disengagement: Future Directions*, ed. Chaim I. Waxman, 373–414. New York: Yeshiva University Press, 2008.
———. "The Hungarian Jewish Congress." In *YIVO Encyclopedia of the Jews in Eastern Europe*, ed. Gershon Hundert, 826–28. New Haven: Yale University Press, 2008.
———. "Religious Zealotry and Religious Law: Reexamining Conflict and Coexistence." *Journal of Religion*, January 2004, 48–77.
———. "Religious Zionism, *Galut*, and Global Jewry: Exploring 'Gush' Exceptionalism." In *How I Love Your Torah: Essays in Honor of Yeshivat Har Etzion on the Forty-fifth Anniversary of Its Founding*, ed. Yitzhak Recanati, Shaul Barth, and Reuven Ziegler, 111–41. Alon Shevut: Yeshivat Har Etzion, 2014.
———. "The Road Not Taken: Rabbi Salamon Zvi Schück and the Legacy of Hungarian Orthodoxy." *Hebrew Union College Annual* 79 (2011): 107–40.
———. "The Role of Reform in Israeli Orthodoxy." In *Between Jewish Tradition and Modernity: Essays in Honor of David H. Ellenson*, ed. Michael A. Meyer and David Myers, 51–66. Detroit: Wayne State University Press, 2014.
———. "On Fragmentary Judaism: The Jewish 'Other' and the Worldview of Rabbi Dr. Aharon Lichtenstein." *Tradition* (forthcoming 2015).
Finkelman, Yoel. "Haredi Isolation in Changing Environments: A Case Study in Yeshivah Immigration." *Modern Judaism* 22, no. 1 (2002): 61–82.
———. "An Ideology for American Yeshiva Students: The Sermons of R. Aharon Kotler, 1942–1962." *Journal of Jewish Studies* 58, no. 2 (2007): 314–32.
———. "On the Irrelevance of Religious-Zionism." *Tradition* 39, no. 1 (2005): 21–44.
———. "Virtual Volozhin: Socialization versus Learning in Israel Yeshiva Programs." In *Wisdom from All My Teachers: Challenges and Initiatives in Contemporary Torah Education*, ed. Jeffrey Saks and Susan Handelman, 360–72. Jerusalem: ATID and Urim, 2003.
Fogel, Joshua. "Illegal Drug Use in Orthodox Jewish Adolescents." *Journal of Ethnicity in Substance Abuse* 3, no. 3 (2004): 17–31.
Friedman, Menachem. "The Changing Role of the Community Rabbinate." *Jerusalem Quar-*

BIBLIOGRAPHY

terly 25 (Fall 1982): 79–99.

———. "The Haredim and the Holocaust." *Jerusalem Quarterly* 53 (Winter 1990): 86–114.

Frimer, Aryeh A., and Dov I. Frimer. "Women's Prayer Services: Theory and Practice." *Tradition* 32, no. 2 (1998): 5–118.

Furstenberg, Rochelle. "The Flourishing of Higher Jewish Learning for Women." *Jerusalem Letter* 429 (May 2000): 1–11.

Garb, Yonatan. "Tehiyatah ha-movnet shel ha-mistikah be-yameinu." In *Tarbut Yehudit be-Ein ha-Se'arah: Sefer ha-Yovel le-Yoseph Ahituv*, ed. Avi Sagi and Nahem Ilan, 172–99. Tel Aviv: Ha-Kibbutz ha-Me'uhad, 2002.

Geiger, Yitzhak. "Ha-Zionut ha-Datit ha-hadashah." *Akdamot* 11 (2002): 51–77.

Gonen, Amiram. "From Yeshiva to Work: The American Experience and Lessons for Israel." *Floersheimer Institute Policy Studies*, nos. 4/5 (2000), www.fips.org.il/Site/p_publications/item_en.asp?doc=&iss=&iid=569.

Grossman, Lawrence. "American Orthodoxy in the 1950s: The Lean Years." In *Rav Chesed: Essays in Honor of Rabbi Dr. Haskel Lookstein*, ed. Rafael Medoff, 251–70. Jersey City, N.J.: Ktav, 2009.

———. "Charles S. Liebman, the Scholar and the Man." *American Jewish History* 80, no. 4 (1991): 465–78.

———. "Decline and Fall: Thoughts on Religious Zionism in America." In *Religious Zionism Post-Disengagement: Future Directions*, ed. Chaim I. Waxman, 31–56. New York: Yeshiva University Press, 2008.

———. "Mainstream Orthodoxy and the American Public Square." In *Jewish Polity and American Civil Society*, ed. Alan Mittleman, Jonathan D. Sarna, and Robert Licht, 283–307. Lanham, Md.: Rowman and Littlefield, 2002.

Gurock, Jeffrey S. "The Emergence of the American Synagogue." In *The American Jewish Experience*, ed. Jonathan D. Sarna, 219–34. New York: Holmes and Meier, 1997.

———. "From Fluidity to Rigidity: The Religious Worlds of Conservative and Orthodox Jews in Twentieth Century America." David W. Belin Lecture in American Jewish Affairs, University of Michigan (2000). Reprinted in *American Jewish Identity Politics*, ed. Deborah Dash Moore, 159–206. Ann Arbor: University of Michigan Press, 2008.

———. "Ha-Irgunim ha-Orthodoksim be-Amerika ve-temikhatam ba-Zionut, 1880–1930." In *Zionut ve-Dat*, ed. Shmuel Almong, Judah Reinharz, and Anita Shapira, 263–85. Jerusalem: Merkaz Shazar, 1994.

———. "An Orthodox Conspiracy Theory: The Travis Family, Bernard Revel, and the Jewish Theological Seminary." *Modern Judaism* 19, no. 3 (1999): 241–53.

———. "The Orthodox Synagogue." In *The American Synagogue: A Sanctuary Transformed*, ed. Jack Wertheimer, 37–84. Cambridge: Cambridge University Press, 1987.

———. "The Ramaz Version of American Orthodoxy." In *Ramaz: School, Community, Scholarship and Orthodoxy*, ed. Jeffrey S. Gurock, 40–82. Hoboken, N.J.: Ktav, 1989.

———. "Resisters and Accommodators: Varieties of Orthodox Rabbis in America, 1886–1983." *American Jewish Archives* 35, no. 2 (1983): 100–187. Reprinted in J. Marcus and A. Peck, eds. *The American Rabbinate: A Century of Continuity and Change, 1883–1983*, 10–97. Hoboken, N.J.: Ktav, 1985.

———. "Twentieth-Century American Orthodoxy's Era of Non-Observance (1900–1960)." *Torah U-Madda Journal* 9 (2000): 87–107.

———. "The Winnowing of American Orthodoxy." In *American Jewish Orthodoxy in Historical Perspective*, 299–316. Hoboken, N.J.: Ktav, 1996.

Haas, Peter. "Reform Judaism and Halacha: A Rapprochement." In *Platforms and Prayer Books*, ed. Dana Evan Kaplan, 233–47. Lanham, Md.: Rowman and Littlefield, 2002.

Hacohen, Aviad. "'Religious Zionist Halakhah': Is It a Reality or Was It a Dream." In *Religious Zionism Post-Disengagement: Future Directions*, ed. Chaim I. Waxman, 342–45. New York: Yeshiva University Press, 2008.

Heilman, Samuel C. "Haredim and the Public Square." In *Jewish Polity and American Civil Society*, ed. Alan Mittleman, Jonathan D. Sarna, and Robert Licht, 311–36. Lanham, Md.: Rowman and Littlefield, 2002.

———. "The Many Faces of Orthodoxy: Part 1." *Modern Judaism* 2, no. 1 (1982): 23–51.

———. "The Many Faces of Orthodoxy: Part 2." *Modern Judaism* 2, no. 2 (1982): 171–98.

Heilman, Uriel. "Can Asher Lopatin Secure Yeshivat Chovevei Torah's Place in the Orthodox World?" *JTA*, September 7, 2013, www.jta.org/2012/09/07/life-religion/can-asher-lopatin-secure-yeshivat-chovevei-torahs-place-in-the-orthodox-world#ixzz2brbpDv7d.

———. "Chabad Outreach Admired by Other Orthodox, Reform." *Jewish Review*, May 12, 2008, www.jewishreview.org/node/7880.

———. "Is Yeshivat Chovevei Torah Kosher Enough?" *JTA*, September 7, 2012, www.jta.org/2012/09/07/news-opinion/the-telegraph/is-yeshivat-chovevei-torah-kosher-enough.

Hellinger, M. "Individualism, datiyut, ruhaniyut, be-idan post-moderni." *Akdamot* 14 (December 2004): 9–14.

Helmreich, William B. "Visits to Europe, Zionist Education, and Jewish Identity: The Case of the March of the Living." *Journal of Jewish Education* 61, no. 3 (1995): 16–20.

Helmreich, William B., and Reuel Shinnar. "Modern Orthodoxy in America: Possibilities for a Movement under Siege." *Jerusalem Letter/Viewpoints*, June 1, 1998, http://jcpa.org/article/modern-orthodoxy-in-america-possibilities-for-a-movement-under-siege/.

Heschel, Susannah. "The Impact of Feminist Theory on Jewish Studies." In *Modern Judaism in Historical Consciousness*, ed. Andreas Gotzmann and Christian Wiese, 528–48. Leiden: Brill, 2007.

Heuberger, R. "Orthodoxy and Reform: The Case of Rabbi Nehemiah Anton Nobel of Frankfurt a. Main." *Leo Baeck Institute Year Book* 37 (1992): 45–58.

Hoffman, Joshua. "The Changing Attitude of Rabbi Gavriel Zev Margolis toward RIETS." *The Commentator*, December 22, 2004, http://admin2.collegepublisher.com/preview/mobile/2.2469/2.2843/1.299300.

Holman Weisbard, Phyllis. "Annotated Bibliography and Guide to Archival Resources on the History of Jewish Women in America." March 1, 2009. http://jwa.org/encyclopedia/article/annotated-bibliography-and-guide-to-archival-resources-on-history-of-jewish-wom.

Jackson, Livia B. "Zionism in Hungary: The First Twenty-Five Years." *Herzl Yearbook* 7 (1971): 285–320.

Jacobson, Daniel. "In Search of Self: Psychological Perspectives on Change." In Shalom Z. Berger, Daniel Jacobson, and Chaim I. Waxman, *Flipping Out? Myth or Fact: The Impact of the "Year in Israel,"* 79–144. New York: Yashar Books, 2007.

Jaephet, Saemy. "The Secession from the Frankfort Community under Samson Raphael Hirsch." *Historia Judaica* 10 (1948): 123–34.

Jelenko, E. W. "Samson Raphael Hirsch." In *Great Jewish Personalities in Modern Times*, ed. Simon Noveck, 69–96. Clinton, Mass.: Bnai Brith, 1960.

Joselit, Jenna W. "Of Manners, Morals, and Orthodox Judaism: Decorum within the Orthodox Synagogue." In *Ramaz: School, Community, Scholarship and Orthodoxy*, ed. Jeffrey S. Gurock, 20–39. Hoboken, N.J.: Ktav, 1989.

———. "The Special Sphere of the Middle-Class American Jewish Woman: The Synagogue Sisterhood, 1890–1940." In *The American Synagogue: A Sanctuary Transformed*, ed. Jack

Wertheimer, 206–30. Cambridge: Cambridge University Press, 1987.
Kahn, Douglas. "Advocacy on a Communal Level." In *A Second Exodus: The American Movement to Free Soviet Jews*, ed. Murray Friedman and Albert D. Chernin, 181–99. Hanover, N.H.: Brandeis University Press, 1999.
Kaplan, Dana E. "The Reform Theological Enterprise at Work: Debating Theory and Practice in the American Market Place." In *Platforms and Prayer Books*, ed. Dana Evan Kaplan, 1–24. Lanham, Md.: Rowman and Littlefield, 2002.
Kaplan, Lawrence. "*Daas Torah*: A Modern Conception of Rabbinic Authority." In *Rabbinic Authority and Personal Autonomy*, ed. Moshe Sokol, 1–60. Northvale, N.J.: Jason Aronson, 1992.
———. "The Multi-Faceted Legacy of the Rav: A Critical Analysis of Hershel Schachter's Nefesh ha-Rav." *BDD* (*Bekhol Derakhekha Daehu: Journal of Torah and Scholarship*) 7 (Summer 1998): 51–85.
———. "Rabbi Abraham Isaac Kook, Rabbi Joseph B. Soloveitchik and Dr. Isaac Breuer on Jewish Identity and the National Jewish Revival." In *Jewish Identity in the Postmodern Age*, ed. Charles Selengut, 47–66. New York: Paragon, 1999.
———. "Revisionism and the Rav: The Struggle for the Soul of Modern Orthodoxy." *Judaism* 48, no. 3 (1999): 291–311.
Kaplan, Zvi J. "Rabbi Joel Teitelbaum, Zionism, and Hungarian Ultra-Orthodoxy." *Modern Judaism* 24, no. 2 (2004): 165–78.
Kapralski, Slawomir. "Battlefields of Memory: Landscape and Identity in Polish-Jewish Relations." *History and Memory* 13, no. 2 (2001): 35–58.
Karp, Abraham J. "The Ridvas: Rabbi Jacob David Wilowsky, 1845–1913." In *Perspectives on Jews and Judaism: Essays in Honor of Wolfe Kelman*, ed. Arthur A. Chiel, 215–39. New York: Rabbinical Assembly, 1978.
Katz, Jacob. "*Da'at Torah*: The Unqualified Authority Claimed for Halachists." The Gruss Lectures: Jewish Law and Modernity, October 26–November 30, 1994, www.law.harvard.edu/programs/Gruss/katz.html.
———. "Ha-Rav Shimshon Raphael Hirsch: Ha-mi-yamin u-mi-sema'iel." In *Torah im Derekh Eretz*, ed. Mordechai Breuer, 13–32. Ramat-Gan: Bar-Ilan University Press, 1987. Reprinted in Jacob Katz, ed., *Ha-Halakhah be-Meizar: Mikhsholim al Derekh ha-Orthodoksiyah be-Hithavutah*, 228–46. Jerusalem: Magnes Press, 1992.
———. "Orthodoxy in Historical Perspective." In *Studies in Contemporary Jewry*, ed. Peter Medding, 2:3–17. Bloomington: Indiana University Press, 1986.
———. "Religion as a Uniting and Dividing Force in Jewish History." In *Jewish Emancipation and Self-Emancipation*, 20–33. Philadelphia: Jewish Publication Society, 1986.
Katz, Steven T. "Irving (Yitzchak) Greenberg." In *Interpreters of Judaism in the Twentieth Century*, ed. Steven T. Katz, 59–90. Washington, D.C.: Bnai Brith Books, 1993.
Katzburg, Nathaniel. "The Hungarian Jewish Congress of 1868–1869." In *Hungarian Jewish Studies*, ed. Randolph Braham, 2:1–34. New York: World Federation of Hungarian Jews, 1969.
Kaufman, Debra R. "Engendering Orthodoxy: Newly Orthodox Women and Hasidism." In *New World Hasidism: Ethnographic Studies of Hasidic Jews in America*, ed. Janet S. Belcove-Shalin, 135–60. Albany: State University of New York Press, 1995.
Kelman, Wolfe. "Moshe Feinstein and Postwar American Orthodoxy." *Survey of Jewish Affairs 1987* (1988): 173–87.
Kelner, Shaul. "Ritualized Protest and Redemptive Politics: Cultural Consequences of the American Mobilization to Free Soviet Jewry." *Jewish Social Studies* 14, no. 3 (2008): 1–37.

Klein Halevi, Yossi. "Jacob Birnbaum and the Struggle for Soviet Jewry." *Azure* 17 (Spring 5764/2004): 27–57.

Koren, Irit. "The Bride's Voice: Religious Women Challenge the Wedding Ritual." *Nashim* 10 (2005): 29–52.

Kosmin, Barry A., and Ariella Keysar. "American Jewish Secularism: Jewish Life beyond the Synagogue." *American Jewish Year Book 2012* (2013): 3–54.

Kranzler, David. "Orthodoxy's Finest Hour." *Jewish Action* 63, no. 1 (2002), www.ou.org/publications/ja/5763/5763fall/ORTHODOX.pdf.

Krasner, Jonathan. "The Rise and Fall of the Progressive Talmud Torah: The Central Jewish Institute and Interwar American Jewish Identity." In *Rav Chesed: Essays in Honor of Rabbi Dr. Haskel Lookstein*, ed. Rafael Medoff, 411–68. Jersey City, N.J.: Ktav, 2009.

Kugelmass, Jack. "Bloody Memories: Encountering the Past in Contemporary Poland." *Cultural Anthropology* 10, no. 3 (1995): 279–301.

———. "The Rites of the Tribe: The Meaning of Poland for American Tourists." *Yivo Annual* 21 (1993): 395–443. Reprinted in C. M. Kreamer and S. D. Lavine, eds., *Museums and Communities: The Politics of Public Culture*, 382–427. Washington, D.C.: Smithsonian Institution Press, 1992.

Lamm, Norman. "The Ideology of the Neturei Karta: According to the Satmarer Version." *Tradition* 13 (1971): 38–53.

Landau, Bezalel. "Ridbaz." Biographical introduction to Ridbaz, *Shu"t ha-Ridbaz*, 5–34. Jerusalem: Mossad ha-Rav Kook, 1995.

Landes, David. "How Lakewood, N.J., Is Redefining What It Means to Be Orthodox in America." *Tablet*, June 5, 2013, www.tabletmag.com/jewish-life-and-religion/133643/lakewood-redefining-orthodoxy?all=1.

Lasoff, Melanie A. "Men in Black: How the Atlanta Scholars Kollel Turns People on to Our 3,000-Year-Old Tradition." *Atlanta Jewish Times*, April 13, 2001.

Lazar, Alon, Julia Chaitin, Tamar Gross, and Dan Bar-On. "Jewish Israeli Teenagers, National Identity, and the Lessons of the Holocaust." *Holocaust and Genocide Studies* 18, no. 2 (2004): 188–204.

Lehrer, Erica, and Hannah Smotrich. "Jewish? Heritage? in Poland? A Brief Manifesto and an Ethnographic Design Intervention into Jewish Tourism to Poland." *Bridges* 12, no. 1 (2007): 36–41.

Leiman, Sid Z. "Rabbi Leopold Greenwald: Tish'ah be-Av at the University of Leipzig." *Tradition* 25, no. 4 (1991): 103–6.

Leon, Nissim, and Aliza Lavie. "*Hizuk*—The Gender Track: Religious Invigoration and Women Motivators in Israel." *Contemporary Jewry* 33, no. 3 (2013): 193–215.

Levi, Leo. "The Relationship of the Orthodox to Heterodox Organizations (From a Halakhic Analysis by Rabbi S. R. Hirsch)." *Tradition* 9, no. 3 (1967): 95–102.

Levine, Yael. "Ha-Tenuah ha-Conservativit ke-fi she-mishtakefet be-teshuvotav shel ha-Rav Moshe Feinstein." In *Sefer Aviad*, ed. Yitzhak Raphael, 281–93. Jerusalem: Mossad ha-Rav Kook, 1986.

Lichtenstein, Aharon. "Symposium: Our Next 100 Years—The Future of American Orthodoxy." *Jewish Action* 59, no. 1 (1998): 51–53.

Liebman, Charles S. "Left and Right in American Orthodoxy." *Judaism* 15, no. 1 (1966): 106–7.

———. "Orthodox Judaism." In *The Encyclopedia of Religion*, ed. Mircea Eliade, 11:114–23. New York: Macmillan, 1987.

———. "Orthodox Judaism Today." *Midstream*, August/September 1979, 19–26.

———. "Orthodoxy in American Jewish Life." *American Jewish Year Book* 66 (1965): 21–97.

———. "A Perspective on My Studies of American Jews." *American Jewish History* 80, no. 4 (1991): 517–34.

———. "Religion and the Chaos of Modernity." In *Take Judaism for Example*, ed. Jacob Neusner, 147–64. Chicago: Chico, 1983.

———. "A Sociological Analysis of Contemporary Orthodoxy." *Judaism* 13, no. 3 (1964): 285–303.

———. "Temurot be-manhigut ruhanit shel Yehudei Arzot ha-Berit." In *Manhigut Ruhanit be-Yisrael*, ed. Ella Belfer, 166–84. Ramat-Gan: Bar-Ilan University Press, 1982.

———. "The Training of American Rabbis." *American Jewish Year Book* 70 (1969): 3–112.

Lightman, N. "A Call to End the Apathy towards Our Brethren." *Hamevasser* 3, no. 2 (1965): 5.

Lipstadt, Debra E. "From Noblesse Oblige to Personal Redemption: The Changing Profile and Agenda of American Jewish Leaders." *Modern Judaism* 4, no. 3 (1984): 295–309.

Loewenthal, Naftali. "'Daughter/Wife of Hasid' or 'Hasidic Woman?'" *Jewish Studies* 40 (2000): 21–28.

———. "From 'Ladies' Auxiliary' to 'Shluhot' Network: Women's Activism in Twentieth-Century Habad." In *A Touch of Grace: Studies in Ashkenazi Culture, Women's History, and the Languages of the Jews Presented to Chava Turniansky*, 69–93. Jerusalem: Zalman Shazar Center for Jewish History; Hebrew University, Center for Research on Polish Jewry, 2013.

———. "Hasidic Woman." *Journal of World Union of Jewish Studies* 40 (2000): 21–28.

———. "Women and the Dialectic of Spirituality in Hasidism." In *Within Hasidic Circles, Studies in Hasidism in Memory of Mordecai Wilensky*, ed. Immanuel Etkes, David Assaf, Israel Bartal, and Elhanan Reiner, 7–65. Jerusalem: Machon Bialik, 1999.

Lupovitch, Howard. "Between Orthodox Judaism and Neology: The Origins of the Status Quo Movement." *Jewish Social Studies* 9, no. 2 (2003): 123–53.

———. "Navigating Rough Waters: Alexander Kohut and the Hungarian Roots of Conservative Judaism." *AJS Review* 32, no. 1 (2008): 49–78.

Mann, Leisah. "Oasis in the Desert." *Jewish News of Greater Phoenix*, December 15, 2000.

Medding, Peter. "The New Jewish Politics in America." In *Terms of Survival: The Jewish World since 1945*, ed. Robert S. Wistrich, 92–93. London: Routledge, 1995.

Meiselman, Moshe. "The Rav, Feminism, and Public Policy: An Insider's View." *Tradition* 33, no. 1 (1998): 5.

———. "Women and Judaism: A Rejoinder." *Tradition* 15, no. 3 (1975): 52–68.

"Mered kadosh be-Kefar Etzion." *Nekudah*, July 1998, 12–13.

Michaelson, H. L. "Plight of Soviet Jewry Arouses Concern, Confusion." *Hamevasser* 2, no. 5 (1964): 3.

Meyer, Michael A. "Mekomo ve-zehuto shel ha-lo-Yehudi be-veit ha-kenesset ha-Reformi." *Gesher* 146 (Winter 2003): 66–74.

Miller, Shmuel. "Ha-Rav Yekutiel Yehudah Greenwald: e had ha-olim." *Apiryon* 4 (Fall 1924): 312.

Mintzberg, Henry. "The Manager's Job: Folklore and Facts." *Harvard Business Review*, July–August 1975, 53.

Mirsky, Norman B. "Categories and Ceremonies: The Rules of the Liebman Method." *American Jewish History* 80, no. 4 (1991): 479–90.

Mirsky, Yehudah. "Modernizing Orthodoxies: The Case of Feminism." In *To Be a Jewish Woman*, ed. Tova Cohen, Kolech Proceedings 4:37–51. Jerusalem: Kolech, 2007.

Miskin, Maayana. "Study: Religious-Zionist World Is Changing." *Arutz Sheva*, May 20, 2011, www.israelnationalnews.com/News/News.aspx/144354#.UnDBe3Ayooc.

Mittleman, Alan. "Fretful Orthodoxy." *First Things* 136 (October 2003): 23–26, www.firstthings.com/article/2007/01/fretful-orthodoxy-30.

Morris, Bonnie. "Agents or Victims of Religious Ideology? Approaches to Locating Hasidic Women in Feminist Studies." In *New World Hasidism: Ethnographic Studies of Hasidic Jews in America*, ed. Janet S. Belcove-Shalin, 161–80. Albany: State University of New York Press, 1995.

Myers, David N. "Commanded War: Three Chapters in the 'Military' History of Satmar Hasidism." *Journal of the American Academy of Religion* 81, no. 2 (2013): 311–56.

Nadler, Allan. "Piety and Politics: The Case of the Satmar Rebbe." *Judaism* 31, no. 2 (1982): 135–52.

———. "The Riddle of Satmar." *Jewish Ideas Daily*, February 17, 2011, www.jewishideasdaily.com/content/module/2011/2/17/main-feature/1/the-riddle-of-the-satmar.

———. "The War on Modernity of R. Hayyim Elazar Schapira of Munkacz." *Modern Judaism* 14, no. 3 (1994): 233–64.

Naftalin, Micha. "The Activist Movement." In *A Second Exodus: The American Movement to Free Soviet Jews*, ed. Murray Friedman and Albert D. Chernin, 224–42. Hanover, N.H.: Brandeis University Press, 1999.

Neuschloss, Simcha A. "Soviet Jewry and Jewish Responsibility: The Historical and Torah Dimensions of the Problem." *Jewish Observer* 11, no. 9 (1965): 3–5.

Oberstein, Elchonon. "Defining the Agenda with Reform: Beyond the Battlefield." *Jewish Observer* 29, no. 8 (1996): 40.

Odenheimer, Micha. "Wise Guy, Wise Man." *Haaretz*, October 10, 2005, www.haaretz.com/news/wise-guy-wise-man-1.171162.

Oppenheimer, Leonard. "Do We Really Have All the Answers." *Jewish Observer* 29, no. 6 (1996): 28–29.

Petuchowski, Jacob J. "Reform Judaism's Diminishing Boundaries: The Grin That Remained." *Journal of Reform Judaism*, Fall 1986, 15–24.

Picard, Ariel. *Ha-Pesikah ha-Hilkhatit bat Zemanenu ve-Hitmodedutah im Ba'ayat ha-Hitbolelut*. Position Paper 3. Ramat-Gan: Rappaport Center for Assimilation Research—Bar-Ilan University, 2003.

Pine, Dan. "Reform-Haredi Collaboration Ends in Bitter Brouhaha." *JWeekly.com*, February 21, 2003, www.jweekly.com/article/full/19371/reform-Haredi-collaboration-ends-in-bitter-brouhaha/.

Polen, Nechemia. "Theological Responses to the Hurban from within the Hurban." In *Jewish Perspectives on the Experience of Suffering*, ed. Robert Hirt and Shalom Carmy, 277–95. Northvale, N.J.: Jason Aronson, 1999.

Rapoport, Louis. "The Refuseniks." In *Encyclopaedia Judaica Year Book, 1988/89*, 76–83. Jerusalem: Keter, 1990.

Rapoport-Albert, Ada. "Hasidism after 1772, Structural Continuity and Change." In *Hasidism Reappraised*, ed. Ada Rapoport-Albert, 76–140. London: Littman Library of Jewish Civilization, 1996.

———. "On Women in Hasidism, S. A. Horodecky, and the Maid of Ludmir Tradition." In *Jewish History: Essays in Honour of Chimen Abramsky*, ed. Ada Rapoport-Albert and Steven J. Zipperstein, 495–525. London: Peter Halban, 1988.

Reinman, Yaakov Yosef. "Remembering Reb Shneur Kotler." In *The Torah Profile*, ed. Nisson Wolpin, 236. Brooklyn: Mesorah, 1988.

Robinson, Avi. "Students Choose between RIETS and Chovevei Torah." *The Commentator* 67, no. 7 (2002), www.yctorah.org/component/option,com_docman/task,doc_view/gid,97/.

Robinson, Ira. "Because of Our Many Sins: The Contemporary Jewish World as Reflected in the Responsa of Moses Feinstein." *Judaism* 35, no. 1 (1987): 364–73.

Romi, Shlomo, and Tamar Lev. "Experiential Learning of History through Youth Journeys to Poland: Israeli Jewish Youth and the Holocaust." *Research in Education* 78 (2007): 88–102.

Rosenblatt, Gary. "Between a Rav and a Hard Place." *Jewish Week*, June 26, 2009, www.thejewishweek.com/editorial_opinion/gary_rosenblatt/between_rav_and_hard_place.

Rosman, Moshe. "Poland: Early Modern, 1500-1795." In *Jewish Women: A Comprehensive Historical Encyclopedia* [online version]. Jerusalem: Shalvi Publishers, 2006, http://jwa.org/encyclopedia/article/poland-early-modern-1500-1795.

Rosner, Shmuel. "Mazav ha-Judaism: Mah bein rav le-ven morah ruhanit." *Ha'aretz*, February 2, 2008, http://cafe.themarker.com/view.php?t=332968.

———. "U.S. Jewish Movement Embraces Mixed Marriages, Reaches Out to Kids." *Ha'aretz*, March 24, 2008, www.haaretz.com/hasen/spages/967339.html.

Roth, Meir. "Ha-Ish she-heekdeem et tekufato." *De'ot* 17 (2003): 31–34, 37.

Rothkoff [Rakefet], A. "The American Sojourns of Ridbaz: Religious Problems within the Immigrant Community." *Proceedings of the American Jewish Historical Society* 57, no. 4 (1968): 557–72.

Rubin, Ronald I. "Student Struggle for Soviet Jewry." *Hadassah Magazine* 48, no. 4 (1966): 7, 34–35.

Rubin Schwartz, Shuli. "Ambassadors without Portfolio? The Religious Leadership of Rebbetzins in Late-Twentieth-Century American Jewish Life." In *Women and American Judaism: Historical Perspectives*, ed. Pamela Suzanne Nadell and Jonathan D. Sarna, 235–67. Hanover, N.H.: Brandeis University Press/University Press of New England, 2001.

Ruby, Walter. "The Role of Nonestablishment Groups." In *A Second Exodus: The American Movement to Free Soviet Jews*, ed. Murray Friedman and Albert D. Chernin, 200–223. Hanover, N.H.: Brandeis University Press, 1999.

Sacks, Jonathan. "The Man Who Turned Judaism Outwards." *Wellsprings* 41 (Summer 1994): 7–8.

———. "Modern Orthodoxy in Crisis." *Le'eyla* 2, no. 17 (1984): 20–25.

Sagi, Avi. "Ha-Orthodoksiyah ke-ba'ayah." In *Ha-Orthodoksiyah ha-Yehudit: Hebetim Hadashim*, ed. Yoseph Salmon, Avi Ravitzky, and Adam S. Ferziger, 21–53. Jerusalem: Magnes Press, 2006.

Salkin, Jeffrey K. "New Age Judaism." In *The Blackwell Companion to Judaism*, ed. Jacob Neusner and Alan J. Avery-Peck, 354–70. Oxford: Blackwell, 2004.

Salmon, Yoseph. "Jacob Katz's Approach to Orthodoxy: The Eastern European Case." *Modern Judaism* 32, no. 2 (2012): 129–54.

Samet, Moshe. "The Beginnings of Orthodoxy." *Modern Judaism* 8, no. 3 (1988): 249–69.

———. "Ha-Shinuyim be-sidrei beit ha-knesset: emdat ha-rabbanim ke-neged 'ha-mehadshim' ha-Reformim." *Assufot* 5 (1991): 253–96.

———. "Kavim nosafim le-biographiah shel ha-Hatam Sofer." In *Torah Im Derekh Eretz*, ed. Mordechai Breuer, 65–74. Ramat-Gan: Bar-Ilan University Press, 1987.

Sarna, Jonathan D. "The Debate over Mixed Seating in the American Synagogue." In *The American Synagogue: A Sanctuary Transformed*, ed. Jack Wertheimer, 363–94. Cambridge: Cambridge University Press, 1987.

———. "The Future of American Orthodoxy." *Shma.Com*, February 2001, http://shma.com/2001/02/the-future-of-american-orthodoxy/.

Schacter, Jacob J. "Holocaust Commemoration and *Tish'a be-Av:* The Debate over *Yom ha-Sho'a.*" *Tradition* 41, no. 2 (2008): 174–79.

———. "Mordecai M. Kaplan's Orthodox Ordination." *American Jewish Archives* 46, no. 2 (1994): 1–11.

Schick, Marvin. "An Essay on Contemporary Jewish Life." *Tradition* 35, no. 2 (2001): 14–35.
———. "The Orthodox Jew and the Negro Revolution: A Hard Look at Religious Jewry's Attitudes." *Jewish Observer* 11, no. 9 (1964): 15–17.
Schiller, Mayer. "Symposium: Our Next 100 Years—The Future of American Orthodoxy." *Jewish Action* 59, no. 1 (1998): 58–64.
Schorsch, Ismar. "Emancipation and the Crisis of Religious Authority." In *Revolution and Evolution: 1848 in German-Jewish History*, ed. W. E. Mosse, 207–14. Tübingen: Mohr Siebeck, 1981.
Schwartz, Julius, and Kaye Solomon, eds. "Isaac Werne." *Who's Who in American Jewry 1926*, 644. New York: Jewish Biographical Bureau, 1927.
Scult, M. "Controversial Beginnings: Kaplan's First Congregation." *The Reconstructionist*, July–August 1985, 21–26.
Selengut, C. "By Torah Alone: Yeshiva Fundamentalism in Jewish Life." In *Accounting for Fundamentalisms*, ed. Martin E. Marty and R. Scott Appleby, 236–63. Chicago: University of Chicago Press, 1994.
Shapiro, Edward S. "Modern Orthodoxy in Crisis: A Test Case." *Judaism* 51, no. 3 (2002): 347–61.
Shapiro, Leon. "Soviet Jewry since the Death of Stalin: A Twenty-Five Year Perspective." *American Jewish Yearbook*, 77–103. New York: American Jewish Committee and Jewish Publication Society, 1979. www.policyarchive.org/handle/10207/bitstreams/17740.pdf.
Shapiro, Marc B. "Hungarian Ultra-Orthodoxy and Its Post–World War II Halakhic Legacy: The Case of *Rabbi Menashe Klein*." Lecture at the Sixteenth World Congress for Jewish Studies, Jerusalem, August 1, 2013.
———. "'Jewish Commitment in a Modern World: Rabbi Hayyim Hirschenson and His Attitude to Modernity' by David Zohar (Jer. 2003)." *Edah Journal* 5, no. 1 (2005), www.edah.org/coldfusion/backend/journalArticle/5_1_shapiro.pdf.
———. "Some Assorted Comments and a Selection from My Memoir, part 2." *The Seforim Blog*, November 1, 2009, http://seforim.blogspot.co.il/2009/11/some-assorted-comments-and-selection.html.
Sharot, Steven. "Assimilating, Coalescing and Spiritual-Seeking: Recent Trends among American Jews." *Studies in Contemporary Jewry* 18 (2002): 240–46.
Sheleg, Yair. "Aliyatah shel Hasidut Ginzburg." *Ha'aretz—Mussaf*, September 9, 1989, 12.
Shemer, Yoram. "Notes on Filming a Hasidic Pilgrimage to Poland." *Jewish Folklore and Ethnology Review* 17 (1995): 53–56.
Sheramy, Rona. "From Auschwitz to Jerusalem: Re-enacting Jewish History on the March of the Living." In *Polin*, vol. 19: *Polish-Jewish Relations in North America*, ed. Mieczslaw B. Biskupski and Antony Polonsky, 307–26. Oxford: Littman Library for Jewish Civilization, 2007.
———. "The March of the Living: Where Is It Now?" *Jewish Educational Leadership* 8, no. 1 (2009), www.lookstein.org/online_journal_toc.php?id=16.
Silber, Micheal K. "The Emergence of Ultra-Orthodoxy: The Invention of a Tradition." In *The Uses of Tradition*, ed. Jack Wertheimer, 23–84. New York: Jewish Theological Seminary of America, 1992.
———. "The Historical Experience of German Jewry and Its Impact on Haskalah and Reforms in Hungary." In *Toward Modernity*, ed. Jacob Katz, 107–57. New Brunswick, N.J.: Transaction Press, 1987.
Singer, David. "Debating Modern Orthodoxy at Yeshiva College: The Greenberg-Lichtenstein Exchange." *Modern Judaism* 26, no. 2 (2006): 113–26.

———. "Emanuel Rackman: Gadfly of Modern Orthodoxy." *Modern Judaism* 28, no. 2 (2008): 134–48.
Soloveitchik, Haym. "Migration, Acculturation, and the New Role of Texts." In *Accounting for Fundamentalisms: The Dynamic Character of Movements*, ed. Martin E. Marty and R. Scott Appleby, 197–235. Chicago: University of Chicago Press, 1994.
———. "Rupture and Reconstruction: The Transformation of Contemporary Orthodoxy." *Tradition* 28, no. 4 (1994): 64–130. Reprinted in Roberta Rosenberg and Chaim I. Waxman, eds., *Jews in America: A Contemporary Reader*, 320–76. Hanover, N.H.: University Press of New England, 1999.
Spiegal, Phil. "Mobilizing a Critical Mass in New York: The Seminal Activity of the Student Struggle for Soviet Jewry (SSSJ), 1964–1966." Typescript. September 18, 2005, 3, 4, 10, 11.
Stavridis, James G. "Closing the Gaps in Naval Leadership." *Proceedings of the U.S. Naval Institute*, July 1982, 76–78.
Stier, Oren B. "Lunch at Majdanek: The March of the Living as a Contemporary Pilgrimage of Memory." *Jewish Folklore and Ethnology Review* 17, nos. 1–2 (1995): 57–66.
Swatos, William H., Jr. "Weber and Troeltsch? Methodology, Syndrome, and the Development of Church-Sect Theory." *Journal for the Scientific Study of Religion* 15, no. 2 (1976): 129–44.
"Symposium: Orthodoxy and the Public Square." *Tradition* 38, no. 1 (2004): 6–52.
Tabory, Ephraim. "The Legitimacy of Reform Judaism: The Impact of Israel on the United States." In *Contemporary Debates in American Reform Judaism: Conflicting Visions*, ed. Dana Evan Kaplan, 221–34. New York: Routledge, 2001.
Tapper, Aaron Joshua. "The 'Cult' of Aish Hatorah: *Ba'alei Teshuva* and the Newly Religious Movement Phenomenon." *Jewish Journal of Sociology* 44, nos. 1–2 (2002): 5–29.
Trugman, Avrum Arieh. "Probing the Carlebach Phenomenon." *Jewish Action* 63 (Winter 2002): 9–12.
Turetsky, Yehuda, and Chaim I. Waxman. "Sliding to the Left? Contemporary American Modern Orthodoxy." *Modern Judaism* 31 (May 2011): 119–41.
Turner, Victor. "The Center Out There: Pilgrim's Goal." *History of Religions* 12, no. 3 (1973): 191–230.
Turner, Yossi. "'Koakh ha-Zibbur' be-mishnato ha-datit Ziyonit shel ha-Rav Hayyim Hirschenson." In *Yahadut Pnim u-Huz—Dialogue bein Olamot*, ed. Avi Sagi, Dudi Schwarz, and Yedidia Stern, 31–57. Jerusalem: Magnes, 2000.
———. "Ma'amad mekorot torat ha-hinukh ha-Yisraeli shel ha-Rav Hayyim Hirschenson." *Hagut be-Hinukh Yehudi* 2 (2000): 201–23.
———. "Samkhut ha-am ve-samkhut ha-Torah be-tefisat ha-Medinah shel ha-Rav Hayyim Hirschenson." In *Dat u-Medinah ba-Hagut ha-Yehudit ba-Me'ah ha-Esrim*, ed. Avi Ravitzky, 195–219. Jerusalem: Israel Democratic Institute, 2005.
———. "Samkhut ve-otonomiyah be-tefisato ha-hilkhatit shel ha-Rav Hayyim Hirschenson." In *Bein Samhut le-Otonomiyah be-Masoret Yisrael*, ed. Avi Sagi and Ze'ev Safrai, 181–95. Tel Aviv: Ha-Kibbutz ha-Meuhad/Ne'emanei Torah va-Avodah, 1997.
Twerski, Benzion. "Orthodox Youth and Drug Abuse: Shattering the Myths." *Jewish Action*, Spring 1998, www.jacsweb.org/article-8.html.
Twersky, Mayer. "Halakhic Values and Halakhic Decisions: Rav Soloveitchik's Pesak Regarding Women's Prayer Groups." *Tradition* 32, no. 3 (1998): 5–18.
Tydor Baumel, Judith. "Kahane in America: An Exercise in Right-Wing Urban Terror." *Studies in Conflict and Terrorism* 22 (1999): 311–29.
Waxman, Chaim I. "An Ambivalent American Jewish Sociologist: The Perspectives of Charles S. Liebman." *American Jewish History* 80, no. 4 (1991): 491–501.

---. "American Modern Orthodoxy: Confronting Cultural Challenges." *Edah Journal* 4, no. 1 (2004), www.bjpa.org/Publications/details.cfm?PublicationID=2024.

---. "Changing Denominational Patterns in the United States." In *American Jewry's Comfort Level: Present and Future*, ed. Steven Bayme and Manfred Gerstenfeld, 133–42. New York: AJC, 2010.

---. "From Institutional Decay to Primary Day: American Orthodox Jewry since World War II." *American Jewish History* 91 (2003): 415–18.

---. "The Haredization of American Orthodox Jewry." *Jerusalem Letter/Viewpoints*, Jerusalem Center for Public Affairs, February 15, 1998, www.bjpa.org/Publications/details.cfm?PublicationID=2373.

---. "Year in Israel and the Orthodox Community." In Shalom Z. Berger, Daniel Jacobson, and Chaim I. Waxman, *Flipping Out? Myth or Fact: The Impact of the "Year in Israel,"* 145–202. New York: Yashar Books, 2007.

Wein, Beryl. "The Sea Change in American Orthodox Judaism: A Symposium." *Tradition* 32, no. 4 (1998): 122–25.

Weissman, Deborah R. "Bais Ya'akov as an Innovation in Jewish Women's Education." *Studies in Jewish Education* 7 (1995): 278–99.

Welte, Carl E. "Management and Leadership: Concepts with an Important Difference." *Personnel Journal* 11 (1990): 57.

Wender, Yonatan. "Ashirim ve-dati'im yozim yoter le-'masaot le-Polin." *Makor Rishon*, January 31, 2008, 24.

Wenger, Beth. "The Politics of Women's Ordination: Jewish Law, Institutional Power, and the Debate over Women in the Rabbinate." In *Tradition Renewed*, ed. Jack Wertheimer, 483–523. New York: Jewish Theological Seminary, 1997.

Wertheimer, Jack. "Between 'West Point Standards' and Life in the Trenches: The Halakhic Dilemmas of Orthodox Outreach Workers." In *Between Jewish Tradition and Modernity: Essays in Honor of David H. Ellenson*, ed. Michael A. Meyer and David Myers, 67–79. Detroit: Wayne State University Press, 2014.

---. "The Outreach Revolution." *Commentary*, April 2013, 20–26, www.commentarymagazine.com/article/the-outreach-revolution/.

---. "What Does Reform Judaism Stand For?" *Commentary*, June 2008, www.commentarymagazine.com/article/what-does-reform-judaism-stand-for/.

---. "Why the Lubavitch Movement Thrives in the Absence of a Living Rebbe." *Jewish Action*, June 16, 2014, www.ou.org/jewish_action/06/2014/lubavitch-movement-thrives-absence-living-rebbe/.

Wodzinski, M. "Hasidism, Shtadlanut, and Jewish Politics in Nineteenth-Century Poland: The Case of Isaac of Warka." *Jewish Quarterly Review* 95, no. 2 (2005): 290–320.

Wolowelsky, Joel. "Rabbis, Rebbetzins and Halakhic Advisors." *Tradition* 36, no. 4 (2002): 54–63.

Wurtzburger, Walter S. "Centrist Orthodoxy: Ideology or Atmosphere?" In *Covenantal Imperatives: Essays by Walter S. Wurzburger on Jewish Law, Thought and Community*, ed. Eliezer L. Jacobs and Shalom Carmy, 212–19. Jerusalem: Urim, 2008.

Zeiger, Malka. "The Student Struggle for Soviet Jewry: The Grassroots Movement to Aid Soviet Jews, 1963–1968." BA paper, Stern College, January 8, 2004.

Zeitz, J. M. "'If I am not for myself...': The American Jewish Establishment in the Aftermath of the Six-Day War." *American Jewish History* 88, no. 2 (2000): 253–86.

Zur, Tovah. "Ha-Masa le-Polin ke-si'o shel tahalikh hinukhi." *Be-Shevilei ha-Zikkaron* 7 (October 1995): 5.

Index

"A Portrait of Jewish Americans" (Pew 2013): American Orthodoxy and, 2, 82; American-born Jews and, 225n6; Chabad critique and, 193–94, 226n6, 295n74; decline in synagogue affiliation and, 2; denominational affiliation and, 2, 225n6; growth of unaffiliated Jewry and, 2; Haredi Orthodoxy and, 9, 13–14; Israel attachment and, 223; Modern Orthodoxy and, 9, 13, 222–23, 230n62, 230n63; Orthodox retention rate and, 2; outreach and, 213, 298n8; percentage of Orthodox college graduates and, 13; sectarian attitudes of Haredi Orthodox and, 13–14. *See also* Demographics

Academic Research: American Orthodoxy and, 1, 2

Adler, Rachel (scholar of Jewish thought): H. Schachter and, 270–71n41

Adlerstein, Yitzchak (Rabbi): internal Orthodox boundaries and, 220–21; Open Orthodoxy and, 218; realignment and, 220–21; H. Schachter and, 220

Agudas Achim Synagogue (Columbus, Ohio), 26, 31

Agudath ha-Rabbonim (Union of Orthodox Rabbis): Conservative Judaism and, 39–40; Y. Y. Greenwald and, 23, 33, 40; H. Hirschenson and, 23; Ramaz Margolies and, 45; Reform Judaism and 39, 40, 131; J. Sarna and, 41, 277n7; women's prayer groups and, 118

Agudath Israel in Europe, 26

Agudath Israel of America: college students and, 257n103; A. Kotler and, 134; *One People, Two Worlds* and, 149–50; Open Orthodoxy and, 216–22; Orthodox feminism and, 123, 208–9; Y. Perlow and, 136–39, 150, 217, 221; public sphere and, 70; Reform and, 131; Soviet Jewry and, 72, 74, 76; A. Weiss and, 209. *See also* Shm. Kamentsky; Moetzes Gedolei ha-Torah; Y. Perlow

Ah le-Zarah (book), 34–35

Aish Hatorah Yeshiva (Jerusalem): outreach in North America and, 160; L. Palatnik and, 201–2; rabbinical training and, 159–61

Aish Kodesh, Congregation (Woodmere, New York), 166n99. *See also* Rabbi Moshe Weinberger; Neo-Hasidism

Alpert, Zalman (Rabbi), 270n41

Amcha–the Coalition for Jewish Concerns: A. Weiss and, 79

American (North American) Orthodoxy (Orthodox Judaism): academic research on, 2, 144; blurring of lines between factions and, 214; Church Orthodoxy and, 2; Conservative Judaism and, 30–31, 36, 38, 133; demographics of, 2; education and 6; focus during the early 20th century, 6; history of, 1, 4–7; C. S. Liebman and, 1, 2, 7–9, 76, 80, 144; M. Sklare on, 1; Modern Orthodoxy and, 2; New York and, 225–26n6; organizational affiliation and, 4, 7; Pew 2013 and, 2, 13–14, 82, 222–23, 230n62, 230n63; public square and, 68–70;

331

INDEX

American Orthodoxy (*continued*)
  Reform Judaism and, 130–50; religious passion and, 1, 144, 223; religious punctiliousness and, 3, 90–91, 109–110; Sectarian Orthodoxy and, 2, 8–9; slide to the right and, 3, 13, 14; Soviet Jewry and, 58–76; varieties of, 4, 7–9. *See also* Haredi Orthodoxy; Modern Orthodoxy
American (U.S.) Jewry: academic research and, 1, 2; demographics of, 2; history of, 4–7; Jewish settlement of, 4. *See also* "A Portrait of Jewish Americans"
American Jewish Conference on Soviet Jewry (AJCSJ), 61, 63
American Jewish Establishment: 1960s and, 68; definition and, 247n3; I. Greenberg and, 249n16; Orthodox and, 69; Soviet Jewry and, 59–62, 64–65
American Jewish History (journal), 229n51
American Labor Movement: Soviet Jewry and, 60
American Public Sphere: Orthodoxy and, 69–70; Soviet Jewry activism and, 59, 61–62, 68–70
Americanization: Agudath ha-Rabbonim and, 41; gap year Israeli yeshivas and, 109; Haredi Orthodoxy and, 9; KJ and, 44, 47; J. Lookstein and, 47, 242–43n27; Modern Orthodoxy and, 7, 9; Sectarian Orthodoxy and, 229n51; Soviet Jewry and, 75
Ansky, Shmuel (author, playright, Shloyme Zanvl Rappoport), 99
Anti-Semitism: Orthodox-Reform relations and, 132
Anusim (conversos, forced converts), 4
Apiryon (rabbinic journal), 21, 27, 28
Artscroll Publishers, 34
Ascent Institute (Houston), 197
Ashkenazi Synagogue: first in America, 5
Ashkenazic Jewry: immigration to America and, 4; in Europe, 4
Assaf, David (historian): Rizhin Hasidic dynasty and, 247n75
Assimilation: Haredi Orthodoxy and, 11
Association of Jewish Outreach Professionals (AJOP): community kollels and, 185; S. Milikowsky and, 158
Atlanta Scholar's Kollel (ASK Kollel): activities and, 183; founding and, 183; introductory service in Reform Temple and, 141; postdenominational posture and, 141; Y. Weinberg and, 142
Auschwitz-Birkenau (Concentration and Death Camp): Poland pilgrimages and, 88, 90–98, 99, 106; "Torah view" and, 96
Avi Chai Foundation, 146
Avraham, Michael (Rabbi): change in Jewish law and, 71

Bacon, Gershon (historian), 15
Bais Yaakov Educational Movement: Chabad and, 206; E. Jungreis and, 204; Poland pilgrimages and, 97, 98; scholarship and, 196
Balkans: Jewish immigration to the United States and, 5
Baltimore, Maryland: Haredi concentration and, 10. *See also* Ner Israel Rabbinical College
Bar-Ilan University: J. Lookstein and, 46
Batei Ungarin (Jerusalem neighborhood), 37
Baumgarten, Albert (historian): Jewish sectarianism and, 11–12
Beginner's Prayer Services: ASK Kollel and, 141; KJ and, 49
Be-Ikvei ha-Zon (book), 120, 126
Beit Yitzhak (journal), 119
Belarus: Haredi pilgrimages and, 96, 97, 98
Belkin, Samuel (Rabbi Dr.): KJ and, 55
Belzec (Nazi death camp), 99
Benor, Sara (social linguist), 7
Ben-Yehudah, Eliezer (Hebraist): Hayyim Hirschenson and, 37
Berger, Shalom Z. (Rabbi Dr., education scholar): gap year yeshiva experience and, 266n100
Berglas, Vicky (educator): Poland pilgrimages and, 93
Berkowitz, Yitzchak (Rabbi): Jerusalem Kollel and, 162; Ner LeElef and, 162
Berl, Michael (educator): Poland pilgrimages and, 89, 90, 91, 92, 93, 112, 161–62n31
Berlin, Naftali Zvi Yehudah (Rabbi, Nez"iv of Volozhin): Volozhin yeshiva and, 243n39

INDEX

Berman, Saul (Rabbi, Jewish law scholar): Edah (organization) and, 134; Solidarity Orthodoxy and, 78–79; Soviet Jewry and, 67; women in Jewish law and, 268n13

Bernstein, David I. (Dr., educator): Haredization and, 93; Pardes Institute and, 261n19; Poland pilgrimages and, 91

Bernstein, Louis (Rabbi), 118

Beth Jacob Congregation, Columbus, Ohio, 25, 31; separate seating and, 26, 35

Beth Medrash Govoha (BMG, Lakewood yeshiva), 7, 283n84; A. Kotler and, 134–35; outreach profession and, 145; rabbinical training and, 285n20; N. Waxman and, 290n2

Bialik, Hayyim Nahman (poet), 25

Billet, Avi (Rabbi): Poland pilgrimages and, 92–93, 105, 106; *Yeshivat Hakhmei Lublin* and, 105

Bin-Nun, Amitai (researcher): SSSJ and, 65

Birnbaum, Jacob (Ya'akov): congressional declaration and, 80; death and, 250n27; founding of Soviet Jewry movement and, 62–65; new Jewish politics and, 69; personal Jewish identity and, 65, 66. *See also* Soviet Jewry; SSSJ

Birnbaum, Nathan (political ideologue), 63

Birthright (Israel trips), 88

Black Hatters: Haredi Orthodoxy and, 6

Black Power movement, 75

Blau (Teitz), Rivka (Dr., educator): Yavne and, 179

Bleich, Judah David (Rabbi): non-Orthodox denominations and, 271n51

Bnai Jeshurun, Congregation (Manhattan): J. Magnes and, 45

Borough Park, Brooklyn: Orthodoxy in the 1920s and, 237n76

Borowitz, Eugene (Rabbi Dr., theologian): Soviet Jewry and, 65

Brander, Kenneth (Rabbi), 169, 259n125

Brill, Alan (religion scholar): Modern Orthodoxy and, 237n35

Bronspigel, Abba (Rabbi): Lander College and, 287n50; women's prayer services and, 270n41

Brooklyn: Haredi concentration and, 10, 222

Budapest, Hungary, 28, 29

Bulka, Reuven (Rabbi), 131

Caplan, Kimmy (historian): Eastern European immigrant rabbis and, 239n4; Haredi family economics and, 296n26

Carlebach Minyanim (Neo-Hasidic style prayer), 109

Carlebach, Shlomo (Rabbi, songwriter): Chabad and, 178–79, 291n14; posthumous legacy and, 258n119; Solidarity Orthodoxy and, 79; Soviet Jewry and, 65

Caro, Joseph (Rabbi), 3

Center for Jewish Future (CJF, YU), 169, 259n125. *See also* YU

Central Conference of American Rabbis (CCAR): Y. Perlow and, 136–37, 150; *Statement of Principles* (1999) and, 136–37. *See also* Reform Judaism

Centrist Orthodoxy: KJ and, 49; terminology and, 238n81

Chabad House: activities and, 180; community kollel and, 178–88; S. Cunin and, 179; description of, 179–80; early Hasidism and, 180; founding and, 179; non-denominationalism and, 180; M. M. Schneerson and, 178, 179, 181

Chabad-Lubavitch Hasidic Movement: community kollel and, 141, 146, 175–94; criticism and, 177, 181; Haredi Orthodoxy and, 7, 141, 146, 175–94; C. S. Liebman and, 177; mitzvah campaigns and, 179; outreach and, 11, 146, 164–65, 199, 212–13; Pew 2013 and, 193–94; public sphere and, 70; rabbinical training and, 164–65, 173; Reform Judaism and, 146–47; Soviet Jewry and, 60, 70–72; women and, 199, 206–10, 297n41. *See also* I. Schneerson; M. M. Schneerson; *Shluchim*; *Shluchos*

Chabon, Michael (novelist): Yorkville (Manhattan) and, 240n7

Charleston, South Carolina: first Reform Synagogue in America and, 5, 133; Spanish and Portuguese Jews and, 4

Chicago Community Kollel, 192–93, 294n70

Chicago: Haredi Orthodoxy and, 182, 222

Christianity, Early: S. Heschel and, 273n64; Orthodox Jewish feminism and, 121, 122,

INDEX

123, 220
Church Orthodoxy: church/sect theory and, 2, 7; Columbus, Ohio and, 31; H. Hirschenson and, 39; KJ and, 43, 56; nonobservant and, 8; non-Orthodox and, 8; rabbinate and, 153; realignment and, 13, 217; Soviet Jewry and, 76; 130; TMZ and, 193
Church/Sect Theory, 2; "Church" Orthodoxy and, 2, 7; Modern Orthodoxy and, 2, 7; realignment and, 13; Sectarian Orthodoxy and, 2, 7, 8; E. Troeltsch and, 2; M. Weber and, 2. *See also* Modern Orthodoxy
Cincinnati, Ohio: Hebrew Union College and, 5; Reform Judaism and, 139
City College of New York, 35
Civil Religion, 242–43n27
Civil Rights Movements: Modern Orthodoxy and, 75; non-Orthodox and, 76; Soviet Jewry movement and, 61; P. Teitz and, 74
CLAL-the National Jewish Center for Learning and Leadership: I. Greenberg and, 79
Cleveland: Haredi concentration and, 222
Cleveland Committee on Soviet Anti-Semitism, 62
Cleveland Torat Tzion Kollel (CTTK), 191
Cohen, Erik (sociologist and education scholar): pilgrimage and, 112
Cohen, Hermann (philosopher), 24
Cold War, 75
Columbia University, 64; Modern Orthodox and, 222
Columbus, Ohio: Y. Y. Greenwald and, 25. *See also* Agudas Achim; Beth Jacob; M. Hirschsprung; D. Stavsky; I. Werner
Coming Cataclysm, The (book), 131
Communism: Soviet Jewry and, 257n106
Community Kollel: Chabad and, 141, 146, 175–91, 293n51; coordination between kollels, 184–85; *daf yomi* and, 184–85; definition of, 140; evolution and, 181–83, 292n35; intermarried Jews and, 143–44; Olney, Maryland and, 158; outreach and, 140–44; positive anti-Hasidism and, 188–91; post-denominational character and, 141–44, 184; religious quest and, 186; study and, 185–86, 293n51

Conference of Presidents of Major Jewish Organizations: M. Hoenlein and, 62; I. Miller and, 77
Confirmation Ceremony, 32
Congress (U.S.): Soviet Jewry and, 64
Conservative Judaism: community kollels and, 140–42; denominationalism and, 3–4; M. Feinstein and, 134–35; female rabbis and, 207; Mechon Hadar and, 221; Homosexuality and, 133; intermarriage and, 278n21; Jewish law and, 3; JTS and, 6; N. Lamm and, 136; J. Lookstein and, 46–47, 133; Orthodox feminism and, 118–22; Orthodoxy and 30–31, 36, 38; 133; Poland pilgrimages and, 88; Reform and, 133; G. Richter and, 66; women and, 119. *See also* Y. Y. Greenwald; JTS
Constituency Definition: modern rabbinate and, 151–52, 154, 228n36
Conversion: Reform Judaism and, 120, 137; non-Orthodox in Israel and, 133
Conversos (anusim, forced converts), 4
Crown Heights, Brooklyn: Chabad and, 177
Cunin, Shlomo (Rabbi), 179

Da'as Torah (supreme rabbinic authority on non-legal matters): J. B. Soloveitchik and, 74, 256n97
Daf Yomi (7 and 1/2 year daily Talmud study cycle): community kollel and, 184–85; popularity and, 265n81; *Yeshivat Hakhmei Lublin* and, 105
Dallas Area Torah Association (DATA Kollel): interdenominational cooperation and, 141
Dallas, Texas: Haredi concentration and, 10
Danzger, M. Herbert (sociologist), 291n14, 293n49, 293n52
Demographics: American Orthodox Jews and, 2; Haredi Orthodox and, 9, 13; mid-nineteenth century American Jewry and, 5; turn of the twentieth century American Jewry and, 5; twenty-first century American Jewry and, 2. *See also* "A Portrait of American Jews"
Deutsch, Menachem (Rabbi), 183
Dietary Laws: Eastern European immi-

grants and supervision of, 6; Spanish-Portuguese communities and, 4
Discovery Seminars (Aish Hatorah), 159
Douglas, Mary (social anthropologist), 15
Drisha Institute for Advanced Torah Study for Women, 221
Dumont, Louis (anthropologist), 15
Durkheim, Emile (sociologist), 15, 221

Eastern European Orthodox Judaism, 4
Economics: Haredi Orthodoxy and, 145–46, 212; Modern Orthodoxy and, 222–23, 300n40
Edah (Modern Orthodox organization), 279n34; S. Berman and, 79, 135; "the courage to be modern and Orthodox" and, 238n80
Edelstein, Avraham (Rabbi), 161, 201. See also Ner LeElef
Edrei, Aryeh (legal scholar): Holocaust remembrance by Haredi Orthodox and, 95–96, 98, 104, 263n41
Education: Eastern European immigrants and, 6; Ramaz and, 54
Eibeschütz, Yonatan (Rabbi), 25
Eisenstadt (Burgenland, Hungary), 125
Eisenstein, Judah David (rabbinic scholar): H. Hirschenson and, 234n23
Eleff, Zev (historian): NCSY and, 229n54, 285n16; Y. Weinberg and, 279n60; A. Weiss and, 289n80; Yeshivat Maharat and, 289n80
Eliezrie, David (Rabbi), 193–94, 226n6, 295n74
Elimelekh of Leżajsk (Rebbe), 106; grave site pilgrimages and, 106, 109, 265n91
Ellenson, David H. (Rabbi Dr.): HUC and, 135; YU and, 135, 279n35
Emergent Jewish Religious Communities, 2
Emory University: outreach and, 190
Engelwood, New Jersey: Modern Orthodox concentration and, 222
Epstein, Louis (Rabbi): Jewish laws of the Agunah (anchored wife) and, 236n71
Etra, Max: Looksteins and, 50, 54; Ramaz and, 54
Ettlinger, Jacob (Rabbi): Sadducees and, 275n83

Farber, Seth (Rabbi Dr., historian, Shaul): J. B. Soloveitchik and, 271n49, 276n30
Feinstein, Moshe (Rabbi): academic scholars and, 273n63; ASK Kollel and, 141; Conservative Judaism and, 134–35, 140; Reform Judaism and, 134–35, 139, 140; Soviet Jewry and, 71–72, 73; women and, 268n13
Feldheim Publishers, 34
Feldman, Emanuel (Rabbi), 156
Feldman, Ilan (Rabbi), 218
Feldman, Jackie (anthropologist): Poland pilgrimages and, 95, 262n34, 267n108
Felsen, Joey (Rabbi), 141–42, 198, 201. See also JSN
Female Cantors, 196
Female Congregational Interns, 196
Female Halakhic Advisors, 196; Orthodox feminism and, 117
Female Haredi Authors, 196
Female Haredi Outreach Activists, 196–210; Chabad shluchos and, 205–8; conflicts and, 200–1; mixed-gender environments and, 197–98, 201; organization and, 199–200; rebbetzin and, 197; training and, 198–99. See also Feminism; Orthodox Feminism; Women
Female Israeli Haredi Preachers, 196
Female Rabbinic Advocates, 196
Female Rabbis, 196, 207
Female Spiritual Leaders: Orthodox feminism and, 117
Female Yeshiva Head, 196
Feminism: American Orthodox Judaism and, 114–29. See also Female Haredi Outreach Activists; Orthodox Feminism; H. Schachter; Women; Yeshivat Maharat
Finkelman, Yoel (religion scholar): Haredization in Israeli gap year yeshivas and, 110; internal distinctions within Haredi Orthodoxy and, 7
Fischer, Elli: economics of Modern Orthodoxy and, 300n40
Folk religion: American Orthodoxy and, 8
Frankel, Abraham (Rabbi, Budapest), 28
Frankfurt am Main (Germany), 24, 28, 47
Frankfurt Yeshiva: Y.Y. Greenwald and, 24
Franz Josef (Kaiser), 27
Freehoff, Solomon (Rabbi, scholar), 26

Frey, Marc (political scientist): beginning of Soviet Jewry movement and, 248n11
Fried, Yehuda (Rabbi): *hurban* and, 96, 97, 98; Poland pilgrimages and, 96
Fried, Yerachmiel (Rabbi), 142, 281n66
Frimer, Aryeh A. (Rabbi, scientist): women's prayer services and, 268n17, 268n19, 270n38, 270n41
Frimer, Dov I. (Rabbi, legal scholar): women's prayer services and, 268n17, 268n19, 270n38, 270n41

Gaon of Vilna (Rabbi Elijah): Hasidism and, 188–89, 190
Gap Year Post High-School Study in Israel, 89–99, 104–12; Americanization and, 109; Haredization and, 9, 87, 109; history and, 259–60n3. *See also* Poland Pilgrimages
Geiger, Abraham (Rabbi, theologian): Sadducees and, 274n75
Gemeindeorthodoxe (non-separatist German Orthodoxy), 24
Gender: Modern Orthodoxy and, 48–49, 115–17, 203–4 216–22; outreach and, 195–210; Poland pilgrimages and, 89–94, 97–98; seating in the synagogue, 26, 29, 152; separation of sexes and Haredization, 9. *See also* Feminism; Homosexuality; Mixed Seating; Women
Generation of Seekers: Chabad house and, 188; community kollel and, 188
German Orthodoxy: immigration to America and, 4
German-Speaking Jewish immigrants: arrival in the United States and, 5, 20; financial success and, 5; Reform Judaism and, 5
Gever, Dara (student): outreach at Emory University and, 190
Gilbert, Sir Martin (historian): Jacob Birnbaum and, 62
Gillman, Neil (philosopher): peoplehood agenda and, 259n124
Goldstein, Warren (Rabbi): Shabbos Project and, 282n77
Gorbachev, Mikhail (statesman), 59
Grade, Chaim (author), 99
Greater New York Conference for Soviet Jewry: M. Hoenlein and, 62; H. Lookstein and, 59
Greece: Jewish immigration to the United States and, 5
Green, Arthur (Rabbi Dr.): JTS and, 65–66; Soviet Jewry and, 65–66
Greenberg, Blu (author, activist): Orthodox feminism and, 117, 119
Greenberg, Irving (Rabbi Dr., Yitz): civil rights and, 257n105; Solidarity Orthodoxy and, 79–80; Soviet Jewry and, 67, 75, 79–80, 249n16; SSSJ and, 67
Greenwald, Yekutiel Yehuda (Leopold, Rabbi), 19–36, 39–41; American Orthodoxy and, 28, 30–36, 237n77; English oratory skills and, 35; Haredi Orthodoxy and, 216; H. Hirschenson and, 22–23, 27, 28; historical writings and, 25; Hungarian Orthodoxy and, 22–23, 27–30; Looksteins and, 42–43, 49; Modern Orthodoxy and, 30–36, 41, 42; papers and, 233n21; rabbinate and, 25–27, 152; Rabbis' March-Washington 1943 and, 253n67; Reform and, 237n77; Sziget (Maramarossziget, Romania) and, 24; wedding ceremonies in synagogues and, 26
Grossman, Lawrence (historian): Orthodoxy in the public square and, 69
Grunblatt, Akiva (Rabbi), 163
Gurock, Jeffrey S. (historian): Americanization at KJ/Ramaz and, 242–43n27; M. M. Kaplan and, 240n9; KJ and, 238–39n2; Ramaz Margolies and, 239n4; Orthodox feminism and, 267n3; YU students protesting Vietnam War and, 123

Hadassah Women: L. Palatnik and, 203
Hair Covering (female), 228–29n49
Hamburg: Spanish and Portuguese community in, 4
Harcsztark, Tully (Rabbi): H. Schachter and, 218–19; women donning tefillin and, 218; YU/RIETS and, 218–19
Haredi Orthodoxy: abandonment of strict norms and, 3; American-born and, 11; assimilation and, 11; at-risk youth and, 148; Bais Yaakov and, 116; S. Benor and, 7; Chabad and, 146–48, 175–91; changing attitudes toward non-Orthodox and, 146–48;

college education and, 230n62; contemporary constituencies and, 6–7; definition of, 6; Eastern Europe and, 95–98; economics and, 145–46, 212, 283n85, 296n26; European-born rabbis and, 73–75; female education and, 116; Y. Finkelman and, 7; geographic concentration and, 222; Y. Y. Greenwald as a forerunner and, 41; Holocaust remembrance and, 96, 98; increased exposure to non-Orthodox society and, 148; Israeli Haredi women activists and, 296n34; Jewish law and, 142–43; A. Kotler and, 134–35; NCSY and, 285n16; off the *derekh* youth and, 213; Open Orthodoxy and, 216–22; Orthodox feminism and, 123–24, 148, 203, 208–10, 274–75n77; outreach and, 11, 134–45, 155–66, 173–74, 181–88, 195–210, 212–14; Y. Perlow and, 136–39, 142, 150; Pew 2013 and, 9, 13–14, 230n63; place of Reform in internal polemics and, 148; postdenominationalism and, 211–16; public sphere and, 70; Reform and, 130–50; reformist sects and, 12; H. Schachter and, 126–29; social problems and, 148; M. Sofer and, 124; Soviet Jewry and, 58–59, 70–76, 80; study in Israel and, 161; survival and, 156; triumphalism and, 144–45, 212; woman's religious roles, 268n10; women's leadership and, 195–210; World War II immigration and, 6, 156; YCT and, 173–74. *See also* Agudat Israel; Slide to the Right; Y. Perlow

Harris, David (Rabbi), 163

Hasidic Rebbe (grand rabbi): dynasty and, 50; finances and, 49–50; immigration to America and, 4; Satmar and, 20. *See also* M. M. Schneerson

Hasidism: Chabad and, 180–81; Elimelekh of Leżajsk and, 106; Europe and, 4, 97; Haredi Orthodoxy and, 6, 7; Hungarian courts of, 20; immigration to America and, 4; Neo-Hasidism and, 107–9; Poland Pilgrimages and, 96–98, 100, 104–9; positive anti-Hasidism and, 188–91; Satmar court of, 20; *Yeshivat Hakhmei Lublin* and, 105; United States and, 20

Hauer, Moshe (Rabbi), 211–16; Jews for Jesus and, 214–15; *Klal Perspectives* and, 211–16; partnership minyan and, 215; postdenominationalism and, 211–16

Havurah Movement, 65–66, 257–58n107

Hayyim of Volozhin (Rabbi): financial management of yeshiva and, 54; fundraising and, 245n55; Lithuanian yeshiva model and, 155; positive anti-Hasidism and, 189; S. Stampfer and, 243n39; *Torah li-Shmah* (Torah study for its own sake) and, 155

Hebrew Institute of Riverdale (synagogue): solidarity Orthodoxy and, 79; YCT and, 171

Hebrew Union College (HUC): D. Ellenson and, 135; founding and, 5; Y. Y. Greenwald and, 26. *See also* Reform Judaism

Hebrew University in Jerusalem: Poland pilgrimages and, 89

Hecht, Eli (Rabbi): Chabad rabbinical training and, 164, 286–87n41

Heilman, Samuel C. (sociologist): definition of Haredi Orthodoxy and, 6; definition of Modern Orthodoxy and, 7; gap year in Israel experience and, 110; H. Schachter and, 117–18; Slide to the Right and, 238n80; syncretist Orthodox and, 33, 236n67; term "Modern Orthodox" and, 238n80; typologies of Orthodoxy and, 33, 241n18

Henderson, John B. (religion scholar): heresiology and, 273n66

Hendler, Aryeh (Rabbi): Hasidism and, 107–9; Poland pilgrimages and, 107–9

Heresy: Orthodox Jewish feminism and, 114–15, 120–24; Reform Judaism and, 137

Heritage Seminars (Eastern Europe), 91–95, 97, 99–113; Haredization and, 94; pilgrimage and, 109–13. *See also* Poland Pilgrimages; Gap Year Post-High School Study in Israel

Herring, Basil (Rabbi), 118

Herzl, Theodor, 25

Heschel, Abraham Joshua (Rabbi Dr.): Soviet Jewry and, 65, 250n30, 251n44, 256n91; Vietnam and, 256n91

Heschel, Susannah (historian): early Christian critique of Jewish law on women and, 273n64

Hevrutah (partnership-oriented Torah study), 293n49

INDEX

Hildesheimer, Esriel (Rabbi): Hungarian schism and, 29, 33; Nehemiah Nobel and, 24; Ultra-Orthodox and, 125
Hineni (organization), 204
Hirsch, Ammiel (Rabbi), 149
Hirsch, Samson Raphael (Rabbi), 28, 36, 275n78; American Modern Orthodoxy and, 124, 275n80; Frankfurt secessionist Orthodoxy and, 246n70; J. Lookstein and, 47, 242–43n17; Reform Judaism and, 126–27, 139, 236–37n74; H. Schachter and, 126–27
Hirschenson, Hayyim (Rabbi), 23–24; E. Ben-Yehudah and, 37; J. D. Eisenstein and, 234n23; excommunication of, 37; Y. Y. Greenwald and, 21–24, 28, 31, 34; Hoboken, New Jersey and, 37; Hungarian Orthodoxy and, 19, 22–24, 29–30, 36–39; Old Yishuv in Palestine and, 36–38; Religious Zionism and, 24; theoretical Jewish Law and, 23
Hirschian Orthodoxy: immigration to America and, 4, 236-37n74
Hirschsprung, Mordechai (Rabbi), 35
Hirt, Robert S. (Rabbi), 279n35
Hoboken, New Jersey: H. Hirschenson and, 37
Hoenlein, Malcolm (national Jewish leader): J. Birnbaum and, 62; Chabad and, 71; M. Feinstein and, 73; Soviet Jewry and, 62, 71; SSSJ and, 66
Holocaust: American Jewish apathy and, 63; commemoration and, 95–99; education and, 87, 94–95; Haredi Orthodoxy and, 95–99, 262n39, 262–63n40; immigration to the United States and, 8; Jewish identity and, 86. *See also* Poland Pilgrimages
Homiletics: H. Lookstein and, 246n68; J. Lookstein and, 46
Homosexuality: training rabbis and, 133. *See also* Gender; Reform
Horn, Elie (philanthropist), 161
Houston Conference for Jewish Women, 197
Houston, Texas: Haredi concentration and, 10
Hungarian Jewish Congress (1868–69), 21, 38
Hungarian Jewry: anti-modernism and, 4; history of, 20–21; immigration to America and, 4, 20; Jewish Congress (of 1868–69), 21, 27. *See also* Y. Y. Greenwald
Hungarian Orthodoxy, 19–41; anti-modernism and, 20; Y. Y. Greenwald and, 22–23, 27–30; H. Hirschenson and, 37–39; immigrant rabbis and, 20; Land of Israel and, 28, 37–39
Hungarian Ultra-Orthodoxy: Y. Y. Greenwald and, 28, 31; E. Hildesheimer and, 125–26; Hungary and, 21, 275n81; M. Klein and, 285n15; H. Schachter and, 126
Hurban (destruction): World War II and, 96. *See also* Haredi Orthodoxy; Holocaust; Poland Pilgrimages,
Hurwitz, Sara (Rabba): ordination and, 172; Yeshivat Maharat and, 173. *See also* Orthodox Feminism; YCT
Hutner, Isaac (Rabbi): M. M. Schneerson and, 290n12

Illowy, Bernard (Rabbi): Reform Judaism and, 133
Immigrant Rabbis (in the United States), 23–30, 73
Immigration of Jews to America: eighteenth century and, 5; Haredi rabbis and, 73; Hungarians, 20; turn of the twentieth century and, 4, 5, 20; seventeenth century and, 4; World War II period and, 4, 6, 8
Inreach: Modern Orthodox rabbinate and, 165–66
Interdenominational Relations: Orthodox feminism and, 119–24; Orthodox-Reform and, 130–50. *See also* Conservative Judaism; Reform Judaism
Intermarriage: community kollels and, 143–44; Conservative rabbis and, 278n21; non-Orthodox Jews and, 2, 143–44; Reform rabbis and, 278n21; Reform synagogues and, 143–44
International Rabbinical Fellowship (IRF): YCT and, 172
Isaiah, Book of, 6
Israel, State of: activism and, 70; KJ and, 57; Ministry of Education and, 88, 89; Modern Orthodox support and, 7; new Jewish politics in America and, 68; Orthodox and, 14; Orthodox-Reform relations and,

INDEX

132; Poland pilgrimages and, 95, 96, 100; Pew 2013 and, 223; Shas political party and, 6. *See also* Zionism

Isserles, Moses (Rabbi), 3

Jackson-Vanek Amendment, 59
Jacobson, Daniel (psychologist): gap year in Israel experience and, 110
Jerusalem: H. Hirschenson and, 36–38; Hungarian Ultra-Orthodox and, 21
Jerusalem Kollel (TJK): outreach rabbinical training and, 162; women's outreach training and, 198
Jesus, 32
Jewish Action (journal), 131
Jewish Daily Forward (newspaper): Y. Perlow and, 138
Jewish Defense League (Boston): Soviet Jewry and, 67
Jewish Defense League (JDL, Kahane): Orthodox Jews and, 67; Soviet Jewry and, 62–63, 67
Jewish law (Halakhah): *agunah* (anchored wife) and, 236n71; change and, 274n71; Y. Y. Greenwald and, 26; KJ rabbi and, 56; KJ Yom Kippur service and, 242n22; J. Lookstein and, 47; Ramaz Margolies and, 44–45; Modern Orthodox and, 9; Orthodox feminism and, 117–24, 203–4; outreach and, 139–44; outreach to women and, 199; Religious Zionism and, 266n101
Jewish Learning Initiative on Campus (JLIC), 172
Jewish Observer (journal): Orthodox feminism and, 123; outreach and, 285n15; Y. Perlow and, 136–39; suspension of denominational hostilities and, 136–39
Jewish Outreach: Halakhic Perspectives (book), 140
Jewish Press (weekly): non-Orthodox and, 138; Y. Perlow and, 138; suspension of denominational hostilities and, 138
Jewish Renewal Movement, 2
Jewish Study Network (JSN, Palo Alto Community Kollel): interdenominational cooperation and, 141–42; mixed-gender activities and, 198
Jewish Theological Seminary (JTS): Agudath ha-Rabbonim and, 40; founding and, 6; Y. Y. Greenwald and, 30, 33; M. M. Kaplan and, 44; KJ and, 44; J. Lookstein and, 47; Soviet Jewry and, 66; Orthodox Union and, 234n54; YCT and, 289n76. *See also* Conservative Judaism

Jewish Women (magazine), 203
Jewish Women's Renaissance Project (JWRP), 201–3, 209; feminism and, 209. *See also* L. Palatnik
Jews for Jesus: M. Hauer and, 214–15
Jews of Silence, The (book), 61
Joel, Richard (YU President), 169, 259n125
Joselit, Jenna (historian): KJ and, 52, 238–39n2; J. Lookstein and, 241n19
Jung, Leo (Rabbi), 231n3
Jungreis, Esther (Rebbetzin): feminism and, 204–6

Kagan, Aaron (Rabbi), 141
Kagan, Yisrael Meir (Rabbi, "Chofetz Chaim"), 162
Kahane, Meir (Rabbi): Soviet Jewry and, 62–63, 67
Kahn, Aharon (Rabbi), 168
Kamenetsky, Shmuel (Rabbi): Jewish law regarding outreach and, 142–43; Moetzes Gedolei ha-Torah and, 142; *One People, Two Worlds* and, 149–50; outreach activities in non-Orthodox synagogues and, 142–43; Philadelphia Yeshiva and, 142, 149
Kamenetsky, Sholom (Rabbi): Jewish law regarding outreach and, 143; *One People, Two Worlds* and, 149; Philadelphia Yeshiva and, 143, 149
Kaplan, Mordecai (Rabbi): Y. Y. Greenwald and, 25, 31; JTS and, 30–31; KJ and, 44, 240n9; Ramaz Margolies and, 240n9; J. D. Willowski and, 240n10
Karaites, 125
Katz, Jacob (historian): S. R. Hirsch and, 128–29; Hungarian Orthodoxy and, 20; methodology and, 15; Pressburg Yeshiva and, 234n27
Katz, Ysoscher (Rabbi): partnership minyanim and, 220
Kaufman, Debra (sociologist), 205–6

INDEX

Kehilath Jeshurun, Congregation (KJ): Americanization and, 43, 242–43n27; appointment of H. Lookstein as assistant rabbi, 54–55; appointment of J. Lookstein as rabbi and, 46; board meetings and, 50–51; church-like Orthodoxy and, 77; constituency and, 43, 47; dignified service and, 47; female synagogue officers and, 270n37; fire and, 53; J. Gurock and, 238–39n2, 239n6; history and, 42–43, 44; intermarriage and, 242n27; liturgical service and, 43; J. Lookstein's vision and, 47; Lookstein dynasty and, 55–56; membership and, 300n39; Modern Orthodoxy and, 43, 56–57, 222; nonobservant Jews and, 47, 242n27; original name and, 239n5; rabbi's salary and, 51; rabbinical search and, 56–57; Ramaz and, 54, 57, 218; role of rabbi and, 56–57, 244n42, 244n43; H. Schachter and, 48, 218, 270n37; Thanksgiving service and, 242–43n27. *See also* H. Lookstein; J. Lookstein; Ramaz Margolies

Kelner, Shaul (sociologist): Soviet Jewry and, 248n6; protest as ritual and, 258n109

Ketubah (Jewish marriage writ): women's recital and, 122, 273–74n70

Ketubot (Tractate, Babylonian Talmud), 73

Kiruv. *See* Outreach to Nonobservant

Klal Perspectives (journal): M. Hauer and, 211–16; L. Palatnik and, 202–3

Klein, Menashe (Rabbi), 285n15

Klein, Phillip (Rabbi), 231n3

Klein-Halevi, Yossi (journalist): J. Birnbaum and, 63, 66

Knesset Yisrael–Slobodka Yeshiva, 162

Kohut, Alexander (Rabbi Dr.), 231n3

Kol Bo al Aveilut (book), 34.

Kollel Elyon (RIETS), 167–68

Kook, Abraham Isaac (Rabbi), 38, 275–76n91

Korn, Eugene (Rabbi): Solidarity Orthodoxy and, 80–81

Kotler, Aharon (Rabbi): Agudath Israel and, 134, 176; American Haredi Orthodox renaissance and, 134–35, 176; American Jewry and, 176; biography of, 134, 175–76; BMG and, 134, 176–77, 278n25; Chabad and, 175–78, 290n10; Conservative Judaism and, 134; Gaon of Vilna and, 190; kollel and, 176, 182, 185; Moetzes Gedolei ha-Torah and, 134; New York Board of Rabbis and, 134, 141; Reform Judaism and, 134, 136, 139, 142; Synagogue Council of America and, 134; N. Waxman and, 290n2. *See also* Beth Medrash Govoha

Kotler, Shneur (Rabbi), 141: community kollel and, 183

Krakow, 98, 116

Kraus, Yitzhak (Rabbi Dr., scholar of Jewish thought): Schneerson family and, 290n8

Kugelmass, Jack (anthropologist): Poland pilgrimages and, 95, 97, 106–7

Lakewood, New Jersey: BMG and, 7; Haredi concentration and, 10, 182, 222

Lamm, Norman (Rabbi Dr.): non-Orthodox and, 135–36; Soviet Jewry and, 65; YU and, 135

Lander College for Men (Touro), 228n44, 287n50

Landes, David (religion scholar): H. Schachter and, 273n67

Late Friday Night Services, 32–33

Latin America: Shas political party and, 6

Lavie, Aliza (communications scholar), 296n34

Lazin, Fred (political scientist), 62–63

Lederhendler, Eli (historian): mid-twentieth century New York Jewry and, 69–70; Soviet Jewry and, 248n6

Lefkowitz, Jay P.: Social Orthodoxy and, 300n36

Leibowitz, Dovid (Rabbi), 162

Leibowitz, Henoch (Rabbi), 163

Leibowitz, Yeshayah (scientist, theologian): women in Judaism and, 114–15

Leningrad Trials (1970–71), 61

Leon, Nissim (sociologist), 296n34

Lerea, Dov (Rabbi): YCT and, 289n76

Levine, Joel: Yavne and, 179

Leżajsk (Poland), 106

Liason Bureau (Israeli, *Lishkat ha-Kesher*): Soviet Jewry and, 60

Liberal Denominations: dominance of American Jewish life and, 1; religious passion and, 2. *See also* Conservative

340

INDEX

Judaism; Haredi Orthodoxy; Open Orthodoxy; Outreach to Nonobservant; Y. Perlow; Reconstructionist Judaism; Reform Judaism

Lichtenstein, Aharon (Rabbi Dr.), 251n44; decline in interdenominational tension and, 131, 271n52; non-Orthodox Jews and, 279n37; Soviet Jewry and, 65, 74

Liebman, Charles S.: application of church/sect theory to American Orthodoxy and, 2, 7–9, 76; Chabad and, 177, 229n53; historical methodology and, 15; Jewish survival and, 293n48; journal *American Jewish History* and, 14–15; A. Kotler and, 177–78; methodology for studying contemporary Jewry and, 15; "Orthodoxy in American Jewish Life" and, 1, 2, 7, 80, 144, (critique of), 229n51; Poland pilgrimages and, 100; rabbinical training and, 153, 154–55, 162; reevaluation of his theory, 10–11, 14, 217, 223; social scientific methodology and, 15; Soviet Jewry and, 80, 248n6; SSSJ and, 80; TMZ and, 193

Li-Felagot Yisrael be-Hungariyah (book), 28, 31, 34

Lincoln Square Synagogue: S. Riskin and, 66

Linzer, Dov (Rabbi), 170, 269n22

Lithuania: Haredi pilgrimages and, 96, 97, 98

Lithuanian Yeshivas: Poland Pilgrimages and, 97–99; rabbinical training and, 152, 154, 155–57. *See also* Hayyim of Volozhin; *Torah li-Shma*

Loewenthal, Naftali (Hasidism scholar): role of women in Chabad and, 206–8

London: Spanish and Portuguese community and, 4

Lookstein Family: CEO and, 49–57; dynasty and, 50–57; rabbinical independence and, 54

Lookstein, Audrey: Soviet Jewry and, 48

Lookstein, Gertrude (Schlang): appointment of H. Lookstein and, 55; J. Lookstein and, 46; Ramaz Margolies and, 46

Lookstein, Haskel (Rabbi Dr.): appointment as rabbi of KJ and, 54–55; arrest and, 48, 78; biography and, 48–49; CEO style and, 49–57; change and, 49; female synagogue officers and, 270n37; fundraising and, 52–53; Jewish law and, 48–49; KJ service and, 49, 242n22, 243n37; J. Lookstein and, 46, 49, 52, 244n42, 244n43, 246n68; *menschliness* and, 49; Modern Orthodoxy and, 48–49, 56; non-Orthodox groups and, 49; public activism and, 43; rabbinical dynasty and, 49; H. Schachter and, 48, 270n37; Solidarity Orthodoxy and, 78; Soviet Jewry and, 48, 58–59, 68, 77, 78; women donning tefillin and, 218; YU and, 48, 246n68. *See also* KJ; Ramaz, Soviet Jewry

Lookstein, Joseph H. (Rabbi): Agudath Israel and, 241n241; American Orthodox synagogue and, 45; Americanization and, 47, 242n27; appointment as KJ rabbi and, 46; biography and, 45–48; CEO style and, 49–57; churchlike Orthodoxy and, 79; civil religion and, 242–43n27; definition of KJ and, 43; founding of Ramaz and, 54, 245n63; fundraising and, 52–54, 245n56; Haredization and, 48, 242n22; S. R. Hirsch and, 242n27; Jewish law and, 47, 242n22; KJ English-speaking rabbi and, 44, 46, 241n19; H. Lookstein and, 46, 49, 52, 242n22; Ramaz Margolies and, 43, 44–45; Modern Orthodox rabbinate and, 48, 152; Modern Orthodoxy and, 46–47; nonobservant Jews and, 47; old Jewish politics and, 79; outreach and, 47; public activism and, 79; rabbinic succession and, 246n69; B. Revel and, 46; RIETS homiletics professor and, 46, 246n68; synagogue aesthetics and, 47, 52; synagogue attendance and, 241n19; teacher/preacher and, 154; Yeshiva College and, 46. *See also* KJ; Ramaz

Lopatin, Asher (Rabbi): "Odyssey Generation" and, 288n67; YCT and, 170–72, 216, 217, 288n67. *See also* YCT

Los Angeles, California: Haredi Orthodoxy and, 10, 182

Lower East Side (Manhattan): 44

Maas, Richard: Soviet Jewry and, 62

Magnes, Judah (Rabbi): KJ and, 45

Majdanek (concentration camp): Poland pilgrimages and, 98, 99, 106

Malki ba-Kodesh (book), 22

Manhigah Hilkhatit Ruhanit Toranit (Maharat), 173; YCT and, 173. *See also* Open Orthodoxy; S. Hurwitz; A. Weiss
Maor (rabbinical training program), 157–58; outreach rabbinate and, 158
March of the Living, 88–90
Margolies, Moses Zebulun (Rabbi, RaMaZ), 44–45, 239n3; Agudath ha-Rabbonim and, 45; J. Gurock and 239n4; H. Hirschenson and, 45; immigration to the United States and, 239n3; Jewish law and, 44–45; KJ and, 43; J. Lookstein and, 43, 44–45; J. Magnes and, 45; nondenominational organizations and, 45; Ramaz School and, 53; RIETS (YU) and, 45; typology of Orthodox rabbis and, 241n18; J. D. Willowski and, 240n10; Zionism and, 45. *See also* KJ; G. Lookstein; J. Lookstein
Masorah (longstanding traditions of handed-down religious behavior): H. Schachter and, 121, 122, 126–27, 272n59; J. B. Soloveitchik and, 272n59; women's ordination and, 289n79
Matanky, Leonard A. (Rabbi): TMZ and, 192
Max Stern Division of Communal Services (MSDCS, YU), 169
Meah She'arim (Jerusalem), 37
Mechon Hadar, 221, 289n77
Medding, Peter (political scientist), 68
Meir (Meyerson, stateswoman), Golda, 25
Meltzer, Isser Zalman (Rabbi), 290n2
Methodology, 14–16; G. Bacon and, 15; M. Douglas and, 15; L. Dumont and, 15; J. Katz and, 15; C. Liebman and, 14–15
Michlalah College for Women: Poland pilgrimages and, 99
Milikowsky, Shaya (Rabbi), 157–58
Miller, Israel (Rabbi): Soviet Jewry and, 61, 78
Mirsky, Yehudah (religion scholar): feminist influence on the boundaries of Orthodoxy and, 269n28
Mishnah, 3
Mitnagedim (non-or anti-Hasidim): Chabad and, 178; community kollel and, 188–91; Eastern Europe and, 4; Haredi Orthodoxy and, 6, 7; ideology and, 279–80n38; immigration to America and, 4; Poland pilgrimages and, 97–98. *See also* Gaon of Vilna; Hasidism; Hayyim of Volozhin; *Torah li-Shmah*
Mitzvah Campaigns: Chabad and, 179
Mixed Seating, 26, 29, 234n36; Agudath ha-Rabbonim and, 40; Y. Y. Greenwald and, 26, 29; Modern Orthodox rabbis and, 152; J. Sarna and, 278n30; D. Stavsky and, 234n36; synagogue and, YCT and, 171; weddings and, 228n48. *See also* Conservative Judaism; Gender; Women
Mizrachi, Yemima (Rabbanit), 296n32
Mizrahi (Religious Zionist) Party: Y. Y. Greenwald and, 24
Modern Orthodoxy: American-born rabbis and, 75; assimilation and, 230n60; church/sect theory and, 2, 7, 8; civil rights movement and, 75, 256n93; college campus and, 230n60; crisis and, 13; decline in level of observance and, 13; definition and, 7; diversity and, 8; economics and, 222–23, 300n40; female education and, 116–17; female public ritual and, 116–17; Y. Y. Greenwald and, 30–36, 38, 41; S. Heilman on, 7; S. R. Hirsch and, 124; inreach and, 165–66; Israeli Religious Zionism and, 109–10, 161n29; KJ and, 49; C. S. Liebman and, 100; nonobservant and, 8; non-Orthodox and, 8; Open Orthodoxy and, 216–22; outreach and, 11; Pew 2013 and, 9, 13, 230n62, 230n63; Poland pilgrimages and, 85–87; 89–95, 100; public sphere and, 70; rabbinate and, 151–53, 154, 166–74; rabbinical training and, 166–72; Reform and, 130–32, 133–34, 135–36; H. Schachter and, 275n89; Soviet Jewry and, 58–82; survivalism and, 13; woman's religious roles, 268n10; YCT and, 216–22. *See also* Church Orthodoxy; Church-Sect Orthodoxy; KJ; Ramaz; RIETS; Social Orthodoxy; YU
Modernity: the rabbinate and, 152
Moetzes Gedolei ha-Torah (Council of Torah Sages of Agudath Israel): Sh. Kamenetsky and, 142; A. Kotler and, 134; *One People, Two Worlds* and, 149–50; Open Orthodoxy and, 217; Soviet Jewry and, 72, 76, 255n87. *See also* Agudath Israel
Morais, Sabato (Rabbi), 231n3

INDEX

Morris, Bonnie (women's studies scholar), 205–6

Mussar (religious ethics): CC and, 163

National Conference for Soviet Jewry, 62

National Council of Synagogue Youth (NCSY): Haredi Orthodoxy and, 229n54, 285n16; Modern Orthodoxy and, 229n54; Y. Weinberg and, 279n60

Nazis, 86, 87, 99

Neo-Hasidism, 107–109; Aish Kodesh and, 266n99; Israeli Religious Zionism and, 108–9, 265n96. *See also* S. Carlebach; Carlebach Minyamin; A. Hendler; Poland Pilgrimages

Neologue movement (Hungary), 20–21, 27, 125

Ner Israel Rabbinical College (Ner Israel Yeshiva, Baltimore), 156; ASK kollel and, 141, 183; college education and, 286n38; Haredi Orthodoxy and, 214; rabbinical training and, 157; realignment and, 218; H. Schachter and, 276n95; Y. Weinberg and, 142

Ner LeElef (NLE, outreach organization): female outreach supervision and, 201; feminism and, 203, 205; Lakewood program and, 162; outreach training and, 142; rabbinical training and, 161–62; RIETS and, 168–69; use of non-Orthodox facilities and, 142; women's training, 161, 198–99

Nesivos of the Gedolim (Easter Europe Pilgrimage), 94, 95–100, 263n54; Legacy Tours and, 99. *See also* Poland Pilgrimages

New Age Judaism, 2

New Amsterdam: settlement of Spanish and Portuguese Jews and, 4

New Jewish Politics: American Jewry and, 68; Orthodoxy and, 69; Soviet Jewry and, 68–69

New York Board of Rabbis: A. Kotler and, 134; Soviet Jewry and, 70

New York University (NYU): 64, 222

New York: community of Spanish and Portuguese Jews and, 4; Orthodox Jews and, 225–26n6; Orthodox religious standards and, 10

Nobel, Nehemiah Anton (Rabbi), 24

Nondenominational Judaism, 2

Nonobservance: Eastern European immigrants and, 5; KJ and, 43; KJ rabbi and, 56; J. Lookstein and, 47; Modern Orthodox synagogues and, 8; Spanish and Portuguese immigrants and, 4. *See also* Outreach to Nonobservant

Non-Orthodox: KJ rabbi and, 56; Soviet Jewry and, 66, 76. *See also* Chabad; Community Kollel; Conservative Judaism; Nonobservance; Reconstructionist Judaism; Reform Judaism; YCT

Northbrook Community Synagogue (Illinois), 171, 288n70

Northern California Council for Soviet Jewry, 67

Oberstein, Elchonon (Rabbi), 139

Ohev Shalom Talmud Torah Congregation (OSTT, Olney, Maryland), 158

Ohr Somayach Yeshiva, 159

Ohr Yerushalayim Yeshiva, 99

One People, Two Worlds: A Reform Rabbi and an Orthodox Rabbi Explore the Issues that Divide Them (book), 149–50

Open Orthodoxy: Haredi Orthodoxy and, 216–22; Modern Orthodoxy and, 216–22; "neo-Conservatism" and, 217–18; Realignment and, 216–22; YCT and, 171. *See also* A. Lopatin; A. Weiss; Women; YCT

Oppenheimer, Leonard (Rabbi), 139

Organ: American synagogues and, 5

Orlev, Zevulun (Israeli politician), 89

Orthodox Community at Penn (OCP), 222

Orthodox Feminism, 115–26; 268n12; Haredi Orthodoxy and, 274–75n77; Jewish law and, 274–75n77; Orthodox boundaries and, 269n28; slippery slope argument and, 271n47. *See also* Female Haredi Outreach Activists; Gender; H. Schachter; Women; YCT; Yeshivat Maharat

Orthodox Judaism: definition and, 3–4; Jewish law and, 3; modern religious trend and, 3; Reform Judaism and, 272n58; religious behavior and, 3; *Shulhan Arukh* and, 3; theology and, 3, 226n12; *Torah min ha-Shamayim* and, 3; *Torah she-be'al peh* and, 3; voluntary character and, 3

INDEX

Orthodox Rabbis: arrival in America, 5
Orthodox Union (OU): history and, 235n54; JTS and, 235n54; public sphere and, 70
Oswiecim (Auschwitz, Polish town), 87
Outreach to Nonobservant (kiruv): activities in non-Orthodox synagogues/institutions and, 139–43; Aish Hatorah and, 159–61; BMG and, 145; Chabad and, 11, 177–81; community kollel and, 181–88; critique and, 298n7; frustration of activists and, 213–14; funding sources and, 146, 213–14; Haredi Orthodox and, 11, 12, 13, 139–44, 181–88; Jewish law and, 139–43, 199; J. Lookstein and, 47; Maor and, 157–58; Modern Orthodox and, 11, 166–72; Orthodox triumphalism and, 145; Pew 2013 and, 213, 298n8; professional careers and, 145; rabbinical training and, 157–66, 168–70, 172–74; realignment and, 11, 223; Reform and, 139; YU and, 166–72

Palatnik, Lori (religious activist): Aish Hatorah and, 201; female outreach and, 201–5, 208–98; JWRP and, 201–3; *Klal Perspectives* and 202–3. See also Female Haredi Outreach Activists; Feminism; Women
Parnes, Yehuda (Rabbi): Lander College and, 287n50; women's prayer services and, 270n41
Partnership Minyanim (egalitarian Orthodox): coalescence of Orthodox mainstream and, 215–16; Haredi Orthodoxy and, 214; Jews for Jesus and, 215; Orthodox feminism and, 117, 195, 203–10; quorum and, 271n45; RIETS/YU and, 219–20; H. Schachter and, 219–20
Passaic, New Jersey: Haredi concentration and, 10, 22
Patrilineal Descent: Reform movement and, 120, 121, 133, 134, 137
Penner, Menachem (Rabbi), 219–20
Peretz, I. L. (author), 99
Perlow, Yaakov (Rabbi), 136; Agudath Israel and, 136–40, 150, 216; Chaim Berlin Yeshiva and, 136; *Daily Jewish Forward* and, 138; Modern Orthodox and, 217, 221; *One People, Two Worlds* and, 150; Open Orthodoxy and, 217, 218, 221; Orthodox triumphalism and, 145; outreach and, 140; Reform and, 136–39, 142, 145, 147, 150, 299n19
Petuchowski, Jacob J. (Rabbi, theologian): Orthodox attitudes toward Reform and, 134
Pharisees: A. Geiger and, 274n75; reformist sect and, 12
Philadelphia Yeshiva, 142, 149
Philadelphia, PA.: community of Spanish and Portuguese Jews and, 4
Phoenix Community Kollel, 141, 184
Pilgrimages: anthropology and, 94–95, 264n64, 266n104
Pittsburgh Kollel Jewish Learning Center: interdenominational cooperation and, 141
Pittsburgh Platform (Reform Judaism, 1885), 137
Plaszow (Nazi concentration camp), 99
Poland Pilgrimages: birthright and, 88; decline of communism and, 87; gender and, 89–94, 97–98; Haredization and, 86, 92–94, 100, 104–9; Hasidism and, 106–9, 265n95; high school tours and, 261–62n31; history and, 87–94, 260n6, 260n7; Jewish identity and, 88, 89; Jewish solidarity and, 88, 93; long-term influence and, 260–61n14; March of the Living and, 88–90; Modern Orthodox groups and, 93, 94, 95; Modern Orthodoxy and, 109–13; Orthodox identity, 94, 108; rites of passage and, 86; Western tourism and, 87. See also Heritage Tours; Nesivos of the Gedolim
Popper, Micha (social psychologist): leadership and, 244n53
Postdenominationalism: Chabad and, 179, 184; community kollel and, 184; Haredi Orthodoxy and, 211–16; J. Wertheimer and, 131
Pressburg Yeshiva: Y. Y. Greenwald and, 24; Y. H. Sonnenfeld and, 38
Public Protest: antagonism to, 70–76; Haredi rabbis and, 70–76; Rabbi's March–Washington 1943, 253n67; Soviet Jewry and, 59, 63–65
Putnam, Robert: *Bowling Alone* (book) and, 81–82, 188, 259n126

INDEX

Queens College, New York, 64
Qumran Community (Dead Sea Sect): introversionist sects and, 12

Rabbinate: American-born and, 154; chief executive officer (CEO) and, 49–57, 154; English-speaking and, 6, 43, 69; grievance counselor and, 154; modernity and, 152; outreach and, 155–65, 168–69, 172–74; pastoral skills and, 56; pre-modern roles and, 151–52, 153–54; religious adjudication and, 153–54; salary and, 51; school principal and, 154; social worker and, 154; synagogue administration and, 51. *See also* Women Rabbis; Maharat
Rabbinical Associations, 6
Rabbinical Council of America (RCA): KJ rabbinical search and, 56; J. Lookstein and, 46; Modern Orthodox identification and, 7; Open Orthodoxy and, 217–18, 221; Orthodoxy feminism and, 209; Reform Judaism and, 131; H. Schachter and, 118; J. B. Soloveitchik and, 135; Soviet Jewry and, 60–61
Rabbinical Ordination Leadership Program (ROLP, Aish Hatorah), 159–61
Rabbinical Seminaries: curriculum of, 153–54; emergence of, 153–54
Rabbinical Seminary of America–Yeshivas Chofetz Chaim (CC): Haredi yeshivas and, 163; history and, 162–63; outreach and, 164; rabbinical training and, 163–64; realignment and, 218; Talmud study and, 163
Rabbinical Training: American Orthodox Judaism and, 151–74; Chabad and, 164–65; Haredi Orthodoxy and, 155–65; history and, 153–55; JTS and, 6; C. S. Liebman and, 153, 154–55; outreach and, 155–65, 168–69, 172–74; Reform Judaism and, 5; RIETS/YU and, 151–53, 154–55, 166–72; textual learning and, 154–55; YCT and, 151, 155, 170–74; 172–74. *See also* Aish Hatorah; CC; Jerusalem Kollel; Maor; Ner LeElef
Rabin Dagi, Lora (student), 75
Raichik, Shmuel David (Rabbi), 179
Ramaz School: Americanization and, 242–43n27; M. Etra and, 54; founding and, 53–54; KJ and, 47, 54; KJ fire and, 53; J. Lookstein and, 46; Ramaz Margolies and, 53; Modern Orthodox education and, 54; Modern Orthodoxy and, 222; Soviet Jewry and, 59, 78; women donning tefillin and, 218. *See also* KJ; H. Lookstein; J. Lookstein
Raphael, Marc Lee (historian): Columbus Jewry and, 32
Rapoport, Chaim (Rabbi): Chabad messianism and, 291n12
Realignment of American Orthodox Judaism, 3, 9, 11, 14, 113, 115, 128, 130, 214, 216
Rebbetzin, 196, 198
Reconformadox, 297–98n6
Reconstructionist Judaism, 44; Poland pilgrimages and, 88; prayer book of, 25. *See also* M. M. Kaplan
Reform Conference in 1869, 5
Reform Judaism: 1869 Conference and, 5; Chabad and, 146–47; Classical Reform Judaism and, 137; community kollel and, 140–42; Conservative Judaism and, 133; M. Feinstein and, 134–35; First Reform Temple and, 5; founding of the Hebrew Union College and, 5; founding of Union of American Hebrew Congregations (UAHC) and, 5; Y. Y. Greenwald and, 28, 32, 34–35, 36, 37; S. R. Hirsch and, 124–25; increased traditional behavior and, 137; intermarriage and, 133, 144, 278n21; A. Kotler and, 134; N. Lamm and, 136; J. Lookstein and, 46–47; mid-nineteenth century Jewish immigrants and, 5; Orthodox and, 130–50, 272n57; Orthodox Jewish feminism and, 114, 120–24; Y. Perlow and, 136–39, 142, 145, 147, 150, 299n19; Pew 2013 and, 144; Pittsburgh Platform (1885) and, 137; Poland pilgrimages and, 88; religious denominations and, 3–4; renewed vibrancy, 2, 144; same-sex marriage and, 133; H. Sofer and, 124–25; *Statement of Principles* (1999) and, 136–37; Synagogues in the 1870s and, 5; universalism and, 137; women and, 119–24. *See also* CCAR; HUC; UAHC
Refuseniks, 58, 72

INDEX

Reinman, Yosef (Rabbi), 149–50

Reisman, Levi (Rabbi): Reform and, 138

Religious Punctiliousness (*humrah*): American Orthodoxy and, 3; Haredi Orthodoxy and, 90–91; Religious Zionism and 90–91, 109–10

Religious Tourism, 262n38

Religious Zionism: American Modern Orthodoxy and, 109; Diaspora and, 108–9; Haredization and, 93, 266n101; H. Hirschenson and, 24; Holocaust remembrance and, 96, 104; Jewish law and, 266n101; Poland pilgrimage and, 88; negation of the exile and, 265–66n97; Neo-Hasidism and, 108–9; H. Schachter and, 127; women and, 268n11, 269n23. *See also* Gap Year Post High-School Study in Israel; Israel, State of

Revel, Bernard (Rabbi Dr.): American Orthodox rabbinate and, 47; J. Lookstein and, 46

Richter, Glenn (activist), 64, 66, 67; Chabad and, 71; Civil Rights and, 75; S. Riskin and, 66; Torah Leadership Seminar and, 66; A. Weiss and, 79. *See also* Soviet Jewry; SSSJ

RIETS (Rabbi Isaac Elchanan Theological Seminary, Yeshiva University), 31; curriculum and, 166–70; inreach and, 166, 169–70; KJ rabbinical search and, 56; Kollel Elyon and, 167–68; J. Lookstein and, 46; Ramaz Margolies and, 45; Modern Orthodoxy and, 166–70; MSDCS and, 169; Ner LeElef and, 168–69; non-Orthodox and, 135; outreach and, 166, 167, 168–69; partnership minyan and, 219–20; professional placement and, 171–72; rabbinical training and, 166–70; H. Schachter and, 118–19, 127–28; D. Sperber and, 273n62; Torahweb.com and, 272n58; YCT and, 171. *See also* YU

Riskin, Shlomo (Rabbi Dr., Steven): Orthodox Feminism and, 267n3; M. M. Schneerson and, 71; Solidarity Orthodoxy and, 78; Soviet Jewry and, 66–67, 252n55

Riverdale (New York): I. Greenberg and, 80; Modern Orthodox concentration and, 222

Rockland County (New York): Haredi concentration and, 10

Rodeph Sholom, Congregation (Manhattan), 44

Rosh Yeshiva (yeshiva head; advanced Talmud teacher): dynasty and, 50; finances and, 50; Hayyim of Volozhin and, 189; Lithuania and, 49–50; RIETS and, 48

Ross, Tamar (philosopher, theologian), 267n3, 268n13

Rubin Schwartz, Shuli (historian), 204

Sacks, Jonathan (Lord Rabbi): Katz award for Halakhah in modern life and, 269n30; Reform Judaism and, 133

Sadducees: J. Ettlinger and, 275n83; A. Geiger and, 274n75 Hungarian Ultra-Orthodoxy and, 126; Orthodox Jewish feminists and, 114, 120–24, 220; prototypes for modern religious deviants, 274n75; A. Y. Schlesinger and, 126; women's inheritance and, 122, 274n75

Safed: H. Hirschenson and, 23

Sages: Mishnah and, 3; Talmud and, 3

SAR (Salanter Akiba Riverdale) High School: Modern Orthodoxy and, 222; women donning tefillin and, 218

Sarna, Jonathan (historian): Agudath ha-Rabbonim and, 41, 277n7; Orthodoxy in America and, 132–33; Reform Judaism in the late nineteenth century and, 5; Soviet Jewry and, 6

Satmar Hasidism: post-World War II immigration and, 20; A. Shafran and, 217

Saturday Night Live (television comedy show), 68

Savannah (Georgia): community of Spanish and Portuguese Jews and, 4

Schachter, Herschel [Zvi] (Rabbi), 117–18, 128; ancient Jewish heretical groups and, 117–24, 217–18, 273n67; change in Jewish law and, 122, 275n90; Conservative Judaism and, 118–24, 218; Gentiles and, 271n44; T. Harcsztark and, 218–19; Haredization and, 126–29, 276n95; S. Heilman on, 117–18; S. R. Hirsch and, 124–26; Hungarian Ultra-Orthodoxy and, 124–26; Katz award for Halakhah in modern life and, 269n30; KJ and, 48, 218; liberal-minded students of J. B. Soloveitchik and, 275n88;

H. Lookstein and, 48, 270n37; *masorah* and, 121, 127, 272n59; Modern Orthodoxy and, 117–18, 126–29, 275n89; Ner Israel Yeshiva and, 276n95; Orthodox feminism and, 117–24, 218–20; partnership minyanim and, 219–20; Religious Zionism and, 127, 275–76n91; J. B. Soloveitchik and, 118, 126, 127, 270n34, 272n59, 275–76n91; D. Sperber and, 273–74n63; Torahweb.com and, 272n58, 274n70; woman's Talmud study and, 127; women donning tefillin and, 218–19; women's prayer groups and, 118–21, 219, 271n51; women's recital of *ketubah* and, 273–74n70; women's recital of *kiddush levanah* (sanctification of the new moon) and, 276n94; YU and, 127–28, 276n95, 276n98. *See also* Orthodox Feminism

Schacter, Herschel (Rabbi), 78

Schacter, Jacob J. (Rabbi Dr.): Holocaust commemoration and, 263n41; M. M. Kaplan and, 240n9

Schachter-Shalomi, Zalman (Rabbi): Chabad and, 179

Schechter, Barton "Bob", 144

Schechter, Solomon (Rabbi Dr.), 40. *See also* Conservative Judaism; JTS

Schenirer, Sarah (educator): Bais Yaakov and, 98, 116, 208; Haredi female education and, 116; Krakow visits and, 98

Schick, Marvin (education scholar): critique of Haredi outreach and, 298n7

Schick, Moses (Rabbi, Maharam Schick): Y. Y. Greenwald and, 29

Schiller, Mayer (Rabbi): feminism and, 272n56

Schlesinger, Akiva Yosef (Rabbi): Sadducees and, 126

Schneerson, Joseph Isaac (Rabbi), 179; America and, 290n8; Chabad women and, 206; outreach and, 290n8; N. Waxman and, 290n2. *See also* S. Carlebach; Z. Schachter-Shalomi

Schneerson, Menachem Mendel (Rabbi), 289n1; American democracy and, 255–56n91; American Jewry and, 177; Chabad women and, 206–7; female empowerment and, 207; I. Hutner and, 291n12; A. Kotler and, 177; messianism and, 178, 291n12; I. Miller and, 71, 254n78; S. Riskin and, 71; 175–79; *shluchim* and, 178–79; J. B. Soloveitchik and, 291n12; Soviet Jewry and, 71; N. Waxman and, 290n12; Yavne and, 179. *See also* Chabad; Chabad House; *Shluchim*; *Shluchos*

Schochetman, Eliav (legal scholar), 267n3

Schöpenhauer, Arthur (philosopher), 35

Schorsch, Ismar (historian): modern rabbinate and, 153–54

Schwartz, Jim (social scientist): Soviet Jewry and, 66

Schwartz, Ze'ev: TMZ and, 191

Sectarian Orthodoxy: acculturation and, 9; church/sect theory and, 2, 7; definition of, 8; M. Hauer and, 212; C. S. Liebman and, 8, 9, 223; nonobservant Jews and, 8; non-Orthodox Jews and, 8. *See also* Haredi Orthodoxy

Sectarianism: study of, 11–12; Haredi Orthodoxy and, 12

Sects: definition of, 11; reformist and, 12; Second Temple period and, 11–12. *See also* Church-Sect Theory

Seed Program–Torah Umesorah, 182

Selma (Alabama) Civil Rights March (1965): S. Riskin and, 66

Shabbos Project: community kollels and, 282n77

Shafran, Avi (Rabbi, Agudath Israel spokesman): Chabad and, 181, 217; definition of American Orthodoxy and, 217, 218; non-Orthodox and, 138–39; Open Orthodoxy and, 216–17; Y. Perlow and, 280n51; RIETS/YU and, 217; Satmar Hasidism and, 217; YCT and, 216

Shapira, Meir (Rabbi), 104

Shapiro, Marc (historian): M. Klein and, 285n15

Shapiro, Mendel (Rabbi): women's public Torah recital and, 121

Shas Political Party: Haredi Orthodoxy and, 6

Shcharansky, Natan (Anatoly, dissident, statesman), 59, 247n4

Sheer, Charles (Rabbi): Columbia University and, 79; Solidarity Orthodoxy and, 79; Soviet Jewry and, 67, 79, 257n102; SSSJ and, 67

INDEX

Sheramy, Rona (historian): March of the Living and, 260n8
Sherer, Moshe (Rabbi), 156
Shluchim (male emissaries, Chabad), 207; convention and, 181; M. M. Schneerson and, 177, 178, 181; training of, 164–65. *See also* Chabad; Rabbinical Training
Shluchos (female emissaries, Chabad): feminism and, 205–8; M. M. Schneerson and, 177; scholarship and, 196, 205–8. *See also* Chabad; Female Haredi Outreach Activists
Shneier, Arthur (Rabbi): Soviet Jewry and, 254n74
Shoah, 96. *See also* Holocaust
Shtadlanut (traditional quiet diplomacy): American Jewish establishment and, 61; Haredi Orthodoxy and, 70–76
Silber, Michael K. (historian), 126
Silver, Abba Hillel (Rabbi), 25
Silver Spring (Maryland): Modern Orthodox concentration and, 222
Simon Wiesenthal Center, 79
Six-Day War (1967, Israel): American Jewry and, 68; Soviet Jewry and, 59, 61–64, 74–76
Sixties (1960s): mixed-dancing and, 9; Soviet Jewry and, 63
Sklare, Marshal (sociologist): on American Orthodoxy, 1
Skokie (Illinois): Modern Orthodox concentration and, 222
Slide [shift] to the Right (Haredization): American Orthodoxy and, 3; *Flipping Out?* (book) and, 87; Gap year in Israel and, 87; S. Heilman and, 228n42; J. Lookstein and, 47; Modern Orthodoxy and, 9, 13, 14; Neo-Hasidism and, 109; Orthodox Jewish feminism and, 114–15; 123–29; Poland Pilgrimages and, 85–113; RIETS and, 167; H. Schachter and, 127–28; strict observance of Halakhah and, 9; C. I. Waxman and, 178; YU and, 81, 118–19, 127–28, 219.
Social Boundaries: institutions and, 12; porous and, 14
Social Capital: Soviet Jewry and, 81–82

Social Orthodoxy, 300n36
Sofer, Hayyim (Rabbi), 125, 275n86
Sofer, Moses (Rabbi; Hatam Sofer), 275n79; American rabbinate and, 275n80; Haredi Orthodoxy and, 124; Reform Judaism and, 132, 139, 277n11; wedding ceremonies in synagogues and, 26
Solidarity Marches for Soviet Jewry, 59, 65
Solidarity Orthodoxy, 58, 76–82
Soloveitchik, Ahron (Rabbi): civil rights and, 75; Soviet Jewry and, 75; Vietnam War and, 75
Soloveitchik, Haym (historian): American Orthodox Judaism and, 81; Haredi Orthodoxy and, 282n70
Soloveitchik, Hayyim (Rabbi, Brisk): Volozhin yeshivah and, 243n39
Soloveitchik, Joseph B. (Rabbi Dr.): *da'as Torah* and, 74; Holocaust and, 258n110, 263n41; Israel and, 256n96; Israeli Haredi Orthodoxy and, 276n97; non-Orthodox denominations and, 120, 139; non-Orthodox synagogues and, 135; H. Schachter and, 118, 126, 127, 272n59, 275–76n91; M. M. Schneerson and, 291n12; Soviet Jewry and, 74–75, 256n95; synagogue seating and, 135; Zionism and, 256n96, 275–76n91
Sonnenfeld, Yosef Hayyim (Rabbi), 37–38
Soviet Jewry: activists profile and, 66; Agudath Israel of America and, 72, 74, 76; American Jewish establishment and, 69; American Labor Movement and, 60; American (North American) Orthodoxy (Orthodox Judaism) and, 58–76; American public sphere and, 59, 61–62, 68–70; Americanization and, 75; S. Berman and, 67; J. Birnbaum and, 62–65, 66, 80; E. Borowitz and, 65; S. Carlebach and, 65; Chabad and, 60, 70–72; Church Orthodoxy and, 76; Civil Rights Movement and, 61; M. Feinstein and, 71–72, 73; A. Green and, 65–66; I. Greenberg and, 67, 75, 79–80; Haredi Orthodoxy and, 58–59, 70–76, 80; A. J. Heschel and, 65; history and, 59–60; M. Hoenlein and, 62, 66, 71, 73; JDL and, 62–63, 67; Jewish Defense League (Bos-

348

ton) and, 67; JTS and, 66; M. Kahane and, 62–63, 67; Liason Bureau (*Lishkat ha-Kesher*), and 60; C. S. Liebman and, 80; A. Lookstein, 48; H. Lookstein and, 48, 58–59, 68, 77, 78; I. Miller and, 61, 78; Modern Orthodoxy and, 58–82; Moetzes Gedolei ha-Torah (Council of Torah Sages of Agudath Israel) and, 72, 76; New York Board of Rabbis and, 70; New York Modern Orthodoxy and, 66; Poland pilgrimages and, 85–86; Public protest and, 59, 63–65; rabbinical delegations and, 60–61; Ramaz School and, 59, 78; RCA and, 60–61; S. Riskin and, 66–67; C. Sheer and, 67, 79; Sixties and, 63, 85; J. B. Soloveitchik and, 74–75; SSSJ and, 62–70; Stern College for Women and, 66; P. Teitz and, 70–74; M. D. Tendler and, 71–72; U.S. Congress and, 64; A. Weiss and, 66, 67; E. Wiesel and, 61; YU and, 66

Spanish and Portuguese Jews: Charleston, South Carolina and, 4; communal religious standards and, 5; membership in the community and, 5; New Amsterdam and, 4; New York and, 4; Philadelphia and, 4; Savannah, Georgia and, 4; settlement in America and, 4; religious observance, 4

Sperber, Daniel (Rabbi, Talmudic scholar and classicist): change in Jewish law and, 274n71; RIETS and, 273n62; H. Schachter, 273n63; women's public Torah recital and, 121, 267n3, 272n60

Spinoza, Benedict de (Barukh), 35

Stampfer, Shaul (historian): Lithuanian yeshivas and, 243n39; Volozhin Yeshiva and, 52, 54, 245n55, 245n67, 247n75

Statement of Principles for Reform Judaism (Pittsburgh, 1999), 136–37. *See also* Reform Judaism

Status Quo Communities (Hungary), 21, 27

Stavridis, James G. (political scientist): typology of leadership and, 244n41

Stavsky, David (Rabbi), 234n36

Stephen Wise Free Synagogue, 149

Stern College for Women (YU): Soviet Jewry and, 66

Student Struggle for Soviet Jewry (SSSJ), 62–70; Modern Orthodoxy and, 65–68; outside New York, 67; profile of activists, 66; religious symbolism and, 64; Solidarity Orthodoxy and, 77. *See also* J. Birnbaum; G. Richter; S. Riskin; Soviet Jewry; A. Weiss

Survivalism: Haredi Orthodox and, 11; Modern Orthodox and, 13

Sussman, Yehuda (Rabbi), 192

Synagogue: attendance, 6; dignified service and, 47, 49; first Ashkenazi synagogue, 5; first Reform Temple, 5; membership and, 225n6; Spanish and Portuguese immigrants and, 4; traditional style and, 234n36; weddings and, 26. *See also* Mixed Seating

Synagogue Council of America: A. Kotler and, 134; J. Lookstein and, 46

Sziget (Maramarossziget, Romania): Y. Y. Greenwald and, 24

Talmud, 3; women's study and, 116

Tchernowitz, Hayyim (Rav Za'ir), 28

Teaneck (New Jersey): Modern Orthodox concentration and, 222

Tefillin (phylacteries): H. Schachter and, 218–19; women and, 218–19

Teitz, Pinchas (Rabbi): J. Birnbaum and, 71; civil rights and, 74; Elizabeth, New Jersey rabbinate and, 245n66; Latvia and, 74; Lithuanian yeshivas and, 74; rabbinical succession and, 245n66; Soviet Jewry and, 70–74, 254n74; YU and, 70, 71

Temple Emanuel (Manhattan), 44; J. Magnes and, 45

Tendler, Moses D. (Rabbi Dr.): Soviet Jewry and, 71–72

Thanksgiving Service: KJ and, 242–43n27

Tolstoy, Leo (author), 34

Torah li-Shmah (Torah study for its own sake): American Haredi yeshivas and, 156, 157; CC and, 163; Hayyim of Volozhin and, 155; Lithuanian yeshivas and, 155–56; rabbinical training and, 155–56, 157

Torah min ha-Shamayim (Divinely dictated Torah), 3

Torah MiTzion (TMZ, organization, Zionist kollels): history of, 191; Modern Orthodox crisis and, 191–93; YU and, 193
Torah she-be'al peh (Oral Torah), 3
Torah Umesorah (organization), 182, 184
Torahweb.com: RIETS and, 272n58; H. Schachter and, 272n58
TORCH Community Kollel (Houston), 197
Toronto, Ontario: Haredi concentration and, 10, 182, 222
Traditional Synagogue (Midwest), 234n36. *See also* Mixed Seating
Treblinka (Nazi death camp), 99
Treife Medina (unkosher state), 152
Triumphalism: Haredi Orthodox and, 144–45, 212, 283n80, 283n81
Troeltsch, Ernst: church/sect theory and, 2
Turkey: H. Hirschenson and, 23, 37; Jewish immigration to the United States and, 5
Turner, Victor (anthropologist): pilgrimage and, 111

Ukeles, Jacob (demographer), 222n6
Unaffiliated Jews: Pew 2013 and, 2, 144
Union of American Hebrew Congregations (UAHC), 5; Atlanta conference 1995 and, 139; Y. Perlow and, 136; N. Wolpin and, 139, 289n52. *See also* Reform Judaism
United States Holocaust Memorial Council: I. Greenberg and, 79
United Synagogue (Conservative Judaism), 40
University of California, Los Angeles (UCLA): Chabad House and, 179
University of Pennsylvania: Modern Orthodox and, 222; OCP and, 222
Upper East Side (Manhattan), 42; 243n35

Vietnam War, 75, 256n91; YU and, 259n123
Volozhin Yeshiva: financial management and, 52; fundraising and, 245–46n67; leadership succession and, 247n75

Warsaw (Poland), 98
Washington Heights (Manhattan), 63
Waxman, Chaim I. (sociologist): Haredi Orthodoxy and, 229n55; Haredization and, 178, 228n42 (with Joshua Turetsky); Open Orthodoxy and, 228n42 (with Turetsky). *See also* N. Waxman
Waxman, Nissan (Rabbi), 290n2
Weber, Max (sociologist): church/sect theory and, 2
Weddings: Modern Orthodox and, 10; Orthodox feminism and, 269n22; synagogues and, 26
Wein, Beryl (Rabbi), 283n81
Weinberg, Noah (Rabbi), 159
Weinberg, Yaakov (Rabbi): ASK kollel and, 142; NCSY and, 281n60; Ner Israel Yeshiva and, 142
Weinberger, Moses (Rabbi), 231n3
Weinberger, Moshe (Rabbi): Aish Kodesh and, 266n99; Jewish laws of outreach and, 140; RIETS and, 266n99
Weiss, Avraham (Rabbi, Avi): ordination of women and, 172; N. Shcharansky and, 247n4; Solidarity Orthodoxy and, 79, 259n125; Soviet Jewry and, 66; SSSJ and, 67; Stern College and, 288n61; YCT and, 135, 170, 171; Yeshivat Maharat and, 172–73, 289n80. *See also* Open Orthodoxy; Soviet Jewry; YCT; Yeshivat Maharat
Weiss, David W. (scientist): Soviet Jewry and, 61
Werne, Isaac (Rabbi), 32, 236n59, 236n65
Wertheimer, Jack (historian): denominational divisions and, 277n3; outreach and, 157, 229n55, 282n72; postdenominationalism and, 131
West Rodgers Park, (Chicago, Illinois): Haredi concentration and, 10
Westchester County (New York): Modern Orthodox concentration and, 222
Western Sephardic Diaspora, 4
Wiesel, Elie (author): Soviet Jewry and, 61
WIK–Women in Kiruv (organization): conference and, 199–200. *See also* Female Haredi Outreach Activists
Willig, Mordechai (Rabbi), 118, 270n41
Willowski, Jacob David (Rabbi, Ridbaz): M. M. Kaplan and, 240n10; Ramaz Margolies and, 240n10
Wilson, Bryan (sociologist), 12

INDEX

Wise, Stephen (Rabbi), 28
Wolfson Family (philanthropists), 161
Wolfson, Elliot R. (scholar of mysticism and Jewish thought): Chabad Messianism and, 291n12
Wolpin, Nissan (Rabbi, editor of *Jewish Observer*): Orthodox feminism and, 123; Reform and, 139, 289n52
Woman's Prayer Groups: KJ and, 48–49; Orthodox feminism and, 117; H. Schachter and, 118–21
Women: Chabad shluchos and, 205–8; M. Feinstein, 268n13; *hakafot* and, 119; halakhic advisors and, 117; Haredi Outreach Activists, 196–210; Haredi preachers and, 196; Jewish law and, 118–24, 218–20, 268n13; new religious trends within American Jewry and, 4; Orthodox education and, 115–17; Orthodox Feminism and, 114–29; outreach and, 195–210; public ritual and, 116–17; Rabbinic Advocates, 196; rabbis and, 122–23, 133, 196, 207; recitation of *kaddish* (mourner's prayer) and, 269n27; recitation of the Book of Esther and, 119; recitation of the *ketubah* (marriage writ) and, 117, 122; religious roles and, 268n10; Religious Zionism and, 268n11; seminaries in Israel and, 87; spiritual leaders and, 117; Talmud study and, 116, 222; tefillin and, 218; Torah recital and, 121
Women Rabbis, 196, 207; Conservative Judaism and, 133; H. Schachter and, 122–23. *See also* Female Haredi Outreach Activists; Feminism; Women
Women's Liberation Movement: H. Schachter and, 119; Yeshiva heads and, 196; Yeshivat Maharat and, 172–73
World War I, 25
Wuthnow, Robert (religion scholar), Chabad and, 188; community kollels and, 188

Yad Vashem (Israel Holocaust Authority), 107
Yammer, Michael (Rabbi): Poland pilgrimages and, 92, 93

Yavne (Orthodox student organization), 63; M. M. Schneerson and, 179
Yeshiva of South Fallsburg, New York, 7
Yeshiva University (YU): alternatives to, 9; J. Birnbaum and, 63, 66; CJF and, 169, 259n125; Haredization and, 9, 118–19, 127–28, 219; E. Jungreis and, 205; H. Lookstein and, 48; J. Lookstein and, 46; Maccabees basketball team and, 9; Modern Orthodox identification with, 7; non-Orthodox and, 81, 135; rabbinical training, 166–70; Yeshiva College and, 30, 31, 35; Soviet Jewry and, 66; H. Schachter and, 118–19, 127–28; student humanitarian programs and, 259n125. *See also* CJF; RIETS; Stern College
Yeshiva University High School: early Soviet Jewry demonstration and, 248n12
Yeshivas: early twentieth century America and, 6; Eastern Europe and, 96–97; Israel and, 87; Poland pilgrimages and, 96–97; world of, 6, 97, 156
Yeshivat Chovevei Torah (YCT): curriculum and, 170–71; Haredi Orthodoxy and, 173–74, 216–22; HUC and, 289n77; JTS and, 289n76, 289n77; D. Linzer and, 170; A. Lopatin and, 170, 216; Mechon Hadar and, 221, 289n77; mission statement and, 170; Modern Orthodoxy and, 216–22; non-Orthodox and, 135, 171; professional placement and, 171–72; rabbinical petition and, 217; RCA and, 172, 217; RIETS and, 170–71; Solidarity Orthodoxy and, 79; A. Weiss and, 135, 170; women and, 170; Yeshivat Maharat and, 172–73
Yeshivat Hakhmei Lublin: *daf yomi* and 105; picture and, 265n79; Poland pilgrimages and, 104–6
Yeshivat Har Etzion (Gush): TMZ and, 191; Poland pilgrimages and, 266n100
Yeshivat Maharat, 172–73, 221, 289n80. *See also* Sarah Hurwitz; Maharat; Open Orthodoxy; Orthodox Feminism; A. Weiss; YCT
Yiddish: Ramaz Margolies and, 44; mid-nineteenth century immigrants and, 5
Yom ha-Shoah (Holocaust Commemoration Day): Poland Pilgrimages and, 88

INDEX

Yorkville (Upper East Side of Manhattan), 240n7; M. Chabon and, 240n7

Young Israel (National Council of): Modern Orthodox identification with, 7; YCT and, 172

Young Jewish Adults in the United States (survey): Orthodoxy in New York and, 225n6

Zionism: gap year students and, 264n73; H. Hirschenson and, 39; Ramaz Margolies and, 45; Modern Orthodoxy and, 7; Orthodox-Reform relations and, 132; Poland pilgrimages and, 95, 100. *See also* Israel, State of; Religious Zionism

Zuroff, Efraim (Nazi hunter, scholar): Solidarity Orthodoxy and, 79

www.ingramcontent.com/pod-product-compliance
Lightning Source LLC
Chambersburg PA
CBHW051556230426
43668CB00013B/1873